Paper 2.4

FINANCIAL MANAGEMENT AND CONTROL

For exams in December 2006 and June 2007

Study Text

ACCA

In this June 2006 new edition

- A user-friendly format for easy navigation
- Exam-centred topic coverage, directly linked to ACCA's syllabus and study guide
- Exam focus points showing you what the examiner will want you to do
- Regular fast forward summaries emphasising key points
- Questions and quick quizzes to test your understanding
- Exam question bank containing exam standard questions with answers
- A full index

BPP's **i-Learn** and **i-Pass** products also support this paper.

FOR EXAMS IN DECEMBER 2006 AND JUNE 2007

First edition 2001
Sixth edition June 2006

ISBN 0 7517 2667 2 (Previous edition 0 7517 2318 5)

British Library Cataloguing-in-Publication Data
A catalogue record for this book
is available from the British Library

Published by

BPP Professional Education
Aldine House, Aldine Place
London W12 8AW

www.bpp.com

Printed in Great Britain by
W M Print
45-47 Frederick Street
Walsall, West Midlands
WS2 9NE

All our rights reserved. No part of this publication may be reproduced, stored in a retrieval system or transmitted, in any form or by any means, electronic, mechanical, photocopying, recording or otherwise, without the prior written permission of BPP Professional Education.

We are grateful to the Association of Chartered Certified Accountants for permission to reproduce past examination questions. The suggested solutions in the exam answer bank have been prepared by BPP Professional Education.

©
BPP Professional Education
2006

Contents

Page

Introduction

> The introduction pages contain lots of valuable advice and information. They include tips on studying for and passing the exam, also the content of the syllabus and what has been examined.

The BPP Effective Study Package – How the BPP Study Text can help you pass – Help yourself study for your ACCA exams – Syllabus and Study Guide – The exam paper – Oxford Brookes BSc (Hons) in Applied Accounting – ACCA professional development requirements – Syllabus mindmap

Part A Costing systems and techniques
1. Cost and management accounting 3
2. Absorption and marginal costing 15
3. Other methods of cost accumulation 39

Part B: Standard costing
4. Introduction to standard costing 79
5. Basic variance analysis 93
6. Further variance analysis 119

Part C: Budgeting and performance measurement
7. Budget planning and control 149
8. Budget preparation 165
9. Budgetary control and the behavioural implications of budgeting 193
10. Alternative budget systems 213
11. Quantitative aids in budgeting 225
12. Index numbers 255
13. Performance measurement 271

Part D: The framework of financial management
14. Financial management and financial objectives 299
15. The financial management framework 321
16. Macroeconomic policy 343
17. Government intervention 365

Part E: Working capital management
18. Management of working capital 381
19. The management of debtors and creditors 397
20. The management of stocks and cash 421

Part F: Sources of finance
21. Equity financing 451
22. Debt financing 479
23. The capital structure decision 493
24. Financing of small and medium-sized enterprises 509

Part G: Investment appraisal

25	Investment decisions	525
26	Investment appraisal using DCF methods	539
27	Allowing for inflation and taxation	567
28	Project appraisal and risk	581
29	Capital rationing	595
30	Leasing decisions	605

Appendix: Mathematical tables 619

Exam question bank 627
Exam answer bank 661

Index 741
Review form and free prize draw

Computer-based learning products from BPP

If you want to reinforce your studies by **interactive** learning, try BPP's **i-Learn** product, covering major syllabus areas in an interactive format. For **self-testing**, try **i-Pass**, which offers a large number of **objective test questions**, particularly useful where objective test questions form part of the exam.

Learn Online

Learn Online uses BPP's wealth of teaching experience to produce a fully **interactive** e-learning resource **delivered via the Internet**. The site offers comprehensive **tutor support** and features areas such as **study, practice, email service, revision** and **useful resources**.

Visit our website www.bpp.com/acca/learnonline to sample aspects of Learn Online free of charge.

Learning to Learn Accountancy

BPP's ground-breaking **Learning to Learn Accountancy** book is designed to be used both at the outset of your ACCA studies and throughout the process of learning accountancy. It challenges you to consider how you study and gives you helpful hints about how to approach the various types of paper which you will encounter. It can help you **focus your studies on the subject and exam**, enabling you to **acquire knowledge, practise and revise efficiently and effectively**.

The BPP Effective Study Package

Recommended period of use	The BPP Effective Study Package
From the outset and throughout	**Learning to Learn Accountancy** Read this invaluable book as you begin your studies and refer to it throughout your studies.
Three to twelve months before the exam	**Study Text and i-Learn** Use the Study Text to acquire knowledge, understanding, skills and the ability to apply techniques. Use BPP's **i-Learn** product to reinforce your learning.
Throughout	**Learn Online** Study, practise, revise and use other helpful resources with BPP's fully interactive e-learning site, including full tutor support.
Throughout	**i-Pass** **i-Pass**, our computer-based testing package, provides objective test questions in a variety of formats and is ideal for self-assessment.
One to six months before the exam	**Practice & Revision Kit** Try the numerous examination-format questions in our Kit and compare your answers with the suggested solutions. Examiners emphasise that tackling exam-standard questions is essential preparation for your exams. Then attempt the two mock exams.
From three months before the exam until the last minute	**Passcards** Work through these short, memorable notes which are focused on the topics most likely to come up in your exam and which you can take anywhere.
One to six months before the exam	**Success CDs** The CDs cover the vital elements of your syllabus in less than 90 minutes per subject. They also contain exam hints to help you fine tune your strategy.

You can purchase these products by visiting www.bpp.com/mybpp

How the BPP Study Text can help you pass

> It provides you with the knowledge and understanding, skills and application techniques that you need to be successful in your exams

This Study Text has been targeted at the **Financial Management and Control** syllabus.

- It is **comprehensive**. It covers the syllabus content. No more, no less.
- It is written at the **right level**. Each chapter is written with ACCA's syllabus and study guide in mind.
- It is aimed at the **exam**. We have taken account of recent exams, guidance the examiner has given and the assessment methodology.

> It allows you to study in the way that best suits your learning style and the time you have available, by following your personal Study Plan (see page (ix))

You may be studying at home on your own or you may be attending a full-time course. You may like to read every word, or you may prefer to skim-read and practise questions the rest of the time. However you study, you will find the BPP Study Text meets your needs in designing and following your personal Study Plan.

> It ties in with the other components of the BPP Effective Study Package to ensure you have the best possible chance of passing the exam (see page (vi))

Help yourself study for your ACCA exams

Exams for professional bodies such as ACCA are very different from those you have taken at college or university. You will be under **greater time pressure before** the exam – as you may be combining your study with work. Here are some hints and tips.

The right approach

1 **Develop the right attitude**

Believe in yourself	Yes, there is a lot to learn. But thousands have succeeded before and you can too.
Remember why you're doing it	You are studying for a good reason: to advance your career.

2 **Focus on the exam**

Read through the Syllabus and Study Guide	These tell you what you are expected to know and are supplemented by **Exam focus points** in the text.
Study the Exam paper section	Past papers are likely to be good guides to what you should expect in the exam.

3 **The right method**

See the whole picture	Keeping in mind how all the detail you need to know fits into the whole picture will help you understand it better. • The **Introduction** of each chapter puts the material in context. • The **Syllabus content**, **Study guide** and **Exam focus points** show you what you need to **grasp**.
Use your own words	To absorb the information (and to practise your written communication skills), you need to **put it into your own words**. • **Take notes.** • Answer the **questions** in each chapter. • Draw **mindmaps**. We have an example for the whole syllabus. • Try **'teaching' a subject** to a colleague or friend.
Give yourself cues to jog your memory	The BPP Study Text uses **bold** to **highlight key points**. • Try **colour coding** with a highlighter pen. • Write **key points** on cards.

4 **The right recap**

Review, review, review	Regularly reviewing a topic in summary form can **fix it in your memory**. The BPP Study Text helps you review in many ways. • **Chapter roundups** summarise the 'Fast forward' key points in each chapter. Use them to recap each study session. • The **Quick quiz** actively tests your grasp of the essentials. • Go through the **Examples** in each chapter a second or third time.

Developing your personal Study Plan

BPP's **Learning to Learn Accountancy** book emphasises the need to use a study plan. Planning and sticking to the plan are key elements of learning successfully.

There are five steps you should work through.

Step 1 **How do you learn?**

First you need to be aware of your style of learning. BPP's **Learning to Learn Accountancy** book commits a chapter to this **self-discovery**. What types of intelligence do you display when learning? You might be advised to brush up on certain study skills before launching into this Study Text.

BPP's **Learning to Learn Accountancy** book helps you to identify what intelligences you show more strongly and then details how you can tailor your study process to your preferences. It also includes handy hints on how to develop intelligences you exhibit less strongly, but which might be needed as you study accountancy.

Step 2 **What do you prefer to do first?**

If you prefer to get to grips with a theory before seeing how it is applied, we suggest you concentrate first on the explanations we give in each chapter before looking at the examples and case studies. If you prefer to see first how things work in practice, skim through the detail in each chapter, and concentrate on the examples and case studies, before supplementing your understanding by reading the detail.

Step 3 **How much time do you have?**

Work out the time you have available per week, given the following.

- The standard you have set yourself
- The time you need to set aside later for work on the Practice & Revision Kit and Passcards
- The other exam(s) you are sitting
- Practical matters such as work, travel, exercise, sleep and social life

	Hours
Note your time available in box A. A	

Step 4 **Allocate your time**

- Take the time you have available per week for this Study Text shown in box A, multiply it by the number of weeks available and insert the result in box B.   **B**

- Divide the figure in box B by the number of chapters in this text and insert the result in box C.   **C**

Remember that this is only a rough guide. Some of the chapters in this book are longer and more complicated than others, and you will find some subjects easier to understand than others.

INTRODUCTION

Step 5   Implement

Set about studying each chapter in the time shown in box C, following the key study steps in the order suggested by your particular learning style.

This is your personal **Study Plan**. You should try to combine it with the study sequence outlined below. You may want to modify the sequence to adapt it to your **personal style**.

> BPP's **Learning to Learn Accountancy** gives further guidance on developing a study plan, and deciding where and when to study.

Tackling your studies

The best way to approach this Study Text is to tackle the chapters in order. Taking into account your individual learning style, you could follow this sequence for each chapter.

Key study steps	Activity
Step 1 **Topic list**	This topic list helps you navigate each chapter; each numbered topic is a numbered section in the chapter.
Step 2 **Introduction**	This sets your objectives for study by giving you the big picture in terms of the context of the chapter. The content is referenced to the Study Guide, and Exam guidance shows how the topic is likely to be examined. The Introduction tells you **why** the topics covered in the chapter need to be studied.
Step 3 **Knowledge brought forward boxes**	These highlight information and techniques that it is assumed you have 'brought forward' with you from your earlier studies. Remember that you may be tested on these areas in the exam. If you are unsure of these areas, you should consider revising your more detailed study material from earlier papers.
Step 4 **Fast forward**	Fast forward boxes give you a quick summary of the content of each of the main chapter sections. They are listed together in the roundup at the end of each chapter to help you review each chapter quickly.
Step 5 **Explanations**	Proceed methodically through each chapter, particularly focussing on areas highlighted as significant in the chapter introduction, or areas that are frequently examined.
Step 6 **Key terms and Exam focus points**	• Key terms can often earn you **easy marks** if you state them clearly and correctly in an exam answer. They are highlighted in the index at the back of this text. • Exam focus points state how the topic has been or may be examined, difficulties that can occur in questions about the topic, and examiner feedback on common weaknesses in answers.
Step 7 **Note taking**	Take brief notes, if you wish. Don't copy out too much. Remember that being able to record something yourself is a sign of being able to understand it. Your notes can be in whatever format you find most helpful; lists, diagrams, mindmaps.
Step 8 **Examples**	Work through the examples very carefully as they illustrate key knowledge and techniques.
Step 9 **Case studies**	Study each one, and try to add flesh to them from your own experience. They are designed to show how the topics you are studying come alive in the real world.
Step 10 **Questions**	Attempt each one, as they will illustrate how well you've understood what you've read.

Key study steps	Activity
Step 11 **Answers**	Check yours against ours, and make sure you understand any discrepancies.
Step 12 **Chapter roundup**	Review it carefully, to make sure you have grasped the significance of all the important points in the chapter.
Step 13 **Quick quiz**	Use the Quick quiz to check how much you have remembered of the topics covered and to practise questions in a variety of formats.
Step 14 **Question practice**	Attempt the Question(s) suggested at the very end of the chapter. You can find these in the Exam Question Bank at the end of the Study Text, along with the answers so you can see how you did. If you have bought i-Pass, use this too.

Short of time: Skim study technique?

You may find you simply do not have the time available to follow all the key study steps for each chapter, however you adapt them for your particular learning style. If this is the case, follow the **skim study** technique below.

Read the **topic list, chapter introduction** and **knowledge brought forward boxes**.

↓

Skim through the **explanations**, focusing on the points highlighted as important in the **fast forward boxes**.

↓

Read the **key terms** and **exam focus points** carefully.

↓

Go through the **examples** and **case studies**.

↓

Prepare outline **answers** to the **questions**.

↓

Revisit the fast forwards in the **chapter roundups**.

↓

Answer the **quick quiz** and look back at any areas where you got questions wrong.

↓

Do a plan for the **question(s) in the exam question bank** and review our answers carefully.

↓

Brief notes may help you skim study, although you may simply rely on the **passcards** for notes you can use for revision.

Moving on...

When you are ready to start revising, you should still refer back to this Study Text.

- As a source of **reference** (you should find the index particularly helpful for this)
- As a way to **review** (the Fast forwards, Exam focus points, Chapter roundups and Quick quizzes help you here)

Remember to keep careful hold of this Study Text – you will find it invaluable in your work.

> More advice on Study Skills can be found in BPP's **Learning to Learn Accountancy** book.

Syllabus

Aim

To develop knowledge and understanding of financial management methods for analysing the benefits of various sources of finance and capital investment opportunities and of the application of management accounting techniques for business planning and control.

Objectives

On completion of this paper, candidates should be able to:

- explain the role and purpose of financial management
- evaluate the overall management of working capital
- evaluate appropriate sources of finance for particular situations
- appraise capital investment through the use of appropriate methods
- identify and discuss appropriate costing systems and techniques
- prepare budgets and use them to control and evaluate organisational performance
- understand the basic principles of performance management
- critically assess the tools and techniques of financial management and control
- demonstrate the knowledge, understanding, skills, abilities and critical evaluation expected in Part 2

Position of the paper in the overall syllabus

Students must have a thorough knowledge of the material in Paper 1.2 **Financial Information for Management** and a good knowledge of other Part 1 papers.

Financial Management and Control is integrated with other Part 2 papers by providing a management decision framework within which some aspects of the Part 2 syllabus are developed. The effects of capital allowances and corporation tax on capital investment appraisal are examinable. Knowledge gained from Paper 2.3 **Business Taxation** (UK) will be useful in this respect.

Financial Management and Control is developed in Part 3 into advanced study of **Performance Management** (Paper 3.3) and **Strategic Financial Management** (Paper 3.7).

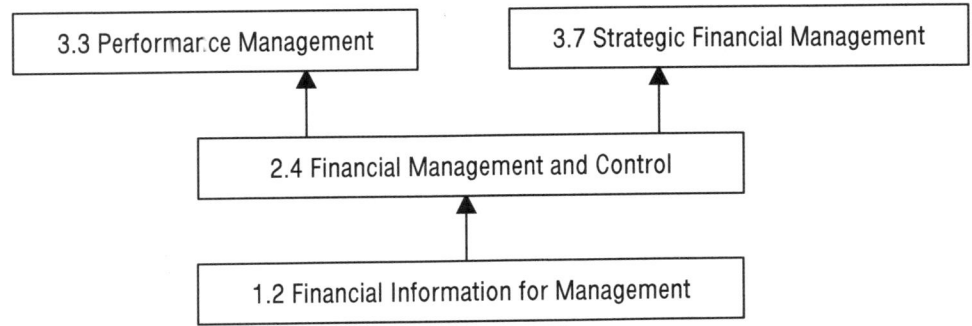

INTRODUCTION

1 **Financial management objectives**

   (a) The nature, purpose and scope of financial management.

   (b) The relationship between financial management, management accounting and financial accounting.

   (c) The relationship of financial objectives and organisational strategy.

   (d) Problems of multiple stakeholders in financial management and the consequent multiple objectives.

   (e) Objectives (financial and otherwise) in not-for-profit organisations.

2 **The financial management environment**

   (a) Financial intermediation and credit creation.

   (b) Money and capital markets.

   (i) Domestic and international
   (ii) Stock markets (both major markets and small firm markets).

   (c) The Efficient Markets Hypothesis.

   (d) Rates of interest and yield curves.

   (e) The impact of fiscal and monetary policy on business.

   (f) Regulation of business (for example, pricing restrictions, green policies and corporate governance).

3 **Management of working capital**

   (a) The nature and scope of working capital management.

   (b) Funding requirements for working capital.

   (c) Working capital needs of different types of business.

   (d) The relationship of working capital management to business solvency.

   (e) Management of stock, debtors, short term funds, cash, overdrafts and creditors.

   (f) Techniques of working capital management (including ratio analysis, EOQ, JIT, credit evaluation, terms of credit, cash discounts, factoring and invoice discounting, debtors cycles, efficient short term fund investing, cash forecasting and budgets, Miller-Orr model, basic foreign exchange methods, probabilities and risk assessment, terms of trade with creditors).

4 **Sources of finance**

   (a) Sources and relative costs (including issue costs) of various types of finance and their suitability to different circumstances and organisations (large and small, listed and unlisted) including:

   (i) Access to funds and the nature of business risk
   (ii) The nature and importance of internally generated funds
   (iii) Capital markets (types of share capital, new issues, rights issues, loan capital, convertibles, warrants)
   (iv) The effect of dividend policy on financing needs
   (v) Bank finance (short, medium and long term, including leasing)
   (vi) Trade credit
   (vii) Government sources: grants, regional and national aid schemes and tax incentives

- (viii) Problems of small company financing (collateral, maturity, funding gap, risk)
- (ix) Problems of companies with low initial earnings (R&D, Internet and other high-technology businesses)
- (x) Venture capital and financial sources particularly suited to the small company
- (xi) International money and capital markets, including an introduction to international banking and the finance of foreign trade.

(b) Requirements of finance (for what purpose, how much and for how long) in relation to business operational and strategic objectives.

(c) The importance of the choice of capital structure: equity versus debt and basic analysis of the term profile of funds.

(d) Financial gearing and other key financial ratios and analysis of their significance to the organisation.

(e) Appropriate sources of finance, taking into account
- (i) Cost of finance
- (ii) Timing of cash payments
- (iii) Business risk and financial risk
- (iv) Effect on gearing and other ratios
- (v) Effect on company's existing investors

5 **Capital expenditure and investment**

(a) Discounted cash flow techniques
- (i) Simple and compound interest
- (ii) Net present value
- (iii) Annuities and perpetuities
- (iv) Internal rate of return
- (v) Future value
- (vi) Nominal interest

(b) Appraisal of domestic capital investment opportunities for profit and non-profit making organisations through the use of appropriate methods and techniques
- (i) The risk/return relationship
- (ii) Return on capital employed
- (iii) Payback
- (iv) Internal rate of return
- (v) Net present value
- (vi) Single and multi-period capital rationing
- (vii) Lease or buy decisions
- (viii) Asset replacement using equivalent annual cost

Including (in categories (i) - (viii)) the effects of taxation, inflation, risk and uncertainty (probabilities, sensitivity analysis, simulation).

6 **Costing systems and techniques**

(a) The purpose of costing as an aid to planning, monitoring and control of business activity.

(b) Different approaches to costing.

(c) Costing information requirements and limitations in not-for-profit organisations.

(d) Behavioural implications of different costing approaches including performance evaluation.

INTRODUCTION

    (e)   Implications of costing approaches for profit reporting, the pricing of products and internal activities/services.

7 Standard costing and variance analysis

(a) Standard costing

    (i)   Determination of standards

    (ii)   Identification and calculation of sales variances (including quantity and mix), cost variances (including mix and yield): absorption and marginal approaches

    (iii)   Significance and relevance of variances

    (iv)   Operating statements

    (v)   Interpretation and relevance of variance calculations to business performance.

(b) Planning and operational variances.

(c) Behavioural implications of standard costing and variance reporting.

8 Budgeting and budgetary control

(a) Objectives of budgetary planning and control systems including aspects of behavioural implications.

(b) Evaluation of budgetary systems such as fixed and flexible, zero based and incremental, periodic, continuous and activity based.

(c) Development, implementation and co-ordination of budgeting systems: functional, subsidiary and master/principal budgets (including cash budgeting): budget review.

(d) Calculation and cause of variances as aids to controlling performance.

(e) Quantitative aids to budgeting and the concepts of correlation, basic time series analysis (seasonality) and forecasting: use of computer-based models.

(f) Behavioural implications of budgeting and budgetary control.

9 Performance measurement

(a) Measurement of productivity, activity, profitability and quality of service.

(b) Relationship of measure to type of entity and range of measures, both monetary and non-monetary.

(c) Indices to allow for price and performance changes through time.

(d) Evaluating performance against objectives and plans, and identifying areas of concern from the information produced.

(e) The impact of cost centres, revenue centres, profit centres and investment centres on management appraisal.

(f) Difference between business performance and management performance.

(g) Benchmarking.

INTRODUCTION

Excluded topics

The following topics are specifically excluded from the syllabus:

- Calculations involving the derivation of cost of capital in discounting problems. Candidates will always be supplied with an appropriate discount rate.
- Calculations relating to Modigliani and Miller propositions.

Key areas of the syllabus

The core of the syllabus is aimed at developing the skills required in supporting managerial decision making. They reflect the core competencies needed for students to satisfy the aim of the paper identified above. The core areas are:

- Financial management objectives
- Management of working capital
- Sources of finance
- Capital investment appraisal
- Costing systems
- Standard costing and variance analysis
- Budgeting and budgetary control
- Performance management

Paper 2.4

Financial Management and Control

Study Guide

1 THE ECONOMIC ENVIRONMENT 1

Syllabus reference 2e

Macroeconomic Objectives

- Identify and explain the main macro-economic policy targets
- Explain how government economic policy may affect planning and decision-making in business
- Define and explain the role of fiscal, monetary, interest rate and exchange rate policy

Fiscal policy

- Identify the main tools of fiscal policy
- Explain how public expenditure is financed and the meaning of PSBR
- Explain how PSBR and taxation policy interact with other economic indicators
- Identify the implications of fiscal policy for business

2 THE ECONOMIC ENVIRONMENT II

Syllabus reference 2d, 2e, 2f

Monetary, inflation and exchange rate policy

- Identify the main tools of monetary policy
- Identify the factors which influence inflation and exchange rates, including the impact of interest rates
- Identify the implications of monetary, inflation and exchange rate policy for business

Aspects of government intervention and regulation

- Explain the requirement for and the role of competition policy
- Explain the requirements for and the role of official aid intervention
- Explain the requirement for and the role of Green policies
- Identify examples of government intervention and regulation

3 THE NATURE AND SCOPE OF FINANCIAL MANAGEMENT

Syllabus reference 1a, 1b, 1c, 1d, 1e

- Broadly describe the relationship between financial management, management accounting and financial accounting
- Discuss the nature and scope of financial objectives for private sector companies in the context of organisational objectives
- Discuss the role of social and non-financial objectives in private sector companies and identify their financial implications
- Identify objectives (financial and otherwise) in not-for-profit organisations and identify the extent to which they differ from private sector companies
- Discuss the problems of multiple stakeholders in financial management and the consequent multiple objectives and scope for conflict

4 THE FINANCIAL MANAGEMENT FRAMEWORK

Syllabus reference 2a, 2b(i), (ii), 2c, 4a(xi), 5b(i)

- Identify the general role of financial intermediaries
- Explain the role of commercial banks as providers of funds (including the creation of credit)
- Discuss the risk/return trade-off
- Identify the international money and capital markets and outline their operation
- Explain the functions of a stock market and corporate bond market
- Explain the key features of different types of security in terms of the risk/return trade-off
- Outline the Efficient Markets Hypothesis and assess its broad implications for corporate policy and financial management
- Explain the Separation Theorem
- Explain the functions of and identify the links between the money and capital markets

INTRODUCTION

5 MANAGEMENT OF WORKING CAPITAL I

Syllabus reference 3a, 3b, 3c, 3d, 3e, 3f

General issues

- Explain the nature and scope of working capital management
- Distinguish between cash flow and profits
- Explain the requirement for effective working capital management
- Explain the relationship between working capital management and business solvency
- Distinguish the working capital needs of different types of business

Management of stock

- Calculate and interpret stock ratios
- Explain the role of stock in the working capital cycle
- Apply the tools and techniques of stock management including the EOQ model
- Analyse and evaluate the results of stock management techniques

6 MANAGEMENT OF WORKING CAPITAL II

Syllabus reference 3e, 3f

Management of creditors

- Explain the role of creditors in the working capital cycle
- Explain the availability of credit
- Identify the risks of taking increased credit and buying under extended credit terms
- Explain how methods of paying suppliers may influence cash flows of both parties
- Discuss the particular problems of managing overseas accounts payable
- Calculate and interpret creditor ratios
- Apply the tools and techniques of creditor management
- Analyse and evaluate the results of creditor management techniques

Management of debtors

- Explain the role of debtors in the working capital cycle
- Explain how the credit-worthiness of customers may be assessed
- Evaluate the balance of risks and costs of customer default against the profitability of marginal business
- Explain the role of factoring and invoice discounting
- Explain the role of early settlement discounts
- Discuss the particular problems of managing overseas debtors
- Calculate and interpret debtor ratios
- Apply the tools and techniques of debtor management
- Analyse and evaluate the results of debtor management techniques

7 MANAGEMENT OF WORKING CAPITAL III

Syllabus reference 3e, 3f

Management of cash

- Explain the role of cash in the working capital cycle
- Calculate optimal cash balances
- Describe the functions of and evaluate the benefits from centralised cash control and Treasury Management
- Calculate and interpret cash ratios
- Apply the tools and techniques of cash management including the Baumol model and the Miller-Orr model
- Analyse and evaluate the results of cash management techniques

8 SOURCES OF FINANCE I: SMALL AND MEDIUM SIZED ENTERPRISES (SMEs)

Syllabus reference 4a(i), (ii), (v), (vi), (vii), (viii), (ix), (x), 4b, 4c, 4d, 4e(i), (ii), (iii), (iv)

- Explain financing in terms of the risk/return trade-off
- Describe the requirements for finance of SME's (purpose, how much, how long)
- Describe the nature of the financing problem for small businesses in terms of the funding gap, the maturity gap and inadequate security
- Identify the role of risk and the lack of information on small companies to help explain the problem of SME financing
- Explain the role of information provision provided by financial statements
- Describe the particular financing problems of low-earning/high growth companies
- Describe the response of government agencies and

xix

INTRODUCTION

- financial institutions to the SME financing problem
- Explain what other measures may be taken to ease the financial problems of SMEs such as trade creditors, factoring, leasing, hire purchase, AIM listing, business angels and venture capital
- Describe how capital structure decisions in SMEs may differ from larger organisations
- Describe appropriate sources of finance for SMEs
- Calculate and interpret appropriate ratios

9 SOURCE OF FINANCE II: EQUITY FINANCING

Syllabus reference 4a(iii), (iv), 4c, 4d, 4e(i), (ii), (iii), (iv)

- Describe ways in which a company may obtain a stock market listing
- Describe how stock markets operate including AIM
- Explain the requirements of stock market investors in terms of returns on investment
- Calculate, analyse and evaluate appropriate financial ratios (eg EPS, PE ratio, dividend yield, etc)
- Outline and apply the dividend valuation model, including the growth adjustment
- Explain the importance of internally generated funds
- Describe the advantages and disadvantages of rights issues
- Calculate the price of rights
- Explain the purpose and impact of a bonus issue, scrip dividends and stock splits

10 SOURCE OF FINANCE III: DEBT AND NEAR-DEBT FINANCING

Syllabus reference 4a(i), (iii), (v), (vi), (xi), 4b, 4c, 4d, 4e (i), (ii), (iii), (iv)

- Explain the features of different types of preference shares and the reasons for their issue
- Explain the features of different types of long-term straight debt and the reasons for their issue
- Explain the features of convertible debt and warrants and the reasons for their issue
- Broadly describe the reasons for the choice of financing between preference shares, debt and near-debt instruments in terms of the risk/return trade-off
- Assess the effect on EPS of conversion and option rights
- Broadly describe international debt markets and the financing of foreign trade
- Calculate and interpret appropriate ratios

11 SOURCE OF FINANCE IV: THE CAPITAL STRUCTURE DECISION

Syllabus reference 4c, 4d, 4e(i), (ii), (iii), (iv)

- Explain and calculate the level of financing gearing
- Distinguish between operational and financial gearing, and business risk and financial risk
- Outline the effects of gearing on the value of shares, company risk and required return
- Explain how a company may determine its capital structure in terms of interest charges, dividends, risk and redemption requirements
- Explain the role of short term financing in the capital structure decision
- Explain the relationship between the management of working capital and the long term capital structure decision
- Calculate and interpret appropriate ratios

12 INVESTMENT DECISIONS

Syllabus reference 5b(ii), (iii)

- Define and distinguish between capital and revenue expenditure
- Compare and contrast fixed asset investment and working capital investment
- Describe the impact of investment projects on financial statements
- Calculate payback and assess its usefulness as a measure of investment worth
- Calculate ROCE and assess its usefulness as a measure of investment worth

13 INTEREST AND DISCOUNTING

Syllabus reference 5a(i), (iii), (v), (vi)

- Explain the difference between simple and compound interest

- Explain the relationship between inflation and interest rates, distinguishing between nominal and real interest rates, and calculate nominal interest rates
- Explain what is meant by future values and calculate future values, including application of the annuity formula
- Explain what is meant by discounting, and calculate present values, including the application of the annuity and perpetuity formula, and the use of present value and annuity tables
- Explain the importance of the time value of money

14 INVESTMENT APPRAISAL USING DCF METHODS

Syllabus reference 5a(ii), (iv), 5b(ii), (iii), (iv), (v), (viii)

- Explain the role of the cost of capital in appraising investments
- Identify and evaluate relevant cash flows of potential investments
- Calculate present values to derive the NPV and IRR measures of investment worth
- Explain the superiority of DCF methods over payback and ROCE
- Assess the merits of IRR and NPV
- Apply DCF methods to asset replacement decisions

15 PROJECT APPRAISAL ALLOWING FOR INFLATION AND TAXATION

Syllabus reference 5b

Inflation

- Distinguish general inflation from specific price increases and assess their impact on cash flows
- Evaluate capital investment projects on a real terms basis
- Evaluate capital investment projects on a nominal terms basis

Taxation

- Calculate the effect of capital allowances and Corporation Tax on project cash flows
- Evaluate the profitability of capital investment projects on a post-tax basis

16 PROJECT APPRAISAL ALLOWING FOR RISK

Syllabus reference 5b

- Distinguish between risk and uncertainty
- Identify the sources of risk affecting project profitability
- Evaluate the sensitivity of project NPV to changes in key variables
- Apply the probability approach to calculating expected NPV of a project and the associated standard deviation
- Explain the role of simulation in generating a probability distribution for the NPV of a project
- Identify risk reduction strategies for projects
- Evaluate the usefulness of risk assessment methods

17 CAPITAL RATIONING

Syllabus reference 5b(vi)

- Distinguish hard and soft capital rationing
- Apply profitability index techniques for single period divisible projects
- Evaluate projects involving single and multi-period capital rationing

18 LEASING DECISIONS

Syllabus reference 5b(vii)

- Distinguish between operating and finance leases
- Apply DCF methods to projects involving buy or lease problems
- Assess the relative advantages and disadvantages of different types of lease
- Describe the impact of leasing on company gearing

19 COSTING SYSTEMS AND TECHNIQUES

Syllabus reference 6a, 6b, 6c, 6d, 6e

- Outline and distinguish between the nature and scope of management accounting and the role of costing in meeting the needs of management
- Describe the purpose of costing as an aid to planning, monitoring and controlling business activity

INTRODUCTION

- Different approaches to costing
  - Marginal costing and absorption costing
  - Service costing
  - Theory of constraints and throughput accounting
  - Activity based costing; use of cost drivers and activities
  - Life cycle costing
  - Target costing
- Describe the costing information requirements and limitations in not-for-profit organisations and small entities
- Broadly outline the behavioural implications of different costing approaches including performance evaluation
- Explain the potential for different costing approaches to influence profit reporting and the pricing of products and internal services
- Explain the role of costing systems in decision making

20 STANDARD COSTING I

Syllabus reference 7a(i), (ii), (iii), (iv), 7c, 8d

- Explain the uses of standard costs and the methods by which they are derived and subsequently reviewed
- Calculate and evaluate capacity limitations when setting standards
- Describe the types of standard (ideal, attainable, current and basic), and their behavioural implications

- Calculate basic labour, material, overhead (variable and fixed) and sales variances, including problems of labour idle time
- Explain the reasons for variances
- Assess appropriate management action arising from the variances identified

21 STANDARD COSTING II

Syllabus reference 7a(ii), (iii), (iv), (v), 7b, 8d

- Prepare reconciliations using operating statements which
  - reconcile budgeted and actual profit figures, and/or
  - reconcile the actual sales less the standard cost of sales with the actual profit
- Calculate and explain operational and planning variances
- Demonstrate how absorption and marginal approaches can be used in standard costing
- Calculate mix and yield variances for materials
- Calculate mix and quantity variances for sales
- Demonstrate an understanding of the inter-relationship between variances
- Explain the reasons for variances
- Assess appropriate management action arising from the variances identified

22 BUDGET PLANNING AND CONTROL I

Syllabus reference 8a, 8c

- Identify the purposes of budgetary planning and control systems
- Describe the planning and control cycle, and the control process
- Explain the implications of controllability for responsibility reporting
- Prepare, review and explain a budget preparation timetable
- Prepare and evaluate functional, subsidiary and master budgets, including cash budgeting
- Explain the processes involved with the development and implementation of budgets
- Explain the process of participation in budget setting and how this can address motivational problems

23 BUDGET PLANNING AND CONTROL II

Syllabus reference 8b, 8f

- Prepare and evaluate fixed and flexible budgets and evaluate the resulting variances
- Prepare flexed budgets when standard fixed overhead absorption is employed
- Assess the behavioural implications of budget control and performance evaluation, including participation in budget setting

24 BUDGET PLANNING AND CONTROL II

Syllabus reference 8b

- Describe and evaluate the main features of zero based budgeting systems
- Describe the areas/organisations in which zero based budgeting may be applied
- Describe and evaluate incremental budgeting and discuss the differences with zero based budgeting
- Describe and evaluate periodic and continuous budgeting systems

25 QUANTITATIVE AIDS TO BUDGETING

Syllabus reference 8e

- Describe and apply the techniques of
  - high low method
  - least squares regression
  - scatter diagrams and correlation
  - forecasting with least squares regression
  - time series to identify trends and seasonality
  - forecasting with time series
- Evaluate the results of quantitative aids

26 INDICES

Syllabus reference 9c

- Explain the purpose of index numbers, and calculate and interpret simple index numbers for one or more variables
- Deflate time-related data using an index
- Construct a chained index series
- Explain the term 'average index', distinguishing between simple and weighted averages
- Calculate Laspeyres and Paasche price and quantity indices
- Describe the relative merits of Laspeyres and Paasche indices

27 PERFORMANCE MEASUREMENT

Syllabus reference 9a, 9b, 9c, 9d, 9e, 9f, 9g

- Outline the essential features of responsibility accounting for various types of entity
- Describe the range of management performance measures available for various types of entity
- Calculate and explain the concepts of return on investment and residual income
- Explain and give examples of appropriate non-monetary performance measures
- Describe the various types of responsibility centre and the impact of these on management appraisal
- Discuss the potential conflict in the use of a measure for both business and management performance
- Analyse the application of financial performance measures including cost, profit, return on capital employed
- Assess and illustrate the measurement of profitability, activity and productivity
- Discuss the measurement of quality and service
- Identify areas of concern from information supplies and performance measures calculated
- Describe the features of benchmarking and its application to performance appraisal

INTRODUCTION

The exam paper

The examination is a **three hour paper** in **two sections**. Financial management issues will always, but not exclusively, be examined in Section A. The Section A question will typically be a scenario based question. Most of the Section B questions will contain a mix of computation and discursive elements although it is intended that at least one question will be entirely discursive. The balance between computation and discursive elements will remain largely constant from one examination to the next.

		Number of Marks
Section A:	One compulsory scenario-based question	50
Section B:	Choice of 2 from 4 questions (25 marks each)	50
		100

Additional information

Present value and annuity tables will be provided in the examination. The Study Guide provides more detailed guidance on the syllabus.

The Study Guide provides more detailed guidance on the syllabus. Examinable documents are listed in the 'Exam Notes' section of the *Students' Newsletter*.

Analysis of past papers

Note: The past papers include certain topics that are no longer in the syllabus.

December 2005

Section A

1   Investment appraisal, report on debt financing, calculation of standard contribution and standard profit

Section B

2   Responsibility centres, return on investment and residual income
3   Activity-based costing, and comparison with absorption costing
4   Lease or purchase using investment appraisal, operating and finance leases, bank borrowing
5   Cash budgets, financing, Baumol cash model

June 2005

Section A

1   Investment appraisal, financing, hedging, bills of exchange

Section B

2   Budgeting (zero based budgets, activity based budgets), not for profit organisations
3   Standard costing, variance analysis
4   Ratio analysis, shareholder return, management remuneration
5   Stock management, EOQ, JIT

December 2004

Section A

1 Planning and operational variances; equivalent annual cost and investment decision; net present value calculation; return on capital employed (ROCE); conflict between corporate objectives; lifestyle and target costing.

Section B

2 Budgeting and variance analysis
3 Rights issues; earnings per share; redemption of debentures; price/earnings ratio; debt/ equity ratio
4 Activity based costing; measurement of performance
5 Investment appraisal; risk and uncertainty; sensitivity analysis; payback period

June 2004

Section A

1 Maximisation of present value of contribution; internal rate of return; return on capital employed; risk and uncertainty in investment appraisal; sources of finance

Section B

2 Rate of interest charged on bank loans; yield curve; long and short term finance; cash operating cycle
3 Activity based costing
4 Preparation of forecast profit and loss account; financial and operational gearing; interest cost; earnings per share; business and financial risk
5 Planning and operational variances; direct labour and direct material variances; investigation of variances

December 2003

Section A

1 Overtrading; debtor management; lease or buy; pricing

Section B

2 Production and cash budgets; periodic and continuous budgeting; budgetary slack
3 Capital rationing; relevant cash flows
4 Monopoly; equity and debt finance
5 Variance analysis; operating statement; motivational effect of standards

June 2003

Section A

1 Net present value; financing of investment; performance analysis

Section B

2 Trend analysis; top-down and bottom-up planning
3 Early payment discounts; financing of working capital; improvement of working capital management
4 Market efficiency; interest rates; value for money; maximisation of shareholder wealth
5 Limiting factor; make-or-buy; marginal costing

INTRODUCTION

December 2002

Section A

1 Cash budgets; just-in-time stock management; financing mix; working capital management

Section B

2 Stakeholders; corporate governance
3 Operating statements; budgets; variances; marginal costing
4 Lease or buy; capital rationing
5 Absorption costing and activity based costing

June 2002

Section A

1 Present value; investment appraisal; demand forecast; regression analysis

Section B

2 Zero-based budgeting; employee participation in budget setting
3 Convertible debentures; intermediation
4 Process costing; service costing
5 Forecast profit and loss account; cash shortage; objectives

December 2001

Section A

1 Net present value; sensitivity analysis; business risk

Section B

2 Standard costing; non-financial objectives
3 Decision making involving opportunity costs; finance for small to medium-size enterprises
4 Working capital funding; factoring; credit control
5 Costing in a not-for-profit organisation

Pilot paper

Section A

1 Working capital management; cash budgeting; cash and treasury management

Section B

2 Assessment of growth and liquidity; sources of finance for small business
3 Replacement of assets; limitations of NPV
4 Basic and more complex variance analysis
5 Activity based costing

Oxford Brookes BSc (Hons) in Applied Accounting

The standard required of candidates completing Part 2 is that required in the final year of a UK degree. Students completing Parts 1 and 2 will have satisfied the examination requirement for an honours degree in Applied Accounting, awarded by Oxford Brookes University.

To achieve the degree, you must also submit two pieces of work based on a **Research and Analysis Project.**

- A 5,000 word **Report** on your chosen topic, which demonstrates that you have acquired the necessary research, analytical and IT skills.

- A 1,500 word **Key Skills Statement**, indicating how you have developed your interpersonal and communication skills.

BPP was selected by the ACCA and Oxford Brookes University to produce the official text *Success in your Research and Analysis Project* to support students in this task. The book pays particular attention to key skills not covered in the professional examinations.

BPP also offers courses and mentoring services.

For further information, please see BPP's website: www.bpp.com/bsc

ACCA professional development requirements

Soon, you will possess a professional qualification. You know its value by the effort you have put in. To uphold the prestige of the qualification, ACCA, with the other professional bodies that form the International Federation of Accountants (IFAC), requires its members to undertake continuous professional development (CPD). This requirement applies to all members, not just those with a practising certificate. Happily, BPP Professional Education is here to support you in your professional development with materials, courses and qualifications.

> For further information, please see ACCA's website: www.accaglobal.com

Professional development with BPP

You do not have to do exams for professional development (PD) – but you need relevant technical updating and you may also benefit from other work-related training. BPP can provide you with both. Visit our professional development website, www.bpp.com/pd for details of our PD courses in accounting, law, general business skills and other important areas. Offering defined hours of structured CPD, and delivered by top professionals throughout the year and in many locations, our courses are designed to fit around your busy work schedule. Our unique PD passport will give you access to these PD services at an attractive discount.

> For further information, please see BPP's website: www.bpp.com/pd

Master of Business Administration (MBA)

ACCA and Oxford Brookes University, a leading UK university, have worked together on an MBA programme. The MBA, accredited by AMBA (the Association of MBAs) lasts 21 months for ACCA members, and is taught by distance learning with online seminars delivered to a global student base over the Internet. BPP provides the user-friendly materials. As an ACCA member, you will receive credits towards this MBA and you can begin your studies when you have completed your ACCA professional exams. Flexibility, global reach and value for money underpin a high quality learning experience.

The qualification features an introductory module (*Foundations of Management*). Other modules include *Global Business Strategy*, *Managing Self Development*, and *Organisational Change and Transformation*.

Research Methods are also taught, as they underpin the **research dissertation**.

> For further information, please visit: www.accaglobal.com, www.brookes.ac.uk or www.bpp.com/mba

Diploma in International Financial Reporting

The ACCA's Diploma in International Financial Reporting is designed for those whose country-specific accounting knowledge needs to be supplemented by knowledge of international accounting standards. BPP offers books and courses in this useful qualification – it also earns you valuable CPD points.

> For further information, please see ACCA's website: www.accaglobal.com and BPP's website: www.bpp.com/dipifr

Tax and financial services

If you are interested in tax, BPP offers courses for the ATT (tax technician) and CTA (Chartered Tax Adviser, formerly ATII) qualifications. You can also buy our user-friendly CTA texts to keep up-to-date with tax practice.

> For further information, please see BPP's website: www.bpp.com/att and www.bpp.com/cta

If your role involves selling financial services products, such as pensions, or offering investment advice, BPP provides learning materials and training for relevant qualifications. BPP also offers training for specialist financial markets qualifications (eg CFA®) and insolvency.

> For further information, please see BPP's website: www.bpp.com/financialadvisers

Other business qualifications

BPP supports many business disciplines, such as market research, marketing, human resources management and law. We are the official provider of distance learning programmes for the Market Research Society. We train for the Chartered Institute of Personnel and Development qualification, with a number of other supporting qualifications in training and personnel management. BPP's law school is an industry leader.

> Visit www.bpp.com for further details of all that we can offer you. BPP's personalised online information service, My BPP, will help you keep track of the details you submit to BPP.

INTRODUCTION

Syllabus mindmap

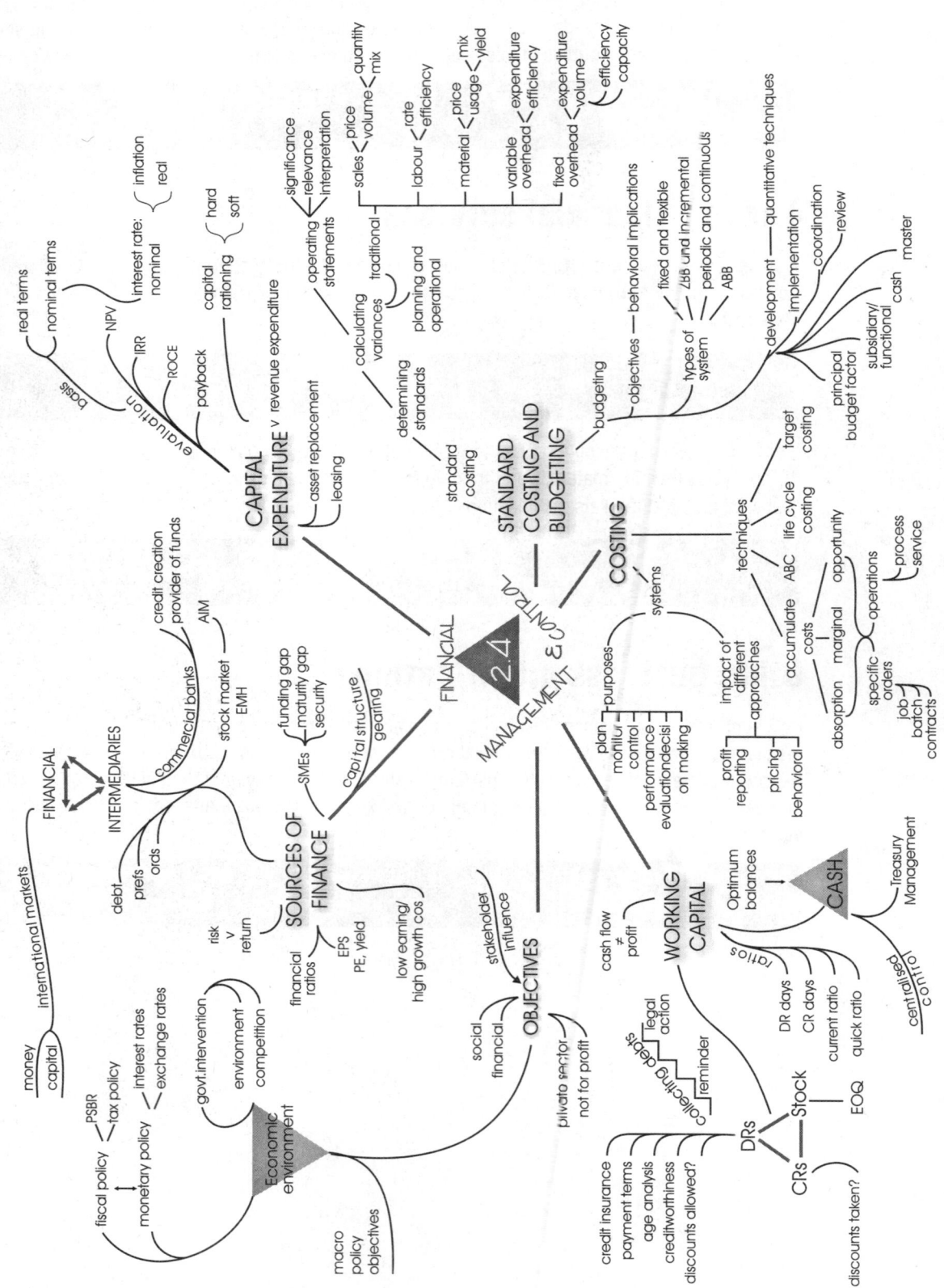

Part A
Costing systems and techniques

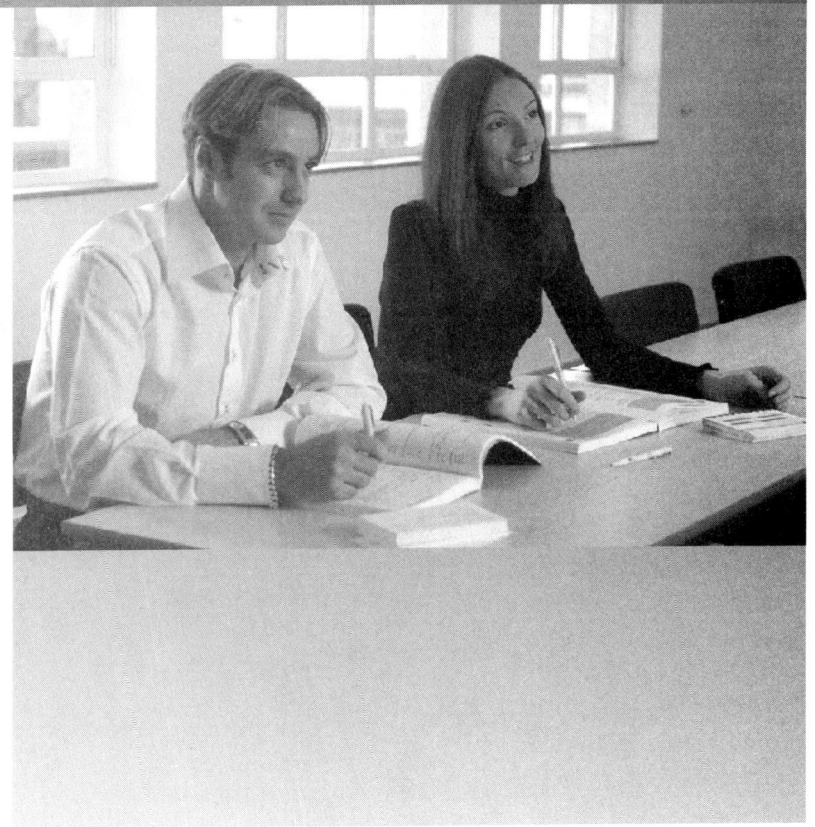

Cost and management accounting

Topic list	Syllabus reference
1 Management accounting and management	6(a)
2 Management accounting	6(a)
3 Cost accounting	6(a)
4 Costing	6(a)

Introduction

Welcome to Financial Management and Control. As you will already be aware if you have read through the introduction to this Study Text (and if you have not, you are strongly advised to do so before going any further), *Financial Management and Control* examines two related subjects, **management accounting** and **financial management**. We will be studying management accounting in the first 13 chapters of this Study Text, financial management being the subject of the remaining part of the text.

This chapter serves as an introduction both to management accounting and the role of the management accountant.

In the following chapters we will be looking at the methods and techniques employed by the management accountant to fulfil that role.

PART A COSTING SYSTEMS AND TECHNIQUES

Study guide

Section 19 – Costing systems and techniques

- Outline and distinguish between the nature and scope of management accounting and the role of costing in meeting the needs of management
- Describe the purpose of costing as an aid to planning, monitoring and controlling business activity
- Explain the role of costing systems in decision making

Exam guide

This chapter serves as an introduction and framework for the remainder of your study of management accounting, but you could get a discursive Section B question on the role of management accounting in a particular type of organisation, say.

The issues covered in this chapter are useful background to the Oxford Brookes degree Research and Analysis Project Topic 10, which requires you to analyse how management accounting techniques are used to support decision making in organisations.

1 Management accounting and management

FAST FORWARD

> The management accountant is involved in the management of a business, ie **planning, controlling, organising, motivating and decision-making.**

1.1 The role of management

Have you ever wondered what those elevated beings do? You know who I mean. Elevated beings. Managers. So, what do they do? Difficult question if you are under their control. Easier, of course, if you just happen to be one of them.

If you are under their control you may think managers take long expensive lunches, have long exotic holidays, make long personal telephone calls, do little work, make little effort and treat you with little more than contempt. But if you are a manager, you probably think you work very hard and nobody who works for you works very hard at all.

If you are having trouble defining the role of management, think about your management role. 'What role?', you may be thinking. Well, we are all managers of our lives. So what should we do to be effective managers of our lives?

1.2 You as a manager

Imagine your normal working day. There is little point in waking up each weekday and just hoping that you will find some washed and ironed clothes in your wardrobe, that some milk will have magically appeared in your fridge, that a bus which might happen to pass will get you to the office on time or that you will be able to fly off to the Caribbean on holiday. **You have to plan** for these things. They don't just happen. You have to plan to ensure that you have the resources (milk, ironed clothes, transport and cash) to enable you to live.

What else do you do while managing your daily life? How many of us can afford to jump in a helicopter to go to work? Most of us are stuck with the bus, tube, train or car. What would happen if you decided to be extremely extravagant and chartered a helicopter every morning to take you to work. Your dream holiday to the Caribbean might then be out of the window. A lack of control over spending means that plans you might have made (for a holiday to the Caribbean) never come to fruition. So **you have to control what you do** to ensure that you can stick to your plans.

Suppose that you share a house with three other friends. What would happen if you made no decision as to who would do the cleaning, who would clean the toilet and who would put the bin bags out for the dustmen to collect. There would be chaos! If you want to be able to walk around your home barefoot without worrying about what you might step in, **you need to organise yourself and others.**

Imagine you really fancy a few drinks in the pub after work. Your work colleagues are totally apathetic about the idea. They would rather go home and watch Coronation Street. How do you get them to do what you want them to do? You entice them with thoughts of good company, tomato juice and packets of crisps. You attempt to make them see that it really would be much better for them to accompany you to the pub than to slump in front of the television. In short **you motivate them**.

There is one common activity running through the various aspects of managing your life, however. You have to decide what mode of transport to take to work, where to go on holiday, who cleans the toilet and who washes up and what drink to have in the pub. A great part of managing your life obviously involves making decisions. Indeed, **it is difficult to plan, control, organise or motivate without making decisions**.

What does managing your life therefore involve?

- Planning
- Controlling
- Motivating
- Organising
- Decision making

This is exactly what those elevated beings have to do to manage you, your organisation's products, your organisation's financial position and your organisation's public image.

(a) **Planning**

Management have to **plan for both the short term and the long term**. A long-range plan is necessary in order to anticipate any future needs or opportunities that require action to be taken either now or in the near future. Management should constantly be **thinking ahead**. They should **never be surprised by any gradual developments**. The organisation's long-term objectives (such as building a new factory) are converted into a succession of short-term plans of action in the form of annual budgets.

(b) **Controlling**

Control enables management to see whether the organisation's long-term objectives are achievable and involves **comparing actual performance with the short-term plans** so that deviations from these short-term plans can be identified and corrective action taken to ensure that the long-term objectives are possible. If it is clear the long-term objectives are not achievable, the objectives can be changed before any serious damage to the company's future occurs.

(c) **Organising**

Organising involves establishing a **framework within which necessary activities can be performed**, designating an individual to be responsible for a particular activity and **defining managers' responsibilities**. It requires a breakdown of the organisation into manageable sections such as departments and the **coordination of activities** in these sections if the organisation's objectives are to be met.

(d) **Motivating**

Managers need to **influence employees to act in such a manner that the employees' objectives and the organisation's objectives are the same.**

(e) **Decision making**

Management is decision taking. Managers of all levels take decisions.

(i) Decisions taken at the **strategic level, set or change the objectives or strategic targets of an organisation**. They include decisions about the selection of products and markets, the required levels of company profitability, the purchase or disposal of major fixed assets and so on.

(ii) **Tactical-level decisions** are concerned with the **efficient and effective use of an organisation's resources** (the '4Ms': men, materials, machines and money). They therefore include setting budgets for sales, production and so on and setting measures of performance by which results can be gauged.

(iii) **Operational-level decisions** are concerned with **ensuring that specific tasks are carried out effectively and efficiently.** They might include decisions concerning the allocation of particular staff to particular tasks or jobs.

1.3 Meeting the needs of management

Just as you manage your life so that you meet your objectives, managers manage the organisation so that the organisation's objectives are achieved. Let us look at how the management accountant can assist the manager to manage.

(a) **Assistance in planning**

The management accountant assists planning **by providing information**. This may be about pricing, product costs or competition. In the short-term planning process of budgeting, the management accountant provides information on past costs and revenues and is deeply involved in the budgeting process itself. He establishes budget procedures, provides a budget timetable, coordinates and ensures the harmonisation of all subsidiary budgets and uses the subsidiary budgets to prepare the master budget.

(b) **Assistance in controlling**

The management accountant **supplies performance reports which compare actual performance with planned performance and which therefore highlight those activities which are not conforming to plan.**

(c) **Assistance in organising**

By **ensuring that the accounting system is tailored to the organisational structure**, the management accountant helps to reinforce the objectives of the organisational framework.

(d) **Assistance in motivating**

Formalised targets are more likely to motivate than vague and uncertain plans. **Budgets prepared by the management accountant should motivate managers and subordinates** to achieve the organisation's objectives. **Performance reports produced by the management accountant** are intended to motivate individuals by communicating performance information in relation to the targets which have been set. As we shall see, however, budgets and performance reports can cause serious behavioural problems and can be demotivating if used without knowledge of the problems which can occur.

(e) **Assistance in decision making**

The **management accountant collects data about the various options available and analyses that data into information so that management can make an informed decision about the most appropriate course of action**. For example, suppose a component that an organisation currently manufactures in-house can now be purchased from a supplier. The management accountant provides information about the various costs and benefits associated with each option so that management can choose whether to buy-in the component or manufacture it in-house.

We will be examining the way in which the management accountant provides this assistance in great detail and so you will have a much fuller understanding of how the management accountant fulfils his role by the time you have completed the text.

> **Question** — Role of managers
>
> Have a chat with some managers in your organisation. What do they do? Do they plan, control, organise, motivate and make decisions? How do they do this? Why do they do this? Are they successful in what they are doing and if not, why not?

2 Management accounting

FAST FORWARD

Management accounting deals principally with the gathering of data from both internal and external sources and analysing, processing, interpreting and communicating the resulting information within the organisation to aid management processes.

Having looked at how management accounting can meet the needs of management, we will now look at the discipline in more general terms.

Key term

Management accounting is the application of the principles of accounting and financial management to create, protect, preserve and increase value so as to deliver that value to the stakeholders of profit and not-for-profit enterprises, both public and private.

Management accounting is an integral part of management, requiring the identification, generation, presentation, interpretation and use of information relevant to:

- Formulating business strategy
- Planning and controlling activities
- Decision-making
- Efficient resource usage
- Performance improvement and value enhancement
- Safeguarding tangible and intangible assets
- Corporate governance and internal control

To assist with management planning, control and decision making, management accounting therefore deals principally with **gathering of data** from both internal and external sources and **analysing, processing, interpreting** and **communicating the resulting information.**

Exam focus point

In the exam you may be asked to describe the role of the management accountant within a particular setting.

PART A   COSTING SYSTEMS AND TECHNIQUES

3 Cost accounting

FAST FORWARD

Cost accounting provides a bank of data for the management accountant to use.

There are many different opinions on the distinction between management accounting and cost accounting.

(a) Drury (*Management and Cost Accounting*) claims that 'Cost accounting is concerned with cost accumulation for stock valuation to meet the requirements of external reporting, whereas management accounting relates to the provision of appropriate information for people within the organisation to help them make better decisions'.

(b) Lucey (*Costing*) states that 'there are similarities between the objectives of both management and cost accounting and indeed in practice there is no true dividing line. In general, management accounting is wider in scope and uses more advanced techniques. However, a fundamental requirement for management accounting is the existence of a sound costing system to provide basic data'.

(c) Horngren, Foster, Datar (*Cost Accounting: A Managerial Emphasis*) are of the opinion that 'Cost accounting provides information for both management accounting and financial accounting. It measures and reports financial and non-financial information that relates to the cost of acquiring or consuming resources by an organisation. Cost accounting includes those parts of management accounting and financial accounting where cost information is collected or analysed'.

There is therefore no right or wrong definition of cost accounting. Here's ours!

Key term

Cost accounting is a management information system which analyses past, present and future data to provide a bank of data for the management accountant to use.

Cost accounting aims **to provide the answers to** the following types of questions.

(a) (i) **What has been the cost** of goods produced or services provided?
    (ii) **What have revenues** been?

Knowing about costs and revenues that are being/have been incurred and earned **enables management** to do the following.

(i) **Assess the profitability** of a product, service or department.
(ii) **Set selling prices** with some regard for the costs of sale.
(iii) Put a **value to stocks of goods** that are still held in store at the end of a period.

(b) **What are the future costs of goods and services** (and operations and so on) likely to be? Costing is an integral part of budgeting (planning) for the future.

(c) **How do actual costs compare with budgeted costs?** If an organisation's revenues and costs turn out to be different from those planned, the differences can be measured and reported. Management can use these reports as a guide to whether corrective or 'control' action is needed to sort out a problem revealed by these differences. This is often referred to as budgetary control.

(d) **What information does management need in order to make sensible decisions about profits and costs?**

(e) **How much has been spent on operations and how much on providing rewards to the providers of financing for those operations?**

We shall consider financing and the cost of financing in the second half of this text. For now you should be aware that the main **financing costs** are **interest on loans and overdrafts** and **dividends**.

> **Exam focus point**
>
> In his report on the June 2003 exam, the examiner commented that many candidates confused operating and financing costs, with some incorrectly stating that there would be a decrease in operating profit because overdraft interest had risen. Remember
>
> Operating profit = (Sales – Operating costs) = Profit *before* interest and tax (also *before* dividends).

4 Costing

> **FAST FORWARD**
>
> **Costing** is the process of determining the costs of products, services or activities.
>
> **Costing systems** must be flexible enough to provide different costs for different purposes.

> **Key term**
>
> **Costing** is the process of determining the costs of products, services or activities.

Given the definition of cost accounting we have adopted above, **use of costing methods** to provide information (such as the estimated cost of job X) is part of **cost accounting. Use of that information** (such as whether or not to proceed with job X given estimated costs) is part of **management accounting.**

In your earlier studies you have seen how to use various costing methods. In this text we will be looking in more detail at how to use those costing methods and considering how to use the resulting information.

> **Exam focus point**
>
> One of the stated aims of the 2.4 syllabus is that you will be able to identify and implement appropriate costing methods. Work through Chapters 1 – 13 of this text and you will!

4.1 The importance of flexibility

The costing systems used by an organisation need to provide information for a **wide variety of purposes** in a **wide range of organisations** (including not-for-profit organisations, covered in Chapter 3).

4.1.1 Flexibility and cost accumulation and profit reporting

In Chapters 2 and 3 we will look at the costing approaches (absorption costing, marginal costing, activity based costing, opportunity costing, life cycle costing, service costing) to accumulating costs and reporting profit and the impact that these can have on the figures produced.

4.1.2 Flexibility and decision making

Management face a wide variety of decisions on an hourly, daily, weekly and monthly basis.

(a) **Routine planning decisions**, for example, budgeting. Budgeting decisions commonly analyse fixed and variable costs, together with revenues, over a one-year period. They are also often concerned with how to make the best use of scarce resources.

(b) **Short-run problem decisions**, typically, unforeseen 'one-off' special decisions of a non-recurring nature, where the costs and benefits are all obtained within a relatively short period. For example, should a contract be accepted or rejected? What price should be quoted in the tender for a contract?

(c) **Investment or disinvestment decisions**, for example should an item of equipment be purchased? Should a department be shut down? Decisions of this nature often have long-term consequences, so that the 'time value of money' must be allowed for, and discounted cash flow techniques applied. We shall consider these decisions in Part G of this text.

(d) **Longer-range decisions**, meaning decisions made once and reviewed infrequently, but which are intended to provide a continuing solution to a continuing or recurring problem. They include decisions about selling and distribution policies (such as whether goods should be sold through middlemen or direct to customers? What type of customer should the sales force attempt to attract? What should the company's discount policies be? Should a new product or service be launched?)

(e) **Control decisions**, for example, should disappointing performance be investigated, given that the benefits expected must exceed the costs from investigation and control?

It should be clear from the examples given that the management accountant will frequently be involved in providing information for business decisions of all kinds. Costing systems therefore need to be sufficiently flexible to provide the required information.

4.1.3 Flexibility and performance evaluation

Performance evaluation entails setting targets, recording actual performance and comparing this to target performance. This sounds straightforward enough, doesn't it? The **identification of appropriate performance measures** to affect the appropriate behavioural response is often **difficult**, however, and **costing systems** are often **unable to provide** the target and actual **information**. For example, if divisional management are appraised using a profit figure which includes non-controllable costs at division level and apportioned group costs and/or the costing system is unable to provide a figure for controllable profit, a negative motivational impact is likely. We consider these issues more fully throughout the text.

What should now be clear is that **costing systems** need to be **flexible** enough to provide **different costs for different purposes**.

Question — Functions

Wilton, Pearce & Co, a medium-sized firm of architects, are about to absorb Butcher & Partners, a similar sized firm. They have engaged you as management accountant. Part of your duties will be to review the cost and management accounting function of the combined practice and to recruit an assistant. You have an appointment with the senior partner to discuss these issues.

Required

Jot down notes to use in tomorrow's meeting which cover the following points.

(a) The functions of cost and management accounting
(b) The personal attributes you would expect the assistant management accountant to possess

Answer

(a) Cost and management accounting involve providing and interpreting internal accounting information for managers to use for the following purposes.

(i) **Planning the organisation's activities in the short, medium and long term**. For example, the management accounting system should provide information which will allow management to plan the future activities of the new, larger business.

(ii) **Controlling the activities of the organisation**. Management will have to learn to control a larger business. They will therefore need control reports so that they can compare actual results against plans or budgets. Action can then be taken to correct any differences between actual and plan and to help the organisation to continue in the direction set out by the plans.

(iii) **Making decisions**. For example, information will be needed for pricing architectural contracts for tendering purposes.

(iv) **Performance appraisal, both financial and non-financial**. For example, information on the percentage of jobs completed on time, percentage of successful tenders and so on should be provided.

(b) (i) Be training for or already possess a professional **qualification** in management accountancy.

(ii) Be highly **numerate**.

(iii) Have excellent knowledge of the cost and management accounting **information requirements** of a large architects' business.

(iv) Be able to critically **appraise the existing systems and information** to ensure their relevance to the future.

(v) Have excellent **communication skills**, particularly because of the uncertainty caused by the changes taking place. He must be able to explain and interpret management accounting information for employees who have little or no financial background.

(vi) Be **flexible** and **self-motivating**. For example he/she must be willing to leave their office desk and visit sites when necessary.

(vii) Possess **management perspective** as well as being technically competent.

Of course you may have thought of completely different points to those noted above. The purpose of this question was to get you thinking about management accounting.

Chapter Roundup

- The management accountant is involved in the management of a business, ie **planning, controlling, organising, motivating and decision-making**.
- **Management accounting** deals principally with the gathering of data from both internal and external sources and analysing, processing, interpreting and communicating the resulting information within the organisation to aid management processes.
- **Cost accounting** provides a bank of data for the management accountant to use.
- **Costing** is the process of determining the costs of products, services or activities.
- **Costing systems** must be flexible enough to provide different costs for different purposes.

PART A COSTING SYSTEMS AND TECHNIQUES

Quick Quiz

1. *Match the type of decision with the appropriate description.*

Reasons		Descriptions	
(a)	Strategic level	(1)	Set or change the objectives of an organisation
(b)	Tactical level	(2)	Ensure that specific tasks are carried out effectively and efficiently
(c)	Operational level	(3)	Concerned with the efficient and effective use of the '4 Ms'

2. Name five management activities with which the management accountant can assist.

3. Should the following tasks be classified as management accounting or cost accounting?

Tasks	Management accounting	Cost accounting
Valuation of stock using absorption costing		
Preparation of budgets		
Analysis of information about various decision options		
Valuation of output of a continuous process		
Setting of standard costs		
Preparation of performance reports		

4. Give six examples of approaches to accumulating costs.

5. Here are some terms you should have encountered in your earlier studies. *Match the term to the definition.*

Terms	Definitions	
Direct cost	(a)	Specific costs of, say, an activity, which would not be incurred if the activity did not exist
Prime cost	(b)	Total of direct costs
Overhead		
Classification by function	(c)	Future cash flow which will be changed as the result of a decision
Fixed cost	(d)	Product produced by an organisation
Variable cost	(e)	Dividing costs into production, administration, selling and distribution, research and development and financing costs
Product cost		
Avoidable cost	(f)	Cost that can be traced in full to whatever is being costed
Controllable cost	(g)	Organisation's departments
Relevant cost	(h)	A cost that varies with the level of output
Cost centre	(i)	A cost that is incurred in the course of making a product but which cannot be traced directly and in full to the product
Cost unit		
	(j)	Cost that is incurred for a particular period of time and which, within certain activity levels, is unaffected by changes in the level of activity
	(k)	Cost identified with goods produced or purchased for resale and initially included in the value of stock
	(l)	Cost which can be influenced by management decisions and actions

6. Give four examples of tasks that management accountants will carry out with the data gathered from different sources.

7. .... is the process of determining the costs of products, activities or services.

8. Give five examples of the decisions faced by managers.

Answers to Quick Quiz

1. (a) (1)
   (b) (3)
   (c) (2)

2. - Planning
   - Controlling
   - Organising
   - Motivating
   - Decision making

3.

Tasks	Management accounting	Cost accounting
Valuation of stock using absorption costing		✓
Preparation of budgets	✓	
Analysis of information about various decision options	✓	
Valuation of output of a continuous process		✓
Setting of standard costs		✓
Preparation of performance reports	✓	

4. - Absorption costing
   - Marginal costing
   - Activity-based costing
   - Opportunity costing
   - Life cycle costing
   - Service costing

5. Direct cost (f)
   Prime cost (b)
   Overhead (i)
   Classification by function (e)
   Fixed cost (j)
   Variable cost (h)
   Product cost (k)
   Avoidable cost (a)
   Controllable cost (l)
   Relevant cost (c)
   Cost centre (g)
   Cost unit (d)

6. - Analysing
   - Processing
   - Interpreting
   - Communicating

7. Costing

8. - Routine planning decisions
   - Short-run problem decisions
   - Investment or divestment decisions
   - Longer-range decisions
   - Control decisions

PART A COSTING SYSTEMS AND TECHNIQUES

Now try the questions below from the Exam Question Bank

Number	Level	Marks	Time
Q1	Examination	25	45 mins

Absorption and marginal costing

Topic list	Syllabus reference
1 The problem of overheads	6(b), (e)
2 A revision of absorption costing	6(b), (e)
3 Overhead apportionment	6(b), (e)
4 Overhead absorption	6(b), (e)
5 Marginal costing	6(b), (e)
6 Reconciling the profit figures given by the two methods	6(b), (e)
7 Absorption costing and marginal costing compared	6(b), (e)

Introduction

As we saw in the previous chapter, cost accounting is used to determine the cost of products, jobs or services (whatever the organisation happens to be involved in). Such costs have to be built up using a process known as **cost accumulation**.

In your earlier studies you will have learnt how to accumulate the various cost elements which make up total cost. If you have forgotten, the diagram of an **absorption costing** cost accumulation system on the following page should jog your memory.

Remember that under a **marginal costing** system the production overhead absorbed would be variable production overhead only.

In this chapter we will be both building on your existing knowledge and seeing how the techniques which you have already learnt can be applied in more complex situations. This is quite a long chapter but much of what we cover will be familiar to you so working through it won't be too arduous.

In Chapter 3 we will be looking at some other techniques for allocating and apportioning costs.

PART A COSTING SYSTEMS AND TECHNIQUES

```
        DIRECT COSTS                      INDIRECT COSTS/
                                             OVERHEADS
    Materials  Labour  Expenses          Production   Non-
                                                      production

                                         Absorbed    Under/over-
                                         overhead    absorbed
                                                     overhead

              PRODUCTION COST

                        TOTAL COST
```

Absorption costing cost accumulation system

Study guide

Section 19 – Costing systems and techniques

- Different approaches to costing – marginal costing and absorption costing

Exam guide

Absorption costing and marginal costing could appear in Section A (with other topics) or in Section B.

A Section B question might cover absorption costing or marginal costing or could ask you to compare and contrast the results of applying both methods. Alternatively they might need to be used as the appropriate cost accumulation methods within a question on another syllabus area.

1 The problem of overheads

FAST FORWARD

> **Indirect costs**, or **overheads**, are costs incurred in making a product or providing a service, but which cannot be traced directly to the product or service. **Absorption costing** is a means of incorporating a fair share of these costs into the cost of a unit of product or service provided.

If a company manufactures a product, the cost of the product will include the cost of the raw materials and components used in it and cost of the labour effort required to make it. These are **direct costs** of the product. The company would, however, incur many other costs in making the product, which are not directly attributable to a single product, but which are incurred generally in the process of manufacturing a large number of product units. These are **indirect costs** or **overheads**. Such costs include the following.

- Factory rent and rates
- Machine depreciation
- Supervision costs
- Heating and lighting

Key terms

> A **direct cost** is a cost that can be traced in full to the product, service or department that is being costed.
>
> An **indirect cost** or **overhead** is a cost that is incurred in the course of making a product, providing a service or running a department, but which cannot be traced directly and in full to the product, service or department.

In some companies, the overheads cost might greatly exceed the direct production costs.

It might seem unreasonable to ignore indirect costs entirely when accumulating the costs of making a product, and yet there **cannot be a completely satisfactory way of sharing out indirect costs** between the many different items of production which benefit from them.

1.1 Using absorption costing to deal with the problem of overheads

Traditionally, the view has been that a fair share of overheads should be added to the cost of units produced. This fair share will **include a portion of all production overhead expenditure** and possibly administration and marketing overheads too. This is the view embodied in the principles of **absorption costing.**

1.1.1 Theoretical justification for using absorption costing

All production overheads are incurred in the production of the organisation's output and so each unit of the product receives some benefit from these costs. Each unit of output should therefore be charged with some of the overhead costs.

1.1.2 Practical reasons for using absorption costing

(a) **Stock valuations**

Stock in hand must be valued for two reasons.

(i) For the closing stock figure in the balance sheet
(ii) For the cost of sales figure in the profit and loss account

The valuation of stocks will affect profitability during a period because of the way in which the cost of sales is calculated.

Cost of goods sold = cost of goods produced + the value of opening stocks
− the value of closing stocks

(b) **Pricing decisions**

Many companies attempt to set selling prices **by calculating the full cost of production or sales** of each product, and then adding a margin for profit. 'Full cost plus pricing' can be particularly useful for companies which do jobbing or contract work, where each job or contract is different, so that a standard unit sales price cannot be fixed. Without using absorption costing, a full cost is difficult to ascertain.

(c) **Establishing the profitability of different products**

This argument in favour of absorption costing states that if a company sells more than one product, it will be difficult to judge **how profitable each individual product is**, unless overhead costs are shared on a fair basis and charged to the cost of sales of each product.

1.1.3 SSAP 9: stock and long-term contracts

Of these three arguments, the problem of valuing stocks is perhaps the most significant. **Absorption costing is recommended in financial accounting** by the *Statement of standard accounting practice* on stocks and long-term contracts (SSAP 9). SSAP 9 deals with financial accounting systems and not with cost accounting systems. The cost accountant is (in theory) free to value stocks by whatever method seems best, but where companies integrate their financial accounting and cost accounting systems into a single system of accounting records, the valuation of closing stocks will be determined by SSAP 9.

SSAP 9 states that costs of all stocks should comprise those costs which have been incurred in the normal course of business in **bringing the product to its 'present location and condition'**. These costs incurred will include all related production overheads, even though these overheads may accrue on a time basis. In other words, in financial accounting, closing stocks should be valued at full factory cost, and it may therefore be convenient and appropriate to value stocks by the same method in the cost accounting system.

1.2 Using marginal costing to deal with the problem of overheads

For many purposes absorption costing is less useful as a costing method than marginal costing. In some situations, **absorption costing can be misleading** in the information it supplies.

Advocates of **marginal costing** take the view that only the variable costs of making and selling a product or service should be identified. **Fixed costs should be dealt with separately** and treated as a cost of the accounting period rather than shared out somehow between units produced. Some overhead costs are, however, variable costs which increase as the total level of activity rises and so the marginal cost of production and sales should include an amount for variable overheads.

2 A revision of absorption costing

FAST FORWARD

Absorption costing is a traditional approach to dealing with overheads, involving three stages: allocation, apportionment and absorption.

Apportionment has two stages, general overhead apportionment and service department cost apportionment.

Key term

Absorption costing is a method of product costing which aims to include in the total cost of a product (unit, job and so on) an appropriate share of an organisation's total overhead, which is generally taken to mean an amount which reflects the amount of time and effort that has gone into producing the product.

You should have covered absorption costing in your earlier studies. We will therefore summarise the simpler points of the topic but will go into some detail on the more complex areas to refresh your memory.

Knowledge brought forward from earlier studies

Absorption costing

- Product costs are built up using absorption costing by a process of **allocation**, **apportionment** and **overhead absorption**.

- **Allocation** is the process by which whole cost items are charged directly to a cost unit or cost centre. **Direct costs** are allocated directly to cost units. **Overheads** clearly identifiable with cost centres are allocated to those cost centres but costs which cannot be identified with one particular cost centre are allocated to general overhead cost centres. The cost of a warehouse security guard would therefore be charged to the warehouse cost centre but heating and lighting costs would be charged to a general overhead cost centre.

- The **first stage of overhead apportionment** involves sharing out (or apportioning) the overheads within **general overhead cost centres** between the other cost centres using a fair basis of apportionment (such as floor area occupied by each cost centre for heating and lighting costs).

- The **second stage of overhead apportionment** is to apportion the costs of **service cost centres** (both directly allocated and apportioned costs) to production cost centres.

- The final stage in absorption costing is the **absorption** into product costs (using overhead absorption rates) of the overheads which have been allocated and apportioned to the production cost centres.

- Costs allocated and apportioned to non-production cost centres are usually deducted from the full cost of production to arrive at the cost of sales.

Question

Cost apportionment

Briefly discuss the type of factors which could affect the choice of the bases an organisation can use to apportion service department costs.

Answer

(a) The type of service being provided
(b) The amount of overhead expenditure involved
(c) The number of departments benefiting from the service
(d) The ability to be able to produce realistic estimates of the usage of the service
(e) The resulting costs and benefits

Question

More cost apportionment

A company is preparing its production overhead budgets and determining the apportionment of those overheads to products. Cost centre expenses and related information have been budgeted as follows.

	Total £	Machine shop A £	Machine shop B £	Assembly £	Canteen £	Maintenance £
Indirect wages	78,560	8,586	9,190	15,674	29,650	15,460
Consumable materials	16,900	6,400	8,700	1,200	600	–
Rent and rates	16,700					
Buildings insurance	2,400					
Power	8,600					
Heat and light	3,400					
Depreciation (machinery)	40,200					
Value of machinery	402,000	201,000	179,000	22,000	–	–
Power usage (%)	100	55	40	3	–	2
Direct labour (hours)	35,000	8,000	6,200	20,800	–	–
Machine usage (hours)	25,200	7,200	18,000	–	–	–
Area (sq ft)	45,000	10,000	12,000	15,000	6,000	2,000

Required

Using the direct apportionment to production departments method and bases of apportionment which you consider most appropriate from the information provided, calculate overhead totals for the three production departments.

Answer

	Total £	A £	B £	Assembly £	Canteen £	Maintenance £	Basis of apportionment
Indirect wages	78,560	8,586	9,190	15,674	29,650	15,460	Actual
Consumable materials	16,900	6,400	8,700	1,200	600	–	Actual
Rent and rates	16,700	3,711	4,453	5,567	2,227	742	Area
Insurance	2,400	533	640	800	320	107	Area
Power	8,600	4,730	3,440	258	–	172	Usage
Heat and light	3,400	756	907	1,133	453	151	Area
Depreciation	40,200	20,100	17,900	2,200	–	–	Val of mach
	166,760	44,816	45,230	26,832	33,250	16,632	
Reallocate	–	7,600	5,890	19,760	(33,250)	–	Direct labour
Reallocate	–	4,752	11,880	–	–	(16,632)	Mach usage
Totals	166,760	57,168	63,000	46,592	–	–	

3 Overhead apportionment

FAST FORWARD

There are three methods of **service department cost apportionment**.

- Direct
- Using algebra
- Repeated distribution method

In Question 2 above, the costs of the canteen were allocated only to production departments, and not to maintenance, even though employees working in maintenance are as likely to use the canteen as anyone else and it is quite possible for the ovens and other machines in the kitchen to require maintenance.

It could therefore be argued that a **fair sharing** of service department costs is not possible unless consideration is given to the work done by each service department for other service department **(reciprocal services) are taken into account.**

For example, suppose a company has two production and two service departments. The following information about activity in the recent costing period is available.

	Production departments		Stores department	Maintenance department
	A	B		
Overhead costs	£10,030	£8,970	£10,000	£8,000
Number of material requisitions	300	500	–	200
Maintenance hours needed	8,000	1,000	1,000	

If service department overheads were apportioned directly to production departments, the apportionment would be as follows.

Service department	Basis of apportionment	Total cost £		A £		B £
Stores	Material requisitions	10,000	(3/8)	3,750	(5/8)	6,250
Maintenance	Maintenance hours	8,000	(8/9)	7,111	(1/9)	889
		18,000		10,861		7,139
Overheads of departments A and B		19,000		10,030		8,970
		37,000		20,891		16,109

Suppose, however, recognition is made of the fact that the stores and maintenance department do work for each other, and the basis of apportionment remains the same.

	Dept A	Dept B	Stores	Maint.
Stores (100%)	30%	50%	–	20%
Maintenance (100%)	80%	10%	10%	–

This may be done using one of the following methods.

(a) **The repeated distribution method**
(b) **The simultaneous equation (algebraic) method**
(c) **The step-wise (elimination) method**

3.1 Repeated distribution method

	Dept A £	Dept B £	Stores £	Maint. £
Overhead costs	10,030	8,970	10,000	8,000
Apportion stores costs * (30%/50%/20%)	3,000	5,000	(10,000)	2,000
			0	10,000
Apportion maintenance costs (80%/10%/10%)	8,000	1,000	1,000	(10,000)
			1,000	0
Repeat: Apportion stores	300	500	(1,000)	200
Repeat: Apportion maintenance	160	20	20	(200)
Repeat: Apportion stores	6	10	(20)	4
Repeat: Apportion maintenance **	4	–	–	(4)
	21,500	15,500	0	0

* The first apportionment could have been the costs of maintenance, rather than stores; there is no difference to the final results.

** When service department costs become small numbers (here £4) the final apportionment is an approximate rounding.

3.2 Simultaneous equation (algebraic) method

(a) Let S be the total stores department overhead for apportionment, after it has been apportioned overhead from Maintenance.

(b) Let M be the total of maintenance department overhead after it has been apportioned overhead from Stores.

We can set up our equations as follows.

$S = 0.1M + £10,000$ (1)
$M = 0.2S + £8,000$ (2)

Multiplying (2) by 5 gives us

$5M = S + £40,000$ (3), which can be rearranged so that
$S = 5M - £40,000$ (4)

Subtracting (1) from (4)

$S = 5M - £40,000$ (4)
$S = 0.1M + £10,000$ (1)
$0 = 4.9M - £50,000$
$M = £50,000/4.9 = £10,204$

Substituting in (1)

$S = 0.1 \times (£10,204) + £10,000 = £11,020$

PART A COSTING SYSTEMS AND TECHNIQUES

These overheads can be apportioned as follows, using the percentages on page 21.

	Dept A £	Dept B £	Stores £	Maintenance £
Overhead costs	10,030	8,970	10,000	8,000
Apportion stores total	3,306	5,510	(11,020)	2,204
Apportion maintenance total	8,164	1,020	1,020	(10,204)
	21,500	15,500	–	–

This is the same result as the one we got using repeated distribution.

3.3 Step-wise (elimination) method

In examination questions you will be told which service department overheads to apportion first. We will start with stores.

	Dept A £	Dept B £	Stores £	Maintenance £
Overhead costs	10,030	8,970	10,000	8,000
Apportion stores (30%/50%/20%)	3,000	5,000	(10,000)	2,000
	13,030	13,970	–	10,000
Apportion maintenance (8/9, 1/9)	8,889	1,111		(10,000)
	21,915	15,081		–

The service department **overheads apportioned first** (stores) **are apportioned across all the other departments**, both production and service. The **other service department's overheads** (maintenance) (which now include an apportionment of those of the stores department) are **apportioned to the production departments only in the ratio of use by the production departments**. In our example the ratio is 80% to 10% or 8:1 or 8/9:1/9 (the denominator of 9 coming from 8 + 1). If the usage percentages had been 30% and 40% (with stores usage at 30%), the ratio would have been 3:4 or 3/7:4/7.

Apportioning service department overheads is only useful if the resulting product costs reflect accurately the amounts expended by service departments. If, however, the apportionment is arbitrary or ill-considered, the absorption of service department costs into product costs may be misleading.

Question — Bases of apportionment

You are the cost accountant of an industrial concern and have been given the following budgeted information regarding the four cost centres within your organisation.

	Dept 1 £	Dept 2 £	Maint. dept. £	Canteen £	Total £
Indirect labour	60,000	70,000	25,000	15,000	170,000
Consumables	12,000	16,000	3,000	10,000	41,000
Heating and lighting					12,000
Rent and rates					18,000
Depreciation					30,000
Supervision					24,000
Power					20,000
					315,000

	Dept 1	Dept 2	Maint. dept.	Canteen	Total
Floor space in sq. metres	10,000	12,000	5,000	3,000	30,000
Book value of machinery (£)	150,000	120,000	20,000	10,000	300,000
Number of employees	40	30	10		80
Kilowatt hours	4,500	4,000	1,000	500	10,000

You are also told that the canteen staff are outside contractors and that departments 1 and 2 are production cost centres and the maintenance department and canteen are service cost centres.

Required

(a) Provide an overhead statement showing the allocation of overheads and apportionment of general overheads to the four cost centres, showing the apportionment bases.

(b) Using the fact that the maintenance department provides 4,000 service hours to department 1, 3,000 service hours to department 2 and 1,000 hours for the canteen, apportion the overheads of the two service departments using the algebraic method.

(c) List the factors which should be considered when choosing bases of apportionment for apportioning the overheads of the service cost centres.

Answer

(a)

	Basis of Apportionment	Dept 1 £	Dept 2 £	Maint. dept £	Canteen £	Total £
Indirect labour	-	60,000	70,000	25,000	15,000	170,000
Consumables	-	12,000	16,000	3,000	10,000	41,000
Heat and light	Space	4,000	4,800	2,000	1,200	12,000
Rent and rates	Space	6,000	7,200	3,000	1,800	18,000
Depreciation	Book value	15,000	12,000	2,000	1,000	30,000
Supervision	Employees	12,000	9,000	3,000	–	24,000
Power	Kilowatt hrs	9,000	8,000	2,000	1,000	20,000
		118,000	127,000	40,000	30,000	315,000

(b) **Let C = canteen overhead including apportioned maintenance overhead.**

Let M = maintenance overhead including apportioned canteen overhead.

$C = 30,000 + \frac{1}{8} M$ (1)

$M = 40,000 + \frac{1}{8} C$ (2)

Re-arrange equation (2) and multiply by 8 to eliminate the fraction and make C the subject

$8(M - 40,000) = C$ (3) (from (2))

We can now substitute equation (1) for the value of C in equation (3), thus eliminating C, leaving M as the only unknown.

$8(M - 40,000) = 30,000 + \frac{1}{8} M$ (4) (sub (1) into (3))

$8M - 320,000 = 30,000 + \frac{1}{8} M$

We solve for M.

$7 \frac{7}{8} M = 350,000$

$M = £44,444$

We substitute the value of M into (1) to solve for C.

$C = 30,000 + \frac{1}{8} (44,444) = £35,556$

	Dept 1 £	Dept 2 £	Maintenance £	Canteen £
Overheads	118,000	127,000	40,000	30,000
Apportion maintenance	22,222	16,666	(44,444)	5,556
Apportion canteen	17,778	13,334	4,444	(35,556)
Total	158,000	157,000	–	–

PART A COSTING SYSTEMS AND TECHNIQUES

(c) (i) Services which the maintenance department and the canteen provide to each other, and to departments 1 and 2.

(ii) Selecting an appropriate basis of apportionment eg space, book value, employees.

(iii) The ability to produce accurate estimates about the usage of the maintenance department and the canteen by each other and by departments 1 and 2.

(iv) The cost of implementing the apportionment as compared with the resulting benefit.

(v) The value of the overhead expenditure incurred by the service and production departments, and how many departments used the service departments.

4 Overhead absorption   12/05

FAST FORWARD

After apportionment, overheads are **absorbed** into products using an appropriate **absorption rate** based on budgeted costs and budgeted activity levels.

Having allocated and/or apportioned all **overheads**, the next stage in absorption costing is to **add them to, or absorb them into**, the cost of production or sales.

4.1 Use of a predetermined absorption rate

Knowledge brought forward from earlier studies

Step 1 The overhead likely to be incurred during the coming year is estimated.

Step 2 The total hours, units or direct costs on which the overhead absorption rates are based (activity levels) are estimated.

Step 3 Absorption rate = estimated overhead ÷ budgeted activity level

4.2 Choosing the appropriate absorption base

Question Absorption bases

List as many possible bases of absorption (or 'overhead recovery rates') which you can think of.

Answer

(a) A percentage of direct materials cost
(b) A percentage of direct labour cost
(c) A percentage of prime cost
(d) A percentage of factory cost (for administration overhead)
(e) A percentage of sales or factory cost (for selling and distribution overhead)
(f) A rate per machine hour
(g) A rate per direct labour hour
(h) A rate per unit

The choice of an absorption basis is a **matter of judgement and common sense**. There are no strict rules or formulae involved. But the basis should realistically reflect the characteristics of a given cost centre, avoid undue anomalies and be 'fair'. The **choice will be significant in determining the cost of individual** products, but the **total cost of production overheads is the budgeted overhead expenditure, no matter what basis of absorption is selected**. It is the relative share of overhead costs borne by individual products and jobs which is affected.

Question — Absorption rates

Using the information in and the results of the question on page 19, determine budgeted overhead absorption rates for each of the production departments using appropriate bases of absorption.

Answer

Machine shop A: £57,168/7,200 = £7.94 per machine hour
Machine shop B: £63,000/18,000 = £3.50 per machine hour
Assembly: £46,592/20,800 = £2.24 per direct labour hour

4.3 Over and under absorption of overheads

FAST FORWARD Under-/over-absorbed overhead occurs when overheads incurred do not equal overheads absorbed.

The rate of overhead absorption is based on estimates (of both numerator and denominator) and it is quite likely that either one or both of the estimates will not agree with what actually occurs. Actual overheads incurred will probably be either greater than or less than overheads absorbed into the cost of production, and so it is almost inevitable that at the end of the accounting year there will have been an over absorption or under absorption of the overhead actually incurred.

- **Over absorption** means that the **overheads charged to the cost of sales are greater than the overheads actually incurred**.
- **Under absorption** means that **insufficient overheads have been included in the cost of sales**.

Suppose that the budgeted overhead in a production department is £80,000 and the budgeted activity is 40,000 direct labour hours, the overhead recovery rate (using a direct labour hour basis) would be £2 per direct labour hour. Actual overheads in the period are, say £84,000 and 45,000 direct labour hours are worked.

	£
Overhead incurred (actual)	84,000
Overhead absorbed (45,000 × £2)	90,000
Over-absorption of overhead	6,000

In this example, the cost of production has been charged with £6,000 more than was actually spent and so the cost that is recorded will be too high. The over-absorbed overhead will be an adjustment to the profit and loss account at the end of the accounting period to reconcile the overheads charged to the actual overhead.

Question — Under and over-absorption

The total production overhead expenditure of the company in the questions above was £176,533 and its actual activity was as follows.

	Machine shop A	Machine shop B	Assembly
Direct labour hours	8,200	6,500	21,900
Machine usage hours	7,300	18,700	–

Required

Using the information in and results of the previous questions, calculate the under– or over-absorption of overheads.

Answer

		£	£
Actual expenditure			176,533
Overhead absorbed			
Machine shop A	7,300 hrs × £7.94	57,962	
Machine shop B	18,700 hrs × £3.50	65,450	
Assembly	21,900 hrs × £2.24	49,056	
			172,468
Under-absorbed overhead			4,065

4.4 The reasons for under-/over-absorbed overhead

The overhead absorption rate is predetermined from budget estimates of overhead cost and activity level. Under or over recovery of overhead will occur in the following circumstances.

- Actual overhead costs are different from budgeted overheads.
- The actual activity level is different from the budgeted activity level.
- Actual overhead costs **and** actual activity level differ from those budgeted.

Question — Over and under-absorption

Elsewhere Ltd has a budgeted production overhead of £180,000 and a budgeted activity of 45,000 machine hours.

Required

Calculate the under-/over-absorbed overhead, and note the reasons for the under-/over-absorption in the following circumstances.

(a) Actual overheads cost £170,000 and 45,000 machine hours were worked.
(b) Actual overheads cost £180,000 and 40,000 machine hours were worked.
(c) Actual overheads cost £170,000 and 40,000 machine hours were worked.

Answer

The overhead recovery rate is £180,000/45,000 = £4 per machine hour.

		£
(a)	Actual overhead	170,000
	Absorbed overhead (45,000 × £4)	180,000
	Over-absorbed overhead	10,000

Reason: Actual and budgeted machine hours are the same but actual overheads cost less than expected.

		£
(b)	Actual overhead	180,000
	Absorbed overhead (40,000 × £4)	160,000
	Under-absorbed overhead	20,000

Reason: Budgeted and actual overhead costs were the same but fewer machine hours were worked than expected.

		£
(c)	Actual overhead	170,000
	Absorbed overhead (40,000 × £4)	160,000
	Under-absorbed overhead	10,000

Reason: A combination of the reasons in (a) and (b).

2: ABSORPTION AND MARGINAL COSTING

Exam focus point

Absorption costing appeared in the first sitting of Paper 2.4. For three marks candidates were asked to briefly assess the reasonableness of particular allocation bases used for fixed and variable overheads.

In December 2002 candidates were asked to assess product profitability under absorption costing and Activity Based Costing (Chapter 3) and evaluate the implications of each approach.

5 Marginal costing   12/05

FAST FORWARD

In **marginal costing**, stocks are valued at variable production cost whereas in absorption costing they are valued at their full production cost.

Key terms

Marginal cost is the cost of one unit of a product/service which could be avoided if that unit were not produced/provided.

Contribution is the difference between sales revenue and variable (marginal) cost of sales.

Marginal costing is an alternative to absorption costing. Only variable costs (marginal costs) are charged as a cost of sales. Fixed costs are treated as period costs and are charged in full against the profit of the period in which they are incurred.

Knowledge brought forward from earlier studies

Marginal costing

- In **marginal costing**, closing **stocks are valued at marginal (variable) production cost** whereas, in **absorption costing**, stocks are **valued at their full production cost** which includes absorbed fixed production overhead.

- If the opening and closing stock levels differ, the **profit reported** for the accounting period **under the two methods** of cost accumulation **will therefore be different**.

- But **in the long run, total profit for a company will be the same** whichever is used because, in the long run, total costs will be the same by either method of accounting. Different accounting conventions merely affect the profit of individual periods.

Question — Absorption and marginal costing

A company makes and sells a single product. At the beginning of period 1, there are no opening stocks of the product, for which the variable production cost is £4 and the sales price £6 per unit. Fixed costs are £2,000 per period, of which £1,500 are fixed production costs. Normal output is 1,500 units per period. In period 1, sales were 1,200 units, production was 1,500 units. In period 2, sales were 1,700 units, production was 1,400 units.

Required

Prepare profit statements for each period and for the two periods in total using both absorption costing and marginal costing.

PART A   COSTING SYSTEMS AND TECHNIQUES

Answer

It is important to notice that although production and sales volumes in each period are different, over the **full period, total production equals sales volume**. The total cost of sales is the same and therefore the **total profit is the same by either method** of accounting. **Differences** in profit in any one period are merely **timing differences** which cancel out over a longer period of time.

(a) **Absorption costing.** The absorption rate for fixed production overhead is £1,500/1,500 units = £1 per unit. The fully absorbed cost per unit = £(4+1) = £5.

		Period 1		Period 2		Total	
		£	£	£	£	£	£
Sales			7,200		10,200		17,400
Production costs							
Variable		6,000		5,600		11,600	
Fixed		1,500		1,400		2,900	
		7,500		7,000		14,500	
Add opening stock b/f	(300×£5)	–		1,500		1,500	
		7,500		8,500		16,000	
Less closing stock c/f	(300×£5)	1,500		–		1,500	
Production cost of sales		6,000		8,500		14,500	
Under-absorbed o/hd		–		100		100	
Total costs			6,000		8,600		14,600
Gross profit			1,200		1,600		2,800
Other costs			(500)		(500)		(1,000)
Net profit			700		1,100		1,800

(b) **Marginal costing**

The marginal cost per unit = £4.

		Period 1		Period 2		Total	
		£	£	£	£	£	£
Sales			7,200		10,200		17,400
Variable production cost		6,000		5,600		11,600	
Add opening stock b/f	(300×£4)	–		1,200		1,200	
		6,000		6,800		12,800	
Less closing stock c/f	(300×£4)	1,200		–		1,200	
Variable prod. cost of sales			4,800		6,800		11,600
Contribution			2,400		3,400		5,800
Fixed costs			2,000		2,000		4,000
Profit			400		1,400		1,800

Question — Marginal and absorption costing

RH Ltd makes and sells one product, which has the following standard production cost.

		£
Direct labour	3 hours at £6 per hour	18
Direct materials	4 kilograms at £7 per kg	28
Production overhead	Variable	3
	Fixed	20
Standard production cost per unit		69

Normal output is 16,000 units per annum. Variable selling, distribution and administration costs are 20 per cent of sales value. Fixed costs are £180,000 per annum. There are no units in finished goods stock at 1 October 20X2. The fixed overhead expenditure is spread evenly throughout the year. The selling price per unit is £140. Production and sales budgets are as follows.

2: ABSORPTION AND MARGINAL COSTING

	Six months ending 31 March 20X3	Six months ending 30 September 20X3
Production	8,500	7,000
Sales	7,000	8,000

Required

Prepare profit statements for each of the six-monthly periods, using the following methods of costing.

(a) Marginal costing
(b) Absorption costing

Answer

(a) **Profit statements for the year ending 30 September 20X3**
Marginal costing basis

	Six months ending 31 March 20X3		Six months ending 30 September 20X3	
	£'000	£'000	£'000	£'000
Sales at £140 per unit		980		1,120
Opening stock			73.5	
Std. variable prod. cost (at £49 per unit)	416.5		343.0	
	416.5		416.5	
Closing stock (W1)	73.5		24.5	
		343		392
		637		728
Variable selling and so on costs		196		224
Contribution		441		504
Fixed costs: production (W2)	160		160	
selling and so on	90		90	
		250		250
Net profit		191		254

(b) **Profit statements for the year ending 30 September 20X3**
Absorption costing basis

	Six months ending 31 March 20X3		Six months ending 30 September 20X3	
	£'000	£'000	£'000	£'000
Sales at £140 per unit		980		1,120
Opening stock			103.5	
Std. cost of prod. (at £69 per unit)	586.5		483.0	
	586.5		586.5	
Closing stock (W1)	103.5		34.5	
	483.0		552.0	
(Over-)/under-absorbed overhead (W3)	(10.0)		20.0	
		473		572
Gross profit		507		548
Selling and so on costs				
Variable	196		224	
Fixed	90		90	
		286		314
Net profit		221		234

PART A COSTING SYSTEMS AND TECHNIQUES

Workings

1

	Six months ending 31 March 20X3	*Six months ending 30 September 20X3*
	Units	Units
Opening stock		1,500
Production	8,500	7,000
	8,500	8,500
Sales	7,000	8,000
Closing stock	1,500	500
Marginal cost valuation (× £49)	£73,500	£24,500
Absorption cost valuation (× £69)	£103,500	£34,500

2 Budgeted fixed production o/hd = 16,000 units × £20 = £320,000 pa = £160,000 per six months

3

	Six months ending 31 March 20X3		*Six months ending 30 September 20X3*	
Normal output (16,000 ÷ 2)	8,000	units	8,000	units
Budgeted output	8,500	units	7,000	units
Difference	500	units	1,000	units
× std. fixed prod. o/hd per unit	× £20		× £20	
(Over-)/under-absorbed overhead	(£10,000)		£20,000	

Exam focus point

> The examiner commented in his report on the June 2003 exam that many answers incorrectly included fixed costs when calculating contribution per unit.

6 Reconciling the profit figures given by the two methods

FAST FORWARD

> If opening and closing stock levels differ profit reported under the two methods will be different.
>
> In the long run, total profit will be the same whatever method is used.

The **difference in profits** reported under the two costing systems is due to the **different stock valuation methods** used.

(a) **If stock levels increase** between the beginning and end of a period, **absorption costing will report the higher profit** because some of the fixed production overhead incurred during the period will be carried forward in closing stock (which reduces cost of sales) to be set against sales revenue in the following period instead of being written off in full against profit in the period concerned.

(b) **If stock levels decrease, absorption costing will report the lower profit** because as well as the fixed overhead incurred, fixed production overhead which had been carried forward in opening stock is released and is also included in cost of sales.

6.1 Example: Reconciling profits

The profits reported for period 1 in the question on page 27 would be reconciled as follows.

	£
Marginal costing profit	400
Adjust for fixed overhead in stock (stock increase of 300 units × £1 per unit)	300
Absorption costing profit	700

Question — Profit reconciliation

Reconcile the profits reported for period 2 of the example in Question 8.

Answer

	£
Marginal costing profit	1,400
Adjust for fixed overhead in stock (stock decrease of 300 units × £1 per unit)	(300)
Absorption costing profit	1,100

7 Absorption costing and marginal costing compared

FAST FORWARD

Marginal costing is more useful for decision-making purposes, but absorption costing is needed for financial reporting purposes to comply with SSAP 9.

Exam focus point

Remember that if opening stock values are greater than closing stock values, marginal costing shows the greater profit.

7.1 Marginal versus absorption costing: reporting to management

We know that the reported profit in any period is likely to differ according to the costing method used, but does one method provide a more reliable guide to management about the organisation's profit position.

With marginal costing, contribution varies in direct proportion to the volume of units sold. Profits will increase as sales volume rises, by the amount of extra contribution earned. Since fixed cost expenditure does not alter, marginal costing gives an accurate picture of how a firm's cash flows and profits are affected by changes in sales volumes.

With absorption costing, in contrast, **there is no clear relationship between profit and sales volume**, and as sales volume rises the total profit will rise by the sum of the gross profit per unit plus the amount of overhead absorbed per unit. Arguably this is a confusing and unsatisfactory method of monitoring profitability.

If sales volumes are the same from period to period, marginal costing reports the same profit each period (given no change in prices or costs). In contrast, using absorption costing, profits can vary with the volume of production, even when the volume of sales is constant. **Using absorption costing there is therefore the possibility of manipulating profit, simply by changing output and stock levels.**

7.2 Example: Manipulating profits

Gloom Ltd budgeted to make and sell 10,000 units of its product in 20X1. The selling price is £10 per unit and the variable cost £4 per unit. Fixed production costs were budgeted at £50,000 for the year. The company uses absorption costing and budgeted an absorption rate of £5 per unit. During 20X1, it became apparent that sales demand would only be 8,000 units. The management, concerned about the apparent effect of the low volume of sales on profits, decided to increase production for the year to 15,000 units. Actual fixed costs were still expected to be £50,000 in spite of the significant increase in production volume.

Required

Calculate the profit at an actual sales volume of 8,000 units, using the following methods.

(a) Absorption costing
(b) Marginal costing

Solution

(a) **Absorption costing**

	£	£
Sales (8,000 × £10)		80,000
Cost of production (15,000 × £9)	135,000	
Less: over-absorbed overhead	(25,000)	
		(110,000)
		(30,000)
Closing stock (7,000 × £9)		63,000
Profit		33,000

(b) **Marginal costing**

	£	£
Sales		80,000
Cost of sales		
Cost of production (15,000 × £4)	60,000	
Closing stock (7,000 × £4)	28,000	
		32,000
Contribution		48,000
Fixed costs		50,000
Loss		(2,000)

The difference in profits of £35,000 is explained by the difference in the increase in stock values (7,000 units × £5 of fixed overhead per unit). With absorption costing, the expected profit will be higher than the original budget of £10,000 (10,000 units × (£10 − 9)) simply because £35,000 of fixed overheads will be carried forward in closing stock values. By producing to absorb overhead rather than to satisfy customers, stock levels will, of course, increase. Unless this stock is sold, however, there may come a point when production has to stop and the inventory has to be sold off at lower prices. Marginal costing would report a contribution of £6 per unit, or £48,000 in total for 8,000 units, which fails to cover the fixed costs of £50,000 by £2,000.

The argument above is not conclusive, however, because **marginal costing is not so useful when sales fluctuate from month to month because of seasonal variations in sales demand**, but production per month is held constant in order to arrange for an even flow of output (and thereby prevent the cost of idle resources in periods of low demand and overtime in periods of high demand).

7.3 Example: Seasonal variations in sales demand

H Ltd budgets to make and sell 3,600 units of its product during 20X2 at a selling price of £5. Production variable costs are £3 per unit and fixed costs for the year are budgeted as £5,400 (divisible equally between the 12 months of the year). Sales demand in the first six months of the year will be only 200 units per month, but monthly demand will double in the second six months. In order to save unnecessary production costs, the company has budgeted to spread production evenly over the year.

Required

Calculate the profits each month using the following costing methods.

(a) Absorption costing
(b) Marginal costing

Solution

(a) **Absorption costing**

The fixed overhead absorption rate is £5,400/3,600 units = £1.50 per unit.

For each of the first six months of the year, profit per month would be as follows.

	£
Sales (200 units × £5)	1,000
Less full cost of sales (200 units × £4.50)	900
	100
Under-/over-absorbed overhead	0
Profit (£0.50 per unit)	100

For each of the second six months of the year, profit per month would be as follows.

	£
Sales (400 units × £5)	2,000
Less full cost of sales (400 units × £4.50)	1,800
	200
Under-/over-absorbed overhead	0
Profit (£0.50 per unit)	200

Total profit for the year would be 3,600 units × £0.50 = £1,800

(b) **Marginal costing**

For each of the first six months of the year, there would be a loss.

	£
Sales (200 units × £5)	1,000
Less variable cost of sales (200 units × £3)	600
Contribution (£2 per unit)	400
Less fixed costs	450
Loss	(50)

For each of the second six months of the year there would be a profit.

	£
Sales (400 units × £5)	2,000
Less variable cost of sales (400 units × £3)	1,200
Contribution (£2 per unit)	800
Less fixed costs	450
Profit	350

Total profit for the year would be £1,800

In this example it might be argued that in view of the deliberate policy of producing goods for stock in the first half of the year, and selling out of stock in the second half absorption costing would provide a better method of reporting profits month by month. At a profit of £0.50 per unit, total monthly profits double when sales double, which would conform to the expectations of the management of H Ltd.

In contrast, marginal costing would report a loss in each of the first six months and a misleadingly large jump into profitability in the second half of the year.

Other **arguments in favour of absorption costing for internal profit reporting** are as follows.

(a) **Marginal costing fails to recognise the importance of working to full capacity**. With absorption costing, the effect of higher production volumes is to reduce unit costs (because the fixed cost per unit is lower) and if sales prices are based on the 'cost-plus' method, the relevance of output capacity to cost/price/sales demand should be clear.

(b) **Selling prices based on marginal costing** might enable the firm to make a contribution on each unit of product it sells, but the **total contribution earned might be insufficient to cover all fixed costs**.

(c) **In the long run, all costs are variable**, and inventory values based on **absorption costing will give recognition to these long-run variable costs**.

There is a further **argument in favour of marginal costing for internal profit reporting: fixed costs** (such as depreciation, rent or salaries) **relate to a period of time and should be charged against the revenues of the period in which they are incurred.**

7.4 Marginal versus absorption costing: external reporting

It **might be argued that absorption costing is preferable** to marginal costing in management accounting, **in order to be consistent with the requirement of SSAP 9** to include production overhead in inventory values in published accounts. This is especially relevant in an integrated accounting system for financial and management accounts.

It is, however, easy for a firm to maintain accounts on a marginal costing basis, and for financial accounts to convert stock values into fully absorbed costs.

7.5 Pricing decisions

Pricing goods on the basis of **marginal costs** plus an **extra mark-up** is a commonly used method of pricing.

The **advantages** of a **marginal cost** plus approach to pricing are as follows.

(a) The mark-up can be **varied**, and so provided that a rigid mark-up is not used, mark-up pricing can be adjusted to reflect demand conditions.

(b) It draws management attention to **contribution** and the effects of **higher or lower sales volume**s on profit. In this way, it helps to create a better awareness of the concepts and implications of marginal costing and breakeven analysis. For example, if a product costs £10 a unit and a mark-up of 150% is added to reach a price of £25 per unit, management will know that every additional £1 of sales revenue would add 60p to contribution and profit.

(c) Mark-up pricing is convenient where there is a **readily identifiable basic variable cost**. Retail industries are the most obvious example, and it is quite common for the prices of goods in shops to be fixed by adding a mark-up (20% or $33^{1}/_{3}$%, say) to the purchase cost.

One of the **drawbacks** to marginal cost plus pricing is that it ignores fixed overheads in the pricing decision, so the price must be high enough to ensure that a profit is made after covering fixed costs.

The main alternative method is **full cost plus pricing**, where the sales price is determined **by calculating the full cost of the product and adding a percentage mark-up for profit**. This method is often used to price contracts or other transactions where separate terms are agreed for each transaction.

Businesses may also wish to know what the **minimum price** is that they can charge. We shall examine this in the context of opportunity costing in the next chapter.

Chapter Roundup

- **Indirect costs**, or **overheads**, are costs incurred in making a product or providing a service, but which cannot be traced directly to the product or service. **Absorption costing** is a means of incorporating a fair share of these costs into the cost of a unit of product or service provided.

- **Absorption costing** is a traditional approach to dealing with overheads, involving three stages: allocation, apportionment and absorption.

- **Apportionment** has two stages, general overhead apportionment and service department cost apportionment.

- There are three methods of **service department cost apportionment**.
    - Direct
    - Using algebra
    - Repeated distribution method

- After apportionment, overheads are **absorbed** into products using an appropriate **absorption rate** based on budgeted costs and budgeted activity levels.

- **Under-/over-absorbed overhead** occurs when overheads incurred do not equal overheads absorbed.

- In **marginal costing**, stocks are valued at variable production cost whereas in absorption costing they are valued at their full production cost.

- If opening and closing stock levels differ **profit reported under the two methods will be different.**

- In the long run, total profit will be the same whatever method is used.

- Marginal costing is more useful for decision-making purposes, but absorption costing is needed for financial reporting purposes to comply with SSAP 9.

PART A   COSTING SYSTEMS AND TECHNIQUES

Quick Quiz

1. How is an overhead absorption rate calculated?

    A   Estimated overhead ÷ actual activity level
    B   Estimated overhead ÷ budgeted activity level
    C   Actual overhead ÷ actual activity level
    D   Actual overhead ÷ budgeted activity level

2. Over absorption means that the overheads charged to the cost of sales are greater than the overheads actually incurred.

    ☐ True

    ☐ False

3. Fill in the blanks in the statements about marginal costing and absorption costing below.

    (a) If stock levels .... between the beginning and end of a period, absorption costing will report the higher profit.

    (b) If stock levels decrease, ... costing will report the lower profit.

4. The overhead cost of service department A is £40,000, while that of B is £25,000. 15% of A's work is for B. 35% of B's work is for A. Which of the following sets of equations could be used to apportion the overhead costs?

    (a)   A = 40,000 − 0.35B   B = 25,000 − 0.15A
    (b)   A = 40,000 − 0.15B   B = 25,000 − 0.35A
    (c)   A = 40,000 + 0.35B   B = 25,000 + 0.15A
    (d)   A = 40,000 + 0.15B   B = 25,000 + 0.35A

5. Fill in the following blanks with either 'marginal' or 'absorption'.

    (a) Using .... costing, profits can be manipulated simply by changing output and stock levels.

    (b) Fixed costs are charged in full against the profit of the period in which they are incurred when .... costing is used.

    (c) .... costing fails to recognise the importance of working to full capacity.

    (d) .... costing could be argued to be preferable to .... costing in management accounting in order to be consistent with the requirements of SSAP9.

    (e) .... costing should not be used when decision-making information is required.

6. Service department Y does 60% of its work for department A, 35% for department B and 5% for service department X. If the step-wise method of apportionment is used, and service department X costs are apportioned first, what proportion of Y's costs are apportioned to A?

7. Under the repeated distribution method, how are service department costs apportioned?

8. Allocation is the process by which whole cost items are charged directly to a cost unit or cost centre.

    ☐ True

    ☐ False

Answers to Quick Quiz

1. B
2. True
3. (a) Increase
   (b) Absorption
4. (c)
5. (a) absorption
   (b) marginal
   (c) marginal
   (d) absorption, marginal
   (e) absorption
6. $60\%/95\% = 12/19$
7. At the first stage, apportioning the costs of one service department to all other departments, and at the next stage apportioning the costs of another service department to all other departments, and repeating the process until the costs of all service departments have been fully apportioned to production departments.
8. True

Now try the questions below from the Exam Question Bank

Number	Level	Marks	Time
Q2	Examination	25	45 mins

Other methods of cost accumulation

Topic list	Syllabus reference
1 Relevant and opportunity costing	6(b), 6(e)
2 Activity based costing	6(b), 6(e)
3 Absorption costing versus ABC	6(b), 6(e)
4 Merits and criticisms of ABC	6(b), 6(e)
5 Life cycle costing	6(b), 6(e)
6 Target costing	6(b), 6(e)
7 Throughput accounting	6(b), 6(e)
8 Service costing	6(b), 6(e)
9 Costing in not-for-profit organisations	6(b), 6(c), 6(e)
10 Service costing for internal services	6(b), 6(e)

Introduction

In this chapter we will be looking at other methods of cost accumulation, firstly for products, then for services.

- **Relevant and opportunity costing** is particularly useful for decision making.
- **Activity based costing** is a modern alternative to absorption costing.
- **Life cycle costing** accumulates costs over a product's life rather than on a periodic basis.

Target costing and throughput accounting, the subjects of Sections 6 and 7, are cost management processes rather than methods of accumulating costs.

In the latter part of the chapter we turn our attention to **service costing** which is concerned with establishing the costs, not of items of production, but of services rendered. It is used by organisations operating in a service industry that wish to cost their services, and by organisations wishing to establish the cost of services carried out by some of their own departments.

PART A COSTING SYSTEMS AND TECHNIQUES

Study guide

Section 19 – Costing systems and techniques

- Different approaches to costing: service costing; theory of constraints and throughput accounting; activity-based costing (use of cost drivers and activities); life cycle costing; target costing
- Explain the potential for different costing approaches to influence profit reporting and the pricing of products and internal services
- Explain the role of costing systems in decision making
- Describe the costing information requirements and limitations in not-for-profit organsiations

Exam guide

There have been whole Section B questions on ABC recently, but it could be examined with other subjects in Section A. The other topics covered in this chapter are likely to be examined with each other or with other topics in either Section A or Section B.

1 Relevant and opportunity costing

FAST FORWARD

Only **relevant costs** are brought into calculations for decision-making purposes. Relevant costs are incremental cash flows occurring as a result of the decision.

The **costs which should be used for decision making** are often referred to as **relevant costs**.

Key term

A **relevant cost** is a future cash flow arising as a direct consequence of a decision.

(a) **Relevant costs are future costs.**

A decision is about the future; it cannot alter what has been done already. A cost that has been incurred in the past is totally irrelevant to the decision.

(b) **Relevant costs are cash flows.**

Costs or charges which do not reflect additional cash spending should be ignored for the purpose of decision making. These include the following.

(i) **Depreciation**, as a fixed overhead incurred.
(ii) **All overheads absorbed**.

(c) **Relevant costs are incremental costs.**

A relevant cost is one which arises as a direct consequence of a decision. Relevant costs are therefore future, incremental cash flows.

(d) **Relevant costs are differential costs.**

When choosing between alternative courses of action, the relevant costs are the ones that will only be incurred by some alternatives. Any costs **incurred by all alternatives**, can be ignored. Be careful however if the business has the alternative of not choosing any of the courses of action, and thus has the choice of doing nothing.

When for example, a business is taking a **make or buy decision,** deciding whether to make a product itself or pay another organisation to make that product, the **relevant costs of making** will be the **variable costs** of production and the fixed costs that would have been saved if the contractor had been used. The monies paid to the contractor will be the relevant costs of the buying option.

1.1 Non-relevant costs

FAST FORWARD

> Non-relevant costs, such as sunk costs, committed costs, notional costs, existing fixed costs and non-cashflows such as depreciation, are excluded from the calculations.

A number of terms are used to describe costs that are **irrelevant for decision making**.

Key term
> A **sunk** cost is a cost which has already been incurred and hence should not be taken account of in decision making.

An **example** of this type of cost is **maintenance**. If the fixed asset has been purchased, maintenance may have been incurred for several years but the cost is a sunk cost, about which nothing can now be done.

Key term
> A **committed cost** is a future cash outflow that will be incurred anyway, whatever decision is taken now about alternative opportunities.

Committed costs may exist because of contracts already entered into by the organisation, which it cannot get out of.

Key term
> A **notional cost** or **imputed cost** is a hypothetical accounting cost to reflect the use of a benefit for which no actual cash expense is incurred.

Examples in cost accounting systems include **notional rent** (such as that charged to a subsidiary of an organisation for the use of accommodation which the organisation owns).

1.2 Fixed and variable costs

Unless you are given an indication to the contrary, you should assume the following.

    (a)   Variable costs will be relevant costs.
    (b)   Fixed costs are irrelevant to a decision.

1.2.1 Attributable fixed costs

There might be occasions when a fixed cost is a relevant cost.

    (a)   **Directly attributable fixed costs** are those costs which, although fixed within a relevant range of activity level, or regarded as fixed because management has set a budgeted expenditure level (for example advertising costs are often treated as fixed), would, in fact, do one of two things.

        (i)   **Increase if certain extra activities were undertaken**

        (ii)   **Decrease/be eliminated entirely if a decision were taken either to reduce the scale of operations or shut down entirely**

    (b)   **General fixed overheads** are those fixed overheads which will be **unaffected** by **decisions to increase or decrease the scale of operations**. An apportioned share of head office charges is an example.

You should appreciate that whereas **directly attributable fixed costs will be relevant** to a decision in hand, **general fixed overheads will not be**.

PART A COSTING SYSTEMS AND TECHNIQUES

1.3 Example: Relevant costs

A company has been making a machine to order for a customer, but the customer has since gone into liquidation, and there is no prospect that any money will be obtained from the winding up of the company. Costs incurred to date in manufacturing the machine are £50,000 and progress payments of £15,000 have been received from the customer prior to the liquidation. The sales department has found another company willing to buy the machine for £34,000 once it has been completed. To complete the work, the following costs would be incurred.

(a) Materials: these have been bought at a cost of £6,000. They have no other use, and if the machine is not finished, they would be sold for scrap for £2,000.

(b) Further labour costs would be £8,000. Labour is in short supply, and if the machine is not finished, the work force would be switched to another job, which would earn £30,000 in revenue, and incur direct costs of £12,000 and absorbed (fixed) overhead of £8,000.

(c) Consultancy fees £4,000. If the work is not completed, the consultant's contract would be cancelled at a cost of £1,500.

(d) General overheads of £8,000 would be added to the cost of the additional work.

Required

Assess whether the new customer's offer should be accepted.

Solution

(a) **Costs incurred in the past, or revenue received in the past are not relevant** because they cannot affect a decision about what is best for the future. Costs incurred to date of £50,000 and revenue received of £15,000 should therefore be ignored.

(b) Similarly, the price paid in the past for the materials is irrelevant. The only relevant cost of materials affecting the decision is the revenue from scrap which would be forgone, £2,000.

(c)
	£
Labour costs required to complete work	8,000
Contribution forgone by losing other work £(30,000 – 12,000)	18,000
Relevant cost of labour	26,000

(d) The **incremental** cost of consultancy from completing the work is the difference between the cost of completing the work and the cost of cancelling the contract (£(4,000 – 1,500) = £2,500).

(e) **Absorbed overhead** is a notional accounting cost and should be **ignored**. Actual overhead incurred is the only overhead cost to consider. General overhead costs (and the absorbed overhead of the alternative work for the labour force) should be ignored.

(f) **Relevant costs** may be summarised as follows.

		£	£
Revenue from completing work			34,000
Relevant costs			
Materials:	scrap foregone	2,000	
Labour:	basic pay	8,000	
	contribution foregone	18,000	
Incremental cost of consultant		2,500	
			30,500
Extra profit to be earned by accepting the completion order			3,500

3: OTHER METHODS OF COST ACCUMULATION

1.4 Opportunity costing

FAST FORWARD

An **opportunity cost** is the value of the benefit sacrificed by not carrying out an alternative course of action.

In a system of cost accumulation using opportunity costing, the costs of resources consumed are valued at their opportunity cost rather than at the amount it actually costs to acquire them.

Key term

The **opportunity cost** is the benefit forgone by choosing one opportunity instead of the next best alternative.

A common feature of both absorption costing and marginal costing is that the costs of the jobs or products or services are built up from the 'purchase' costs of the resources that are used up in making them. For example, suppose that a company manufactures a product at each of two sites, one in London and one in North East England. The factory rental in London is very cheap by London standards, because the company has occupied the premises for many years. The actual rental in London is £40,000 pa, which is exactly the same as for the similar-sized factory in the North East, where a full commercial rental is being paid. The company could sub-let the London factory, if it wished, for £100,000 pa.

(a) If absorption costing were used to cost the output from each factory, the rental cost allocated to production overhead would be £40,000 pa for each factory.

(b) If marginal costing were used instead, the rental cost of £40,000 pa at each factory would be charged as a period cost against profits.

Neither method of costing recognises the opportunity cost of the London factory, which is the revenue that could be earned from sub-letting the factory (but which has been sacrificed in favour of using the factory to make the company's own product). There is an argument that £100,000 should be charged as the cost of the London factory, to reflect the true value to the company of the resource – factory space – that it is using in London.

In a system of cost accumulation using **opportunity costing**, the **costs of resources consumed are valued at their opportunity cost rather than at the amount it actually costs to acquire them**.

(a) **If no alternative use for a resource exists then the opportunity cost is zero.**

(b) **If a resource is not scarce, no sacrifice exists from using the resource and so the opportunity cost is zero.**

In the relevant cost in example 1.3 above the **receipts from scrap** and the **contribution foregone** by losing other work are examples of opportunity costs.

The main argument in favour of opportunity costing is that management are made more aware of how well they are using resources to make products, and whether resources could be used better in other ways.

The main drawback to opportunity costing is a practical one. It is not always easy to recognise alternative uses for certain resources, nor to put an accurate value on opportunity cost. It is only likely to be accurate if resources have an alternative use which can be valued at an external market price, such as factory rental, or staff time in the case of professional firms of accountants and so on.

1.5 Example: Opportunity costing

An information technology consultancy firm has been asked to do an urgent job by a client, for which a price of £2,500 has been offered. The job would require 30 hours' work from one member of staff, who is paid on an hourly basis, at a rate of £20 per hour, but who would normally be employed on work for clients where the charge-out rate is £45 per hour. No other member of staff is able to do the member of staff in question's work.

The job would also require 5 hours of mainframe computer time, which the firm normally charges out to external users at a rate of £50 per hour. Mainframe computer time is currently used 24 hours a day, 7 days a week. Supplies and incidental expenses would be £200.

The opportunity cost of the job would be calculated as follows.

	£
Labour (30 hours × £45)	1,350
Computer time opportunity cost (5 hours × £50)	250
Supplies and expenses	200
	1,800

The opportunity cost of labour and computer time is the normal charge-out rate, of £45 and £50 per hour respectively. A further addition to cost might be added for 'general overhead' depending on the system of costing being used. The opportunity cost of the job shows that the firm would increase profits by accepting the job, by £(2,500 – 1,800) = £700.

1.6 Imputed interest (notional interest)

There is a view that costs should include an interest charge which is based on the opportunity cost of the capital value of resources tied up. For example, if a production department employs assets valued at £100,000, and the company's cost of borrowing is 12% pa, it might be considered appropriate to charge interest of £12,000 pa to the department, to reflect the cost of the assets.

Another reason for charging jobs or services with notional interest is to assist comparability. Suppose that there are two departments, A and B, each producing the same finished product with the same item of machinery. However, A has purchased its machine, whereas B leases its machine. Costs for period 1 are as follows.

	Dept A	Dept B
Output (units)	10,000	10,000
	£	£
Variable costs	10,000	10,000
Depreciation	2,000	–
Lease charge	–	2,500
Other fixed costs	8,000	8,000
	20,000	20,500

The costs in each department are identical, except that Dept A is charged with depreciation (a share of the original capital cost) whereas Dept B's lease charge will include an element for capital cost and an element for the finance or interest charge in the lease. To make the costs of the two departments properly comparable, it could be argued that Dept A ought to be charged a notional amount for interest on the capital value of its machine.

1.7 Opportunity costing and decision making

As we will see later in this Text, opportunity costing must be used in decisions such as investment appraisals.

1.7.1 Minimum pricing

Another area in which opportunity costing can be useful is in determining the **minimum price** that a business should charge for its output. A minimum price is the price that would have to be charged so that the **following costs are just covered.**

- The incremental costs of producing and selling the item
- The opportunity costs of the resources consumed in making and selling the item

A minimum price would leave the business no better or worse off in financial terms than if it did not sell the item. Key features are:

(a) It is based on **relevant costs**.

(b) It is **unlikely that a minimum price would actually be charged** because if it were, it would not provide the business with any incremental profit. However, the minimum price for an item **shows** the following.

(i) **an absolute minimum below which the price should not be set.**

(ii) **The incremental profit that would be obtained from any price that is actually charged in excess of the minimum.**

If there are **no scarce resources and a company has spare capacity, the minimum price of a product is the incremental cost of making it**. Any price in excess of this minimum would provide an incremental contribution towards profit.

If there are scarce resources and a company makes more than one product, minimum prices **must include an allowance for the opportunity cost** of using the scarce resources to make and sell the product (instead of using the resources on the next most profitable product).

2 Activity based costing   12/02, 6/04, 12/04, 06/05, 12/05

FAST FORWARD

An alternative to absorption costing is **activity based costing (ABC).**

ABC involves the identification of the factors **(cost drivers)** which cause the costs of an organisation's major activities. Support overheads are charged to products on the basis of their usage of an activity.

- For costs that vary with production level in the short term, the cost driver will be volume related (labour or machine hours).

- Overheads that vary with some other activity (and not volume of production) should be traced to products using transaction-based cost drivers such as production runs or number of orders received.

2.1 Reasons for the development of ABC

The traditional cost accumulation system of **absorption costing** was developed in a time when most organisations produced only a **narrow range of products** (so that products underwent **similar operations** and consumed **similar proportions of overheads**). And **overhead costs were only a very small fraction of total costs**, direct labour and direct material costs accounting for the largest proportion of the costs. The **benefits** of **more accurate systems for overhead allocation** would probably have been relatively **small**. In addition, **information processing costs were high.**

In **recent** years, however, there has been a **dramatic fall** in the **costs** of **processing information**. And, with the advent of **advanced manufacturing technology (AMT)**, **overheads** are likely to be far **more important** and in fact direct labour may account for as little as 5% of a product's cost. It therefore now appears difficult to justify the use of direct labour or direct material as the basis for absorbing overheads or to believe that errors made in attributing overheads will not be significant.

Many resources are used in **non-volume related support activities**, (which have increased due to AMT) such as setting-up, production scheduling, inspection and data processing. These support activities assist the efficient manufacture of a wide range of products and are **not, in general, affected by changes in production volume**. They tend to **vary in the long term according to the range and complexity** of the products manufactured rather than the volume of output.

The wider the range and the more complex the products, the more support services will be required. Consider, for example, factory X which produces 10,000 units of one product, the Alpha, and factory Y which produces 1,000 units each of ten slightly different versions of the Alpha. Support activity costs in the factory Y are likely to be a lot higher than in factory X but the factories produce an identical number of units. For example, factory X will only need to set-up once whereas Factory Y will have to set-up the production run at least ten times for the ten different products. Factory Y will therefore incur more set-up costs for the same volume of production.

Traditional costing systems, which assume that all products consume all resources in proportion to their production volumes, tend to **allocate too great a proportion of overheads to high volume products** (which cause relatively little diversity and hence use fewer support services) and **too small a proportion of overheads to low volume products** (which cause greater diversity and therefore use more support services). **Activity based costing (ABC)** attempts to overcome this problem.

2.2 Definition of ABC

Key term

> **Activity based costing (ABC)** involves the identification of the factors which cause the costs of an organisation's major activities. Support overheads are charged to products on the basis of their usage of the factor causing the overheads.

The **major ideas** behind activity based costing are as follows.

(a) **Activities cause costs.** Activities include ordering, materials handling, machining, assembly, production scheduling and despatching.

(b) **Producing products creates demand for the activities.**

(c) Costs are **assigned** to a product **on the basis of the product's consumption of the activities.**

2.3 Outline of an ABC system

An ABC system operates as follows.

Step 1 Identify an organisation's major activities.

Step 2 Identify the **factors which determine the size of the costs of an activity/cause the costs of an activity**. These are known as **cost drivers**.

Key term

> A **cost driver** is a factor which causes a change in the cost of an activity.

Look at the following examples.

Costs	Possible cost driver
Ordering costs	Number of orders
Materials handling costs	Number of production runs
Production scheduling costs	Number of production runs
Despatching costs	Number of despatches

Step 3 Collect the **costs associated with each cost driver** into what are known as **cost pools**.

Step 4 Charge costs to products on the basis of their usage of the activity. A product's usage of an activity is measured by the number of the activity's cost driver it generates.

3: OTHER METHODS OF COST ACCUMULATION

Question
Cost driver

Which of the following definitions best describes a cost driver?

A   Any activity which causes an increase in costs
B   A collection of costs associated with a particular activity
C   A cost that varies with production levels
D   Any factor which causes a change in the cost of an activity

Answer

D. Any factor which causes a change in the cost of an activity.

2.4 Cost drivers

For those **costs that vary with production levels in the short term**, ABC uses **volume-related cost drivers** such as labour or machine hours. The cost of oil used as a lubricant on the machines would therefore be added to products on the basis of the number of machine hours, since oil would have to be used for each hour the machine ran.

Kaplan and Cooper argue that long-term variable overhead costs are related to the transactions undertaken by the support departments where the costs are incurred.

(a) **Logistical transactions** are those activities concerned with organising the flow of resources throughout the manufacturing process.

(b) **Balancing transactions** are those activities which ensure that demand for and supply of resources are matched.

(c) **Quality transactions** are those activities which relate to ensuring that production is at the required level of quality.

(d) **Change transactions** are those activities associated with ensuring that customers' requirements (delivery date, changed design etc) are met.

These transactions in the support departments are the appropriate cost drivers to use.

Exam focus point

ABC was the topic of a question in the pilot paper. It has since been examined five more times.

The examiner commented that when asked to *discuss* the advantages and disadvantages of ABC, candidates would not gain full credit by merely listing these. He also commented that statements such as "ABC gives more accurate product cost" raise the question 'more accurate than what?' A full discussion and explanation is expected.

3 Absorption costing versus ABC

The following example illustrates the point that traditional cost accounting techniques result in a misleading and inequitable division of costs between low-volume and high-volume products, and that ABC can provide a more meaningful allocation of costs.

3.1 Example: Activity based costing

Suppose that Cooplan Ltd manufactures four products, W, X, Y and Z. Output and cost data for the period just ended are as follows.

	Output units	Number of production runs in the period	Material cost per unit £	Direct labour hours per unit	Machine hours per unit
W	10	2	20	1	1
X	10	2	80	3	3
Y	100	5	20	1	1
Z	100	5	80	3	3
		14			

Direct labour cost per hour £5

Overhead costs	£
Short run variable costs	3,080
Set-up costs	10,920
Expediting and scheduling costs	9,100
Materials handling costs	7,700
	30,800

Required0

Prepare unit costs for each product using conventional costing and ABC.

Solution

Using a **conventional absorption costing approach** and an absorption rate for overheads based on either direct labour hours or machine hours, the product costs would be as follows.

	W £	X £	Y £	Z £	Total £
Direct material	200	800	2,000	8,000	
Direct labour	50	150	500	1,500	
Overheads *	700	2,100	7,000	21,000	
	950	3,050	9,500	30,500	44,000
Units produced	10	10	100	100	
Cost per unit	£95	£305	£95	£305	

* £30,800 ÷ 440 hours = £70 per direct labour or machine hour.

Using **activity based costing** and assuming that the number of production runs is the cost driver for set-up costs, expediting and scheduling costs and materials handling costs and that machine hours are the cost driver for short-run variable costs, unit costs would be as follows.

	W £	X £	Y £	Z £	Total £
Direct material	200	800	2,000	8,000	
Direct labour	50	150	500	1,500	
Short-run variable overheads (W1)	70	210	700	2,100	
Set-up costs (W2)	1,560	1,560	3,900	3,900	
Expediting, scheduling costs (W3)	1,300	1,300	3,250	3,250	
Materials handling costs (W4)	1,100	1,100	2,750	2,750	
	4,280	5,120	13,100	21,500	44,000
Units produced	10	10	100	100	
Cost per unit	£428	£512	£131	£215	

Workings

1 £3,080 ÷ 440 machine hours = £7 per machine hour
2 £10,920 ÷ 14 production runs = £780 per run
3 £9,100 ÷ 14 production runs = £650 per run
4 £7,700 ÷ 14 production runs = £550 per run

Summary

Product	Conventional costing unit cost £	ABC unit cost £	Difference per unit £	Difference in total £
W	95	428	+ 333	+3,330
X	305	512	+ 207	+2,070
Y	95	131	+ 36	+3,600
Z	305	215	− 90	−9,000

The figures suggest that the **traditional volume-based absorption costing system is flawed**.

(a) It **underallocates overhead costs to low-volume products** (here, W and X) and **over-allocates overheads to higher-volume products** (here Z in particular).

(b) It **underallocates overhead costs to smaller-sized products** (here W and Y with just one hour of work needed per unit) and **over allocates overheads to larger products** (here X and particularly Z).

3.2 ABC versus traditional costing methods

Both traditional absorption costing and ABC systems adopt the two stage allocation process.

3.2.1 Allocation of overheads

ABC establishes **separate cost pools for support activities** such as despatching. As the costs of these activities are assigned directly to products through cost driver rates, **reapportionment of service department costs is avoided**.

3.2.2 Absorption of overheads

The principal difference between the two systems is the way in which overheads are absorbed into products.

(a) **Absorption costing** most commonly uses two **absorption bases** (labour hours and/or machine hours) to charge overheads to products.

(b) **ABC** uses **many cost drivers** as absorption bases (eg. number of orders or despatches).

Absorption rates under **ABC** should therefore be **more closely linked to the causes of overhead costs**.

3.3 Cost drivers

The **principal idea** of ABC is to **focus attention on what causes costs to increase**, ie the **cost drivers**.

(a) The **costs that vary with production volume**, such as power costs, should be traced to products using production **volume-related cost drivers**, such as direct labour hours or direct machine hours.

Overheads which do not **vary** with output but **with some other activity** should be traced to products using **transaction-based cost drivers**, such as number of production runs and number of orders received.

(b) Traditional costing systems allow overheads to be related to products in rather more arbitrary ways producing, it is claimed, less accurate product costs.

PART A COSTING SYSTEMS AND TECHNIQUES

Question — Traditional costing versus ABC

A company manufactures two products, L and M, using the same equipment and similar processes. An extract of the production data for these products in one period is shown below.

	L	M
Quantity produced (units)	5,000	7,000
Direct labour hours per unit	1	2
Machine hours per unit	3	1
Set-ups in the period	10	40
Orders handled in the period	15	60

Overhead costs	£
Relating to machine activity	220,000
Relating to production run set-ups	20,000
Relating to handling of orders	45,000
	285,000

Required

Calculate the production overheads to be absorbed by one unit of each of the products using the following costing methods.

(a) A traditional costing approach using a direct labour hour rate to absorb overheads
(b) An activity based costing approach, using suitable cost drivers to trace overheads to products

Answer

(a) **Traditional costing approach**

	Direct labour hours
Product L = 5,000 units × 1 hour	5,000
Product M = 7,000 units × 2 hours	14,000
	19,000

∴ Overhead absorption rate = $\frac{£285,000}{19,000}$

= £15 per hour

Overhead absorbed would be as follows.

Product L	1 hour × £15 =	£15 per unit
Product M	2 hours × £15 =	£30 per unit

(b) **ABC approach**

		Machine hours
Product L	= 5,000 units × 3 hours	15,000
Product M	= 7,000 units × 1 hour	7,000
		22,000

Using ABC the overhead costs are absorbed according to the **cost drivers**.

	£			
Machine-hour driven costs	220,000	÷	22,000 m/c hours	= £10 per m/c hour
Set-up driven costs	20,000	÷	50 set-ups	= £400 per set-up
Order driven costs	45,000	÷	75 orders	= £600 per order

Overhead costs are therefore as follows.

		Product L £		Product M £
Machine-driven costs	(15,000 hrs × £10)	150,000	(7,000 hrs × £10)	70,000
Set-up costs	(10 × £400)	4,000	(40 × £400)	16,000
Order handling costs	(15 × £600)	9,000	(60 × £600)	36,000
		163,000		122,000
Units produced		5,000		7,000
Overhead cost per unit		£32.60		£17.43

These figures suggest that product M absorbs an unrealistic amount of overhead using a direct labour hour basis. Overhead absorption should be based on the activities which drive the costs, in this case machine hours, the number of production run set-ups and the number of orders handled for each product.

4 Merits and criticisms of ABC

FAST FORWARD

ABC has both advantages and disadvantages, and tends to be more widely used by larger organisations and the service sector.

As you will have discovered when you attempted the question above, there is nothing difficult about ABC. Once the necessary information has been obtained it is similar to traditional absorption costing. This simplicity is part of its appeal. Further merits of ABC are as follows.

(a) The **complexity of manufacturing has increased**, with wider product ranges, shorter product life cycles and more complex production processes. **ABC recognises this complexity with its multiple cost drivers.**

(b) In a more competitive environment, companies must be able to assess product profitability realistically. **ABC facilitates a good understanding of what drives overhead costs**.

(c) In modern manufacturing systems, overhead functions include a lot of non-factory-floor activities such as product design, quality control, production planning and customer services. **ABC is concerned with all overhead costs** and so it takes management accounting beyond its 'traditional' factory floor boundaries.

4.1 Criticisms of ABC

It has been suggested by critics that **activity based costing has some serious flaws.**

(a) Some measure of (arbitrary) cost apportionment may still be required at the cost pooling stage for items like rent, rates and building depreciation.

(b) Can a single cost driver explain the cost behaviour of all items in its associated pool?

(c) Unless costs are caused by an activity that is measurable in quantitative terms and which can be related to production output, cost drivers will not be usable. What drives the cost of the annual external audit, for example?

(d) ABC is sometimes introduced because it is fashionable, not because it will be used by management to provide meaningful product costs or extra information. If management is not going to use ABC information, an absorption costing system may be simpler to operate.

(e) The cost of implementing and maintaining an ABC system can exceed the benefits of improved accuracy.

(f) **Implementing** ABC is often **problematic**. Recent journal articles have highlighted the following issues.

(i) The incorrect belief that ABC can solve all an organisation's problems
(ii) Lack of the correct type of data
(iii) Difficulty in determining appropriate cost drivers

'World wide adoption rates for ABC have peaked at 20 per cent and a declining number of firms are giving it further consideration.' (Tom Kennedy, *Financial Management,* May 2000). Recent UK studies have found ABC usage rates of about 25%, with larger organisations and service sector companies being most likely to use it.

> **Exam focus point**
>
> Questions on activity based costing often require a comparison with more traditional methods, as in the December 2002 question. The implications for the business of each approach is often required.

4.2 Other uses of ABC

The information provided by analysing activities can support the management functions of planning, control and decision making, provided it is used carefully and with full appreciation of its implications.

4.2.1 Planning

Before an ABC system can be implemented, management must analyse the organisation's activities, determine the extent of their occurrence and establish the relationships between activities, products/services and their cost.

The **information database** produced from such an exercise can then be **used as a basis for forward planning and budgeting**. For example, once an organisation has set its budgeted production level, the database can be used to determine the number of times that activities will need to be carried out, thereby establishing necessary departmental staffing and machine levels. Financial budgets can then be drawn up by multiplying the budgeted activity levels by cost per activity.

This activity-based approach may not produce the final budget figures but it can **provide the basis for different possible planning scenarios**.

4.2.2 Control

The information database also provides an **insight into the way in which costs are structured and incurred in service and support departments**. Traditionally it has been difficult to control the costs of such departments because of the lack of relationship between departmental output levels and departmental cost. With ABC, however, it is possible to **control or manage the costs by managing the activities which underlie them** by monitoring a number of key performance measures.

4.2.3 Decision making

Many of ABC's supporters claim that it can assist with decision making in a number of ways.

- **Provides accurate and reliable cost information**
- Establishes a long-run product cost
- Provides data which can be used to evaluate different ways of delivering business.

It is therefore particularly suited to the following types of decision.

- Pricing
- Promoting or discontinuing products or parts of the business
- Redesigning products and developing new products or new ways to do business

Note, however, that an ABC cost is **not a true cost**, it is **simply an average cost** because some costs such as depreciation are still arbitrarily allocated to products. An ABC cost is therefore **not a relevant cost** for all decisions.

The traditional cost behaviour patterns of fixed cost and variable cost are felt by advocates of ABC to be unsuitable for longer-term decisions, when resources are not fixed and changes in the volume or mix of business can be expected to have an impact on the cost of all resources used, not just short-term variable costs. A **five-level hierarchy** has therefore been suggested to facilitate the analysis of costs.

Level	Basis	Cost are dependent on ...	Example
1	Unit	volume of production	Machine power
2	Batch	number of batches	Set-up costs
3	Process	existence of a process	Quality control
4	Product	existence of a product group/line	Product management
5	Facility	existence of a production facility	Rent and rates

As Innes and Mitchell (*Activity Based Costing: A Review with Case Studies*, CIMA 1990) say:

'This analysis of cost highlights the decision level at which each element of cost can be influenced. For example, the reduction of production cost levels will not simply depend on a general reduction in output volumes, but also on reorganising production to perhaps increase *batch* size and reduce batch volume, on eliminating or modifying a *process*, on cutting out or merging product lines or on altering or removing *facility* capacity'.

Raiborn *et al* explain how a product cost is determined using such an analysis.

'Traditionally, accounting has assumed that if costs did not vary until changes in production at the unit level, those costs were fixed rather than variable. Such an assumption is not true. Batch level, product level, and organizational level costs are all variable, but these types of costs vary for reasons other than changes in production volume. For this reason, to determine an accurate estimate of product or service cost, **costs should be accumulated at each successively higher level of costs**. Because unit, batch and product level costs are all related to units of products (merely at different levels), these **costs can be gathered together at the product level to match with the revenues generated by product sales. Organisational level costs**, however, are not product related and, thus, should **only be subtracted in total from net product revenues**.'

Such an analysis provides an alternative method of determining product profitability which may be used for management decision making.

For example, suppose an organisation was deciding whether to withdraw a product. The withdrawal of the product could result in a **reduction in the number of some activities** and hence in a cost saving. This cost saving might **apply to unit level, batch level and product level costs but not to facility level costs**, which represent fixed infrastructure costs which would be incurred anyway.

4.3 Conclusion

The examiner of the equivalent paper to 2.4 under the old syllabus provided a useful conclusion to the ABC debate in a recent article. [Emphasis is BPP's own.]

'It can offer considerable benefits to some companies but a **decision to adopt ABC should not be taken lightly**. The staff time involved in developing and getting the system into operation is conservatively estimated at two person years, costs are at least £100,000 though it depends on the system being implemented and the size of the company.

It requires **serious commitment of resources** and top management support.

It is not a system that the accountant can do in his/her spare time.

Indeed it is **not a system that should focus exclusively on the accountant**. It is common for a project team to develop the ABC system on which the accountant can play a part, but not necessarily a dominating part.

Its **implementation** is not easy but is **made easier by the availability of IT support** within the organisation. Existing IT facilities can make it possible, at little extra cost, to obtain useful cost driver data. There is now a range of PC based packages on which to develop stand alone ABC systems, or they can be integrated with existing systems, though the former seem advisable at the prototype stage.

There are cases of companies claiming significant benefit from adopting ABC (changing the way they do business) but also **examples of companies trying but rejecting the activity-based approach**.

To be effective, cost management must be based on a sound knowledge of an organisation's cost structure, the proportion of its overheads, the degree of competition, its information needs within the organisation, an appreciation of how costs are determined and how they may be influenced. Only after **consideration of these factors can a judgement be made on the potential for an organisation of ABC**.'

Evaluating the Potential of Activity-Based Costing, Mike Tayles, ACCA Students' Newsletter

Exam focus point

As well as being able to establish activity based costs, you must be prepared to answer a discursive question on ABC on, for example, its value in planning, control and decision making.

The June 2004 question required a discussion as to whether information provided was *suitable* for use in ABC analysis.

5 Life cycle costing   12/04

5.1 What are life cycle costs?

FAST FORWARD

Life cycle costing tracks and accumulates costs and revenues attributable to each product over the entire product life cycle.

A product's life cycle costs are incurred **from its design stage through development to market launch, production and sales, and finally to its eventual withdrawal from the market**. The component elements of a product's cost over its life cycle could therefore include the following.

- **Research & development costs**
- The **cost of purchasing any technical data** required
- **Training costs** (including initial operator training and skills updating)
- **Production costs**
- **Distribution costs**
- **Marketing costs**
- **Inventory costs** (holding spare parts, warehousing and so on)
- **Retirement and disposal costs**

Life cycle costs can apply to services, customers and projects as well as to physical products.

Traditional cost accumulation systems are based on the financial accounting year and tend to dissect a product's life cycle into a series of 12-month periods. This means that traditional management accounting systems **do not accumulate costs over a product's entire life cycle** and **do not** therefore **assess a product's profitability over its entire life**. Instead they do it on a periodic basis.

Life cycle costing, on the other hand, **tracks and accumulates actual costs and revenues** attributable to each product **over the entire product life cycle.** Hence the total profitability of any given product can be determined.

Key term

> **Life cycle costing** is the accumulation of costs over a product's entire life.

5.2 The product life cycle

FAST FORWARD

> A **product life cycle** can be divided into four phases.
> - Introduction
> - Growth
> - Maturity
> - Decline

Every product goes through a life cycle.

(a) **Introduction**. The product is introduced to the market. Potential customers will be unaware of the product or service, and the organisation may have to spend further on advertising to bring the product or service to the attention of the market.

(b) **Growth**. The product gains a bigger market as demand builds up. Sales revenues increase and the product begins to make a profit.

(c) **Maturity**. Eventually, the growth in demand for the product will slow down and it will enter a period of relative maturity. It will continue to be profitable. The product may be modified or improved, as a means of sustaining its demand.

(d) **Decline**. At some stage, the market will have bought enough of the product and it will therefore reach 'saturation point'. Demand will start to fall. Eventually it will become a loss-maker and this is the time when the organisation should decide to stop selling the product or service.

The level of sales and profits earned over a life cycle can be illustrated diagrammatically as follows.

The horizontal axis measures the duration of **the life cycle**, which **can last** from, say, **18 months to several hundred years.** Children's crazes or fad products have very short lives while some products, such as binoculars (invented in the eighteenth century) can last a very long time.

5.3 Problems with traditional cost accumulation systems

Traditional cost accumulation systems do not tend to relate **research and development costs** to the products that caused them. Instead they **write off** these costs on an annual basis **against** the **revenue** generated by existing products. This makes the existing products seem **less profitable** than they really are. If research and development costs are not related to the causal product the true profitability of that product cannot be assessed.

Traditional cost accumulation systems usually **total all non-production costs** and record them as a **period expense**.

5.4 The value of life cycle costing

With life cycle costing, non-production costs are traced to individual products over complete life cycles.

(a) The total of these costs for each individual product can therefore be reported and compared with revenues generated in the future.

(b) The visibility of such costs is increased.

(c) **Individual product profitability can be better understood** by attributing *all* costs to products.

(d) As a consequence, **more accurate feedback information** is available on the organisation's success or failure in developing new products. In today's competitive environment, where the ability to produce new or updated versions of products is paramount to the survival of an organisation, this information is vital.

6 Target costing 12/04

FAST FORWARD

Target costing involves setting a target cost by subtracting a desired profit margin from a competitive market price.

To compete effectively, organisations must continually redesign their products in order to shorten **product life cycles**. The **planning, development and design stage** of a product is therefore **critical** to an organisation's cost management process. Considering possible **cost reductions at this stage** of a product's life cycle (rather than during the production process) is now one of the most **important** issues facing management accountants in industry.

Here are some examples of **decisions made at the design stage** which **impact on the cost of a product**.

- The number of different components
- Whether the components are standard or not
- The ease of changing over tools

Japanese companies have developed **target costing** as a **response to the problem of controlling and reducing costs over the product life cycle**.

Key terms

Target costing involves setting a target cost by subtracting a desired profit margin from a competitive market price.

Target cost is an estimate of a product cost which is determined by subtracting a desired profit margin from a competitive market price. This target cost may be less than the planned initial product cost but it is expected to be achieved by the time the product reaches the maturity stage of the product life cycle.

Target costing has its **greatest impact at the design stage** because a large percentage of a product's **life cycle costs are determined by decisions made early in its life cycle**.

Exam focus point

In December 2004 eight marks were available for a discussion of how lifecycle costing and target costing may assist the company in question in controlling costs and pricing engineering products.

Case Study

A number of countries, including Holland, Sweden and Norway, have passed or proposed legislation that will require manufacturers of certain goods to take back a product at the end of its life for safe disposal or salvage. The European Commission has also developed proposals to force manufacturers of electrical and electronic goods to take back obsolete products.

Any requirements to take back products will affect post-production costs and ultimately overall projected lifecycle costs. To cut these costs, the design could, for example, make the product easy to dismantle and its raw materials easy to recycle. Or it may be possible to design a product for use over several lifecycles rather than just one. (Xerox has been doing this for several years.)

The technique requires managers to **change** the way they think about the **relationship between cost, price and profit**.

(a) **Traditionally** the approach is to **develop a product, determine the production cost** of that product, **set a selling price**, with a **resulting profit** or loss.

(b) The **target costing approach** is to **develop a product, determine the market selling price and desired profit margin**, with a **resulting cost** which must be achieved.

In 'Product costing/pricing strategy' (*ACCA Students Newsletter*, August 1999), one of the examiners provided a useful summary of the **steps in the implementation of the target costing process**.

Step 1 Determine a product specification of which an adequate sales volume is estimated.

Step 2 Set a selling price at which the organisation will be able to achieve a desired market share.

Step 3 Estimate the required profit based on return on sales or return on investment.

Step 4 Calculate the target cost = target selling price – target profit.

Step 5 Compile an estimated cost for the product based on the anticipated design specification and current cost levels.

Step 6 Calculate cost gap = estimated cost – target cost.

Step 7 Make efforts to close the gap. This is more likely to be successful if efforts are made to 'design out' costs prior to production, rather than to 'control out' costs during the production phase. (See next paragraph.)

Step 8 Negotiate with the customer before making the decision about whether to go ahead with the project.

When a product is first manufactured, its target cost may well be much lower than its currently-attainable cost, which is determined by current technology and processes. Management can then set **benchmarks for improvement** towards the target costs, by improving technologies and processes. Various techniques can be employed.

- Reducing the **number of components**
- Using **standard components** wherever possible
- **Training** staff in more efficient techniques
- Using **different materials**
- Using **cheaper staff**
- Acquiring new, more efficient **technology**
- Cutting out **non-value-added activities** (identified using **activity analysis** etc)

Even if the product can be produced within the target cost the story does not end there. Target costing can be applied throughout the entire life cycle. **Once the product goes into production target costs will therefore gradually be reduced**. These reductions will be **incorporated into the budgeting process**. This means that **cost savings** must be **actively sought** and made **continuously** over the life of the product.

PART A COSTING SYSTEMS AND TECHNIQUES

Case Study

The following comments appeared in an article in the Financial Times. (Emphasis is BPP's.)

'Mercedes-Benz, one of the world's most prestigious and tradition-laden carmakers, has taken its time to wake up to the daunting dimensions of the challenges it faces in the **rapidly-changing world car market** of the 1990s.

The company has accepted that radical changes in the world car market mean that Mercedes-Benz will no longer be able to demand premium prices for its products based on an image of effortless superiority and a content of the ultimate in automotive engineering.

Instead of developing the ultimate car and then charging a correspondingly sky-high price as in the past, Mercedes-Benz is taking the dramatic and radical step of moving to '**target pricing**'. **It will decide what the customer is willing to pay** in a particular product category – priced against its competitors – it will **add its profit margin** and then the real work will begin to **cost every part and component to bring in the vehicle at the target price**.

The following extracts are from an article which appeared three months later.

'The marketing motto for the Mercedes-Benz compact C-class is that it offers customers more car for their money.

It is the first practical example of the group's new pricing policy. The range embodies a principle new to Mercedes which states that **before any work starts a new product will be priced according to what the market will bear and what the company considers an acceptable profit. Then each component and manufacturing process will be costed to ensure the final product is delivered at the target price**.

Under the old system of building the car, adding up the costs and then fixing a price, the C-class would have been **between 15 per cent and 20 per cent dearer** than the 10-year-old outgoing 190 series, Mr Vöhringer said.

Explaining the practical workings of the new system, he explained that project groups for each component and construction process were instructed without exception to increase productivity by between 15 and 25 per cent. And they had to reach their targets in record time.

One result was that development time on the new models was cut to 40 months, about a third less than usual. But the most important effect, according to Mr Vöhringer, has been to **reduce** the **company's cost disadvantages vis-à-vis Japanese competitors in this class from 35 per cent to only 15 per cent**.'

7 Throughput accounting

FAST FORWARD

> **Throughput accounting** is a product management system which aims to maximise throughput, and therefore cash generation from sales, rather than profit. A **just in time (JIT)** environment is operated, with buffer stock kept only when there is a **bottleneck resource**.

7.1 Theory of constraints

The theory of constraints (TOC) is an **approach to production management**. Its key financial concept is to turn materials into sales as quickly as possible, thereby maximising the net cash generated from sales. This is achieved by striving for balance in production processes, and so evenness of production flow is also an important aim.

Key term

> **Theory of constraints (TOC)** is an approach to production management which aims to maximise sales revenue less material and variable overhead cost. It focuses on factors such as bottlenecks which act as constraints to this maximisation.
>
> **Bottleneck resource** or **binding constraint** – an activity which has a lower capacity than preceding or subsequent activities, thereby limiting throughput.

One process will inevitably act as a bottleneck (or limiting factor) and constrain throughput – this is known as the **binding constraint** in TOC terminology. Steps should be taken to remove this by buying more equipment, improving production flow and so on. But ultimately there will always be a binding constraint, unless capacity is far greater than sales demand or all processes are totally in balance, which is unlikely.

Output through the binding constraint should never be delayed or held up otherwise sales will be lost. To avoid this happening a **buffer stock should be built up immediately prior to the bottleneck** or binding constraint. **This is the only stock that the business should hold**, with the exception of possibly a very small amount of finished goods stock and raw materials that are consistent with the JIT approach.

Operations prior to the binding constraint should operate at the same speed as the binding constraint, otherwise work in progress (other than the buffer stock) will be built up. According to TOC, stock costs money in terms of storage space and interest costs, and so **stock is not desirable**.

The overall aim of TOC is to maximise throughput contribution (sales revenue – material cost) while keeping conversion cost (all operating costs except material costs) and investment costs (stock, equipment and so on) to the minimum. A strategy for increasing throughput contribution will only be accepted if conversion and investment costs increase by a lower amount than the increase in contribution.

7.2 Throughput accounting

The concept of throughput accounting has been developed from TOC as an **alternative system of cost and management accounting in a JIT environment.** (A JIT or just in time environment is one where material purchases and production are matched with demand as closely as possible, so that stock levels are minimised. It is discussed further in Chapter 20.)

Key term

> **Throughput accounting (TA)** is an approach to accounting which is largely in sympathy with the JIT philosophy. In essence, TA assumes that a manager has a given set of resources available. These comprise existing buildings, capital equipment and labour force. Using these resources, purchased materials and parts must be processed to generate sales revenue. Given this scenario the most appropriate financial objective to set for doing this is the maximisation of throughput (Goldratt and Cox, 1984) which is defined as: sales revenue *less* direct material cost.
>
> (Tanaka, Yoshikawa, Innes and Mitchell, *Contemporary Cost Management*)

TA for JIT is said to be based on three concepts.

(a) **Concept 1**

In the short run, **most costs in the factory (with the exception of materials costs)** are fixed (the opposite of ABC, which assumes that all costs are variable). These fixed costs include direct labour. It is useful to group all these *costs* together and call them **Total Factory Costs (TFC).**

(b) **Concept 2**

In a JIT environment, all stock is a 'bad thing' and the **ideal inventory level is zero.** Products should not be made unless a customer has ordered them. When goods are made, the factory effectively operates at the rate of the slowest process, and there will be unavoidable idle capacity in other operations.

Work in progress should be **valued at material cost only** until the output is eventually sold, so that no value will be added and no profit earned until the sale takes place. Working on output just to add to work in progress or finished goods stock creates no profit, and so should not be encouraged.

(c) **Concept 3**

Profitability is determined by the rate at which 'money comes in at the door' (that is, sales are made) and, in a JIT environment, this depends on **how quickly goods can be produced to satisfy customer orders**. Since the goal of a profit-orientated organisation is to make money, stock must be sold for that goal to be achieved. The **bottleneck resource slows the process** of making money.

Question — Throughput accounting (1)

How are these concepts a direct contrast to the fundamental principles of conventional cost accounting?

Answer

Conventional cost accounting	Throughput accounting
Stock is an asset.	Stock is not an asset. It is a result of unsynchronised manufacturing and is a barrier to making profit.
Costs can be classified either as direct or indirect.	Such classifications are no longer useful.
Product profitability can be determined by deducting a product cost from selling price.	Profitability is determined by the rate at which money is earned.
Profit can be increased by reducing cost elements.	Profit is a function of material cost, total factory cost and throughput.

7.2.1 Bottleneck resources

The aim of modern manufacturing approaches is to match production resources with the demand for them. This implies that there are **no constraints, termed bottleneck resources** in TA, within an organisation. The throughput philosophy entails the identification and elimination of these bottleneck resources by **overtime, product changes** and **process alterations** to reduce **set-up** and waiting times.

Where throughput cannot be eliminated by say prioritising work, and to avoid the build-up of work in progress, **production must be limited to the capacity of the bottleneck resource** but this capacity must be **fully** utilised. If a rearrangement of existing resources or buying-in resources does not alleviate the bottleneck, investment in new equipment may be necessary.

The elimination of one bottleneck is likely to lead to the creation of another at a previously satisfactory location, however. The management of bottlenecks therefore becomes a primary concern of the manager seeking to increase throughput.

3: OTHER METHODS OF COST ACCUMULATION

There are other factors which might limit throughput other than a lack of production resources (bottlenecks) and these need to be addressed as well.

- (a) The **existence** of an **uncompetitive selling price**
- (b) The **need to deliver on time to particular customers**
- (c) The **lack of product quality and reliability**
- (d) The **lack of reliable material suppliers**
- (e) The **shortage of production resources**

7.2.2 Performance measures in throughput accounting

Performance measures are based around the concept that only direct materials are regarded as variable costs.

- (a) **Return per factory hour**

$$\frac{\text{Sales} - \text{direct material costs}}{\text{Usage of bottleneck resource in hours (factory hours)}}$$

This enables businesses to take short-term decisions when a resource is in scarce supply.

- (b) **Efficiency of bottleneck use**

$$\frac{\text{Throughput cost per day}}{\text{Total conversion cost per day}} \times 100\%$$

where throughput cost per day =

No of units produced × Conversion cost per time taken to produce one unit

Conversion costs are all factory costs other than material costs.

This should be as close to 100% as possible.

- (c) **Throughput accounting ratio**

$$\frac{\text{Return per factory hour}}{\text{Total conversion cost per factory hour}}$$

Again factory hours are measured in terms of use of the bottleneck resource. Businesses should try to maximise the throughput accounting ratio.

Question — Throughput accounting (2)

Growler Ltd manufactures computer components. Health and safety regulations mean that one of its processes can only be operated 8 hours a day. The hourly capacity of this process is 500 units per hour. The selling price of each component is £100 and the unit material cost is £40. The daily total of all factory costs (conversion costs) is £144,000, excluding materials. Expected production is 3,600 units per day.

Required

Calculate

- (a) Total profit per day
- (b) Return per factory hour
- (c) Efficiency of bottleneck use
- (d) Throughput accounting ratio

Answer

(a) Total profit per day = Throughput contribution − Conversion costs
= (3,600 × (100 − 40) − 144,000)
= £72,000

(b) Return per factory hour $= \dfrac{\text{Sales} - \text{direct material costs}}{\text{Usage of bottleneck resource in hours (factory hours)}}$

$= \dfrac{100 - 40}{1/500}$

= £30,000

(c) Throughput cost per day = No of units produced × Conversion cost per time taken to produce one unit

= 3,600 × (144,000/(8 × 500))

= 129,600

Efficiency of bottleneck resource usage $= \dfrac{\text{Throughput cost per day}}{\text{Total conversion cost per day}}$

$= \dfrac{129,600}{144,000} \times 100\%$

= 90%.

(d) Throughput accounting ratio $= \dfrac{\text{Return per factory hour}}{\text{Total conversion cost per factory hour}}$

$= \dfrac{30,000}{144,000/8}$

= 1.67

7.2.3 Is it good or bad?

TA is seen by some as **too short term**, as all costs other than direct material are regarded as fixed. Moreover, it **concentrates on direct material costs** and does nothing for the control of other costs such as overheads. These characteristics make throughput accounting a **good complement for ABC**, however, since ABC focuses on labour and overhead costs.

TA attempts to maximise throughput whereas traditional systems attempt to maximise profit. By attempting to maximise throughput an organisation could be producing in excess of the profit-maximising output. **Production scheduling** problems inevitably mean that the throughput-maximising output is never attained, however, and so a **throughput maximising approach** could well **lead to the profit-maximising output** being achieved.

TA helps to direct attention to bottlenecks and focus management on the key elements in making profits, inventory reduction and reducing the response time to customer demand.

8 Service costing   6/02

FAST FORWARD

> **Service costing** can be used by companies operating in a service industry or by companies wishing to establish the cost of services carried out by some of their departments.

8.1 What are service organisations?

Service organisations do not make or sell tangible goods. Profit-seeking service organisations include accountancy firms, law firms, management consultants, transport companies, banks, insurance companies and hotels. Non-profit-seeking organisations – hospitals, schools, libraries – are also normally service organisations.

Key term

> **Service/function costing** is the application of cost accounting principles and techniques to services and functions.

Service costing differs from product costing methods for a number of reasons.

(a) With many services, the **cost of direct materials** consumed will be **relatively small** compared to the labour, direct expenses and overheads cost. In product costing the direct materials are often a greater proportion of the total cost. Catering and hospitality is a service, however, but in restaurants and canteens up to 40% of the cost relates to materials (food). And hospitals hold large stocks of medicines, equipment and consumables.

(b) The **output** of most service organisations is **difficult to define** and hence a **unit cost is difficult to calculate**.

(c) The service industry includes such a **wide range of organisations** which provide such different services and have such **different cost structures** that costing will vary considerably from one to another.

Tom Sheridan, in his article 'Costing in the service sector' (*Management Accounting*, May 1996), expands on these differences between service costing and product costing.

> 'Britain has a powerful service economy but nonetheless costing has only become a talking point in the service sector in the last decade. The service sector is wide-ranging. It not only covers a whole variety of business areas but also includes the head office administrative element of manufacturing companies...
>
> **In theory, costing should be easier in the service sector**: there are **no stocks** or work-in-progress to be valued while, secondly, being a Johnny-come-lately in costing, it has been possible to ... **take advantage of the new concepts** ... Not a few new businesses in the service sector have been able to introduce ABC or incorporate ABC concepts, right from the start without going through the trauma and expense of dismantling their previous costing systems.
>
> **But there are disadvantages too.** The products are so **subjective**. **Simultaneity** and **perishability** are also key factors. One cannot build for stock. A lawyer without clients loses billable time for ever, a hotel with rooms unoccupied or an airline with seats unsold cannot recoup the costs after the event...
>
> If management's bottom-line objective is – as it usually is – cost management through cost understanding and traceability, the task is not made any easier because in most service industries one is dealing with intangibles. Everything is **intangible**. You cannot touch the product as you can in manufacturing. So, how do you measure it? How does one define a product or service? How does one cost it? Everything seems to be an overhead and therefore, try as one will, one cannot get away from that bugbear of the management accountant's life – allocations ...
>
> A key to unravelling the complexities is to **take an ABC approach** ...'

8.2 Cost control and service organisations

The cost control techniques used by manufacturing organisations may not be entirely suitable for service organisations due to difficulties set out above and to the following service organisation characteristics.

Characteristic	Example
Most services are intangible	The customer on an aeroplane will be influenced by the comfort of the seat, the meal served, the attitudes of the cabin staff, the boarding process and so on. Managing and controlling the operation is therefore complex because it is difficult to establish exactly what the customer is buying, the journey or the treatment.
Service outputs vary from day to day	Services are provided by individuals whose performance can affect the quality of service provided, such as the service provided by hairdressers.
Production and consumption of many services are inseparable	A plane journey is produced and consumed simultaneously.
Services are perishable and cannot be stored	If an airline seat is unoccupied, the sales opportunity is lost forever and the service is wasted.

8.3 Unit cost measures

We mentioned above that the output of most service organisations is difficult to define. This is a particular problem with service costing: the difficulty in defining a realistic cost unit that represents a suitable measure of the service provided. Frequently, a **composite cost unit may be deemed more appropriate** if the service is a function of two activity variables. Hotels, for example, may use the 'occupied bed night' as an appropriate unit for cost ascertainment and control.

Typical cost units used by companies operating in a service industry are shown as follows.

Service	Cost unit
Road, rail and air transport services	Passenger/kilometre
Hotels	Occupied bed-night
Education	Full-time student
Hospitals	Patient

Each organisation will need to ascertain the cost unit most appropriate to its activities. If a number of organisations within an industry use a common cost unit, valuable comparisons can be made between similar establishments. This is particularly applicable to hospitals, educational establishments and local authorities.

8.4 Management accounting in service industries

The difficulties of costing service businesses that we have been looking at mean that attention should be directed on to other measures rather than the traditional 'cost per unit'.

(a) **Competitive performance** should focus on factors such as sales growth and market share.

(b) Like any other business, a service business needs to monitor its **financial performance** and to plan, and its short-term plans can be drawn up for service activities in the form of a budget. (Budgeting is covered in Chapters 7 to 11.)

 (i) There might be a budgeted expenditure limit for activities within the business.
 (ii) Standard performance measures can be established as targets for efficiency.

(c) **Service quality** is measured principally by qualitative measures, although quantitative measures are used by some businesses. If it were able to obtain the information, a retailer, for example, might use number of lost customers in a period as an indicator of service quality. Lawyers use the proportion of time spent with clients.

(d) **Flexibility** has three aspects.

   (i) **Speed of delivery** in the sense of punctuality is vital in some service industries like passenger transport: indeed punctuality is currently one of the most widely-publicised performance measures in the UK, because organisations like London Underground are making a point of it. Measures include waiting time in queues, as well as late trains.

   (ii) The **ability** of a service organisation **to respond to customers' specifications** is vital in a professional service such as legal advice where assistance must be tailored exactly to the customers' needs.

   (iii) **Coping with demand** is clearly measurable in quantitative terms in a mass service like London Underground which can ascertain the extent of overcrowding. It can also be very closely monitored in service shops: customer queuing time can be measured for example, and this is highly relevant for banks.

(e) **Resource utilisation** is usually measured in terms of productivity, which is the ratio of inputs to outputs. As usual, the ease with which this may be measured varies according to the service being delivered.

   (i) The main resource of a firm of accountants, for example, is the *time* of various grades of staff. The main output of an accountancy firm is chargeable hours.

   (ii) In a restaurant it is not nearly so straightforward. Inputs are the ingredients for the meal, the chef's time and expertise, the waiter's time and expertise, the surroundings, the other customers, and the customers' own likes and dislikes. A customer attitude survey might show whether or not a customer enjoyed the food, but it could not ascribe the enjoyment or lack of it to the quality of the ingredients, say, rather than the skill of the chef or the speed of the waiter.

(f) Companies do not have to **innovate** to be successful, but it helps! Others will try to steal their market, and so others' innovations must at least be matched. In a modern environment in which product quality, product differentiation and continuous improvement are the order of the day, a company that can find innovative ways of satisfying customers' needs has an important competitive advantage.

8.5 Non-financial indicators

There is a danger in service organisations of focusing excessively on financial performance measures, which can be easily quantified, thus placing an undue emphasis on maximising short-term performance even if this conflicts with maximising long-term performance. It is therefore more important in service organisations that a range of **non-financial indicators** be developed to provide better predictors for the attainment of long-term profitability goals. Here are some examples.

- Quality
- Number of customer complaints
- Lead times
- Delivery to time
- Non-productive hours
- System (machine) down time, and so on

Unlike traditional variance reports, measures such as these can be **provided quickly** for managers, per shift or on a daily or hourly basis. They are likely to be **easy to calculate**, and **easier** for non-financial managers **to understand** and therefore to use effectively.

The beauty of non-financial indicators is that **anything can be compared if it is meaningful to do so**. The measures should be **tailored to the circumstances** so that number of coffee breaks per 20 pages of text might indicate to you how hard you are studying!

Some service organisations, notably banks, are using **activity-based profitability analysis** to analyse and thus measure profits of different segments of the business.

9 Costing in not-for-profit organisations 6/05

> **FAST FORWARD**
>
> **Not-for- profit organisations** need to produce non-financial performance indicators that demonstrate the level and quality of the service they provide.

Not-for-profit organisations include private sector organisations like **charities** and **churches** and much of the **public sector**.

The **purpose** of such organisations is to **serve the broader community interests** rather than to pursue profit. Commercial organisations generally have market competition and the profit motive to guide the process of managing resources economically, efficiently and effectively. Not-for-profit organisations **cannot by definition be judged by profitability nor do they generally have to be successful against competition**. They are more concerned with providing an appropriate level of service. They therefore tend to use **non-financial indicators** as measures, profit margin and return on capital employed having little relevance.

A major problem with many not-for-profit organisations, particularly government bodies, is that it is extremely **difficult to define their objectives** at all, let alone find *one* which can serve as a yardstick function in the way that profit does for commercial bodies. This is in part due to the fact that they usually need to **satisfy** a **wide group** of people (**stakeholders**). A hospital, for example, has stakeholders which include the government (the provider of funds), the employees (the providers of services) and the general public (the customers).

9.1 Example: Costing an educational establishment

A university organisation structure consists of three faculties each with a number of teaching departments. In addition, there is a university administrative/management function and a central services function.

(a) The following cost information is available for the year ended 30 June 20X3.

(i) **Occupancy costs.** Costs of £1,500,000 are apportioned on the basis of area used, which is as follows.

	Square metres
Faculties	7,500
Teaching departments	20,000
Administration/management	7,000
Central services	3,000

(ii) **Administrative/management costs**. Direct costs of £1,775,000 and indirect costs (an apportionment of occupancy costs) are charged to degree courses on a percentage basis.

(iii) **Faculty costs**. Direct costs of £700,000 and indirect costs (an apportionment of occupancy costs and central service costs) are charged to teaching departments.

(iv) **Teaching departments**. Direct costs of £5,525,000 and indirect costs (an apportionment of occupancy costs and central service costs plus all faculty costs) are charged to degree courses on a percentage basis.

(v) **Central services.** Direct costs total £1,000,000. Indirect costs are an apportion-ment of occupancy costs.

(b) Direct and indirect costs of central services have been charged to users on a percentage basis. A recent study has estimated what user areas would have paid external suppliers for the same services on an individual basis. For the year ended 30 June 20X3, the apportionment of the central services cost is to be recalculated in a manner which recognises the cost savings achieved by using the central services facilities instead of using external service companies. This is to be done by apportioning the overall savings to user areas in proportion to their share of the estimated external costs, which are as follows.

	£'000
Faculties	240
Teaching departments	800
Degree courses:	
Business studies	32
Mechanical engineering	48
Catering studies	32
All other degrees	448
	1,600

(c) Additional data relating to the degree courses is as follows.

	Business studies	Degree course Mechanical engineering	Catering studies
Number of graduates	80	50	120
Apportioned costs (as % of totals)			
Teaching departments	3.0%	2.5%	7%
Administration/management	2.5%	5.0%	4%

Central services are to be apportioned as detailed in (a)(v) above. The total number of undergraduates from the university in the year to 30 June 20X3 was 2,500.

Required

(a) Calculate the average cost per undergraduate for the year ended 30 June 20X3 and discuss the relevance of this information to the university management.

(b) Calculate the average cost per undergraduate for each of the three degrees detailed, showing all relevant cost analysis.

(c) Suggest reasons for any differences in the average cost per undergraduate from one degree to another, and discuss briefly the usefulness of such information to the university management.

Solution

(a) The **average cost per undergraduate** is as follows.

	Total costs £'000
Occupancy	1,500
Admin/management	1,775
Faculty	700
Teaching departments	5,525
Central services	1,000
	10,500
Number of undergraduates	2,500
Average cost per undergraduate for year ended 30 June 20X3	£4,200

The average cost per undergraduate is not particularly relevant for the university management. It is a figure that can be monitored from year to year. If it becomes too high then control action needs to be taken to bring costs down.

PART A COSTING SYSTEMS AND TECHNIQUES

(b) **Average cost per undergraduate for specified course** is as follows.

	Business studies £	Mechanical engineering £	Catering studies £
Teaching department costs (W1 and using % in question)	241,590	201,325	563,710
Admin/management costs (W1 and using % in question)	51,375	102,750	82,200
Central services (W2)	22,400	33,600	22,400
	315,365	337,675	668,310
Number of undergraduates	80	50	120
Average cost per undergraduate for year ended 30 June 20X3	£3,942	£6,754	£5,569

Workings

1 **Cost allocation and apportionment**

Cost item	Basis of apportionment	Teaching departments £'000	Admin/ management £'000	Central services £'000	Faculties £'000
Direct costs	allocation	5,525	1,775	1,000	700
Occupancy costs	area used	800	280	120	300
Central services Reapportioned	(W2)	560	–	(1,120)	168
Faculty costs Reallocated	allocation	1,168	–	–	(1,168)
		8,053	2,055	–	–

2 Apportioning savings to user areas on the basis given in the question gives the same result as apportioning internal costs in proportion to the external costs.

	External costs £'000	Apportionment of internal central service costs £'000
Faculties	240	168.0
Teaching	800	560.0
Degree courses:		
Business studies	32	22.4
Mechanical engineering	48	33.6
Catering studies	32	22.4
All other degrees	448	313.6
	1,600	1,120.0

(c) **Possible reasons for the differences in the average cost per undergraduate**

(i) Some of the courses may require lecturers of greater skill, who command higher rates of pay.

(ii) Teaching methods may be different on the various courses. Some may be split into small groups, each needing a separate tutor. Others may be taught by one lecturer in a large group, or two or more lecturers simultaneously.

(iii) Teaching aids in use will vary from course to course. Both mechanical engineering and catering studies require specialist equipment.

(iv) Some courses may take longer to complete than others.

(v) Some courses may feature intensive one-to-one tuition as a matter of routine, whereas others will operate on the basis of seminars or lectures.

(vi) Management and administration charges will vary from course to course. Catering studies is likely to require extensive space for kitchens.

(vii) The students for each course may be drawn from different years. The overall size of each year may be different.

Usefulness of the information

(i) Monitoring the cost per graduate for each degree course on a year by year basis will prove useful. Such information will allow an assessment of how well the costs relating to particular disciplines are being controlled.

(ii) Consideration should be given to the costs actually included in the analysis. The management should consider whether unavoidable costs should be incorporated.

(iii) The information may prove more useful if it is used in conjunction with qualitative information such as pass rates and student satisfaction.

The key findings of Paul Cropper and Professor Colin Drury's recent survey of management accounting practices within UK university management are as follows.

(i) 'The costing method considered the most appropriate for determining the cost of running *degree courses* was identified as the calculation of '**full costs**' (35 per cent of institutions favoured this method). A significant number of institutions (27 per cent) stated that they believed '**activity-based costing**' was the most appropriate method. 'Direct cost plus a fixed percentage overhead' was preferred by only 21 per cent of institutions despite the fact that 56 per cent of respondents said they currently used this method 'often or always'.

These findings indicate that institutions would like to move towards a **more accurate basis for costing their principal activities**.'

(ii) '... 100 per cent of higher-education institutions indicating that they operated a system of **budgetary control** ... where the cost estimates submitted by managers were perceived to be excessive, 57 per cent of respondents indicated that budgets were reduced through negotiation. A further 9 per cent said that a reduction was achieved through a combination of negotiation and cuts deemed appropriate by upper management. ... Of the budgetary control methods available, by far the most popular were '**previous year plus inflation**' and '**incremental budgeting**'.'

(iii) 'The majority of respondents (73 per cent) do place a strong emphasis on a manager's ability to attain the budget as a major factor in judging performance ... **non-financial measures** are used and that institutions do attempt to measure student/customer satisfaction and student achievement on a regular basis ... Most respondents placed an emphasis on **measuring and evaluating their performance relative to that of other institutions**.'

('Management Accounting Practices in Universities', *Management Accounting,* February 1996)

Exam focus point

The application of costing information and principles in a not-for-profit organisation was examined in June 2005 in Section B.

10 Service costing for internal services

FAST FORWARD

Service costing for internal services adds to the administrative burdens of an organisation because it costs time and money. The benefits of the system should therefore exceed the costs of its operation.

Service costing can be used to establish a **specific cost for an 'internal service'** which is a service provided by one department for another, rather than sold externally. Service departments therefore include canteens and data processing departments.

10.1 The purposes of service costing for internal services

(a) **To control the costs and efficiency in the service department.** If we establish a distribution cost per tonne/km, a canteen cost per employee or a mainframe computer operating cost per hour, we can do the following.

   (i) Compare actual costs against a target or standard
   (ii) Compare actual costs in the current period against the in previous periods

(b) **To control the costs of the user departments, and prevent the unnecessary use of services.** If the costs of services are charged to the user departments so that the charges reflect the use actually made by each user department of the services then the following will occur.

   (i) The overhead costs of user departments will be established more accurately. Variable costs might be identified as costs which are directly attributable to the user department.

   (ii) If the service department's charges for a user department are high, the user department might consider it is making an excessively costly and wasteful use of the service department's service.

   (iii) The user department might decide that it can obtain a similar service at a lower cost from an external service company. This is clearly not satisfactory from the point of view of the organisation as a whole.

Service costing also provides a **fairer basis for charging service costs to user departments**, instead of charging service costs as overheads on a broad direct labour hour basis, or similar arbitrary apportionment basis. This is because service **costs are related more directly to use**, particularly if an **ABC** system is used.

(a) If repair costs in a factory are costed as jobs with each bit of repair work being given a job number and costed accordingly, repair costs can be charged to the departments on the basis of repair jobs actually undertaken, instead of on a more generalised basis, such as apportionment according to machine hour capacity in each department. Departments with high repair costs could then consider their high incidence of repairs, the age and reliability of their machines, or the skills of the machine operators.

(b) If mainframe computer costs are charged to a user department on the basis of a cost per hour, the user department would make the following assessment.

   (i) Whether it was getting good value from its use of the mainframe computer

   (ii) Whether it might be better to hire the service of a computer bureau, or perhaps install a stand-alone microcomputer system in the department

10.2 The bases for charging service costs to user departments

The 'cost' of support services charged to user departments could be based on any of the following.

(a) **No charge at all**

Service costs are either apportioned on a more arbitrary basis between production departments in a system of absorption costing, or charged against profit as a period charge in a system of marginal costing, without any attempt to recognise that some departments might be using services more than others.

(b) **Total actual cost**

The total costs of the service department are accumulated over a period of time. No distinction is made between fixed and variable costs in the department. The charge to the user departments is then:

(total actual cost/total activity (eg hours worked)) × work done for user department

This method might be suitable if it is difficult to separate fixed and variable costs or if it is difficult to establish standard costs, but there are several problems associated with it.

(i) User departments are charged for any overspending and inefficiency in the service departments.

(ii) If the service department is not working at full capacity, the charge per unit of service is higher than if the department is more busy. This might discourage user departments from using the service, to avoid high service charges.

(iii) The fluctuating charges which can result from the use of actual costs could make it difficult for the user departments to plan and control costs.

(c) **Standard absorption cost**

The charge to user departments is based on a standard, predetermined cost for the service, consisting of the service department's variable costs plus a share of its fixed costs. The standard cost is based on (standard total costs ÷ standard (budgeted) service activity). The user departments are therefore *not* penalised for either overspending and inefficiency or under-capacity in the service department. There are, however, two problems with this method.

(i) It is necessary to review the standard cost regularly and frequently, so that user departments do not get a false impression of the cost of the service.

(ii) There is a problem in deciding what the standard activity level ought to be.

(d) **Variable cost**

Support services are costed at marginal or variable cost only. This could be either standard or actual variable cost. The advantage of this method is that user departments are charged for the extra costs incurred by using more of the service. There are, however, a number of weaknesses or problems with this system.

(i) The user departments are under a false impression as to the true full cost of the service, because they are charged with just the marginal costs.

(ii) If actual variable costs are used, there is no control of overspending and inefficiency in the service department because the service department simply 'passes on' its overspending in higher charges to the user department.

(iii) If standard costs are used, the standard needs to be revised regularly.

PART A COSTING SYSTEMS AND TECHNIQUES

(e) **Opportunity cost**

This method is appropriate if the service department is working at full capacity and is also providing services outside the company. This means that profit is forgone every time the service department provides a service internally, which should be reflected in an opportunity cost charge. The main problem associated with this method is that it is difficult to establish the opportunity cost.

Question — Service department costs

Identify three different reasons for the charging of service department costs to user departments and comment on the charging methods which may be relevant in the case of maintenance, computer services, and health, safety and welfare service departments.

Answer

Service department costs are charged to user departments for the following **reasons**.

(a) User departments which use most of the services are made responsible for them.
(b) Service costs are included in production costs, where appropriate.
(c) The 'true' cost of each user department is known to management.
(d) User departments are encouraged to use the service as opposed to external contractors.

Maintenance might be easy to allocate. The machines are in definite locations, and there is a distinct chain of responsibility. Maintenance costs could be charged out in the budget as part of production overhead at a predetermined rate, or in an activity based costing system. This would be for budgetary purposes only. In practice, during the budget period, maintenance jobs could be charged out on an individual basis, directly to user departments.

Computer services cost would be charged on the basis of computer time for normal processing, and any computer projects which are directly attributable to user departments would be charged directly. Some estimate would be needed of any system enhancements required during the year.

The **health, safety and welfare department's** cost will be allocated to user departments on a basis of employee numbers in the case of nursing care, or floorspace in the case of fire prevention equipment, alarm systems and so forth. Both the number of employees and the floor area might therefore be a means of allocating the cost.

Exam focus point

Service costing in a not-for-profit organisation was examined in the first sitting of the 2.4 syllabus. A fee charging hospital provided the scenario and candidates were required to prepare budgeted profit/loss statements and to evaluate a proposal. Neither requirement demanded more than the most basic of techniques or knowledge.

In June 2002 part of a question required the candidates to write a memorandum explaining the nature of service organisations compared to production based companies and to suggest appropriate cost unit measures for consulting activities.

Chapter Roundup

- Only **relevant costs** are brought into calculations for decision-making purposes. Relevant costs are incremental cash flows occurring as a result of the decision.

- **Non-relevant costs**, such as **sunk costs, committed costs, notional costs, existing fixed costs** and non-cashflows such as **depreciation**, are excluded from the calculations.

- An **opportunity cost** is the value of the benefit sacrificed by not carrying out an alternative course of action.

- In a system of cost accumulation using opportunity costing, the costs of resources consumed are valued at their opportunity cost rather than at the amount it actually costs to acquire them.

- An alternative to absorption costing is **activity based costing (ABC).**

- ABC involves the identification of the factors **(cost drivers)** which cause the costs of an organisation's major activities. Support overheads are charged to products on the basis of their usage of an activity.

    - For costs that vary with production level in the short term, the cost driver will be volume related (labour or machine hours).

    - Overheads that vary with some other activity (and not volume of production) should be traced to products using transaction-based cost drivers such as production runs or number of orders received

- ABC has both advantages and disadvantages, and it tends to be more widely used by larger organisations and the service sector.

- **Life cycle costing** tracks and accumulates costs and revenues attributable to each product over the entire product life cycle.

- A **product life cycle** can be divided into four phases.

    - Introduction
    - Growth
    - Maturity
    - Decline

- **Target costing** involves setting a target cost by subtracting a desired profit margin from a competitive market price.

- **Throughput accounting** is a product management system which aims to maximise throughput, and therefore cash generation from sales, rather than profit. A **just in time (JIT)** environment is operated, with buffer stock kept only when there is a **bottleneck resource**.

- **Service costing** can be used by companies operating in a service industry or by companies wishing to establish the cost of services carried out by some of their departments.

- **Not-for-profit organisations** need to produce non-financial performance indicators that demonstrate the level and quality of the service they provide.

- **Service costing for internal services** adds to the administrative burdens of an organisation because it costs time and money. The benefits of the system should therefore exceed the costs of its operation.

PART A COSTING SYSTEMS AND TECHNIQUES

Quick Quiz

1. Material X costs £20 per kg and is in short supply. 100 kgs are needed for job Y but those 100 kgs could be used on job Z, where they will earn contribution of £5 per kg. What is the opportunity cost per kg of using material X on job Y?

2. *Choose the correct phrases.*

   Traditional costing systems tend to allocate **too great/too small** a proportion of overheads to high volume products and **too great/too small** a proportion of overheads to low volume products.

3. *Fill in the blanks.*

   The major ideas behind ABC are as follows.

   (a) Activities cause ....
   (b) Producing products creates demand for the ....
   (c) Costs are assigned to a product on the basis of the product's consumption of the ....

4. *Match the most appropriate cost driver to each cost.*

Costs		Cost driver
(a)	Set-up costs	Number of machine hours
(b)	Short-run variable costs	Number of production runs
(c)	Materials handling and despatch	Number of orders executed

5. *Match the following costs to the appropriate life cycle cost classification.*

Costs	Classifications
Design	Inventory costs
Energy costs	Acquisition costs
Warehousing	Maintenance costs
Transportation	Operation costs
Customer service	Product distribution costs

6. Life cycle costing is the profiling of cost over a product's production life.

   ☐ True
   ☐ False

7. *Fill in the blanks using words from the list (a) to (h).*

   Target cost = ... – ....

   Cost gap = ... – ....

   (a) target cost
   (b) cost gap
   (c) budgeted selling price
   (d) production cost
   (e) target selling price
   (f) estimated cost
   (g) estimated selling price
   (h) target profit

8. Give five examples of bases on which the cost of support services could be charged to user departments.

Answers to Quick Quiz

1 £(20 ÷ 5) = £25

2 Too great
   Too small

3 (a) Costs
   (b) Activities
   (c) Activities

4 (a) Number of production runs
   (b) Number of machine hours
   (c) Number of orders executed

5
Cost	Classification
Design	Acquisition costs
Energy costs	Operation costs
Warehousing	Inventory costs
Transportation	Product distribution costs
Customer service	Maintenance costs

6 False. It also looks at development costs and so on which are incurred prior to production, and any dismantling costs, which are incurred once production ceases.

7 Target cost = estimated selling price − target profit
   Cost gap = estimated cost − target cost

8 (a) No charge at all
   (b) Total actual cost
   (c) Standard absorption cost
   (d) Variable cost
   (e) Opportunity cost

Now try the questions below from the Exam Question Bank

Number	Level	Marks	Time
Q3	Introductory	n/a	30 mins
Q4	Examination	25	45 mins

Part B
Standard costing

Introduction to standard costing

Topic list	Syllabus reference
1 Standard costs	7(a)(i)
2 Standard costing	7(a)(i)
3 Deriving standards	7(a)(i)
4 Types of standard and their behavioural impact	7(a)(i), 7(c)
5 Reviewing standards	7(a)(i)

Introduction

Just as there are standards for most things in our daily lives (cleanliness in hamburger restaurants, educational achievement of nine year olds, number of underground trains running on time) there are **standards** for the costs of products and services. And just as the standards in our daily lives are not always met, the standards for the costs of products and services are not always met. We will not, however, be considering the cleanliness of hamburger restaurants in this chapter but we will be looking at standard costs and standard costing.

In the next chapter we will see how standard costing forms the basis of a process called **variance analysis**, a vital management control tool.

PART B STANDARD COSTING

Study guide

Section 20 – Standard costing I

- Explain the uses of standard costs and the methods by which they are derived and subsequently reviewed
- Calculate and evaluate capacity limitations when setting standards
- Describe the types of standard (ideal, attainable current and basic) and their behavioural implications

Exam guide

The contents of this chapter are likely to be examined in conjunction with variance analysis, covered in Chapters 5 and 6.

1 Standard costs

06/05

FAST FORWARD

A **standard cost** is an estimated unit cost built up of standards for each cost element (standard resource price and standard resource usage).

Key term

A **standard cost** is an estimated unit cost.

The standard cost of product 12345 is set out below on a **standard cost card**.

```
                       STANDARD COST CARD
              Product: the Splodget, No 12345

                              Cost          Requirement
                                                           £         £
Direct materials
    A                     £2.00 per kg        6 kgs      12.00
    B                     £3.00 per kg        2 kgs       6.00
    C                     £4.00 per litre     1 litre     4.00
Others                                                    2.00
                                                                   24.00
Direct labour
  Grade I                 £4.00 per hour      3 hrs      12.00
  Grade II                £5.40 per hour      5 hrs      27.00
                                                                   39.00
Variable production overheads  £1.00 per hour  8 hrs      8.00
Fixed production overheads     £3.00 per hour  8 hrs     24.00
Standard full cost of production                         95.00
```

Notice how it is **built up from standards for each cost element**: standard quantities of materials at standard prices, standard quantities of labour time at standard rates and so on. It is therefore determined by management's estimates of the following.

- The expected prices of materials, labour and expenses
- Efficiency levels in the use of materials and labour
- Budgeted overhead costs and budgeted volumes of activity

We will see how management arrives at these estimates later in the chapter.

But why should management want to prepare standard costs? Obviously to assist with standard costing, but what is the point of standard costing?

2 Standard costing

FAST FORWARD

Standard costing is principally used to value stocks and cost production and to act as a control device.

2.1 The uses of standard costing

Standard costing has two principal **uses**.

- **To value stocks and cost production** for cost accounting purposes. It is an alternative method of valuation to methods like FIFO and LIFO which you will have covered in your earlier studies.
- **To act as a control device** by establishing standards (expected costs) and comparing actual costs with the expected costs, thus highlighting areas of the organisation which may be out of control

It can also be used in the following circumstances.

(a) To assist in setting **budgets** and **evaluating managerial performance**.

(b) To enable the principle of **'management by exception'** to be practised. A standard cost, when established, is an average expected unit cost. Because it is only an average, actual results will vary to some extent above and below the average. Only significant differences between actual and standard should be reported.

(c) To provide a prediction of future costs to be used in **decision-making** situations.

(d) To **motivate** staff and management by the provision of challenging targets.

(e) To provide guidance on possible ways of **improving efficiency**.

Exam focus point

An outline of the uses of standard costing was worth eight marks in the December 2001 exam.

Although the various uses of standard costing should not be overlooked, we will be concentrating on the control aspect.

2.2 Standard costing as a control technique

Key terms

Standard costing involves the establishment of predetermined estimates of the costs of products or services, the collection of actual costs and the comparison of the actual costs with the predetermined estimates. The predetermined costs are known as standard costs and the difference between standard and actual cost is known as a **variance**. The process by which the total difference between standard and actual results is analysed in known as **variance analysis**.

Question
Standard costing

What are the possible advantages for the control function of an organisation of having a standard costing system?

Answer

(a) Carefully planned standards are an aid to more accurate **budgeting**.

(b) Standard costs provide a **yardstick** against which actual costs can be measured.

(c) The setting of standards involves determining the **best** materials and methods which may lead to economies.

(d) A **target of efficiency** is set for employees to reach and **cost-consciousness** is stimulated.

(e) Variances can be calculated which enable the principle of **'management by exception'** to be operated. Only the variances which exceed acceptable tolerance limits need to be investigated by management with a view to control action.

(f) Standard costs and variance analysis can provide a way of **motivation** to managers to achieve better performance. However, care must be taken to distinguish between controllable and non-controllable costs in variance reporting.

2.3 Where standard costing should be used

FAST FORWARD

Standard costing is most suited to mass production and repetitive assembly work.

Although standard costing can be used in a variety of costing situations (batch and mass production, process manufacture, jobbing manufacture (where there is standardisation of parts) and service industries (if a realistic cost unit can be established)), the **greatest benefit from its use can be gained if there is a degree of repetition in the production process** so that average or expected usage of resources can be determined. It is therefore **most suited to mass production and repetitive assembly work** and less suited to organisations which produce to customer demand and requirements.

Question — Standard service costing

Can you think of a service organisation that could apply standard costing?

Answer

In an *ACCA Students' Newsletter* article (December 1998), the examiner of the equivalent paper under the old syllabus provided the example of restaurants which deal with standard recipes for meals. If a large number of meals are produced, say, for conference delegates, mass production systems will apply. Standards may not be calculated with the same accuracy as in manufacturing environments, but the principles are still relevant. Other examples are equally valid.

3 Deriving standards

FAST FORWARD

The **responsibility for deriving standard costs** should be shared between **managers able to provide the necessary information** about levels of expected efficiency, prices and overhead costs.

3.1 Setting standards for materials costs

Direct materials costs per unit of raw material will be estimated by the purchasing department from their knowledge of the following.

- Purchase contracts already agreed
- Pricing discussions with regular suppliers
- The forecast movement of prices in the market
- The availability of bulk purchase discounts
- The quality of material required by the production departments

The standard cost ought to include an allowance for **bulk purchase discounts**, if these are available on all or some of the purchases, and it may have to be a weighted average price of the differing prices charged for the same product by alternative suppliers.

A decision must also be taken as to how to deal with price **inflation**. Suppose that a material costs £10 per kilogram at the moment, and during the course of the next 12 months, it is expected to go up in price by 20% to £12 per kilogram. What standard price should be selected?

(a) If the **current price** of £10 per kilogram **were used in the standard**, the reported price variance would become adverse as soon as prices go up, which might be very early in the year. If prices go up gradually rather than in one big jump, it would be difficult to select an appropriate time for revising the standard.

(b) If an **estimated mid-year price** of, say, £11 per kilogram **were used**, price variances should be favourable in the first half of the year and adverse in the second half, again assuming that prices go up gradually. Management could only really check that in any month, the price variance did not become excessively adverse (or favourable) and that the price variance switched from being favourable to adverse around month six or seven and not sooner.

Standard costing is therefore more **difficult in times of inflation but it is still worthwhile**.

- Usage and efficiency variances will still be meaningful.
- Inflation is measurable: there is no reason why its effects cannot be removed.
- Standard costs can be revised, so long as this is not done too frequently.

3.2 Setting standards for labour costs

Direct labour rates per hour will be set by reference to the payroll and to any agreements on pay rises with trade union representatives of the employees. A separate hourly rate or weekly wage will be set for each different labour grade/type of employee and an average hourly rate will be applied for each grade (even though individual rates of pay may vary according to age and experience).

Similar problems to those which arise when setting material standards in times of high inflation can be met when setting labour standards.

3.3 Setting standards for material usage and labour efficiency

To estimate the materials required to make each product (material usage) and also the labour hours required (labour efficiency), technical specifications must be prepared for each product by production experts (either in the production department or the work study department).

3.4 Setting standards for overheads

When standard costs are fully absorbed costs (standard costs can be used in both marginal and absorption costing systems), the **absorption rate** of fixed production overheads will be **predetermined** and **based on budgeted** fixed production **overhead** and planned **production volume**.

Production volume will depend on two factors.

(a) **Production capacity** (or 'volume capacity') measured perhaps in standard hours of output (a standard hour being the amount of work achievable at standard efficiency levels in an hour), which in turn reflects direct production labour hours.

(b) **Efficiency of working**, by labour or machines, allowing for rest time and contingency allowances.

Suppose that a department has a work force of ten men, each of whom works a 36 hour week to make standard units, and each unit has a standard time of two hours to make. The expected efficiency of the work-force is 125%.

(a) Budgeted capacity, in direct labour hours, would be 10 × 36 = 360 production hours per week.

(b) Budgeted efficiency is 125% so that the work-force should take only 1 hour of actual production time to produce 1.25 standard hours of output.

(c) This means in our example that budgeted output is 360 production hours × 125% = 450 standard hours of output per week. At 2 standard hours per unit, this represents production activity or volume of 225 units of output per week.

Question — Budgeted output

ABC Ltd carries out routine office work in a sales order processing department, and all tasks in the department have been given standard times. There are 40 clerks in the department who work on average 140 hours per month each. The efficiency ratio of the department is 110%.

Required

Calculate the budgeted output in the department.

Answer

Capacity = 40 × 140 = 5,600 hours per month
Efficiency = 110%
Budgeted output = 5,600 × 110% = 6,160 standard hours of work per month.

3.4.1 Capacity levels

FAST FORWARD

There are four **capacity levels** you need to be aware of.

- Full
- Practical
- Budgeted
- Idle

Capacity levels are needed to establish a standard absorption rate for production overhead, when standard absorption costing is used. **Capacity ratios** can also be calculated.

4: INTRODUCTION TO STANDARD COSTING

Key terms

- **Full capacity** is the theoretical capacity, assuming continuous production without any stoppages due to factors such as machine downtime, supply shortages or labour shortages. Full capacity would be associated with ideal standards.

- **Practical capacity** is an output level below full capacity, and is associated with attainable standards, since it takes account of known, unavoidable stoppages.

- **Budgeted capacity** is the capacity (labour hours, machine hours) needed to produce the budgeted output. It is associated with current standards, which relate to current conditions but may not be representative of normal practical capacity over a longer period of time.

- **Idle capacity** is the practical capacity in a period less the budgeted capacity measured in standard hours of output. It represents unused capacity that ought to be available, but which is not needed because the budgeted volume is lower than the practicable volume that could be achieved.

Question — Capacity ratios

Given the following information, calculate an idle capacity ratio, a production volume/ratio, a capacity ratio and an efficiency ratio and explain their meanings.

Full capacity	10,000 standard hours
Practical capacity	8,000 standard hours
Budgeted capacity	7,500 standard hours
Standard hours produced	6,500
Actual hours worked	7,000

Answer

Idle capacity ratio = ((practical capacity − budgeted capacity)/practical capacity) × 100%
= ((8,000 − 7,500)/8,000) × 100% = 6.25%.

This means that 6.25% of practical capacity will be unused because budgeted volume is lower than the volume that could be achieved.

Production volume ratio = (actual output measured in expected or standard hours/budgeted capacity) × 100%

= (6,500/7,500) × 100% = 86.67%

This means actual output was only 86.67% of budgeted output.

Capacity ratio = (actual hours worked/budgeted capacity) × 100%
= (7,000/7,500) × 100% = 93.33%

This means that only 93.33% of budgeted capacity was actually used.

Efficiency ratio = (actual output measured in standard or expected hours/actual hours worked) × 100%
= (6,500/7,000) × 100% = 92.86%

This means that the labour force were working at 92.86% efficiency.

PART B STANDARD COSTING

The production volume ratio shows the overall effect of the capacity and efficiency ratio. In the question above we have:

Production volume ratio	= capacity ratio	×	efficiency ratio
ie 86.67%	= 93.33%	×	92.86%

3.5 Setting standards for sales price and margin

The **standard selling price** will depend on a number of factors including the following.

- Anticipated market demand
- Competing products
- Manufacturing costs
- Inflation estimates

The **standard sales margin** is the difference between the standard cost and the standard selling price.

Question — Standard setting

What problems do you think could occur when standards are being set?

Answer

The following problems can occur when setting standards.

(a) Deciding how to incorporate **inflation** into planned unit costs

(b) Agreeing on a **performance standard** (attainable or ideal)

(c) Deciding on the **quality** of materials to be used (a better quality of material will cost more, but perhaps reduce material wastage)

(d) Estimating materials prices where **seasonal price variations** or **bulk purchase discounts** may be significant

(e) Finding sufficient **time** to construct standards as standard setting can be time consuming

(f) Incurring the **cost** of setting up and maintaining a system for establishing standards

4 Types of standard and their behavioural impact   12/03

FAST FORWARD

There are four **types of standard: ideal, attainable, current** and **basic**. These can have an impact on employee motivation.

How demanding should a standard be? Should the standard represent perfect performance or easily attainable performance? There are four types of standard.

Key terms

- An **ideal standard** is a standard which can be attained under perfect operating conditions: no wastage no inefficiencies, no idle time, no breakdowns.

- An **attainable standard** is a standard which can be attained if production is carried out efficiently, machines are properly operated and/or materials are properly used. Some allowance is made for wastage and inefficiencies.

- A **current standard** is standard based on current working conditions (current wastage, current inefficiencies).

- A **basic standard** is a long-term standard which remains unchanged over the years and is used to show trends.

The **different types of standard have a number of advantages and disadvantages.**

(a) **Ideal standards** can be seen as **long-term targets** but are not very useful for day-to-day control purposes.

(b) **Ideal standards cannot be achieved**. If such standards are used for budgeting, an allowance will have to be included to make the budget realistic and attainable.

(c) **Attainable standards** can be used for **product costing**, cost control, stock valuation, estimating and as a basis for budgeting.

(d) **Current standards** or attainable standards provide the **best basis for budgeting**, because they represent an achievable level of productivity.

(e) Current standards **do not attempt to improve** on current levels of efficiency.

(f) **Current standards** are useful during **periods when inflation is high**. They can be set on a month by month basis.

(g) **Basic standards** are used to show **changes in efficiency or performance** over a long period of time. They are perhaps the least useful and least common type of standard in use.

4.1 The impact on employee behaviour of the type of standard set

The type of standard set can have an impact on the behaviour of the employees trying to achieve those standards.

Type of standard	Impact
Ideal	Some say that they provide employees with an **incentive to be more efficient** even though it is highly unlikely that the standard will be achieved. Others argue that they are likely to have an unfavourable effect on employee motivation because the differences between standards and actual results will always be adverse. The **employees may feel that the goals are unattainable** and so **they will not work so hard**.
Attainable	Might be an **incentive to work harder** as they provide a **realistic but challenging target of efficiency**.
Current	**Will not motivate employees to do anything more than they are currently doing**.
Basic	May have an **unfavourable impact** on the motivation of employees. Over time they will discover that they are easily able to achieve the standards. They may become bored and lose interest in what they are doing if they have nothing to aim for.

Exam focus point

We will return to the behavioural implications of different costing approaches in Chapter 9 so try to link what you have covered here with the behavioural aspects of budgetary control systems when you get to that point in the Text.

In the December 2003 paper, seven marks were available for critically discussing the types of standard costing and their effect on employee motivation.

PART B STANDARD COSTING

5 Reviewing standards

> **FAST FORWARD**
>
> Standards should be revised whenever there are changes of a permanent and reasonably long-term nature.

Although standards are developed from past and current information, they should reflect technical and current factors expected for the period in which they are to be applied. Management should not think that once standards are set they will remain useful for ever. **Standards must evolve to reflect an organisation's changing methods and processes**. Comparing out-of-date standards with actual results will provide misleading information.

Consider a computer manufacturer. Suppose that the standard price for computer chips was set in 1995 and not changed until 2001. In the six-year period, however, the price of chips would have dramatically decreased. Consistently favourable material price variances would have been reported, giving the appearance that the purchasing department was performing very well, buying chips at well below the standard price. What's more, if stocks are valued at standard cost, the stock value of the chips would have been too high. The price reductions occurring since the standard was set would therefore render the standard obsolete and worthless.

It has been argued that **standard costing is unhelpful and potentially misleading in the modern organisation**, and causes managers to focus their attention on the wrong issues. **Continuous improvement and cost reduction programmes** are widespread but can they co-exist with systems of standard costing?

(a) Efforts to improve the efficiency of operations or reduce costs will **alter quantities of inputs**, **prices** and so on whereas standard costing is best used in a stable, standardised, repetitive environment.

(b) Predetermined standards conflict with a **philosophy of continual improvement**.

(c) Standard costs often incorporate a **planned level of scrap in material standards**. This is at odds with the aim of 'zero defects' inherent in continuous improvement programmes.

If standard costing is to be adopted in conjunction with cost reduction and continuous improvement programmes it is therefore vital that management **review standards on a regular basis and revise them if necessary**.

Some argue that standards should be revised as soon as there is any change in the basis upon which they were set. Clearly, if a standard is based on the cost of a material that is no longer available, it is meaningless to compare actual performance using a new material with the old standard. Or if an existing standard is discovered to be incorrectly set, the use of the incorrect standard is pointless.

Others believe that frequent changes in standards make them ineffective as motivators and measures of performance, since those trying to achieve the targets will feel that the **goal posts** are constantly being moved. It is also argued that frequent changes to standards are **too time-consuming** in terms of administration, although the introduction of computer systems makes this objection less forceful.

In practice, standard costs are **usually revised once a year** to allow for the new overheads budget, inflation in prices and wage rates, and any changes in the expected efficiency of material usage, labour or machinery. One research study showed that most organisations revise their standards annually.

The **most suitable approach** would therefore appear to be a policy of **revising the standards whenever changes of a permanent and reasonably long-term nature occur,** but not in response to temporary 'blips' in price or efficiency.

Exam focus point

There were eight marks available in the December 2001 exam for a discussion on the reasons why standards have to be reviewed.

4: INTRODUCTION TO STANDARD COSTING

Chapter Roundup

- A **standard cost** is an estimated unit cost built up of standards for each cost element (standard resource price and standard resource usage).
- **Standard costing** is principally used to value stocks and cost production and to act as a control device.
- Standard costing is most suited to mass production and repetitive assembly work.
- The responsibility for setting standards should be shared between the managers able to provide the necessary information about levels of expected efficiency, prices and overhead costs.
- There are four **capacity levels** you need to be aware of.
  - Full
  - Practical
  - Budgeted
  - Idle
- There are four **types of standard: ideal, attainable, current** and **basic**. These can have an impact on employee motivation.
- Standards should be revised whenever there are changes of a permanent and reasonably long-term nature.

PART B STANDARD COSTING

Quick Quiz

1   Choose the appropriate words from those highlighted.

   The **greatest/least** benefit from the use of standard costing can be gained if there is a degree of repetition in the production process.

   Standard costing is therefore **most/less** suited to organisations which produce to customer demand and requirements and **most/less** suited to mass production.

2   Fill in the blanks using phrases from the list below.

   (a) Idle capacity ratio = ((........................ – ....)/..........................) × 100%

   (b) Production volume ratio = (.........................../..........................) × 100%

   (c) Capacity ratio = (.........................../..........................) × 100%

   (d) Efficiency ratio = (.........................../..........................) × 100%

   Missing phrases
   Actual hours worked   Budgeted capacity
   Budgeted capacity   Practical capacity
   Practical capacity   Budgeted capacity
   Actual hours worked   Actual output measured in expected hours
   Actual output measured in standard hours

3   *Match the type of standard with the correct definition.*

Types of standard		Definitions
Ideal	(a)	Can be attained under perfect operating conditions
Attainable	(b)	Can be attained if production is carried out efficiently, machines are properly operated and/or materials are properly used
Current		
Basic	(c)	Based on current working conditions
	(d)	Remains unchanged over the years and is used to show trends

4   *Fill in the blanks.*

   Standard costing is difficult in times of inflation but it is still worthwhile.

   - .... and .... variances will still be meaningful.
   - Inflation is .... : there is no reason why its effects cannot be removed.
   - Standard costs can be ...., as long as this is not done ....

5   Provide three reasons why standard costing conflicts with schemes of continuous improvement and cost reduction programmes.

6   Standard costing is often used as an alternative to FIFO and LIFO in stock valuation.

   ☐ True
   ☐ False

7   With what kind of standards is practical capacity associated?

8   Ideal standards are long-term targets.

   ☐ True
   ☐ False

Answers to Quick Quiz

1. greatest
   less
   most

2. (a) ((practical capacity – budgeted capacity)/practical capacity) x 100%
   (b) (actual output measured in expected hours/budgeted capacity) x 100%
   (c) (actual hours worked/budgeted capacity) x 100%
   (d) (actual output measured in standard hours/actual hours worked) x 100%

3. Ideal   (a)
   Attainable (b)
   Current   (c)
   Basic   (d)

4. (a) Usage and efficiency variances will still be meaningful.
   (b) Inflation is measurable: there is no reason why its effects cannot be removed.
   (c) Standard costs can be reviewed, as long as this is not done too frequently.

5. (a) Efforts to improve the efficiency of operations or reduce costs will alter quantities of inputs, prices and so on whereas standard costing is best used in a stable, standardised, repetitive environment.
   (b) Predetermined standards conflict with a philosophy of continual improvement.
   (c) Standard costs often incorporate a planned level of scrap in material standards. This is at odds with the aim of 'zero defects' inherent in continuous improvement programmes.

6. True

7. Attainable standards

8. True

Now try the questions below from the Exam Question Bank

Number	Level	Marks	Time
Q5	Examination	25	45 mins

Basic variance analysis

Topic list	Syllabus reference
1 Variances	7(a)(ii)
2 Material variances	7(a)(ii)
3 Labour variances	7(a)(ii)
4 Variable production overhead variances	7(a)(ii)
5 Fixed production overhead variances	7(a)(ii)
6 Sales variances	7(a)(ii)
7 Working backwards approach	7(a)(ii)
8 The reasons for variances	7(a)(iii), (v)
9 Investigating variances	7(a)(iii), (v)

Introduction

The **actual results** achieved by an organisation will, more than likely, be **different from the expected results** (the expected results being the standard costs and revenues which we looked at in the previous chapter). Such differences may occur between individual items, such as the cost of labour or the volume of sales, and between the total expected profit/contribution and the total actual profit/contribution. These differences are **variances**.

In this chapter and the next we will be looking at the way in which variances are calculated and analysed.

We take each type of cost and compare the expected cost with the actual cost. Any variation is then analysed into a difference in the price of that item and a difference in the quantity used. Sales variances are also calculated.

You will see that it is important to compare like with like in these calculations, which means taking the original budget and **flexing** it to the level of actual output before comparing it to the actual results. Otherwise, you might be comparing the actual cost of producing 3,000 units with the expected cost of producing the budgeted 2,000 units and finding huge variances!

The management accountant would not stop at the calculation of variances. The next step would be to identify which warrant investigation and then to look into the reasons behind them. We suggest reasons for different types of variances and also highlight the way in which they inter-relate; the cause of a variance on one cost can often have an impact on another cost variance.

PART B STANDARD COSTING

Study guide

Section 20 – Standard costing I

- Calculate basic labour, material, overhead (variable and fixed) and sales variances, including problems of labour idle time
- Explain the reasons for variances
- Assess appropriate management action arising from the variances identified

Section 21 – Standard costing II

- Demonstrate an understanding of the inter-relationships between variances

Exam guide

Expect to see Section B questions based entirely on the contents of this chapter. Of course, Section A questions could also include variance analysis. The examiner has stressed that **discussion** of variances is a core topic in this paper.

1 Variances

FAST FORWARD

Variances measure the difference between actual results and expected results.

Key terms

- A **variance** is the difference between an actual result and an expected result.
- **Variance analysis** is the process by which the *total* difference between standard and actual results is analysed.

When actual results are better than expected results, we have a **favourable variance (F)**. If actual results are worse than expected results, we have an **adverse variance (A)**.

Exam focus point

Since December 2002, variances have been examined in every paper. Although this has tended to be in a Section B question, in December 2004 these were examined in the compulsory Section A.

2 Material variances   12/02, 6/04, 12/04

FAST FORWARD

The **direct material total variance** can be subdivided into the direct material **price** variance and the direct material **usage** variance. Direct material price variances are extracted at the time of receipt of the materials, not the time of usage.

Key terms

- The material **total variance** is the difference between what the output actually cost and what it should have cost, in terms of material. It can be divided into the following two sub-variances.
- The **material price variance** is the difference between what the material did cost and what it should have cost.
- The **material usage variance** is the difference between the standard cost of the material that should have been used and the standard cost of the material that was used.

2.1 Example: Material variances

Product X has a standard direct material cost of 10 kilograms of material Y at £10 per kilogram (= £100 per unit of X). During period 4, 1,000 units of X were manufactured, using 11,700 kilograms of material Y which cost £98,600.

Required

Calculate the following variances.

(a) The material total variance
(b) The material price variance
(c) The material usage variance

Solution

(a) The **material total variance**. This is the difference between what 1,000 units should have cost and what they did cost.

	£
1,000 units should have cost (× £100)	100,000
but did cost	98,600
Material total variance	1,400 (F)

The variance is favourable because the units cost less than they should have cost.

(b) The **material price variance**. This is the difference between what 11,700 kgs should have cost and what 11,700 kgs did cost.

	£
11,700 kgs of Y should have cost (× £10)	117,000
but did cost	98,600
Material Y price variance	18,400 (F)

The variance is favourable because the material cost less than it should have.

(c) The **material usage variance**. This is the difference between how many kilograms of Y should have been used to produce 1,000 units of X and how many kilograms were used, valued at the standard cost per kilogram.

1,000 units should have used (× 10 kgs)	10,000 kgs
but did use	11,700 kgs
Usage variance in kgs	1,700 kgs (A)
× standard cost per kilogram	× £10
Usage variance in £	£17,000 (A)

The variance is adverse because more material than should have been used was used.

(d) **Summary**

	£
Price variance	18,400 (F)
Usage variance	17,000 (A)
Total variance	1,400 (F)

2.2 Materials variances and opening and closing stock

Suppose that raw material P has a standard price of £3 per metre. During one month 6,000 metres are bought for £18,600, and 5,000 metres are used in production. At the end of the month, stock will have been increased by 1,000 metres. Should the material price variance be calculated on the basis of materials purchased (6,000 metres) or on the basis of materials used (5,000 metres)?

PART B STANDARD COSTING

The answer depends on how **closing stocks** of the raw materials will be valued.

(a) If they are **valued at standard cost**, (1,000 units at £3 per unit) the **price variance** is **calculated on material purchases** in the period.

(b) If they are **valued at actual cost** (FIFO) (1,000 units at £3.10 per unit) the **price variance is calculated on materials used in production** in the period.

A full standard costing system is usually in operation and therefore the price variance is calculated on purchases in the period. The variance on the full 6,000 metres will be written off to the costing profit and loss account, even though only 5,000 metres are included in the cost of production.

There are two main **advantages** in extracting the material price variance at the time of receipt.

(a) Variances will be brought to the attention of managers earlier than if they are extracted as the material is used. If it is necessary to correct any variances then management action can be more timely.

(b) All stocks will be valued at standard price. This is administratively easier than using FIFO, LIFO or a weighted average method and it means that all issues from stocks can be made at standard price. If stocks are held at actual cost it is necessary to calculate a separate price variance on each batch as it is issued. This can be a time consuming task, especially with a manual system.

The price variance would be calculated as follows.

	£
6,000 metres of material P purchased should cost (× £3)	18,000
but did cost	18,600
Price variance	600 (A)

Note that there are **disadvantages** to doing this, however.

(a) If variances are extracted at the time of receipt, revenues will be matched with the standard cost of the materials used plus the variances on the materials purchased rather than the true cost of sales, which does not comply with the matching concept.

(b) The usage variance may be calculated on a different amount to that on which the price variance is calculated and so the two variances may not sum to the materials total variance.

(c) SSAP 9 requires that stocks are valued at the lower of cost and net realisable value but by extracting variances upon receipt stocks are valued at standard. This may require an inventory adjustment for financial accounting purposes.

In practice, most organisations calculate materials price variances **when the material is purchased**. As far as your exam is concerned, David Cornes provides the following guidance in the June 1996 edition of *ACCA Students' Newsletter*.

'In examination questions the wording of the question should make clear what method is to be used. If both variances are to be calculated on the same quantity the examiner may say that the company uses a method of just-in-time purchasing or even that a system of Backflush Accounting ensures that purchases are not accounted for until the materials are used.'

3 Labour variances   12/02, 12/03, 6/04, 12/04

FAST FORWARD

The **direct labour total variance** can be subdivided into the direct labour **rate** variance and the direct labour **efficiency** variance.

If idle time arises, it is usual to calculate a separate **idle time variance**, and to base the calculation of the efficiency variance on active hours (when labour actually worked) only. It is always an adverse variance.

5: BASIC VARIANCE ANALYSIS

Key terms

> - The **labour total variance** is the difference between what the output should have cost and what it did cost, in terms of labour. It can be divided into two sub-variances.
> - The **labour rate variance** is the difference between what the labour did cost and what it should have cost.
> - The **labour efficiency variance** is the difference between the standard cost of the hours that should have been worked and the standard cost of the hours that were worked.

The calculation of labour variances is very similar to the calculation of material variances. The calculation of the labour rate variance is similar to that for the material price variance while the calculation of the labour efficiency variance is similar to that for the material usage variance.

3.1 Example: Labour variances

The standard direct labour cost of product X is 2 hours of grade Z labour at £5 per hour (= £10 per unit of product X). During period 4, 1,000 units of product X were made, and the direct labour cost of grade Z labour was £8,900 for 2,300 hours of work.

Required

Calculate the following variances.

(a) The labour total variance
(b) The labour rate variance
(c) The labour efficiency (productivity) variance

Solution

(a) **The labour total variance.** This is the difference between what 1,000 units should have cost and what they did cost.

	£
1,000 units should have cost (× £10)	10,000
but did cost	8,900
Labour total variance	1,100 (F)

The variance is favourable because the units cost less than they should have done.

(b) **The labour rate variance.** This is the difference between what 2,300 hours should have cost and what 2,300 hours did cost.

	£
2,300 hours of work should have cost (× £5 per hr)	11,500
but did cost	8,900
Labour rate variance	2,600 (F)

The variance is favourable because the labour cost less than it should have cost.

(c) **The labour efficiency variance.** This is the difference between the number of hours it should have taken to produce 1,000 units of X, and the number of hours it did take, valued at the standard rate per hour.

1,000 units of X should have taken (× 2 hrs)	2,000 hrs
but did take	2,300 hrs
Efficiency variance in hours	300 hrs (A)
× standard rate per hour	×£5
Efficiency variance in £	£1,500 (A)

The variance is adverse because more hours were worked than should have been worked.

PART B STANDARD COSTING

(d) **Summary**

	£
Rate variance	2,600 (F)
Efficiency variance	1,500 (A)
Total variance	1,100 (F)

3.2 Idle time variance

Key term

> The **idle time variance** is the number of hours that labour were idle valued at the standard rate per hour.

Idle time may be caused by machine breakdowns or not having work to give to employees, perhaps because of bottlenecks in production or a shortage of orders from customers. When it occurs, the labour force is still paid wages for time at work, but no actual work is done. Such time is unproductive and therefore inefficient. **In variance analysis, idle time is an adverse efficiency variance**.

The idle time variance is shown as a separate part of the total labour efficiency variance. The remaining **efficiency variance will then relate only to the productivity of the labour force during the hours spent actively working**.

3.3 Example: Labour variances with idle time

During period 5, 1,500 units of product X were made and the cost of grade Z labour was £17,500 for 3,080 hours. During the period, however, there as a shortage of customer orders and 100 hours were recorded as idle time.

Required

Calculate the following variances.

(a) The labour total variance
(b) The labour rate variance
(c) The idle time variance
(d) The labour efficiency variance

Solution

(a) **The labour total variance**

	£
1,500 units of product X should have cost (× £10)	15,000
but did cost	17,500
Labour total variance	2,500 (A)

Actual cost is greater than standard cost. The variance is therefore adverse.

(b) **The labour rate variance.** This is a comparison of what the hours paid should have cost and what they did cost.

	£
3,080 hours of grade Z labour should have cost (× £5)	15,400
but did cost	17,500
Labour rate variance	2,100 (A)

Actual cost is greater than standard cost. The variance is therefore adverse.

(c) **The idle time variance.** This is the hours of idle time, *valued* at the standard rate per hour. Idle time is *always* an adverse variance.

Idle time variance = 100 hours (A) × £5 = £500 (A)

(d) **The labour efficiency variance.** This considers the hours actively worked (the difference between hours paid for and idle time hours) and is calculated by taking the amount of output produced and comparing the time it should have taken to make them, with the actual time spent *actively* making them (3,080 – 100 = 2,980 hours). The variance in hours is valued at the standard rate per labour hour.

1,500 units of product X should take (× 2 hrs)	3,000 hrs
but did take (3,080 – 100)	2,980 hrs
Labour efficiency variance in hours	20 hrs (F)
× standard rate per hour	× £5
Labour efficiency variance in £	£100 (F)

(e) **Summary**

	£
Labour rate variance	2,100 (A)
Idle time variance	500 (A)
Labour efficiency variance	100 (F)
Labour total variance	2,500 (A)

Remember that, if idle time is recorded, the actual hours used in the efficiency variance calculation are the hours worked and not the hours paid for.

4 Variable production overhead variances 12/02

FAST FORWARD

> The **variable production overhead total variance** can be subdivided into the variable production overhead **expenditure** variance and the variable production overhead **efficiency** variance (based on active hours).

Suppose that the variable production overhead cost of product X is 2 hours at £1.50 (= £3 per unit). During period 6, 400 units of product X were made. The labour force worked 820 hours, of which 60 hours were recorded as idle time. The variable overhead cost was £1,230.

Required

Calculate the following variances.

(a) The variable production overhead total variance
(b) The variable production overhead expenditure variance
(c) The variable production overhead efficiency variance

Since this **example relates to variable production costs, the total variance is based on actual units of production**. (If the overhead had been a variable selling cost, the variance would be based on sales volumes.)

	£
400 units of product X should cost (× £3)	1,200
but did cost	1,230
Variable production overhead total variance	30 (A)

In many variance reporting systems, the variance analysis goes no further, and expenditure and efficiency variances are not calculated. However, the adverse variance of £30 may be explained as the sum of two factors.

(a) The **hourly rate of spending on variable production overheads was higher** than it **should have been**, that is there is an **expenditure variance**.

(b) The **labour force worked inefficiently**, and took longer to make the output than it should have done. This means that spending on variable production overhead was higher than it should have been, in other words there is an **efficiency (productivity) variance**. The **variable production overhead efficiency variance is exactly the same, in hours, as the direct labour efficiency variance, and occurs for the same reasons.**

PART B STANDARD COSTING

It is usually **assumed that variable overheads are incurred during active working hours**, but are not incurred during idle time (for example the machines are not running, therefore power is not being consumed). This means in our example that although the labour force was paid for 820 hours, they were actively working for only 760 of those hours, therefore variable production overhead spending occurred during 760 hours.

Key terms

> - The **variable production overhead total variance** is the difference between what the output should have cost and what it did cost, in terms of variable production overhead. It can be divided into two sub-variances.
> - The **variable production overhead expenditure variance** is the difference between the amount of variable production overhead that should have been incurred in the actual hours actively worked, and the actual amount of variable production overhead incurred.
> - The **variable production overhead efficiency variance** is the difference between the standard cost of the hours that should have been worked for the number of units actually produced, and the standard cost of the actual number of hours worked.

In our example, the expenditure and efficiency variances would be as follows.

		£
(a)	760 hours of variable production overhead should cost (× £1.50)	1,140
	but did cost	1,230
	Variable production overhead expenditure variance	90 (A)
(b)	400 units of product X should take (× 2 hrs)	800 hrs
	but did take (active hours)	760 hrs
	Variable production overhead efficiency variance in hours	40 hrs (F)
	× standard rate per hour	× £1.50
	Variable production overhead efficiency variance in £	£60 (F)
(c)	*Summary*	£
	Variable production overhead expenditure variance	90 (A)
	Variable production overhead efficiency variance	60 (F)
	Variable production overhead total variance	30 (A)

Note that **if variances change in line with production volume rather than labour hours, only a total variance can be calculated.**

5 Fixed production overhead variances   12/02, 12/04

FAST FORWARD

> The **fixed production overhead total variance** can be subdivided into an **expenditure** variance and a **volume** variance. The volume variance can be subdivided into an **efficiency** variance and a **capacity** variance.

You may have noticed that the method of calculating cost variances for variable cost items is essentially the same for labour, materials and variable overheads. Fixed production overhead variances are very different. In an absorption costing system, they are simply an **attempt to explain the under or over absorption of fixed overheads.**

The **fixed production overhead total variance may be broken down into two parts** as usual.

(a) An **expenditure variance**

(b) A **volume variance**. This in turn may be split into two parts.

   (i) **A volume efficiency variance**
   (ii) **A volume capacity variance**

The fixed production overhead volume variance sometimes causes confusion and may need more explanation. The most important point is that the volume variance applies to fixed production overhead costs only and not to variable production overheads.

(a) Variable production overheads **incurred change** with the volume of activity. If the master budget is to work for 300 hours and variable production overheads are incurred and absorbed at a rate of £6 per hour, the variable production overhead budget will be £1,800. If only 200 hours are actually worked, the variable production overhead absorbed will be £1,200, but the expected expenditure will also be £1,200, so that there will be **no under– or over-absorption** of production overhead because of volume changes.

(b) Fixed production overheads are different because the level of expenditure does not change as the **number of hours worked varies**. If the master budget is to work for 300 hours and fixed production overheads are budgeted to be £2,400, the fixed production overhead absorption rate will be £8 per hour. If actual hours worked are only 200 hours, the fixed production overhead absorbed will be £1,600, whereas expected expenditure will be unchanged at £2,400. There is an under-absorption of £800 because of the volume variance of 100 hours shortfall multiplied by the absorption rate of £8 per hour.

You will find it easier to calculate and understand fixed production overhead variances if you keep in mind the whole time the fact that you are trying to explain the reasons for any under– or over-absorbed production overhead. Remember that the absorption rate is calculated as (budgeted fixed production overhead ÷ budgeted level of activity).

Generally the level of activity used in the overhead absorption rate will be units of production or hours of activity. More often than not, if just one product is being produced, the level of activity is in terms of units produced. If, however, more than one product is produced, units of output are converted to standard hours.

As you should remember, if either the budgeted overhead or the budgeted activity level or both are incorrect then we will have under– or over-absorbed fixed production overhead.

(a) The fixed production overhead **expenditure variance** measures the under– or over-absorption caused by the **actual production overhead expenditure being different from budget**.

(b) There are two reasons why the actual production or hours of activity may be different from the budgeted production or budgeted number of hours used in calculating the absorption rate.

(i) The **work force may have been working at a more or less efficient rate than standard** to produce a given output. This is measured by the fixed production overhead **volume efficiency variance**, which is similar to the variable production overhead efficiency variance.

(ii) Regardless of the level of efficiency, the **total number of hours worked could have been less or more than was originally budgeted** (employees may have worked a lot of overtime or there may have been a strike). Other things being equal, this could lead to under– or over-absorbed fixed overhead and the effect is measured by the fixed production overhead **volume capacity variance**.

PART B STANDARD COSTING

5.1 How to calculate the variances

Key terms

- **Fixed production overhead total variance** is the difference between fixed production overhead incurred and fixed production overhead absorbed. In other words, it is the under– or over-absorbed fixed production overhead.
- **Fixed production overhead expenditure variance** is the difference between the budgeted fixed production overhead expenditure and actual fixed production overhead expenditure.
- **Fixed production overhead volume variance** is the difference between actual and budgeted production/volume multiplied by the standard absorption rate per *unit*.
- **Fixed production overhead volume efficiency variance** is the difference between the number of hours that actual production should have taken, and the number of hours actually taken (that is, worked) multiplied by the standard absorption rate per *hour*.
- **Fixed production overhead volume capacity variance** is the difference between budgeted hours of work and the actual hours worked, multiplied by the standard absorption rate per *hour*.

5.2 Example: Fixed production overhead variances

Suppose that a company budgets to produce 1,000 units of product E during August. The expected time to produce a unit of E is five hours, and the budgeted fixed production overhead is £20,000. The standard fixed production overhead cost per unit of product E will therefore be 5 hours at £4 per hour (= £20 per unit). Actual fixed production overhead expenditure in August turns out to be £20,450. The labour force manages to produce 1,100 units of product E in 5,400 hours of work.

Required

Calculate the following variances.

(a) The fixed production overhead total variance
(b) The fixed production overhead expenditure variance
(c) The fixed production overhead volume variance
(d) The fixed production overhead volume efficiency variance
(e) The fixed production overhead volume capacity variance

Solution

(a) **Fixed production overhead total variance**

	£
Fixed production overhead incurred	20,450
Fixed production overhead absorbed (1,100 units × £20 per unit)	22,000
Fixed production overhead expenditure variance	1,550 (F)
(= under-/over-absorbed overhead)	

The variance is favourable because more overheads were absorbed than budgeted.

(b) **Fixed production overhead expenditure variance**

	£
Budgeted fixed production overhead expenditure	20,000
Actual fixed production overhead expenditure	20,450
Fixed production overhead expenditure variance	450 (A)

The variance is adverse because actual expenditure was greater than budgeted.

(c) **Fixed production overhead volume variance**. The production volume achieved was greater than expected. The fixed production overhead volume variance measures the difference at the standard rate.

	£
Actual production at standard rate (1,100 × £20 per unit)	22,000
Budgeted production at standard rate (1,000 × £20 per unit)	20,000
Fixed production overhead volume variance	2,000 (F)

The variance is favourable because output was greater than expected.

(i) The labour force may have worked efficiently, and produced output at a faster rate than expected. More overhead will be absorbed if units are produced more quickly. This **efficiency variance** is exactly the same in hours as the direct labour efficiency variance (and the variable production overhead efficiency variance), but is valued in £ at the standard absorption rate for fixed overhead.

(ii) The labour force may have worked longer hours than budgeted, and therefore produced more output, so there may be a *capacity variance*.

(d) **Fixed production overhead volume efficiency variance.** The volume efficiency variance is calculated in the same way as the labour efficiency variance.

1,100 units of product E should take (× 5 hrs)	5,500 hrs
but did take	5,400 hrs
Fixed overhead production volume efficiency variance in hours	100 hrs (F)
× standard fixed production overhead absorption rate per hour	× £4
Fixed production overhead volume efficiency variance in £	£400 (F)

The labour force has produced 5,500 standard hours of work in 5,400 actual hours and so output is 100 standard hours (or 20 units of product E) higher than budgeted for this reason and the variance is favourable.

(e) **Fixed production overhead volume capacity variance.** The volume capacity variance is the difference between the budgeted and actual active hours of work (excluding any idle time).

Budgeted hours of work	5,000 hrs
Actual hours of work	5,400 hrs
Fixed production overhead volume capacity variance	400 hrs (F)
× standard fixed production overhead absorption rate per hour	× £4
Fixed production overhead volume capacity variance in £	£1,600 (F)

Since the labour force worked 400 hours longer than budgeted, we should expect output to be 400 standard hours (or 80 units of product E) higher than budgeted and hence the variance is favourable.

Question — Various variances

Brain Ltd produces and sells one product only, the Blob, the standard cost for one unit being as follows.

	£
Direct material A – 10 kilograms at £20 per kg	200
Direct material B – 5 litres at £6 per litre	30
Direct wages – 5 hours at £6 per hour	30
Fixed production overhead	50
Total standard cost	310

The fixed overhead included in the standard cost is based on an expected monthly output of 900 units. Fixed production overhead is absorbed on the basis of direct labour hours.

PART B STANDARD COSTING

During April the actual results were as follows.

Production	800 units
Material A	7,800 kg used, costing £159,900
Material B	4,300 litres used, costing £23,650
Direct wages	4,200 hours worked for £24,150

Fixed production overhead   £47,000

Required

(a) Calculate price and usage variances for each material.

(b) Calculate labour rate and efficiency variances.

(c) Calculate fixed production overhead expenditure and volume variances and then subdivide the volume variance.

Answer

(a) **Price variance – A**

	£
7,800 kgs should have cost (× £20)	156,000
but did cost	159,900
Price variance	3,900 (A)

Usage variance – A

800 units should have used (× 10 kgs)	8,000 kgs
but did use	7,800 kgs
Usage variance in kgs	200 kgs (F)
× standard cost per kilogram	× £20
Usage variance in £	£4,000 (F)

Price variance – B

	£
4,300 litres should have cost (× £6)	25,800
but did cost	23,650
Price variance	2,150 (F)

Usage variance – B

800 units should have used (× 5 l)	4,000 l
but did use	4,300 l
Usage variance in litres	300 (A)
× standard cost per litre	× £6
Usage variance in £	£1,800 (A)

(b) **Labour rate variance**

	£
4,200 hours should have cost (× £6)	25,200
but did cost	24,150
Rate variance	1,050 (F)

104

Labour efficiency variance

800 units should have taken (× 5 hrs)	4,000 hrs
but did take	4,200 hrs
Efficiency variance in hours	200 hrs (A)
× standard rate per hour	× £6
Efficiency variance in £	£1,200 (A)

(c) **Fixed overhead expenditure variance**

	£
Budgeted expenditure (£50 × 900)	45,000
Actual expenditure	47,000
Expenditure variance	2,000 (A)

Fixed overhead volume variance

	£
Budgeted production at standard rate (900 × £50)	45,000
Actual production at standard rate (800 × £50)	40,000
Volume variance	5,000 (A)

Fixed overhead volume efficiency variance

	£
800 units should have taken (× 5 hrs)	4,000 hrs
but did take	4,200 hrs
Volume efficiency variance in hours	200 hrs
× standard absorption rate per hour	× £10
Volume efficiency variance	£2,000 (A)

Fixed overhead volume capacity variance

Budgeted hours	4,500 hrs
Actual hours	4,200 hrs
Volume capacity variance in hours	300 hrs (A)
× standard absorption rate per hour (£50 ÷ 5)	× £10
	£3,000 (A)

6 Sales variances   12/03, 6/04, 6/05

6.1 Selling price variance

> **FAST FORWARD**
>
> The **selling price variance** measures the effect on expected profit of a selling price different to the standard selling price. It is calculated as the difference between what the sales revenue should have been for the actual quantity sold, and what it was.

Suppose that the standard selling price of product X is £15. Actual sales in March were 2,000 units at £15.30 per unit. The selling price variance is calculated as follows.

	£
Revenue from 2,000 units should be (× £15)	30,000
but was (× £15.30)	30,600
Selling price variance	600 (F)

The variance is favourable because the price was higher than expected.

6.2 Sales volume variance

FAST FORWARD

The **sales volume variance** measures the increase or decrease in expected profit as a result of the sales volume being higher or lower than budgeted.

Suppose that a company budgets to sell 8,000 units of product J for £12 per unit. The standard full cost per unit is £7. Actual sales were 7,700 units, at £12.50 per unit. The sales volume variance is calculated as follows.

Budgeted sales volume	8,000 units
Actual sales volume	7,700 units
Sales volume variance in units	300 units (A)
× standard profit per unit (£(12–7))	× £5
Sales volume variance	£1,500 (A)

The variance is adverse because actual sales were less than budgeted.

6.3 Example: Sales variances

Jasper Ltd has the following budget and actual figures for May.

	Budget	Actual
Sales units	600	620
Selling price per unit	£30	£29

Standard full cost of production = £28 per unit.

Required

Calculate the selling price variance and the sales volume variance.

Solution

		£
(a)	Sales revenue for 620 units should have been (× £30)	18,600
	but was (× £29)	17,980
	Selling price variance	620 (A)
(b)	Budgeted sales volume	600 units
	Actual sales volume	620 units
	Sales volume variance in units	20 units (F)
	× standard profit per unit (£(30 – 28))	× £2
	Sales volume variance	£40 (F)

Exam focus point

A common mistake when computing the sales volume variance is to multiply the variance in units by the standard selling price rather than by the standard profit per unit. In effect this is calculating the sales value variance.

7 Working backwards approach

Exam questions often provide you with data about expected and actual results and you have to calculate variances. One way in which your understanding of the topic can be tested, however, is if you are provided with **information about variances from which you have to 'work backwards' to determine the expected and actual results.**

5: BASIC VARIANCE ANALYSIS

7.1 Example: Working backwards

The standard direct material cost of Product X is £96 (16 kgs × £6 per kg) and the standard direct labour cost is £72 (6 hours × £12 per hour). The following variances were among those reported in control period 10 in relation to Product X.

Direct material price: £18,840 favourable
Direct material usage: £480 adverse
Direct labour rate: £10,598 adverse
Direct labour efficiency: £8,478 favourable

Actual direct wages cost £171,320 and £5.50 was paid for each kg of direct material. There was no opening or closing stocks of the material.

Required

Calculate the following.

(a) Actual output
(b) Actual hours worked
(c) Average actual wage rate per hour
(d) Actual number of kilograms purchased and used

Solution

(a)

	£
Total direct wages cost	171,320
Adjust for variances:	
labour rate	(10,598)
labour efficiency	8,478
Standard direct wages cost	169,200

∴ Actual output = Total standard cost ÷ unit standard cost
= £169,200 ÷ £72
= 2,350 units

(b)

	£
Total direct wages cost	171,320.0
Less rate variance	(10,598.0)
Standard rate for actual hours	160,722.0
÷ standard rate per hour	÷ £12.0
Actual hours worked	13,393.5 hrs

(c) Average actual wage rate per hour = actual wages/actual hours = £171,320/13,393.5 = £12.79 per hour.

(d) Number of kgs purchased and used = x

	£
x kgs should have cost (× £6)	6.0x
but did cost (× £5.50)	5.5x
Direct material price variance	0.5x

∴ £0.5x = £18,840
∴ x = 37,680 kgs

Question — Working backwards

XYZ Ltd uses standard costing. The following data relates to labour grade II.

Actual hours worked = 10,400 hours
Standard allowance for actual production = 9,800 hours
Standard rate per hour = £5
Rate variance (adverse) = £416

What was the actual rate of pay per hour?

PART B STANDARD COSTING

> **Answer**
>
> Rate variance per hour worked = £416/10,400 = £0.04(A)
>
> Actual rate per hour = £(5.00 + 0.04) = £5.04

8 The reasons for variances   12/02, 12/03, 12/04

Exam focus point

> In an examination, always be prepared to be able to explain the reasons why variances have occurred, and their significance.

There now follows a list of a few possible causes of variances. This is not an exhaustive list and in an examination question you should review the information given and use your imagination and common sense to suggest possible reasons for variances.

Variance	Favourable	Adverse
Material price	Unforeseen discounts received Greater care in purchasing Change in material standard	Price increase Careless purchasing Change in material standard
Material usage	Material used of higher quality than standard More effective use made of material Errors in allocating material to jobs	Defective material Excessive waste Theft Stricter quality control Errors in allocating material to jobs
Labour rate	Use of workers at a rate of pay lower than standard	Wage rate increase
Idle time	*The idle time variance is always adverse.*	Machine breakdown Non-availability of material Illness or injury to worker
Labour efficiency	Output produced more quickly than expected, because of work motivation, better quality of equipment or materials Errors in allocating time to jobs	Lost time in excess of standard allowed Output lower than standard set because of lack of training, sub-standard material etc Errors in allocating time to jobs
Overhead expenditure	Savings in costs incurred More economical use of services	Increase in cost of services Excessive use of services Change in type of services used
Overhead volume	Production or level of activity greater than budgeted	Production or level of activity less than budgeted
Selling price	Unplanned price increase	Unplanned price reduction
Sales volume	Additional demand	Unexpected fall in demand Production difficulties

9 Investigating variances

6/04

> **FAST FORWARD**
>
> **Materiality**, **controllability**, the **type** of standard being used, variance **trend**, **interdependence** and **costs** should be taken into account when deciding on the significance of a variance.

9.1 The decision whether or not to investigate

Before management decide whether or not to investigate the reasons for the occurrence of a particular variance, there are a number of factors which should be considered in assessing the significance of the variance.

9.1.1 Materiality

Because a standard cost is really only an *average* expected cost, small variations between actual and standard are bound to occur and are unlikely to be significant. Obtaining an 'explanation' of the reasons why they occurred is likely to be time consuming and irritating for the manager concerned. The explanation will often be 'chance', which is not, in any case, particularly helpful. For such variations **further investigation is not worthwhile** since such variances are not controllable.

9.1.2 Controllability

This must also influence the decision about whether to investigate. If there is a general worldwide increase in the price of a raw material there is nothing that can be done internally to control the effect of this. If a central decision is made to award all employees a 10% increase in salary, staff costs in division A will increase by this amount and the variance is not controllable by division A's manager. **Uncontrollable variances call for a change in the plan, not an investigation into the past.**

9.1.3 The type of standard being used

The efficiency variance reported in any control period, whether for materials or labour, will depend on the **efficiency level set**. If, for example, an ideal standard is used, variances will always be adverse. A similar problem arises if average price levels are used as standards. If **inflation** exists, favourable price variances are likely to be reported at the beginning of a period, to be offset by adverse price variances later in the period.

9.1.4 Variance trend

Although small variations in a single period are unlikely to be significant, small variations that occur consistently may need more attention. Variance trend is probably more important that a single set of variances for one accounting period. The trend **provides an indication of whether the variance is fluctuating within acceptable control limits or becoming out of control.**

(a) If, say, an efficiency variance is £1,000 adverse in month 1, the obvious conclusion is that the process is out of control and that corrective action must be taken. This may be correct, but what if the same variance is £1,000 adverse every month? The *trend* indicates that the process is in control and the standard has been wrongly set.

(b) Suppose, though, that the same variance is consistently £1,000 adverse for each of the first six months of the year but that production has steadily fallen from 100 units in month 1 to 65 units by month 6. The variance trend in absolute terms is constant, but relative to the number of units produced, efficiency has got steadily worse.

Individual variances should therefore not be looked at in isolation; variances should be scrutinised for a number of successive periods if their full significance is to be appreciated.

9.1.5 Interdependence between variances

Individual variances should not be looked at in isolation. One variance might be inter-related with another, and much of it might have occurred only because the other variance occurred too. **When two variances are interdependent (interrelated) one will usually be adverse and the other one favourable.** Here are some examples.

Interrelated variances	Explanation
Materials price and usage	If **cheaper materials** are purchased for a job in order to obtain a favourable price variance, materials wastage might be **higher** and an **adverse usage variance** may occur.
	If the cheaper materials are more difficult to handle, there might be an **adverse labour efficiency variance** too.
	If more expensive materials are purchased, the **price variance** will be **adverse** but the **usage variance** might be **favourable** if the material is easier to use or of a higher quality.
Labour rate and efficiency	If employees are paid higher rates for experience and skill, using a highly skilled team might lead to an **adverse rate variance** and a **favourable efficiency variance** (experienced staff are less likely to waste material, for example).
	In contrast, a favourable rate variance might indicate a larger-than-expected proportion of inexperienced workers, which could result in an **adverse labour efficiency variance**, and perhaps **poor materials handling and high rates of rejects** too (and hence an adverse materials usage variance).
Selling price and sales volume	A reduction in the selling price might stimulate bigger sales demand, so that an **adverse selling price variance** might be counterbalanced by a **favourable sales volume variance**.
	Similarly, a price rise would give a **favourable price variance**, but possibly cause an **adverse sales volume variance**.

9.1.6 Costs of investigation

The costs of an investigation should be weighed against the benefits of correcting the cause of a variance.

Exam focus point

When asked to provide a commentary on variances you have calculated, make sure that you *interpret* your calculations rather than simply detail them.

9.2 Variance investigation models

FAST FORWARD

The **rule-of-thumb** and **statistical significance** variance investigation models and/or statistical **control charts** can be used to determine whether a variance should be investigated.

9.2.1 Rule-of-thumb model

This involves **deciding a limit** and if the size of a **variance is within the limit**, it should be considered **immaterial**. Only if it exceeds the limit is it considered materially significant, and worthy of investigation.

In practice many managers believe that this approach to deciding which variances to investigate is perfectly adequate. However, it has a number of **drawbacks**.

(a) Should variances be investigated if they exceed 10% of standard? Or 5%? Or 15%?

(b) Should a **different fixed percentage be applied to favourable and unfavourable variances**?

(c) Suppose that the fixed percentage is, say, 10% and an important category of expenditure has in the past been very closely controlled so that adverse variances have never exceeded, say, 2% of standard. Now if adverse variances suddenly shoot up to, say, **8% or 9%** of standard, there might well be **serious excess expenditures incurred that ought to be controlled**, but with the fixed percentage limit at 10%, the variances would not be 'flagged' for investigation.

(d) **Unimportant categories** of low-cost expenditures might be loosely controlled, with variances commonly exceeding 10% in both a favourable and adverse direction. These would be regularly – and **unnecessarily – flagged for investigation**.

(e) Where actual expenditures have **normal and expected wide fluctuations** from period to period, but the 'standard' is a fixed expenditure amount, variances will be **flagged for investigation unnecessarily often**.

(f) There is **no attempt to consider the costs and potential benefits of investigating variances** (except insofar as the pre-set percentage is of 'material significance').

(g) The **past history of variances in previous periods is ignored**. For example, if the pre-set percentage limit is set at 10% and an item of expenditure has regularly exceeded the standard by, say, 6% per month for a number of months in a row, in all probability there is a situation that ought to warrant control action. Using the pre-set percentage rule, however, the variance would never be flagged for investigation in spite of the cumulative adverse variances.

Some of the difficulties can be overcome by **varying the pre-set percentage from account to account** (for example 5% for direct labour efficiency, 2% for rent and rates, 10% for salesmen's expenditure, 15% for postage costs, 5% for direct materials price, 3% for direct materials usage and so on). On the other hand, some difficulties, if they are significant, can only be overcome with a different cost-variance investigation model.

9.2.2 Statistical significance model

Historical data are used to **calculate** both a standard as **an expected average** and the **expected standard deviation** around this average when the process is under control. An **in-control process** (process being material usage, fixed overhead expenditure and so on) is one in which any resulting **variance is simply due to random fluctuations** around the expected outcome. An **out-of-control process**, on the other hand, is one in which **corrective action can be taken to remedy any variance**.

By assuming that variances that occur are normally distributed around this average, a **variance will be investigated if it is *more* than a distance from the expected average that the estimated normal distribution suggests is likely if the process is in control**. (Note that such a variance would be deemed significant.)

(a) A 95% or 0.05 significance level rule would state that variances should be investigated if they exceed 1.96 standard deviations from the standard.

(b) A 99% or 0.01 significance level rule would state that variances should be investigated if they exceed 2.58 standard deviations from the standard. This is less stringent than a 0.05 significance level rule.

(c) For simplicity, 1.96 and 2.58 standard deviations can be rounded up to 2 and 3 standard deviations respectively.

For example data could be collected and analysed to reveal the following pattern.

Standard hours per unit   6 hours
Standard deviation per unit   0.5 hours

Assume that a **0.05 significance level** rule is in use.

Suppose that 100 units are made and take 640 hours. The efficiency variance would be 40 hours (A). The standard deviation is 0.5 hours for one unit and $0.5 \times \sqrt{100} = 5$ hours for 100 units. Since 40 hours (A) is **8 standard deviations** from the standard of 600 hours, the efficiency variance should be **investigated**.

Question — Investigation of variances

Data has been collected and analysed and reveals that transport costs per month are £25,000, with a standard deviation of £2,000. A 0.01 significance rule is in use. Actual travel expenses are £28,750. Should the resulting variance be investigated?

Answer

Variance = £3,750 (A) = 1.875 standard deviations

The variance would not be investigated.

The statistical significance rule has two principal **advantages** over the rule of thumb approach.

(a) **Important costs** that normally vary by only a small amount from standard will be **signalled for investigation if variances increase significantly**.

(b) Costs that **usually fluctuate by large amounts will not be signalled** for investigation unless variances are extremely large.

The main **disadvantage** of the statistical significance rule is the problem of assessing standard deviations in expenditure.

9.2.3 Statistical control charts

By marking variances and control limits on a control chart, **investigation** is signalled not only when a particular **variance exceeds the control limit** (since it would be non-random and worth investigating) but also when the **trend of variances shows a progressively worsening movement** in actual results (even though the variance in any single control period has not yet overstepped the control limit).

The $\bar{x}$ **control chart** is based on the principle of the statistical significance model. For each cost item, a chart is kept of monthly variances and **tolerance limits are set at 1, 2 or 3 standard deviations**.

In this example, variances do not exceed the tolerance limits in any month, but the chart shows a worsening of variances over time, and so management might decide that an investigation is warranted, perhaps when it exceeds an inner warning limit.

Using a **cusum chart, the cumulative sum of variances** over a long period of time **is plotted**. If the variances are not significant, these 'sums' will simply fluctuate in a random way above and below the average to give a total or cumulative sum of zero. But if significant variances occur, the cumulative sum will start to develop a positive or negative drift, and when it exceeds a set tolerance limit, the situation must be investigated.

The **advantage** of the multiple period approach over the single period approach is that **trends are detectable earlier**, and control action would be introduced sooner than might have been the case if only current-period variances were investigated.

9.3 Possible control action

FAST FORWARD

Measurement errors and **out of date standards**, as well as **efficient/inefficient operations** and **random fluctuations**, can cause differences between standard and actual performance.

There are few basic reasons why variances occur and the **control action which may be taken will depend on the reason why the variance occurred**.

9.3.1 Measurement errors

In exam questions there is generally no question of the information that you are given being wrong. In practice, however, it may be extremely difficult to establish that 1,000 units of product A used 32,000 kg of raw material X. Scales may be misread, the pilfering or wastage of materials may go unrecorded, items may be wrongly classified (as material X3, say, when material X8 was used in reality), or employees may make 'cosmetic' adjustments to their records to make their own performance look better than it really was. An investigation may show that **control action is required to improve the accuracy of the recording system** so that measurement errors do not occur.

9.3.2 Out of date standards

Price standards are likely to become out of date quickly when frequent changes to the costs of material, power, labour and so on occur, or in **periods of high inflation**. In such circumstances an **investigation of variances is likely to highlight a general change in market prices** rather than efficiencies or inefficiencies in acquiring resources. Standards may also be out of date where operations are subject to **technological development** or if **learning curve effects** have not been taken into account. Investigation of this type of variance will provide information about the inaccuracy of the standard and **highlight the need to frequently review and update standards**.

9.3.3 Efficient or inefficient operations

Spoilage and better quality material/more highly skilled labour than standard are all likely to affect the efficiency of operations and hence cause variances. **Investigation** of variances in this category should **highlight the cause of the inefficiency or efficiency and will lead to control action to eliminate the inefficiency being repeated** or action to **compound the benefits of the efficiency**. For example, stricter supervision may be required to reduce wastage levels and the need for overtime working. The purchasing department could be encouraged to continue using suppliers of good quality materials.

9.3.4 Random or chance fluctuations

A standard is an average figure and so **actual results are likely to deviate unpredictably within the predictable range.** As long as the variance falls within this range, it will be classified as a random or chance fluctuation and **control action will not be necessary**.

Chapter Roundup

- **Variances** measure the difference between actual results and expected results.

- The **direct material total variance** can be subdivided into the direct material **price** variance and the direct material **usage** variance. Direct material price variances are extracted at the time of receipt of the materials, not the time of usage.

- The **direct labour total variance** can be subdivided into the direct labour **rate** variance and the direct labour **efficiency** variance.

- If idle time arises, it is usual to calculate a separate **idle time variance**, and to base the calculation of the efficiency variance on active hours (when labour actually worked) only. It is always an adverse variance.

- The **variable production overhead total variance** can be subdivided into the variable production overhead **expenditure** variance and the variable production overhead **efficiency** variance (based on active hours).

- The **fixed production overhead total variance** can be subdivided into an **expenditure** variance and a volume variance. The volume variance can be subdivided into an **efficiency** variance and a **capacity** variance.

- The **selling price variance** measures the effect on profit of a selling price different to the standard selling price. It is calculated as the difference between what the sales revenue should have been for the actual quantity sold, and what it was.

- The **sales volume variance** measures the effect on profit of actual sales volume being higher or lower than budgeted.

- **Materiality**, **controllability**, the **type** of standard being used, variance **trend**, **interdependence** and **costs** should be taken into account when deciding on the significance of a variance.

- The **rule-of-thumb** and **statistical significance** variance investigation models and/or statistical **control charts** can be used to determine whether a variance should be investigated.

- **Measurement errors** and **out of date standards**, as well as **efficient/inefficient operations** and **random fluctuations**, can cause differences between standard and actual performance.

Quick Quiz

1   *Fill in the blanks.*

    The material price variance is the difference between .... and ....

    The material usage variance is the difference between .... and ....

2   If closing stocks of raw materials are valued at standard cost, the material price variance is calculated on material purchases in the period.

    True ☐

    False ☐

3   *Choose the appropriate words from those highlighted.*

    The idle time variance is an **efficiency/price** variance which is **adverse/favourable**.

4   Are variable production overhead variances based on hours paid or hours worked?

5   *Fill in the boxes in the diagram with the names of the variances and add the appropriate definition number from the list below.*

    Fixed production overhead total variance
    (Definition ....)

    ☐ variance
    (Definition ....)

    ☐ variance
    (Definition ....)

    ☐ variance
    (Definition ....)

    ☐ variance
    (Definition ....)

Definitions

1   The difference between actual and budgeted production, multiplied by the standard absorption rate per unit

2   The difference between budgeted hours of work and the actual hours worked, multiplied by the standard absorption rate per hour

3   The under or over absorption of fixed production overhead

4   The difference between budgeted fixed production overhead expenditure and actual fixed production overhead expenditure

5   The difference between the number of hours that actual production should have taken, and the number of hours actually taken, multiplied by the standard absorption rate per hour

PART B STANDARD COSTING

6 The sales volume variance is valued at the standard selling price per unit.

True ☐

False ☐

7 *Match the following causes of variances to the appropriate variance.*

Variances
- (a) Favourable labour efficiency
- (b) Adverse sales volume
- (c) Adverse material price
- (d) Adverse selling price
- (e) Adverse fixed production overhead volume
- (f) Idle time

Causes
- (1) Inexperienced staff in the purchasing department
- (2) Materials of higher quality than standard
- (3) Unexpected slump in demand
- (4) Production difficulties
- (5) Strike
- (6) Poor machine maintenance

8 *Match the three pairs of interrelated variances.*
- (a) Adverse selling price
- (b) Favourable labour rate
- (c) Adverse materials usage
- (d) Favourable sales volume
- (e) Adverse materials price
- (f) Favourable materials usage
- (g) Adverse sales volume
- (h) Idle time

Answers to Quick Quiz

1. The material price variance is the difference between what the material did cost and what it should have cost.

   The material usage variance is the difference between the standard cost of the material that should have been used and the standard cost of the material that was used.

2. True

3. The idle time variance is an adverse efficiency variance.

4. Variable production overhead variances are based on hours worked.

5.
```
                Fixed production overhead total variance
                           (Definition 3)
                          /              \
                  Expenditure            Volume
                   variance             variance
                 (Definition 4)        (Definition 1)
                                      /            \
                              Volume              Volume
                             efficiency           capacity
                              variance            variance
                            (Definition 5)     (Definition 2)
```

6. False. It is valued at the standard profit margin per unit.

7. (a) (2)
   (b) (3) or (4) or (5)
   (c) (1)
   (d) (3)
   (e) (4) or (5) or (6)
   (f) (5) or (6)

8. (a) and (d)
   (b) and (c)
   (e) and (f)

Now try the question below from the Exam Question Bank			
Number	**Level**	**Marks**	**Time**
Q6	Examination	25	45 mins

Further variance analysis

Topic list	Syllabus reference
1 Operating statements	7(a)(iv)
2 Variances in a standard marginal costing system	7(a)(ii)
3 Materials mix and yield variances	7(a)(ii)
4 Sales mix and quantity variances	7(a)(ii)
5 Planning and operational variance	7(b)

Introduction

In this chapter we build on the knowledge you have gained from Chapters 4 and 5 and examine a number of further variance analysis topics. We begin by considering the way in which individual variances can be **summarised** so as to show how budgeted profit/contribution differs from actual profit/contribution.

We then move on to looking at the **differences** between variances in an **absorption** costing system (which we have been concentrating on so far) and those in a **marginal** costing system.

The final three topics of the chapter deal with slightly more complex variance analysis.

When a product requires two or more materials in its make-up, the **materials usage variance** can be split into a materials **mix variance** and a materials **yield variance**. Likewise, if a company sells more than one product, it is possible to analyse the overall **sales volume variance** into a sales **mix variance** and a sales **quantity variance**. Don't be put off by these new terms. The basic principles of variance calculation covered in the previous chapter still applies: an actual result is compared with an original standard result.

In the last section of the chapter we will be moving away from this approach to variance calculation with a study of **planning and operational variances.**

PART B   STANDARD COSTING

Study guide

Section 21 – Standard costing II

- Prepare reconciliations using operating statements which reconcile budgeted and actual profit figures, and/or reconcile the actual sales less the standard cost of sales with the actual profit
- Calculate and explain operational and planning variances
- Demonstrate how absorption and marginal approaches can be used in standard costing
- Calculate mix and yield variances for materials
- Calculate mix and quantity variances for sales
- Demonstrate an understanding of the inter-relationships between variances
- Explain the reasons for variances
- Assess appropriate management action arising from the variances identified

Exam guide

Section B questions on the topics covered in this chapter are likely to be set regularly but variances may also be included in Section A. The topics in Chapter 6 may be examined, either on their own or in conjunction with more straightforward variance analysis covered in Chapter 5. The examiner has stated that the variance calculations set are likely to be the more complicated variances covered in this chapter.

1 Operating statements   12/02, 12/03, 6/04

FAST FORWARD

> **Operating statements** show how cost and revenue variances combine to reconcile budgeted profit to actual profit.

So far, we have considered how variances are calculated without considering how they combine to reconcile the difference between budgeted profit and actual profit during a period. This reconciliation is usually presented as a report to senior management at the end of each control period. The report is called an **operating statement** or **statement of variances**.

Key term

> An **operating statement** is a regular report for management which compares actual costs and revenues with budgeted figures and shows variances.

An extensive example will now be introduced, both to revise the variance calculations already described, and also to combine them into an operating statement.

1.1 Example: Variances and operating statements

Armoured Kangaroo Ltd manufactures one product, and the entire product is sold as soon as it is produced. There are no opening or closing stocks and work in progress is negligible. The company operates a standard costing system and analysis of variances is made every month. The standard cost card for the product, a boomerang, is as follows.

STANDARD COST CARD – BOOMERANG

		£
Direct materials	0.5 kilos at £4 per kilo	2.00
Direct wages	2 hours at £2.00 per hour	4.00
Variable overheads	2 hours at £0.30 per hour	0.60
Fixed overhead	2 hours at £3.70 per hour	7.40
Standard cost		14.00
Standard profit		6.00
Standing selling price		20.00

Budgeted output for June was 5,100 units. Actual results for June were as follows.

Production of 4,850 units was sold for £95,600
Materials consumed in production amounted to 2,300 kilos at a total cost of £9,800
Labour hours paid for amounted to 8,500 hours at a cost of £16,800
Actual operating hours amounted to 8,000 hours
Variable overheads amounted to £2,600
Fixed overheads amounted to £42,300

Required

Calculate all variances and prepare an operating statement for June.

Solution

			£
(a)	2,300 kg of material should cost (× £4)		9,200
	but did cost		9,800
	Material price variance		600 (A)
(b)	4,850 boomerangs should use (× 0.5 kgs)		2,425 kg
	but did use		2,300 kg
	Material usage variance in kgs		125 kg (F)
	× standard cost per kg		× £4
	Material usage variance in £		£ 500 (F)
(c)	8,500 hours of labour should cost (× £2)		17,000
	but did cost		16,800
	Labour rate variance		200 (F)
(d)	4,850 boomerangs should take (× 2 hrs)		9,700 hrs
	but did take (active hours)		8,000 hrs
	Labour efficiency variance in hours		1,700 hrs (F)
	× standard cost per hour		× £2
	Labour efficiency variance in £		£3,400 (F)
(e)	Idle time variance 500 hours (A) × £2		£1,000 (A)
(f)	8,000 hours incurring variable o/hd expenditure should cost (× £0.30)		2,400
	but did cost		2,600
	Variable overhead expenditure variance		200 (A)
(g)	Variable overhead efficiency variance is the same as the labour efficiency variance:		
	1,700 hours (F) × £0.30 per hour		£ 510 (F)

PART B STANDARD COSTING

(h)		Budgeted fixed overhead (5,100 units × 2 hrs × £3.70)		37,740
		Actual fixed overhead		42,300
		Fixed overhead expenditure variance		4,560 (A)
	(i)	Actual production at standard rate (4,850 units × £7.40)		35,890
		Budgeted production at standard rate (5,100 units × £7.40)		37,740
		Fixed overhead volume variance		1,850 (A)
	(j)	4,850 boomerangs should have sold for (× £20)		97,000
		but did sell for		95,600
		Selling price variance		1,400 (A)
(k)		Budgeted sales volume		5,100 units
		Actual sales volume		4,850 units
		Sales volume variance in units		250 units
		× standard profit per unit		× £6 (A)
		Sales volume variance in £		£1,500 (A)

There are several ways in which an operating statement may be presented. Perhaps the most **common format** is one which **reconciles budgeted profit to actual profit. Sales variances are reported first,** and the **total of the budgeted profit and the two sales variances** results in a figure for **'actual sales minus the standard cost of sales'** as follows.

	£	£
Budgeted profit (5,100 units × £6 profit)		30,600
Selling price variance	1,400	(A)
Sales volume variance	1,500	(A)
		2,900 (A)
Actual sales (£95,600) less the standard cost of sales (4,850 × £14)		27,700

The cost variances are then reported, and an actual profit calculated.

ARMOURED KANGAROO LTD – OPERATING STATEMENT FOR JUNE

	£	£	£
Budgeted profit			30,600
Sales variances: price		1,400 (A)	
volume		1,500 (A)	
			2,900 (A)
Actual sales minus the standard cost of sales			27,700

Cost variances

	(F) £	(A) £	£
Material price		600	
Material usage	500		
Labour rate	200		
Labour efficiency	3,400		
Labour idle time		1,000	
Variable overhead expenditure		200	
Variable overhead efficiency	510		
Fixed overhead expenditure		4,560	
Fixed overhead volume		1,850	
	4,610	8,210	3,600 (A)
Actual profit for June			24,100

Check

	£	£
Sales		95,600
Materials	9,800	
Labour	16,800	
Variable overhead	2,600	
Fixed overhead	42,300	
		71,500
Actual profit		24,100

Another way in which an operating statement can be presented is to reconcile the actual sales minus the standard cost of sales with the actual profit. In other words, only the cost variances are shown on the face of the operating statement.

2 Variances in a standard marginal costing system 12/02

FAST FORWARD

There are two main differences between the variances calculated in an absorption costing system and the **variances calculated in a marginal costing system**. In a marginal costing system the only fixed overhead variance is an expenditure variance and the sales volume variance is valued at standard contribution margin, not standard profit margin.

Exam focus point

Before tackling variances in a standard marginal costing system, it is vital that you are happy with the principles of marginal costing.

If an organisation uses standard marginal costing instead of standard absorption costing, there will be two differences in the way the variances are calculated.

(a) In marginal costing, fixed costs are not absorbed into product costs and so there are no fixed cost variances to explain any under– or over-absorption of overheads. There will, therefore, be *no* **fixed overhead volume variance**. There will be a fixed overhead expenditure variance which is calculated in exactly the same way as for absorption costing systems.

(b) The **sales volume variance will be valued at standard contribution margin**, **not standard profit margin** (that is, sales price per unit minus variable costs of sale per unit).

2.1 Example: Marginal costing operating statement

Returning once again to the example of Armoured Kangaroo Ltd, the variances in a system of standard marginal costing would be as follows.

(a) There is no fixed overhead volume variance.

(b) The standard contribution per unit of boomerang is £(20 – 6.60) = £13.40, therefore the sales volume variance of 250 units (A) is valued at (× £13.40) = £3,350 (A).

The other variances are unchanged, therefore an operating statement might appear as follows.

PART B STANDARD COSTING

ARMOURED KANGAROO – OPERATING STATEMENT FOR JUNE

	£	£	£
Budgeted profit		30,600	
Budgeted fixed production costs		37,740	
Budgeted contribution		68,340	
Sales variances: volume		3,350 (A)	
price		1,400 (A)	
			4,750 (A)
Actual sales (£95,600) minus the standard			
variable cost of sales (4,850 × £6.60)			63,590
	(F)	(A)	
Variable cost variances	£	£	£
Material price		600	
Material usage	500		
Labour rate	200		
Labour efficiency	3,400		
Labour idle time		1,000	
Variable overhead expenditure		200	
Variable overhead efficiency	510		
	4,610	1,800	
			2,810 (F)
Actual contribution			66,400
Budgeted fixed production overhead		37,740	
Expenditure variance		4,560 (A)	
Actual fixed production overhead			42,300
Actual profit			24,100

Note. The profit here is the same on the profit calculated by standard absorption costing because there were no changes in stock levels. Absorption costing and marginal costing do not always produce an identical profit figure.

Question — Operating statements

Hides of March Ltd manufacture a standard leather walking boot, model number M25, for which the standard unit cost and selling price are as follows.

		£
Direct materials		
Leather	3 units at £5 per unit	15
Other materials		3
		18
Direct labour	1½ hours at £4 per hour	6
Variable production overheads	1½ hours at £2 per hour	3
Fixed production overheads	1½ hours at £6 per hour	9
Standard cost		36
Selling price		48
Standard profit, before marketing and administrative expenses		12

Budgeted production and sales for period 7 of 20X8 were 3,000 units of M25.

During period 7 the actual results were as follows.

Production of M25	3,200 units
Sales of M25	2,850 units
Sales revenue	£141,000
Leather purchased: quantity	9,200 units
cost	£45,400

6: FURTHER VARIANCE ANALYSIS

Leather used	9,750 units
Other materials purchased and used	£9,500
Direct labour: hours paid for	5,850 hours
production time	5,100 hours
labour cost	£24,100
Variable production overheads	£10,650
Fixed production overheads	£31,500

Stocks of leather are valued at standard cost, and stocks of finished goods are valued at standard full production cost.

Required

Prepare an operating statement for period 7 reconciling budgeted and actual profit and specifying all the relevant variances. Ignore marketing and administration costs.

Answer

Budgeted profit. This is clearly 3,000 units × standard profit of £12 per unit = £36,000.

(a) Stocks are valued at standard costs, and so price variances must be calculated on quantities purchased, rather than quantities used.

	£
9,200 units of leather were purchased and cost	45,400
but should cost (× £5)	46,000
Leather price variance	600 (F)

(b)
3,200 units of M25 were made and used	9,750 units of materials
but 3,200 units should use (× 3)	9,600 units of materials
Usage variance in units	150 units (A)
× standard cost per unit of leather	× £5
Leather usage variance in £	£750 (A)

(c) **Other materials**. We are not given a breakdown into units of material and price per unit of material, and so the only materials variance we can calculate is the total cost variance.

	£
3,200 units of M25 did cost	9,500 in other materials
but should cost (× £3)	9,600
Other materials cost variance	100 (F)

(d)
	£
5,850 hours were paid for and cost	24,100
but should cost (× £4)	23,400
Direct labour rate variance	700 (A)

(e) The efficiency variance is based on production hours, excluding idle time.

3,200 units of M25 took	5,100 hours
but should take (× 1 1/2 hrs)	4,800 hours
Efficiency variance, in hours	300 hours (A)
× standard cost per labour hour	× £4
Direct labour efficiency variance in £	£1,200 (A)

(f) **Idle time variance** = 750 hours × £4 per hr = £3,000 (A)

This is a large variance compared to the others calculated so far, and the existence of this variance would raise control questions about how such a large amount of idle time occurred, and if it is normal downtime, why an allowance for idle time has not been built into the standard cost itself.

(g)
	£
5,100 hours of working did cost	10,650
but should cost (× £2)	10,200
Variable overhead expenditure variance	450 (A)

(h) The **variable overhead efficiency variance** is exactly the same in hours as the direct labour efficiency variance, ignoring idle time hours = 300 hours (A) × £2 per hour = £600 (A).

(i)
	£
Actual fixed overheads absorbed (3,200 × £9)	28,800
Actual fixed overheads incurred	31,500
Total fixed overhead variance	2,700 (A)

(j) **Fixed overhead expenditure variance.** This is under– or over-absorption of overhead because actual fixed overhead expenditure differed from budgeted expenditure.

	£
Budgeted fixed overhead	27,000
Actual fixed overhead	31,500
Expenditure variance	4,500 (A)

The expenditure variance also indicates over-spending above budget by £4,500, and a control report should attempt to pinpoint the source of this excessive overhead spending more specifically.

(k) **Fixed overhead volume variance.** This is under– or over-absorbed overhead caused by a difference between actual and budgeted production volume.

	In terms of units	Alternatively standard hours
Budgeted production volume of M25	3,000 (× 1.5)	4,500
Actual production volume	3,200 (× 1.5)	4,800
Total volume variance, in units or std hours	200 (F)	300 (F)
× standard fixed overhead cost per unit or per std hr	× £9	× £6
Total **volume variance** in £	£1,800 (F)	£1,800 (F)

Producing a bigger quantity than budgeted will create over absorption of fixed overhead, and so is a favourable variance. The fixed overhead total volume variance of 300 standard hours (F) means that the company produced 300 standard hours worth of output more than budgeted in period 7. The reason for this must have been either working more efficiently than expected (a volume efficiency variance) or working more production hours than expected (a volume capacity variance).

(l) **Fixed overhead volume efficiency variance.** This is the same variance in hours as the direct labour efficiency variance (ignoring idle time) = 300 hrs (A) × £6 per hour = £1,800 (A)

(m) **Fixed overhead volume capacity variance.** This is the difference between actual and budgeted production hours.

Budgeted production hours (3,000 units × 1.5 hrs)	4,500 hours
Actual production hours, ignoring idle time	5,100 hours
Volume capacity variance in hours	600 hours (F)
× standard fixed overhead rate per hour	× £6
Volume capacity variance in £	£3,600 (F)

The capacity and efficiency variances add up to the total volume variance of £1,800(F).

(n)
		£
2,850 units of M25 should have sold for (× £48)		136,800
but did sell for		141,000
Selling price variance		4,200 (F)

(o)
Budgeted sales volume of M25	3,000 units
Actual sales volume	2,850 units
Sales volume variance	150 units (A)
× standard profit margin per unit	× £12
Sales volume variance	£1,800 (A)

The variances can now be summarised in an operating statement.

HIDES OF MARCH LTD
OPERATING STATEMENT FOR PERIOD 7

			£	£	£
Budgeted profit					36,000
Sales variances:	price variance			4,200 (F)	
	volume variance			1,800 (A)	
					2,400 (F)
					38,400

Cost variances

		(F) £	(A) £	£
Leather:	price	600		
	usage		750	
Other materials		100		
Direct labour:	rate		700	
	efficiency		1,200	
Idle time			3,000	
Variable overhead expenditure			450	
Variable overhead efficiency			600	
Fixed overhead expenditure			4,500	
Fixed overhead volume		1,800		
		2,500	11,200	
Total cost variances				8,700 (A)
Actual profit				29,700

3 Materials mix and yield variances   Pilot paper, 12/03

FAST FORWARD

> The **materials usage variance** can be subdivided into a materials **mix** variance and a materials **yield** variance when more than one material is used in the product.

When a product requires two or more raw materials in its make-up, it is often possible to **sub-analyse the materials usage variance into a materials mix and a materials yield variance**.

Adding a greater proportion of one material (therefore a smaller proportion of a different material) might make the materials mix cheaper or more expensive. For example the standard mix of materials for a product might consist of the following.

	£
(²/₃) 2 kg of material A at £1.00 per kg	2.00
(¹/₃) 1 kg of material B at £0.50 per kg	0.50
	2.50

It may be possible to change the mix so that one kilogram of material A is used and two kilograms of material B. The new mix would be cheaper.

		£
(¹/₃)	1 kg of material A	1
(²/₃)	2 kg of material B	1
		2

By changing the proportions in the mix, the efficiency of the combined material usage may change. In our example, in making the proportions of A and B cheaper, at 1:2, the product may now require more than three kilograms of input for its manufacture, and the new materials requirement per unit of product might be 3.6 kilograms.

		£
(¹/₃)	1.2 kg of material A at £1.00 per kg	1.20
(²/₃)	2.4 kg of material B at £0.50 per kg	1.20
		2.40

In establishing a materials usage standard, management may therefore have to balance the cost of a particular mix of materials with the efficiency of the yield of the mix.

Once the standard has been established it may be possible for management to exercise control over the materials used in production by calculating and reviewing mix and yield variances.

Key terms

> A **mix variance** occurs when the materials are not mixed or blended in standard proportions and it is a measure of whether the actual mix is cheaper or more expensive than the standard mix.
>
> A **yield variance** arises because there is a difference between what the input should have been for the output achieved and the actual input.

3.1 Calculating the variances

The **mix variance** is calculated as the **difference between** the **actual total quantity used** in the **standard mix** and the **actual quantities used in the actual mix**, valued at standard costs.

The **yield variance** is calculated as the **difference between the standard input for what was actually output, and the actual total quantity input (in the standard mix), valued at standard costs.**

3.2 When to calculate the mix and yield variance

A mix variance and yield variance are only appropriate in the following situations.

  (a)   **Where proportions of materials in a mix are changeable and controllable**

  (b)   Where the **usage variance of individual materials is of limited value because of the variability of the mix**, and a combined yield variance for all the materials together is more helpful for control

It would be totally inappropriate to calculate a mix variance where the materials in the 'mix' are discrete items. A chair, for example, might consist of wood, covering material, stuffing and glue. These materials are separate components, and it would not be possible to think in terms of controlling the proportions of each material in the final product. The usage of each material must be controlled separately.

3.3 Example: Materials usage, mix and yield variances

A company manufactures a chemical, Dynamite, using two compounds Flash and Bang. The standard materials usage and cost of one unit of Dynamite are as follows.

		£
Flash	5 kg at £2 per kg	10
Bang	10 kg at £3 per kg	30
		40

In a particular period, 80 units of Dynamite were produced from 500 kg of Flash and 730 kg of Bang.

Required

Calculate the materials usage, mix and yield variances.

Solution

(a) **Usage variance**

	Std usage for actual output kgs	Actual usage kgs	Variance kgs	Standard cost per kg £	Variance £
Flash	400	500	100 (A)	2	200 (A)
Bang	800	730	70 (F)	3	210 (F)
	1,200	1,230	30 (A)		10 (F)

The total usage variance of £10 (F) can be analysed into a mix variance and a yield variance.

(b) **Mix variance**

To calculate the mix variance, it is first necessary to decide how the total quantity of materials used (500 kg + 730 kg) should have been divided between Flash and Bang. In other words, we need to **calculate the standard mix of the actual quantity of materials used.**

	kg
Total quantity used (500 + 730)	1,230

	kg
Standard mix of actual use: $1/3$ Flash	410
$2/3$ Bang	820
	1,230

The differences between what should have been used in the mix (as calculated above) and what was actually used is the mix variance (in kg) which should be converted into money values at standard cost.

	Mix should have been kgs	but mix was kgs	Variance kgs	Standard cost per kg £	Variance £
Flash	410	500*	90 (A)	2	180 (A)
Bang	820	730	90 (F)	3	270 (F)
	1,230	1,230	–		90 (F)

* When actual use exceeds standard use the variance is always adverse.

Note that the **total mix variance in quantity is zero**. This must always be the case since the expected mix is based on the total quantity actually used and hence the difference between the total expected and total actual is zero.

The favourable money variance is due to the greater use in the mix of the relatively cheap material, Flash.

PART B STANDARD COSTING

(c) **Yield variance**

The yield variance can be calculated in total or for each individual material input.

In total

Each unit of output (Dynamite) requires

	5 kg of Flash, costing	£10
	10 kg of Bang, costing	£30
	15 kg	£40

1,230 kg should have yielded (÷ 15 kg)	82 units of Dynamite
but did yield	80 units of Dynamite
Yield variance in units	2 units (A)
× standard cost per unit of output	× £40
Yield variance in £	£80 (A)

The adverse yield variance is due to the output from the input being less than standard.

For individual materials

This is calculated as the **difference between what the usage should have been for the output actually achieved and the actual usage in the standard mix**, converted into money values at standard cost.

	Standard usage for actual output	Actual usage in standard mix	Variance	Standard cost per kg	Variance
	kgs	kgs	kgs	£	£
Flash	400	410	10 (A)	2	20 (A)
Bang	800	820	20 (A)	3	60 (A)
	1,200	1,230	30 (A)		80 (A)

Question — Mix and yield variances

The standard materials cost of product D456 is as follows.

		£
Material X	3 kg at £2.00 per kg	6
Material Y	5 kg at £3.60 per kg	18
		24

During period 2, 2,000 kgs of material X (costing £4,100) and 2,400 kgs of material Y (costing £9,600) were used to produce 500 units of D456.

Required

Calculate the following variances.

(a) Price variances
(b) Mix variances
(c) Yield variances – in total and for each individual material

Answer

(a)

	£
2,000 kg of X should cost (× £2)	4,000
but did cost	4,100
Material X price variance	100 (A)

	£
2,400 kg of Y should cost (× £3.60)	8,640
but did cost	9,600
Material Y price variance	960 (A)

(b)

	kg
Total quantity used (2,000 + 2,400) kgs	4,400

Standard mix for actual use:		kg
	3/8 X	1,650
	5/8 Y	2,750
		4,400

	Mix should have been kgs	but mix was kgs	Variance kgs	Standard cost per kg £	Variance £
X	1,650	2,000	350 (A)	2.00	700 (A)
Y	2,750	2,400	350 (F)	3.60	1,260 (F)
	4,400	4,400	–		560 (F)

(c) **In total**

Each unit of D456 requires	3 kg of X, costing	£6
	5 kg of Y, costing	£18
	8 kg	£24

4,400 kg should have yielded (÷ 8 kg)	550 units
But did yield	500 units
Yield variance in units	50 units (A)
× standard cost per unit of output	× £24
Yield variance in £	£1,200 (A)

For individual materials

	Std usage for actual output kgs	Actual usage in std mix kgs	Variance kgs	Standard cost per kg £	Variance £
X	1,500	1,650	150 (A)	2.00	300 (A)
Y	2,500	2,750	250 (A)	3.60	900 (A)
	4,000	4,400	400 (A)		1,200 (A)

Exam focus point

With all variance calculations, it is vital that you do not simply learn formulae. You must have a thorough understanding of what your calculations are showing. This is especially true of the variances we will look at in this section and in Section 4.

The next example is similar to the pilot paper question in that it incorporates losses.

3.4 Example: Losses, mix and yield

Coope and Sorcerer Ltd make product T42 in a continuous process, for which standard and actual quantities in month 10 were as follows.

	Quantity kg	Standard Price per kg £	Value £	Quantity kg	Actual Price per kg £	Std cost of actual usage £
Material P	40,000	2.50	100,000	34,000	2.50	85,000
Material Q	20,000	4.00	80,000	22,000	4.00	88,000
	60,000		180,000	56,000		173,000

Losses occur at an even rate during the processing operation and are expected to be 10% of materials input. Actual output during the month was 53,000 kgs.

Required

Calculate total usage, mix and yield variances.

Solution

Usage variance

Output of 53,000 kgs should have used input of 53,000/90% = 58,889 kgs.

∴ Standard input should have been as follows.

			Kg
P	$2/3 \times 58,889$	=	39,259
Q	$1/3 \times 58,889$	=	19,630
			58,889

	P	Q
53,000 kg of T42 should need	39,259 kg	19,630 kg
but did need	34,000 kg	22,000 kg
Usage variance in kg	5,259 kg (F)	2,370 kg (A)
× standard price per kg	× £2.50	× £4
Usage variance in £	£13,148 (F)	£9,480 (A)
Total usage variance	£3,668 (F)	

Yield variance

Each kg of T42 requires (1 × $^{100}/_{90}$) kg of input costing £3.33 (£180,000/(60,000 × 90%))

56,000 kg should have yielded (÷ 100/90)	50,400 kg
but did yield	53,000 kg
Yield variance in kgs	2,600 kg (F)
× standard cost per kg of T42	× £3.33
Yield variance in £	£8,667 (F)

Mix variance

Total quantity used	Kg 56,000.00

Standard mix for actual use:	2/3 P	Kg 37,333.33
	1/3 Q	18,666.67
		56,000.00

	P	Q
Mix should have been	37,333.33 kg	18,666.67 kg
but was	34,000.00 kg	22,000.00 kg
Mix variance in kg	3,333.33 kg (F)	3,333.33 kg (A)
× standard cost per kg	× £2.50	× £4.00
Mix variance in £	£8,333.00 (F)	£13,333.00 (A)
Total mix variance	£5,000 (A)	

(Note that there is a difference between the sum of the mix and yield variances and the usage variance due to rounding.)

4 Sales mix and quantity variances   12/03, 06/05

FAST FORWARD

The **sales volume variance** can be subdivided into a **mix** variance and a **quantity** variance when more than one product is sold.

Just as it is possible to subdivide the materials usage variance into mix and yield variances, the **sales volume variance** can be subdivided into a **mix variance** and a **quantity variance**.

If a company sells more than one product, the **volume variance can be caused by two factors**.

(a) The **quantity** of product sold is **different than budgeted**. For example, suppose Nilats Ltd sells two products, the Trot and the Sky.

	Budget Units	Actual Units
Trots	100 (50%)	175 (70%)
Skys	100 (50%)	75 (30%)
	200	250

Notice that the total quantity is 50 greater than budget and that the relative proportions of the products to the total are also different than budgeted.

(b) The **mix** of products sold can be **different than budgeted**. For example if product A earned a standard profit of £10 per unit and product B earned a standard profit of £8 a unit, a change in the relative numbers of each product sold will change the total profit.

	Budgeted sales		Actual sales	
	Units	£	Units	£
A	100	1,000	75	750
B	50	400	75	600
	150	1,400	150	1,350

If management cannot control the proportions of products sold then there is **little point in calculating sales mix and sales quantity variances** since their causes are uncontrollable.

4.1 Example: Sales quantity and sales mix variances

Tardis Ltd manufactures three products, the Dalek, the Yeti and the Cyberman. The budget relating to period 1 is given below.

	Unit sales price £	Unit full cost of product £	Profit per unit £	Budgeted sales Units	Standard mix %
Dalek	5	3	2	500	50
Yeti	7	4	3	300	30
Cyberman	10	6	4	200	20

Actual sales in period 1 were as follows.

	Units	%
Dalek	700	46.7
Yeti	300	20.0
Cyberman	500	33.3
	1,500	100.0

Solution

(a) **Sales quantity variance**

Product	Actual sales in standard mix Units	Budgeted sales Units	Variance Units	Standard profit per unit £	Variance £
Dalek	750	500	250 (F)	2	500 (F)
Yeti	450	300	150 (F)	3	450 (F)
Cyberman	300	200	100 (F)	4	400 (F)
	1,500	1,000	500 (F)		1,350 (F)

(b) **Sales mix variance**

Product		Mix should have been Units	but mix was Units	Variance Units	Standard profit per unit £	Variance £
Dalek	(1,500 × 50%) =	750	700	(50) (A)	2	(100) (A)
Yeti	(1,500 × 30%) =	450	300	(150) (A)	3	(450) (A)
Cyberman	(1,500 × 20%) =	300	500	200 (F)	4	800 (F)
		1,500	1,500	0		250 (F)

(c) **Total sales volume variance**

			£
Dalek	£500(F) quantity + £100(A) mix	=	400 (F)
Yeti	£450(F) quantity + £450(A) mix	=	0
Cyberman	£400(F) quantity + £800(F) mix	=	1,200 (F)
Total sales volume variance			1,600 (F)

5 Planning and operational variances   6/04, 12/04

> **FAST FORWARD**
>
> A planning and operational approach to variance analysis divides the total variance into those variances which have arisen because of inaccurate planning or faulty standards (**planning variances**) and those variances which have been caused by adverse or favourable operational performance, compared with a standard which has been revised in hindsight (**operational variances**).

So far in this text we have been looking at variances which are calculated using what we will call the conventional approach to variance analysis, whereby an actual cost is compared with an original standard cost. In this section of the chapter we will be examining planning and operational variances. They are not really alternatives to the conventional approach, they merely provide a much more detailed analysis.

Basically, the planning and operational approach attempts to divide a total variance (which has been calculated conventionally) into a group of variances which have arisen because of inaccurate planning or faulty standards (planning variances) and a group of variances which have been caused by adverse or favourable operational performance (operational variances, surprisingly enough!).

Planning and operational variances may seem confusing if you do not have a really good grasp of the conventional approach and so, before you go any further, make sure that you understand everything that we covered so far in this Text. Go back over any areas you are unsure about. Only when you are happy that you have mastered the basics should you begin on this section.

6: FURTHER VARIANCE ANALYSIS

Key terms

> A **planning variance** (or **revision variance**) compares an original standard with a revised standard that should or would have been used if planners had known in advance what was going to happen.
>
> An **operational variance** (or **operating variance**) compares an actual result with the revised standard.

Planning and operational variances are based on the principle that variances ought to be reported by taking as the **main starting point**, not the original standard, but a **standard** which can be seen, in hindsight, to be the **optimum** that should have been **achievable**.

Exponents of this approach argue that the monetary value of variances ought to be a realistic reflection of what the **causes** of the variances have cost the organisation. In other words they should show the cash (and profit) gained or lost as a consequence of operating results being different to what should have been achieved. Variances can be valued in this way by **comparing actual results with a realistic standard or budget**. Such variances are called **operational variances**.

Planning variances arise because the **original standard and revised more realistic standards are different** and have nothing to do with operational performance. In most cases, it is unlikely that anything could be done about planning variances: they are **not controllable by operational managers but by senior management**.

In other words the **cause of a total variance** might be one or both of:

- Adverse or favourable operational performance (**operational variance**)
- Inaccurate planning, or faulty standards (**planning variance**)

5.1 Calculating total planning and operational variances

We will begin by looking at how to split a total cost variance into its planning and operational components.

5.2 Example: Total cost planning and operational variances

At the beginning of 20X0, WB Ltd set a standard marginal cost for its major product of £25 per unit. The standard cost is recalculated once each year. Actual production costs during August 20X0 were £304,000, when 8,000 units were made.

With the benefit of hindsight, the management of WB Ltd realises that a more realistic standard cost for current conditions would be £40 per unit. The planned standard cost of £25 is unrealistically low.

Required

Calculate the planning and operational variances.

Solution

With the benefit of hindsight, the **realistic standard should have been £40**. The variance caused by favourable or adverse **operating** performance should be calculated by comparing actual results against this realistic standard.

	£
Revised standard cost of actual production (8,000 × £40)	320,000
Actual cost	304,000
Total **operational** variance	16,000 (F)

The variance is favourable because the actual cost was lower than would have been expected using the revised basis.

The **planning** variance reveals the extent to which the original standard was at fault.

		£
Revised standard cost	8,000 units × £40 per unit	320,000
Original standard cost	8,000 units × £25 per unit	200,000
Planning variance		120,000 (A)

It is an adverse variance because the original standard was too optimistic, overestimating the expected profits by understating the standard cost. More simply, it is adverse because the revised cost is much higher than the original cost.

	£
Planning variance	120,000 (A)
Operational variance	16,000 (F)
Total	104,000 (A)

If **traditional variance analysis** had been used, the total cost variance would have been the same, but **all the 'blame' would appear to lie on actual results** and operating inefficiencies (rather than some being due to faulty planning).

	£
Standard cost of 8,000 units (× £25)	200,000
Actual cost of 8,000 units	304,000
Total cost variance	104,000 (A)

Question — Planning and operational variances

Suppose a budget is prepared which includes a raw materials cost per unit of product of £2 (2 kg of copper at £1 per kg). Due to a rise in world prices for copper during the year, the average market price of copper rises to £1.50 per kg. During the year, 1,000 units were produced at a cost of £3,250 for 2,200 kg of copper.

What are the planning and operational variances?

Answer

Operational variance

	£
Actual cost (for 1,000 units)	3,250
Revised standard cost (for 1,000 units) (2,000 kg × £1.50)	3,000
Total operational variance	250 (A)

Planning variance

	£
Revised standard cost (1,000 × 2 kg × £1.50)	3,000
Original standard cost (1,000 × 2 kg × £1)	2,000
Total planning variance	1,000 (A)

5.3 Operational price and usage variances

So far we have only considered planning and operational variances in total, without carrying out the usual two-way split. In the question above, for instance, we identified a total operational variance for materials of £250 without considering whether this operational variance could be split between a usage variance and a price variance.

This is not a problem so long as you retain your grasp of knowledge you already possess. You know that a **price** variance measures the difference between the actual amount of money paid and the amount of money that should have been paid for that quantity of materials (or whatever). Thus, in our example:

	£
Actual price of actual materials (2,200 kg)	3,250
Revised standard price of actual materials (£1.50 × 2,200 kg)	3,300
Operational price variance	50 (F)

The variance is favourable because the materials were purchased more cheaply than would have been expected.

Similarly, a **usage** variance measures the difference between the actual physical quantity of materials used or hours taken and the quantities that should have been used or taken for the actual volume of production. Those physical differences are then converted into money values by applying the appropriate standard cost.

In our example we are calculating **operational variances**, so we are not interested in planning errors. This means that the **appropriate standard cost is the revised standard cost** of £1.50.

Actual quantity should have been	2,000 kgs
but was	2,200 kgs
Operational usage variance in kgs	200 kgs (A)
× revised standard cost per kg	× £1.50
Operational usage variance in £	£300 (A)

The two variances of course reconcile to the total variance as previously calculated.

	£
Operational price variance	50 (F)
Operational usage variance	(300) (A)
Total operational variance	250 (A)

Exam focus point

> There are a number of ways of doing these calculations but the examiner has stated that **revised standard cost** should be used not the original standard cost.

5.4 Operational variances for labour and overheads

Precisely the same argument applies to the calculation of operational variances for labour and overheads, and the examples already given should be sufficient to enable you to do the next question.

Question — Operational and planning variances

A new product requires three hours of labour per unit at a standard rate of £6 per hour. In a particular month the budget is to produce 500 units. Actual results were as follows.

Hours worked	1,700
Production	540 units
Wages cost	£10,500

Within minutes of production starting it was realised that the job was extremely messy and the labour force could therefore claim an extra 25p per hour in 'dirty money'.

Required

Calculate planning and operational variances in as much detail as possible.

Answer

Keep calm and calculate the *total* variance in the normal way to begin with. Then you will understand what it is that you have to analyse. Next follow through the workings shown above, substituting the figures in the exercise for those in the example.

Total labour variance

	£
540 units should have cost (× 3 hrs × £6)	9,720
but did cost	10,500
	780 (A)

Planning variance

	£
Revised standard cost (540 × 3 hrs × £6.25)	10,125
Original standard cost (540 × 3 hrs × £6.00)	9,720
	405 (A)

Operational rate variance

	£
Actual cost of actual units	10,500
Revised cost of actual units (1,700 × £6.25)	10,625
	125 (F)

Operational efficiency variance

540 units should have taken (× 3 hrs)	1,620 hrs
but did take	1,700 hrs
Operational efficiency variance in hours	80 hrs
× revised standard rate per hour	× £6.25
Operational efficiency variance in £	£500 (A)

5.5 Planning variances and sub-variances

In the examples described so far, there has only been one 'planning error' in the standard cost. When two planning errors occur, there may be some difficulty in deciding how much of the total planning variance is due to each separate error.

5.6 Example: Two planning errors

A company estimates that the standard direct labour cost for a product should be £20 (4 hours × £5 per hour). Actual production of 1,000 units took 6,200 hours at a cost of £23,800. In retrospect, it is realised that the standard cost should have been 6 hours × £4 per hour = £24 per unit.

Required

Calculate the planning and operational variances.

Solution

(a) **Operational variances**

(i)
1,000 units should take (× 6 hours)	6,000 hrs
but did take	6,200 hrs
Efficiency variance in hours	200 hrs (A)
× revised standard cost per hour	× £4 (A)
Efficiency variance in £	£800 (A)

(ii)
	£
6,200 hours should cost (× £4)	24,800
but did cost	23,800
Rate variance	1,000 (F)

(iii) *Check:*
	£
Actual costs	23,800
Revised standard cost (1,000 units × £24)	24,000
Total operational variance (800 (A) + 1,000 (F))	200 (F)

(b) **Planning variance**

	£
Revised standard cost 1,000 units × 6 hours × £4	24,000
Original standard cost 1,000 units × 4 hours × £5	20,000
Planning variance	4,000 (A)

Commentary

Within the total planning variance, there are two separate variances.

- A **planning efficiency variance** of 1,000 units × (6 – 4) hours or 2,000 hours (A).
- A **planning rate variance** of £1 per hour (F).

The problem, however, is to put a **value** to these sub-variances. This can be done in either of **two ways**.

			£
(a)	Planning efficiency variance	2,000 hours (A) × original price of £5	10,000 (A)
	Planning rate variance	£1 per hour (F) × revised standard efficiency of 6,000 hours	6,000 (F)
	Total		4,000 (A)
(b)	Planning efficiency variance	2,000 hours (A) × revised rate of £4	8,000 (A)
	Planning rate variance	£1 per hour (F) × original efficiency of 4,000 hours	4,000 (F)
	Total		4,000 (A)

Since the analysis can be done either way, it is **doubtful whether there is much value in splitting the total planning variance**. However, this point may be examinable and is worth learning. The following exercise provides an example of when there may be some point in carrying out the analysis.

Question — Planning variance analysis

The standard materials cost of a product is 3 kg × £1.50 per kg = £4.50. Actual production of 10,000 units used 28,000 kg at a cost of £50,000. In retrospect it was realised that the standard materials cost should have been 2.5 kg per unit at a cost of £1.80 per kg (so that the *total* cost per unit was correct).

Required

Calculate the planning and operational variances in as much detail as possible, giving alternative analyses of planning variances.

Answer

As always, calculate the *total* materials variance first, to give you a point of reference. Then follow through the workings above.

Total materials variance

	£
10,000 units should have cost (× £4.50)	45,000
but did cost	50,000
	5,000 (A)

Operational price variance

	£
28,000 kg should cost (× £1.80)	50,400
but did cost	50,000
	400 (F)

PART B STANDARD COSTING

Operational usage variance		
10,000 units should use (× 2.5 kgs)		25,000 kgs
but did use		28,000 kgs
		3,000 kgs (A)
× standard rate per kg		× £1.80
		£5,400 (A)
Planning variance		
Either		£
Planning usage variance (5,000 kgs (F) × £1.50)		7,500 (F)
Planning price variance (£0.30(A) × 25,000 kgs)		7,500 (A)
		–
or		£
Planning usage variance (5,000 kgs (F) × £1.80)		9,000 (F)
Planning price variance (£0.30 (A) × 30,000 kgs)		9,000 (A)
		–

5.7 Planning and operational sales variances

Our final calculations in this section deal with planning and operational sales variances.

5.8 Example: Planning and operational sales variances

Dimsek Ltd budgeted to make and sell 400 units of its product, the role, in the four-week period no 8, as follows.

	£
Budgeted sales (100 units per week)	40,000
Variable costs (400 units × £60)	24,000
Contribution	16,000
Fixed costs	10,000
Profit	6,000

At the beginning of the second week, production came to a halt because stocks of raw materials ran out, and a new supply was not received until the beginning of week 3. As a consequence, the company lost one week's production and sales. Actual results in period 8 were as follows.

	£
Sales (320 units)	32,000
Variable costs (320 units × £60)	19,200
Contribution	12,800
Fixed costs	10,000
Actual profit	2,800

In retrospect, it is decided that the optimum budget, given the loss of production facilities in the third week, would have been to sell only 300 units in the period.

Required

Calculate appropriate planning and operational variances.

Solution

The **planning** variance **compares the revised budget** with the **original budget**.

Revised sales volume, given materials shortage	300 units
Original budgeted sales volume	400 units
Planning variance in units of sales	100 units(A)
× standard contribution per unit	× £40
Planning variance in £	£4,000 (A)

Arguably, **running out of raw materials is an operational error** and so the loss of sales volume and contribution from the materials shortage is an opportunity cost that could have been avoided with better purchasing arrangements. The operational variances are variances calculated in the usual way, except that actual results are compared with the revised standard or budget. There is a sales volume variance which is an **operational variance**, as follows.

Actual sales volume	320 units
Revised sales volume	300 units
Operational sales volume variance in units	20 units (F)
(possibly due to production efficiency or marketing efficiency)	
× standard contribution per unit	× £40
	£800 (F)

These variances can be used as **control information** to reconcile budgeted and actual profit.

Operating statement, period 8

	£	£
Budgeted profit		6,000
Planning variance	4,000 (A)	
Operational variance – sales volume	800 (F)	
		3,200 (A)
Actual profit in period 8		2,800

You will have noticed that in this example sales volume variances were **valued at contribution forgone**, and there were no fixed cost volume variances. This is because contribution forgone, in terms of lost revenue or extra expenditure incurred, is the nearest equivalent to **opportunity cost** which is readily available to management accountants (who assume linearity of costs and revenues within a relevant range of activity).

Question — More planning and operational variances

KSO Ltd budgeted to sell 10,000 units of a new product during 20X0. The budgeted sales price was £10 per unit, and the variable cost £3 per unit.

Although actual sales in 20X0 were 10,000 units and variable costs of sales were £30,000, sales revenue was only £5 per unit. With the benefit of hindsight, it is realised that the budgeted sales price of £10 was hopelessly optimistic, and a price of £4.50 per unit would have been much more realistic.

Required

Calculate planning and operational variances.

PART B STANDARD COSTING

Answer

The only variances are selling price variances.

Planning (selling price) variance

	Total £
Revised budget (10,000 × £4.50)	45,000
Original budget (10,000 × £10.00)	100,000
Planning variance	55,000 (A)

The original variance was too optimistic and so the planning variance is an adverse variance.

Operational (selling price) variance

	£
Actual sales (10,000 × £5)	50,000
Revised sales (10,000 × £4.50)	45,000
Operational (selling price) variance	5,000 (F)

The total difference between budgeted and actual profit of £50,000 (A) is therefore analysed as follows.

	£
Operational variance (selling price)	5,000 (F)
Planning variance	55,000 (A)
	50,000 (A)

5.9 The value of planning and operational variances

Advantages of a system of planning and operational variances

- The analysis highlights those variances which are **controllable** and those which are **non-controllable**.

- **Managers' acceptance** of the use of variances for performance measurement, and their **motivation**, is likely to increase if they know they will not be held responsible for poor planning and faulty standard setting.

- The **planning and standard-setting processes** should improve; standards should be more accurate, relevant and appropriate.

- Operational variances will provide a **'fairer' reflection of actual performance**.

The limitations of planning and operational variances, which must be overcome if they are to be applied in practice.

- It is difficult to **decide in hindsight** what the **realistic standard** should have been.

- It may become **too easy to justify all the variances as being due to bad planning**, so no operational variances will be highlighted.

- Establishing realistic revised standards and analysing the total variance into planning and operational variances can be a **time consuming** task, even if a spreadsheet package is devised.

- Even though the intention is to provide more meaningful information, **managers may be resistant** to the very idea of variances and refuse to see the virtues of the approach. Careful presentation and explanation will be required until managers are used to the concepts.

5.10 Management reports involving planning and operational variances

The format of a management report that includes planning and operational variances should be tailored to the information requirements of the managers who receive it.

From the **point of view of senior management** reviewing performance as a whole, a layout that identifies **all of the planning variances together**, and then **all of the operational variances** may be most illuminating. The difference due to planning is the responsibility of the planners, and the remainder of the difference is due to functional managers.

One possible layout is shown below.

X LTD Operating statement period 1

	£	£
Original budget contribution		X
Planning variances		
Material usage	X	
Material price	X	
Labour efficiency	X	
Labour idle time	X	
Labour rate	X	
Selling price	X	
		X
Revised budget contribution		X
Sales volume variance		X
Revised standard contribution from sales achieved		X
Operational variances		
Selling price	X	
Material usage	X	
Material price	X	
Labour efficiency	X	
Labour rate	X	
Variable overhead expenditure	X	
Variable overhead efficiency	X	
		X
Actual contribution		X
Less: fixed costs budget	X	
expenditure variance	X	
		X
Actual margin		X

PART B   STANDARD COSTING

Chapter Roundup

- **Operating statements** show how cost and revenue variances combine to reconcile budgeted profit to actual profit.

- There are two main differences between the variances calculated in an absorption costing system and the **variances calculated in a marginal costing system**. In a marginal costing system the only fixed overhead variance is an expenditure variance and the sales volume variance is valued at standard contribution margin, not standard profit margin.

- The **materials usage variance** can be subdivided into a materials **mix** variance and a materials **yield** variance when more than one material is used in the product.

- The **sales volume variance** can be subdivided into a **mix** variance and a **quantity** variance when more than one product is sold.

- A planning and operational approach to variance analysis divides the total variance into those variances which have arisen because of inaccurate planning or faulty standards (**planning variances**) and those variances which have been caused by adverse or favourable operational performance, compared with a standard which has been revised in hindsight (**operational variances**).

Quick Quiz

1. By what two variances does budgeted profit need to be adjusted to get actual sales minus the standard cost of sales?

2. *Fill in the blanks.*

   If an organisation uses standard marginal costing, there will be no .... variance and the .... variance will be valued at ....

3. *Choose the appropriate words from those highlighted.*

   The materials mix variance is calculated as the difference between the **standard/actual** total quantity used in the **standard/actual** mix and the **standard/actual** quantities used in the **standard/actual** mix, valued at **standard/actual** costs.

4. *Choose the appropriate words from those highlighted.*

   The materials yield variance is calculated on the difference between the **standard/actual** input for **standard/actual** output, and the **standard/actual** total quantity input (in the **standard/actual** mix), valued at **standard/actual** costs.

5. The total yield variance in quantity is zero.

   ☐ True
   ☐ False

6. *Fill in the boxes using three of the following words.*

   Possible words

   quantity, rate, mix, volume, price, efficiency, usage, total

	Sales	[ ]	variance
+	Sales	[ ]	variance
=	Sales	[ ]	variance

7. A revision variance compares what with what?

8. If a planning efficiency variance is valued at an original standard rate, the planning rate variance is valued at the original efficiency level.

   ☐ True
   ☐ False

PART B STANDARD COSTING

Answers to Quick Quiz

1   Sales volume and selling price

2   There will be no fixed production overhead volume variance and the sales volume variance will be valued at standard contribution margin.

3   The materials mix variance is calculated as the difference between the actual total quantity used in the standard mix, and the actual quantities used in the actual mix, valued at standard costs.

4   The materials yield variance is calculated as the difference between the standard input for actual output, and the actual total quantity input (in the standard mix), valued at standard costs.

5   False. It is the total mix variance in quantity which is zero.

6   Sales   mix   variance
    + Sales   quantity   variance
    = Sales   volume   variance

7   A revision or planning variance compares an original standard with a revised standard that should or would have been used if planners had known in advance what was going to happen.

8   False. It is valued at the revised efficiency level.

Now try the questions below from the Exam Question Bank

Number	Level	Marks	Time
Q7	Examination	25	45 mins
Q8	Examination	25	45 mins
Q34	Examination	25	45 mins

Question 34 has been fully analysed to help you get to grips with the more complex aspects of variance analysis.

Part C
Budgeting and performance measurement

Budget planning and control

Topic list	Syllabus reference
1 The planning and control cycle	8(a)
2 The control process	8(a)
3 Feedback and feedforward control	8(a)
4 Controllability and responsibility reporting	8(a)
5 Budgetary planning and control systems	8(a)

Introduction

This chapter serves as an **introduction** to Part C of the Study Text and looks at the **overall planning and control system**.

We look at the various stages in the planning process, and where the annual budget fits in to this. We also see how the budget is used in the control process, a large part of which involves variance analysis which we studied in the previous two chapters.

The idea that different managers are held responsible for different costs and cost variances is introduced. This means that we must also identify which costs are **controllable** and which are not, so that managers are only answerable for costs and variances that they are able to influence.

In the next chapter we go on to consider budget preparation.

PART C BUDGETING AND PERFORMANCE MEASUREMENT

Study guide

Section 22 – Budget planning and control I

- Identify the purposes of budgetary planning and control systems
- Describe the planning and control cycle, and the control process
- Explain the implications of controllability for responsibility reporting

Exam guide

Topics covered in this chapter could form the basis of part or all of a Section B discursive question. Section A questions could well require you to apply what you learn in this chapter given the wide context of the subject.

1 The planning and control cycle

FAST FORWARD

Planning involves making choices between alternatives and is primarily a decision-making activity.

The **planning and control cycle** has seven steps.

- *Step 1.* Identify **objectives**
- *Step 2.* Identify potential **strategies**
- *Step 3.* Evaluate strategies
- *Step 4.* Choose alternative courses of action
- *Step 5.* Implement the long-term plan
- *Step 6.* Measure actual results and compare with the plan
- *Step 7.* Respond to divergences from the plan

The diagram below represents the planning and control cycle. The first five steps cover the planning process. **Planning** involves making choices between alternatives and is primarily a decision-making activity. The last two steps cover the **control** process, which involves measuring and correcting actual performance to ensure that the alternatives that are chosen and the plans for implementing them are carried out.

The planning and control cycle

Planning process	Step
Identify objectives	Step 1
Identify alternative courses of action (strategies) which might contribute towards achieving the objectives	Step 2
Evaluate each strategy	Step 3
Choose alternative courses of action	Step 4
Implement the long-term plan in the form of the annual budget	Step 5
Measure actual results and compare with the plan	Step 6
Respond to divergences from plan	Step 7

Steps 1–5: Planning process
Steps 6–7: Control process

7: BUDGET PLANNING AND CONTROL

Step 1 **Identify objectives**

Objectives establish the direction in which the management of the organisation wish it to be heading. Typical objectives include the following.

- To maximise profits
- To increase market share
- To produce a better quality product than anyone else

Objectives answer the question: **'where do we want to be?'**

Step 2 **Identify potential strategies**

Once an organisation has decided 'where it wants to be', the next step is to identify a range of possible courses of action or **strategies that might enable the organisation to get there.** The organisation must therefore carry out an **information-gathering exercise** to ensure that it has a full **understanding of where it is now.** This is known as a **'position audit'** or **'strategic analysis'** and involves looking both **inwards** and **outwards**.

(a) The organisation must **gather information from all of its internal parts** to find out what resources it possesses: what its manufacturing capacity and capability is, what is the state of its technical know-how, how well it is able to market itself, how much cash it has in the bank and so on.

(b) It must also **gather information externally** so that it can assess its position in the environment. Just as it has assessed its **own strengths and weaknesses**, it must do likewise for its competitors (**threats**). Current and potential markets must be analysed to identify possible new **opportunities**. The 'state of the world' must be considered. Is it in recession or is it booming? What is likely to happen in the future?

Having carried out a strategic analysis, alternative strategies can be identified. An organisation might decide to be the lowest cost producer in the industry, perhaps by withdrawing from some markets or developing new products for sale in existing markets. This may involve internal development or a joint venture.

Step 3 **Evaluate strategies**

The strategies must then be evaluated **in terms of suitability, feasibility and acceptability**. Management should select those strategies that have the greatest potential for achieving the organisation's objectives.

Step 4 **Choose alternative courses of action**

The next step in the process is to collect the **chosen strategies** together and **co-ordinate them into a long-term financial plan.** Typically this would show the following.

- Projected cash flows
- Projected long-term profits
- A description of the long-term objectives and strategies in words
- Capital expenditure plans
- Balance sheet forecasts

Step 5 **Implement the long-term plan**

The **long-term plan** should then be **broken down into smaller parts**. It is unlikely that the different parts will fall conveniently into successive time periods. Strategy A may take two and a half years, while Strategy B may take five months, but not start until year three of the plan. It is usual, however, to break down the plan as a whole into equal time periods (usually one year). The resulting **short-term plan** is called a **budget**.

PART C BUDGETING AND PERFORMANCE MEASUREMENT

> **Question** — Planning and control cycle
>
> Is your organisation's planning and control cycle similar to the one described here? If it differs, how does it differ? Why does it differ? Try to find out your organisation's objectives and the strategies being adopted to attain these objectives.
>
> Answers to this question could be usefully employed in the exam.

2 The control process

FAST FORWARD

> **Control** is achieved through the **control cycle**. Actual performance is compared with planned performance and the appropriate action is taken for those items that are not proceeding according to plan.

Control is achieved through what is known as a control cycle. The elements in the control cycle are as follows.

Step 1 **Plans and targets are set for the future**. These could be long; medium; or short-term. Examples include budgets, profit targets and standard costs.

Step 2 **Plans are put into operation**. As a consequence, materials and labour are used, and other expenses are incurred.

Step 3 **Actual results are recorded and analysed.**

Step 4 **Information about actual results is fed back** to the management concerned, often in the form of accounting reports. This reported information is **feedback**.

Step 5 **The feedback is used by management to compare** actual results with the plan or targets (what should be or should have been achieved). See also Section 3 below.

Step 6 By comparing actual and planned results, management can then do one of three things, depending on how they see the situation.

  (a) **They can take control action**. By identifying what has gone wrong, and then finding out why, corrective measures can be taken.

  (b) **They can decide to do nothing**. This could be the decision when actual results are going better than planned, or when poor results were caused by something which is unlikely to happen again in the future.

  (c) **They can alter the plan or target** if actual results are different from the plan or target, and there is nothing that management can do (or nothing, perhaps, that they want to do) to correct the situation.

It may be helpful at this stage to relate the control system to a **practical example, such as monthly sales**.

Step 1 A **sales budget** or plan is prepared for the year.

Step 2 Management **organises the business's resources** to achieve the budget targets.

Step 3 At the end of each month, **actual results** are **reported back to management**.

Step 4 Managers **compare actual results against the plan.**

Step 5 Where necessary, they **take corrective action to adjust the workings of the system**, probably by amending the inputs to the system.

- Salesmen might be asked to work longer hours.
- More money might be spent on advertising.
- Some new price discounts might be decided.
- Delivery periods to customers might be reduced by increasing output.

Where appropriate the sales plan may be revised, up or down.

In this example, however, we have **not allowed for several factors**.

(a) The **influence of the environment** (such as government legislation about safety standards, changing consumer demand, an unexpected rise in raw material prices, or a long strike in a supplier industry).

(b) **Whether control action is possible**. A sales manager might not be able to increase sales if the production department can't produce the desired output fast enough.

(c) **How much information should be measured and compared with planned results.** Not all output is measured, either because it would not have any useful value, or because the system does not provide for its measurement. The reasons why customers buy or don't buy from the company might be reported back, but they might not.

(d) The **plan might need to be changed** and a **comparison of actual results against the existing plan might be invalid.** Environmental influences could be responsible for the need to change the sales plan.

(e) **Not all inputs to the system are controllable**; a rise in raw material prices is outside the scope of management control. Other inputs might be controllable, but are **not controlled due to lax or inattentive management** (for example poor labour morale and a high labour turnover amongst sales staff).

In an article in the *ACCA Students' Newsletter* ('Budgetary control - the organisational aspects, December 1998), the examiner of the equivalent paper under the old syllabus provided the following diagram of the management control process.

Phases of management control

'To elaborate on the features of [the diagram] *programming* is the link with strategic planning. It identifies the products a company intends to develop, projects which management intend to pursue to meet the organisation's overall goals. *Budgets* are derived from these and are specified in terms of a manager's responsibility. *Operating and measurement* is the collecting of actual costs and outcomes identified to both programmes and responsibility centres. Finally, *reporting and analysis* takes place as a basis for control to the budget, for the co-ordination of activities and as a basis for future decisions perhaps to change the original plan.

Budgets as they are generally understood form the cornerstone of management control and the management control system...'

3 Feedback and feedforward control

> **Feedback** is the process of reporting back control information to management and the control information itself.
>
> **Feedforward control** is control based on comparing original targets or actual results with a forecast of future results.

3.1 Feedback

Key term

> **Feedback** is both the process of reporting back control information to management and the control information itself. In a business organisation, it is information produced from within the organisation (management control reports) with the purpose of helping management and other employees with control decisions.

(a) **Single loop feedback**, normally expressed as feedback, is the feedback of relatively small variations between actual and plan in order that corrective action can bring performance in line with planned results. This implies that the existing plans will not change. This type of feedback is associated with budgetary control and standard costing.

(b) **Double loop feedback**, also known as **higher level feedback**, ensures that plans, budgets, organisational structures and the control systems themselves are revised to meet changes in conditions.

(c) Feedback will most often be **negative:** targets were missed and this was **not** what was required. It may, however, be **positive:** targets were missed, but other targets were hit which were better than those we were aiming at. Negative feedback would result in control action to get back onto target. Positive feedback means that the target should be moved.

The feedback loop in the control cycle is illustrated by the following diagram.

Feedback loop in the control cycle

3.2 Feedforward control

Most control systems make use of a comparison between results of the current period (historical costs) and the planned results. Past events are therefore used as a means of controlling or adjusting future activity.

Consider, however, a **cash budget** (which we cover in depth in the next chapter). This is used to identify likely peaks and troughs in cash balances, and if it seems probable that, say, a higher overdraft facility will be needed later in the year, control action will be taken in advance of the actual need, to make sure that the facility will be available. This is an example of **feedforward control**

Key term

> **Feedforward control** is control based on comparing original targets or actual results with a forecast of future results.

The 'information revolution', which has arisen from computer technology, management information systems theory and the growing use of quantitative techniques has widened the scope for the use of this control technique. Forecasting models can be constructed which enable regular revised forecasts to be prepared about what is now likely to happen in view of changes in key variables (such as sales demand, wage rates and so on).

If regular forecasts are prepared, managers will have both the current forecast and the original plan to guide their action. The original plan may or may not be achievable in view of the changing circumstances. The current forecast indicates what is expected to happen in view of these circumstances.

3.2.1 Examples of control comparisons

Step 1 **Current forecast versus plan.** What action must be taken to get back to the plan, given the differences between the current forecast and the plan? Is any control action worthwhile?

Step 2 If **control action** is **planned**, the current forecast will need to be amended to take account of the effects of the control action and a **revised forecast** prepared.

Step 3 The next comparison should then be **revised forecast versus plan** to determine whether the plan is now expected to be achieved.

Step 4 A comparison between the **original current forecast** and the **revised forecast** will show what the expected effect of the control action will be.

Step 5 At the **end of a control period**, actual results will be analysed and two comparisons may be made.

- **Actual results versus the revised forecast.** Why did differences between the two occur?
- **Actual results so far in the year versus the plan.** How close are actual results to the plan?

Step 6 At the same time, a **new current forecast** should be prepared, and the cycle of comparisons and control action may begin again.

It is in this way that costs are constantly controlled and monitored.

PART C BUDGETING AND PERFORMANCE MEASUREMENT

4 Controllability and responsibility reporting

FAST FORWARD

> The selection of **budget centres** in an organisation is a key first step in setting up a control system. A system of **responsibility accounting** must be established.
>
> **Responsibility centres** include **cost centres**, **profit centres** and **investment centres**.

In order to prepare a budget for an organisation as a whole, individual budgets have to be prepared for sub-sections of the organisation, such as individual subsidiaries within the group and individual departments, products or activities within each subsidiary.

Key term

Each section of an organisation for which a budget is prepared is a **budget centre**.

Since budgets will be made for each of these budget centres, **control reporting** (the comparison of actual results against plan) will also be **based on budget centres**.

The **selection of budget centres** in an organisation is therefore a **key first step in setting up a control system**. What should the budget centres be? What income, expenditure and/or capital employment plans should each budget centre prepare? And how will measures of performance for each budget centre be made?

A well-organised system of control should have the following features.

Feature	Explanation
A hierarchy of budget centres	If the organisation is quite large a hierarchy is needed. Subsidiary companies, departments and work sections might be budget centres. Budgets of each section would then be consolidated into a departmental budget, departmental budgets in turn would be consolidated into the subsidiary's budget, and the budgets of each subsidiary would be combined into a master budget for the group as a whole.
Clearly identified responsibilities for achieving budget targets	Individual managers should be made responsible for achieving the budget targets of a particular budget centre.
Responsibilities for revenues, costs and capital employed	Budget centres should be organised so that all the revenues earned by an organisation, all the costs it incurs, and all the capital it employs are made the responsibility of someone within the organisation, at an appropriate level of authority in the management hierarchy.

Exam focus point

A description of these features was worth up to six marks in the December 2001 exam.

Budgetary control and budget centres are therefore part of the overall system of **responsibility accounting** within an organisation.

Key terms

Responsibility accounting is a system of accounting that segregates revenue and costs into areas of personal responsibility in order to monitor and assess the performance of each part of an organisation.

A **responsibility centre** is a unit of an organisation headed by a manager who has direct responsibility for its performance.

Responsibility centres might be a mixture of cost centres, profit centres and investment centres.

7: BUDGET PLANNING AND CONTROL

The following table should help to highlight the differences between cost centres, profit centres and investment centres.

Type of responsibility centre	Manager has control over . . .	Principal performance measure
Cost centre	Controllable costs	Variance analysis
Profit centre	Controllable costs Sales volumes Sales prices	Profit
Investment centre	Controllable costs Sales prices Output volumes Investment in fixed and current assets	Return on investment and residual income

Question — Cost centres

Find out if your organisation has a system of cost, profit and investment centres. What is the scope of planning and control within each centre?

Exam focus point

The difficulty in implementing responsibility accounting in not-for-profit organisations was examined in December 2001. Would you have been able to earn the possible six marks available? Try the question below to find out.

Question — Responsibility accounting

Why might responsibility accounting be difficult to implement in a not-for-profit organisation?

Answer

(a) Objectives are often unclear, so there is no obvious link between inputs and outputs. Responsibility is then hard to define.

(b) Budget holders may have to monitor costs rather than control them. For example, budget holders in a hospital are often not medical staff but medical decisions control the extent to which costs are incurred.

(c) The value for money objective of effectiveness is not measurable in money terms.

4.1 Controllable and non-controllable costs

FAST FORWARD

Controllable costs are items of expenditure which can be directly influenced by a given manager within a given time span. A particular cost might be the responsibility of two or more managers (**dual responsibility**). A reporting system must allocate responsibility appropriately.

A cost which is not controllable by a junior manager might be controllable by a senior manager. For example, there may be high direct labour costs in a department caused by excessive overtime working. The junior manager may feel obliged to continue with the overtime to meet production schedules, but his senior may be able to reduce costs by hiring extra full-time staff, thereby reducing the requirements for overtime.

A cost which is not controllable by a manager in one department may be controllable by a manager in another department. For example, an increase in material costs may be caused by buying at higher prices than expected (controllable by the purchasing department) or by excessive wastage (controllable by the production department) or by a faulty machine producing rejects (controllable by the maintenance department).

Some costs are **non-controllable**, such as increases in expenditure items due to inflation. Other costs are **controllable, but in the long term rather than the short term**. For example, production costs might be reduced by the introduction of new machinery and technology, but in the short term, management must attempt to do the best they can with the resources and machinery at their disposal.

4.2 The controllability of fixed costs

It is often assumed that all fixed costs are non-controllable in the short run. This is not so.

(a) **Committed fixed costs** are those costs arising from the possession of plant, equipment, buildings and an administration department to **support the long-term needs of the business**. These costs (depreciation, rent, administration salaries) are largely **non-controllable in the short term** because they have been committed by longer-term decisions affecting longer-term needs. When a company decides to cut production drastically, the long-term committed fixed costs will be reduced, but only after redundancy terms have been settled and assets sold.

(b) **Discretionary fixed costs**, such as advertising and research and development costs, are incurred as a result of a top management decision, but could be **raised or lowered at fairly short notice** (irrespective of the actual volume of production and sales).

4.3 Controllability and apportioned costs

Managers should only be held accountable for costs over which they have some influence. This may seem quite straightforward in theory, but it is not always so easy in practice to distinguish controllable from uncontrollable costs. **Apportioned overhead costs provide a good example.**

Suppose that a manager of a production department in a manufacturing company is made responsible for the costs of his department. These costs include **directly attributable overhead items** such as the costs of indirect labour employed in the department and indirect materials consumed in the department. The department's overhead costs also include an apportionment of costs from other costs centres, such as rent and rates for the building it shares with other departments and a share of the costs of the maintenance department.

Should the production manager be held accountable for any of these apportioned costs?

(a) Managers should **not be held accountable** for costs over which they have **no control**. In this example, apportioned rent and rates costs would not be controllable by the production department manager.

(b) Managers should be held **accountable for** costs over which they have **some influence**. In this example, it is the responsibility of the maintenance department manager to keep maintenance costs within budget. But their costs will be partly variable and partly fixed, and the variable cost element will depend on the volume of demand for their services. If the production department's staff treat their equipment badly we might expect higher repair costs, and the production department manager should therefore be made accountable for the repair costs that his department makes the maintenance department incur on its behalf.

7: BUDGET PLANNING AND CONTROL

Question — Fixed costs

Try to discover some of your organisation's committed fixed costs and discretionary fixed costs. You will then be able to use them as examples in the exam.

4.4 Controllability and dual responsibility

Quite often a particular cost might be the **responsibility of two or more managers**. For example, raw materials costs might be the responsibility of the purchasing manager (prices) and the production manager (usage). A **reporting system must allocate responsibility appropriately**. The purchasing manager must be responsible for any increase in raw materials prices whereas the production manager should be responsible for any increase in raw materials usage.

4.5 Control reporting

Feedback periods ought to be planned, especially for routine control reporting.

(a) It is important to **avoid excessive reporting**. There is no point in producing control reports weekly if it takes several days to find out the cause of a variance and put it right. There has to be a reasonable interval between control reports so that managers can make a reasonable judgement about the effects of their past control actions. If reports are too frequent, they might well be thrown into the wastepaper basket unread.

(b) It is also important to **avoid unnecessary delays** in control reporting, by making the feedback period too long, or by taking too much time to put a feedback report together.

The most suitable frequency of routine control reporting will vary from operation to operation.

Control reports should be **clear** and **understandable** to the person receiving them. **Highlighting key results** and **exception reporting** are ways of improving clarity. Several reports will be prepared, all relating in some way to the same actual results. This is because reports will go to managers at different levels in the chain of command.

5 Budgetary planning and control systems   12/04

FAST FORWARD

Here are the objectives of a budgetary planning and control system.

- Ensure the achievement of the organisation's objectives
- Compel planning
- Communicate ideas and plans
- Coordinate activities
- Provide a framework for responsibility accounting
- Establish a system of control
- Motivate employees to improve their performance

A budgetary planning and control system is essentially a system for ensuring **communication**, **coordination** and **control** within an organisation. Communication, coordination and control are general objectives: more information is provided by an inspection of the specific objectives of a budgetary planning and control system.

PART C BUDGETING AND PERFORMANCE MEASUREMENT

Objective	Comment
Ensure the achievement of the organisation's objectives	Objectives are set for the organisation as a whole, and for individual departments and operations within the organisation. Quantified expressions of these objectives are then drawn up as targets to be achieved within the timescale of the budget plan.
Compel planning	This is probably the most important feature of a budgetary planning and control system. Planning forces management to **look ahead**, to set out **detailed plans** for achieving the targets for each department, operation and (ideally) each manager and to anticipate problems. It thus prevents management from relying on ad hoc or uncoordinated planning which may be detrimental to the performance of the organisation.
Communicate ideas and plans	A formal system is necessary to ensure that each person affected by the plans is aware of what he or she is **supposed to be doing**. Communication might be one-way, with managers giving **orders to subordinates**, or there might be a two-way dialogue and exchange of ideas.
Coordinate activities	The activities of different departments or sub-units of the organisation need to be coordinated to ensure **maximum integration** of effort towards common goals. This concept of coordination implies, for example, that the purchasing department should base its budget on production requirements and that the production budget should in turn be based on sales expectations. Although straightforward in concept, coordination is remarkably difficult to achieve, and there is often **'sub-optimality'** and conflict between departmental plans in the budget so that the efforts of each department are not fully integrated into a combined plan to achieve the company's best targets.
Provide a framework for responsibility accounting	Budgetary planning and control systems require that managers of **budget centres** are made responsible for the achievement of budget targets for the operations under their personal control.
Establish a system of control	A budget is a **yardstick** against which actual performance is measured and assessed. Control over actual performance is provided by the comparisons of actual results against the budget plan. Departures from budget can then be investigated and the reasons for the departures can be divided into **controllable** and **uncontrollable** factors.
Motivate employees to improve their performance	The interest and commitment of employees can be retained via a system of **feedback of actual results**, which lets them know how well or badly they are performing. The identification of controllable reasons for departures from budget with managers responsible provides an incentive for improving future performance.

Exam focus point

An exam question could well ask you to explain a number of these objectives in the context of a particular scenario such as a not-for-profit organisation.

Chapter Roundup

- **Planning** involves making choices between alternatives and is primarily a decision-making activity.
- The **planning and control cycle** has seven steps.
    - *Step 1.* Identify **objectives**
    - *Step 2.* Identify potential **strategies**
    - *Step 3.* Evaluate strategies
    - *Step 4.* Choose alternative courses of action
    - *Step 5.* Implement the long-term plan
    - *Step 6.* Measure actual results and compare with the plan
    - *Step 7.* Respond to divergences from the plan
- **Control** is achieved through the **control cycle**. Actual performance is compared with planned performance and the appropriate action is taken for those items that are not proceeding according to plan.
- **Feedback** is the process of reporting back control information to management and the control information itself.
- **Feedforward control** is control based on comparing original targets or actual results with a forecast of future results.
- The selection of **budget centres** in an organisation is a key first step in setting up a control system. A system of **responsibility accounting** must be established.
- **Responsibility centres** include **cost centres**, **profit centres** and **investment centres**.
- **Controllable costs** are items of expenditure which can be directly influenced by a given manager within a given time span.
- A particular cost might be the responsibility of two or more managers (**dual responsibility**). A reporting system must allocate responsibility appropriately.
- Here are the **objectives of a budgetary planning and control system.**
    - Ensure the achievement of the organisation's objectives
    - Compel planning
    - Communicate ideas and plans
    - Coordinate activities
    - Provide a framework for responsibility accounting
    - Establish a system of control
    - Motivate employees to improve their performance

PART C BUDGETING AND PERFORMANCE MEASUREMENT

Quick Quiz

1   Put the following steps in the planning cycle in the correct order.

   - Evaluate strategies
   - Implement the long-term plan
   - Identify objectives
   - Choose alternative courses of action
   - Identify potential strategies

2   A 'strategic audit' or 'position analysis' is an information gathering exercise carried out by an organisation to ensure that it has a full understanding of where it is now.

   ☐ True
   ☐ False

3   What question does an objective answer?

4   Complete the following steps in the control cycle.

   Step 1..

   Step 2..

   Step 3..

   Step 4..

   Step 5..

   Step 6..

   (a) ....

   (b) ....

   (c) ....

5   Match the following terms to the correct description.

Terms		Descriptions
• Programming	(a)	The cornerstone of management control and the management control system
• Operating and measurement	(b)	Collection of actual costs and outcomes identified to both programmes and responsibility centres
• Reporting and analysis	(c)	Identification of the products a company intends to develop and projects which management intend to pursue to meet the organisation's overall goals
• Feedback	(d)	Used to compare actual results with targets
• Budgets	(e)	Used as a basis for control, for the coordination of activities and as a basis for future decisions perhaps to change the original plan

6   Fill in the blanks.

   A well-organised system of control should have the following features.

   (a)   A hierarchy of ....

   (b)   Clearly identified .... for achieving budget targets

   (c)   Responsibilities for ...., ... and ....

7   Which of the following are not controllable by a production department manager?

    (a)   Direct labour rate
    (b)   Variable production overheads
    (c)   Apportioned canteen costs
    (d)   Increases in raw material costs due to inflation
    (e)   Increases in overall material costs due to high levels of wastage caused by poor supervision of production workers
    (f)   An increase in the level of idle time because of poorly-maintained machines
    (g)   Depreciation
    (h)   Advertising for production workers

8   What elements would typically make up a long-term financial plan?

Answers to Quick Quiz

1. Identify objectives
   Identify potential strategies
   Evaluate strategies
   Choose alternative courses of action
   Implement the long-term plan

2. False. A 'position audit' or 'strategic analysis' is being described.

3. 'Where do we want to be?'

4. Step 1. Plans and targets are set for the future.
   Step 2. Plans are put into operation.
   Step 3. Actual results are recorded and analysed.
   Step 4. Information about actual results is fed back to management.
   Step 5. Management uses the feedback to compare actual results and targets.
   Step 6. The comparison leads management to do one of three things.

   (a) Take control action
   (b) Decide to do nothing
   (c) Alter the plan or target

5. Programming — (c)
   Operating and measurement — (b)
   Reporting and analysis — (e)
   Feedback — (d)
   Budgets — (a)

6. (a) budget centres
   (b) responsibilities
   (c) revenues
       costs
       capital employed

7. (a)
   (c)
   (d)
   (f) (if there is a maintenance department)
   (g)
   (h)

8. - Projected cash flows
   - Projected long-term profits
   - Capital expenditure plans
   - Balance sheet forecasts
   - Description of long-term objectives and strategies in words

Now try the questions below from the Exam Question Bank

Number	Level	Marks	Time
Q9	Examination	25	45 mins

Budget preparation

Topic list	Syllabus reference
1 Administration of the budget	8(c)
2 The budget preparation timetable	8(c)
3 Functional budgets	8(c)
4 Cash budgets	8(c)
5 Budgeted P&L account and balance sheet	8(c)
6 The master budget	8(c)

Introduction

In Chapter 7 we looked at how **budgeting** fits into organisational planning. Budgeting is a topic which you will meet at all stages of your examination studies and so it is vital that you get a firm grasp of the basics now.

The chapter begins by looking at the **budgeting process**. The process is broken down and the individual stages looked at in detail. We will see how the sales budget and the production and related budgets (the **functional budgets**) are prepared, as well as the **cash budget.** The culmination of the budget process is the **master budget**, which comprises the budgeted profit and loss account, budgeted balance sheet and the cash budget. You will have the opportunity to see how a master budget is prepared in Section 6 of the chapter.

Chapter 9 builds on the general awareness of budgeting which you will have gained in this chapter and considers the control function of budgets.

PART C BUDGETING AND PERFORMANCE MEASUREMENT

Study guide

Section 22 – Budget planning and control I

- Prepare, review and explain a budget preparation timetable
- Prepare and evaluate functional, subsidiary and master budgets, including cash budgeting
- Explain the processes involved with the development and implementation of budgets

Exam guide

As well as discursive questions on the topics of this chapter, Section B questions could require you to prepare budgets including various functional budgets, a master budget and/or a cash budget.

Budget preparation may also appear in conjunction with financial management topics in Section A; a cash budget is particularly likely to be set in Section A.

1 Administration of the budget

FAST FORWARD

A budget is a **quantified plan of action** for a forthcoming accounting period.

The **budget manual** is a collection of instructions governing the responsibilities of persons and the procedures, forms and records relating to the preparation and use of budgetary data.

The **budget committee** is the coordinating body in the preparation and administration of budgets.

Key term

A **budget** is an organisation's plan for a forthcoming period, expressed in money term.

Having seen why organisations prepare budgets in the previous chapter, we will now turn our attention to the administrative procedures that ensure that the budget process works effectively.

1.1 The budget period

Key term

The **budget period** is the time period to which the budget relates.

Except for capital expenditure budgets, the budget period is commonly the accounting year (sub-divided into 12 or 13 control periods).

1.2 Budget documentation: the budget manual

Key term

The **budget manual** is a collection of instructions governing the responsibilities of persons and the procedures, forms and records relating to the preparation and use of budgetary data.

As one of the functions of the budget is to improve communication, a manual should be produced so that everyone can refer to it for information and guidance about the budgeting process. The budget manual does *not* contain the actual budgets for the forthcoming period; it is more of an **instruction/information manual about the way budgeting operates** in a particular organisation.

A budget manual will usually be prepared by the management accountant and although its contents will vary from organisation to organisation, it may contain the following.

Content	Detail
Explanation of the objectives of the budgeting process	• The purpose of budgetary planning and control • The objectives of the various stages of the budgeting process • The importance of budgets in the long-term planning and administration of the enterprise
Organisational structures	• An organisation chart • A list of staff holding budget responsibilities
Outline of the principal budgets	• Relationship between them
Administrative details	• Membership, and terms of reference, of the budget committee • Sequence in which budgets are to be prepared • A timetable
Procedural matters	• Specimen forms and instructions for completing them • Specimen reports • Account codes (or a chart of accounts) • Budget officer to whom to send enquiries

1.3 Responsibility for the preparation of budgets

Ideally the **managers (and their subordinates) responsible for preparing budgets should be the managers (and their subordinates) who are responsible for carrying out the budgets**. For example, the sales manager should draft the sales budget and selling overhead cost centre budget and the purchasing manager should draft the material purchases budget.

1.4 Budget committee

The **coordination** and **administration of budgets** is usually the **responsibility of a budget committee** (with the managing director as chairman). The budget committee is **assisted by a budget officer** who is usually an accountant. Every part of the organisation should be represented on the committee, so there should be a **representative from sales, production, marketing** and so on. Functions of the budget committee include the following.

- **Coordination of budget preparation**, including the issue of the budget manual
- **Issuing of timetables** for the preparation of functional budgets
- **Allocation of responsibilities** for the preparation of functional budgets
- **Provision of information** to assist in the preparation of budgets
- **Communication of final budgets** to the appropriate managers
- **Comparison of actual results** with budget and the investigation of variances
- **Continuous assessment** of the budgeting and planning process

2 The budget preparation timetable

FAST FORWARD

The **budget preparation** process is as follows.
- Communicating details of the budget policy and budget guidelines.
- Determining the factor that restricts output
- Preparation of the sales budget
- Initial preparation of budgets
- Negotiation of budgets with superiors
- Coordination and review of budgets
- Final acceptance of the budgets
- Budget review

Let us now look at the steps involved in the **development, preparation and implementation of a budget**. The procedures will differ from organisation to organisation, but the step-by-step approach described here is indicative of the steps followed by many organisations. The preparation of a budget may take weeks or months and the budget committee may meet several times before an organisation's budget is finally agreed.

Step 1 Communicating details of the budget policy and budget guidelines

The long-term plan is the starting point for the preparation of the annual budget. Managers responsible for preparing the budget must be aware of the way it is affected by the long-term plan so that it becomes part of the process of meeting the organisation's objectives. For example, if the long-term plan calls for a more aggressive pricing policy, the budget must take this into account. Managers should also be provided with important guidelines for wage rate increases, changes in productivity and so on, as well as information about industry demand and output.

Step 2 Determining the factor that restricts output

Key term

The **principal budget factor** (or **key budget factor** or **limiting budget factor**) is the factor that limits an organisation's performance for a given period and is often the starting point in budget preparation.

For example, a sales department might estimate that it could sell 1,000 units of product X, which would require 5,000 hours of grade A labour. If there are no units of product X already in stock, and only 4,000 hours of grade A labour available in the period, the company would be unable to sell 1,000 units of X because of the shortage of labour hours. Grade A labour would be a limiting budget factor, and management must choose one of the following options.

- Reduce budgeted sales by 20%
- Try to increase the availability of grade A labour by 1,000 hours (25%) by recruitment or overtime working
- Try to sub-contract the production of 1,000 units to another manufacturer, but still profit on the transaction

In most organisations the principal budget factor is sales demand: a company is usually restricted from making and selling more of its products because there would be no sales demand for the increased output at a price which would be acceptable to the company. The principal budget factor may also be machine capacity, distribution and selling resources, the availability of key raw materials or cash. Once this factor is defined then the rest of the budget can be prepared. For example, if sales are the principal budget factor then the production manager can only prepare his budget after the sales budget is complete.

Management may not know what the limiting budget factor is until a draft budget has been attempted. The first draft budget will therefore usually begin with the preparation of a draft sales budget.

Step 3 Preparation of the sales budget

We have already established that, for many organisations, the principal budget factor is sales volume. The sales budget is therefore often the primary budget from which the majority of the other budgets are derived. Before the sales budget can be prepared a **sales forecast** has to be made. Sales forecasting is complex and difficult and involves the consideration of a number of factors.

- Past sales patterns
- The economic environment
- Results of market research
- Anticipated advertising
- Competition
- Changing consumer taste
- New legislation
- Distribution
- Pricing policies and discounts offered
- Legislation
- Environmental factors

As well as bearing in mind the above factors, management can use a number of forecasting methods, which we will return to in Chapter 11.

On the basis of the sales forecast and the production capacity of the organisation, a sales budget will be prepared. This may be subdivided, possible subdivisions being by product, by sales area, by management responsibility and so on.

Step 4 Initial preparation of budgets

Budget	Detail
Finished goods stock budget	Decides the planned increase or decrease in finished stock levels.
Production budget	Stated in units of each product and is the sales budget in units plus the budgeted increase in finished goods stocks **or** minus the budgeted decrease in finished goods stocks.
Budgets of resources for production	**Materials usage budget** is stated in quantities and perhaps cost for each type of material used. It should take into account budgeted losses in production. **Machine utilisation budget** shows the operating hours required on each machine or group of machines. **Labour budget or wages budget** will be expressed in hours for each grade of labour and in terms of cost. It should take into account budgeted idle time.
Overhead cost budgets	**Production, administration, selling and distribution and research and development department overheads**
Raw materials stock budget	Decides the planned increase or decrease of the level of stocks.
Raw materials purchase budget	Can be prepared in quantities and value for each type of material purchased once the raw material usage requirements and the raw materials stock budget are known.
Overhead absorption rate	Can be calculated once the production volumes are planned, and the overhead cost centre budgets prepared.

Step 5 Negotiation of budgets with superiors

Once a manager has prepared his draft budget he should submit it to his superior for approval. The superior should then incorporate this budget with the others for which he or she is responsible and then submit this budget for approval to his or her superior. This process continues until the final budget is presented to the budget committee for approval.

At each stage, the **budget** would be **negotiated between the manager who had prepared the budget and his/her superior** until agreed by both parties.

Step 6 Co-ordination of budgets

Remember that it is unlikely that the execution of the above steps will be problem-free. The budgets must be reviewed in relation to one another. Such a **review may indicate that some budgets are out of balance with others and need modifying** so that they will be compatible. The budget officer must identify such inconsistencies and bring them to the attention of the manager concerned. The **revision of one budget may lead to the revision of all budgets**.

During this process the budgeted profit and loss account and budgeted balance sheet and cash budget should be prepared to ensure that all of the individual parts of the budget combine into an acceptable master budget.

PART C BUDGETING AND PERFORMANCE MEASUREMENT

Step 7 **Final acceptance of the budget**

When all the budgets are in harmony with one another they are summarised into a **master budget** consisting of a budgeted profit and loss account, budgeted balance sheet and cash budget.

Step 8 **Budget review**

The budgeting process does not stop once the budgets have been agreed. Actual results should be compared on a regular basis with the budgeted results. Management should receive a report detailing the differences and should investigate the reasons for the differences. **If the differences are within the control of management, corrective action should be taken** to bring the reasons for the difference under control and to ensure that such inefficiencies do not occur in the future.

The **differences may have occurred, however, because the budget was unrealistic to begin with or because the actual conditions did not reflect those anticipated (or could have possibly been anticipated).** This would therefore invalidate the remainder of the budget.

The **budget committee**, who should meet periodically to evaluate the organisation's actual performance, **may need to reappraise the organisation's future plans in the light of changes to anticipated conditions and to adjust the budget to take account of such changes**.

The important point to note is that the budgeting process does not end for the current year once the budget period has begun: budgeting should be seen as a continuous and dynamic process.

Question — Budgets

A company that manufactures and sells a range of products, with sales potential limited by market share, is considering introducing a system of budgeting.

Required

(a) List (in order of preparation) the functional budgets that need to be prepared.

(b) State which budgets the master budget will comprise.

(c) Consider how the work outlined in (a) and (b) can be coordinated in order for the budgeting process to be successful.

Answer

(a) The **sequence** of budget preparation will be roughly as follows.

  (i) **Sales budget**. (The market share limits demand and so sales is the principal budget factor. All other activities will depend upon this forecast.)

  (ii) **Finished goods stock budget** (in units)

  (iii) **Production budget** (in units)

  (iv) **Production resources budgets** (materials, machine hours, labour)

  (v) **Overhead budgets** for production, administration, selling and distribution, research and development and so on

  Other budgets required will be the capital expenditure budget, and, very importantly, the cash budget.

(b) The master budget is the summary of all the functional budgets. It often includes a **summary profit and loss account and balance sheet.**

(c) Procedures for preparing budgets can be contained in a **budget manual** which shows which budgets must be prepared when and by whom, what each functional budget should contain and detailed directions on how to prepare budgets including, for example, expected price increases, rates of interest, rates of depreciation and so on.

The formulation of budgets can be coordinated by a **budget committee** comprising the senior executives of the departments responsible for carrying out the budgets: sales, production, purchasing, personnel and so on.

The budgeting process may also be assisted by the use of a **spreadsheet/computer budgeting package**.

3 Functional budgets

FAST FORWARD

The **principal budget factor** should be identified at the beginning of the budgetary process, and the budget for this is prepared before all the other **functional budgets**.

Exam focus point

You must be able to prepare budgets from information provided in examination questions and comment on those budgets, perhaps giving recommendations about management action required.

Key term

Functional (or **departmental**) **budgets** are the budgets for the various functions and departments of an organisation. They therefore include production budgets, marketing budgets, sales budgets, personnel budgets, purchasing budgets and research and development budgets.

We will look at the preparation of a number of types of functional budget in this chapter but the general principles covered can be applied in most situations.

3.1 Production cost budget   12/03

If the principal budget factor was production capacity then the production cost budget would be the first to be prepared.

To assess whether production is the principal budget factor, the **production capacity available** must be determined. This should take into account the following factors.

- **Available labour**, including idle time, overtime and standard output rates per hour
- **Availability of raw materials** including allowances for losses during production
- **Maximum machine hours available**, including expected idle time and expected output rates per machine hour

It is, however, normally sales volume that is the constraint and therefore the production budget is prepared after the sales budget and the finished goods stock budget.

The **production cost budget** will show the **quantities** and **costs** for **each product** and product group and will tie in with the sales and stock budgets. This co-ordinating process is likely to show any shortfalls or excesses in capacity at various times over the budget period. If there is likely to be a shortfall then consideration should be given to overtime, subcontracting, machine hire, new sources of raw materials or some other way of increasing output. A significant shortfall means that production capacity is, in fact, the limiting factor. If capacity exceeds sales volume for a length of time then consideration should be given to product diversification, a reduction in selling price (if demand is price elastic) and so on.

Once the production budget has been finalised, the labour, materials and machine budgets can be drawn up. These budgets will be based on budgeted activity levels, existing stock positions and projected labour and material costs.

3.2 Example: The preparation of the production budget and direct labour budget

Pearson Ltd manufactures two products, P and L, and is preparing its budget for 20X3. Both products are made by the same grade of labour, grade G. The company currently holds 800 units of P and 1,200 units of L in stock, but 250 of these units of L have just been discovered to have deteriorated in quality, and must therefore be scrapped. Budgeted sales of P are 3,000 units and of L 4,000 units, provided that the company maintains finished goods stocks at a level equal to three months' sales.

Grade G labour was originally expected to produce one unit of P in two hours and one unit of L in three hours, at an hourly rate of £2.50 per hour. In discussions with trade union negotiators, however, it has been agreed that the hourly wage rate should be raised by 50p per hour, provided that the times to produce P and L are reduced by 20%.

Required

Prepare the production budget and direct labour budget for 20X3.

Solution

The expected time to produce a unit of P will now be 80% of 2 hours = 1.6 hours, and the time for a unit of L will be 2.4 hours. The hourly wage rate will be £3, so that the direct labour cost will be £4.80 for P and £7.20 for L (thus achieving a saving for the company of 20p per unit of P produced and 30p per unit of L).

(a) **Production budget**

		Product P		Product L	
		Units	Units	Units	Units
Budgeted sales			3,000		4,000
Closing stocks	($^3/_{12}$ of 3,000)	750		($^3/_{12}$ of 4,000) 1,000	
Opening stocks (minus stocks scrapped)		800		950	
(Decrease)/increase in stocks			(50)		50
Production			2,950		4,050

(b) **Direct labour budget**

	Grade G Hours	Cost £
2,950 units of product P	4,720	14,160
4,050 units of product L	9,720	29,160
Total	14,440	43,320

It is assumed that there will be no idle time among grade G labour which, if it existed, would have to be paid for at the rate of £3 per hour.

3.3 Labour budget

A useful concept in budgeting for labour requirements is the standard hour.

Key term

> A **standard hour** is the quantity of work achievable at standard performance, expressed in terms of a standard unit of work done in a standard period of time.

Budgeted output of different products or jobs in a period can be converted into standard hours of production, and a labour budget constructed accordingly.

Standard hours are particularly useful when management wants to monitor the production levels of a variety of dissimilar units. For example product A may take five hours to produce and product B, seven hours. If four units of each product are produced, instead of saying that total output is eight units, we could state the production level as $(4 \times 5) + (4 \times 7)$ standard hours = 48 standard hours.

3.4 Example: Direct labour budget based on standard hours

Canaervon Ltd manufactures a single product, the close, with a single grade of labour. Its sales budget and finished goods stock budget for period 3 are as follows.

Sales	700 units
Opening stocks, finished goods	50 units
Closing stocks, finished goods	70 units

The goods are inspected only when production work is completed, and it is budgeted that 10% of finished work will be scrapped. The standard direct labour hour content of the close is three hours. The budgeted productivity ratio for direct labour is only 80% (which means that labour is only working at 80% efficiency). The company employs 18 direct operatives, who are expected to average 144 working hours each in period 3.

Required

(a) Prepare a production budget.

(b) Prepare a direct labour budget.

(c) Comment on the problem that your direct labour budget reveals, and suggest how this problem might be overcome.

Solution

(a) **Production budget**

	Units
Sales	700
Add closing stock	70
	770
Less opening stock	50
Production required of 'good' output	720
Wastage rate	10%

Total production required* = 720/0.9 = 800 units

* Output = 90% × input and so 720 = 0.9 × input and therefore 720/0.9 = input.

(b) Now we can prepare the **direct labour budget.**

Standard hours per unit		3
Total standard hours required	= 800 units × 3 hours	2,400 hours
Productivity ratio		80%
Actual hours required	= 2,400/0.8 = 3,000 hours	

(c) If we look at the direct labour budget against the information provided, we can identify the **problem**.

	Hours
Budgeted hours available (18 operatives × 144 hours)	2,592
Actual hours required	3,000
Shortfall in labour hours	408

The (draft) budget indicates that there will not be enough direct labour hours to meet the production requirements. This problem might be **overcome** in one, or a combination, of the following ways.

(i) Reduce the closing stock requirement below 70 units. This would reduce the number of production units required.

(ii) Persuade the workforce to do some overtime working.

(iii) Perhaps recruit more direct labour if long-term prospects are for higher production volumes.

(iv) Discuss with the workforce (or their union representatives) the following possibilities.

(1) Improve the productivity ratio, and so reduce the number of hours required to produce the output.

(2) If possible, reduce the wastage rate below 10%.

3.5 Cost of sales budget

This is based on the **production cost budget** but **adjusted by the opening and closing stock positions**.

3.6 Coordination of functional budgets

It is vital that the functional budgets are prepared in the correct order (for example, the material usage budget should be prepared after the production budget) and that the **overall process is coordinated** to ensure that the budgets are all in balance with each other. There is little point in the material usage budget being based on a budgeted production level of 10,000 units if the budgeted production level specified in the production budget is 15,000 units.

4 Cash budgets   12/02, 12/03, 12/05

Cash budgets show the expected receipts and payments during a budget period and are a vital management control tool, especially during times of recession.

Key term

A **cash budget** is a detailed budget of cash inflows and outflows incorporating both revenue and capital items.

A cash budget is thus a statement in which estimated future cash receipts and payments are tabulated in such a way as to show the forecast cash balance of a business at defined intervals. For example, in December 20X2 an accounts department might wish to estimate the cash position of the business during the three following months, January to March 20X3. A cash budget might be drawn up in the following format.

	Jan £	Feb £	Mar £
Estimated cash receipts			
From credit customers	14,000	16,500	17,000
From cash sales	3,000	4,000	4,500
Proceeds on disposal of fixed assets		2,200	
Total cash receipts	17,000	22,700	21,500
Estimated cash payments			
To suppliers of goods	8,000	7,800	10,500
To employees (wages)	3,000	3,500	3,500
Purchase of fixed assets		16,000	
Rent and rates			1,000
Other overheads	1,200	1,200	1,200
Repayment of loan	2,500		
	14,700	28,500	16,200
Net surplus/(deficit) for month	2,300	(5,800)	5,300
Opening cash balance	1,200	3,500	(2,300)
Closing cash balance	3,500	(2,300)	3,000

In the example above (where the figures are purely for illustration) the accounts department has calculated that the cash balance at the beginning of the budget period, 1 January, will be £1,200. Estimates have been made of the cash which is likely to be received by the business (from cash and credit sales, and from a planned disposal of fixed assets in February). Similar estimates have been made of cash due to be paid out by the business (payments to suppliers and employees, payments for rent, rates and other overheads, payment for a planned purchase of fixed assets in February and a loan repayment due in January).

From these estimates it is a simple step to calculate the excess of cash receipts over cash payments in each month. In some months cash payments may exceed cash receipts and there will be a deficit for the month; this occurs during February in the above example because of the large investment in fixed assets in that month.

The last part of the cash budget above shows how the business's estimated cash balance can then be rolled along from month to month. Starting with the opening balance of £1,200 at 1 January a cash surplus of £2,300 is generated in January. This leads to a closing January balance of £3,500 which becomes the opening balance for February. The deficit of £5,800 in February throws the business's cash position into overdraft and the overdrawn balance of £2,300 becomes the opening balance for March. Finally, the healthy cash surplus of £5,300 in March leaves the business with a favourable cash position of £3,000 at the end of the budget period.

Exam focus point

When preparing budgets, it is vital that your work is clearly laid out, and referenced to workings where appropriate.

4.1 The usefulness of cash budgets

The cash budget is one of the most important planning tools that an organisation can use. It shows the cash effect of all plans made within the budgetary process and hence its preparation can lead to a modification of budgets if it shows that there are insufficient cash resources to finance the planned operations.

It can also **give management an indication of potential problems that could arise and allows them the opportunity to take action to avoid such problems**. A cash budget can show four positions. Management will need to take appropriate action depending on the potential position.

PART C   BUDGETING AND PERFORMANCE MEASUREMENT

Cash position	Appropriate management action
Short-term surplus	Pay creditors early to obtain discount Attempt to increase sales by increasing debtors and stocks Make short-term investments
Short-term deficit	Increase creditors Reduce debtors Arrange an overdraft
Long-term surplus	Make long-term investments Expand Diversify Replace/update fixed assets
Long-term deficit	Raise long-term finance (such as via issue of share capital) Consider shutdown/disinvestment opportunities

Exam focus point

A cash budgeting question could ask you to prepare the cash budget and then recommend appropriate action for management. Ensure your advice takes account both of whether there is a surplus or deficit and whether the position is long or short term.

4.2 What to include in a cash budget

A cash budget is prepared to show the **expected receipts of cash and payments of cash** during a budget period.

It should be obvious that the **profit or loss made by an organisation during an accounting period does not reflect its cash flow position for the following reasons.**

(a) Not all cash receipts affect profit and loss account income.

(b) Not all cash payments affect profit and loss account expenditure.

(c) Some costs in the profit and loss account such as profit or loss on sale of fixed assets or depreciation are not cash items but are costs derived from accounting conventions.

(d) The timing of cash receipts and payments may not coincide with the recording of profit and loss account transactions. For example, a dividend might be declared in the results for 20X6 and shown in the profit and loss account for that year, but paid in 20X7.

To ensure that there is sufficient cash in hand to cope adequately with budgeted activities, management should therefore prepare and pay close attention to a cash budget rather than a profit and loss account. Cash budgets are most effective if they are treated as rolling budgets. **Rolling budgets** involve a process of continuous budgeting whereby regularly each period (week month, quarter) a new future period is added to the budget whilst the earliest period is deleted. In this way the budget is **constantly revised** to reflect the most up to date position. We consider rolling budgets in Chapter 10.

Exam focus point

Clear workings and assumptions are very important in a cash budget.

4.3 Example: Cash budget

Peter Blair has worked for some years as a sales representative, but has recently been made redundant. He intends to start up in business on his own account, using £15,000 which he currently has invested with a building society. Peter maintains a bank account showing a small credit balance, and he plans to approach his bank for the necessary additional finance. Peter provides the following additional information.

(a) Arrangements have been made to purchase fixed assets costing £8,000. These will be paid for at the end of September and are expected to have a five-year life, at the end of which they will possess a nil residual value.

(b) Stocks costing £5,000 will be acquired on 28 September and subsequent monthly purchases will be at a level sufficient to replace forecast sales for the month.

(c) Forecast monthly sales are £3,000 for October, £6,000 for November and December, and £10,500 from January 20X4 onwards.

(d) Selling price is fixed at the cost of stock plus 50%.

(e) Two months' credit will be allowed to customers but only one month's credit will be received from suppliers of stock.

(f) Running expenses, including rent but excluding depreciation of fixed assets, are estimated at £1,600 per month.

(g) Blair intends to make monthly cash drawings of £1,000.

Required

Prepare a cash budget for the six months to 31 March 20X4.

Solution

The opening cash balance at 1 October is £7,000 which consists of Peter's initial £15,000 less the £8,000 expended on fixed assets purchased in September. Cash receipts from credit customers arise two months after the relevant sales.

Payments to suppliers are a little more tricky. We are told that cost of sales is 100/150 × sales. Thus for October cost of sales is 100/150 × £3,000 = £2,000. These goods will be purchased in October but not paid for until November. Similar calculations can be made for later months. The initial stock of £5,000 is purchased in September and consequently paid for in October.

Depreciation is not a cash flow and so is *not* included in a cash budget.

CASH BUDGET FOR THE SIX MONTHS ENDING 31 MARCH 20X4

	Oct £	Nov £	Dec £	Jan £	Feb £	Mar £
Payments						
Suppliers	5,000	2,000	4,000	4,000	7,000	7,000
Running expenses	1,600	1,600	1,600	1,600	1,600	1,600
Drawings	1,000	1,000	1,000	1,000	1,000	1,000
	7,600	4,600	6,600	6,600	9,600	9,600
Receipts						
Debtors	–	–	3,000	6,000	6,000	10,500
Surplus/(shortfall)	(7,600)	(4,600)	(3,600)	(600)	(3,600)	900
Opening balance	7,000	(600)	(5,200)	(8,800)	(9,400)	(13,000)
Closing balance	(600)	(5,200)	(8,800)	(9,400)	(13,000)	(12,100)

PART C   BUDGETING AND PERFORMANCE MEASUREMENT

4.4 Cash budgets and an opening balance sheet

You might be given a cash budget question in which you are required to analyse an opening balance sheet to decide how many outstanding debtors will pay what they owe in the first few months of the cash budget period, and how many outstanding creditors must be paid.

Suppose that a balance sheet as at 31 December 20X4 shows debtors of £150,000 and trade creditors of £60,000. The following information is also relevant.

- Debtors are allowed two months to pay.
- 1½ months' credit is taken from trade creditors.
- Sales and materials purchases were both made at an even monthly rate.

Let's try to ascertain the months of 20X5 in which the debtors will eventually pay and the creditors will be paid.

(a) Since debtors take two months to pay, the £150,000 of debtors in the balance sheet represents credit sales in November and December 20X4, who will pay in January and February 20X5 respectively. Since sales in 20X4 were at an equal monthly rate, the cash budget should plan for receipts of £75,000 each month in January and February from the debtors in the opening balance sheet.

(b) Similarly, since creditors are paid after 1½ months, the balance sheet creditors will be paid in January and the first half of February 20X5, which means that budgeted payments will be as follows.

	£
In January (purchases in 2nd half of Nov. and 1st half of Dec.20X4)	40,000
In February (purchases in 2nd half of December 20X4)	20,000
Total creditors in the balance sheet	60,000

(The balance sheet creditors of £60,000 represent 1½ months' purchases, so that purchases in 20X4 must be £40,000 per month, which is £20,000 per half month.)

4.5 Example: A month by month cash budget

From the following information which relates to George and Zola Ltd you are required to prepare a month by month cash budget for the second half of 20X5 and to append such brief comments as you consider might be helpful to management.

(a) The company's only product, a vest, sells at £40 and has a variable cost of £26 made up of material £20, labour £4 and overhead £2.

(b) Fixed costs of £6,000 per month are paid on the 28th of each month.

(c) Quantities sold/to be sold on credit

May	June	July	Aug	Sept	Oct	Nov	Dec
1,000	1,200	1,400	1,600	1,800	2,000	2,200	2,600

(d) Production quantities

May	June	July	Aug	Sept	Oct	Nov	Dec
1,200	1,400	1,600	2,000	2,400	2,600	2,400	2,200

(e) Cash sales at a discount of 5% are expected to average 100 units a month.

(f) Customers settle their accounts by the end of the second month following sale.

(g) Suppliers of material are paid two months after the material is used in production.

(h) Wages are paid in the same month as they are incurred.

8: BUDGET PREPARATION

(i) 70% of the variable overhead is paid in the month of production, the remainder in the following month.

(j) Corporation tax of £18,000 is to be paid in October.

(k) A new delivery vehicle was bought in June. It cost £8,000 and is to be paid for in August. The old vehicle was sold for £600, the buyer undertaking to pay in July.

(l) The company is expected to be £3,000 overdrawn at the bank at 30 June 20X5.

(m) No increases or decreases in raw materials, work in progress or finished goods are planned over the period.

(n) No price increases or cost increases are expected in the period.

Solution

Cash budget for 1 July to 31 December 20X5

	July £	Aug £	Sept £	Oct £	Nov £	Dec £	Total £
Receipts							
Credit sales	40,000	48,000	56,000	64,000	72,000	80,000	360,000
Cash sales	3,800	3,800	3,800	3,800	3,800	3,800	22,800
Sale of vehicle	600	–	–	–	–	–	600
	44,400	51,800	59,800	67,800	75,800	83,800	383,400
Payments							
Materials	24,000	28,000	32,000	40,000	48,000	52,000	224,000
Labour	6,400	8,000	9,600	10,400	9,600	8,800	52,800
Variable overhead (W)	3,080	3,760	4,560	5,080	4,920	4,520	25,920
Fixed costs	6,000	6,000	6,000	6,000	6,000	6,000	36,000
Corporation tax				18,000			18,000
Purchase of vehicle		8,000					8,000
	39,480	53,760	52,160	79,480	68,520	71,320	364,720
Receipts less payments	4,920	(1,960)	7,640	(11,680)	7,280	12,480	18,680
Balance b/f	(3,000)	1,920	(40)	7,600	(4,080)	3,200	(3,000)
Balance c/f	1,920	(40)	7,600	(4,080)	3,200	15,680	15,680

Working

	June £	July £	Aug £	Sept £	Oct £	Nov £	Dec £
Variable overhead production cost	2,800	3,200	4,000	4,800	5,200	4,800	4,400
70% paid in month		2,240	2,800	3,360	3,640	3,360	3,080
30% in following month		840	960	1,200	1,440	1,560	1,440
		3,080	3,760	4,560	5,080	4,920	4,520

Comments

(a) There will be a small overdraft at the end of August but a much larger one at the end of October. It may be possible to delay payments to suppliers for longer than two months or to reduce purchases of materials or reduce the volume of production by running down existing stock levels.

(b) If neither of these courses is possible, the company may need to negotiate overdraft facilities with its bank.

(c) The cash deficit is only temporary and by the end of December there will be a comfortable surplus. The use to which this cash will be put should ideally be planned in advance.

Exam focus point

You may be asked to prepare a cash budget, and also consider the effects on the budget or particular figures in it of the original assumptions changing.

PART C BUDGETING AND PERFORMANCE MEASUREMENT

Question — Cash budget

You are presented with the following budgeted cash flow data for your organisation for the period November 20X1 to June 20X2. It has been extracted from functional budgets that have already been prepared.

	Nov X1 £	Dec X1 £	Jan X2 £	Feb X2 £	Mar X2 £	Apr X2 £	May X2 £	June X2 £
Sales	80,000	100,000	110,000	130,000	140,000	150,000	160,000	180,000
Purchases	40,000	60,000	80,000	90,000	110,000	130,000	140,000	150,000
Wages	10,000	12,000	16,000	20,000	24,000	28,000	32,000	36,000
Overheads	10,000	10,000	15,000	15,000	15,000	20,000	20,000	20,000
Dividends		20,000						40,000
Capital expenditure			30,000			40,000		

You are also told the following.

(a) Sales are 40% cash 60% credit. Credit sales are paid two months after the month of sale.
(b) Purchases are paid the month following purchase.
(c) 75% of wages are paid in the current month and 25% the following month.
(d) Overheads are paid the month after they are incurred.
(e) Dividends are paid three months after they are declared.
(f) Capital expenditure is paid two months after it is incurred.
(g) The opening cash balance is £15,000.

The managing director is pleased with the above figures as they show sales will have increased by more than 100% in the period under review. In order to achieve this he has arranged a bank overdraft with a ceiling of £50,000 to accommodate the increased stock levels and wage bill for overtime worked.

Required

(a) Prepare a cash budget for the six-month period January to June 20X2.
(b) Comment on your results in the light of the managing director's comments and offer advice.

Answer

(a)

	January £	February £	March £	April £	May £	June £
Cash receipts						
Cash sales	44,000	52,000	56,000	60,000	64,000	72,000
Credit sales	48,000	60,000	66,000	78,000	84,000	90,000
	92,000	112,000	122,000	138,000	148,000	162,000
Cash payments						
Purchases	60,000	80,000	90,000	110,000	130,000	140,000
Wages: 75%	12,000	15,000	18,000	21,000	24,000	27,000
Wages: 25%	3,000	4,000	5,000	6,000	7,000	8,000
Overheads	10,000	15,000	15,000	15,000	20,000	20,000
Dividends				20,000		
Capital expenditure			30,000			40,000
	85,000	114,000	178,000	152,000	181,000	235,000
b/f	15,000	22,000	20,000	(36,000)	(50,000)	(83,000)
Net cash flow	7,000	(2,000)	(56,000)	(14,000)	(33,000)	(73,000)
c/f	22,000	20,000	(36,000)	(50,000)	(83,000)	(156,000)

(b) The overdraft arrangements are quite inadequate to service the cash needs of the business over the six-month period. If the figures are realistic then action should be taken now to avoid difficulties in the near future. The following are **possible courses of action**.

   (i) **Activities** could be **curtailed**.

   (ii) **Other sources of cash** could be explored, for example a long-term loan to finance the capital expenditure and a factoring arrangement to provide cash due from debtors more quickly.

   (iii) Efforts to increase the **speed of debt collection** could be made.

   (iv) **Payments to creditors** could be delayed.

   (v) The **dividend payments** could be **postponed** (the figures indicate that this is a small company, possibly owner-managed).

   (vi) Staff might be persuaded to work at a **lower rate** in return for, say, an annual bonus or a profit-sharing agreement.

   (vii) **Extra staff** might be taken on to reduce the amount of overtime paid.

   (viii) The **stockholding policy** should be **reviewed**; it may be possible to meet demand from current production and minimise cash tied up in stocks.

5 Budgeted P&L account and balance sheet

FAST FORWARD

The profit or loss made by an organisation during an accounting period does not reflect its cash flow position.

As well as wishing to forecast its cash position, a business might want to estimate its profitability and its financial position for a coming period. This involves the preparation of a budgeted P&L account and balance sheet, along with the cash budget which form the master budget.

Just like historical financial statements, **budgeted accounts are based on the accruals concept**. The example of Peter Blair above will be used to illustrate the procedure.

5.1 Example: Preparing a budgeted P&L account and balance sheet

Using the information in the Peter Blair example, prepare Peter Blair's budgeted P&L account for the six months ending on 31 March 20X4 and a budgeted balance sheet as at that date.

Solution

The profit and loss account is straightforward. The first figure is sales, which can be computed very easily from the information in Paragraph 4.3(c). It is sufficient to add up the monthly sales figures given there; for the profit and loss account there is no need to worry about any closing debtor. Similarly, cost of sales is calculated directly from the information on gross margin contained in Paragraph 4.3(d).

PART C BUDGETING AND PERFORMANCE MEASUREMENT

FORECAST TRADING AND PROFIT AND LOSS ACCOUNT
FOR THE SIX MONTHS ENDING 31 MARCH 20X4

	£	£
Sales (3,000 + (2 × 6,000) + (3 × 10,500))		46,500
Cost of sales (2/3 × £46,500)		31,000
Gross profit		15,500
Expenses: Running expenses (6 × £1,600)	9,600	
Depreciation (£8,000 × 20% × 6/12)	800	
		10,400
Net profit		5,100

Items will be shown in the balance sheet as follows.

(a) Stock will comprise the initial purchases of £5,000.
(b) Debtors will comprise sales made in February and March (paid in April and May).
(c) Creditors will comprise purchases made in March (not paid for until April).
(d) The bank overdraft is the closing cash figure computed in the cash budget.

FORECAST BALANCE SHEET AT 31 MARCH 20X4

	£	£
Fixed assets £(8,000 – 800)		7,200
Current assets		
Stocks	5,000	
Debtors (2 × £10,500)	21,000	
	26,000	
Current liabilities		
Bank overdraft	12,100	
Trade creditors (March purchases)	7,000	
	19,100	
Net current assets		6,900
		14,100
Proprietor's interest		
Capital introduced		15,000
Profit for the period	5,100	
Less drawings	6,000	
Deficit retained		(900)
		14,100

Budget questions are often accompanied by a large amount of sometimes confusing detail. This should not blind you to the fact that many figures can be entered very simply from the logic of the trading situation described. For example in the case of Blair you are told that debtors take two months to pay. Closing debtors will equal total credit sales in the last two months of the period.

Similarly, you may be given a simple statement that a business pays rates at £1,500 a year, followed by a lot of detail to enable you to calculate a prepayment at the beginning and end of the year. If you are preparing a budgeted profit and loss account for the year the rates expense can be entered as £1,500 without any calculation at all.

6 The master budget

FAST FORWARD

When all the functional budgets have been prepared, they are summarised and consolidated into a **master budget** which consists of the budgeted profit and loss account, budgeted balance sheet and cash budget and which provides the overall picture of the planned performance for the budget period.

8: BUDGET PREPARATION

6.1 Example: A master budget

Plagued Engineering Limited produces two products, Niks and Args. The budget for the forthcoming year to 31 March 20X8 is to be prepared. Expectations for the forthcoming year include the following.

(a) **PLAGUED ENGINEERING LTD**
BALANCE SHEET AS AT 1 APRIL 20X7

	£	£
Fixed assets		
Land and buildings		45,000
Plant and equipment at cost	187,000	
Less accumulated depreciation	75,000	
		112,000
Current assets		
Raw materials	7,650	
Finished goods	23,600	
Debtors	19,500	
Cash	4,300	
	55,050	
Current liabilities		
Creditors	6,800	
		48,250
		205,250
Financed by		
Share capital		150,000
Retained profit		55,250
		205,250

(b) **Finished products**

The sales director has estimated the following.

			Niks	Args
(i)	Demand for the company's products		4,500 units	4,000 units
(ii)	Selling price per unit		£32	£44
(iii)	Closing stock of finished products at 31 March 20X8		400 units	1,200 units
(iv)	Opening stock of finished products at 1 April 20X7		900 units	200 units
(v)	Unit cost of this opening stock		£20	£28
(vi)	Amount of plant capacity required for each unit of product			
	Machining		15 min	24 min
	Assembling		12 min	18 min
(vii)	Raw material content per unit of each product			
	Material A		1.5 kilos	0.5 kilos
	Material B		2.0 kilos	4.0 kilos
(viii)	Direct labour hours required per unit of each product		6 hours	9 hours

Finished goods are valued on a FIFO basis at full production cost.

(c) **Raw materials**

		Material A	Material B
(i)	Closing stock requirement in kilos at 31.3.X8	600	1,000
(ii)	Opening stock at 1 April 20X7 in kilos	1,100	6,000
(iii)	Budgeted cost of raw materials per kilo	£1.50	£1.00

Actual costs per kilo of opening stocks are as budgeted cost for the coming year.

PART C BUDGETING AND PERFORMANCE MEASUREMENT

(d) **Direct labour**

The standard wage rate of direct labour is £1.60 per hour.

(e) **Production overhead**

Production overhead is absorbed on the basis of machining hours, with separate absorption rates for each department. Overheads in the machining department are anticipated to be £39,500, while in the assembling department they are anticipated to be £18,650.

Depreciation is taken at 5% straight line on plant and equipment. A machine costing the company £20,000 is due to be installed on 1 October 20X7 in the machining department, which already has machinery installed to the value of £100,000 (at cost). Land worth £180,000 is to be acquired in December 20X7.

(f) Selling and administration expenses are expected to be £30,400.

(g) There is no opening or closing work in progress and inflation should be ignored.

(h) **Budgeted cash flows** are as follows.

	Quarter 1	Quarter 2	Quarter 3	Quarter 4
Receipts from customers	70,000	100,000	100,000	40,000
Payments:				
Materials	7,000	9,000	10,000	5,000
Wages	33,000	20,000	11,000	15,000
Other costs and expenses	10,000	100,000	205,000	5,000

Required

Prepare the following for the year ended 31 March 20X8 for Plagued Engineering Ltd.

(a) Sales budget
(b) Production budget (in quantities)
(c) Plant utilisation budget
(d) Direct materials usage budget
(e) Direct labour budget
(f) Production overhead budget
(g) Computation of the factory cost per unit for each product
(h) Direct materials purchases budget
(i) Cost of goods sold budget
(j) Master budget

Solution

(a) **Sales budget**

	Market demand Units	Selling price £	Sales value £
Niks	4,500	32.00	144,000
Args	4,000	44.00	176,000
			320,000

(b) **Production budget**

	Niks Units	Args Units
Sales requirement	4,500	4,000
(Decrease)/increase in finished goods stock	(500)	1,000
Production requirement	4,000	5,000

(c) **Plant utilisation budget**

Product	Units	Machining Hours per unit	Total hours	Assembling Hours per unit	Total hours
Niks	4,000	0.25	1,000	0.20	800
Args	5,000	0.40	2,000	0.30	1,500
			3,000		2,300

(d) **Direct materials usage budget**

	Material A kg	Material B kg
Required for production:		
Niks: 4,000 × 1.5 kilos	6,000	–
4,000 × 2.0 kilos	–	8,000
Args: 5,000 × 0.5 kilos	2,500	–
5,000 × 4.0 kilos	–	20,000
Material usage	8,500	28,000
Unit cost	£1.50 per kilo	£1.00 per kilo
Cost of materials used	£12,750	£28,000

(e) **Direct labour budget**

Product	Production Units	Hours required per unit	Total hours	Rate per hour £	Cost £
Niks	4,000	6	24,000	1.60	38,400
Args	5,000	9	45,000	1.60	72,000
				Total direct wages	110,400

(f) **Production overhead budget**

	Machining dept £	Assembling dept £
Production overhead allocated and apportioned (excluding depreciation)	39,500	18,650
Depreciation costs		
(i) Existing plant: (5% of £100,000 in machining)	5,000	
(5% of £87,000 in assembly)		4,350
(ii) Proposed plant: (5% of 6/12 × £20,000)	500	
Total production overhead	45,000	23,000
Total machine hours (see (c))	3,000 hrs	2,300 hrs
Absorption rate per machine hour	£15	£10

(g) **Cost of finished goods**

			Niks £		Args £
Direct material A	1.5 kg × £1.50		2.25	0.5 kg × £1.50	0.75
B	2.0 kg × £1.00		2.00	4.0 kg × £1.00	4.00
Direct labour	6 hrs × £1.60		9.60	9 hrs × £1.60	14.40
Production overhead					
Machining department	15 mins at £15 per hr		3.75	24 min at £15 per hr	6.00
Assembling department	12 mins at £10 per hr		2.00	18 mins at £10 per hr	3.00
Production cost per unit			19.60		28.15

PART C BUDGETING AND PERFORMANCE MEASUREMENT

(h) **Direct material purchases budget**

	A kg	B kg
Closing stock required	600	1,000
Production requirements	8,500	28,000
	9,100	29,000
Less opening stock	1,100	6,000
Purchase requirements	8,000	23,000
Cost per unit	£1.50	£1.00
Purchase costs	£12,000	£23,000

(i) **Cost of goods sold budget** (Using FIFO)

	Units		Niks £	Units		Args £
Opening stocks	900	(× £20.00)	18,000	200	(× £28.00)	5,600
Cost of production	4,000	(× £19.60)	78,400	5,000	(× £28.15)	140,750
	4,900		96,400	5,200		146,350
Less closing stocks	400	(× £19.60)	7,840	1,200	(× £28.15)	33,780
Cost of sales	4,500		88,560	4,000		112,570

Notes

(i) The cost of sales of Niks = 900 units at £20 each plus 3,600 units at £19.60 each.
(ii) The cost of sales of Args = 200 units at £28 each plus 3,800 units at £28.15 each.

(j) **MASTER BUDGET**

Cash budget for year to 31.3.X8

	Quarter 1 £	Quarter 2 £	Quarter 3 £	Quarter 4 £	Total £
Receipts	70,000	100,000	100,000	40,000	310,000
Payments					
Materials	7,000	9,000	10,000	5,000	31,000
Labour	33,000	20,000	11,000	15,000	79,000
Other costs and expenses	10,000	100,000	205,000	5,000	320,000
	50,000	129,000	226,000	25,000	430,000
Receipts less payments	20,000	(29,000)	(126,000)	15,000	(120,000)
Opening cash balance b/f	4,300	24,300	(4,700)	(130,700)	4,300
Closing cash balance c/f	24,300	(4,700)	(130,700)	(115,700)	(115,700)

Budgeted profit and loss account for year to 31.3.X8

	Niks £	Args £	Total £
Sales	144,000	176,000	320,000
Less cost of sales	88,560	112,570	201,130
Gross profit	55,440	63,430	118,870
Less selling and administration			30,400
Net profit			88,470

Note. There will be no under-/over-absorbed production overhead in the budgeted profit and loss account.

Budgeted balance sheet at 31.3.X8

	£	£	£
Fixed assets			
Land and buildings (W1)			225,000
Plant and equipment at cost (W2)		207,000	
Less accumulated depreciation (W3)		84,850	
			122,150
			347,150
Current assets			
Raw materials (W4)		1,900	
Finished goods (W5)		41,620	
Debtors (W6)		29,500	
		73,020	
Current liabilities			
Creditors (W7)	10,750		
Bank overdraft (W8)	115,700		
		126,450	
Net current liabilities			(53,430)
			293,720
			£
Financed by			
Share capital			150,000
Retained profit (W9)			143,720
			293,720

Workings

1. Opening balance at 1.4.X7 + addition = cost at 31.3.X8

    ∴ £(45,000 + 180,000) = £225,000

2. Opening balance at 1.4.X7 + addition = cost at 31.3.X8

    ∴ £(187,000 + 20,000) = £207,000

3. Opening balance at 1.4.X7 + addition in period ((f)(i) and (ii) of solution) = accumulated depreciation at 31.3.X8

    ∴ £(75,000 + 5,000 + 4,350 + 500) = £84,850

4.

	A	B	Total
Closing stock (kgs)	600	1,000	
Cost per kg	× £1.50	× £1.00	
Value of closing stock	£900	£1,000	£1,900

5.

	Niks	Args	Total
Closing stock (units)	400	1,200	
Cost per unit ((g) of solution)	× £19.60	× £28.15	
	£7,840	£33,780	£41,620

6. Opening balance + sales ((a) of solution) – receipts (from cash budget) = closing balance

    ∴ £(19,500 + 320,000 – 310,000) = £29,500

PART C BUDGETING AND PERFORMANCE MEASUREMENT

7

		£	£	£
Opening balance at 1.4.X7				6,800
Land			180,000	
Machine			20,000	
Labour			110,400	
Production overhead		39,500		
		18,650		
			58,150	
Materials		12,000		
		23,000		
			35,000	
Expenses			30,400	
				433,950
				440,750
Cash payments (from cash budget)				(430,000)
Closing balance at 31.3.X8				10,750

8   From cash budget £115,750 overdrawn

9   Retained profit b/f + profit for year = retained profit c/f

∴ £(55,250 + 88,470) = £143,720.

Exam focus point   You need to be able to transfer **accurate** information **quickly** when building up a master budget so make sure that you are happy with the techniques covered in this section.

Chapter Roundup

- A budget is a **quantified plan of action** for a forthcoming accounting period.

- The **budget manual** is a collection of instructions governing the responsibilities of persons and the procedures, forms and records relating to the preparation and use of budgetary data.

- The **budget committee** is the coordinating body in the preparation and administration of budgets.

- The **budget preparation process** is as follows.
  - Communicating details of the budget policy and budget guidelines.
  - Determining the factor that restricts output
  - Preparation of the sales budget
  - Initial preparation of budgets
  - Negotiation of budgets with superiors
  - Coordination and review of budgets
  - Final acceptance of the budgets
  - Budget review

- The **principal budget factor** should be identified at the beginning of the budgetary process, and the budget for this is prepared before all the other **functional budgets**.

- **Cash budgets** show the expected receipts and payments during a budget period and are a vital management control tool, especially during times of recession.

- The profit or loss made by an organisation during an accounting period does not reflect its cash flow position.

- When all the functional budgets have been prepared, they are summarised and consolidated into a **master budget** which consists of the budgeted profit and loss account, budgeted balance sheet and cash budget and which provides the overall picture of the planned performance for the budget period.

PART C BUDGETING AND PERFORMANCE MEASUREMENT

Quick Quiz

1. List six functions of the budget committee.

2. *Put the following steps involved in the preparation of a budget in the correct order.*

   - Negotiation of budgets with superiors
   - Determining the factor that restricts output
   - Final acceptance of the budget
   - Initial preparation of other budgets
   - Communicating details of budget policy and budget guidelines
   - Preparation of the budget for the principal budget factor
   - Coordination of budgets
   - Budget review

3. Which of the following could not be a principal budget factor?

(a)	Cash	(b)	Machine capacity
(c)	Sales demand	(d)	Selling price
(e)	Labour	(f)	Premises

4. *Fill in the blanks.*

   When preparing a production budget, the quantity to be produced is equal to sales .... opening stock .... closing stock.

5. A production process is set up to manufacture product X. 10% of total output is rejected because of quality problems. Sales demand is 17,500 units. How many units must be produced?

6. Which of the following should be included in a cash budget?

	Include	Do not include
Funds from the issue of share capital		
Revaluation of a fixed asset		
Receipts of dividends from outside the business		
Depreciation of production machinery		
Bad debts written off		
Repayment of a bank loan		

7. *Match the appropriate management action to the cash position shown by a cash budget.*

Position		Action	
(a)	Short-term surplus	1	Diversify
(b)	Short-term deficit	2	Issue share capital
(c)	Long-term surplus	3	Reduce debtors
(d)	Long-term deficit	4	Increase debtors
		5	Increase creditors
		6	Expand

8. Which budget provides the overall picture of the planning performance for the budget period?

Answers to Quick Quiz

1.
   - Co-ordination of budget preparation, including the issue of the budget manual
   - Issuing of timetables for the preparation of functional budgets
   - Allocation of responsibilities for the preparation of functional budgets
   - Provision of information to assist in the preparation of budgets
   - Communication of final budgets to the appropriate managers
   - Comparison of actual results with budget and the investigation of variances
   - Continuous assessment of the budgeting and planning process

2.
   - Communicating details of budget policy and budget guidelines
   - Determining the factor that restricts output
   - Preparation of the budget for the principal budget factor
   - Initial preparation of other budgets
   - Negotiation of budgets with superiors
   - Coordination of budgets
   - Final acceptance of the budget
   - Budget review

3. (d)

4. Quantity to be produced = sales – opening stock + closing stock

5. Good output = 90% of total production
   ∴ 17,500 = 0.9 × total production
   ∴ 17,500/0.9 = total production
   ∴ 19,445 units = total production

6.

	Include	Do not include
Funds from the issue of share capital	✓	
Revaluation of a fixed asset		✓
Receipts of dividends from outside the business	✓	
Depreciation of production machinery		✓
Bad debts written off		✓
Repayment of a bank loan	✓	

7. (a) 4
   (b) 3, 5
   (c) 1, 6
   (d) 2

8. The master budget.

Now try the questions below from the Exam Question Bank

Number	Level	Marks	Time
Q10	Examination	25	45 mins

Budgetary control and the behavioural implications of budgeting

Topic list	Syllabus reference
1 Fixed and flexible budgets	8(b)
2 Flexible budgets and budgetary control	8(b), 8(d)
3 Behavioural implications of budgeting	6(d), 8(f)
4 Participation and performance evaluation	6(d), 8(f)
5 The use of budgets as targets	6(d), 8(f)
6 The management accountant and motivation	6(d), 8(f)

Introduction

You should now be able to prepare functional budgets and a master budget and have a firm grasp of the budgeting process. This chapter continues the budgeting theme and looks at two particular issues.

Flexible budgets are vital in management planning and control and this chapter shows how they are constructed and their use in the overall budgetary control process.

The chapter then moves on to consider the **behavioural implications** of operating a budgetary control system. There has been a great deal of research into the behavioural implications of budgeting and, as in all studies of human behaviour, it is difficult to draw concrete conclusions. There is, however, one point which is agreed: budgeting is more than a mathematical technique.

While Chapter 11 details the **quantitative techniques** which the management accountant can use in the budgeting process, Chapter 10 examines alternative budgeting systems to the traditional one outlined in Chapter 8.

PART C BUDGETING AND PERFORMANCE MEASUREMENT

Study guide

Section 19 – Costing systems and techniques

- Different approaches to costing

Section 22 – Budget planning and control I

- Explain the process of participation in budget setting and how this can address motivational problems

Section 23 – Budget planning and control II

- Prepare and evaluate fixed and flexible budgets and evaluate the resulting variances
- Prepare flexed budgets when standard fixed overhead absorption is employed
- Assess the behavioural implications of budget control and performance evaluation, including participation in budget setting

Exam guide

Given that the behavioural implications of budgeting and budgetary control is a key area of the syllabus, a discursive Section B question could focus on the behavioural aspects of budgeting. A computational question could require you to produce a flexible budget.

1 Fixed and flexible budgets

FAST FORWARD

> **Fixed budgets** remain unchanged regardless of the level of activity; **flexible budgets** are designed to flex with the level of activity.

1.1 Fixed budgets

Key term

> A **fixed budget** is a budget which is designed to remain unchanged regardless of the volume of output or sales achieved.

The master budget prepared before the beginning of the budget period is known as the **fixed budget**. The term 'fixed' means the following.

(a) The budget is **prepared on the basis of an estimated volume of production** and an **estimated volume of sales**, but no plans are made for the event that actual volumes of production and sales may differ from budgeted volumes.

(b) When actual volumes of production and sales during a control period (month or four weeks or quarter) are achieved, a fixed budget is **not adjusted (in retrospect) to the new levels of activity.**

The major purpose of a fixed budget is at the planning stage, when it seeks to define the broad objectives of the organisation.

1.2 Flexible budgets

Key term

> A **flexible budget** is a budget which, by recognising different cost behaviour patterns, is designed to change as volumes of output change.

9: BUDGETARY CONTROL AND THE BEHAVIOURAL IMPLICATIONS OF BUDGETING

Flexible budgets may be used in one of two ways.

(a) **At the planning stage**. For example, suppose that a company expects to sell 10,000 units of output during the next year. A master budget (the fixed budget) would be prepared on the basis of these expected volumes. However, if the company thinks that output and sales might be as low as 8,000 units or as high as 12,000 units, it may prepare **contingency flexible budgets**, at volumes of, say 8,000, 9,000, 11,000 and 12,000 units and then assess the possible outcomes.

(b) **Retrospectively**. At the end of each month (control period) or year, the results that should have been achieved given the actual circumstances (the flexible budget) can be compared with the actual results. As we shall see, flexible budgets are an essential factor in **budgetary control**.

1.3 Example: Preparing a flexible budget

(a) Prepare a budget for 20X6 for the direct labour costs and overhead expenses of a production department at the activity levels of 80%, 90% and 100%, using the information listed below and ignoring inflation.

　(i)　The direct labour hourly rate is expected to be £3.75.

　(ii)　100% activity represents 60,000 direct labour hours.

　(iii)　
Variable indirect labour cost	£0.75 per direct labour hour
Variable consumable supplies cost	£0.375 per direct labour hour
Variable canteen cost	6% of direct and indirect labour costs

　(iv)　Semi-variable costs are expected to relate to the direct labour hours in the same manner as for the last five years. They consist of a fixed element of £8,000, and a variable element of 20p per hour.

　(v)　*Fixed costs*

	£
Depreciation	18,000
Maintenance	10,000
Insurance	4,000
Rates	15,000
Management salaries	25,000

(b) Calculate the **budget cost allowance (ie expected expenditure)** or **flexed budget** for 20X6 assuming that 57,000 direct labour hours are worked.

Solution

(a)

	80% level 48,000 hrs £'000	90% level 54,000 hrs £'000	100% level 60,000 hrs £'000
Direct labour	180.00	202.50	225.0
Other variable costs			
Indirect labour	36.00	40.50	45.0
Consumable supplies	18.00	20.25	22.5
Canteen etc	12.96	14.58	16.2
Total variable costs (£5.145 per hour)	246.96	277.83	308.7
Semi-variable costs (W)	17.60	18.80	20.0
Fixed costs			
Depreciation	18.00	18.00	18.0
Maintenance	10.00	10.00	10.0
Insurance	4.00	4.00	4.0
Rates	15.00	15.00	15.0
Management salaries	25.00	25.00	25.0
Budgeted costs	336.56	368.63	400.7

Working

Semi-variable costs are calculated as follows.

			£
60,000 hours	(60,000 × £0.20) + £8,000	=	20,000
54,000 hours	(54,000 × £0.20) + £8,000	=	18,800
48,000 hours	(48,000 × £0.20) + £8,000	=	17,600

(b) The **budget cost allowance** for 57,000 direct labour hours of work would be as follows.

		£
Variable costs	(57,000 × £5.145)	293,265
Semi-variable costs	(£8,000 + (57,000 × £0.20))	19,400
Fixed costs		72,000
		384,665

2 Flexible budgets and budgetary control

FAST FORWARD

Comparison of a fixed budget with the actual results for a different level of activity is of little use for control purposes. Flexible budgets should be used to show what cost and revenues should have been for the actual level of activity. The differences between the components of the fixed budget and the actual results are known as **budget variances**.

Key term

Budgetary control involves drawing up budgets for the areas of responsibility for individual managers (for example production managers, purchasing managers and so on) and of regularly comparing actual results against expected results. The differences between actual results and expected results are called **variances** and these are used to provide a guideline for control action by individual managers.

Note that individual managers are held responsible for investigating differences between budgeted and actual results, and are then expected to take corrective action or amend the plan in the light of actual events.

9: BUDGETARY CONTROL AND THE BEHAVIOURAL IMPLICATIONS OF BUDGETING

The wrong approach to budgetary control is to compare actual results against a fixed budget. Suppose that Windy Ltd manufactures a single product, the cloud. Budgeted results and actual results for June 20X2 are shown below.

	Budget	Actual results	Variance
Production and sales of the cloud (units)	2,000	3,000	
	£	£	£
Sales revenue (a)	20,000	30,000	10,000 (F)
Direct materials	6,000	8,500	2,500 (A)
Direct labour	4,000	4,500	500 (A)
Maintenance	1,000	1,400	400 (A)
Depreciation	2,000	2,200	200 (A)
Rent and rates	1,500	1,600	100 (A)
Other costs	3,600	5,000	1,400 (A)
Total costs (b)	18,100	23,200	5,100
Profit (a) – (b)	1,900	6,800	4,900 (F)

(a) Here the variances are meaningless for control purposes. Costs were higher than budget because the output volume was also higher; variable costs would be expected to increase above the costs budgeted in the fixed budget. There is no information to show whether control action is needed for any aspect of costs or revenue.

(b) For control purposes, it is necessary to know the following.

(i) Were actual costs higher than they should have been to produce and sell 3,000 clouds?

(ii) Was actual revenue satisfactory from the sale of 3,000 clouds?

The **correct approach to budgetary control** is as follows.

(a) **Identify fixed and variable costs**
(b) **Produce a flexible budget using marginal costing techniques**

Let's suppose that we have the following estimates of cost behaviour for Windy Ltd.

(a) Direct materials, direct labour and maintenance costs are variable.
(b) Rent and rates and depreciation are fixed costs.
(c) Other costs consist of fixed costs of £1,600 plus a variable cost of £1 per unit made and sold.

Now that the cost behaviour patterns are known, a **budget cost allowance** can be calculated for each item of expenditure. This allowance is shown in a flexible budget as the expected expenditure on each item for the relevant level of activity. The budget cost allowances are calculated as follows.

(a) Variable cost allowances = original budgets × (3,000 units/2,000 units)

eg material cost allowance = £6,000 × $^3/_2$ = £9,000

(b) Fixed cost allowances = as original budget

(c) Semi-fixed cost allowances = original budgeted fixed costs
+ (3,000 units × variable cost per unit)

eg other cost allowances = £1,600 + (3,000 × £1) = £4,600

The budgetary control analysis should be as follows.

PART C BUDGETING AND PERFORMANCE MEASUREMENT

	Fixed budget (a)	Flexible budget (b)	Actual results (c)	Budget variance (b) – (c)
Production and sales (units)	2,000	3,000	3,000	
	£	£	£	£
Sales revenue	20,000	30,000	30,000	0
Variable costs				
Direct materials	6,000	9,000	8,500	500 (F)
Direct labour	4,000	6,000	4,500	1,500 (F)
Maintenance	1,000	1,500	1,400	100 (F)
Semi-variable costs				
Other costs	3,600	4,600	5,000	400 (A)
Fixed costs				
Depreciation	2,000	2,000	2,200	200 (A)
Rent and rates	1,500	1,500	1,600	100 (A)
Total costs	18,100	24,600	23,200	1,400 (F)
Profit	1,900	5,400	6,800	1,400 (F)

Note. **(F)** denotes a favourable variance and **(A)** an adverse or unfavourable variance.

We can **analyse** the above as follows.

(a) In selling 3,000 units the expected profit should have been, not the fixed budget profit of £1,900, but the flexible budget profit of £5,400. Instead, actual profit was £6,800 ie £1,400 more than we should have expected. One of the reasons for the improvement is that, **given output and sales** of 3,000 units, **costs were lower than expected** (and sales revenue exactly as expected).

	£
Direct materials cost variance	500 (F)
Direct labour cost variance	1,500 (F)
Maintenance cost variance	100 (F)
Other costs variance	400 (A)
Fixed cost variances	
Depreciation	200 (A)
Rent and rates	100 (A)
	1,400 (F)

(b) Another reason for the improvement in profit above the fixed budget profit is the **sales volume**. Windy Ltd sold 3,000 clouds instead of 2,000 clouds.

	£	£
Sales revenue increased by		10,000
Variable costs increased by:		
direct materials	3,000	
direct labour	2,000	
Maintenance	500	
variable element of other costs	1,000	
Fixed costs are unchanged		6,500
Profit increased by		3,500

Profit was therefore increased by £3,500 because sales volumes increased.

(c) A full variance analysis statement would be as follows.

	£	£
Fixed budget profit		1,900
Variances		
Sales volume	3,500 (F)	
Direct materials cost	500 (F)	
Direct labour cost	1,500 (F)	
Maintenance cost	100 (F)	
Other costs	400 (A)	
Depreciation	200 (A)	
Rent and rates	100 (A)	
		4,900 (F)
Actual profit		6,800

If management believes that any of these variances are large enough to justify it, they will investigate the reasons for them to see whether any corrective action is necessary or whether the plan needs amending in the light of actual events.

Question — Budget preparation

The budgeted and actual results of Crunch Ltd for September were as follows. The company uses a marginal costing system. There were no opening or closing stocks.

	Fixed budget 1,000 units		Actual 700 units	
	£	£	£	£
Sales		20,000		14,200
Variable cost of sales				
Direct materials	8,000		5,200	
Direct labour	4,000		3,100	
Variable overhead	2,000		1,500	
		14,000		9,800
Contribution		6,000		4,400
Fixed costs		5,000		5,400
Profit/(loss)		1,000		(1,000)

Required

Prepare a budget that will be useful for management control purposes.

Answer

We need to prepare a **flexible budget for 700 units**.

	Budget 1,000 units	Per unit	Flexed budget 700 units	Actual 700 units	Variances
	£	£	£	£	£
Sales	20,000	(20)	14,000	14,200	200 (F)
Variable costs					
Direct material	8,000	(8)	5,600	5,200	400 (F)
Direct labour	4,000	(4)	2,800	3,100	300 (A)
Variable production overhead	2,000	(2)	1,400	1,500	100 (A)
	14,000	(14)	9,800	9,800	
Contribution	6,000		4,200	4,400	
Fixed costs	5,000	(N/A)	5,000	5,400	400 (A)
Profit/(loss)	1,000		(800)	(1,000)	200 (A)

By **flexing** the budget in the exercise above we **removed the effect on sales revenue of the difference between budgeted sales volume and actual sales volume.** But there is still a variance of £200 (F). This means that the actual *selling price* must have been different to the budgeted selling price, resulting in a £200 (F) **selling price variance**.

2.1 Preparing a flexible budget – absorption costing

Flexible budgeting allows you to see what total costs should be at differing levels of output. Since fixed costs are the same at all levels of output (within a normal or relevant range of activity), only variable costs vary with increases or decreases in the level of activity.

Although **fixed costs *incurred* do not change as the level of activity increases or decreases**, if an organisation uses absorption costing the **amount of fixed costs absorbed will vary**. This is because the fixed overhead **absorption rate** is predetermined at the start of the budget period, and is **based on the expected level of activity in the *fixed* budget**.

Suppose that a company which has an absorption costing system budgets for fixed production overhead of £4,000 and output of 1,000 units. The overhead absorption rate will therefore be £4 per unit. If the company decides to prepare a fixed master budget and also flexible budgets at output levels of 900 units and 1,100 units, the overhead costs in the budget would be as follows.

	Flexible budget 900 units £	Fixed budget 1,000 units £	Flexible budget 1,100 units £
Overhead cost of production (× £4 per unit) – absorbed	3,600	4,000	4,400
(Under-)/over-absorbed overhead	(400)	–	400
Overhead incurred	4,000	4,000	4,000

2.2 Example: Flexible budgets and absorption costing

An organisation's management requires a flexible overhead budget for levels of output of 20,000, 24,000 and 32,000 units respectively. The standard of activity has been set at 28,000 units. Total overhead incurred at this level would be £42,000 of which variable overhead would be £1.20 per unit.

Task

Calculate the under-/over-absorbed fixed overheads at each level of activity.

Solution

If the total overheads incurred at 28,000 units of output are £42,000, and variable overhead incurred is £1.20 per unit, fixed overheads must be £42,000 minus £(28,000 × 1.20) = £8,400.

The overhead absorption rate (OAR) is based on the standard level of activity, 28,000 units.

OAR = budgeted fixed overheads ÷ budget output = £8,400 ÷ 28,000 units = £0.30 per unit

	Level of output and sales			
	20,000 units £	24,000 units £	28,000 units £	32,000 units £
Overheads absorbed (at £0.30 per unit)	6,000	7,200	8,400	9,600
Overheads incurred	8,400	8,400	8,400	8,400
(Under-)/over-absorbed overheads	(2,400)	(1,200)	0	1,200

2.3 Factors to consider when preparing flexible budgets

The mechanics of flexible budgeting are, in theory, fairly straightforward but in practice there are a number of points to consider before figures are simply flexed.

(a) Splitting mixed costs is not always straightforward.

(b) Fixed costs may behave in a step-line fashion as activity levels increase/decrease.

(c) Account must be taken of the assumptions upon which the original fixed budget was based. Such assumptions might include the constraint posed by limiting factors, the rate of inflation, judgements about future uncertainty, the demand for the organisation's products and so on.

(d) 'Flexing ... can incorporate changes for any factor which differs from what applied when the budget was prepared, for example different states of the economy. In this way, flexing is saying "If I knew then what I know now what budget would I set?" It is a useful concept but can lead to some concern, if taken to extremes, because managers can be confused and frustrated if faced throughout the year with a possibly moving target.'

(Mike Tayles, *ACCA Students Newsletter*, December 1998)

3 Behavioural implications of budgeting

FAST FORWARD

Used correctly, a budgetary control system can **motivate** but it can also produce undesirable **negative reactions**.

The purpose of a budgetary control system is to assist management in planning and controlling the resources of their organisation by providing appropriate control information. The information will only be valuable, however, if it is interpreted correctly and used purposefully by managers *and* employees.

The correct use of control information therefore depends not only on the content of the information itself, but also on the behaviour of its recipients. This is because control in business is exercised by people. Their attitude to control information will colour their views on what they should do with it and a number of behavioural problems can arise.

(a) The **managers who set the budget** or standards are **often not the managers** who are then made **responsible for achieving budget targets.**

(b) The **goals of the organisation as a whole**, as expressed in a budget, **may not coincide with the personal aspirations of individual managers.**

(c) **Control is applied at different stages by different people.** A supervisor might get weekly control reports, and act on them; his superior might get monthly control reports, and decide to take different control action. Different managers can get in each others' way, and resent the interference from others.

3.1 Motivation

Motivation is what makes people behave in the way that they do. It comes from individual attitudes, or group attitudes. Individuals will be motivated by personal desires and interests. These may be in line with the objectives of the organisation, and some people 'live for their jobs'. Other individuals see their job as a chore, and their motivations will be unrelated to the objectives of the organisation they work for.

It is therefore vital that the goals of management and the employees harmonise with the goals of the organisation as a whole. This is known as goal congruence. Although obtaining goal congruence is essentially a behavioural problem, **it is possible to design and run a budgetary control system which will** go some way towards ensuring that goal congruence is achieved. Managers and employees must therefore be favourably disposed towards the budgetary control system so that it can operate efficiently.

The management accountant should therefore try to ensure that employees have positive attitudes towards **setting budgets, implementing budgets** (that is, putting the organisation's plans into practice) and feedback of results (**control information**).

3.2 Poor attitudes when setting budgets

But poor attitudes or hostile behaviour towards the budgetary control system can begin at the **planning stage. If managers are involved in preparing a budget** the following may happen.

(a) Managers may **complain that they are too busy** to spend much time on budgeting.

(b) They may **build 'slack' into their expenditure estimates**.

(c) They may argue that **formalising a budget plan on paper is too restricting** and that managers should be allowed flexibility in the decisions they take.

(d) They may set budgets for their budget centre and **not coordinate** their own plans with those of other budget centres.

(e) They may **base future plans on past results**, instead of using the opportunity for formalised planning to look at alternative options and new ideas.

On the other hand, **managers may not be involved in the budgeting process**. Organisational goals may not be communicated to them and they might have their budget decided for them by senior management or administrative decision. It is **hard for people to be motivated to achieve targets set by someone else.**

3.2.1 Poor attitudes when putting plans into action

Poor attitudes also arise **when a budget is implemented**.

(a) Managers might **put in only just enough effort** to achieve budget targets, without trying to beat targets.

(b) A formal budget might **encourage rigidity and discourage flexibility**.

(c) **Short-term planning** in a budget **can draw attention away from the longer-term consequences** of decisions.

(d) There might be **minimal cooperation and communication** between managers.

(e) Managers will often try to make sure that they **spend up to their full budget allowance, and do not overspend**, so that they will not be accused of having asked for too much spending allowance in the first place.

3.2.2 Poor attitudes and the use of control information

The **attitude of managers towards the accounting control information** they receive **might reduce the information's effectiveness**.

(a) Management accounting control reports could well be seen as having a relatively **low priority** in the list of management tasks. Managers might take the view that they have more pressing jobs on hand than looking at routine control reports.

(b) Managers might **resent control information**; they may see it as **part of a system of trying to find fault with their work**. This resentment is likely to be particularly strong when budgets or standards are imposed on managers without allowing them to participate in the budget-setting process.

(c) If budgets are seen as **pressure devices** to push managers into doing better, control reports will be resented.

(d) Managers **may not understand the information** in the control reports, because they are unfamiliar with accounting terminology or principles.

(e) Managers might have a **false sense of what their objectives should be**. A production manager might consider it more important to maintain quality standards regardless of cost. He would then dismiss adverse expenditure variances as inevitable and unavoidable.

(f) **If there are flaws in the system of recording actual costs**, managers will dismiss control information as unreliable.

(g) **Control information** might be **received weeks after the end of the** period to which it relates, in which case managers might regard it as out-of-date and no longer useful.

(h) Managers might be **held responsible for variances outside their control**.

It is therefore obvious that accountants and senior management should try to implement systems that are acceptable to budget holders and which produce positive effects.

3.2.3 Pay as a motivator

Many researchers agree that **pay can be an important motivator**, when there is a formal link between higher pay (or other rewards, such as promotion) and achieving budget targets. Individuals are likely to work harder to achieve budget if they know that they will be rewarded for their successful efforts. There are, however, problems with using pay as an incentive.

(a) A serious problem that can arise is that **formal reward and performance evaluation systems can encourage dysfunctional behaviour**. Many investigations have noted the tendency of managers to pad their budgets either in anticipation of cuts by superiors or to make the subsequent variances more favourable. And there are numerous examples of managers making decisions in response to performance indices, even though the decisions are contrary to the wider purposes of the organisation.

(b) The targets must be challenging but fair, otherwise individuals will become dissatisfied. **Pay can be a demotivator as well as a motivator**!

4 Participation and performance evaluation 6/03

4.1 Participation

FAST FORWARD

A budget can be set from the **top down (imposed** budget) or from the **bottom up (participatory** budget). Many writers refer to a third style, the negotiated budget.

It has been argued that **participation** in the budgeting process **will improve motivation** and so will improve the quality of budget decisions and the efforts of individuals to achieve their budget targets (although obviously this will depend on the personality of the individual, the nature of the task (narrowly defined or flexible) and the organisational culture).

There are basically two ways in which a budget can be set: from the **top down** (imposed budget) or from the **bottom up** (participatory budget).

4.2 Imposed style of budgeting (top-down budgeting)

In this approach to budgeting, **top management prepare a budget with little or no input from operating personnel** which is then imposed upon the employees who have to work to the budgeted figures.

The times when imposed budgets are effective are as follows.

- In newly-formed organisations
- In very small businesses
- During periods of economic hardship
- When operational managers lack budgeting skills
- When the organisation's different units require precise coordination

They are, of course, advantages and disadvantages to this style of setting budgets.

Advantages

- **Strategic plans** are likely to be incorporated into planned activities.
- They **enhance** the **coordination** between the plans and objectives of divisions.
- They use **senior management's awareness** of total resource availability.
- They **decrease the input from inexperienced or uninformed lower-level employees**.
- They **decrease the period of time taken** to draw up the budgets.

Disadvantages

- **Dissatisfaction**, **defensiveness** and **low morale** amongst employees.
- The **feeling of team spirit** may disappear.
- The **acceptance of organisational goals** and **objectives** could be limited
- The feeling of the budget as a **punitive device** could arise.
- **Unachievable budgets** for overseas divisions could result if consideration is not given to local operating and political environments.
- **Lower-level management initiative** may be **stifled**.
- Participative style of budgeting (bottom-up budgeting)

In this approach to budgeting, **budgets are developed by lower-level managers who then submit the budgets to their superiors**. The budgets are based on the lower-level managers' perceptions of what is achievable and the associated necessary resources.

Participative budgets are effective in the following circumstances.

- In **well-established organisations**
- In **very large businesses**
- During periods of **economic affluence**
- When operational managers have **strong budgeting skills**
- When the organisation's different units act **autonomously**

The **advantages** of participative budgets are as follows.

- They are based on **information from employees** most familiar with the department.
- **Knowledge spread** among several levels of management is pulled **together**.
- **Morale** and **motivation** is improved.
- They **increase operational managers' commitment** to organisational objectives.
- In general they are **more realistic**.
- **Co-ordination** between units is **improved**.
- **Specific resource requirements** are **included**.
- **Senior managers' overview** is mixed with operational level details.

There are, on the other hand, a number of **disadvantages** of participative budgets.

- They **consume more time**.
- **Changes implemented** by senior management may **cause dissatisfaction**.
- Budgets may be **unachievable** if managers' are not qualified to participate.
- They may cause managers to introduce **budgetary slack**.
- They can support **'empire building'** by subordinates.
- An **earlier start** to the budgeting process could be required.

4.2.1 Negotiated style of budgeting

At the two extremes, budgets can be dictated from above or simply emerge from below but, in practice, different levels of management often agree budgets by a process of negotiation. In the imposed budget approach, operational managers will try to negotiate with senior managers the budget targets which they consider to be unreasonable or unrealistic. Likewise senior management usually review and revise budgets presented to them under a participative approach through a process of negotiation with lower level managers. **Final budgets are therefore most likely to lie between what top management would really like and what junior managers believe is feasible.** The budgeting process is hence a **bargaining process** and it is this bargaining which is of vital importance, **determining whether the budget is an effective management tool or simply a clerical device**.

4.3 Performance evaluation

FAST FORWARD

There are three ways of using budgetary information to evaluate managerial performance (**budget constrained style, profit conscious style, non-accounting style**).

A very important **source of motivation to perform well** (to achieve budget targets, perhaps, or to eliminate variances) is, not surprisingly, being **kept informed about how actual results are progressing, and how actual results compare with target**. Individuals should not be kept in the dark about their performance.

The information fed back about actual results should have the qualities of good information.

- (a) Reports should be **clear** and **comprehensive**.
- (b) **Significant variances** should be **highlighted** for investigation.
- (c) Reports should be **timely**, which means they must be produced in good time to allow the individual to take control action before any adverse results get much worse.

Surprisingly research evidence suggests that **all too often accounting performance measures lead to a lack of goal congruence**. Managers seek to improve their performance on the basis of the indicator used, even if this is not in the best interests of the organisation as a whole. For example, a production manager may be encouraged to achieve and maintain high production levels and to reduce costs, particularly if his or her bonus is linked to these factors. Such a manager is likely to be highly motivated. But the need to maintain high production levels could lead to high levels of slow-moving stock, resulting in an adverse effect on the company's cash flow.

The **impact of an accounting system on managerial performance** depends ultimately on how the information is used. Research by Hopwood has shown that there are three distinct ways of using budgetary information to evaluate managerial performance.

- (a) **A budget constrained style of evaluation**

    'The **manager's performance** is primarily evaluated upon the basis of his **ability to meet the budget** continually on a short-term basis. This criterion of performance is stressed at the expense of other valued and important criteria and the manager will receive unfavourable feedback from his superior if, for instance, his actual costs exceed the budgeted costs, regardless of other considerations.'

(b) **A profit conscious style of evaluation**

'The manager's performance is evaluated on the basis of his ability to **increase the general effectiveness** of his unit's operations in relation to the long-term purposes of the organisation. For instance, at the cost centre level one important aspect of this ability concerns the **attention** which he devotes to reducing long-run costs. For this purpose, however, the budgetary information has to be used with great care in a rather flexible manner.'

(c) **A non-accounting style of evaluation**

'The **budgetary information** plays a relatively **unimportant part** in the superior's evaluation of the manager's performance.'

A summary of the effects of the three styles of evaluation is as follows.

	Style of evaluation		
	Budget constrained	Profit conscious	Non-accounting
Involvement with costs	HIGH	HIGH	LOW
Job-related tension	HIGH	MEDIUM	MEDIUM
Manipulation of the accounting reports	EXTENSIVE	LITTLE	LITTLE
Relations with the supervisor	POOR	GOOD	GOOD
Relations with colleagues	POOR	GOOD	GOOD

Research has shown no clear preference for one style over another.

4.4 Budgetary slack   12/03

Budgetary slack is the difference between the minimum necessary costs and the costs built into the budget or actually incurred.

In the process of preparing budgets, managers might **deliberately overestimate costs and underestimate sales**, so that they will not be blamed in the future for overspending and poor results.

In controlling actual operations, managers must then **ensure that their spending rises to meet their budget**, otherwise they will be 'blamed' for careless budgeting.

A typical situation is for a manager to **waste money** on **non-essential expenses** so that he uses all his budget allowances. The reason behind his action is the fear that unless the allowance is fully spent it will be **reduced in future periods** thus making his job more difficult as the future reduced budgets will not be so easy to attain. Because inefficiency and slack are allowed for in budgets, achieving a budget target means only that costs have remained within the accepted levels of inefficient spending.

Conversely, it has been noted that, after a run of mediocre results, some managers **deliberately overstate revenues** and **understate cost estimates**, no doubt feeling the need to make an immediate favourable impact by promising better performance in the future. They may merely delay problems, however, as the managers may well be censured when they fail to hit these optimistic targets.

5 The use of budgets as targets

In certain situations it is useful to prepare an **expectations budget** and an **aspirations budget**.

Once decided budgets become targets. As targets, they can motivate managers to achieve a high level of performance. But **how difficult should targets be**? And how might people react to targets of differing degrees of difficulty in achievement?

(a) There is likely to be a **demotivating** effect where an **ideal standard** of performance is set, because adverse efficiency variances will always be reported.

(b) A **low standard of efficiency** is also **demotivating**, because there is no sense of achievement in attaining the required standards.

(c) A **budgeted level of attainment** could be 'normal': that is, the **same as the level that has been achieved in the past**. Arguably, this level will be **too low**. It might **encourage budgetary slack**.

It has been argued that **each individual has a personal 'aspiration level'**. This is a level of performance in a task with which the individual is familiar, which the individual undertakes for himself to reach. This aspiration level might be quite challenging and if individuals in a work group all have similar aspiration levels it should be possible to incorporate these levels within the official operating standards.

Some care should be taken, however, in applying this.

(a) If a manager's **tendency to achieve success is stronger than the tendency to avoid failure**, budgets with **targets of intermediate levels of difficulty** are the most **motivating**, and stimulate a manager to better performance levels. Budgets which are either too easy to achieve or too difficult are de-motivating, and managers given such targets achieve relatively low levels of performance.

(b) A manager's **tendency to avoid failure might be stronger than the tendency to achieve success**. (This is likely in an organisation in which the budget is used as a pressure device on subordinates by senior managers). Managers might then be discouraged from trying to achieve budgets of intermediate difficulty and tend to avoid taking on such tasks, resulting in poor levels of performance, worse than if budget targets were either easy or very difficult to achieve.

It has therefore been suggested that in a situation where budget targets of an intermediate difficulty *are* motivating, such targets ought to be set if the purpose of budgets is to motivate; however, although budgets which are set for **motivational purposes** need to be stated in terms of **aspirations rather than expectations**, budgets for planning and decision purposes need to be stated in terms of the best available estimate of expected actual performance. The **solution** might therefore be to have **two budgets**.

(a) A **budget for planning and decision making** based on reasonable expectations.

(b) A second **budget for motivational purposes**, with **more difficult targets of performance** (that is, targets of an intermediate level of difficulty).

These two budgets might be called an **'expectations budget'** and an **'aspirations budget'** respectively.

6 The management accountant and motivation

FAST FORWARD

Management and the management accountant require strategies and methods for dealing with the **tensions** and **conflict** resulting from the **conflicting purposes** of budget.

As we have seen, budgets serve many purposes, but in some instances their purposes can conflict and have an effect on management behaviour. Management and the management accountant therefore require strategies and methods for dealing with the resulting tensions and conflict. For example, should targets be adjusted for uncontrollable and unforeseeable environmental influence? But what is then the effect on motivation if employees view performance standards as changeable?

Can performance measures and the related budgetary control system ever motivate managers towards achieving the organisation's goals?

(a) Accounting measures of performance **can't provide a comprehensive assessment** of what a person has achieved for the organisation.

(b) It is usually **impossible to segregate controllable and uncontrollable components of performance**. This can lead to unfairness in evaluating performance.

(c) Accounting **reports tend to concentrate on short-term achievements**, to the exclusion of the long-term effects.

(d) Many accounting **reports try to serve several different purposes**, and in trying to satisfy several needs actually satisfy none properly.

The management accountant does not have the authority to do much on his or her own to improve hostile or apathetic attitudes to control information. There has to be support, either from senior management or from cost and profit centre managers. However, the management accountant can do quite a lot to improve and then maintain the standard of a budgetary control reporting system.

(a) **Senior management can offer support** by doing the following.

- Making sure that a **system of responsibility accounting is adopted**.
- Allowing **managers to have a say in formulating their budgets**.
- Offering **incentives** to managers who meet budget targets.
- **Not regarding budgetary control information as a way of apportioning blame**.

(b) **Cost centre/profit centre managers should accept their responsibilities**. In-house training courses could be held to encourage a collective, cooperative and positive attitude amongst managers.

(c) The **management accountant should improve** (or maintain) the **quality of the budgetary control system** by doing the following.

(i) **Developing a working relationship with operational managers**, going out to meet them and discussing the control reports.

(ii) **Explaining the meaning of budgets and control reports**.

(iii) **Keeping accounting jargon in these reports to a minimum.**

(iv) Making **reports clear and to the point**, for example using the principle of reporting by exception.

(v) Providing control information with a **minimum of delay.**

(vi) **Making control information as useful as possible**, by distinguishing between directly attributable costs over which a manager should have influence and apportioned or fixed costs which are unavoidable or uncontrollable.

(vii) Trying to make sure that **actual costs are recorded accurately**.

(viii) Trying to ensure that **budgets are up-to-date**, either by having a system of rolling budgets, or else by updating budgets or standards as necessary, and ensuring that standards are 'fair' so that control information is realistic.

9: BUDGETARY CONTROL AND THE BEHAVIOURAL IMPLICATIONS OF BUDGETING

Exam focus point

There are no ideal solutions to the conflicts caused by the operation of a budgetary control system. Management and the management accountant have to develop their own ways of dealing with them, taking into account their organisation, their business and the personalities involved. You should think about how the budgetary control system operates in your organisation and the conflicts, if there are any, caused by it. How are the conflicts dealt with? Real life examples can be usefully incorporated into solutions in the exam.

Question — Behavioural aspects of participation

Discuss the behavioural aspects of participation in the budgeting process and any difficulties you might envisage.

Answer

The level of participation in the budgeting process can vary from zero participation to a process of group decision making. There are a number of behavioural aspects of participation to consider.

(a) **Communication**. Managers cannot be expected to achieve targets if they do not know what those targets are. Communication of targets is made easier if managers have participated in the budgetary process from the beginning.

(b) **Motivation**. Managers are likely to be better motivated to achieve a budget if they have been involved in compiling it, rather than having a dictatorial budget imposed on them.

(c) **Realistic targets**. A target must be achievable and accepted as realistic if it is to be a motivating factor. A manager who has been involved in setting targets is more likely to accept them as realistic. In addition, managers who are close to the operation of their departments may be more aware of the costs and potential savings in running it.

(d) **Goal congruence**. One of the best ways of achieving goal congruence is to involve managers in the preparation of their own budgets, so that their personal goals can be taken into account in setting targets.

Although participative budgeting has many advantages, difficulties might also arise.

(a) **Pseudo-participation**. Participation may not be genuine, but merely a pretence at involving managers in the preparation of their budgets. Managers may feel that their contribution is being ignored, or that the participation consists of merely obtaining their agreement to a budget which has already been decided. If this is the case then managers are likely to be more demotivated than if there is no participation at all.

(b) **Coordination**. If participative budgeting is well managed it can improve the coordination of the preparation of the various budgets. There is, however, a danger that too many managers will become involved so that communication becomes difficult and the process become complex.

(c) **Training**. Some managers may not possess the necessary skill to make an effective contribution to the preparation of their budgets. Additional training may be necessary, with the consequent investment of money and time. It may also be necessary to train managers to understand the purposes and advantages of participation.

(d) **Slack**. If budgets are used in a punitive fashion for control purposes then managers will be tempted to build in extra expenditure to provide a 'cushion' against overspending. It is easier for them to build in slack in a participative system.

PART C BUDGETING AND PERFORMANCE MEASUREMENT

Chapter Roundup

- **Fixed budgets** remain unchanged regardless of the level of activity; **flexible budgets** are designed to flex with the level of activity.

- Comparison of a fixed budget with the actual results for a different level of activity is of little use for control purposes. Flexible budgets should be used to show what cost and revenues should have been for the actual level of activity. The differences between the components of the fixed budget and the actual results are known as **budget variances**.

- Used correctly a budgetary control system can **motivate** but it can also produce undesirable **negative reactions**.

- A budget can be set from the **top down** (**imposed** budget) or from the **bottom up** (**participatory** budget). Many writers refer to a third style (negotiated).

- There are three ways of using budgetary information to evaluate managerial performance (**budget constrained style**, **profit conscious style**, **non-accounting style**).

- **Budgetary slack** is the difference between the minimum necessary costs and the costs built into the budget or actually incurred.

- In certain situations it is useful to prepare an **expectations budget** and an **aspirations budget**.

- Management and the management accountant require strategies and methods for dealing with the **tensions** and **conflict** resulting from the **conflicting purposes** of budget.

Quick Quiz

1 *Fill in the gaps.*

   A flexible budget is a budget which, by recognising ...., is designed to .... as the level of activity changes.

2 An extract of the costs incurred at two different activity levels is shown. Classify the costs according to their behaviour patterns and show the budget cost allowance for an activity of 1,500 units.

	1,000 units £	2,000 units £	Type of cost	Budget cost allowance for 1,500 units £
Fuel	3,000	6,000	....	....
Photocopying	9,500	11,000	....	....
Heating	2,400	2,400	....	....
Direct wages	6,000	8,000	....	....

3 *Choose the appropriate words from those highlighted.*

   A fixed budget is based on output of 500 units.

   - A flexible budget for 550 units is produced. This will show overheads as being **under/over** absorbed.

   - A flexible budget is also produced for 450 units. This will show overheads as being **under/over** absorbed.

4   Match the descriptions to the budgeting style.

    Description

    (a)   Budget allowances are set without the involvement of the budget holder

    (b)   All budget holders are involved in setting their own budgets

    (c)   Budget allowances are set on the basis of discussions between budget holders and those to whom they report

    Budgeting style

    Negotiated budgeting
    Participative budgeting
    Imposed budgeting

5   Budgetary slack is necessary to ensure that managers are able to meet their targets.

    ☐ True

    ☐ False

6   Fill in the gaps.

    An expectations budget would be most useful for the purposes of ...., whereas an aspirations budget is more appropriate for ....

7   Which of the following actions could be used by a management accountant to improve/maintain the quality of the budgetary control system?

    (a)   Ensure that relationships are not built up with operational managers.

    (b)   Ensure that control reports use the appropriate technical vocabulary understood by accounting personnel only.

    (c)   Do not provide control information too soon after a period end as operational managers need time to reflect on events before being inundated with volumes of control information.

    (d)   Do not distinguish between controllable and uncontrollable costs as this will give operational managers the opportunity to abdicate responsibility for everything.

    (e)   Do not change the budget once it has been set at the beginning of the year.

8   A system where managers aim to improve their performance judged by the performance indicators used, even if what they do is not in the best interests of the organisation, lacks ....

PART C BUDGETING AND PERFORMANCE MEASUREMENT

Answers to Quick Quiz

1. cost behaviour patterns
   flex or change

2. Variable £4,500
   Semi-variable £10,250
   Fixed £2,400
   Semi-variable £7,000

3. The budget for 550 units will show over absorption, the other under absorption.

4. (a) Imposed budgeting
   (b) Participative budgeting
   (c) Negotiated budgeting

5. False. Budgets should be reviewed to ensure that operational managers have not included slack.

6. (a) planning and decision making based on reasonable expectations
   (b) improving motivation by setting targets of an intermediate level of difficulty

7. None of the suggestions should be used.

   (a) A working relationship with operational managers should be developed.
   (b) Accounting jargon in reports should be kept to a minimum so that they are easily understood.
   (c) Control information should be provided with a minimum of delay. Beware of information overload.
   (d) Managers should only be responsible for costs over which they have control.
   (e) Budgets should be kept as up to date as possible.

8. Goal congruence.

Now try the questions below from the Exam Question Bank

Number	Level	Marks	Time
Q11	Examination	25	45 mins
Q12	Examination	25	45 mins

Alternative budget systems

Topic list	Syllabus reference
1 Incremental budgeting and zero based budgeting	8(b)
2 The main features of zero based budgeting systems	8(b)
3 Using zero based budgeting	8(b)
4 Continuous budgets	8(b)
5 Activity based budgeting	8(b)
6 The future of budgeting	8(b)

Introduction

So far in this text we have concentrated on budgeting systems based on standard costing. We have also hinted at the traditional approach of **incremental budgeting** which bases next year's budget on this year's, with increases for inflation and changes in activity levels. However, this may not always be appropriate for certain organisations or for certain types of cost and revenue. **Zero based budgeting** and **continuous budgets** are alternative budget systems which can be applied in certain circumstances and situations. **Activity based budgets** may use bases other than volume of output for flexing budgets. This chapter looks in detail at these systems.

In the next chapter we will look at quantitative aids to budgeting, in other words, different ways of forecasting future figures for use in budgets.

PART C   BUDGETING AND PERFORMANCE MEASUREMENT

Study guide

Section 24 – Budget planning and control III

- Describe and evaluate the main features of zero based budgeting systems
- Describe the areas/organisations in which zero based budgeting may be applied
- Describe and evaluate incremental budgeting and discuss the differences with zero based budgeting
- Describe and evaluate periodic and continuous budgeting systems

Exam guide

The topics covered in this chapter are likely to be examined in conjunction with other topics in both Section A and Section B.

1 Incremental budgeting and zero based budgeting

FAST FORWARD

> The traditional approach to budgeting, known as **incremental budgeting**, bases the budget on the current year's results plus an extra amount for estimated growth or inflation next year. It encourages slack and wasteful spending to creep into budgets.

Key term

> **Incremental budgeting** is the traditional approach to budgeting and involves basing next year's budget on the current year's results plus an extra amount for estimated growth or inflation next year.

Incremental budgeting is so called because it is concerned mainly with the increments in costs and revenues which will occur in the coming period.

Incremental budgeting is a reasonable procedure if current operations are as effective, efficient and economical as they can be. It is also appropriate for budgeting for costs such as staff salaries, which may be estimated on the basis of current salaries plus an increment for inflation and are hence administratively fairly easy to prepare.

In general, however, it is an **inefficient form of budgeting** as it **encourages slack** and **wasteful spending** to creep into budgets. Past inefficiencies are perpetuated because cost levels are rarely subjected to close scrutiny.

To ensure that inefficiencies are not concealed, however, alternative approaches to budgeting have been developed. One such approach is **zero based budgeting (ZBB)**.

Question — Incremental budgeting

Can incremental budgeting be used to budget for rent? What about for advertising expenditure?

Answer

Incremental budgeting is appropriate for budgeting for rent, which may be estimated on the basis of current rent plus an increment for the annual rent increase. Advertising expenditure, on the other hand, is not so easily quantifiable and is more discretionary in nature. Using incremental budgeting for advertising expenditure could allow slack and wasteful spending to creep into the budget.

10: ALTERNATIVE BUDGET SYSTEMS

2 The main features of zero based budgeting systems
6/02, 6/05

2.1 The principles of zero based budgeting (ZBB)

FAST FORWARD

The principle behind **zero based budgeting (ZBB)** is that the budget for each cost centre should be made from 'scratch' or zero. Every item of expenditure must be justified in its entirety in order to be included in the next year's budget.

ZBB rejects the assumption inherent in incremental budgeting that this year's activities will continue at the same level or volume next year, and that next year's budget can be based on this year's costs plus an extra amount, perhaps for expansion and inflation.

Key term

Zero based budgeting involves preparing a budget for each cost centre from a zero base. Every item of expenditure has then to be justified in its entirety in order to be included in the next year's budget.

In reality, however, managers do not have to budget from zero, but can **start from their current level of expenditure and work downwards**, asking what would happen if any particular aspect of current expenditure and current operations were removed from the budget. In this way, every aspect of the budget is examined in terms of its cost and the benefits it provides and the selection of better alternatives is encouraged.

2.2 Implementing zero based budgeting

FAST FORWARD

There is a three-step approach to ZBB.

- Define decision units
- Evaluate and rank packages
- Allocate resources

The implementation of ZBB involves a number of steps but of greater importance is the **development of a questioning attitude** by all those involved in the budgetary process. Existing practices and expenditures must be challenged and searching questions asked.

- Does the activity need to be carried out?
- What would be the consequences if the activity was not carried out?
- Is the current level of provision current?
- Are there alternative ways of providing the function?
- How much should the activity cost?
- Is the expenditure worth the benefits achieved?

The basic approach of ZBB has three steps.

Step 1 **Define decision packages**, comprehensive **descriptions of specific organisational activities which management can use to evaluate the activities and rank them in order of priority against other activities.** There are two types.

    (a) **Mutually exclusive packages** contain **alternative methods of getting the same job done**. The best option among the packages must be selected by comparing costs and benefits and the other packages are then discarded.

    (b) **Incremental packages divide one aspect of an activity into different levels of effort.** The 'base' package will describe the minimum amount of work that must be done to carry out the activity and the other packages describe what additional work could be done, at what cost and for what benefits.

Suppose that a cost centre manager is preparing a budget for maintenance costs. He might first consider two mutually exclusive packages.

- Package A might be to keep a maintenance team of two men per shift for two shifts each day at a cost of £60,000 per annum
- Package B might be to obtain a maintenance service from an outside contractor at a cost of £50,000

A cost-benefit analysis will be conducted because the quicker repairs obtainable from an in-house maintenance service might justify its extra cost. If we now suppose that package A is preferred, the budget analysis must be completed by describing the incremental variations in this chosen alternative.

(a) The 'base' package would describe the minimum requirement for the maintenance work. This might be to pay for one man per shift for two shifts each day at a cost of £30,000.

(b) Incremental package 1 might be to pay for two men on the early shift and one man on the late shift, at a cost of £45,000. The extra cost of £15,000 would need to be justified, for example by savings in lost production time, or by more efficient machinery.

(c) Incremental package 2 might be the original preference, for two men on each shift at a cost of £60,000. The cost-benefit analysis would compare its advantages if any, over incremental package 1; and so on.

Step 2 **Evaluate and rank each activity (decision package)** on the basis of its benefit to the organisation. This can be a lengthy process. Minimum work requirements (those that are essential to get a job done) will be given high priority and so too will work which meets legal obligations. In the accounting department these would be minimum requirements to operate the payroll, purchase ledger and sales ledger systems, and to maintain and publish a set of accounts.

Step 3 **Allocate resources** in the budget according to the funds available and the evaluation and ranking of the competing packages.

Question — Base and incremental packages

What might the base and incremental packages for a personnel department cover?

Answer

The base package might cover the recruitment and dismissal of staff. Incremental packages might cover training, pension administration, trade union liaison, staff welfare and so on.

2.3 The advantages and limitations of implementing ZBB

The **advantages** of zero based budgeting are as follows.

- It is possible to identify and **remove inefficient or obsolete operations.**
- It forces employees to **avoid wasteful expenditure**.
- It can **increase motivation**.

- It **responds to changes** in the business environment.
- **ZBB documentation provides** an in-depth **appraisal of an organisation's operations.**
- It **challenges the status quo**.
- In summary, ZBB should result in a **more efficient allocation of resources**.

The major **disadvantage** of zero based budgeting is the **volume of extra paperwork** created. The assumptions about costs and benefits in each package must be continually updated and new packages developed as soon as new activities emerge. The following problems might also occur.

(a) **Short-term benefits** might be **emphasised** to the detriment of long-term benefits.

(b) It might give the impression **that all decisions have to be made in the budget**. Management must be able to meet unforeseen opportunities and threats at all times, however, and must not feel restricted from carrying out new ideas simply because they were not approved by a decision package, cost benefit analysis and the ranking process.

(c) It may **call for management skills** both in constructing decision packages and in the ranking process **which the organisation does not possess**. Managers may have to be trained in ZBB techniques.

(d) The organisation's **information systems may not be capable of providing suitable information**.

(e) **The ranking process can be difficult**. Managers face three common problems.

   (i) A large number of packages may have to be ranked.

   (ii) It can be difficult to rank packages which appear to be equally vital, for legal or operational reasons.

   (iii) It is difficult to rank activities which have qualitative rather than quantitative benefits – such as spending on staff welfare and working conditions.

In summary, perhaps the **most serious drawback to ZBB is that it requires a lot of management time and paperwork**. One way of obtaining the benefits of ZBB but of overcoming the drawbacks is to apply it selectively on a rolling basis throughout the organisation. This year finance, next year marketing, the year after personnel and so on. In this way all activities will be thoroughly scrutinised over a period of time.

3 Using zero based budgeting

> **FAST FORWARD**
>
> ZBB is particularly useful for budgeting for discretionary costs and for rationalisation purposes.

ZBB is not particularly suitable for direct manufacturing costs, which are usually budgeted using standard costing, work study and other management planning and control techniques. It is best applied to **support expenses**, that is expenditure incurred in departments which exist to support the essential production function. These support areas include marketing, finance, quality control, personnel, data processing, sales and distribution. In many organisations, these expenses make up a large proportion of the total expenditure. These activities are less easily quantifiable by conventional methods and are more **discretionary** in nature.

ZBB can also be successfully applied to **service industries** and **non-profit-making organisations** such as local and central government departments, educational establishments, hospitals and so on, and in any organisation where alternative levels of provision for each activity are possible and where the costs and benefits are separately identifiable.

ZBB can also be used to make rationalisation decisions. 'Rationalisation' is a euphemism for cutting back on production and activity levels, and cutting costs. The need for service departments to operate above a minimum service level or the need for having a particular department at all can be questioned, and ZBB can be used to make rationalisation decisions when an organisation is forced to make spending cuts.

4 Continuous budgets   12/03

FAST FORWARD

Continuous budgets (rolling budgets) are budgets which are continuously updated by adding a further period (say a month or a quarter) and deducting the earliest period.

4.1 Dynamic conditions

Actual conditions may differ from those anticipated when the budget was drawn up for a number of reasons.

(a) **Organisational changes** may occur.

    (i) A change in structure, from a functional basis, say, to a process-based one

    (ii) New agreements with the workforce about flexible working or safety procedures

    (iii) The reallocation of responsibilities following, say, the removal of tiers of middle management and the 'empowerment' of workers further down the line

(b) Action may be needed to **combat an initiative by a competitor.**

(c) **New technology** may be introduced to improve productivity, reduce labour requirements or enhance quality.

(d) **Environmental conditions** may change: there may be a general boom or a recession, an event affecting supply or demand, or a change in government or government policy.

(e) The level of **inflation** may be higher or lower than that anticipated.

(f) The **level of activities** may be different from the levels planned.

Any of these changes **may make the original budget quite inappropriate**, either in terms of the numbers expected, or the way in which responsibility for achieving them is divided, or both.

Exam focus point

Dynamic conditions and rolling/continuous budgets are key syllabus areas.

If management need the chance to revise their plans, they may decide to introduce a system of **continuous budgets** (also called **rolling budgets**).

Key term

A **continuous** or **rolling budget** is a budget which is continuously updated by adding a further accounting period (a month or quarter) when the earlier accounting period has expired.

Continuous budgets are an attempt to prepare targets and plans which are **more realistic and certain**, particularly with a regard to price levels, by **shortening the period between preparing budgets**.

Instead of preparing a **periodic budget** annually for the full budget period, there would be **budgets every one, two, three or four months** (three to six, or even twelve budgets each year). **Each of these budgets would plan for the next twelve months** so that the current budget is extended by an extra period as the current period ends: hence the name rolling budgets.

Suppose, for example, that a continuous budget is prepared every three months. The first three months of the budget period would be planned in great detail, and the remaining nine months in lesser detail, because of the greater uncertainty about the longer-term future. If a first continuous budget is prepared for January to March in detail and April to December in less detail, a new budget will be prepared towards the end of March, planning April to June in detail and July to March in less detail. Four rolling budgets would be prepared every 12 months on this 3 and 9 month basis, requiring, inevitably, greater administrative effort.

4.2 The advantages and disadvantages of continuous budgets

The **advantages** are as follows.

(a) They **reduce the element of uncertainty** in budgeting because they concentrate detailed planning and control on short-term prospects where the degree of uncertainty is much smaller.

(b) They force managers to reassess the budget regularly, and to **produce budgets** which are **up to date in the light of current events and expectations.**

(c) **Planning and control will be based on a recent plan** which is likely to be far more realistic than a fixed annual budget made many months ago.

(d) Realistic budgets are likely to have a **better motivational influence** on managers.

(e) There is **always a budget which extends for several months ahead**. For example, if rolling budgets are prepared quarterly there will always be a budget extending for the next 9 to 12 months. This is not the case when fixed annual budgets are used.

The **disadvantages** of continuous budgets can be a deterrent to using them.

(a) They involve **more time, effort and money** in budget preparation.

(b) Frequent budgeting might have an **off-putting effect on managers** who doubt the value of preparing one budget after another at regular intervals.

(c) Revisions to the budget might involve revisions to standard costs too, which in turn would involve revisions to stock valuations. This could replace a large **administrative effort** from the accounts department every time a rolling budget is prepared.

4.3 Continuous budgets or updated annual budgets

If the expected changes are not likely to be continuous there is a strong argument that routine updating of the budget is unnecessary. **Instead the annual budget could be updated whenever changes become foreseeable,** so that a budget might be updated once or twice, and perhaps more often, during the course of the year.

When a fixed budget is updated, a 'rolling' budget would probably not be prepared. If a budget is updated in month 8 of the year, the updated budget would relate to months 8 – 12. It would not be extended to month 7 of the following year.

5 Activity based budgeting 6/04, 6/05

> **FAST FORWARD**
>
> At its simplest, **activity based budgeting (ABB)** is merely the use of costs determined using ABC as a basis for preparing budgets.
>
> More formally, ABB involves defining the activities that underlie the financial figures in each function and using the level of activity to decide how much resource should be allocated, how well it is being managed and to explain variances from budget.

Implementing ABC leads to the realisation that the **business as a whole** needs to be **managed** with far more reference to the behaviour of activities and cost drivers identified. For example, traditional budgeting may make managers 'responsible' for activities which are driven by factors beyond their control: the cost of setting-up new personnel records and of induction training would traditionally be the responsibility of the personnel manager even though such costs are driven by the number of new employees required by managers other than the personnel manager.

5.1 Claimed results of using ABB

(a) **Different activity levels** will provide a **foundation** for the base package and incremental packages of ZBB.

(b) The organisation's **overall strategy** and any actual or likely changes in that strategy will be taken into account because ABB attempts to manage the business as the sum of its interrelated parts.

(c) **Critical success factors** (an activity in which a business must perform well if it is to succeed) will be identified and performance measures devised to monitor progress towards them.

(d) The focus is on the **whole of an activity**, not just its separate parts, and so there is more likelihood of getting it right first time. For example, what is the use of being able to produce goods in time for their despatch date if the budget provides insufficient resources for the distribution manager who has to deliver them.

5.2 Flexing budgets using cost drivers

There may be a considerable **case for flexing budgets on the basis of differences between budgeted and actual cost-driving activities**. For example, if inspection costs are driven by the number of inspections that take place (rather than varying in relation to production volume, which is the normal basis for flexing), then the budget should be flexed on this basis.

	Budget		Actual		Variance	
	No	£'000	No	£	No	£'000
Inspections/inspection costs	1,000	140	1,100	165	100	25

The adverse variance of £25,000 may be analysed as an activity level variance of $(100 \times £140) = £14,000$ and an expenditure variance of $(1,100 \times £(150 - 140)) = £11,000$.

This kind of analysis simply requires you to be more flexible (if you will forgive the pun) in your application of basic techniques.

> **Exam focus point**
> Although ABB is not mentioned in the Study Guide, it is specifically mentioned in the syllabus and so you would be advised to have an awareness of the topic and to recognise how it offers an alternative approach to flexing budgets.

6 The future of budgeting

Recent research shows that **80%** of companies are **dissatisfied** with their planning and budgeting processes.

Criticisms of traditional budgeting

- **Time consuming** and **costly**
- **Major barrier** to **responsiveness**, flexibility and change
- **Adds little value** given the amount of management time required
- **Rarely strategically focused**

- Makes people feel **undervalued**
- **Reinforces departmental barriers** rather than encouraging knowledge sharing
- Based on **unsupported assumptions** and guesswork as opposed to sound, well-constructed performance data
- **Developed** and **updated infrequently**

Ways in which companies are adapting planning and budgeting processes

- Use of **rolling forecasts**
- **Separation** of the **forecasting process** from the budget to increase speed and accuracy and reduce management time
- **Focus on the future** rather than past performance
- Use of the **balanced scorecard** (discussed in Chapter 13)

Some companies such as the Swedish bank Svenska Handelsbanken (now one of Europe's most successful banks) have abandoned budgeting completely.

Chapter Roundup

- The traditional approach to budgeting, known as **incremental budgeting**, bases the budget on the current year's results plus an extra amount for estimated growth or inflation next year. It encourages slack and wasteful spending to creep into budgets.

- The principle behind **zero based budgeting (ZBB)** is that the budget for each cost centre should be made from 'scratch' or zero. Every item of expenditure must be justified in its entirety in order to be included in the next year's budget.

- There is a three-step approach to ZBB.
    - Define decision units
    - Evaluate and rank packages
    - Allocate resources

- ZBB is particularly useful for budgeting for discretionary costs and for rationalisation purposes.

- **Continuous budgets (rolling budgets)** are budgets which are continuously updated by adding a further period (say a month or a quarter) and deducting the earliest period.

- At its simplest, **activity based budgeting (ABB)** is merely the use of costs determined using ABC for preparing budgets. More formally, it involves defining the activities that underlie the financial figures in each function and using the level of activity to decide how much resource should be allocated, how well it is being managed and to explain variances from budget.

Quick Quiz

1. Incremental budgeting is widely used and is a particularly efficient form of budgeting.

    ☐ True

    ☐ False

2. What are the three steps of ZBB?

    Step 1 ....

    Step 2 ....

    Step 3 ....

3. To which of the following can ZBB be usefully applied?

	Use ZBB	Do not use ZBB
Personnel		
Social services department of local government		
Direct material costs		
Sales department		
Schools		
An inefficient production department		
An efficient production department		

4. *Choose the appropriate word from those highlighted.*

    A continuous budget is also known as a **periodic/rolling** budget.

5. If a system of a ABB is in use, how might the cost of scheduling production be flexed?

    A   Number of items produced
    B   Number of set-ups
    C   Number of direct labour hours
    D   Number of parts used in production

6. A system of zero-based budgeting forces employees to remove wasteful expenditure.

    ☐ True

    ☐ False

7. *Choose the appropriate word from those highlighted.*

    Zero-based budgeting can highlight **short/long**-term benefits at the expense of **short/long**-term advantages.

8. Use of zero-based budgeting implies flexing budgets on the basis of differences between budgeted and actual cost-driving activities.

    ☐ True

    ☐ False

10: ALTERNATIVE BUDGET SYSTEMS

Answers to Quick Quiz

1 False. Incremental budgeting is inefficient.

2 Step 1. Define decision packages
  Step 2. Evaluate and rank activities (decision package)
  Step 3. Allocate resources

3

	Use ZBB	Do not use ZBB
Personnel	✓	
Social services department of local government	✓	
Direct material costs		✓
Sales department	✓	
Schools	✓	
An inefficient production department	✓	
An efficient production department		✓

4 It is also known as a rolling budget.

5 B Number of set-ups

6 True

7 short
  long

8 False. This is a common feature of **activity-based** budgeting.

Now try the questions below from the Exam Question Bank

Number	Level	Marks	Time
Q13	Introductory	n/a	20 mins

Quantitative aids in budgeting

Topic list	Syllabus reference
1 Forecasting using historical data	8(e)
2 The high-low method	8(e)
3 Linear regression analysis	8(e)
4 Scatter diagrams and correlation	8(e)
5 Sales forecasting	8(e)
6 Regression and forecasting	8(e)
7 The components of time series	8(e)
8 Finding the trend	8(e)
9 Finding the seasonal variations	8(e)
10 Time series analysis and forecasting	8(e)
11 Forecasting problems	8(e)
12 Using spreadsheet packages to build business models	8(e)

Introduction

In this chapter we will look at where the figures which go into the budgets come from. To produce a budget calls for the **preparation of forecasts of costs and revenues**. Various quantitative techniques can assist with these **'number-crunching' aspects of budgeting.** This chapter aims to provide an understanding of those techniques within their budgetary context.

There is a certain amount of truth in the comment that **budgeting is more a test of forecasting skill than anything else** and. Forecasts need to be made of sales volumes and prices, wage rates, material availability and prices, rates of inflation, the cost of bought-in services and overheads such as power. It is not sufficient to simply add a percentage to last year's budget in the hope of achieving a realistic forecast.

A **forecast** is a **best estimate** of what might happen in the future, based on certain assumptions about the conditions that are expected to apply. A **budget**, in contrast, is a **plan** of what the organisation is aiming to achieve and what it has set as a target. A budget should be **realistic** and so it will be based to some extent on forecasts prepared. In formulating a budget, management will try to establish some control over the conditions that will apply in the future.

PART C BUDGETING AND PERFORMANCE MEASUREMENT

Study guide

Section 25 – Quantitative aids to budgeting

- Describe and apply the following techniques
    - High-low method
    - Least squares regression
    - Scatter diagrams and correlation
    - Forecasting with least squares regression
    - Time series to identify trends and seasonality
    - Forecasting with time series
- Evaluate the results of quantitative aids

Exam guide

Budget techniques and quantitative aims are a key area of the syllabus. You might be required to employ one or more of the techniques in either a Section A or a Section B question. Alternatively you may face an entire Section B question on, say, time series analysis.

1 Forecasting using historical data

FAST FORWARD

Two important quantitative methods the management accountant can use to obtain information for inclusion in budgets based on historical data, are the high-low method and linear regression analysis.

Numerous techniques have been developed for using past costs incurred as the basis for forecasting future values. These techniques range from simple arithmetic and visual methods to advanced computer-based statistical systems. With all techniques, however, there is the **presumption that the past will provide guidance to the future**. Before using any extrapolation techniques, the **past data** must therefore be critically examined to **assess their appropriateness for the intended purpose**. The following checks should be made.

(a) The **time period** should be long enough to include any periodically paid costs but short enough to ensure that averaging of variations in the level of activity has not occurred.

(b) The **data** should be examined to ensure that any non-activity level factors affecting costs were roughly the same in the past as those forecast for the future. Such factors might include changes in technology, changes in efficiency, changes in production methods, changes in resource costs, strikes, weather conditions and so on. Changes to the past data are frequently necessary.

(c) The **methods of data collection** and the accounting policies used should not introduce bias. Examples might include depreciation policies and the treatment of by-products.

(d) Appropriate choices of **dependent** and **independent variables** must be made.

The two forecasting methods which we are going to look at (the scatter diagram method and linear regression analysis) are based on the assumption that a **linear relationship** links levels of cost and levels of activity.

11: QUANTITATIVE AIDS IN BUDGETING

> **Knowledge brought forward from earlier studies**
>
> *Linear relationships*
>
> - A **linear relationship** can be expressed in the form of an equation which has the general form $y = a + bx$
>
>   where y is the **dependent** variable, depending for its value on the value of x
>
>   x is the **independent** variable, whose value helps to determine the value of y
>
>   a is a **constant**, a fixed amount
>
>   b is a constant, being the **coefficient of x** (that is, the number by which the value of x should be multiplied to derive the value of y)
>
> - If there is a linear relationship between total costs and level of activity, y = total costs, x = level of activity, a = fixed cost (the cost when there is no activity level) and b = variable cost per unit.
>
> - The graph of a linear equation is a **straight line** and is determined by two things, the **gradient** (or slope) of the straight line and the point at which the straight line crosses the y axis (the **intercept**).
>
>   – Gradient = b in the equation $y = a + bx = (y_2 - y_1)/(x_2 - x_1)$ where (x_1, y_1), (x_2, y_2) are two points on the straight line
>
>   – Intercept = a in the equation $y = a + bx$

2 The high-low method

FAST FORWARD

The **high-low method** is a relatively simple way of determining the **fixed** and **variable** cost elements of **semi-variable** costs.

You may have encountered the high-low method in your earlier studies. It is used to identify the fixed and variable elements of costs that are **semi-variable**.

2.1 High-low method

Follow the steps below to estimate the fixed and variable elements of semi-variable costs.

Step 1 Review records of costs in previous periods.

- Select the period with the **highest** activity level.
- Select the period with the **lowest** activity level.

Step 2 If inflation makes it difficult to compare costs, adjust by indexing up or down.

Step 3 Determine the following.

- Total cost at high activity level
- Total costs at low activity level
- Total units at high activity level
- Total units at low activity level

Step 4 Calculate the following.

$$\frac{\text{Total cost at high activity level} - \text{total cost at low activity level}}{\text{Total units at high activity level} - \text{total units at low activity level}}$$

= variable cost per unit (v)

Step 5 The fixed costs can be determined as follows. (Total cost at high activity level) – (total units at high activity level × variable cost per unit)

The following graph demonstrates the high-low method.

Demonstration of high-low method

2.2 Example: The high-low method with inflation

DG Ltd has recorded the following total costs during the last five years.

Year	Output volume Units	Total cost £	Average price level index
20X0	65,000	145,000	100
20X1	80,000	179,200	112
20X2	90,000	209,100	123
20X3	60,000	201,600	144
20X4	75,000	248,000	160

Required

Calculate the total cost that should be expected in 20X5 if output is 85,000 units and the average price level index is 180.

Solution

Step 1
- Period with highest activity = 20X2
- Period with lowest activity = 20X3

Step 2
- Adjust costs so that they can be compared.
- 20X2 indexed cost = £209,100 × $\frac{100}{123}$ = £170,000
- 20X0 indexed cost = £201,600 × $\frac{100}{144}$ = £140,000

Step 3
- Total cost at high activity level = 170,000
- Total cost at low activity level = 140,000
- Total units at high activity level = 90,000
- Total units at low activity level = – 60,000

Step 4 Variable cost per unit

$$= \frac{\text{total cost at high activity level} - \text{total cost at low activity level}}{\text{total units at high activity level} - \text{total units at low activity level}}$$

$$= \frac{170,000 - 140,000}{90,000 - 60,000} = \frac{30,000}{30,000} = £1 \text{ per unit}$$

Step 5 Fixed costs = (total cost at high activity level) − (total units at high activity level × variable cost per unit)

= 170,000 − (90,000 × 1) = 170,000 − 90,000 = £80,000

Therefore the costs in 20X5 for output of 85,000 units are as follows.

		£
Variable costs =	85,000 × £1 =	85,000
Fixed costs =		80,000
		165,000

However, we must now index up the 20X5 costs to reflect 20X5 price levels.

$$£165,000 \times \frac{180}{100} = £297,000$$

The step-by-step guide has been covered in order that you fully understand the process involved.

Question — High-low method

The Valuation Department of a large firm of surveyors wishes to develop a method of predicting its total costs in a period. The following past costs have been recorded at two activity levels.

	Number of valuations (V)	Total cost (TC)
Period 1	420	82,200
Period 2	515	90,275

The total cost model for a period could be represented by what equation?

Answer

Although we only have two activity levels in this question we can still apply the high-low method.

	Valuations V	Total cost £
Period 2	515	90,275
Period 1	420	82,200
Change due to variable cost	95	8,075

∴ Variable cost per valuation = £8,075/95 = £85.

Period 2: fixed cost = £90,275 − (515 × £85)
= £46,500

Therefore total costs = 46,500 + (85 × number of valuations)

PART C BUDGETING AND PERFORMANCE MEASUREMENT

3 Linear regression analysis

FAST FORWARD

Linear regression analysis (least squares technique) involves determining a **line of best fit**.

Linear regression analysis, also known as the **'least squares technique'**, is a **statistical method** of estimating costs using historical data from a number of previous accounting periods.

Linear regression analysis is used to derive a **line of best fit which has the general form**

y = a + bx where

y, the dependent variable = total cost
x, the independent variable = the level of activity
a, the intercept of the line on the y axis = the fixed cost
b, the gradient of the line = the variable cost per unit of activity.

Historical data is collected from previous periods and adjusted to a common price level to remove inflationary differences. This provides a number of readings for activity levels (x) and their associated costs (y). Then, by substituting these readings into the formulae below for a and b, estimates of the fixed cost and variable cost per unit are provided.

Formula to learn

If $y = a + bx$, $b = \dfrac{n\Sigma xy - \Sigma x \Sigma y}{n\Sigma x^2 - (\Sigma x)^2}$ and $a = \dfrac{\Sigma y}{n} - \dfrac{b\Sigma x}{n}$

where n is the number of pair of data for x and y.

Exam focus point

Note that you don't need to learn this formula, or the one in Section 4, as they are provided in the exam. But it would be very easy to make a mistake when copying them down so always double check back to the exam paper.

3.1 Example: Least squares method

The transport department of Norwest Council operates a large fleet of vehicles. These vehicles are used by the various departments of the Council. Each month a statement is prepared for the transport department comparing actual results with budget. One of the items in the transport department's monthly statement is the cost of vehicle maintenance. This maintenance is carried out by the employees of the department. To facilitate control, the transport manager has asked that future statements should show vehicle maintenance costs analysed into fixed and variable costs.

Data from the six months from January to June inclusive are given below.

	Vehicle maintenance cost £	Vehicle running hours
January	13,600	2,100
February	15,800	2,800
March	14,500	2,200
April	16,200	3,000
May	14,900	2,600
June	15,000	2,500

Required

Analyse the vehicle maintenance costs into fixed and variable costs, based on the data given, utilising the least squares method.

Solution

If y = a + bx, where y represent costs and x represents running hours (since costs depend on running hours) then b= (nΣxy − ΣxΣy)/ (nΣx² − (Σx)²), when n is the number of pairs of data, which is 6 in this problem.

x '000 hrs	y £'000	xy	x²
2.1	13.6	28.56	4.41
2.8	15.8	44.24	7.84
2.2	14.5	31.90	4.84
3.0	16.2	48.60	9.00
2.6	14.9	38.74	6.76
2.5	15.0	37.50	6.25
15.2	90.0	229.54	39.10

Variable cost per hour, b = (6(229.54) − (15.2)(90.00))/(6(39.1) − (15.2)²)
= (1,377.24 − 1,368)/(234.6 − 231.04) = 9.24/3.56 = £2.60

Fixed costs (in £'000), a = (Σy/n) − (bΣx/n) = (90/6) − (2.6(15.2)/6) = 8.41 approx, say £8,400

Question — Cost levels

You are given the following data for output at a factory and costs of production over the past five months.

Month	Output '000 units x	Costs £'000 y
1	20	82
2	16	70
3	24	90
4	22	85
5	18	73

Required

(a) Calculate an equation to determine the expected cost level for any given output volume.
(b) Prepare a budget for total costs if output is 22,000 units.

Answer

(a) *Workings*

x	y	xy	x²	y²
20	82	1,640	400	6,724
16	70	1,120	256	4,900
24	90	2,160	576	8,100
22	85	1,870	484	7,225
18	73	1,314	324	5,329
Σx = 100	Σy = 400	Σxy = 8,104	Σx² = 2,040	Σy² = 32,278

n = 5 (There are five pairs of data for x and y values)

b = (nΣxy − ΣxΣy)/(nΣx2 − (Σx)2) = ((5 × 8,104) − (100 × 400))/ ((5 × 2,040) − 100²)
= (40,520 − 40,000)/(10,200 − 10,000) = 520/200 = 2.6

a = $\bar{y} - b\bar{x}$ = (400/5) − (2.6 × (100/5)) = 28

y = 28 + 2.6x

where y = total cost, in thousands of pounds and x = output, in thousands of units.

(b) If the output is 22,000 units, we would expect costs to be 28 + 2.6 × 22 = 85.2 = £85,200.

3.2 The conditions suited to the use of linear regression analysis

The conditions which should apply if linear regression analysis is to be used to estimate costs are as follows.

(a) **A linear cost function should be assumed.** This assumption can be tested by measures of reliability, such as the correlation coefficient and the coefficient of determination (which ought to be reasonably close to 1). We will be looking at these concepts later in the chapter.

(b) When calculating a line of best fit, there will be a range of values for x. In Question 1, the line y = 28 + 2.6x was predicted from data with output values ranging from x = 16 to x = 24. Depending on the degree of correlation between x and y, we might safely use the estimated line of best fit to forecast values for y, provided that the value of x remains within the range 16 to 24. We would be on less safe ground if we used the equation to predict a value for y when x = 10, or 30, or any other value outside the range 16 to 24, because we would **have to assume that costs behave in the same way outside the range of x values used to establish the line in the first place.**

> **Key terms**
>
> **Interpolation** means using a line of best fit to predict a value within the two extreme points of the observed range.
>
> **Extrapolation** means using a line of best fit to predict a value outside the two extreme points.

(c) The **historical data** for cost and output should be **adjusted to a common price level** (to overcome cost differences caused by inflation) and the historical data should also be **representative of current technology, current efficiency levels and current operations** (products made).

(d) As far as possible, **historical data should be accurately recorded** so that variable costs are properly matched against the items produced or sold, and fixed costs are properly matched against the time period to which they relate. For example, if a factory rental is £120,000 per annum, and if data is gathered monthly, these costs should be charged £10,000 to each month instead of £120,000 in full to a single month.

(e) Management should either be **confident that conditions** which have existed in the past **will continue into the future or amend the estimates** of cost produced by the linear regression analysis to **allow for expected changes** in the future.

(f) As with any forecasting process, the **amount of data available is very important.** Even if correlation is high, if we have fewer than about ten pairs of data, we must regard any forecast as being somewhat unreliable.

(g) It must be assumed that the **value of one variable, y, can be predicted or estimated from the value of one other variable, x.**

Question — Linear regression model

The relationship between total operating cost and quantity produced (in a manufacturing company) is given by the linear regression model TC = 5,000 + 500Q, where TC = total operating cost (in £) per annum and Q = quantity produced per annum (kg).

What reservations might you have about relying on the above model for decision-making purposes?

Answer

(a) The reliability of the model is unknown if we do **not know the correlation coefficient**. A low correlation would suggest that the model may be unreliable.

(b) The model is probably **valid only over a certain range** of quantity produced. Outside this range, the relationship between the two variables may be very different.

(c) The model is **based on past data**, and assumes that what has happened in the past will happen in the future.

(d) The model **assumes that a linear relationship exists** between the quantity produced per annum and the total operating costs per annum. It is possible that a non-linear relationship may exist.

(e) The **fixed costs** of £5,000 per annum may be **misleading** if they include an element of allocated costs.

4 Scatter diagrams and correlation

4.1 The scatter diagram method of forecasting

FAST FORWARD

Scatter diagrams can be used to estimate the fixed and variable components of costs.

By this method of cost estimation, cost and activity data are plotted on a graph. A **'line of best fit'** is then drawn. This line should be drawn through the middle of the plotted points as closely as possible so that the distance of points above the line are equal to distances below the line. Where necessary costs should be adjusted to the same indexed price level to allow for inflation.

Scatter diagram method of estimating costs

The fixed cost is the intercept of the line of best fit on the vertical axis. Suppose the fixed cost is £500 and that one of the plotted points (which is very close to the line or actually on it) represents output of 100 units and total cost of £550. The variable cost of 100 units is therefore calculated as £(550 − 500) = £50 and so the variable cost per unit is £0.50. The equation of the line of best fit is therefore *approximately*

y = 500 + 0.5x.

If the company to which this data relate wanted to forecast total costs when output is 90 units, a forecast based on the equation would be 500 + (0.5 × 90) = £545. Alternatively the **forecast could be read directly from the graph using the line of best fit.**

PART C BUDGETING AND PERFORMANCE MEASUREMENT

The disadvantage of the scatter diagram method is that the cost line is drawn by visual judgement and so is a **subjective approximation**.

4.2 Correlation

FAST FORWARD

> **Correlation** describes the extent to which the values of two variables are related. Two variables might be **perfectly** correlated, **partly** correlated or **uncorrelated**. The correlation may be **positive** or **negative**.

(a)

(b)

In the scatter diagrams above, you should agree that a line of best fit is more likely to reflect the 'real' relationship between x and y in (b) than in (a). In (b), the pairs of data are all close to the line of best fit, whereas in (a), there is much more scatter around the line.

In the situation represented in scatter diagram (b), forecasting the value of y from a given value for x would be more likely to be accurate than in the situation represented in (a). This is because there would be greater correlation between x and y in (b) than in (a).

Key term

> **Correlation** is the degree to which change in one variable is related to change in another – in other words, the interdependence between variables.

4.3 Degrees of correlation

Two variables might be **perfectly correlated**, **partly correlated**, **uncorrelated** or subject to **non-linear correlation**.

(a)   **Perfect correlation**

(a)

(b)

All the pairs of values lie on a straight line. An **exact linear relationship** exists between the two variables.

(b) **Partial correlation**

(a)

(b)

In the left hand diagram, although there is no exact relationship, **low values of x tend to be associated with low values of y, and high values of x with high values of y.**

In the right hand diagram, there is no exact relationship, but **low values of x tend to be associated with high values of y and vice versa.**

(c) **No correlation**

The values of these two variables are not correlated with each other.

(d) **Non-linear or curvilinear correlation**

There is a relationship between x and y since the points are on an obvious curve but it is not a linear relationship.

4.3.1 Positive and negative correlation

Correlation, whether perfect or partial, can be **positive** or **negative**.

Key terms

- **Positive correlation** is the type of correlation where low values of one variable are associated with low values of the other, and high values of one variable are associated with high values of the other.
- **Negative correlation** is the type of correlation where low values of one variable are associated with high values of the other, and high values of one variable with low values of the other.

PART C BUDGETING AND PERFORMANCE MEASUREMENT

> **Question** — Positive correlation
>
> Which of the diagrams in Paragraph 4.8 demonstrate positive correlation?
>
> **Answer**
>
> The left hand diagrams for perfect and partial correlation.

4.4 Measures of correlation

FAST FORWARD

> The degree of correlation between two variables can be measured using the **Pearsonian coefficient of correlation, r**. The **coefficient of determination** indicates the variations in the dependent variable that can be explained by variations in the independent variable.

4.4.1 The coefficient of correlation, r

The **degree of correlation between two variables** can be measured using the **Pearsonian coefficient of correlation** (also called the **product moment correlation coefficient**).

r has a value between −1 (perfect negative correlation) and +1 (perfect positive correlation). If r = 0 then the variables are uncorrelated.

Formula to learn

The **coefficient of correlation**, r, is calculated as follows.

$$r = \frac{n\Sigma xy - \Sigma x \Sigma y}{\sqrt{[n\Sigma x^2 - (\Sigma x)^2][n\Sigma y^2 - (\Sigma y)^2]}}$$

Look back at the example in Paragraph 3.4. Suppose that we wanted to know the correlation between vehicle maintenance costs and vehicle running hours. We can use a lot of the calculation in Paragraph 3.5 to determine r.

$$r = \frac{6(229.54) - (15.2)(90.0)}{\sqrt{[6(39.1) - (15.2)^2][6\Sigma y^2 - (90.0)^2]}} = \frac{1{,}377.24 - 1{,}368}{\sqrt{(234.6 - 231.04)(6\Sigma y^2 - 8{,}100)}}$$

All we need to calculate is Σy^2.

							Total
y (£'000)	13.60	15.80	14.50	16.20	14.90	15.00	90.00
y^2	184.96	249.64	210.25	262.44	222.01	225.00	1,354.30

$$r = \frac{9.24}{\sqrt{(3.56)(6 \times 1{,}354.30 - 8{,}100)}} = 0.96$$

A **fairly high degree of positive correlation** between x (vehicle running hours) and y (vehicle maintenance cost) is indicated here **because r is quite close to +1**.

4.4.2 The coefficient of determination, r^2

Key term

> The **coefficient of determination** is a measure of the proportion of the change in the value of one variable that can be explained by variations in the value of the other variable.

In our example, $r^2 = (0.96)^2 = 0.9216$, and so 92% of variation in the value of y (cost) can be explained by a linear relationship with x (running hours). This leaves only 8% of variations in y to be predicted from other factors. It is therefore **likely that vehicle** running hours could be used with a high degree of confidence to predict costs during a period.

4.5 Correlation and causation

If two variables are well correlated this may be due to pure chance or there may be a reason for it. The **larger the number of pairs of data**, the **less likely it is that the correlation is due to chance**, though that possibility should never be ignored.

If there is a reason, it may not be causal. Monthly net income is well correlated with monthly credit to a person's bank account, for the logical (rather than causal) reason that for most people the one equals the other. **Even if there is a causal explanation** for a correlation, it **does not follow that variations in the value of one variable cause variations in the value of the other**. Sales of ice cream and of sunglasses are well correlated, not because of a direct causal link but because the weather influences both variables.

Having said this, it is of course possible that where two variables are correlated, there is a direct causal link to be found.

4.6 The interactions of r^2 and r with linear regression

The successful application of linear regression models depends on x and y being closely linearly related. r measures the strength of the linear relationship between two variables but **what numerical value of r is suggestive of sufficient linearity in data to allow one to proceed with linear regression?** The lower the value of r, the less chance of forecasts made using linear regression being adequate.

If there is a perfect linear relationship between the two variables ($r = \pm 1$), we can predict y from any given value of x with great confidence. If correlation is high (for example $r = 0.9$), the actual values will all be quite close to the regression line and so predictions should not be far out. If correlation is below about 0.7, predictions will only give a very rough guide to the likely value of y.

If $r = 0.75$, say, you may feel that the linear relationship between the two variables is fairly strong. But $r^2 = 56.25\%$ indicates that only just over half of the variations in the dependent variable can be explained by a linear relationship with the independent variable. The low figure could be because a non-linear relationship is a better model for the data or because extraneous factors need to be considered (and hence multiple regression analysis should be used). It is a **common rule of thumb that $r^2 \geq 80\%$ indicates that linear regression may be applied for the purpose of forecasting.**

5 Sales forecasting

FAST FORWARD

Sales are often the **principal budget factor**. Forecasting sales requires marketing information, and makes use of such techniques as **time series** and **'What if?'** analysis.

The sales budget is frequently the first budget prepared since **sales is usually the principal budget factor**, but before the sales budget can be prepared a sales forecast has to be made. Sales forecasting is complex *and* difficult and involves the consideration of a number of factors detailed in Chapter 8.

As well as bearing in mind those factors, management can use a number of forecasting methods, often combining them to reduce the level of uncertainty.

(a) **Sales personnel** can be asked to provide estimates.

(b) **Market research** can be used (especially for new products or services).

PART C BUDGETING AND PERFORMANCE MEASUREMENT

(c) **Mathematical** models can be set up so that repetitive computer simulations can be run which permit managers to review the results that would be obtained in various circumstances.

(d) Various **mathematical techniques** can be used to estimate sales levels. We will cover these in the remainder of the chapter.

6 Regression and forecasting

FAST FORWARD

Regression can be used to find a **trend line**, such as the trend in sales over a number of periods.

The same regression techniques as those considered earlier in the chapter can be used to **calculate a regression line (a trend line) for a time series**. A time series is simply a series of figures or values recorded over time (such as total annual costs for the last ten years). The determination of a trend line is particularly useful in forecasting. (We will be looking at time series and trend lines in more detail in the next section.)

The **years (or days or months) become the x variables in the regression formulae** by **numbering them from 0 upwards**.

6.1 Example: Regression and forecasting

Sales of product B over the seven year period from 20X1 to 20X7 were as follows.

Year	20X1	20X2	20X3	20X4	20X5	20X6	20X7
Sales of B ('000 units)	22	25	24	26	29	28	30

There is high correlation between time and the volume of sales.

Required

Calculate the trend line of sales, and forecast sales in 20X8 and 20X9.

Solution

Workings

Year	x	y	xy	x^2
20X1	0	22	0	0
20X2	1	25	25	1
20X3	2	24	48	4
20X4	3	26	78	9
20X5	4	29	116	16
20X6	5	28	140	25
20X7	6	30	180	36
	$\Sigma x = 21$	$\Sigma y = 184$	$\Sigma xy = 587$	$\Sigma x^2 = 91$

n = 7

Where y = a + bx

b = ((7 × 587) − (21 × 184))/((7 × 91) − (21 × 21)) = 245/196 = 1.25
a = (184/7) − ((1.25 × 21)/7) = 22.5357, say 22.5
y = 22.5 + 1.25x where x = 0 in 20X1, x = 1 in 20X2 and so on.

Using this trend line, predicted sales in 20X8 (year 7) would be 22.5 + 1.25 × 7 = 31.25 = 31,250 units.

Similarly, for 20X9 (year 8) predicted sales would be 22.5 + 1.25 × 8 = 32.50 = 32,500 units.

7 The components of time series

FAST FORWARD

A **time series** is a series of figures or values recorded over time. A time series has four components: a **trend**, **seasonal variations**, **cyclical variations** and **random variations**.

Key term

A **time series** is a series of figures or values recorded over time.

The following are examples of time series.

- Output at a factory each day for the last month
- Monthly sales over the last two years
- The Retail Prices Index each month for the last ten years

Key term

A graph of a time series is called a **historigram**.

(Note the letters 'ri'; this is not the same as a histogram.) For example, consider the following time series.

Year	20X0	20X1	20X2	20X3	20X4	20X5	20X6
Sales (£'000)	20	21	24	23	27	30	28

The historigram is as follows.

The horizontal axis is always chosen to represent time, and the vertical axis represents the values of the data recorded.

There are several **components of a time series** which it may be necessary to identify.

(a) A **trend**

(b) **Seasonal variations** or fluctuations

(c) Cycles, or **cyclical variations**

(d) Non-recurring, **random variations**. These may be caused by unforeseen circumstances such as a change in government, a war, technological change or a fire.

7.1 The trend

Key term

The **trend** is the underlying long-term movement over time in values of data recorded.

PART C BUDGETING AND PERFORMANCE MEASUREMENT

In the following examples of time series, there are three types of trend.

	Output per labour hour Units	Cost per unit £	Number of employees
20X4	30	1.00	100
20X5	24	1.08	103
20X6	26	1.20	96
20X7	22	1.15	102
20X8	21	1.18	103
20X9	17	1.25	98
	(A)	(B)	(C)

(a) In time series **(A)** there is a **downward trend** in the output per labour hour. Output per labour hour did not fall every year, because it went up between 20X5 and 20X6, but the long-term movement is clearly a downward one.

(b) In time series **(B)** there is an **upward trend** in the cost per unit. Although unit costs went down in 20X7 from a higher level in 20X6, the basic movement over time is one of rising costs.

(c) In time series **(C)** there is **no clear movement** up or down, and the number of employees remained fairly constant. The trend is therefore a static, or level one.

7.2 Seasonal variations

Key term

Seasonal variations are short-term fluctuations in recorded values, due to different circumstances which affect results at different times of the year, on different days of the week, at different times of day, or whatever.

Here are two examples of seasonal variations.

(a) Sales of ice cream will be higher in summer than in winter.

(b) The telephone network may be heavily used at certain times of the day (such as mid-morning and mid-afternoon) and much less used at other times (such as in the middle of the night).

'Seasonal' is a term which may appear to refer to the seasons of the year, but its meaning in time series analysis is somewhat broader, as the examples given above show.

7.3 Example: A trend and seasonal variations

The number of customers served by a company of travel agents over the past four years is shown in the following historigram.

In this example, there would appear to be large seasonal fluctuations in demand, but there is also a basic upward trend.

7.4 Cyclical variations

Cyclical variations are **medium-term changes in results caused by circumstances which repeat in cycles**. In business, cyclical variations are commonly associated with economic cycles, successive booms and slumps in the economy. Economic cycles may last a few years. Cyclical variations are longer term than seasonal variations.

7.5 Summarising the components

In practice a time series could incorporate all of the four features we have been looking at and, to make reasonably accurate forecasts, the four features often have to be isolated. We can begin the process of isolating each feature by summarising the components of a time series as follows.

The **actual time series, Y = T + S + C + R**

where   Y = the actual time series   C = the cyclical component
        T = the trend series   R = the random component
        S = the seasonal component

Though you should be aware of the cyclical component, it is unlikely that you will be expected to carry out any calculation connected with isolating it. The mathematical model which we will use, the **additive model**, therefore excludes any reference to C and is **Y = T + S + R**.

Key term

> The **additive model** expresses a time series as Y = T + S + R.

We will begin by looking at how to find the trend in a time series.

8 Finding the trend

FAST FORWARD

> **Trend** values can be determined by a process of **moving averages**.

Look at these monthly sales figures.

	August	September	October	November	December
Sales (£'000)	0.02	0.04	0.04	3.20	14.60

It looks as though the business is expanding rapidly – and so it is, in a way. But when you know that the business is a Christmas card manufacturer, then you see immediately that the January sales will no doubt slump right back down again.

It is obvious that the business will do better in the Christmas season than at any other time – that is the seasonal variation. Using the monthly figures, how can he tell whether or not the business is doing well overall – whether there is a rising sales trend over time other than the short-term rise over Christmas?

One possibility is to compare figures with the equivalent figures of a year ago. However, many things can happen over a year to make such a comparison misleading – new products might now be manufactured and prices will probably have changed.

In fact, there are a number of ways of overcoming this problem of distinguishing trend from seasonal variations. One such method is called **moving averages**. This method attempts to **remove seasonal (or cyclical) variations from a time series by a process of averaging so as to leave a set of figures representing the trend**.

A **moving average** is an average of the results of a fixed number of periods. Since it is an average of several time periods, it is **related to the mid-point of the overall period**.

8.1 Example: Moving averages

Year	Sales Units
20X0	390
20X1	380
20X2	460
20X3	450
20X4	470
20X5	440
20X6	500

Required

Take a moving average of the annual sales over a period of three years.

Solution

(a) Average sales in the three year period 20X0 – 20X2 were (390 + 380 + 460)/3 = 1,230/3 = 410. This average relates to the middle year of the period, 20X1.

(b) Similarly, average sales in the three year period 20X1 – 20X3 were (380 + 460 + 450)/3 = 1,290/3 = 430. This average relates to the middle year of the period, 20X2.

(c) The average sales can also be found for the periods 20X2 – 20X4, 20X3 – 20X5 and 20X4 – 20X6, to give the following.

Year	Sales	Moving total of 3 years sales	Moving average of 3 years sales (÷ 3)
20X0	390		
20X1	380	1,230	410
20X2	460	1,290	430
20X3	450	1,380	460
20X4	470	1,360	453
20X5	440	1,410	470
20X6	500		

Note the following points.

(i) The **moving average series has five figures** relating to the years 20X1 to 20X5. The **original series had seven figures** for the years from 20X0 to 20X6.

(ii) There is an upward trend in sales, which is more noticeable from the series of moving averages than from the original series of actual sales each year.

The above example averaged over a three-year period. Over what period should a moving average be taken? The answer to this question is that the **moving average which is most appropriate will depend on the circumstances and the nature of the time series**.

(a) A moving average which takes an **average of the results in many time periods will represent results over a longer term** than a moving average of two or three periods.

(b) On the other hand, with a moving average of results in many time periods, the **last figure in the series will be out of date by several periods**. In our example, the most recent average related to 20X5. With a moving average of five years' results, the final figure in the series would relate to 20X4.

(c) When there is a **known cycle** over which seasonal variations occur, such as all the days in the week or all the seasons in the year, the **most suitable moving average would be one which covers one full cycle**.

8.2 Moving averages of an even number of results

In the previous example, **moving averages were taken of the results in an *odd* number of time periods**, and the **average then related to the mid-point of the overall period**.

If a **moving average** of results was taken in an **even number of time periods**, the basic technique would be the same, but the mid-point of the overall period would not relate to a single period. For example, suppose an average were taken of the following four results.

Spring	120	
Summer	90	Average 115
Autumn	180	
Winter	70	

The average would relate to the mid-point of the period, between summer and autumn.

The trend line average figures need to relate to a particular time period; otherwise, seasonal variations cannot be calculated. To overcome this difficulty, we take a **moving average of the moving average**. An example will illustrate this technique.

8.3 Example: Moving averages over an even number of periods

Calculate a moving average trend line of the following results of Linden Ltd.

Year	Quarter	Volume of sales '000 units
20X5	1	600
	2	840
	3	420
	4	720
20X6	1	640
	2	860
	3	420
	4	740

Solution

A moving average of four will be used, since the volume of sales would appear to depend on the season of the year, and each year has four quarterly results. The moving average of four does not relate to any specific period of time; therefore a second moving average of two will be calculated on the first moving averages.

Year	Quarter	Actual volume of sales '000 units (A)	Moving total of 4 quarters' sales '000 units (B)	Moving average of 4 quarters' sales '000 units (B ÷ 4)	Mid-point of 2 moving averages Trend line '000 units (C)
20X5	1	600			
	2	840			
	3	420	2,580	645.0	650.00
	4	720	2,620	655.0	657.50
20X6	1	640	2,640	660.0	660.00
	2	860	2,640	660.0	662.50
	3	420	2,660	665.0	
	4	740			

By taking a mid point (a moving average of two) of the original moving averages, we can relate the results to specific quarters (from the third quarter of 20X5 to the second quarter of 20X6).

PART C   BUDGETING AND PERFORMANCE MEASUREMENT

9 Finding the seasonal variations

FAST FORWARD

Seasonal variations can be estimated using the **additive** model or the **proportional (multiplicative)** model.

Once a trend has been established we can find the seasonal variations. As we saw earlier, the additive model for time series analysis is Y = T + S + R. We can therefore write Y – T = S + R. In other words, if we deduct the trend series from the actual series, we will be left with the seasonal and residual components of the time series. If we assume that the random component is relatively small, and hence negligible, the **seasonal component can be found as S = Y – T, the de-trended series.**

The actual and trend sales for Linden Ltd (as calculated in Paragraph 9.14) are set out below. The **difference between the actual results for any one quarter (Y) and the trend figure for that quarter (T)** will be the seasonal variation for that quarter.

Year	Quarter	Actual	Trend	Seasonal variation
20X5	1	600		
	2	840		
	3	420	650.00	–230.00
	4	720	657.50	62.50
20X6	1	640	660.00	–20.00
	2	860	662.50	197.50
	3	420		
	4	740		

Suppose that seasonal variations for the third and fourth quarters of 20X6 and the first and second quarters of 20X7 are –248.75, 62.50, –13.75 and 212.50 respectively. The variation between the actual result for a particular quarter and the trend line average is not the same from year to year, but an **average of these variations can be taken**.

	Q_1	Q_2	Q_3	Q_4
20X5			–230.00	62.50
20X6	–20.00	197.50	–248.75	62.50
20X7	–13.75	212.50		
Total	–33.75	410.00	–478.75	125.00
Average (÷ 2)	–16.875	205.00	–239.375	62.50

Variations around the basic trend line should cancel each other out, and add up to zero. At the moment, they do not. We therefore **spread the total of the variations** (11.25) **across the four quarters** (11.25 ÷ 4) **so that the final total of the variations sum to zero.**

	Q_1	Q_2	Q_3	Q_4	Total
Estimated quarterly variations	–16.8750	205.0000	–239.3750	62.5000	11.250
Adjustment to reduce variations to 0	–2.8125	–2.8125	–2.8125	–2.8125	–11.250
Final estimates of quarterly variations	–19.6875	202.1875	–242.1875	59.6875	0

These might be rounded as follows   Q1: –20,   Q2: 202,   Q3: –242,   Q4: 60,   Total: 0

9.1 Seasonal variations using the proportional model

The method of estimating the seasonal variations in the above example was to use the differences between the trend and actual data. This model **assumes that the components of the series are independent** of each other, so that an increasing trend does not affect the seasonal variations and make them increase as well, for example.

The alternative is to use the **proportional model** whereby each actual figure is expressed as a proportion of the trend. Sometimes this method is called the **multiplicative model**.

Key term

> The **proportional (multiplicative) model** summarises a time series as $Y = T \times S \times R$.

The **trend component** will be the **same whichever model is used** but the values of the **seasonal and random components** will **vary according to the model being applied**.

The example on Linden Ltd can be reworked on this alternative basis. The trend is calculated in exactly the same way as before but we need a different approach for the seasonal variations. The proportional model is $Y = T \times S \times R$ and, just as we calculated $S = Y - T$ for the additive model above we can calculate $S = Y/T$ for the proportional model.

Year	Quarter	Actual (Y)	Trend (T)	Seasonal percentage (Y/T)
20X5	1	600		
	2	840		
	3	420	650.00	0.646
	4	720	657.50	1.095
20X6	1	640	660.00	0.970
	2	860	662.50	1.298
	3	420		
	4	740		

Suppose that seasonal variations for the next four quarters are 0.628, 1.092, 0.980 and 1.309 respectively. The summary of the seasonal variations expressed in proportional terms is therefore as follows.

	Q_1 %	Q_2 %	Q_3 %	Q_4 %
20X5			0.646	1.095
20X6	0.970	1.298	0.628	1.092
20X7	0.980	1.309		
Total	1.950	2.607	1.274	2.187
Average	0.975	1.3035	0.637	1.0935

Instead of summing to zero, as **with the additive approach**, the **averages should sum (in this case) to 4.0, 1.0 for each of the four quarters**. They actually sum to 4.009 so 0.00225 has to be deducted from each one.

	Q_1	Q_2	Q_3	Q_4
Average	0.97500	1.30350	0.63700	1.09350
Adjustment	−0.00225	−0.00225	−0.00225	−0.00225
Final estimate	0.97275	1.30125	0.63475	1.09125
Rounded	0.97	1.30	0.64	1.09

Note that the **proportional model is better than the additive model when the trend is increasing or decreasing over time**. In such circumstances, seasonal variations are likely to be increasing or decreasing too. The additive model simply adds absolute and unchanging seasonal variations to the trend figures whereas the proportional model, by multiplying increasing or decreasing trend values by a constant seasonal variation factor, takes account of changing seasonal variations.

10 Time series analysis and forecasting 6/03

FAST FORWARD

Forecasts can be made by calculating a **trend line** (using moving averages or linear regression), using the trend line to forecast future trend line values, and adjusting these values by the **average seasonal variation** applicable to the future period.

By extrapolating a trend and then adjusting for seasonal variations, forecasts of future values can be made.

Forecasts of future values should be made as follows.

(a) **Find a trend line using moving averages or using linear regression analysis (see Section 5).**

(b) **Use the trend line to forecast future trend line values.**

(c) **Adjust these values by the average seasonal variation applicable to the future period, to determine the forecast for that period.** With the additive model, add (or subtract for negative variations) the variation. With the multiplicative model, multiply the trend value by the variation proportion.

Extending a trend line outside the range of known data, in this case forecasting the future from a trend line based on historical data, is known as **extrapolation**.

10.1 Example: Forecasting

The sales (in £'000) of swimwear by a large department store for each period of three months and trend values found using moving averages are as follows.

Quarter	20X4 Actual £'000	20X4 Trend £'000	20X5 Actual £'000	20X5 Trend £'000	20X6 Actual £'000	20X6 Trend £'000	20X7 Actual £'000	20X7 Trend £'000
First			8		20	40	40	57
Second			30	30	50	45	62	
Third			60	31	80	50	92	
Fourth	24		20	35	40	54		

Using the additive model, seasonal variations have been determined as follows.

Quarter 1	Quarter 2	Quarter 3	Quarter 4
−£18,250	+£2,750	+£29,750	−£14,250

Required

Predict sales for the last quarter of 20X7 and the first quarter of 20X8, stating any assumptions.

Solution

We might guess that the trend line is rising steadily, by (57 − 40)/4 = 4.25 per quarter in the period 1st quarter 20X6 to 1st quarter 20X7 (57 being the prediction in 1st quarter 20X7 and 40 the prediction in 1st quarter 20X6). Since the trend may be levelling off a little, a quarterly increase of +4 in the trend will be assumed.

		Trend	Seasonal variation	Forecast
1st quarter	20X7	57		
4th quarter	20X7 (+ (3 × 4))	69	−14.25	54.75
1st quarter	20X8 (+ (4 × 4))	73	−18.25	54.75

Rounding to the nearest thousand pounds, the forecast sales are £55,000 for each of the two quarters.

Note that you could actually plot the trend line figures on a graph, extrapolate the trend line into the future and read off forecasts from the graph using the extrapolated trend line.

If we had been using the proportional model, with an average variation for (for example) quarter 4 of 0.8, our prediction for the fourth quarter of 20X7 would have been 69 × 0.8 = 55.2, say £55,000.

Question — Sales forecast

The trend in a company's sales figures can be described by the linear regression equation y = 780 + 4x, where x is the month number (with January 20X3 as month 0) and y is sales in thousands of pounds. The average seasonal variation for March is 106%.

Required

Forecast the sales for March 20X5.

Answer

x = 26

Forecast = 1.06 × [780 + (4 × 26)] = 937.04 = £937,040 or about £937,000.

11 Forecasting problems

FAST FORWARD

> Errors can be expected in forecasting due to unforeseen changes. This is more likely to happen the further into the future the forecast is for, and the smaller the quantity of data on which the forecast is based.

All forecasts are subject to error, but the likely errors vary from case to case.

- The **further into the future** the forecast is for, the **more unreliable** it is likely to be.
- The **less data** available on which to base the forecast, the **less reliable** the forecast.
- The historic **pattern** of trend and seasonal variations **may not continue** in the future.
- **Random variations** may upset the pattern of trend and seasonal variation.
- **Extrapolation** of the **trend line** is done by judgment and can introduce errors.

There are a number of changes that also may make it difficult to forecast future events.

Type of change	Examples
Political and economic changes	Changes in interest rates, exchange rates or inflation can mean that future sales and costs are difficult to forecast.
Environmental changes	The opening of high-speed rail links might have a considerable impact on some companies' markets.
Technological changes	These may mean that the past is not a reliable indication of likely future events. For example new faster machinery may make it difficult to use current output levels as the basis for forecasting future production output.
Technological advances	Advanced manufacturing technology is changing the cost structure of many firms. Direct labour costs are reducing in significance and fixed manufacturing costs are increasing. This causes forecasting difficulties because of the resulting changes in cost behaviour patterns, breakeven points and so on.
Social changes	Alterations in taste, fashion and the social acceptability of products can cause forecasting difficulties.

Management should have reasonable **confidence** in their estimates and forecasts. The assumptions on which the forecasts/estimates are based should be properly understood and the methods used to make a forecast or estimate should be in keeping with the nature, quantity and reliability of the data on which the forecast or estimate will be based. There is no point in using a 'sophisticated' technique with unreliable data; on the other hand, if there is a lot of accurate data about historical costs, it would be a waste of the data to use the scatter diagram method for cost estimating.

12 Using spreadsheet packages to build business models

FAST FORWARD

Spreadsheet packages can be used to build business **models** to assist the forecasting and planning process. They are particularly useful for 'what if?' analysis.

A spreadsheet is a type of general purpose software package with **many business applications**, not just accounting ones. It **can be used to build a model**, in which data is presented in these **rows and columns**, and it is up to the model builder to determine what data or information should be presented in it, how it should be presented and how the data should be manipulated by the spreadsheet program. The most widely used spreadsheet packages are Lotus 1-2-3 and Excel.

The idea behind a spreadsheet is that the model builder should **construct a model as follows**.

(a) Identify what data goes into each row and column and by **inserting text** (for example, column headings and row identifications).

(b) **Specify how the numerical data in the model should be derived**. Numerical data might be derived using one of the following methods.

- **Insertion into the model via keyboard input**.

- **Calculation from other data in the model** by means of a formula specified within the model itself. The model builder must insert these formulae into the spreadsheet model when it is first constructed.

- **Retrieval from data on a disk file** from another computer application program or module.

12.1 The advantages of spreadsheets

The uses of spreadsheets are really only limited by your imagination, and by the number of rows and columns in the spreadsheet, but some of the more **common accounting applications** are listed below.

- Balance sheets
- Cash flow analysis/forecasting
- General ledger
- Inventory records
- Job cost estimates
- Market share analysis and planning
- Profit projections
- Profit statements
- Project budgeting and control
- Sales projections and records
- Tax estimation

The great value of spreadsheets derives from their **simple format** of rows, columns and worksheets of data, and the ability of the data **users to have direct access themselves** to their spreadsheet model via their own PC. For example, an accountant can construct a cash flow model with a spreadsheet package on the PC on his desk: he can **create** the model, **input** the data, **manipulate** the data and **read or print the output** direct. He will also have fairly **instant access** to the model whenever it is needed, in just the time it takes to load the model into his PC. Spreadsheets therefore bring computer modelling within the everyday reach of data users.

12.2 The disadvantages of spreadsheets

Spreadsheets have disadvantages if they are not properly used.

(a) A **minor error in the design** of a model at any point can **affect the validity of data** throughout the spreadsheet. Such errors can be very difficult to trace.

(b) Even if it is properly designed in the first place, it is very **easy to corrupt** a model by accidentally changing a cell or inputting data in the wrong place.

(c) It is possible to **become over-dependent on them**, so that simple one-off tasks that can be done in seconds with a pen and paper are done on a spreadsheet instead.

(d) The possibility for experimentation with data is so great that it is possible to **lose sight of the original intention** of the spreadsheet.

(e) Spreadsheets **cannot take account of qualitative factors** since they are invariably difficult to quantify. Decisions should not be made on the basis of quantitative information alone.

In summary, spreadsheets should be seen as a **tool in planning and decision making**. The user must make the decision.

12.3 'What if' analysis

Once a model has been constructed the consequences of changes in any of the variables may be tested by asking **'what if' questions, a form of sensitivity analysis**. For example, a spreadsheet may be used to develop a cash flow model, such as that shown below.

PART C BUDGETING AND PERFORMANCE MEASUREMENT

	A	B	C	D
1		Month 1	Month 2	Month 3
2	Sales	1,000	1,200	1,440
3	Cost of sales	(650)	(780)	(936)
4	Gross profit	350	420	504
5				
6	Receipts:			
7	Current month	600	720	864
8	Previous month		400	480
9		–	–	–
10		600	1,120	1,344
11	Payments	(650)	(780)	(936)
12		(50)	340	408
13	Balance b/f	–	(50)	290
14	Balance c/f	(50)	290	698

Typical 'what if' questions for sensitivity analysis

(a) What if the cost of sales is 68% of sales revenue, not 65%?

(b) What if payment from debtors is received 40% in the month of sale, 50% one month in arrears and 10% two months in arrears, instead of 60% in the month of sale and 40% one month in arrears?

(c) What if sales growth is only 15% per month, instead of 20% per month?

Using the spreadsheet model, the answers to such questions can be obtained simply and quickly, using the editing facility in the program. The information obtained should **provide management with a better understanding of what the cash flow position in the future might be**, and **what factors are critical to ensuring that the cash position remains reasonable**. For example, it might be found that the cost of sales must remain less than 67% of sales value to achieve a satisfactory cash position.

Chapter Roundup

- Two important quantitative methods the management accountant can use to obtain information for inclusion in budgets based on historical data, are the high-low method and linear regression analysis.

- The **high-low method** is a relatively simple way of determining the **fixed** and **variable** cost elements of **semi-variable** costs.

- **Linear regression analysis** (least squares technique) involves determining a **line of best fit.**

- **Scatter diagrams** can be used to estimate the fixed and variable components of costs.

- **Correlation** describes the extent to which the values of two variables are related. Two variables might be **perfectly** correlated, **partly** correlated or **uncorrelated**. The correlation may be **positive** or **negative**.

- The degree of correlation between two variables can be measured using the **Pearsonian coefficient of correlation**, r. The **coefficient of determination** indicates the variations in the dependent variable that can be explained by variations in the independent variable.

- Sales are often the **principal budget factor**. Forecasting sales requires marketing information, and makes use of such techniques as **time series** and **'What if?'** analysis.

- Regression can be used to find a **trend line**, such as the trend in sales over a number of periods.

- A **time series** is a series of figures or values recorded over time. A time series has four components: a **trend**, **seasonal variations**, **cyclical variations** and **random variations**.

- **Trend** values can be determined by a process of **moving averages**.

- **Seasonal variations** can be estimated using the **additive** model or the **proportional (multiplicative)** model.

- **Forecasts** can be made by calculating a **trend line** (using moving averages or linear regression), using the trend line to forecast future trend line values, and adjusting these values by the **average seasonal variation** applicable to the future period.

- Errors can be expected in forecasting due to unforeseen changes. This is more likely to happen the further into the future the forecast is for, and the smaller the quantity of data on which the forecast is based.

- **Spreadsheet packages** can be used to build business **models** to assist the forecasting and planning process. They are particularly useful for 'what if?' analysis.

Quick Quiz

1. If the relationship between production costs and output is connected by the linear relationship $y = 75x + 47,000$, what is 47,000?

    A   The number of units produced
    B   Total production costs
    C   The production cost if 75 units are produced
    D   The fixed production costs

2. The costs of production runs consist of a mix of fixed and variable elements. The lowest number of production runs during the year was 120 during February, the highest number 150 during October. If the total costs of production runs in February were £80,000 and in October were £95,000, calculate the fixed and variable cost elements.

3. *Fill in the missing words.*

    Extrapolation involves using a .... of best .... to predict a value .... the two extreme points of the observed range.

4. Between sales of suntan cream and sales of cold drinks, one would expect (assuming spending money to be unlimited)

    A   positive, but spurious, correlation
    B   negative, but spurious, correlation
    C   positive correlation indicating direct causation
    D   negative correlation indicating direct causation

5. Which of the following statements is/are true of the coefficient of determination?

		True	False
(a)	It is the square of the Pearsonian coefficient of correlation		
(b)	It can never quite equal 1		
(c)	If it is high, this proves that variations in one variable cause variations in the other		

6. What variable is used to signify 'time' in the regression equation $y = a + bx$ when regression analysis is used for forecasting?

    A   x
    B   a
    C   b
    D   y

7. Which of the four components of a time series is missing from the list below?

    Trend
    Seasonal variations
    Random variations

8. *Fill in the gaps with the appropriate mathematical symbols.*

    Additive model of time series $Y = T$ .... S .... R
       Seasonal component, S $S = Y$ .... T
    Proportional model of time series $Y = T$ .... S .... R
       Seasonal component, S $S = Y$ .... T

Answers to Quick Quiz

1. D The fixed production costs

2.
	Number of runs	Total costs £
High	150	95,000
Low	120	80,000
	30	15,000

   Variable costs per run = $\frac{15,000}{30}$ = £500

   Fixed costs = 95,000 − (500 × 150) = £20,000

3. line
   fit
   outside

4. A. When cold drinks sell well, so will suntan cream. Neither sales level causes the other; both are caused by the weather.

5. Statement (a) is true. The coefficient of determination is r2.
   Statement (b) is false. r can reach 1 or −1, so r2 can reach 1.
   Statement (c) is false. Correlation does not prove a causal link.

6. A The correct answer is x.

7. Cyclical variations

8. Additive model of time series = T + S + R
   Seasonal component, S = Y − T
   Proportional model of time series = T x S x R
   Seasonal component, S = Y ÷ T

Now try the questions below from the Exam Question Bank

Number	Level	Marks	Time
Q14	Introductory	n/a	35 mins

Index numbers

Topic list	Syllabus reference
1 Basic terminology	9(c)
2 Simple indices	9(c)
3 Index relatives	9(c)
4 Time series deflation	9(c)
5 Composite index numbers	9(c)
6 Weighted index numbers	9(c)
7 Laspeyre and Paasche indices	9(c)

Introduction

Index numbers provide a **standardised way of comparing the values**, over time, of prices, wages, volumes and so on. They are used extensively in business, government and commerce in order to **measure performance**.

No doubt you will be aware of some index numbers – the RPI, the Financial Times All Share Index and so on. This chapter will explain how to construct indices and will look at associated issues such as their relative merits.

Study guide

Section 26 – Indices

- Explain the purpose of index numbers, and calculate and interpret simple index numbers for one or more variables
- Deflate time related data using an index
- Construct a chained index series
- Explain the term 'average index', distinguishing between simple and weighted averages
- Calculate Laspeyre and Paasche price and quantity indices
- Describe the relative merits of the Laspeyre and Paasche indices

Exam guide

Index numbers have just been introduced into the 2.4 syllabus. Be prepared to answer questions on this topic in both sections of your examination. Note that you might be required to use your knowledge of index numbers when answering exam questions covering other topics.

1 Basic terminology

FAST FORWARD

An **index** is a measure, over time, of the average changes in the values (prices or quantities) of a group of items. **An index comprises a series of index numbers** and may be a **price index** or a **quantity index**.

1.1 Price indices and quantity indices

Key term

- A **price index** measures the change in the money value of a group of items over time.
- A **quantity index** (also called a volume index) measures the change in the non-monetary values of a group of items over time.

It is possible to prepare an index for a single item, but such an index would probably be unnecessary. **An index is a most useful measure of comparison when there is a group of items**.

1.2 Index points

The term 'points' refers to the difference between the index values in two years.

1.3 Example: Index points

For example, suppose that the index of food prices in 20X1 – 20X6 was as follows.

20X1	180
20X2	200
20X3	230
20X4	250
20X5	300
20X6	336

The index has risen 156 points between 20X1 and 20X6 (336 – 180). This is an increase of (156/180) × 100 = 86.7%.

Similarly, the index rose 36 points between 20X5 and 20X6 (336 – 300), a rise of 12%.

1.4 The base period, or base year

Index numbers normally take the value for a base date as 100. The base period is usually the starting point of the series, though this is not always the case.

2 Simple indices

FAST FORWARD

A **simple index** is an index which includes only one commodity in its calculation.

When one commodity only is under consideration, we have the following formulae.

Formula to learn

- **Price index** = $100 \times \dfrac{P_1}{P_0}$

- **Quantity index** = $100 \times \dfrac{Q_1}{Q_0}$

where P_1 = the price for the period under consideration
P_0 = the price for the base period
Q_1 = the quantity for the period under consideration
Q_0 = the quantity for the base period

2.1 Example: Single-item indices

(a) **Price index number**

If the price of a cup of coffee was 40p in 20X0, 50p in 20X1 and 76p in 20X2, then using 20X0 as a base year the **price index numbers** for 20X1 and 20X2 would be as follows.

20X1 price index = $100 \times \dfrac{50}{40} = 125$

20X2 price index = $100 \times \dfrac{76}{40} = 190$

(b) **Quantity index number**

If the number of cups of coffee sold in 20X0 was 500,000, in 20X1 700,000 and in 20X2 600,000, then using 20X0 as a base year, the **quantity index numbers** for 20X1 and 20X2 would be as follows.

20X1 quantity index = $100 \times \dfrac{700,000}{500,000} = 140$

20X2 quantity index = $100 \times \dfrac{600,000}{500,000} = 120$

PART C BUDGETING AND PERFORMANCE MEASUREMENT

3 Index relatives

FAST FORWARD

An **index relative** (sometimes just called a relative) is the name given to an index number which measures the change in a single distinct commodity.

Simple price indices and **simple quantity indices** are examples of price and quantity relatives respectively.

Index relatives can be calculated using the **fixed base method** or the **chain base method**.

We calculated price and quantity relatives for cups of coffee in Paragraph 2.2.

3.1 Time series of relatives

There are two ways in which index relatives can be calculated.

- The **fixed base method**
- The **chain base method**

3.2 Fixed base method

The **fixed base method**. A base year is selected (index 100), and all subsequent changes are measured against this base. Such an approach should only be used if **the basic nature of the commodity is unchanged over time**.

3.3 Example: Fixed base method

The price of a commodity was £2.70 in 20X0, £3.11 in 20X1, £3.42 in 20X2 and £3.83 in 20X3. Construct a **fixed base index** for the years 20X0 to 20X3 using 20X0 as the base year.

Solution

Fixed base index			
	20X0	100	
	20X1	115	
	20X2	127	$(3.42/2.70 \times 100)$
	20X3	142	$(3.83/2.70 \times 100)$

3.4 Chain base method

The **chain base method**. Changes are calculated with respect to the value of the commodity in the period immediately before. This approach can be used for any set of commodity values but must be used if **the basic nature of the commodity is changing over time**.

3.5 Example: Chain base method

Using the information in Paragraph 3.3 construct a chain base index for the years 20X0 to 20X3 using 20X0 as the base year.

Solution

Chain base index			
	20X0	100	
	20X1	115	$(3.11/2.70 \times 100)$
	20X2	110	$(3.42/3.11 \times 100)$
	20X3	112	$(3.83/3.42 \times 100)$

The chain base relatives show the rate of change in prices from year to year, whereas the fixed base relatives show changes relative to prices in the base year.

3.6 Rebasing

It is sometimes necessary to change the base of a time series (to **rebase**) of fixed base relatives, perhaps because the **base time point is too far in the past**. The following time series has a base date of 1970 which would probably be considered too out of date.

	1997	1998	1999	2000	2001	2002
Index (1977 = 100)	451	463	472	490	499	505

To change the base date, divide each relative by the relative corresponding to the new base time point and multiply the result by 100.

Question — Rebasing an index

Rebase the index in Paragraph 3.6 to 2000.

Answer

		1997	1998	1999	2000	2001	2002
Index (2000 = 100)	92*	94	96	100**	102***	103

* $451/490 \times 100$
** $490/490 \times 100$
*** $499/490 \times 100$

3.7 Comparing sets of fixed base relatives

FAST FORWARD

In order to compare two time series of relatives, each series should have the same base period and hence one (or both) may need **rebasing**.

You may be required to compare two sets of time series relatives. For example, an index of the annual number of advertisements placed by an organisation in the press and the index of the number of the organisation's product sold per annum might be compared. If the base years of the two indices differ, however, comparison is extremely difficult (as the illustration below shows).

	20W8	20W9	20X0	20X1	20X2	20X3	20X4
Number of advertisements Placed (20X0 = 100)	90	96	100	115	128	140	160
Volumes of sales (20W0 = 100)	340	347	355	420	472	515	572

From the figures above it is impossible to determine whether sales are increasing at a greater rate than the number of advertisements placed, or vice versa. This difficulty can be overcome by **rebasing** one set of relatives so that the **base dates are the same**. For example, we could rebase the index of volume of sales to 20X0.

	20W8	20W9	20X0	20X1	20X2	20X3	20X4
Number of advertisements Placed (20X0 = 100)	90	96	100	115	128	140	160
Volumes of sales (20X0 = 100)	96	98*	100	118	133**	145	161

* $347/355 \times 100$
** $472/355 \times 100$

The two sets of relatives are now much easier to compare. They show that volume of sales is increasing at a slightly faster rate, in general, than the number of advertisements placed.

PART C BUDGETING AND PERFORMANCE MEASUREMENT

4 Time series deflation

FAST FORWARD

The **real value** of a commodity can only be measured in terms of some **'indicator'** (such as the RPI).

Time series deflation is a technique used to obtain a set of index relatives that measure the changes in the real value of some commodity with respect to some given indicator.

The real value of a commodity can only be measured in terms of some **'indicator'** such as the **rate of inflation** (normally represented by the Retail Prices Index (RPI)). For example the cost of a commodity may have been £10 in 20X0 and £11 in 20X1, representing an increase of 10%. However, if we are told the prices **in general** (as measured by the RPI) increased by 12% between 20X0 and 20X1, we can argue that the **real** cost of the commodity has decreased.

An alternative measure of the rate of inflation is the Consumer Price Index (CPI) which is used in inflation targeting by the UK government and the Bank of England Monetary Policy Committee.

4.1 Example: Deflation

James Connolly works for W Watkins plc. Over the last five years he has received an annual salary increase of £500. Despite his employer assuring him that £500 is a reasonable annual salary increase, James is unhappy because, although he agrees £500 is a lot of money, he finds it difficult to maintain the standard of living he had when he first joined the company.

Consider the figures below.

Year	(a) Wages £	(b) Inflation index	(c) Inflated wages £	(d) Actual wages	(e) Real increase/(decrease) in wages
1	12,000	250	12,000	12,000	
2		260	12,480	12,500	
3		275	13,200	13,000	
4		295	14,160	13,500	
5		315	15,120	14,000	–7.4%

(a) This column shows James's wages when he first joined the company.

(b) This column shows the current inflation index.

(c) This column shows the inflated wages figures. The inflated wages represent what wages should be in order for James to keep up the standard of living he enjoyed when he first joined the company. These figures are calculated as follows.

Year 2

$$£12,000 \times \frac{260}{250} = £12,480$$

Year 3

$$£12,000 \times \frac{275}{250} = £13,200$$

Year 4

$$£12,000 \times \frac{295}{250} = £14,160$$

Year 5

$$£12,000 \times \frac{315}{250} = £15,120$$

(d) This column shows the actual wages James Connolly was paid in years 1 to 5.

(e) By year 5, James would expect to be earning £15,120 if his starting salary had increased in line with inflation. In year 5, James is earning £14,000 per annum, and this represents a '**real decrease**' in wages of 7.4% ((£15,120 − £14,000) ÷ £15,120 × 100% = 7.4%).

The real decrease in wages shows that the real value of James' wages has fallen by 7.4% over the five-year period. In order to keep up with inflation, James expects to earn £15,120 in year 5, but he is only earning £14,000. He is probably justified, therefore, in being unhappy.

Question — Time series

The mean weekly take-home pay of the employees of Staples Ltd and a price index for the 11 years from 20X0 to 20Y0 are as follows.

Year	Weekly wage £	Price index (20X0 = 100)
20X0	150	100
20X1	161	103
20X2	168	106
20X3	179	108
20X4	185	109
20X5	191	112
20X6	197	114
20X7	203	116
20X8	207	118
20X9	213	121
20Y0	231	123

Required

Construct a time series of real wages for 20X0 to 20Y0 using a price index with 20X6 as the base year.

Answer

The index number for each year with 20X6 as the base year will be the original index number divided by 114 (the price index in the base year). The real wages for each year will be (money wages × 100)/index number for the year).

Year	Index	Real wage £
20X0	88	170
20X1	90	179
20X2	93	181
20X3	95	188
20X4	96	193
20X5	98	195
20X6	100	197
20X7	102	199
20X8	104	199
20X9	106	201
20Y0	108	214

PART C BUDGETING AND PERFORMANCE MEASUREMENT

5 Composite index numbers

FAST FORWARD

Composite indices cover more than one item.

Most practical indices cover more than one item and are hence termed **composite index numbers**.

Suppose that the cost of living index is calculated from only three commodities: bread, tea and caviar, and that the prices for 20X1 and 20X2 were as follows.

	20X1	20X2
Bread	20p a loaf	40p a loaf
Tea	25p a packet	30p a packet
Caviar	450p a jar	405p a jar

A simple index could be calculated by adding the prices for single items in 20X2 and dividing by the corresponding sum relating to 20X1 (if 20X1 is the base year). In general, if the sum of the prices in the base year is ΣP_0 and the sum of the prices in the new year is ΣP_1, the index is $100 \times \dfrac{\Sigma P_1}{\Sigma P_0}$.

(The sign Σ (sigma) means sum of.) The index, known as a **simple aggregate price index**, would therefore be calculated as follows.

	P_0 20X1 £	P_1 20X2 £
Bread	0.20	0.40
Tea	0.25	0.30
Caviar	4.50	4.05
	$\Sigma P_0 = 4.95$	$\Sigma P_1 = 4.75$

Year	$\Sigma P_1 / \Sigma P_0$	Simple aggregate price index
20X1	4.95/4.95 = 1.00	100
20X2	4.75/4.95 = 0.96	96

The simple aggregate price index has a number of **disadvantages**.

(a) It ignores the **amounts** of bread, tea and caviar consumed (and hence the importance of each item).

(b) It ignores the **units** to which the prices refer. If, for example, we had been given the price of a cup of tea rather than a packet of tea, the index would have been different.

5.1 Average indices

To overcome the problem of different units we consider the changes in prices as **ratios** rather than absolutes so that all price movements, whatever their absolute values, are treated as equally important. Price changes are considered as ratios rather than absolutes by using the **average price relatives index**. Quantity changes are considered as ratios by using the **average quantity relatives index**.

Formula to learn

- **Average price relatives index** = $100 \times \dfrac{1}{n} \times \Sigma(P_1/P_0)$

- **Average quantity relatives index** = $100 \times \dfrac{1}{n} \times \Sigma(Q_1/Q_0)$

where n is the number of goods.

The price relative P_1/P_0 (so called because it gives the new price level of each item relative to the base year price) for a particular commodity will have the same value whatever the unit for which the price is quoted.

Using the cost of living indices given above, we can construct the **average price relatives index** as follows.

Commodity	P_0 £	P_1 £	P_1/P_0
Bread	0.20	0.40	2.00
Tea	0.25	0.30	1.20
Caviar	4.50	4.05	0.90
			4.10

Year	$\frac{1}{n}\Sigma(P_1/P_0)$	Average price relatives index
20X1	⅓ × 3.00 = 1.00	100
20X2	⅓ × 4.10 = 1.37	137

There has therefore been an average price increase of 37% between 20X1 and 20X2.

No account has been taken of the **relative importance** of each item in this index. Bread is probably more important than caviar. To overcome both the problem of quantities in different units and the need to attach importance to each item, we can use **weighting** which reflects the **importance of each item**. To decide the weightings of different items in an index, it is necessary to obtain information, perhaps by market research, about the **relative importance** of each item. The next section of this chapter shall look at **weighted index numbers**, the most important composite index number that you need to know about.

6 Weighted index numbers

FAST FORWARD

Weighting is used to reflect the importance of each item in the index.

Weighted average of relatives indices are found by calculating indices and then applying weights.

There are two types of index which give different weights to different items.

- Weighted average of relatives indices
- Weighted aggregate indices

6.1 Weighted average of relatives indices

This method of weighting involves calculating index relatives for each of the components and using the weights given to obtain a weighted average of the relatives.

Formula to learn

- Weighted average of price relative index = $\dfrac{\Sigma W \times P_1/P_0}{\Sigma W}$

- Weighted average of quantity relative index = $\dfrac{\Sigma W \times Q_1/Q_0}{\Sigma W}$

  where W = the weighting factor

6.2 Example: Weighted average of relatives indices

Use both the information in Section 5 and the following details about quantities purchased by each household in a week in 20X1 to determine a weighted average of price relatives index number for 20X2 using 20X1 as the base year.

	Quantity
Bread	12
Tea	5
Caviar	3

PART C BUDGETING AND PERFORMANCE MEASUREMENT

Solution

Price relatives (P_1/P_0)	Bread	40/20 =	2.00
	Tea	30/25 =	1.20
	Caviar	405/450 =	0.90
Weightings (W)	Bread		12.00
	Tea		5.00
	Caviar		3.00
		$\Sigma W =$	20.00
Index	Bread	2 × 12 =	24.00
	Tea	1.2 × 5 =	6.00
	Caviar	0.9 × 3 =	2.70
		$\Sigma W \times P_1/P_0 =$	32.70

Index number = $\dfrac{32.7}{20.0} \times 100 =$ 163.5

Question — Weighted average of relatives

The average prices of three commodities and the number of units used annually by a company are given below.

Commodity	20X1 Price per unit (P_0) £	20X2 Price per unit (P_1) £	Quantity Units
X	20	22	20
Y	40	48	2
Z	100	104	10

The price for 20X2 based on 20X1, calculated using the weighted average of relatives method is (to the nearest whole number)

A 107
B 108
C 109
D 110

Answer

Commodity	Price $\dfrac{P_1}{P_0}$	Weight (W)	Relative weight $\left(W \times \dfrac{P_1}{P_0}\right)$
X	$\dfrac{22}{20} = 1.1$	20	22.0
Y	$\dfrac{48}{40} = 1.2$	2	2.4
Z	$\dfrac{104}{100} = 1.04$	10	10.4
		$\Sigma W = 32$	34.8

Index = $\dfrac{34.8}{32} \times 100 = 108.75 = 109$

The correct answer is therefore C.

7 Laspeyre and Paasche indices

FAST FORWARD

There are two types of weighted aggregate index
- The Laspeyre
- The Paasche

The **Laspeyre** index uses quantities/prices from the **base period** as weights.

The **Paasche** index uses quantities/prices from the **current** period as weights.

Laspeyre and **Paasche** indices are special cases of **weighted aggregate indices**.

7.1 Laspeyre indices

Laspeyre indices use weights from the base period and are therefore sometimes called base weighted indices.

Exam formula

- Laspeyre price index = $100 \times \dfrac{\Sigma Q_0 P_1}{\Sigma Q_0 P_0}$

- Laspeyre quantity index = $100 \times \dfrac{\Sigma Q_1 P_0}{\Sigma Q_0 P_0}$

A Laspeyre price index uses quantities consumed in the base period as weights. A Laspeyre quantity index uses prices from the base period as weights.

7.2 Paasche indices

Paasche indices use current time period weights. In other words the weights are changed every time period.

Exam formula

- Paasche price index = $100 \times \dfrac{\Sigma Q_1 P_1}{\Sigma Q_1 P_0}$

- Paasche quantity index = $100 \times \dfrac{\Sigma Q_1 P_1}{\Sigma Q_0 P_1}$

A Paasche price index uses quantities consumed in the current period as weights. A Paasche quantity index uses prices from the current period as weights.

7.3 Example: Laspeyre and Paasche price indices

The wholesale price index in Ruritania is made up from the prices of five items. The price of each item, and the average quantities purchased by manufacturing and other companies each week were as follows, in 20X0 and 20X2.

Item	Quantity 20X0 '000 units	Price per unit 20X0 Roubles	Quantity 20X2 '000 units	Price per unit 20X2 Roubles
P	60	3	80	4
Q	30	6	40	5
R	40	5	20	8
S	100	2	150	2
T	20	7	10	10

Required

Calculate the price index in 20X2, if 20X0 is taken as the base year, using the following.

(a) A Laspeyre index
(b) A Paasche index

PART C BUDGETING AND PERFORMANCE MEASUREMENT

Solution

Workings

Item						Laspeyre		Paasche	
	Q_o	P_o	Q_1	P_1	Q_oP_o	Q_oP_1	Q_1P_1	Q_1P_o
P	60	3	80	4	180	240	320	240
Q	30	6	40	5	180	150	200	240
R	40	5	20	8	200	320	160	100
S	100	2	150	2	200	200	300	300
T	20	7	10	10	140	200	100	70
					900	1,110	1,080	950

20X2 index numbers are as follows.

(a) **Laspeyre index** $= 100 \times \dfrac{1,110}{900} = 123.3$

(b) **Paasche index** $= 100 \times \dfrac{1,080}{950} = 113.7$

The Paasche index for 20X2 reflects the decline in consumption of the relatively expensive items R and T since 20X0. The Laspeyre index for 20X2 fails to reflect this change.

Question — Laspeyre and Paasche

A baker has listed the ingredients he used and their prices, in 20X3 and 20X4, as follows.

	Kgs used 20X3 '000s	Price per kg 20X3 £	Kgs used 20X4 '000s	Price per kg 20X4 £
Milk	3	1.20	4	1.50
Eggs	6	0.95	5	0.98
Flour	1	1.40	2	1.30
Sugar	4	1.10	3	1.14

Required

Calculate the following quantity indices for 20X4 (with 20X3 as the base year).

(a) A Laspeyre index
(b) A Paasche index

Answer

Workings

	Q_0	P_0	Q_1	P_1	Q_0P_0	Laspeyre Q_1P_0	Q_1P_1	Paasche Q_0P_1
Milk	3	1.20	4	1.50	3.60	4.80	6.00	4.50
Eggs	6	0.95	5	0.98	5.70	4.75	4.90	5.88
Flour	1	1.40	2	1.30	1.40	2.80	2.60	1.30
Sugar	4	1.10	3	1.14	4.40	3.30	3.42	4.56
					15.10	15.65	16.92	16.24

Quantity index numbers for 20X4 are as follows.

(a) **Laspeyre method** = $100 \times \dfrac{15.65}{15.10} = 103.64$

(b) **Paasche method** = $100 \times \dfrac{16.92}{16.24} = 104.19$

7.4 Relative merits of the Laspeyre and Paasche indices

Both patterns of consumption and prices change and a decision therefore has to be made as to whether a Paasche or a Laspeyre index should be used.

The following points should be considered when deciding which type of index to use.

PAASCHE INDICES	LASPEYRE INDICES
(use weights from the current time period)	(use weights from the base period)
(a) Requires quantities to be ascertained each year which may be costly.	Requires quantities to be ascertained for base year only.
(b) The denominator has to be recalculated each year. The index cannot be calculated until the end of a period when the current prices/quantities are known.	The denominator is fixed. The index may therefore be calculated as soon as current prices/quantities are known.
(c) Because the denominator has to be recalculated each year, comparisons can only be drawn directly between the current year and the base year.	Because the denominator is fixed, the Laspeyre index numbers for several years can be directly compared.
(d) Paasche indices are updated each year.	The weights for a Laspeyre index become out of date.
(e) The effect of current year weighting means that greater importance is placed on goods that are relatively cheaper now than they were in the base year. Inflation could therefore be understated.	Assumes that whatever the price changes, the quantities purchased will remain the same. It therefore assumes that as goods become relatively more expensive, the same quantities will be purchased. Inflation could therefore be overstated.

In practice, it is common to use a Laspeyre index and revise the weights every few years. (Where appropriate, a new base year may be created when the weights are changed.)

PART C BUDGETING AND PERFORMANCE MEASUREMENT

Exam focus point

If you get confused between **Laspeyre** and **Paasche** indices remember that 'L' (for Laspeyre) comes **before** 'P' (for Paasche) in the alphabet and that Laspeyre indices use weights from the **base** year which comes **before** the **current** year (the provider of weights for Paasche indices).

Chapter Roundup

- An **index** is a measure, over time, of the average changes in the values (prices or quantities) of a group of items. **An index comprises a series of index numbers** and may be a **price index** or a **quantity index**.

- A **simple index** is an index which includes only one commodity in its calculation.

- An **index relative** (sometimes just called a relative) is the name given to an index number which measures the change in a single distinct commodity.

- **Simple price indices** and **simple quantity indices** are examples of price and quantity relatives respectively.

- Index relatives can be calculated using the **fixed base method** or the **chain base method**.

- In order to compare two time series of relatives, each series should have the same base period and hence one (or both) may need **rebasing**.

- The **real value** of a commodity can only be measured in terms of some '**indicator**' (such as the RPI).

- **Time series deflation** is a technique used to obtain a set of index relatives that measure the changes in the real value of some commodity with respect to some given indicator.

- **Composite indices** cover more than one item.

- **Weighting** is used to reflect the importance of each item in the index.

- **Weighted average of relatives indices** are found by calculating indices and then applying weights.

- There are two types of weighted aggregate index
    - The Laspeyre
    - The Paasche

- The **Laspeyre** index uses quantities/prices from the **base period** as weights.

- The **Paasche** index uses quantities/prices from the **current** period as weights.

Quick Quiz

1. What does a price index measure?

2. What does a quantity index measure?

3. Complete the following equations using the symbols in the box below.

    (a) **Price index** =   × 100

    (b) **Quantity index** =   × 100

P_1	P_0
Q_1	Q_0

4. An index relative is the name given to an index number which measures the change in a group of items.

    ☐ True

    ☐ False

5.
    Fixed base method   ?   Changes are measured against base period

    Chain base method   Changes are measured against the previous period

6. What is a composite index number?

7. There are two types of index which give different weights to different items.

    - Weighted average of relatives indices
    - Weighted aggregate indices
    - What is the general form of a weighted average of quantity relative index number?

8. Laspeyre indices use quantities/prices from the (1) .... period as weights whilst the Paasche indices use quantities/prices from the (2) .... period as weights.

PART C BUDGETING AND PERFORMANCE MEASUREMENT

Answers to Quick Quiz

1. The change in the money value of a group of items over time.

2. The change in the non-monetary values of a group of items over time.

3. (a) Price index = $\dfrac{P_1}{P_0} \times 100$

   (b) Quantity index = $\dfrac{Q_1}{Q_0} \times 100$

4. False. An index relative is an index number which measures the change in a **single distinct commodity.**

5. Fixed base method → Changes are measured against the base period
   Chain base method → Changes are measured against the previous period

6. A composite index number is an index covering more than one item.

7. $\dfrac{\sum W \times \dfrac{Q_1}{Q_0}}{\sum W}$

   Where W = the weighing factor

   $\dfrac{Q_1}{Q_0}$ = the index relative

8. (1) base
   (2) current

Now try the questions below from the Exam Question Bank

Number	Level	Marks	Time
Q15	Introductory	n/a	15 mins

Performance measurement

Topic list	Syllabus reference
1 Performance measurement	9
2 Responsibility centres	9
3 Measuring profitability, productivity and activity	9
4 Performance measures for manufacturing businesses	9
5 Performance measures for services	9
6 Performance measures for non-profit making organisations	9
7 Benchmarking	9(g)
8 Management performance measures	9

Introduction

Performance measurement is the final chapter in the management accounting section of this Study Text. The chapter begins by introducing the term **performance measurement** and then describes the various performance measures that are used by various types of entity. Variances are an important measure of performance that you have already met.

It is important that the performance of an organisation is monitored, and this is most commonly done by calculating a number of ratios. **Benchmarking** is a type of comparison exercise through which an organisation attempts to improve performance.

Finally we shall be looking at **management performance measures**. We introduced this idea in Chapter 7 when we discussed the controllability of costs and responsibility accounting. It is important that you are able to distinguish between measures of performance of **individual managers** and measures of performance of **what it is they manage**.

PART C BUDGETING AND PERFORMANCE MEASUREMENT

Study guide

Section 28 – Performance measurement

- Outline the essential features of responsibility accounting for various types of entity
- Describe the range of management performance measures available for various types of entity
- Calculate and explain the concepts of return on investment and residual income
- Explain and give examples of appropriate non-monetary performance measures
- Describe the various types of responsibility centre and the impact of these on management appraisal
- Discuss the potential conflict in the use of a measure for both business and management performance
- Analyse the application of financial performance measures including cost, profit, return on capital employed
- Assess and illustrate the measurement of profitability, activity and productivity
- Discuss the measurement of quality and service
- Identify areas of concern from information supplied and performance measures calculated
- Describe the features of benchmarking and its application to performance appraisal

Exam guide

Make sure that you can calculate all of the ratios covered in this chapter – they could well be tested in Section A of your examination.

1 Performance measurement   12/04

> **FAST FORWARD**
>
> **Performance measurement** aims to establish how well something or somebody is doing in relation to a plan.
>
> Performance measures may be divided into two groups.
>
> - Financial performance measures
> - Non-monetary performance measures

Performance measurement aims to establish how well something or somebody is doing in relation to a plan. The 'thing' may be a machine, a factory, a subsidiary company or an organisation as a whole. The 'body' may be an individual employee, a manager or a group of people.

Performance measurement is a **vital part of** the **control process.**

1.1 Performance measures

Different measures are appropriate for different businesses. Factors to consider:

(a) **Measurement needs resources** – people, equipment and time to collect and analyse information. The costs and benefits of providing resources to produce a performance indicator must be carefully weighed up.

(b) **Performance must be measured in relation to something**, otherwise measurement is meaningless. Overall performance should be measured against the **objectives** of the organisation and the **plans** that result from those objectives. If the organisation has no clear objectives, the first step in performance measurement is to set them. The second is to identify the factors that are critical to the success of those objectives.

(c) **Measures must be relevant**. This means finding out what the organisation does and how it does it so that measures reflect what actually occurs.

(d) **Short** and **long-term achievement** should be measured. Short-term targets can be valuable, but exclusive use of them may direct the organisation away from opportunities that will mean success for the business in the long-term.

(e) Measures should be **fair**. They should only include factors which managers can control by their decisions, and for which they can be held **responsible**. Measuring controllable costs, revenues and assets may prove controversial however.

(f) A **variety** of measures should be used. Managers may be able to find ways to distort a single measure, but should not be able to affect a variety of measures. The balanced scorecard (Section 7) provides a method of measuring performance from a number of perspectives.

(g) **Realistic estimates** may be required for measures to be employed. These include estimates of financial items whose value is not certain, such as the cost of capital, and estimates of the impact of non-financial items.

(h) Measurement needs **responses,** above all managers to make decisions in the best interests of the organisation. Managers will only respond to measures that they find useful. The management accountant therefore needs to adopt a modern marketing philosophy to the provision of performance measures: satisfy customer wants, not pile 'em high and sell 'em cheap.

Once suitable performance measures have been selected they must be **monitored on a regular basis** to ensure that they are providing useful information. There is little point in an organisation devoting considerable resources to measuring market share if an increase in market share is not one of the organisation's objectives.

Performance measures may be divided into two groups.

- Financial performance measures
- Non-monetary performance measures.

1.2 Financial performance measures

Financial measures (or **monetary** measures) include:

Measure	Example
Profit	**Profit** is the commonest measure of all. Profit maximisation is usually cited as the main objective of most business organisations: 'ICI increased pre-tax profits to £233m'; 'General Motors... yesterday reported better-than-expected first-quarter net income of $513 (£333m) ... Earnings improved $680m from the first quarter of last year when GM lost $167m.
Revenue	'the US businesses contributed £113.9m of total group turnover of £409m'.
Costs	'Sterling's fall benefited pre-tax profits by about £50m while savings from the cost-cutting programme instituted in 1991 were running at around £100m a quarter'; 'The group interest charge rose from £48m to £61m'.
Share price	'The group's shares rose 31p to 1,278p despite the market's fall'.
Cash flow	'Cash flow was also continuing to improve, with cash and marketable securities totalling $8.4bn on March 31, up from $8bn at December 31'.

Note that the monetary amounts stated are **only given meaning in relation to something else**. Financial results should be compared against a **yard-stick** such as:

- Budgeted **sales**, **costs** and **profits**
- **Standards** in a standard costing system
- The **trend** over time (last year/this year, say)
- The results of **other parts of the business**
- The results of **other businesses**
- The **economy** in general
- **Future potential** (for example the performance of a new business may be judged in terms of nearness to breaking even).

1.3 Non-monetary performance measures

> **FAST FORWARD**
>
> Performance measures can be **quantitative** or **qualitative**.
>
> **Non-financial indicators (NFIs)** are useful in a modern business environment.
>
> **Ratios** and **percentages** are useful performance measurement techniques.

1.3.1 Quantitative and qualitative performance measures

Quantitative information is capable of being expressed in numbers. Qualitative information is not numeric. Qualitative information can sometimes be converted into numeric through tools such as ranking scales. For example 1 = Good, 2 = Average, 3 = Poor.

(a) An example of a **quantitative** performance measure is 'You have been late for work **twice** this week and it's only Tuesday!'.

(b) An example of a **qualitative** performance measure is 'My bed is **very** comfortable'.

The first measure is likely to find its way into a **staff appraisal report**. The second would feature in a bed manufacturer's **customer satisfaction survey**. Both are indicators of whether their subjects are doing as good a job as they are required to do.

Qualitative measures are by nature **subjective** and **judgmental** but they can still be useful. They are especially valuable when they are derived from several **different sources**, as the likelihood of an unreliable judgement is reduced.

Consider the statement.

'Seven out of ten customers think our beds are very comfortable.'

This is a **quantitative measure** of customer satisfaction (7 out of 10), as well as a **qualitative measure** of the perceived performance of the beds (very comfortable).

1.3.2 Non-financial indicators

Financial measures do not convey the full picture of a company's performance, especially in a **modern business environment**. In today's global environment, organisations are **competing** in terms of product quality, delivery, reliability, after-sales service and customer satisfaction. None of these variables is directly measured by a traditional accounting system.

Organisations are increasingly using quantitative and qualitative **non-financial indicators (NFIs)** such as:

- Quality rating
- Number of customer complaints
- Number of warranty claims
- Lead times
- Rework
- Delivery to time
- Non-productive hours
- System (machine) down time

Unlike traditional variance reports, measures such as these can be **provided quickly** for managers, per shift or on a daily or even hourly basis as required. They are likely to be **easy to calculate**, and **easier** for non-financial managers **to understand** and therefore to use effectively.

Anything can be compared if it is meaningful to do so. The measures should be **tailored to the** circumstances. For example, the number of coffee breaks per 20 pages of text might indicate to you how hard you are studying!

Exam focus point

If you are asked to suggest suitable performance measures in an exam, think about NFIs. Remember that anything can be compared if it is meaningful to do so.

1.3.3 Ratios

Ratios are a useful performance measurement technique.

(a) It is **easier to look at changes over time** by comparing ratios in one time period with the corresponding ratios for periods in the past.

(b) Ratios are often **easier to understand than absolute measures** of physical quantities or money values. For example, it is easier to understand that 'productivity in March was 94%' than 'there was an adverse labour efficiency variance in March of £3,600'.

(c) Ratios **relate one item to another, and so help to put performance into context**. For example the profit/sales ratio sets profit in the context of how much has been earned per £1 of sales, and so shows how wide or narrow profit margins are.

(d) Ratios can be used as **targets,** for example for productivity. Managers will then take decisions which will enable them to achieve their targets.

(e) Ratios provide a way of **summarising** an organisation's results, and **comparing** them with similar organisations.

1.3.4 Percentages

A percentage expresses one number as a proportion of another and **gives meaning to absolute numbers**. Market share, capacity levels, wastage and staff turnover are often expressed using percentages.

2 Responsibility centres   12/05

FAST FORWARD

Responsibility accounting is a system of accounting that segregates revenue and costs into areas of personal responsibility in order to monitor and assess the performance of each part of an organisation.

A **responsibility centre** is a function or department of an organisation that is headed by a manager who has direct responsibility for its performance.

A **cost centre** is any unit of an organisation to which costs can be separately attributed.

A **profit centre** is any unit of an organisation to which both revenues and costs are assigned, so that the profitability of the unit may be measured.

A **revenue centre** is where managers only have control over maximising of revenues.

> An **investment centre** is a profit centre whose performance is measured by its return on capital employed.

We had a brief introduction to responsibility centres (cost centres, profit centres and investment centres) in Chapter 3 when we studied cost classification. We are now going to look at these centres in more detail as we continue our study of **performance measurement**.

Key term

> **Responsibility accounting** is a system of accounting that segregates revenue and costs into areas of personal responsibility in order to monitor and assess the performance of each part of an organisation.

If a manager is to bear responsibility for the performance of his area of the business he will need information about its performance. In essence, a manager needs to know three things.

Requirements	Examples of information
What are his resources?	Finance, stocks of raw materials, spare machine capacity, labour availability, the balance of expenditure remaining for a certain budget, target date for completion of a job.
At what rate are his resources being consumed?	How fast is his labour force working, how quickly are his raw materials being used up, how quickly are other expenses being incurred, how quickly is available finance being consumed?
How well are the resources being used?	How well are his objectives being met?

Decisions must also be made as to the level of detail that is provided and the frequency with which information is provided. Moreover the cost of providing information must be weighed against the benefit derived from it.

In a traditional system managers are given monthly reports, but there is no logical reason for this except that it ties in with financial reporting cycles and may be administratively convenient. With modern systems, however, there is a danger of **information overload**, since information technology allows the information required to be made available much more frequently.

The task of the management accountant, therefore, is to learn from the managers of responsibility centres what information they need, in what form and at what intervals, and then to design a planning and control system that enables this to be provided.

It is to this end that responsibility centres are usually divided into different categories. Here we shall describe cost centres, profit centres and investment centres.

2.1 Cost centres

To charge actual costs to a cost centre, each cost centre will have a **cost code**. Items of expenditure will be recorded with the appropriate cost code. When costs are eventually analysed, there may well be some apportionment of the costs of one cost centre to other cost centres. If this happens:

(a) The costs of those cost centres which receive an apportionment of shared costs should be divided into directly attributable costs (for which the cost centre manager is responsible) and shared costs (for which another cost centre is directly accountable).

(b) The **control system** should **trace shared costs back to the cost centres from which the costs have been apportioned**, so that their **managers can be made accountable** for the costs incurred.

Information about cost centres might be collected in terms of **total actual costs, total budgeted costs** and **total cost variances** (the differences between actual and budgeted costs) sub-analysed perhaps into efficiency, usage and expenditure variances. In addition, the information might be analysed in terms of **ratios**, such the following.

- Cost per unit produced (budget and actual)
- Hours per unit produced (budget and actual)
- Efficiency ratio
- Selling costs per £ of sales (budget and actual)
- Transport costs per tonne/kilometre (budget and actual)

Problems with using variances include:

- They focus on **short-term cost minimisation** rather than longer-term quality or delivery.
- It may be difficult to determine who is **responsible** for which variance.
- The variance levels are dependent upon the **standards** that were set originally.

2.2 Profit centres

Profit centres differ from cost centres in that they **account for both costs and revenues** and the **key performance measure** of a profit centre is therefore **profit**.

For profit centres to have any validity in a planning and control system based on responsibility accounting, **the manager of the profit centre must have some influence over both revenues and costs**, that is, a say in both sales and production policies.

A profit centre manager is likely to be a fairly senior person within an organisation, and a profit centre is likely to cover quite a large area of operations. A profit centre might be an entire division within the organisation, or there might be a separate profit centre for each product, product range, brand or service that the organisation sells.

In the hierarchy of responsibility centres within an organisation, there are likely to be several cost centres within a profit centre.

When reporting performance, profit centres should clearly distinguish controllable costs from other costs that are relevant to that centre.

	£	£
Sales		X
Controllable variable costs	X	
Controllable fixed costs	X	X
Controllable profit		X
Other traceable variable costs	X	
Other traceable fixed costs	X	X
Traceable profit		X
Apportioned costs		X
Net profit		X

2.3 Revenue centres

Revenue centres are where managers only have control over maximising of revenues. All decisions about costs are taken elsewhere, possibly centrally.

2.4 Investment centres

An **investment centre** is a profit centre whose performance is measured by its return on capital employed. (We shall be studying this performance measure in detail in the next section of this chapter.)

This implies that the **investment centre manager has some say in investment policy** in his area of operations as well as being responsible for costs and revenues.

Several profit centres might share the same capital items, for example the same buildings, stores or transport fleet, and so investment centres are likely to include several profit centres, and provide a basis for control at a very senior management level, like that of a subsidiary company within a group.

PART C   BUDGETING AND PERFORMANCE MEASUREMENT

3 Measuring profitability, productivity and activity

12/05

> **FAST FORWARD**
>
> **Return on investment (ROI)** or **return on capital employed (ROCE)** shows how much profit has been made in relation to the amount of resources invested.
>
> The **profit margin** (profit to sales ratio) is calculated as (profit ÷ sales) × 100%.
>
> **Residual income (RI)** is an alternative way of measuring the performance of an investment centre. It is a measure of the centre's profits after deducting a notional or imputed interest cost.

3.1 Profitability

3.1.1 Return on investment (ROI)

Key term

> **Return on investment (ROI)** (also called **return on capital employed (ROCE)**) is calculated as (profit before interest and tax/capital employed) × 100% and shows how much profit has been made in relation to the amount of resources invested.

Profits alone do not show whether the return is sufficient, in view of the value of assets committed. Thus if company A and company B have the following results, company B would have the better performance.

	A	B
	£	£
Profit	5,000	5,000
Sales	100,000	100,000
Capital employed	50,000	25,000
ROI	10%	20%

The profit of each company is the same but company B only invested £25,000 to achieve that profit whereas company A invested £50,000.

Overall ROI may be calculated in a number of ways, but management accountants prefer to exclude from profits all revenues and expenditures not related to the core operation of the business (such as interest payable and income from trade investments). **Profit before interest and tax** is therefore often used.

Similarly **all assets of a non-operational nature** (for example trade investments and intangible assets such as goodwill) **should be excluded** from capital employed.

Profits should be related to average capital employed. In practice many companies calculate the ratio **using year-end assets**. This can be misleading. If a new investment is undertaken near to year end and financed, for example, by an issue of shares, the capital employed will rise by the finance raised but profits will only have a month or two of the new investment's contribution.

What does the ROI tell us? What should we be looking for? There are **two principal comparisons** that can be made.

- The change in ROI from one year to the next
- The ROI being earned by other entities

If the ROI is being measured for an investment centre, it is important to compare like-with-like, so that **controllable profit** is compared with **controllable investment**.

3.1.2 Residual income

Key term

> **Residual income (RI)** is 'Pretax profits less an imputed interest charge for invested capital. Used to assess divisional performance'.

Residual income (RI) is an alternative way of measuring the performance of an investment centre, instead of using ROI.

(a) The centre's profit is **after deducting depreciation** on capital equipment.

(b) The imputed cost of capital might be the organisation's cost of borrowing or its weighted average cost of capital.

3.1.3 ROI v residual income

ROI and residual income can sometimes give different indications if they are being used for decision-making.

3.1.4 Example: ROI vs residual income

Division S is part of Paul plc. It currently has net assets of £5 million and makes an annual profit of £1 million. Its cost of capital is 8%.

The division's manager is considering a proposed investment which will involve £2.5 million expenditure on fixed assets and generate a net profit of £250,000.

Required

Calculate the return on investment and residual income under the current situation and assuming the investment takes place, and comment on your results.

Solution

Under the current arrangement:

Return on investment = 1/5 = 20%

Assuming new investment is undertaken:

Return on investment = 1 + 0.25/5 + 2.5 = 16.7%

Under the current arrangement:

Residual income = 1 − (0.08 × 5) = £0.6 m

Assuming new investment is undertaken:

Residual income = 1 + 0.25 − 0.08 (5 + 2.5) = £0.65m.

The two measures give different results; residual income has increased, but return on investment has fallen. As the project generates a return, 10% $\frac{£250,000}{£2.5 \text{ million}}$, that is greater than the cost of capital, it should be accepted, even though return on investment has fallen.

ROI is also a **relative measure**; if two projects are being compared, the project with the higher ROI may give the smaller absolute return. RI measures absolute values, although this may cause problems where investment centres of different sizes are being compared. The fact that one centre has a higher RI than another may be due to its original size rather than better performance.

The RI versus ROI comparison is similar to the comparison between **net present value** and **internal rate of return**, which we shall cover in Chapter 26. However ROI and RI are often both used as short-term measures (an investment should exceed X%/£X in the next three years), and both measures may therefore conflict with the net present value method which focuses on **long-term** positive returns.

Other problems with ROI and RI include the following:

(a) The values are dependent on the **accounting polices** used and the way assets are measured.

(b) Depreciation can cause distortions, both in terms of the **accounting policies** applied, and for ROI in its effect on book value. ROI may improve solely because an asset is being depreciated, and hence the capital employed appears to be falling.

3.1.5 Profit margin

The **profit margin** (profit to sales ratio) is calculated as (profit ÷ sales) × 100%.

The profit margin provides a simple measure of performance for management. Investigation of unsatisfactory profit margins enables control action to be taken, either by reducing excessive costs or by raising selling prices.

Profit margin is usually calculated using operating profit.

3.1.6 Example: The profit to sales ratio

A company compares its year 2 results with year 1 results as follows.

	Year 2 £	Year 1 £
Sales	160,000	120,000
Cost of sales		
Direct materials	40,000	20,000
Direct labour	40,000	30,000
Production overhead	22,000	20,000
Marketing overhead	42,000	35,000
	144,000	105,000
Profit	16,000	15,000
Profit to sales ratio	10%	12½%

Ratio analysis on the above information shows that there is a decline in profitability in spite of the £1,000 increase in profit, because the profit margin is less in year 2 than year 1.

3.1.7 Gross profit margin

The profit to sales ratio above was based on a profit figure which included non-production overheads. The **pure trading activities of a business can be analysed** using the gross profit margin, which is calculated as (gross profit ÷ turnover) × 100%.

For the company in Paragraph 3.8 the gross profit margin in year 1 would be:

((16,000 + 42,000)/160,000) × 100% = 36.25% in year 2 and ((15,000 + 35,000)/120,000) × 100% = 41.67%

3.1.8 Cost/sales ratios

There are three principal ratios for analysing profit and loss account information.

- Production cost of sales ÷ sales
- Distribution and marketing costs ÷ sales
- Administrative costs ÷ sales

When particular areas of weakness are found subsidiary ratios are used to examine them in greater depth. For example, for production costs the following ratios might be used.

- Material costs ÷ sales value of production
- Works labour costs ÷ sales value of production
- Production overheads ÷ sales value of production

3.1.9 Example: Cost/sales ratios

Look back to the example in Paragraph 3.8. A more detailed analysis would show that higher direct materials are the probable cause of the decline in profitability.

	Year 2	Year 1
Material costs/sales	25%	16.7%

Other cost/sales ratios have remained the same or improved.

3.2 Productivity

This is the quantity of the product or service produced **(output) in relation to** the resources put in **(input)**. For example so many units produced per hour, or per employee, or per tonne of material. It measures **how efficiently resources are being used**.

3.3 Activity

Indices can be used in order to measure activity. We studied index numbers in the previous chapter.

You will remember that indices show **how a particular variable has changed relative to a base value**. The base value is usually the level of the variable at an earlier date. The 'variable' may be just one particular item, such as material X, or several items may be incorporated, such as 'raw materials' generally.

In its simplest form an index is calculated as **(current value ÷ base value) × 100%**.

Thus if materials cost £15 per kg in 20X0 and now (20X3) cost £27 per kg the 20X0 value would be expressed in index form as 100 (15/15 × 100) and the 20X3 value as 180 (27/15 × 100). If you find it easier to think of this as a percentage, then do so.

3.4 Example: Work standards and indices

Standards for work done in a service department could be expressed as an index. For example, suppose that in a sales department, there is a standard target for sales representatives to make 25 customer visits per month each. The budget for May might be for ten sales representatives to make 250 customer visits in total. Actual results in May might be that nine sales representatives made 234 visits in total. Performance could then be measured as:

Budget	100	(Standard = index 100)
Actual	104	(234 ÷ (9 × 25)) × 100)

This shows that 'productivity' per sales representative was actually 4% over budget.

Question — Residual income

A division with capital employed of £400,000 currently earns a ROI of 22%. It can make an additional investment of £50,000 for a 5 year life with nil residual value. The average net profit from this investment would be £12,000 after depreciation. The division's cost of capital is 14%.

Required

Calculate the residual income before and after the investment.

Answer

	Before investment £	After investment £
Divisional profit	88,000	100,000
Imputed interest		
(400,000 × 0.14)	56,000	
(450,000 × 0.14)		63,000
Residual income	32,000	37,000

4 Performance measures for manufacturing businesses

FAST FORWARD

Performance measures for **materials** and **labour** include variances. Performance can also be measured using the **standard hour**.

4.1 Performance measures for sales

Traditionally sales performance is measured in terms of price and volume variances, and a sales mix variance. Other possible measures include revenue targets and target market share. They may be analysed in detail: by country, by region, by individual products, by salesperson and so on.

In a customer-focused organisation the basic information 'Turnover is up by 14%' can be supplemented by a host of other indicators.

(a) **Customer rejects/returns: total sales**. This ratio helps to monitor customer satisfaction, providing a check on the efficiency of quality control procedures.

(b) **Deliveries late: deliveries on schedule**. This ratio can be applied both to sales made to customers and to receipts from suppliers. When applied to customers it provides an indication of the efficiency of production and production scheduling.

(c) **Flexibility measures** indicate how well able a company is to respond to customers' requirements. Measures could be devised to measure how quickly and efficiently **new products** are launched, and how well procedures meet **customer needs**.

(d) **Number of people served and speed of service**, in a shop or a bank for example. If it takes too long to reach the point of sale, future sales are liable to be lost.

(e) **Customer satisfaction questionnaires,** for input to the organisation's management information system.

4.2 Performance measures for materials

Traditional measures are **standard costs,** and price and usage **variances**. Many traditional systems also analyse **wastage**.

Measures used in **modern manufacturing environments** include the number of **rejects** in materials supplied, and the **timing and reliability of deliveries** of materials.

4.3 Performance measures for labour

Labour costs are traditionally measured in terms of **standard performance** (ideal, attainable and so on) and rate and efficiency **variances**.

Qualitative measures of labour performance concentrate on matters such as **ability to communicate**, **interpersonal relationships** with colleagues, **customers' impressions** and **levels of skills** attained.

Managers can expect to be judged to some extent by the performance of their staff. High profitability or tight cost control are not the only indicators of managerial performance!

4.4 Performance measures for overheads

Standards for variable overheads and efficiency variances are traditional measures. Various time based measure are also available, such as:

(a) **Machine down time: total machine hours**. This ratio provides a measure of machine usage and efficiency.

(b) **Value added time: production cycle time**. Value added time is the direct production time during which the product is being made. The production cycle time includes non-value-added times such as set-up time, downtime, idle time and so on. The 'perfect' ratio is 100%, but in practice this optimum will not be achieved. A high ratio means non-value-added activities are being kept to a minimum.

4.5 Measures of performance using the standard hour

Sam Ltd manufactures plates, mugs and eggcups. Production during the first two quarters of 20X5 was as follows.

	Quarter 1	Quarter 2
Plates	1,000	800
Mugs	1,200	1,500
Eggcups	800	900

The fact that 3,000 products were produced in quarter 1 and 3,200 in quarter 2 does not tell us anything about Sam Ltd's performance over the two periods because plates, mugs and eggcups are so different. The fact that the production mix has changed is not revealed by considering the total number of units produced. The problem of how to **measure output when a number of dissimilar products are manufactured** can be overcome, however, by the **use of the standard hour**.

The standard hour (or standard minute) is the **quantity of work achievable at standard performance, expressed in terms of a standard unit of work done in a standard period of time.**

The standard time allowed to produce one unit of each of Sam Ltd's products is as follows.

	Standard time
Plate	½ hour
Mug	⅓ hour
Eggcup	¼ hour

By measuring the standard hours of output in each quarter, a more useful output measure is obtained.

Product	Standard hours per unit	Quarter 1 Production	Standard hours	Quarter 2 Production	Standard hours
Plate	½	1,000	500	800	400
Mug	⅓	1,200	400	1,500	500
Eggcup	¼	800	200	900	225
			1,100		1,125

The output level in the two quarters was therefore very similar.

4.6 Efficiency, activity and capacity ratios

Standard hours are useful in computing levels of **efficiency, activity and capacity**. Any management accounting reports involving budgets and variance analysis should incorporate control ratios. The three main control ratios are the **efficiency, capacity** and **activity** ratios.

(a) The **capacity ratio compares actual hours worked and budgeted hours**, and measures the **extent to which planned utilisation has been achieved.**

(b) The **activity or production volume ratio compares the number of standard hours equivalent to the actual work produced and budgeted hours.**

(c) **The efficiency ratio** measures the **efficiency of the labour force** by **comparing equivalent standard hours for work produced and actual hours worked.**

4.7 Example: Ratios and standard hours

Given the following information about Sam Ltd for quarter 1 of 20X5, calculate a capacity ratio, an activity ratio and an efficiency ratio and explain their meaning.

Budgeted hours   1,100 standard hours
Standard hours produced   1,125 standard hours
Actual hours worked   1,200

Solution

Capacity ratio $= \dfrac{\text{Actual hours worked}}{\text{Budgeted hours}} \times 100\% = \dfrac{1{,}200}{1{,}100} \times 100\% = 109\%$

Activity ratio $= \dfrac{\text{Standard hours produced}}{\text{Budgeted hours}} \times 100\% = \dfrac{1{,}125}{1{,}100} \times 100\% = 102\%$

The overall activity or production volume for the quarter was 2% greater than forecast. This was achieved by a 9% increase in capacity.

Efficiency ratio $= \dfrac{\text{Standard hours produced}}{\text{Actual hours worked}} \times 100\% = \dfrac{1{,}125}{1{,}200} \times 100\% = 94\%$

The labour force worked 9% below standard levels of efficiency.

5 Performance measures for services

> **FAST FORWARD**
>
> Performance measures covering the following six 'dimensions' have been suggested for service organisations.
>
> - Competitive performance
> - Financial performance
> - Quality of service
> - Flexibility
> - Resource utilisation
> - Innovation

5.1 Service businesses

A service business does not produce a physical product. Instead it provides a service, for example a haircut, or insurance.

13: PERFORMANCE MEASUREMENT

(a) A service is **intangible**. The actual benefit being bought can not be touched.

(b) The production and consumption of a service are **simultaneous**, and therefore it cannot be inspected for quality in advance.

(c) Services are **perishable**, that is, they cannot be stored. For example a hairdresser cannot do haircuts in advance and keep them stocked away in case of heavy demand.

(d) A service is **heterogeneous**. The service received will vary each time. Services are more reliant on people. People are not robots, so how the service is delivered will not be identical each time.

5.2 'Dimensions' of performance measurement

Performance measurement in service businesses is made more difficult because of the four factors listed above. However, performance measurement is possible, the key being to ensure what you are measuring has been clearly enough defined. A range of performance measures covering **six 'dimensions'** are used.

5.2.1 Competitive performance

Competitive performance focuses on factors such as sales growth, market share and ability to obtain new business.

5.2.2 Financial performance

Like any other business, a service business needs to plan, and its short-term plans can be drawn up in the form of a **budget**.

(a) There might be a **budgeted expenditure limit** for individual activities within the business.

(b) **Standard performance measures** (such as standard cost per unit of activity or standard quantity of 'output' per unit of resource used up (ie productivity)) can be established as targets.

5.2.3 Quality of service

Service quality is measured principally by **qualitative measures**, although some quantitative measures are used by some businesses. An equipment hire company used a 'successful hire indicator'. This was expressed as a percentage. All hires has to be classified as successful or unsuccessful (based on equipment performance) when equipment was returned.

The following table shows the measures used to assess 4 quality factors and the means of obtaining the information by British Airports Authority (BAA), a transport facility service provider.

Service quality factors	Measures	Mechanisms
Access	Walking distances Ease of finding way around	Customer survey and internal operational data
Cleanliness/tidiness	Cleanliness of environment and equipment	Customer survey and management inspection
Comfort	Crowdedness of airport	Customer survey and management inspection
Friendliness	Staff attitude and helpfulness	Customer survey and management inspection

5.2.4 Flexibility

Flexibility has three aspects.

(a) **Speed of delivery** is vital in some service industries. Measures include factors such as waiting time in queues.

In other types of service it may be more a question of timeliness. Does the auditor turn up to do the annual audit during the appointed week? Is the audit done within the time anticipated by the partner or does it drag on for weeks? These aspects are all easily measurable in terms of 'days late'. Depending upon the circumstances 'days late' may also reflect on inability to cope with fluctuations in demand.

(b) The ability of a service organisation to **respond to customers' specifications** will depend on the type of service. A professional service such as legal advice must be tailored exactly to the customer's needs. Performance is partly a matter of customer perception. Customer attitude surveys may be appropriate. Performance also depends on the diversity of skills possessed by the service organisation. This can be measured in terms of the mix of staff skills and the amount of time spent on training.

(c) **Coping with demand** is measurable in quantitative terms. For example train companies can measure the extent of overcrowding. Customer queuing time can be for banks and retailers. Professional services can measure levels of overtime worked.

5.2.5 Resource utilisation measures

Resource utilisation is usually measured in terms of **productivity**. The ease with which this may be measured varies according to the service being delivered. The main input resource of a firm of accountants, for example, is the **time** of staff. The main output of an accountancy firm is **chargeable hours**. Productivity will therefore be measured as the ratio of chargeable hours to total hours.

Here are some resource utilisation ratios.

Business	Input	Output
Consulting firm	Man hours available	Chargeable hours
Hotel	Rooms available	Rooms occupied
Railway company	Train miles available	Passenger miles
Bank	Number of staff	Number of accounts

5.2.6 Innovation

Companies do not have to innovate to be successful, but it helps! Others will try to steal their market, and so others' innovations must at least be matched. In a modern environment in which product quality, product differentiation and continuous improvement are the order of the day, a company that can find innovative ways of satisfying customers' needs has an important **competitive advantage**.

The **innovating process can be measured** in terms of **how much it costs to develop a new service, how effective the process is** (that is, how innovative is the organisation, if at all?), and **how quickly it can develop new services**. In more concrete terms this might translate into:

(a) The **amount of spending on research and development**, and whether these costs are recovered from new service sales (and how quickly).

(b) The **proportion of new services to total services** provided.

(c) The **time between identification of the customer need for a new service and making it available**.

6 Performance measures for non-profit-making organisations

6/03, 6/05

FAST FORWARD

Performance of NPOs can be measured as follows.

- In terms of inputs and outputs
- By judgement
- By comparison

6.1 Non-profit-making organisations (NPMOs)

NPMOs include private sector organisations such as charities and churches and much of the public sector. Commercial organisations generally have market competition and the profit motive to guide the process of managing resources economically, efficiently and effectively. However, NPMOs **cannot** by definition **be judged by profitability** nor do they generally have to be successful against competition, so other methods of assessing performance have to be used.

A major problem, as we have seen, with many NPMOs, particularly government bodies, is that it is **difficult to define their objectives**.

6.2 How can performance be measured?

It is reasonable to argue that such organisations **best serve society's interests** when the **gap** between the **benefits** they provide and **the cost** of providing those benefits is **greatest**. This is commonly termed 'value for money' and is not dissimilar from the concept of profit maximisation, apart from the fact that society's interests are being maximised rather than profit.

Value for money can be defined as **'getting the best possible combination of services from the least resources'**, which means maximising the benefits for the lowest possible cost. This is usually accepted as requiring the application of economy, effectiveness and efficiency.

(a) **Economy** (spending money frugally)
(b) **Efficiency** (getting out as much as possible for what goes in)
(c) **Effectiveness** (getting done, by means of (a) and (b), what was supposed to be done)

More formally, these criteria can be defined as follows.

Key terms

Effectiveness is the extent to which declared objectives/goals are met.

Efficiency is the relationship between inputs and outputs.

Economy is attaining the appropriate quantity and quality of inputs at lowest cost to achieve a certain level of outputs.

6.3 Example: Economy, efficiency, effectiveness

(a) **Economy.** The economy with which a school purchases equipment can be measured by comparing actual costs with budgets, with costs in previous years, with government/ local authority guidelines or with amounts spent by other schools.

(b) **Efficiency.** The efficiency with which a school's IT laboratory is used might be measured in terms of the proportion of the school week for which it is used.

(c) **Effectiveness.** The effectiveness of a school's objective to produce quality teaching could be measured by the proportion of students going on to higher or further education.

Value for money as a concept **assumes** that there is a **yardstick** against which to measure the achievement of objectives. It can be **difficult to determine where there is value for money**, however.

(a) Not-for-profit organisations tend to have **multiple objectives**, so that even if they can all be clearly identified it is impossible to say which is the overriding objective.

(b) **Outputs can seldom be measured** in a way that is generally agreed to be meaningful. (Are good exam results alone an adequate measure of the quality of teaching? How does one quantify the easing of pain following a successful operation?) For example, in the National Health Service success is measured in terms of fewer patient deaths per hospital admission, shorter waiting lists for operations, average speed of patient recovery and so on.

Here are a number of possible solutions to these problems.

(a) Performance can be judged in terms of **inputs**. This is very common in everyday life. If somebody tells you that their suit cost £750, for example, you would generally conclude that it was an extremely well-designed and good quality suit, even if you did not think so when you first saw it. The **drawback**, of course, is that you might also conclude that the person wearing the suit had been cheated or was a fool, or you may think that no piece of clothing is worth £750. So it is with the inputs and outputs of a non-profit-seeking organisation.

(b) Accept that performance measurement must to some extent be subjective. **Judgements** can be made **by experts**.

(c) Most not-for-profit organisations do not face competition but this does not mean that they are all unique. Bodies like local governments, health services and so on can **compare** their performance **against each other** and **against the historical results** of their predecessors. **Unit cost measurements** like 'cost per patient day' or 'cost of borrowing one library book' can be established to allow organisations to assess whether they are doing better or worse than their counterparts. Care must be taken not to read too much into limited information, however.

6.3.1 Performance measures

Although output of not-for-profit organisations can seldom be measured in a way that is generally agreed to be meaningful, outputs of a university might be measured in terms of the following.

Broader performance measures

- Proportion of total undergraduate population attending the university (by subject)
- Proportion of students graduating and classes of degrees obtained
- Amount of private sector research funds attracted
- Number of students finding employment after graduation
- Number of publications/articles produced by teaching staff

Operational performance measures

- Unit costs for each operating 'unit'
- Staff: student ratios; staff workloads
- Class sizes
- Availability of computers; good library stock
- Courses offered

6.4 Example: Inputs and outputs

Suppose that at a cost of £40,000 and 4,000 hours (**inputs**) in an average year, two policemen travel 8,000 miles and are instrumental in 200 arrests (**outputs**). A large number of **possibly meaningful measures** can be derived from these few figures, as the table below shows.

		£40,000	4,000 hours	8,000 miles	200 arrests
Cost (£)	£40,000		£40,000/4,000 = £10 per hour	£40,000/8,000 = £5 per mile	£40,000/200 = £200 per arrest
Time (hours)	4,000	4,000/£40,000 = 6 minutes patrolling per £1 spent		4,000/8,000 = ½ hour to patrol 1 mile	4,000/200 = 20 hours per arrest
Miles	8,000	8,000/£40,000 = 0.2 of a mile per £1	8,000/4,000 = 2 miles patrolled per hour		8,000/200 = 40 miles per arrest
Arrests	200	200/£40,000 = 1 arrest per £200	200/4,000 = 1 arrest every 20 hours	200/8,000 = 1 arrest every 40 miles	

These measures do not necessarily identify cause and effect or personal responsibility and accountability. Actual performance needs to be **compared**:

- With **standards**, if there are any
- With similar **external activities**
- With similar **internal activities**
- With **targets**
- With **indices**
- Over time – **as trends**

7 Benchmarking

FAST FORWARD

Benchmarking is a type of comparison exercise through which an organisation attempts to improve performance.

We have seen how standard costing achieves control by the comparison of actual results with a pre-determined standard. **Benchmarking** is another type of comparison exercise through which an organisation attempts to improve performance. The idea is to seek the best available performance against which the organisation can monitor its own performance.

Key term

Benchmarking is 'The establishment, through data gathering, of targets and comparators, through whose use relative levels of performance (and particularly areas of underperformance) can be identified. By the adoption of identified best practices it is hoped that performance will improve.'

There are four types of benchmarking.

(a) **Internal benchmarking:** a method of comparing one operating unit or function with another within the same industry.

(b) **Functional benchmarking:** in which internal functions are compared with those of the best external practitioners of those functions, regardless of the industry they are in (also known as **operational** or **generic** benchmarking).

(c) **Competitive benchmarking**: in which information is gathered about direct competitors, through techniques such as reverse engineering.

(d) **Strategic benchmarking**: a type of competitive benchmarking aimed at strategic action and organisational change.

From this list you can see that a benchmarking exercise **does not necessarily have to involve the comparison of operations with those of a competitor**. Indeed, it might be difficult to persuade a direct competitor to part with any information which is useful for comparison purposes. Functional benchmarking, for example, does not always involve direct competitors. For instance a railway company may be identified as the 'best' in terms of on-board catering, and an airline company that operates on different routes could seek opportunities to improve by sharing information and comparing their own catering operations with those of the railway company.

The types of organisation most likely to use benchmarking techniques are **customer services, manufacturing, human resources and information services**.

7.1 Benefits of benchmarking?

Benefits of benchmarking include the following.

(a) Its flexibility means that it can be used in both the **public and private sector** and by people at different levels of responsibility.

(b) **Cross comparisons** (as opposed to comparisons with similar organisations) are more likely to expose radically different ways of doing things.

(c) It is an **effective method of implementing change**, people being involved in identifying and seeking out different ways of doing things in their own areas.

(d) It **identifies** the **processes to improve**.

(e) It helps with **cost reduction**.

(f) It **improves the effectiveness** of operations.

(g) It **delivers services** to a defined standard.

(h) It **provides a focus on planning**.

Benchmarking works, it is claimed, for the following reasons.

(a) The comparisons are carried out by the managers who have to live with any changes implemented as a result of the exercise.

(b) Benchmarking focuses on improvement in key areas and sets targets which are challenging but 'achievable'. What is *really* achievable can be discovered by examining what others have achieved: managers are thus able to accept that they are not being asked to perform miracles.

Benchmarking has other advantages: it can provide **early warning of competitive disadvantage** and should lead to a greater incidence of **teamworking** and **cross-functional learning.**

Limitations of benchmarking exercises

- **Difficulties in deciding** which activities to benchmark
- **Identifying** the **'best in class'** for each activity
- **Persuading other organisations** to share information
- **Successful practices** in one organisation may not transfer successfully to another
- The danger of **drawing incorrect conclusions** from inappropriate comparisons

8 Management performance measures

> **FAST FORWARD**
>
> Management performance measures include the following.
> - Subjective measures
> - Judgement of outsiders
> - Upward appraisal
> - Accounting measures

We have not so far **distinguished between measures of performance of individual managers** and **measures of performance of what it is they manage**.

The distinction is very important. A manager may improve performance of a poorly performing division, but the division could still rank as one of the poorest performing divisions within the organisation. If the manager is assessed purely on the division's results then he will not appear to be a good performer.

The problem is deciding which performance measures should be used to measure management performance and which should be used to measure the performance of the business.

It is difficult to devise performance measures that relate specifically to a manager to judge his or her performance **as a manager**. It is possible to calculate statistics to assess the manager as an **employee** (days absent, professional qualifications obtained, personality and so on), but this does not measure managerial performance.

It is necessary to consider a manger in relation to his or her **area of responsibility** depending on whether it is a **cost**, **revenue**, **profit** or **investment** centre. If we want to know how good a manager is at marketing, the marketing performance of his or her division is the **starting point**. Then we must consider to what extent the manager is able to **influence** the performance, and the performance **trend**.

It is unreasonable to assess managers' performance in relation to matters that are beyond their control. Management performance measures should therefore **only include those items that are directly controllable by the manager in question.**

Possible management performance measures

(a) **Subjective measures**, for example ranking performance on a scale of 1 to 5. This approach is imprecise but does measure managerial performance rather than divisional performance. The process must be perceived by managers to be fair. The judgement should be made by somebody impartial, but close enough to the work of each manager to appreciate the efforts he has made and the difficulties he faces.

(b) The **judgement of outsiders.** An organisation might, for example, set up a bonus scheme for directors under which they would receive a bonus if the share price outperforms the FT-SE 100 index for more than three years. This is fair in that the share price reflects many aspects of performance, but it is questionable whether they can all be influenced by the directors concerned.

(c) **Upward appraisal**. This involves staff giving their opinions on the performance of their managers. To be effective this requires healthy working relationships.

(d) **Accounting measures** can be used, but must be tailored according to what or whom is being judged.

Chapter Roundup

- **Performance measurement** aims to establish how well something or somebody is doing in relation to a plan.
- Performance measures may be divided into two groups.
    - Financial performance measures
    - Non-monetary performance measures
- Performance measures can be **quantitative** or **qualitative**.
- **Non-financial indicators (NFIs)** are useful in a modern business environment.
- **Ratios** and **percentages** are useful performance measurement techniques.
- **Responsibility accounting** is a system of accounting that segregates revenue and costs into areas of personal responsibility in order to monitor and assess the performance of each part of an organisation.
- A **responsibility centre** is a function or department of an organisation that is headed by a manager who has direct responsibility for its performance.
- A **cost centre** is any unit of an organisation to which costs can be separately attributed.
- A **profit centre** is any unit of an organisation to which both revenues and costs are assigned, so that the profitability of the unit may be measured.
- A **revenue centre** is where managers only have control over maximising of revenues.
- An **investment centre** is a profit centre whose performance is measured by its return on capital employed.
- **Return on investment (ROI)** or **return on capital employed (ROCE)** shows how much profit has been made in relation to the amount of resources invested.
- The **profit margin** (profit to sales ratio) is calculated as (profit ÷ sales) × 100%.
- **Residual income (RI)** is an alternative way of measuring the performance of an investment centre. It is a measure of the centre's profits after deducting a notional or imputed interest cost.
- Performance measures for **materials** and **labour** include variances. Performance can also be measured using the **standard hour**.
- Performance measures covering the following six 'dimensions' have been suggested for service organisations.
    - Competitive performance
    - Financial performance
    - Quality of service
    - Flexibility
    - Resource utilisation
    - Innovation
- Performance of NPOs can be measured as follows.
    - In terms of inputs and outputs
    - By judgement
    - By comparison
- **Benchmarking** is a type of comparison exercise through which an organisation attempts to improve performance.

- Management performance measures include the following.
    - Subjective measures
    - Judgement of outsiders
    - Upward appraisal
    - Accounting measures

PART C BUDGETING AND PERFORMANCE MEASUREMENT

Quick Quiz

1. Give five examples of a financial performance measure.

   - ....
   - ....
   - ....
   - ....
   - ....

2. How do quantitative and qualitative performance measures differ?

3. ROI = $\dfrac{A}{B} \times 100\%$

   A = ...

   B = ...

4. If X = Actual hours worked
       Y = Budgeted hours
       Z = Standard hours produced

   What is $\dfrac{Z}{Y}$?

   A Capacity ratio
   B Activity ratio
   C Efficiency ratio
   D Standard hours produced ratio

5. **Service quality** is measured principally by quantitative measures.

   ☐ True
   ☐ False

6. Match up the following correctly.

   (1) Effectiveness =

   (2) Efficiency =

   (3) Economy =

   A = Relationship between an organisation's outputs and its objectives

   B = Controlling expenditure

   C = Relationship between inputs and outputs

7. What are the three most important features of the balanced scorecard approach?

8. List four types of benchmarking

   - ....
   - ....
   - ....
   - ....

Answers to Quick Quiz

1.
   - Profit
   - Revenue
   - Costs
   - Share price
   - Cash flow

2. Quantitative measures are expressed in numbers whereas qualitative measures are not.

3. A = profit

   B = capital employed

4. B   Activity ratio

5. False. Service quality is measured principally by **qualitative** measures.

6. (1) A
   (2) C
   (3) B

7.
   - It looks at both internal and external matters concerning the organisation
   - It is related to the key elements of a company's strategy
   - Financial and non-financial measures are linked together

8.
   - Internal
   - Functional
   - Competitive
   - Strategic

Now try the questions below from the Exam Question Bank

Number	Level	Marks	Time
Q16	Examination	12	22 mins

PART C BUDGETING AND PERFORMANCE MEASUREMENT

Part D
The framework of financial management

Financial management and financial objectives

Topic list	Syllabus reference
1 The scope of financial management	1(a), (b)
2 Objectives of private sector companies	1(c)
3 Non-financial objectives	1(c)
4 Stakeholders in a company	1(d)
5 Bodies which are not purely commercial	1(e)
6 Ratio analysis	1(a)

Introduction

Starting with this chapter and in the remaining chapters of this Text, we examine the work of the financial manager and the framework within which the financial manager operates. After introducing the **scope of financial management**, we consider the **objectives** of organisations. We go on to examine **performance indicators** for both business enterprises and non-commercial organisations.

In later chapters, we will be studying the **resources** available for an organisation to meet objectives and the methods available for doing so.

PART D   THE FRAMEWORK OF FINANCIAL MANAGEMENT

Study guide

Section 3 – The nature and scope of financial management

- Broadly describe the relationship between financial management, management accounting and financial accounting
- Discuss the nature and scope of financial objectives for private sector companies in the context of organisational objectives
- Discuss the role of social and non-financial objectives in private sector companies and identify their financial implications
- Identify objectives (financial and otherwise) in not-for-profit organisations and identify the extent to which they differ from private sector companies
- Discuss the problems of multiple stakeholders in financial management and the consequent multiple objectives and scope for conflict

Exam guide

Remember that most of the compulsory questions will be about financial management topics, as well as two of the optional questions.

This chapter is important for the 2.4 exam: a number of questions or part questions have been set on it. The examiner has stressed that the topics in chapters 14 –15 are important knowledge.

In the exam you may be asked to explain the role and purpose of financial management. You may be tested on the objectives of stakeholders other than shareholders, and non-profit making organisations, so do not neglect these areas. When assessing the desirability of undertaking an investment project you may need to discuss non-financial objectives. The Oxford Brookes Degree Research and Analysis Project Topic 8 requires you to analyse a financial situation of your choice.

Exam focus point

> As we begin coverage of the financial management part of the syllabus, bear in mind the format of the paper (as set out in the Introduction to this Study Text). You cannot pass Paper 2.4 without knowing the financial management areas thoroughly. It is not possible to scrape through largely on management accounting knowledge without paying much attention to financial management.

1 The scope of financial management

FAST FORWARD

> Financial management decisions cover **investment** decisions **financing** and **dividend** decisions.

1.1 What is financial management?

Financial management can be defined as the management of the finances of an organisation in order to achieve the financial objectives of the organisation. The usual assumption in financial management for the private sector is that the objective of the company is to **maximise shareholders' wealth**. Broadly, there are two aspects of financial management: **financial planning** and **financial control**.

1.2 Financial planning

The financial manager will need to **plan** to ensure that enough funding is available at the right time to meet the needs of the organisation for short, medium and long-term capital.

(a) In the short term, funds may be needed to pay for purchases of stocks, or to smooth out changes in debtors, creditors and cash: the financial manager is here ensuring that **working capital requirements** are met.

(b) In the medium or long term, the organisation may have planned purchases of **fixed assets** such as plant and equipment, for which the financial manager must ensure that **funding** is available.

The financial manager contributes to decisions on the uses of funds raised by **analysing financial data** to **determine uses** which meet the **organisation's financial objectives.** Is project A to be preferred to Project B? Should a new asset be bought or leased?

1.3 Financial control

The **control** function of the financial manager becomes relevant for funding which has been raised. Are the various activities of the organisation meeting its objectives? Are assets being used efficiently? To answer these questions, the financial manager may **compare data** on **actual performance** with **forecast performance**. Forecast data will have been prepared in the light of past performance (historical data) modified to reflect expected future changes. Future changes may include the effects of economic development, for example an economic recovery leading to a forecast upturn in revenues.

1.4 Financial management decisions

The financial manager makes decisions relating to **investment**, **financing** and **dividends**.

Investments in assets must be **financed** somehow. Financial management is also concerned with the **management of short-term funds** and with how funds can be raised over the long term.

Retention of profits was mentioned above as a financing decision. The other side of this decision is that if profits are retained, there is less to pay out to shareholders as dividends, which might deter investors. An appropriate balance needs to be struck in addressing the **dividend decision**: how much of its profits should the company pay out as dividends and how much should it retain for investment to provide for future growth and new investment opportunities?

We shall be looking at various aspects of the investment, financing and dividend decisions of financial management over the remaining chapters of this Study Text.

	Examples of different types of investment decision
Decisions **internal** to the business enterprise	• Whether to undertake new projects • Whether to invest in new plant and machinery • Research and development decisions • Investment in a marketing or advertising campaign
Decisions involving **external parties**	• Whether to carry out a takeover or a merger involving another business • Whether to engage in a joint venture with another enterprise
Disinvestment decisions	• Whether to sell off unprofitable segments of the business • Whether to sell old or surplus plant and machinery • The sale of subsidiary companies

Question: Disposal of surplus assets

'The financial manager should identify surplus assets and dispose of them'. Why?

Answer

A surplus asset earns no return for the business. The business is likely to be paying the 'cost of capital' in respect of the money tied up in the asset, ie the money which it can realise by selling it.

If surplus assets are sold, the business may be able to invest the cash released in more productive ways, or alternatively it may use the cash to cut its liabilities. Either way, it will enhance the return on capital employed for the business as a whole.

Although selling surplus assets yields short-term benefits, the business should not jeopardise its activities in the medium or long term by disposing of productive capacity until the likelihood of it being required in the future has been fully assessed.

1.5 Management accounting, financial accounting and financial management

Of course, it is not just people *within* an organisation who require information. Those external to the organisation such as banks, shareholders, the Inland Revenue, creditors and government agencies all desire information too.

Management accountants provide internally-used information. The financial accounting function provides externally-used information. The management accountant is not concerned with the calculation of earnings per share and the financial accountant is not concerned with the variances between budgeted and actual labour expenditure.

Management information provides a common source from which are prepared financial accounts and management accounts. The **differences** between the two types of accounts **arise in the manner in which the common source of data is analysed.**

Financial accounts	Management accounts
Financial accounts **detail the performance of an organisation over a defined period and the state of affairs at the end of that period.**	Management accounts are **used to aid management record**, plan and **control activities and to help the decision-making process.**
Limited companies must, **by law**, prepare financial accounts.	There is **no legal requirement** to prepare management accounts.
The **format** of published financial accounts is **determined by law**, by SSAPs and by FRSs. In principle the accounts of different organisations can therefore be easily compared.	The **format** of management accounts is entirely at management discretion: **no strict rules** govern the way they are prepared or presented.
Financial accounts **concentrate on the business as a whole**, aggregating revenues and costs from different operations, and are an end in themselves.	Management accounts can **focus on specific areas** of an organisation's activities. Information may aid a decision rather than be an end product of a decision.
Most financial accounting information is of a **monetary** nature.	Management accounts incorporate **non-monetary** measures.
Financial accounts present an essentially **historic** picture of **past** operations.	Management accounts are both a **historical** record and a **future** planning tool.

As we have seen financial management is **the management of finance**. Finance is used by an organisation just as, for example, labour is used by an organisation. Finance therefore needs management in a similar way to labour. The management accounting function provides information to ensure the effective management of labour and, in the same way, the financial management function provides information on, for example, projected cash flows to aid the effective management of finance.

2 Objectives of private sector companies 6/02, 6/03

FAST FORWARD

Financial targets may include targets for: **earnings; earnings per share; dividend per share; gearing level; profit retention; operating profitability**.

The usual assumption in financial management for the private sector is that the primary financial objective of the company is to **maximise shareholders' wealth**.

In much of economic theory, it is assumed that the firm behaves in such a way as to maximise **profits**, where profit is viewed in an economist's sense. Unlike the accountant's concept of cost, total costs by this economist's definition includes an element of reward for the risk-taking of the entrepreneur, called 'normal profit'.

2.1 Profit maximisation

Where the entrepreneur is in full managerial control of the firm, as in the case of a small owner-managed company or partnership, the **economist's assumption of profit maximisation** would seem to be very reasonable. Remember though that the economist's concept of profits is broadly in terms of **cash**, whereas accounting profits may not equate to cash flows.

Even in companies owned by shareholders but run by non-shareholding managers, if the manager is serving the company's (ie the shareholders') interests, we might expect that the profit maximisation assumption should be close to the truth.

2.2 Managerial objectives

Managers are paid to make the decisions about prices and output, but it is the shareholders who expect to benefit from the profits. Managers, it is argued, will not necessarily make pricing decisions that will maximise profits.

(a) They have **no personal interests** at stake in the size of profits earned, except in so far as they are accountable to the shareholders for the profits they make.

(b) There is **no competitive pressure** in the market to be efficient, minimise costs and maximise profits.

(c) Managers may be more concerned with ensuring **survival**, and hence safeguarding their own jobs, rather than increasing profits and attracting investors.

Given the **divorce of management from ownership**, price and output decisions may be taken by managers with a **managerial aim** rather than the **aim of profit maximisation**. However, there is the constraint that managers must take some account of shareholders' interests because they are formally responsible for them and so are accountable to shareholders for their decisions.

(a) One 'managerial model' of the firm, Baumol's **sales maximisation model**, assumes that the firm acts to maximise sales revenue rather than profits, in order to maintain or increase its market share, to ensure survival and to discourage competition. Managers benefit personally because of the prestige of running a large and successful company, and also because salaries and other perks are likely to be higher in bigger companies than smaller ones.

(b) Another managerial model, Williamson's **management discretion model**, assumes that managers act to **further their own interests** and so **maximise their own utility**, subject to a **minimum profit** requirement. The model states that utility, which a manager aims to maximise, is a function of several different things.

  (i) The manager's own salary

  (ii) Expenditure on his or her staff (prestige and influence depend on the numbers and pay levels of subordinate staff)

  (iii) The amount of perquisites (luxurious office, personal secretary, company car, expense account etc)

  (iv) The authority to make 'discretionary investments' (ie new investments other than straightforward replacement decisions)

The profit aimed for will not be maximum profit, because of management's wishes for expenditure on themselves, their staff and the perquisites of management.

Cyert and March's **consensus theory** suggested that a firm is an **organisational coalition** of shareholders, managers, employees and customers, with each group having different goals. Thus there is a need for **political compromise** in establishing the goals of the firm. Each group must settle for less than it would ideally want to have - shareholders must settle for less than maximum profit, and managers for less than maximum utility, and so on.

The assumptions of economic theory and various theories of the firm all contain an element of truth. However, they do not provide the financial manager with an easy yardstick with which to work.

In the theory of company finance, such a yardstick is provided in the assumption that the financial manager's job is to **maximise the market value** of the company. Specifically, the main financial objective of a company should be to maximise the wealth of its ordinary shareholders. Within this context, the financial manager seeks to ensure that investments earn a **return**, for the benefit of shareholders.

2.3 How are the wealth of shareholders and the value of a company measured?

If the financial objective of a company is to maximise the value of the company, and in particular the value of its ordinary shares, we need to be able to put values on a company and its shares. How do we do it?

Three possible methods for the valuation of a company might occur to us.

(a) **Balance sheet valuation**

Here assets will be valued on a **going concern basis**. Certainly, investors will look at a company's balance sheet. If retained profits rise every year, the company will be a profitable one. Balance sheet values are not a measure of 'market value', although retained profits might give some indication of what the company could pay as dividends to shareholders.

(b) **Break-up basis**

This method of valuing a business is only of interest when the business is threatened with **liquidation**, or when its management is thinking about selling off individual assets to raise cash.

(c) **Market values**

The market value is the price at which buyers and sellers will trade stocks and shares in a company. This is the method of valuation which is most relevant to the financial objectives of a company.

(i) When shares are traded on a recognised stock market, such as the Stock Exchange, the market value of a company can be measured by the **price** at which shares are currently being traded.

(ii) When shares are in a private company, and are not traded on any stock market, there is no easy way to measure their market value. Even so, the financial objective of these companies should be to **maximise** the **wealth** of their **ordinary shareholders**.

The wealth of the shareholders in a company comes from:

- **Dividends** received
- **Market value** of the shares

A shareholder's **return** on investment is obtained in the form of:

- **Dividends** received
- **Capital gains** from increases in the market value of his or her shares

Total shareholder return is the sum of the percentage capital gain and dividend yield over a one year holding period. For example, an individual who sees the share price increase from 50p to 55p over one year and receives a dividend yield of 5% would see a total shareholder return of 15% (10% capital gain and 5% dividend yield).

2.4 How is the value of a business increased?

If a company's shares are traded on a stock market, the wealth of shareholders is increased when the share price goes up. The price of a company's shares will go up when the company makes attractive profits, which it pays out as **dividends** or **re-invests** in the business to achieve future profit growth and dividend growth. However, to increase the share price the company should achieve its attractive profits without taking business risks and financial risks which worry shareholders.

If there is an increase in earnings and dividends, management can hope for an increase in the share price too, so that shareholders benefit from both **higher revenue** (dividends) and also **capital gains** (higher share prices). Management should set targets for factors which they can influence directly, such as profits and dividend growth. A financial objective might be expressed as the aim of increasing profits, earnings per share and dividend per share by, say, 10% a year for each of the next five years.

2.5 Other financial targets

In addition to targets for earnings, EPS, and dividend per share, a company might set **other financial targets**, such as:

(a) A restriction on the company's level of **gearing**, or debt. For example, a company's management might decide:

(i) The ratio of long-term debt capital to equity capital should never exceed, say, 1:1.

(ii) The cost of interest payments should never be higher than, say, 25% of total profits before interest and tax.

(b) A target for **profit retentions**. For example, management might set a target that dividend cover (the ratio of distributable profits to dividends actually distributed) should not be less than, say, 2.5 times.

(c) A target for **operating profitability**. For example, management might set a target for the profit/sales ratio (say, a minimum of 10%) or for a return on capital employed (say, a minimum ROCE of 20%).

PART D THE FRAMEWORK OF FINANCIAL MANAGEMENT

These financial targets are not primary financial objectives, but they can act as subsidiary targets or constraints which should help a company to achieve its main financial objective without incurring excessive risks. They are usually measured over a year rather than over the long term.

Remember however that short-term measures of return can encourage a company to pursue **short-term** objectives at the expense of **long-term** ones, for example by deferring new capital investments, or spending only small amounts on research and development and on training.

A major problem with setting a number of different financial targets, either primary targets or supporting secondary targets, is that they might not all be consistent with each other. When this happens, some compromises will have to be accepted.

2.6 Example: Financial targets

Lion Grange Ltd has recently introduced a formal scheme of long range planning. Sales in the current year reached £10,000,000, and forecasts for the next five years are £10,600,000, £11,400,000, £12,400,000, £13,600,000 and £15,000,000. The ratio of net profit after tax to sales is 10%, and this is expected to continue throughout the planning period. Total assets less current liabilities will remain at around 125% of sales.

It was suggested at a recent board meeting that:

(a) If profits rise, dividends should rise by at least the same percentage

(b) An earnings retention rate of 50% should be maintained

(c) The ratio of long-term borrowing to long-term funds (debt plus equity) is limited (by the market) to 30%, which happens also to be the current gearing level of the company

You are required to prepare a financial analysis of the draft long range plan.

Solution

The draft financial plan, for profits, dividends, assets required and funding, can be drawn up in a table, as follows.

	Current Year £m	Year 1 £m	Year 2 £m	Year 3 £m	Year 4 £m	Year 5 £m
Sales	10.00	10.60	11.40	12.40	13.60	15.00
Net profit after tax	1.00	1.06	1.14	1.24	1.36	1.50
Dividends (50% of profit after tax)	0.50	0.53	0.57	0.62	0.68	0.75
Total assets less current liabilities	12.50	13.25	14.25	15.50	17.00	18.75
Equity (increased by retained earnings)	8.75	9.28	9.85	10.47	11.15	11.90
Maximum debt (30% of long-term funds, or 3/7 × equity)	3.75	3.98	4.22	4.49	4.78	5.10
Funds available	12.50	13.26	14.07	14.96	15.93	17.00
(Shortfalls) in funds *	0	0	(0.18)	(0.54)	(1.07)	(1.75)

* Given maximum gearing of 30% and no new issue of shares = funds available minus net assets required.

Question — Dividends and gearing

Suggest policies on dividends, retained earnings and gearing for Lion Grange Limited, using the data above.

Answer

The financial objectives of the company are not compatible with each other. Adjustments will have to be made.

(a) Given the assumptions about sales, profits, dividends and net assets required, there will be an **increasing shortfall of funds** from year 2 onwards, unless new shares are issued or the gearing level rises above 30%.

(b) In years 2 and 3, the shortfall can be eliminated by **retaining a greater percentage** of profits, but this may have a serious **adverse effect** on the share price. In year 4 and year 5, the shortfall in funds cannot be removed even if dividend payments are reduced to nothing.

(c) The **net asset turnover** appears to be **low**. The situation would be eased if investments were able to generate a higher volume of sales, so that fewer fixed assets and less working capital would be required to support the projected level of sales.

(d) If asset turnover cannot be improved, it may be possible to **increase the profit to sales ratio** by reducing costs or increasing selling prices.

(e) If a new issue of shares is proposed to make up the shortfall in funds, the amount of funds required must be considered very carefully. Total **dividends** would have to be **increased** in order to pay dividends on the new shares. The company seems unable to offer prospects of suitable dividend payments, and so raising new equity might be difficult.

(f) It is conceivable that extra funds could be raised by issuing new debt capital, so that the level of gearing would be over 30%. It is uncertain whether investors would be prepared to lend money so as to increase gearing. If more funds were borrowed, profits after interest and tax would fall so that the share price might also be reduced.

3 Non-financial objectives   12/01, 6/02

FAST FORWARD

Non-financial objectives may include: **employee welfare; management welfare; the welfare of society; service provision objectives; fulfilment of responsibilities to customers and suppliers**.

A company may have important **non-financial objectives**, which will limit the achievement of financial objectives. Examples of non-financial objectives are as follows.

(a) **The welfare of employees**

A company might try to provide **good wages and salaries**, comfortable and safe working conditions, good training and career development, and good pensions. If redundancies are necessary, many companies will provide generous redundancy payments, or spend money trying to find alternative employment for redundant staff.

(b) **The welfare of management**

Managers will often take decisions to improve their **own circumstances**, even though their decisions will incur expenditure and so reduce profits. High salaries, company cars and other perks are all examples of managers promoting their own interests.

(c) **The provision of a service**

The major objectives of some companies will include fulfilment of a responsibility to **provide a service** to the public. Examples are the privatised British Telecom and British Gas. Providing a service is of course a key responsibility of government departments and local authorities.

PART D THE FRAMEWORK OF FINANCIAL MANAGEMENT

(d) **The fulfilment of responsibilities towards customers**

Responsibilities towards **customers** include providing in good time a product or service of a **quality** that customers expect, and dealing **honestly and fairly** with customers. **Reliable supply arrangements,** also **after-sales service arrangements,** are important.

(e) **The fulfilment of responsibilities towards suppliers**

Responsibilities towards **suppliers** are expressed mainly in terms of **trading relationships**. A company's size could give it considerable power as a buyer. The company should not use its power unscrupulously. Suppliers might rely on getting prompt payment, in accordance with the agreed terms of trade.

(f) **The welfare of society as a whole**

The management of some companies is aware of the role that their company has to play in exercising **corporate social responsibility**. This includes **compliance with applicable laws and regulations** but is wider than that. Companies may be aware of their responsibility to minimise pollution and other harmful 'externalities' (such as excessive traffic) which their activities generate. In delivering 'green' environmental policies, a company may improve its corporate image as well as reducing harmful externality effects. Companies also may consider their **'positive' responsibilities**, for example to make a contribution to the community by local sponsorship.

Other non-financial objectives are **growth**, **diversification** and **leadership in research and development**.

> **Exam focus point**
>
> Twelve marks were available in December 2001 for a general discussion of organisations' non-financial objectives.

3.1 Financial and non-financial objectives

Non-financial objectives do not negate financial objectives, but they do suggest that the simple theory of company finance, that the objective of a firm is to maximise the wealth of ordinary shareholders, is too simplistic. Financial objectives may have to be compromised in order to satisfy non-financial objectives.

4 Stakeholders in a company   6/02, 12/02

> **FAST FORWARD**
>
> **Stakeholders** are individuals or groups who are affected by the activities of the firm. They can be classified as **internal** (employees and managers), **connected** (shareholders, customers and suppliers) and **external** (local communities, pressure groups, government).

> **Key term**
>
> There is a variety of different groups or individuals whose interests are directly affected by the activities of a firm. These groups or individuals are referred to as **stakeholders** in the firms.

The various stakeholder groups in a firm can be classified as follows.

Stakeholder groups	
Internal	Employees and pensioners Managers
Connected	Shareholders Debtholders Customers Bankers Suppliers Competitors
External	Government Pressure groups Local and national communities Professional and regulatory bodies

4.1 Objectives of stakeholder groups

The various groups of stakeholders in a firm will have different goals which will depend in part on the particular situation of the enterprise. Some of the more important aspects of these different goals are as follows.

(a) **Ordinary (equity) shareholders**

Ordinary (equity) shareholders are the providers of the risk capital of a company. Usually their goal will be to **maximise the wealth which they have** as a result of the ownership of the shares in the company.

(b) **Trade creditors**

Trade creditors have supplied goods or services to the firm. Trade creditors will generally be profit-maximising firms themselves and have the objective of **being paid the full amount due by the date agreed**. On the other hand, they usually wish to ensure that they continue their trading relationship with the firm and may sometimes be prepared to accept later payment to avoid jeopardising that relationship.

(c) **Long-term creditors**

Long-term creditors, which will often be banks, have the objective of **receiving payments of interest and capital** on the loan by the due date for the repayments. Where the loan is secured on assets of the company, the creditor will be able to appoint a receiver to dispose of the company's assets if the company defaults on the repayments. To avoid the possibility that this may result in a loss to the lender if the assets are not sufficient to cover the loan, the lender will wish to **minimise the risk of default** and will not wish to lend more than is prudent.

(d) **Employees**

Employees will usually want to **maximise their rewards** paid to them in salaries and benefits, according to the particular skills and the rewards available in alternative employment. Most employees will also want **continuity of employment**.

(e) **Government**

Government has objectives which can be formulated in political terms. Government agencies impinge on the firm's activities in different ways including through taxation of the firm's profits, the provision of grants, health and safety legislation, training initiatives and so on. Government policies will often be related to macroeconomic objectives such as **sustained economic growth** and **high levels of employment**.

(f) **Management**

Management has, like other employees (and managers who are not directors will normally be employees), the objective of **maximising** their **own rewards**. Directors and the managers to whom they delegate responsibilities must manage the company for the benefit of shareholders. The objective of reward maximisation might conflict with the exercise of this duty.

4.2 Stakeholder groups and strategy

The actions of stakeholder groups in pursuit of their various goals can exert influence on strategy. The greater the power of the stakeholder, the greater his influence will be. Each stakeholder group will have different expectations about what it wants, and the **expectations of the various groups may conflict**. Each group, however, will influence strategic decision-making.

4.3 Shareholders and management 06/05

Although ordinary shareholders (equity shareholders) are the owners of the company to whom the board of directors are accountable, the actual powers of shareholders tend to be restricted, except in companies where the shareholders are also the directors. The **day-to-day** running of a company is the responsibility of **management**. Although the company's results are submitted for shareholders' approval at the annual general meeting (AGM), there is often apathy and acquiescence in directors' recommendations.

Shareholders are often ignorant about their company's current situation and future prospects. They have no right to inspect the books of account, and their forecasts of future prospects are gleaned from the annual report and accounts, stockbrokers, investment journals and daily newspapers. The relationship between management and shareholders is sometimes referred to as an **agency relationship**, in which managers act as agents for the shareholders.

Key term

> **Agency relationship**: a description of the relationship between management and shareholders expressing the idea that managers act as agents for the shareholder, using delegated powers to run the company in the shareholders' best interests.

However, if managers hold none or very few of the equity shares of the company they work for, what is to stop them from working inefficiently? or not bothering to look for profitable new investment opportunities? **or** giving themselves high salaries and perks?

One power that shareholders possess is the right to **remove** the **directors** from office. But shareholders have to take the initiative to do this, and in many companies, the shareholders lack the energy and organisation to take such a step. Even so, directors will want the company's report and accounts, and the proposed final dividend, to meet with shareholders' approval at the AGM.

Another reason why managers might do their best to improve the financial performance of their company is that managers' pay is often related to the size or profitability of the company. Managers in very big companies, or in very profitable companies, will normally expect to earn higher salaries than managers in smaller or less successful companies. There is also an argument for giving managers some **profit-related pay**, or providing incentives which are related to profits or share price.

The **advantages** of having a **wide range of shareholders** include the following.

(a) There is likely to be **greater activity** in the market in the firm's shares.

(b) There is less likelihood of one shareholder having a **controlling interest**.

(c) Since shareholdings are smaller on average, there is likely to be **less effect** on the **share price** if one shareholder sells his holding.

(d) There is a **greater likelihood** of a **takeover** bid being **frustrated**.

Disadvantages of a large number of shareholders include the following.

(a) **Administrative costs** will be **high**. These include the costs of sending out copies of the annual report and accounts, counting proxy votes, registering new shareholders and paying dividends.

(b) Shareholders will have **differing tax positions** and **objectives** in holding the firm's shares, which makes a dividend/retention policy more difficult for the management to decide upon.

4.4 Shareholders, managers and the company's long-term creditors

The relationship between long-term creditors of a company, the management and the shareholders of a company encompasses the following factors.

(a) Management may decide to raise finance for a company by taking out long-term or medium-term loans. They might well be taking **risky investment decisions** using outsiders' money to finance them.

(b) Investors who provide debt finance will rely on the company's management to generate enough net cash inflows to make **interest payments on time**, and eventually to repay loans.

However, long-term creditors will often take **security** for their loan, perhaps in the form of a fixed charge over an asset (such as a mortgage on a building). Debentures are also often subject to certain restrictive covenants, which restrict the company's rights to borrow more money until the debentures have been repaid.

If a company is unable to pay what it owes its creditors, the creditors may decide to **exercise their security** or to apply for the company to be **wound up**.

(c) The money that is provided by long-term creditors will be invested to earn profits, and the profits (in excess of what is needed to pay interest on the borrowing) will provide **extra dividends** or retained profits for the shareholders of the company. In other words, shareholders will expect to increase their wealth using creditors' money.

4.5 Shareholders, managers and government

The government does not have a direct interest in companies (except for those in which it actually holds shares). However, the government does often have a strong indirect interest in companies' affairs.

(a) **Taxation**

The government raises taxes on sales and profits and on shareholders' dividends. It also expects companies to act as tax collectors for income tax and VAT. The **tax structure** might influence investors' preferences for either dividends or capital growth.

(b) **Encouraging new investments**

The government might provide **funds** towards the cost of some investment projects. It might also encourage private investment by offering **tax incentives.**

(c) **Encouraging a wider spread of share ownership**

In the UK, the government has made some attempts to encourage more private individuals to become company shareholders, by means of **attractive privatisation issues** (such as in the electricity, gas and telecommunications industries) and tax incentives, such as PEPs (personal equity plans) to encourage individuals to invest in shares.

PART D THE FRAMEWORK OF FINANCIAL MANAGEMENT

(d) **Legislation**

The government also influences **companies**, and the **relationships** between shareholders, creditors, management, employees and the general public, through legislation, including the Companies Acts, legislation on employment, health and safety regulations, legislation on consumer protection and consumer rights and environmental legislation.

(e) **Economic policy**

A government's economic policy will affect business activity. For example, **exchange rate policy** will have implications for the revenues of exporting firms and for the purchase costs of importing firms. Policies on **economic growth, inflation, employment, interest rates** and so on are all relevant to business activities.

5 Bodies which are not purely commercial   6/03

FAST FORWARD

The **objectives of non-commercial organisations** such as nationalised industries and charities are aimed at the provision of a certain level and quality of service, and giving value for money, rather than profit oriented.

5.1 Nationalised industries

Following the privatisation programme of the 1980s and early 1990s, the UK's nationalised industries are much fewer in number than they were. The largest nationalised industry remaining is the Post Office. London Transport is another.

5.1.1 Strategic objectives for the nationalised industries

Nationalised industries are financed by government loans, and some borrowing from the capital markets. They do not have equity capital, and there is no stock exchange to give a day-by-day valuation of the business.

The financial objective cannot be to maximise the wealth of its owners, the government or the general public, because this is not a concept which can be applied in practice. Financial objectives will generally be subordinated to a number of political and social considerations.

(a) A nationalised industry may be expected to provide a certain **standard of service** to all customers, regardless of the fact that some individuals will receive a service at a charge well below its cost. For example, the postal service must deliver letters to remote locations for the price of an ordinary first or second class stamp.

(b) The need to provide a service may be of such overriding social and political importance that the government is prepared to **subsidise** the industry. For example transport can be viewed as a social necessity and a certain level of service must be provided, with losses made up by government subsidies.

5.1.2 Investment plans and investment appraisal in nationalised industries

Nationalised industries in the UK have generally been expected to aim at a **rate of return** (before interest and tax) on their new investment programmes of **5% in real terms**. This is required so that the industries do not divert resources away from those areas where they could be used to best effect.

14: FINANCIAL MANAGEMENT AND FINANCIAL OBJECTIVES

5.1.3 Corporate plans, targets and aims for nationalised industries

Each nationalised industry has **financial targets** and a series of **performance aims**. These targets and performance aims are set for a period of three to five years ahead, and may be included within a broader corporate plan.

5.1.4 External financing limits (EFLs) for nationalised industries

External financing limits (EFLs) control the flow of finance to and from nationalised industries. They set a limit on the amount of finance the industry can obtain from the government, and in the case of very profitable industries, they set requirements for the net repayment of finance to the government.

5.2 Not-for-profit organisations

Some organisations, such as **charities,** are set up with a prime objective which is not related to making profits. These organisations exist to pursue non-financial aims, such as providing a service to the community. However, there will be financial constraints which limit what any such organisation can do.

(a) A not-for-profit organisation **needs finance** to pay for its operations, and the major financial constraint is the amount of funds that it can obtain.

(b) Having obtained funds, a not-for-profit organisation should seek to get **value for money** from use of the funds, by considering the 3Es.
  (i) **Economy**: not spending £2 when the same thing can be bought for £1
  (ii) **Efficiency**: getting the best use out of what money is spent on
  (iii) **Effectiveness**: spending funds so as to achieve the organisation's objectives

The nature of financial objectives in a not-for-profit organisation can be explained in more detail, using **government departments** in the UK as an illustration.

Since managing government is different from managing a company, a different framework is needed for **planning and control**. This is achieved by

- Setting **objectives** for each
- **Careful planning** of public expenditure proposals
- Emphasis on getting **value for money**

A development in recent years has been the creation of agencies to carry out specific functions (such as vehicle licensing). These **executive agencies** are answerable to the government for providing a certain level of service, but are independently managed on business principles.

> **Exam focus point**
> In June 2003 candidates were asked to compare the objective of value for money in the public sector with profit maximisation in the private sector.

6 Ratio analysis   06/05

> **FAST FORWARD**
> **Performance measurement** is a part of the system of financial control of an enterprise as well as being important to investors.

6.1 Measuring financial performance

We have discussed profitability measurement in the context of management accounting in Chapter 13. As part of the system of financial control in an organisation, it will also be necessary to have ways of measuring the progress of the enterprise, so that managers know how well the company is doing. A common means of doing this is through ratio analysis, which is concerned with comparing and quantifying relationships between financial variables, such as those variables found in the balance sheet and profit and loss account of the enterprise.

Exam focus point

> The examiner has said, more than once, that knowledge of how to calculate and interpret key ratios is a weak point for many candidates. Make sure that it is one of your strong points. In reviewing ratio analysis below, we are in part revising material included in previous units.

6.2 The broad categories of ratios

Ratios can be grouped into the following four categories:

- **Profitability and return**
- **Debt and gearing**
- **Liquidity**
- **Shareholders' investment ratios ('stock market ratios')**.

The key to obtaining meaningful information from ratio analysis is **comparison**: comparing ratios **over a number of periods** within the same business to establish whether the business is improving or declining, and **comparing ratios between similar businesses** to see whether the company you are analysing is better or worse than average within its own business sector.

6.3 Ratio pyramids

The Du Pont system of ratio analysis involves constructing a pyramid of interrelated ratios like that below.

```
                        Return on equity
                               |
              ┌────────────────┴────────────────┐
        Return on investment    ×    Total assets ÷ equity
              |
      ┌───────┴───────┐
  Return on sales  ×  Asset turnover
      |                     |
  ┌───┴───┐             ┌───┴───┐
Net income ÷ Sales    Sales ÷ Total assets
      |                           |
  ┌───┴───┐                   ┌───┴───┐
Sales - Total costs        Fixed + Current
                           assets   assets
```

Such ratio pyramids help in providing for an overall management plan to achieve profitability, and allow the interrelationships between ratios to be checked.

6.4 Profitability

A company ought of course to be profitable if it is to maximise shareholder wealth, and obvious checks on profitability are:

(a) Whether the company has made a profit or a loss on its ordinary activities
(b) By how much this year's profit or loss is bigger or smaller than last year's profit or loss

Profit before taxation is generally thought to be a better figure to use than profit after taxation, because there might be unusual variations in the tax charge from year to year which would not affect the underlying profitability of the company's operations

Another profit figure that should be considered is **profit before interest and tax (PBIT)**. This is the amount of profit which the company earned before having to pay interest to the providers of loan capital. By

14: FINANCIAL MANAGEMENT AND FINANCIAL OBJECTIVES

providers of loan capital, we usually mean **longer term** loan capital, such as debentures and medium-term bank loans.

6.5 Profitability and return: the return on investment (ROI)

You cannot assess profits or profit growth properly without relating them to the amount of funds (the capital) employed in making the profits. The most important profitability ratio is therefore **return on capital employed (ROCE)**, also called **return on investment (ROI)**, which we encountered in Chapter 13.

> **Key terms**
>
> **Return on Capital Employed** = $\dfrac{\text{PBIT}}{\text{Capital employed}}$
>
> **Capital employed** = Shareholders' funds *plus* 'creditors: amounts falling due after more than one year' *plus* any long-term provisions for liabilities and charges.
>
> = Total assets less current liabilities.

6.6 Evaluating the ROCE

What does a company's ROCE tell us? What should we be looking for? There are three comparisons that can be made.

(a) The **change** in ROCE from one year to the next

(b) The ROCE being **earned** by **other companies**, if this information is available

(c) A comparison of the ROCE with **current market borrowing rates**

   (i) What would be the **cost of extra borrowing** to the company if it needed more loans, and is it earning a ROCE that suggests it could make high enough profits to make such borrowing worthwhile?

   (ii) Is the company making a ROCE which suggests that it is making **profitable use** of its **current borrowing**?

6.7 Secondary ratios

We may analyse the ROCE by looking at the kinds of interrelationships between ratios used in ratio pyramids, which we mentioned earlier. We can thus find out why the ROCE is high or low, or better or worse than last year. Profit margin and asset turnover together explain the ROCE, and if the ROCE is the primary profitability ratio, these other two are the secondary ratios. The relationship between the three ratios is as follows.

Profit margin × asset turnover = ROCE

$$\dfrac{\text{PBIT}}{\text{Sales}} \times \dfrac{\text{Sales}}{\text{Capital employed}} = \dfrac{\text{PBIT}}{\text{Capital employed}}$$

It is also worth commenting on the **change in turnover** from one year to the next. Strong sales growth will usually indicate volume growth as well as turnover increases due to price rises, and volume growth is one sign of a prosperous company.

> **Exam focus point**
>
> Remember that capital employed is **not just** shareholders' funds; this was highlighted as a frequent mistake in the examiners' report on the June 2003 exam.

6.8 Gross profit margin, the net profit margin and profit analysis

Depending on the format of the profit and loss account, you may be able to calculate the **gross profit margin** (covered in Chapter 13) and also the **net profit margin**. Looking at the two together can be quite informative.

6.9 Example: Profit margins

A company has the following summarised profit and loss accounts for two consecutive years.

	Year 1 £	Year 2 £
Turnover	70,000	100,000
Less cost of sales	42,000	55,000
Gross profit	28,000	45,000
Less expenses	21,000	35,000
Net profit	7,000	10,000

Although the net profit margin is the same for both years at 10%, the gross profit margin is not.

In year 1 it is: $\frac{28,000}{70,000} = 40\%$ and in year 2 it is: $\frac{45,000}{100,000} = 45\%$

Is this good or bad for the business? An increased profit margin must be good because this indicates a wider gap between selling price and cost of sales. However, given that the net profit ratio has stayed the same in the second year, expenses must be rising. In year 1 expenses were 30% of turnover, whereas in year 2 they were 35% of turnover. This indicates that administration or selling and distribution expenses may require tighter control.

A percentage analysis of profit between year 1 and year 2 is as follows.

	Year 1 %	Year 2 %
Cost of sales as a % of sales	60	55
Gross profit as a % of sales	40	45
	100	100
Expenses as a % of sales	30	35
Net profit as a % of sales	10	10
Gross profit as a % of sales	40	45

6.10 Debt and gearing ratios

Debt ratios are concerned with how much the company owes in relation to its size and whether it is getting into heavier debt or improving its situation.

(a) When a company is heavily in debt, and seems to be getting even more heavily into debt, banks and other would-be lenders are very soon likely to **refuse further borrowing** and the company might well find itself in trouble.

(b) When a company is earning only a modest profit before interest and tax, and has a heavy debt burden, there will be **very little profit** left over for shareholders after the interest charges have been paid.

The main debt and gearing ratios are covered in Chapter 23.

6.11 Liquidity ratios: cash and working capital

Profitability is of course an important aspect of a company's performance, and debt or gearing is another. Neither, however, addresses directly the key issue of **liquidity**. A company needs liquid assets so that it can meet its debts when they fall due. The main liquidity ratios will be described later in this text.

6.12 Shareholders' investment ratios

A further set of ratios of importance to the financial manager are the ratios which help equity shareholders and other investors to assess the value and quality of an investment in the ordinary shares of a company. These ratios will be described later in this text.

> **Exam focus point**
>
> The examiner has stated that ratio analysis questions will not require you to calculate all possible ratios, nor tell you what ratios to calculate. You will have to select for yourself the ratios that are relevant.

6.13 Selection of ratios

You should bear in mind the following guidelines when deciding which ratios to select and what comments you should make.

(a) **Remember the key areas**

If you are asked for a general analysis, you will need to **calculate ratios** covering each of the main areas. If however you are looking at the company from the viewpoint of a likely purchaser, and the target does not appear to be in financial difficulty, you should concentrate on profitability and shareholder ratios.

(b) **Be wary of single comparisons**

Comparisons just with the previous period may be **misleading** if one set of figures is unusually good or poor. Trends over a number of years will be more reliable. Likewise comparisons with a single similar company may be of limited use if the figures of one of the companies are extreme.

6.14 Environmental reporting

As well as tracking financial performance, managers of organisations need to understand the impact of the operations of the organisation on the environment. This is important, not just because of external pressures, but also so that organisations can gain from opportunities and avoid necessary penalties or costs. It has been argued that environmental reports should become a part of the regular process of financial reporting. Norsk Hydro was a pioneer in this field when it produced an environmental report in 1990.

Environmental reporting has become fairly widespread, with the majority of large UK companies now mentioning the environment in their annual report and accounts. In other countries, Dow Chemicals, Danish Steelworks, Kunert and BSO Origin are among those that have experimented with green reporting. Many companies include statements of **environmental policy** in their annual reports. A smaller number include quantified **indicators** of **environmental performance**.

For example, ICI plc includes statements reporting progress against targets, one of which relates to the reduction of hazardous wastes. However, environmental reporting is relatively rare among smaller companies.

The development of environmental reporting occurred in a period of increasing regulatory requirements in the UK and in the rest of the EU to report more specific data on environmental matters. Over the same period, many large companies sought ways of promoting their corporate image as well as their individual products. Provided the data presents the company's efforts in a positive light, reporting of environmental data should help to enhance people's perception of a company's qualities.

Chapter Roundup

- Financial management decisions cover **investment** decisions **financing** and **dividend** decisions.
- Financial targets may include targets for: **earnings; earnings per share; dividend per share; gearing level; profit retention; operating profitability**.
- The usual assumption in financial management for the private sector is that the primary financial objective of the company is to **maximise shareholders' wealth**.
- Non-financial objectives may include: **employee welfare; management welfare; the welfare of society; service provision objectives; fulfilment of responsibilities to customers and suppliers**.
- **Stakeholders** are individuals or groups who are affected by the activities of the firm. They can be classified as **internal** (employees and managers), **connected** (shareholders, customers and suppliers) and **external** (local communities, pressure groups, government).
- The **objectives of non-commercial organisations** such as nationalised industries and charities are aimed at the provision of a certain level and quality of service, and giving value for money, rather than profit oriented.
- **Performance measurement** is a part of the system of financial control of an enterprise as well as being important to investors.

Quick Quiz

1. Give a definition of financial management.

2. What three broad types of decision does financial management involve?

3. What main financial objective does the theory of company finance assume that a business organisation has?

4. If earnings per share fall from one year to the next, so will the level of dividends.

    ☐ True

    ☐ False

5. Tick which are stakeholder groups for a company.

    Employees ☐

    Ordinary shareholders ☐

    The Board of Directors ☐

    Trade creditors ☐

6. Return on capital employed = $\dfrac{?}{?}$

7. Which of the following are examples of financial objectives that a company might choose to pursue?

    A Provision of good wages and salaries
    B Restricting the level of gearing to below a specified target level
    C Dealing honestly and fairly with customers on all occasions
    D Producing environmentally friendly products

8. Which of the following decisions is not an investment decision?

    A Whether to go ahead with an advertising campaign
    B Whether to retain more profits for reinvestment in the business
    C Whether to carry out a takeover of another company
    D Whether to initiate a new research project

PART D   THE FRAMEWORK OF FINANCIAL MANAGEMENT

Answers to Quick Quiz

1   The management of the finances of an organisation in order to achieve the financial objectives of the organisation.

2   Investment decisions, financing decisions, dividend decisions.

3   To maximise the wealth of the company's ordinary shareholders.

4   False. Dividends may still be maintained from payments out of profits retained in earlier periods.

5   You should have ticked all four boxes.

6   $\dfrac{\text{Profit before interest and tax}}{\text{Capital employed}}$

7   B   This is a financial objective that relates to the level of risk that the company accepts.

8   B   This is the correct answer. Decisions on the level of retentions are financing decisions, not investment decisions.

    A   This is a decision that will involve the expenditure of funds in anticipation of earning additional profits. It is therefore an investment decision.

    C   A takeover would involve the outlay of additional funds with the aim of increasing group profits. It is therefore an investment decision.

    D   The research project would involve the outlay of funds now with the aim of increasing future company profits. It is therefore an investment decision.

Now try the questions below from the Exam Question Bank

Number	Level	Marks	Time
Q17	Introductory	n/a	20 mins

The financial management framework

Topic list	Syllabus reference
1 Financial intermediation and credit creation	2(a)
2 Commercial banks as providers of funds	2(b)
3 Money markets and capital markets	2(b)
4 The efficient market hypothesis	2(c)
5 Rates of interest and rates of return	2(d)
6 The separation theorem	5(b)(i)
7 International money and capital markets	2(b), 4(a)(xi)

Introduction

Having discussed the scope of financial management and the objectives of firms and other organisations in Chapter 14, we now introduce the framework of **markets** and **institutions** through which the financing of a business takes place. We also look at some theoretical aspects of how this framework operates including the **efficient market hypothesis**, which tries to account for why share prices behave as they do.

PART D THE FRAMEWORK OF FINANCIAL MANAGEMENT

Study guide

Section 4 – The financial management framework

- Identify the general role of financial intermediaries
- Explain the role of commercial banks as providers of funds (including the creation of credit)
- Discuss the risk/return trade-off
- Identify the international money and capital markets and outline their operation
- Explain the functions of a stock market and corporate bond market
- Explain the key features of different types of security in terms of the risk/return trade-off
- Outline the Efficient Markets Hypothesis and assess its broad implications for corporate policy and financial management
- Explain the Separation Theorem
- Explain the functions of, and identify the links between, the money and capital markets

Exam guide

You would not get a complete question on the topics covered in this chapter. You might however be asked a part question that relates to the circumstances of a particular company, for instance how an AIM listing can benefit it.

1 Financial intermediation and credit creation   6/02

FAST FORWARD

A **financial intermediary** links those with surplus funds (eg **lenders**) to those with funds deficits (eg potential **borrowers**) thus providing **aggregation** and **economies of scale**, **risk pooling** and **maturity transformation**.

1.1 Financial intermediation

Key term

Financial intermediary is a party bringing together providers and users of finance, either as broker or as principal.

A **financial intermediary** is an institution which links lenders with borrowers, by obtaining deposits from lenders and then re-lending them to borrowers.

Person	Surplus unit
↓ Funds	Savings
Bank	Financial intermediary
↓ Funds	Collective deposits of savings
Company	Deficit unit

15: THE FINANCIAL MANAGEMENT FRAMEWORK

Not all intermediation takes place between savers and investors. Some institutions (such as the discount houses which intermediate between the Bank of England and the commercial banks) act mainly as **intermediaries** between **other institutions**. Financial intermediaries may also lend abroad or borrow from abroad.

> **Exam focus point**
>
> Bear in mind that *financial markets* and *institutions* are topic areas on which the examiner is not expected to set full questions. These topics could, however, be examined in subsections of a question.

1.1.1 Examples of financial intermediaries   6/02

- Commercial banks
- Finance houses
- Building societies
- Government's National Savings department
- Institutional investors eg pension funds and investment trusts

1.2 The benefits of financial intermediation

Financial intermediaries perform the following functions.

(a) They provide obvious and **convenient** ways in which a lender can save money. Instead of having to find a suitable borrower for his money, the lender can deposit his money with a financial intermediary. All the lender has to do is decide for **how long** he might want to lend the money, and **what sort of return** he requires, and he can then choose a financial intermediary that offers a **financial instrument** to suit his requirements.

(b) Financial intermediaries also provide a **ready source of funds** for **borrowers**. Even when money is in short supply, a borrower will usually find a financial intermediary prepared to lend some.

(c) They can **aggregate** or **'package'** the amounts lent by savers and lend on to borrowers in different amounts.

(d) **Risk** for individual lenders is reduced by **pooling**. Since financial intermediaries lend to a large number of individuals and organisations, any losses suffered through default by borrowers or capital losses are effectively pooled and **borne** as **costs** by the intermediary. Such losses are **shared among lenders in general**.

(e) By pooling the funds of large numbers of people, some financial institutions are able to give investors access to **diversified portfolios** covering a varied range of different securities, such as unit trusts and investment trusts.

(f) Financial intermediaries, most importantly, provide **maturity transformation**; ie they bridge the gap between the wish of most lenders for **liquidity** and the desire of most borrowers for **loans** over longer periods.

1.3 Bank deposits and the creation of money ('credit creation')

Banks create money when they lend because when a bank lends money, most of the money will find its way back into the banking system as **new customer deposits**. This means that the amount lent by the bank adds to the money supply.

Suppose, for example, that in a country with a single bank, a customer C deposits £100,000. The bank, we will assume, re-lends all these deposits to another customer D. This customer D uses the money he has borrowed to buy goods and services from firm Y. If firm Y, after receiving payment, then puts the money into its own account with the bank, the bank's deposits will have doubled.

Liabilities of the bank		Assets of the bank	
	£		£
Deposit of customer C	100,000	Loan to customer D	100,000
Deposit of firm Y	100,000		
	200,000		

This will enable the bank to re-lend more money (another £100,000), to bring its assets up to £200,000 and this in turn will create even more bank deposits. This cycle could go on and on, with the bank making more and more loans, and the people who are paid for goods and services bought with the loans putting all their receipts back into the bank as extra deposits. In short, **'every loan creates a deposit'**.

Extra bank lending (and building society lending) therefore has a dual effect. It **increases the money supply**. It **provides credit** which borrowers use to increase their amount of spending. Lending adds to spending in the economy.

Key term

> **Credit creation** is the process whereby banks and other deposit-taking and lending institutions can, on the basis of an increase in reserve assets, expand the volume of lending and deposit liabilities by more than the initial increase in reserves.

2 Commercial banks as providers of funds   12/05

FAST FORWARD

> **Commercial banks** can provide
> - a payment mechanism
> - notes and coins
> - bank accounts
> - loans and overdrafts
> - for individuals and businesses.

An important grouping of financial intermediaries is the **commercial banks**, which include:

(a) The retail banks, which include the well known 'High Street' banks

(b) The wholesale banks, which offer services mainly to larger customers, including large companies (The wholesale banks include merchant banks and overseas banks.)

2.1 The functions of the commercial banks

The functions of the commercial banks include the following.

(a) They provide a **payments mechanism** - a way in which individuals, firms and government can make payments to each other. The **'clearing system'** of the clearing banks enables individuals and firms to make payments by cheque.

(b) The banks are also a source from which individuals and firms can **obtain notes and coin**.

(c) They provide a place for individuals, firms and government to **store their wealth**. Banks compete with other financial institutions to attract the funds of individuals and firms.

(d) They act as **providers of funds** by lending money in the form of loans or overdrafts.

2.2 Bank borrowing

Borrowings from banks are an important source of finance to companies as well as to unincorporated businesses. Bank lending is still mainly short-term although medium-term lending has grown considerably in recent years.

Short-term borrowing may take various forms.

(a) An **overdraft**, which a company should keep within a limit set by the bank. Interest is charged (at a variable rate) on the amount by which the company is overdrawn from day to day.

(b) A **short-term loan**. This may last for up to three years.

(c) **Medium-term loans**. These are loans for a period of from three to ten years.

The rate of interest charged on medium-term bank lending to large companies will typically be a set margin above the **London Inter-Bank Offered Rate (LIBOR)**, with the size of the margin depending on the **credit standing** and **riskiness** of the borrower.

Lending to **smaller companies** will typically be at a margin **above the bank's base rate** and at either a variable or a fixed rate of interest.

Lending on **overdraft** is always at a **variable rate**.

A loan at a variable rate of interest is sometimes referred to as a **floating rate loan**.

Longer term bank loans will sometimes be available, usually for the purchase of property, where the loan takes the form of a mortgage.

3 Money markets and capital markets

> **FAST FORWARD**
>
> The **capital markets** and **money markets** are markets for long-term and short-term capital respectively.
>
> A stock market (in the UK: the **main market** plus the **AIM**) acts as a **primary market** for raising finance, and as a **secondary market** for the trading of existing securities (ie stocks and shares).

The **capital markets**, being markets for long-term capital, are distinguished from the **money markets**, which are markets for:

- Trading short-term financial instruments
- Short-term lending and borrowing

Key terms

> **Short-term capital** is capital that is lent or borrowed for a period which might range from as short as overnight up to about one year, and sometimes longer.
>
> **Long-term capital** is capital invested or lent and borrowed for a period of five years or more.

There is a 'grey area' between long-term and short-term capital, which is lending and borrowing for a period from about a year up to about five years, which may be referred to as **medium-term capital**.

3.1 The money markets

The money markets are **operated** by the **banks** and other **financial institutions**. Although the money markets largely involve borrowing and lending by banks, some large companies and nationalised industries, as well as the government, are involved in money market operations. The building societies have also become major participants in the money markets since liberalisation of the building societies has allowed them to raise wholesale funds.

The primary market is known as the **official market**, the other markets as the **parallel** or **wholesale markets**.

PART D   THE FRAMEWORK OF FINANCIAL MANAGEMENT

Types of market	
Primary market	Approved institutions deal in financial instruments with Bank of England (UK Central bank) Bank of England uses trading to control short-term interest rates
Interbank market	Banks lend short-term funds to each other
Eurocurrency market	Banks lend and borrow in foreign currencies
Certificate of deposit market	Market for trading in Certificates of Deposit (negotiable instruments acknowledging deposits)
Local authority market	Local authorities borrow short-term funds by issuing and selling short-term debt instruments
Finance house market	Dealing in short-term loans raised from money markets by finance houses
Inter-company market	Direct short-term lending between treasury departments of large companies

3.2 The capital markets

Capital markets are markets for trading in long-term finance, in the form of long-term financial instruments such as equities and debentures. In the UK, the principal capital markets are:

(a) The Stock Exchange **'main market'** (for companies with a full Stock Exchange listing)
(b) The more loosely regulated 'second tier' **Alternative Investment Market (AIM)**

The Stock Exchange is also the market for dealings in **government securities**.

Firms obtain long-term or medium-term capital in one of the following ways.

(a) They may raise **share capital**. Most new issues of share capital are in the form of ordinary share capital. Firms that issue ordinary share capital are inviting investors to take an **equity stake** in the business, or to increase their existing equity stake.

(b) They may raise **loan capital**. Long-term loan capital might be raised in the form of a mortgage or debenture.

The stock markets serve two main purposes.

(a) As **primary markets** they enable organisations to **raise new finance**, by issuing new shares or new debentures. In the UK, a company must **have public company status** (be a plc) to be allowed to raise finance from the public on a capital market.

(b) As **secondary markets** they enable existing investors to **sell their investments**, should they wish to do so. The marketability of securities is a very important feature of the capital markets, because investors are more willing to buy stocks and shares if they know that they could sell them easily, should they wish to.

These are the main functions of a stock market, but we can add two more important ones.

(a) When a company comes to the stock market for the first time, and 'floats' its shares on the market, the owners of the company can **realise** some of the **value of their shares** in cash, because they will offer a proportion of their personally-held shares for sale to new investors.

(b) When one company wants to **take over** another, it is common to do so by issuing shares to finance the takeover. Takeovers by means of a share exchange are only feasible if the shares that are offered can be readily traded on a stock market, and so have an identifiable market value.

Question — Financial Times

Get hold of a copy of the Companies and Markets section of the weekday *Financial Times*, and look out for points relevant to your studies. Note the various London Money Rates in the Money Markets section, the parts covering the London Stock Exchange, and the share prices quotations on the London Share Service pages. This may help to put some of the topics covered here into context.

3.3 The Alternative Investment Market (AIM)

The London Stock Exchange launched the AIM in 1995 as a market for smaller, growing, companies that cannot qualify for or do not wish to join the Official List (or 'main market').

AIM companies might be new business 'start-ups' or well established family businesses, from high technology firms to traditional manufacturers. The AIM is designed to attract companies which wish to **cut the cost** of a **stock market** quotation.

The main advantages of an **AIM listing** are:

- Wider access to capital
- Enhanced credibility among financial institutions
- A higher public profile

3.4 OFEX

An unquoted company might choose to seek finance from investors, including members of the general public, through **OFEX**, a facility allowing trading in the securities of unquoted companies. OFEX is not a regulated market; it is a mechanism whereby stock exchange member firms in effect match business 'off exchange'; in the securities of certain unquoted companies.

3.5 Institutional investors

Institutional investors are institutions which have large amounts of funds which they want to invest, and they will invest in stocks and shares or any other assets which offer satisfactory returns and security or lend money to companies directly. The institutional investors are now the biggest investors on the stock market.

The major institutional investors in the UK are **pension funds, insurance companies, investment trusts, unit trusts** and **venture capital organisations**. Of these, pension funds and insurance companies have the largest amounts of funds to invest.

PART D THE FRAMEWORK OF FINANCIAL MANAGEMENT

3.6 Capital market participants

The various participants in the capital markets are summarised in the diagram below.

```
                          Capital markets
Demand for funds                                         Suppliers
comes from...         INTERMEDIARIES                     of funds

INDIVIDUALS      ←─── Banks                    ←───  INDIVIDUALS
(eg housing/consumer                                 (as savers and
goods finance)   ←─── Building societies       ←───  investors)

                      Insurance companies
                 ←─── and pension funds        ←───
FIRMS                                                FIRMS
(share capital;                                      (with long-term
loans)           ←─── Unit trust/investment    ←───  funds to invest)
                      trust companies

                 ←─── Stock exchanges          ←───

GOVERNMENT                                           GOVERNMENT
(budget deficit) ←─── Venture capital          ←───  (budget surplus)
                      organisations
```

4 The efficient market hypothesis   6/03

> **FAST FORWARD**
>
> The **efficient market hypothesis** suggests that **share prices reflect** the **type of information** which is available to investors.

The UK and US stock markets are perhaps efficient capital markets. An 'efficient capital market' in this context is one in which:

(a) The prices of securities bought and sold **reflect all** the **relevant information** which is available to the buyers and sellers - in other words, share prices change quickly to reflect all new information about future prospects.

(b) **No individual dominates** the market.

(c) **Transaction costs** of buying and selling are **not so high** as to discourage trading significantly.

If the stock market is efficient, share prices should vary in a rational way.

(a) If a company makes a **profitable investment**, shareholders will get to know about it, and the **market price** of its shares will **rise** in anticipation of future dividend increases.

(b) If a company makes a **bad investment** shareholders will find out and so the **price** of its shares will **fall**.

(c) If **interest rates rise**, shareholders will want a **higher return** from their investments, so **market prices** will **fall**.

An efficient market is one in which the market prices of all the securities traded on it reflect all the available information. In such a market, there would be no possibility of 'speculative bubbles' in which share prices are pushed up or down by speculative pressure to unrealistically high or low levels. Investors will be reassured that the prices they pay for shares and loan stock are a **fair reflection** of value.

4.1 The definition of efficiency

Different types of efficiency can be distinguished in the context of the operation of financial markets.

TYPES OF EFFICIENCY	
Operational	Minimisation of transaction costs such as commissions, interest rate margins and loan arrangement fees
Informational	Reflects ability of stock market to absorb information widely at minimum cost
Pricing	Market prices of all securities reflect all available information. It has three forms: • Weak • Semi-strong • Strong It arises out of operational and informational efficiency
Allocative	Direction of funds towards firms making best use of them, arises out of pricing efficiency

Under the **weak form** hypothesis of **market efficiency**, current share prices **reflect all information available from past changes in the price**.

Research to prove that the stock market displays weak form efficiency has been based on the principle that:

- If share price changes are random, and
- If there is no connection between past price movements and new share price changes,

then it should be possible to prove statistically there is no correlation between successive changes in the price of a share, that is, that **trends** in prices **cannot be detected**. Proofs of the absence of trends have been claimed in the work of various writers.

Semi-strong form tests attempt to show that the stock market displays semi-strong efficiency, by which we mean that current share prices reflect both:

- All **relevant information** about **past price movements** and their implications, and
- All **knowledge** which is **available publicly** in the financial press, annual accounts, company announcements.

Research in both the UK and the USA has suggested that market prices anticipate mergers several months before they are formally announced, and the conclusion drawn is that the stock markets in these countries *do* exhibit semi-strong efficiency.

Strong form efficiency means that share prices reflect all information available:

- From past price changes
- From public knowledge or anticipation, and
- From insider knowledge available to experts such as investment managers

If strong form efficiency applies, management should concentrate simply on **maximising** the **net present value** of its **investments.** It need not worry, for example, about the effect on share prices of financial results in the published accounts. Investors will make allowances for low profits or dividends in the current year if higher profits or dividends are expected in the future.

Exam focus point

Market efficiency is likely to be tested in the context of how a company's assessment of market efficiency would influence the company's actions.

4.2 The implications of the efficient market hypothesis

If the strong form of the efficient market hypothesis is correct, a company's **real financial position** will be **reflected in its share price**. Its real financial position includes both its **current position** and its expected **future profitability**.

The implication for an investor is that if the market shows **strong form** or **semi-strong form** efficiency, he can **rarely spot shares** at a **bargain price** that will soon rise sharply in value. This is because the market will already have anticipated future developments, and will have reflected these in the share price. All an investor can do, instead of looking for share bargains, is to concentrate on building up a **good spread of shares** (a portfolio) in order to achieve a satisfactory balance between **risk and return**.

The main consequences of efficient markets for financial managers will be that they simply need to **concentrate** on **maximising the net present value** of the **company's investments** in order to maximise the wealth of shareholders. Managers need not worry, for example, about the effect on share prices of financial results in the published accounts because investors will make **allowances** for **low profits** or **dividends** in the current year if higher profits or dividends are expected in the future. A company's real financial position will be reflected in its share price.

If the market is strongly efficient, there is little point in financial managers attempting strategies that attempt to mislead the markets.

(a) There is no point for example in trying to identify a correct date when **shares** should be **issued**, since share prices will always reflect the true worth of the company – they will not be over or under valued at any point in time.

(b) The market will identify any attempts to **window dress the accounts** and put an optimistic spin on the figures.

(c) The market will decide what **level of return** it requires for the risk involved in making an investment in the company. It is pointless for the company to try to change the market's view by issuing different types of capital instruments.

Similarly if the company is looking to expand, the directors will be wasting their time if they seek as **takeover targets** companies whose shares are undervalued, since the market will fairly value all companies' shares.

Only if the market is semi-strongly efficient and the financial managers possess **inside information** that would significantly alter the price of the company's shares if released to the market could they perhaps gain an advantage. However, attempts to take account of this inside information may breach insider dealing laws.

Question
Efficient market hypothesis

In the share price crash of October 1987, share prices on the world's stock markets fell suddenly by 20% to 40%. Why does this raise a question about the validity of the efficient market hypothesis?

Answer

The question is: if EMH is correct, how can shares that were valued at one level on one day suddenly be worth 40% less the next day, without any change in expectations of corporate profits and dividends? It would appear that speculation must have caused share prices to rise to levels which were unsustainable in the longer term.

Exam focus point

The examiner has noted that market efficiency is often poorly understood, so this topic will be examined frequently in this paper.

5 Rates of interest and rates of return 6/04

Interest rates are effectively the 'prices' governing lending and borrowing. The borrower pays interest to the lender at a certain percentage of the capital sum, as the price for the use of the funds borrowed. As with other prices, supply and demand effects apply. For example, the higher the rates of interest that are charged, the lower will be the demand for funds from borrowers.

5.1 The pattern of interest rates

FAST FORWARD

The **pattern of interest rates** on financial assets is influenced by the **risk** of the assets, the **duration** of the lending, and the **size** of the loan.

The pattern of interest rates refers to the variety of interest rates on different financial assets, and the margin between interest rates on lending and deposits that are set by banks. Note that the **pattern of interest rates** is a different thing from the **general level of interest rates.**

Why are there such a large number of interest rates? In other words, how is the **pattern** of interest rates to be explained? The answer to this question relates to several factors.

(a) **Risk**

There is a trade-off between risk and return. Higher-risk borrowers must pay higher yields on their borrowing, to compensate lenders for the greater risk involved. Banks will assess the creditworthiness of the borrower, and set a rate of interest on its loan at a certain mark-up above its base rate or the LIBOR.

(b) **Need to make a profit on re-lending**

Financial intermediaries make their profits from re-lending at a higher rate of interest than the cost of their borrowing. For example, the interest rate charged on bank loans exceeds the rate paid on deposits and the mortgage rate charged by building societies exceeds the interest rate paid on deposits.

(c) **Duration of the lending**

The term of the loan or asset will affect the rate of interest charged on it. In general, longer-dated assets will earn a higher yield than similar short-dated assets but this is not always the case. The differences are referred to as the **term structure** of interest rates.

(d) **Size of the loan or deposit**

The yield on assets might vary with the size of the loan or deposit. Administrative cost savings help to allow **lower rates of interest** to be charged by banks **on larger loans** and **higher rates of interest** to be paid on **larger time deposits**.

(e) **Different types of financial asset**

Different types of financial asset attract **different rates of interest**. This is partly because different types of asset attract different sorts of lender/investor. For example, bank deposits attract individuals and companies, whereas long-dated government securities are particularly attractive to various institutional investors.

PART D   THE FRAMEWORK OF FINANCIAL MANAGEMENT

The rates of interest paid on government borrowing (the **Treasury bill rate** for short-term borrowing and the **gilt-edged rate** for long-dated government stocks) provide benchmarks for other interest rates. For example:

(a) Clearing banks might set the three months inter-bank rate (LIBOR) at about 1% above the Treasury bill rate.

(b) Banks in turn lend (wholesale) at a rate higher than LIBOR.

5.2 The term structure of interest rates: the yield curve

In addition interest rates depend on the term to maturity of the asset. For example, government stock might be short-dated, medium-dated, or long-dated. The **term structure of interest rates** refers to the way in which the yield on a security varies according to the term of the borrowing, that is the length of time until the debt will be repaid as shown by the **yield curve**. Normally, the longer the term of an asset to maturity, the higher the rate of interest paid on the asset.

The reasons why, in theory, the yield curve will normally be upward sloping, so that long-term financial assets offer a higher yield than short-term assets, are as follows.

(a) The investor must be **compensated** for **tying up** his **money** in the asset for a **longer period of time**.

(b) There is a **greater risk** in lending long-term than in lending short-term. To compensate investors for this risk, they might require a higher yield on longer dated investments.

So why might a yield curve slope downwards, with short-term rates higher than longer-term rates?

(a) **Expectations** about the way that interest rates will move in the future affect the term structure of interest rates. When interest rates are expected to fall, short-term rates might be higher than long-term rates, and the yield curve would be downward sloping.

(b) **Government policy** on interest rates might be significant too. A policy of keeping interest rates relatively high might therefore have the effect of forcing short-term interest rates higher than long-term rates.

(c) The **market segmentation theory** of interest rates suggests that the slope of the yield curve will reflect conditions in **different segments** of the market. This theory holds that the major investors are confined to a particular segment of the market and will not switch segment even if the forecast of likely future interests rates changes.

5.3 The general level of interest rates

Interest rates on any one type of financial asset will vary over time. In other words, the general level of interest rates might go up or down. The general level of interest rates is affected by several factors.

(a) **Need for a real return**

Investors normally want to **earn a 'real' rate of return** on their investment. The appropriate 'real' rate of return will depend on factors such as investment risk.

(b) **Inflation**

Nominal rates of interest should be sufficient to **cover expected rates of inflation** over the term of the investment and to provide a real return.

(c) **Uncertainty about future rates of inflation**

When investors are uncertain about inflation and therefore about what future nominal and real interest rates will be, they are likely to require **higher interest yields** to persuade them to take the risk of investing, especially in the longer term.

(d) **Liquidity preference of investors and the demand for borrowing**

Higher interest rates have to be offered to persuade savers to invest their surplus money. When the demand to borrow increases, interest rates will rise.

(e) **Balance of payments**

When a country has a continuing deficit on the current account of its balance of payments, and the authorities are unwilling to allow the exchange rate to depreciate by more than a certain amount, interest rates may have to be raised to **attract capital** into the country. The country can then finance the deficit by borrowing from abroad.

(f) **Monetary policy**

From mid-1997, decisions over UK interest rate policy have been made by the Monetary Policy Committee of the Bank of England. The Bank of England influences very short-term money market rates by means of **open market operations**. Usually longer term money market rates, and then banks' base rates, will respond to the authorities' wish for interest rate changes. We shall discuss monetary policy in more detail in the next chapter.

(g) **Interest rates abroad**

The rate of interest in one country will be influenced by **external factors**, such as interest rates in other countries and expectations about the exchange rate. When interest rates in overseas countries are high, interest rates on domestic currency investments must also be comparably high, to avoid capital transfers abroad and a fall in the exchange rate of the domestic currency.

5.4 The risk-return trade-off

> **FAST FORWARD**
>
> There is a **trade-off** between **risk and return**. Investors in riskier assets expect to be compensated for the risk. In the case of ordinary shares, investors hope to achieve their return in the form of an increase in the share price (a capital gain) as well as from dividends.

We have explained how rates of interest, and therefore rates of return to lenders, will be affected by the risk involved in lending. The idea of a risk-return trade-off can, however, be extended beyond a consideration of interest rates.

An investor has the choice between different forms of investment. The investor may earn interest by depositing funds with a financial intermediary who will lend on to, say, a company, or it may invest in loan stock of a company. Alternatively, the investor may invest directly in a company by purchasing shares in it.

The current market price of a security is found by discounting the future expected earnings stream at a rate suitably adjusted for risk. This means that investments carrying a higher degree of risk will demand a higher rate of return. This rate of return or yield has two components:

- **Annual income** (dividend or interest)
- **Expected capital gain**

In general, the higher the risk of the security, the more important is the capital gain component of the expected yield.

Some of the main forms of investment are listed below in ascending order of risk.

(a) **Government stock**

The risk of default is negligible. Hence this tends to form the **base level** for returns in the market. The only uncertainty concerns the movement of interest rates over time, and hence longer dated stocks will tend to carry a higher rate of interest.

(b) **Company loan stock**

Although there is some risk of default on company loan stock (also called corporate bonds), the stock is usually **secured** against corporate assets.

(c) **Preference shares**

These are generally riskier than loan stock since they rank behind debt in the event of a liquidation, although they rank ahead of **ordinary shares**. The return takes the form of a **fixed percentage dividend** based on the par value of the share.

(d) **Ordinary shares**

Ordinary shares carry a high level of risk. Dividends are paid out of distributable profits after all other liabilities have been paid and can be subject to **large fluctuations** from year to year. However, there is the potential for significant **capital appreciation** in times of growth. In general, the level of risk will vary with the operational and financial **gearing** of the company and the nature of the markets in which it operates.

5.5 The reverse yield gap

Because debt involves lower risk than equity investment, we might expect yields on debt to be lower than yields on shares. More usually, however, the opposite applies and the yields on shares are lower than on low-risk debt; this situation is known as a **reverse yield gap**. A reverse yield gap can occur because shareholders may be willing to accept lower returns on their investment in the short term, in anticipation that they will make capital gains in the future.

5.6 Interest rates and shareholders' required rates of return

Given that equity shares and interest-earning investments stand as alternatives from the investor's point of view, changes in the general level of interest rates can be expected to have an effect on the rates of return which shareholders will expect.

If the return expected by an investor from an equity investment (ie an investment in shares) is 11% and the dividend paid on the shares is 15 pence, the market value of one share will be 15 pence / 11% = £1.36.

Suppose that interest rates then fall. Because the option of putting the funds on deposit has become less attractive, the shareholders' required return will fall, to say, 9%. Then the market value of one share will increase to 15 pence / 9% = £1.67.

You can see from this that an **increase** in the shareholders' **required rate of return** (perhaps resulting from an increase in the general level of interest rates) will lead to a **fall** in the **market value** of the share.

6 The separation theorem

FAST FORWARD

The **separation theorem** implies that companies should concentrate on **maximisation of present value**, since the stock market will enable individuals to obtain the income pattern from their investments that corresponds to their consumption requirements.

The essence of the separation theorem is that **financial decisions of investors** are made **independently of companies' decisions to invest in assets.**

To illustrate why this is so, we need to consider how investors use the capital market.

When investing, investors must choose a portfolio which gives them a satisfactory **balance** between the **expected returns** from the portfolio and the **risk** that actual returns from the portfolio will be higher or lower than expected. Some portfolios will be more risky than others.

Traditional investment theory suggests that rational investors wish to maximise return and minimise risk. Thus if two portfolios have the same element of risk, the investor will choose the one yielding the higher return. Similarly, if two portfolios offer the same return the investor will select the portfolio with the lesser risk. This is illustrated by Figure 1.

Figure 1 An investor's indifference curve

Portfolio A will be preferred to portfolio B because it offers a higher expected return for the same level of risk. Similarly, portfolio C will be preferred to portfolio B because it offers the same expected return for lower risk. But whether an investor chooses portfolio A or portfolio C will depend on the individual's attitude to risk, whether he wishes to accept a greater risk for a greater expected return.

The curve I_1 is an investor's indifference curve. The investor will have no preference between any portfolios which give a mix of risk and expected return which lies on the curve, since he derives equal **utility** from each of them. Thus, to the investor the portfolios A, C, D, E and F are all just as good as each other, and all of them are better than portfolio B.

An investor would prefer combinations of return and risk on **indifference curve** A to those on curve B (Figure 2) because curve A offers higher returns for the same degree of risk (and less risk for the same expected returns). For example, for the same amount of risk x, the expected return on curve A is y_1, whereas on curve B it is only y_2.

Figure 2 Indifference curves compared

6.1 Efficient portfolios

If we drew a graph (Figure 3) to show the expected return and the risk of the many possible portfolios of investments, we could (according to portfolio theory) plot an egg-shaped cluster of dots on a scattergraph. In this graph, there are some portfolios which would not be as good as others. However, there are other portfolios which are neither better nor worse than each other, because they have either a higher expected return but a higher risk, or a lower expected return but a lower risk. These 'efficient' portfolios lie along the so-called **efficient frontier of portfolios** which is shown as a dotted line in Figure 3.

Figure 3 The efficient frontier of available investment portfolios

We can now place an investor's indifference curves on the same graph as the possible portfolios of investments (the **egg-shaped scatter graph**), as in Figure 4. An investor would prefer a portfolio of investments on indifference curve A to a portfolio on curve B, which in turn is preferable to a portfolio on curve C which in turn is preferable to curve D. No portfolio exists, however, which is on curve A or curve B.

Figure 4 The optimum portfolio (ignoring risk-free securities)

The optimum portfolio (or portfolios) to select is one where an indifference curve touches the efficient frontier of portfolios at a tangent. In Figure 4, this is the portfolio marked M, where indifference curve C touches the efficient frontier at a tangent. Any portfolio on an indifference curve to the right of curve C, such as one on curve D, would be worse than M.

Risk-free investments

Figure 5 The capital market line

The efficient frontier is a curved line, not a straight line. This is because the additional return for accepting a greater level of risk will not be constant. The curve eventually levels off because a point will be reached where no more return can be offered to an investor for accepting more risk.

All the portfolios under consideration carry some degree of risk. But some investments are risk-free. It is extremely unlikely that the British Government would default on any payment of interest and capital on its stocks. Thus government stocks can be taken to be risk-free investments. If we introduce a **risk-free investment** into the analysis we can see that the old efficient frontier is superseded (Figure 5).

The straight line XZME is drawn at a tangent to the efficient frontier and cuts the y axis at the point of the risk-free investment's return. The line (known as the **capital market line** (CML)) becomes the new efficient frontier.

Portfolio M is the same as in Figure 4. It is the efficient portfolio which will appeal to the investor most, ignoring risk-free investments. Portfolio Z is a mixture of the investments in portfolio M and risk-free investments. Investors will prefer portfolio Z (a mixture of risky portfolio M and the risk-free investment) to portfolio P because a higher return is obtained for the same level of risk. The only portfolio consisting entirely of **risky investments** a rational investor should want to hold is portfolio M. All other risky portfolios are inefficient (because they are below the CML).

As with the curvilinear frontier, one portfolio on the capital market line is as attractive as another to a rational investor. One investor may wish to hold portfolio Z, which lies 2/3 of the way along the CML between risk-free investment X and portfolio M (that is, a holding comprising 2/3 portfolio M and 1/3 risk-free securities). Another investor may wish to hold portfolio E, which entails putting all his funds in portfolio M and borrowing money at the risk-free rate to acquire more of portfolio M.

We have said that investors will only want to hold one portfolio of risky investments: portfolio M. This may be held in conjunction with a holding of the risk-free investment (as with portfolio Z). Alternatively, an investor may borrow funds to augment his holding of M (as with portfolio E). Therefore, since all investors wish to hold portfolio M, and all shares quoted on the Stock Exchange must be held by investors, it follows that **all shares quoted on the Stock Exchange must be in portfolio M**.

Thus portfolio M is the **market portfolio** and each investor's portfolio will contain a proportion of it.

The implication of the **separation theorem** is that investing in the stock market enables individuals to obtain the distribution that meets their personal time pattern of consumption requirements. Therefore a company's managers do not need to worry about how their investments can match the consumption preferences of their shareholders. What managers have to do is **invest in projects offering positive net present values** when **discounted at the capital market rate**, and the market will do the rest.

7 International money and capital markets

> **FAST FORWARD**
>
> **International money and capital markets** are available for larger companies wishing to raise larger amounts of finance.

Larger companies are able to borrow funds on the **eurocurrency markets** (which are international money markets) and on the markets for **eurobonds** (international capital markets).

> **Exam focus point**
>
> Don't suggest these international markets as possible sources of finance for a *smaller* business in an exam answer.

7.1 Eurocurrency markets

A UK company might borrow money from a bank or from the investing public, in sterling. But it might also borrow in a foreign currency, especially if it trades abroad, or if it already has assets or liabilities abroad denominated in a foreign currency.

When a company borrows in a foreign currency, the loan is known as a **eurocurrency loan**.

> **Key term**
>
> **Eurocurrency** is currency which is held by individuals and institutions outside the country of issue of that currency.

For example, if a UK company borrows US $50,000 from its bank, the loan will be a 'eurodollar' loan. London is a major centre for eurocurrency lending and companies with foreign trade interests might choose to borrow from their bank in another currency.

The **eurocurrency markets** involve the depositing of funds with a bank outside the country of the currency in which the funds are denominated and re-lending these funds for a fairly short term, typically three months. Most eurocurrency transactions in fact takes place between banks of different countries and take the form of negotiable certificates of deposit.

7.2 International capital markets

Large companies may arrange borrowing facilities from their bank, in the form of bank loans or bank overdrafts. Instead, however, they might prefer to borrow from private investors. In other words, instead of obtaining a £10,000,000 bank loan, a company might issue 'bonds', or 'paper' in order to borrow directly from investors, with:

(a) The bank merely **arranging the transaction**, finding investors who will take up the bonds or paper that the borrowing company issues

(b) **Interest** being payable to the **investors themselves**, not to a bank

In recent years, a strong international market has built up which allows very large companies to borrow in this way, long-term or short-term. As well as eurobonds, there is also a less highly developed market in international equity share issues (**'euro-equity'**).

Key term

> A **eurobond** is a bond denominated in a currency which often differs from that of the country of issue.

Eurobonds are long-term loans raised by international companies or other institutions and sold to investors in several countries at the same time. Such bonds can be sold by one holder to another. The term of a eurobond issue is typically ten to 15 years.

Eurobonds may be the most suitable source of finance for a large organisation with an excellent credit rating, such as a large successful multinational company, which:

(a) Requires a **long-term loan** to **finance a big capital expansion** programme. The loan may be for at least five and up to 20 years.

(b) Requires **borrowing** which is **not subject to the national exchange** controls of any government.

In addition, domestic capital issues may be regulated by the government or central bank, with an orderly queue for issues. In contrast, eurobond issues can be made whenever market conditions seem favourable.

A borrower who is contemplating a eurobond issue must consider the **exchange risk** of a long-term foreign currency loan. If the money is to be used to purchase assets which will earn revenue in a currency **different to that of the bond issue**, the borrower will run the risk of exchange losses.

If the money is to be used to purchase assets which will earn revenue in the **same currency**, the borrower can match these revenues with payments on the bond, and so remove or reduce the exchange risk.

An **investor** subscribing to a bond issue will be concerned about the following factors.

(a) **Security**

The borrower must be of **high quality**.

(b) **Marketability**

Investors will wish to have a **ready market** in which bonds can be bought and sold. If the borrower is of high quality the bonds or notes will be readily negotiable.

(c) **Anonymity**

Investors in eurobonds tend to be attracted to the **anonymity** of this type of issue, as the bonds are generally issued to bearer.

(d) The **return on the investment**

This is paid tax-free.

Chapter Roundup

- A **financial intermediary** links those with surplus funds (eg **lenders**) to those with funds deficits (eg potential **borrowers**) thus providing **aggregation** and **economies of scale**, **risk pooling** and **maturity transformation**.

- **Commercial banks** can provide
    - a payment mechanism
    - notes and coins
    - bank accounts
    - loans and overdrafts
    - for individuals and businesses.

- The **capital markets** and **money markets** are markets for long-term and short-term capital respectively.

- A stock market (in the UK: the **main market** plus the **AIM**) acts as a **primary market** for raising finance, and as a **secondary market** for the trading of existing securities (ie stocks and shares).

- The **efficient market hypothesis** suggests that **share prices reflect** the **type of information** which is available to investors.

- The **pattern of interest rates** on financial assets is influenced by the **risk** of the assets, the **duration** of the lending, and the **size** of the loan.

- There is a **trade-off** between **risk and return**. Investors in riskier assets expect to be compensated for the risk. In the case of ordinary shares, investors hope to achieve their return in the form of an increase in the share price (a capital gain) as well as from dividends.

- The **separation theorem** implies that companies should concentrate on **maximisation of present value**, since the stock market will enable individuals to obtain the income pattern from their investments that corresponds to their consumption requirements.

- **International money and capital markets** are available for larger companies wishing to raise larger amounts of finance.

Quick Quiz

1 For short-term borrowing, a company will go to the **money markets/capital markets.** (Which?)

2 (a) From which does the **demand** for capital markets funds come: Individuals/Firms/Government? (Delete any that do not apply).

   (b) From which does the **supply** of capital market funds come: Individuals/Firms/Government? (Delete any that do not apply).

3 Identify five types of capital market intermediaries.

4 Is the Stock Exchange a money market?

5 Which of the following is not a function of the London Stock Exchange?

   A   Enabling organisations to raise new finance
   B   Enabling shareholders to realise the value of their shares
   C   Enabling companies to become public companies
   D   Enabling takeovers by share exchanges

6 The semi-strong form of the hypothesis implies that share prices will reflect information such as earning forecasts and announcements of acquisitions.

☐ True

☐ False

7 Which of the following statements is true of the Alternative Investment market (AIM)?

   A   AIM shares are treated as quoted for tax purposes.
   B   Companies wishing to have their shares traded on AIM must meet eligibility criteria in terms of size and profitability.
   C   There are more obligations to issue shareholder circulars than on the main market.
   D   There are no Stock Exchange requirements for the percentage of shares in public hands.

8 What is meant by efficiency in the context of the efficient market hypothesis?

PART D   THE FRAMEWORK OF FINANCIAL MANAGEMENT

Answers to Quick Quiz

1. Money markets.

2. (a) and (b): You should have deleted none.

3. Any five of: banks; building societies; insurance companies; pension funds; unit trust companies; investment trusts; Stock Exchanges; venture capital organisations.

4. No.   The Stock Exchange is a capital market, not a money market.

5. C   Not every public company is listed on the London Stock Exchange.

6. True.

7. D   This is the correct answer. There are no minimum requirements, although if too few shares are freely available there will be no realistic market price.

   A   AIM shares are treated as unquoted for tax purposes, meaning that a number of reliefs are available to investors.

   B   There are no eligibility criteria for new entrants.

   C   This is incorrect; public announcements will generally be sufficient.

8. Efficiency in processing information in the pricing of stocks and shares.

Now try the questions below from the Exam Question Bank

Number	Level	Marks	Time
Q18	Introductory	n/a	30 mins

Macroeconomic policy

Topic list	Syllabus reference
1 Outline of macroeconomic policy	2(e)
2 Fiscal policy	2(e)
3 Monetary and interest rate policy	2(d), (e)
4 Exchange rates	2(e)
5 Inflation	2(e)
6 The balance of payments	2(e)

Introduction

A business will strive to achieve its objectives, but it has to do so in an economy which the government will try to steer to achieve its own objectives. In this chapter we're moving away from the **microeconomics** of the individual business to the **macroeconomics** of the economy as a whole. The business (and you as an individual) will need to understand how government policies can impact on different aspects of the economy, and the implications for the business's own activities and future plans.

The main **macroeconomic policy** tools we will look at are **fiscal policy, monetary and interest rate policy, prices and incomes policy,** and **exchange rate policy**. We will also look at inflation; many of the government's economic policies will be aimed at keeping inflation down and prices stable.

The next chapter goes on to discuss other aspects of the wider economy.

PART D   THE FRAMEWORK OF FINANCIAL MANAGEMENT

Study guide

Section 1 – The economic environment I

Macroeconomic objectives

- Identify and explain the main macro-economic policy targets
- Explain how government economic policy may affect planning and decision-making in business
- Define and explain the role of fiscal, monetary, interest rate and exchange rate policy

Fiscal policy

- Identify the main tools of fiscal policy
- Explain how public expenditure is financed and the meaning of PSBR
- Explain how PSBR and taxation policy interact with other economic indicators
- Identify the implications of fiscal policy for business

Section 2 – The economic environment II

- Identify the main tools of monetary policy
- Identify the factors which influence inflation and exchange rates, including the impact of interest rates
- Identify the implications of monetary, inflation and exchange rate policy for business

Exam guide

The emphasis in the exam will be discussing how economic conditions or policies affect particular businesses, for example the impact of a change in interest rates.

The examiner has stated that the economic environment, topics covered in Chapters 16 – 17 won't be examined in a full question; however they may be part of a question that also covers sources of finance.

1 Outline of macroeconomic policy

FAST FORWARD

Macroeconomic policy involves

- Policy **objectives** – the ultimate aims of economic policy
- Policy **targets** – quantified levels or ranges which policy is intended to achieve
- Policy **instruments** – the tools used to achieve objectives

Achievement of **economic growth, low inflation, full employment** and a **trade balance** are policy objectives.

Policy targets might be set for **money supply growth** or the **rate of inflation**, for example.

Exam focus point

Topics in economics will be tested in parts of longer questions only. But the economics in the paper should not be neglected – examiners often criticise students' lack of knowledge of economics.

1.1 Microeconomics, macroeconomics and economic policy

Key terms

Microeconomics is concerned with the behaviour of individual firms and consumers or households. **Macroeconomics** is concerned with the economy at large, and with the behaviour of large aggregates such as the national income, the money supply and the level of employment.

A government will of course be concerned with how the economy is behaving as a whole, and therefore with **macroeconomic variables**.

Macroeconomic policy can affect planning and decision making in various ways, for example via interest rate changes, which affect borrowing costs and required rates of return, as we saw earlier.

Note also that a government might adopt policies which try to exert influence at the **microeconomic** level. Examples include policies to remove regulations which restrict competition in particular labour markets or goods markets and policies to bring state-owned businesses into private ownership.

1.2 Economic policies and objectives

The policies pursued by a government may serve various objectives.

AIMS:
- Economic growth
- Control inflation
- Balance of payments
- Full employment

(a) **Economic growth**

'Growth' implies an increase in national income in 'real' terms – ie increases caused by price inflation are not real increases at all.

(b) **Control price inflation**

This means achieving **stable prices**. This has become a central objective of UK economic policy in recent years.

(c) **Full employment**

Full employment does not mean that everyone who wants a job has one all the time, but it does mean that unemployment levels are low, and involuntary unemployment is short-term.

(d) **Balance of payments**

The wealth of a country relative to others, a country's creditworthiness as a borrower, and the goodwill between countries in international relations might all depend on the achievement of an external trade balance over time. Deficits in external trade, with imports exceeding exports, might also be damaging for the prospects of economic growth.

Policies diagram: POLICIES (central) connected to Monetary, Fiscal, External trade, Exchange rate, and Prices and income.

To try to achieve its intermediate and overall objectives, a government will use a number of different policy tools or policy instruments. These include the following.

(a) **Monetary policy**

Monetarist economists believe that control over the growth of the money supply is necessary to reduce inflation and that inflation is harmful to the economy because it creates economic uncertainty which deters growth.

(b) **Fiscal policy**

Keynesian economists believe that when an economy has spare production capacity and unemployment, investment and output can be stimulated (through government spending or tax cuts) so as to reduce unemployment without creating more inflation.

(c) **Prices and incomes policy**

Some economists argue that inflation must be tackled directly through government controls over prices and incomes.

(d) **Exchange rate policy**

Some economists argue that economic objectives can be achieved through management of the exchange rate by the government. The strength or weakness of sterling's value, for example, will influence the volume of UK imports and exports, the balance of payments and interest rates.

(e) **External trade policy**

A government might have a policy for promoting economic growth by stimulating exports. Another argument is that there should be import controls to provide some form of protection for domestic manufacturing industries by making the cost of imports higher and the volume of imports lower. Protection could encourage domestic output to rise, stimulating the domestic economy.

These **policy tools** are not mutually exclusive and a government might adopt a policy mix of monetary policy, fiscal policy and exchange rate policy in an attempt to achieve its intermediate and ultimate economic objectives.

1.3 Conflicts in policy objectives and instruments

Macroeconomic policy aims cannot necessarily all be sustained together for a long period of time; attempts to achieve one objective will often have adverse effects on others, sooner or later.

(a) There may be a **conflict** between **steady balanced growth** in the economy and **full employment**. Although a growing economy should be able to provide more jobs, there is some concern that since an economy must be modernised to grow and modern technology is labour-saving, it might be possible to achieve growth without creating many more jobs, and so keeping unemployment at a high level.

(b) In the UK, **problems** with **creating more employment** and a **steady growth** in the economy have been the balance of payments, the foreign exchange value of sterling, inflation and the money supply. The objectives of lower unemployment and economic growth have been difficult to achieve because of the problems and conflicts with secondary objectives.

  (i) To create jobs and growth, there must be an **increase in aggregate demand**. When demand picks up there will be a surge in imports, with foreign goods bought by UK manufacturers (eg raw materials) and consumers.

  (ii) The high rate of imports creates a **deficit in the balance of payments**, which in turn will weaken sterling and raise the cost of imports, thus giving some impetus to price rises.

  (iii) To maintain the value of sterling, **interest rates** in the UK might need to be kept **high**, and high interest rates appear to **deter** companies from **investing**.

In practice, achieving the best mix of economic policies also involves a number of problems, such as the following.

- Inadequate **information**
- **Time lags** between use of policy and effects being noticeable
- **Political pressures** for short-term solutions
- Unpredictable **side-effects** of policies
- The influence of **other countries**
- **Conflict** between policy instruments

1.4 Effects of economic policy on business enterprises

Economic policy affects business enterprises in both service and manufacturing industries in various ways, for example as follows.

(a) By influencing the level of **aggregate demand (AD)** for goods and services in the economy, macroeconomic policy **affects** the **environment** for business. Business planning should take account of the likely effect of changes in AD for sales growth. Business planning will be easier if government policy is relatively stable.

(b) Tax changes brought about by **fiscal policy** affect businesses. For example, labour costs will be affected by changes in **employer's national insurance contributions**. If indirect taxes such as VAT or excise duty rise, either the additional cost will have to be absorbed or the rise will have to be passed on to consumers in higher prices.

(c) **Interest rate changes** brought about by government policy affect the borrowing costs of business. Increases in interest rates will mean that **fewer investments** show positive returns, deterring companies from expanding. Increases in interest rates will also exert a downward pressure on share prices, making it more difficult for companies to raise monies from new share issues. Businesses will also be squeezed by **decreases in consumer demand** that result from increases in interest rates.

(d) **Inflation**, perhaps induced by policies to boost demand, can **create uncertainty** for business as well as consumers. Businesses will be affected variously, depending on the relative price inflation on its input prices and output prices. A manufacturing industry may indeed make gains from increasing selling prices on stocks it has built up when its purchase prices were lower.

(e) Membership of an **exchange rate system** may reduce uncertainties for businesses involved in international trade because exchange rate fluctuations will be reduced. A service industry is less likely to be affected because it is less likely to be involved in substantial international trade.

2 Fiscal policy

> **FAST FORWARD**
>
> **Fiscal policy** seeks to influence the economy by managing the amounts which the government spends and the amounts it collects through taxation. Fiscal policy can be used as an instrument of **demand management**.

2.1 Fiscal policy, national income and demand management

Key term

> **Fiscal policy** is action by the government to spend money, or to collect money in taxes, with the purpose of influencing the condition of the national economy.

A government might intervene in the economy by:

(a) **Spending more money** and **financing this expenditure** by **borrowing**

(b) **Collecting more in taxes without increasing public spending**

(c) **Collecting more in taxes** in order to **increase public spending**, thus diverting income from one part of the economy to another

Government spending is an **'injection'** into the economy, adding to aggregate demand and therefore national income, whereas taxes are a 'withdrawal' from the economy. Fiscal policy can thus be used as an instrument of demand management.

2.2 Budget surplus; budget deficit; balanced budget

To the extent that a government's expenditure exceeds its income, it must borrow to make up the difference. The amount that the government must borrow each year is the **public sector borrowing requirement** or PSBR.

When a government's income exceeds its expenditure, and there is a negative PSBR – ie a public sector debt repayment or 'PSDR' – we say that the government is running a **budget surplus.** When a government's expenditure exceeds its income, so that it must borrow to make up the difference, there is a PSBR and we say that the government is running a **budget deficit**. When a government's expenditure and income are the same, so that the PSBR is nil, there is a **balanced budget**.

2.3 The broad aims of fiscal policy

Key term

> **Demand management** is an approach to economic policy which seeks to control the level of aggregate demand through fiscal policy and/or monetary policy.

Fiscal policy appears to offer a method of managing aggregate demand in the economy.

(a) If the government spends more – for example, on public works such as hospitals, roads and sewers – without raising more money in taxation (ie by borrowing more) it will **increase expenditure** in the economy, and so **raise demand**.

(b) If the government kept its own spending at the same level, but **reduced** the levels of taxation, it would **also stimulate demand** in the economy because firms and households would have more of their own money after tax for consumption or saving/investing.

(c) In the same way, a government can **reduce demand** in the economy by **raising taxes** or **reducing its expenditure**.

The Keynesian (**demand management**) view is that a depressed economy can be **revived by increases in public expenditure** (ie through fiscal policy). Increasing investment, an initial stimulus to expenditure, will result in an even bigger increase in national income.

Monetarists disagree. They believe that a depressed economy cannot be successfully revived by an increase in public expenditure. Any increase in expenditure will normally have to be financed by increased borrowing which will further depress the economy through a **'crowding out' effect**, and higher interest rates; and it will increase the money supply and will cause more inflation.

2.4 The UK Labour government's fiscal policy approach

The UK Labour government elected in 1997 set out five principles which were to lie at the heart of its fixed policy framework.

(a) **Transparency** in the setting of fiscal policy objectives, the implementation of fiscal policy and in the presentation of the public accounts

(b) **Stability** in the fiscal policy-making process and in the way fiscal policy impacts on the economy

(c) **Responsibility** in the management of the public finances

(d) **Fairness,** including between generations

(e) **Efficiency** in the design and implementation of fiscal policy and in managing both sides of the public sector balance sheet

Fiscal policy is said to be based on the following two fiscal rules announced in the July 1997 Budget.

(a) The **golden rule**: over the economic cycle, the government will borrow only to invest and not to fund current spending, and

(b) **Public debt** as a proportion of national income will be held over the economic cycle at a **stable and prudent level**

2.5 The Private Finance Initiative (PFI)

Under the UK's **Private Finance Initiative**, launched in 1992, no public expenditure is approved without private sector options being explored first.

The PFI is intended to promote the use of private sector finance for public projects, so as to **transfer some of the risks** associated with the projects to the private sector, and to **make use of the skills**, experience and risk management expertise of the private sector.

The PFI applies to various types of public expenditure, from relatively simple catering or cleaning contracts to complex contracts such as a new train system or roadway involving design, construction and long-term operation and maintenance.

From its launch in 1992 up to October 1997, the total of PFI signed deals was £7.5 billion. Over this period, this total is not very large. The new Labour Government has reviewed the Initiative during 1997, and has introduced simplified procedures in an attempt to improve the level of take-up.

PART D THE FRAMEWORK OF FINANCIAL MANAGEMENT

3 Monetary and interest rate policy

FAST FORWARD

A government may use **monetary policies** to pursue its economic aims. Tools for implementing monetary policy include:

- Influence over interest rates
- Fiscal policy
- Exchange rate policy
- The regulation of banks and other financial institutions

Money is important because:

(a) It **'oils the wheels'** of **economic activity**, providing an easy method for exchanging goods and services (ie buying and selling).

(b) The total amount of money in a national economy may have a **significant influence** on **economic activity and inflation.**

3.1 The role and aims of monetary policy

Key term

Monetary policy is the regulation of the economy through control of the monetary system by operating on such variables as the money supply, the level of interest rates and the conditions for availability of credit.

The **effectiveness** of monetary policy will depend on:

(a) Whether the **targets** of **monetary policy** are **achieved successfully**

(b) Whether the **success** of **monetary policy** leads on to the **successful achievement** of the **intermediate target** (eg lower inflation), and

(c) Whether the **successful achievement** of the **intermediate target** (eg lower inflation) leads on to the **successful achievement** of the **overall objective** (eg strong economic growth)

3.2 Targets of monetary policy

Targets of monetary policy are likely to relate to the volume of national income and expenditure.

- Growth in the size of the money stock (money supply)
- The level of interest rates
- The volume of credit or growth in the volume of credit
- The exchange rate against other currencies
- The volume of expenditure in the economy (ie national income or GNP itself)

3.3 The money stock as a target of monetary policy

To monetarist economists, the money stock is a possible intermediate target of economic policy. This is because they claim that an increase in the money supply will raise prices and money incomes, and this in turn will raise the demand for money to spend.

3.4 The growth in the volume of credit as a target for monetary policy

The government might decide to restrict credit lending (impose a 'credit squeeze') and so set targets for limited growth of credit in the economy. An increase in bank lending (ie in the volume of credit) is likely to lead to a rise in the level of expenditure in the economy because people borrow money in order to spend it. Higher bank lending is also likely to result in higher bank deposits and thus an increase in the money stock.

3.5 Fiscal policy as an instrument of monetary policy

Fiscal policy can work in co-operation with monetary policy. For example, a fiscal policy of reducing government expenditure and cutting the PSBR will have the effect of reducing the growth in M4 (a measure of the amount of money in the economy).

3.6 Reserve requirements on banks as a means of controlling the money supply

As another technique for controlling money supply growth, the government might impose reserve requirements on banks.

(a) One type of reserve requirement is a compulsory **minimum cash reserve ratio** (ie the ratio of cash to total assets).

(b) Another form of reserve requirement is that banks should have a minimum ratio of **reserve assets** to total deposits. Reserve assets are types of short-term liquid assets.

3.7 Direct controls as a technique of monetary control

Yet another way of controlling the growth of the money supply is to impose direct controls on bank lending. Direct controls may be either quantitative or qualitative.

(a) **Quantitative controls** might be imposed on either **bank lending** (assets) or **bank deposits** (liabilities).

(b) **Qualitative controls** might be used to alter the **type of lending** by banks. For example, the government (via the Bank) can ask the banks to limit their lending to the personal sector.

3.8 Exchange rate control as an instrument or target of monetary policy

The **exchange rates** between the domestic currencies and other currencies, and changes in exchange rates, have implications for the **balance of payments**, **inflation**, and **economic growth**. The government might seek to achieve a target exchange rate for its currency.

3.9 Interest rates as a target for monetary policy

The authorities may decide that interest rates themselves should be a target of monetary policy. This would be appropriate if it is considered that there is a direct relationship between interest rates and the level of expenditure in the economy.

It certainly seems logical that interest rates should have a strong influence on economic activity.

(a) However firms choose to raise funds, their **cost of capital** will be determined by interest rates. Corporate borrowing rates are normally linked to bank base rate. The exact rate will depend upon the risk element involved.

(b) We shall see later in this text how the cost of capital matters when determining the **viability of commercial investments**.

However although empirical evidence suggests there is some connection between interest rates and investment (by companies) and consumer expenditure, the connection is not a stable and predictable one. Some economists argue that the key element affecting investment is **business confidence** rather than the level of interest rates. Interest rate changes are only likely to affect the level of expenditure after a considerable time lag.

PART D THE FRAMEWORK OF FINANCIAL MANAGEMENT

In 1997 the new Labour Government of the UK gave responsibility for setting short-term interest rates to the central bank, the Bank of England. The Bank now sets rates at a level which it considers appropriate, given the inflation rate target set by the Government. The purpose of having the central bank setting interest rates is to remove the risk of **political influence** over the decisions. If the UK joins **European monetary union** and therefore adopts the **Euro** as its currency, the interest rates that prevail will effectively be set at the European level.

Exam focus point

Because interest rates are a major tool of UK policy, the topic is important for 2.4. See how you get on with the question below.

Question
Interest rate levels

Outline the effects on the economy of a policy of high interest rates to dampen demand and inflation.

Answer

An increase in interest rates is thought to reduce the money supply in the economy and thereby to reduce the level of effective demand which will, in turn, decrease inflation and improve the balance of payments (the latter by decreasing the demand for imports, and freeing more domestic output for sale abroad). Aggregate expenditure in the economy will decrease, for various reasons.

(a) A higher interest rate **encourages savings** at the expense of consumer expenditure.

(b) Higher interest rates will **increase mortgage payments** and will thus reduce the amount of disposable income in the hands of home buyers for discretionary spending.

(c) The higher cost of consumer credit will **deter borrowing** and **spending** on consumer durables.

(d) Higher prices of goods due to higher borrowing costs for industry will also **reduce some consumer expenditure** in the economy.

Investment expenditure may also decline for two reasons.

(a) Higher interest rates **deter some investment** due to increased borrowing costs.

(b) Higher interest rates may make the **corporate sector pessimistic** about future business prospects and confidence in the economy. This may further reduce investment in the economy.

To the extent that higher domestic interest rates lead to an appreciation of the exchange rate, this should reduce inflation by lowering the cost of imported items. Exporters will experience pressure on their costs as the result of the more competitive price conditions they face, and may be less willing to concede high wage demands, and thus wage inflation may be constrained. The desired outcomes of the authorities' interest rate policy noted above may be negated by the following effects of higher interest rates.

(a) Higher interest results in **greater interest income** for savers, who may increase their spending due to this interest windfall.

(b) Since **mortgage payments** are the single largest constituent of the Retail Prices Index (RPI), any increase in them will be reflected immediately in **RPI increases**. This could lead to higher wage demands in the economy, and may result in a wage-price spiral.

(c) By encouraging capital inflows, higher interest rates will tend to lead to an **appreciation of the currency's exchange rate**. This makes exports less competitive and imports more attractive.

(d) A reduction in investment may **decrease the pressure of demand** in the economy but at the same time it will set in motion a process which in the future could reduce the economy's potential for production.

(e) To the extent that higher interest rates do squeeze demand in the economy, they will **reduce employment**, decreasing the proceeds of taxation and increasing the government expenditure on the unemployed.

4 Exchange rates

FAST FORWARD

Exchange rates are determined by **supply and demand**, even under fixed exchange rate systems.

Governments can intervene to influence the exchange rate by, for example, **adjusting interest rates**. Government policies on exchange rates might be **fixed or floating exchange rates** as two extreme policies, but 'in-between' schemes have been more common.

Key term

An **exchange rate** is the rate at which one country's currency can be traded in exchange for another country's currency.

Dealers in foreign exchange – ie banks – make their profit by buying currency at one exchange rate, and selling it at a different rate. This means that there is a selling rate and a buying rate for a currency.

4.1 Factors influencing the exchange rate for a currency

The exchange rate between two currencies is determined primarily by supply and demand in the foreign exchange markets. Demand comes from individuals, firms and governments who want to buy a currency and supply comes from those who want to sell it.

Supply and demand in turn are subject to a number of influences.

- The rate of inflation, compared with the rate of inflation in other countries
- Interest rates, compared with interest rates in other countries
- The balance of payments
- Speculation
- Government policy on intervention to influence the exchange rate

Other factors influence the exchange rate through their relationship with the items identified above.

(a) **Total income and expenditure** (demand) in the **domestic economy** determines the demand for goods. This includes imported goods and demand for goods produced in the country which would otherwise be exported if demand for them did not exist in the home markets.

(b) **Output capacity** and the **level of employment** in the domestic economy might influence the balance of payments, because if the domestic economy has full employment already, it will be unable to increase its volume of production for exports.

(c) The **growth** in the **money supply** influences interest rates and domestic inflation.

4.2 Inflation and the exchange rate

If the rate of inflation is higher in one country than in another country, the value of its currency will tend to weaken against the other country's currency.

Purchasing power parity theory states that an exchange rate varies according to relative price changes, so that:

$$\text{'Old' exchange rate} \times \frac{\text{Price level in country A}}{\text{Price level in country B}} = \text{'New' exchange rate}$$

Although this influence is obvious, it is not predominant. This is apparent from the fact that if exchange rates did respond to demand and supply for current account items, then the balance of payments on the current account of all countries would tend towards equilibrium. This is not so, and **in practice other factors influence exchange rates more strongly**.

Demand for currency to invest in overseas capital investments and supply of currency from firms disinvesting in an overseas currency have more influence on the exchange rate, in the short term at least, than the demand and supply of goods and services.

If a country has a persistent deficit in its balance of payments current account, international confidence in that country's currency will eventually be eroded, and in the long term, its exchange rate will fall as capital inflows are no longer sufficient to counterbalance the country's trade deficit.

4.3 Consequences of an exchange rate policy

Reasons for a policy of controlling the exchange rate

(a) To **rectify a balance of trade deficit**, by trying to bring about a fall in the exchange rate.

(b) To **prevent a balance of trade surplus** from getting too large, by trying to bring about a limited rise in the exchange rate.

(c) To **emulate economic conditions** in other countries. The UK's membership of the ERM (from October 1990 until suspended in 1992) had as one of its aims that of emulating the conditions of lower inflation which exist in other ERM member countries.

(d) To **stabilise the exchange rate** of its currency. Exporters and importers will then face less risk of exchange rate movements wiping out their profits. A stable currency increases confidence in the currency and promotes international trade.

4.4 Fixed exchange rates

A government might try to keep the exchange rate at its fixed level, but if it cannot control inflation, the **real value** of its currency would not remain fixed. If one country's rate of inflation is higher than others, its export prices would become uncompetitive in overseas markets and the country's trade deficit would grow. Devaluation of the currency would be necessary for a recovery.

If exchange rates are fixed, any changes in **(real) interest rates** in one country will create pressure for the **movement of capital** into or out of the country. Capital movements would put pressure on the country's exchange rate to change. It follows that if exchange rates are fixed and capital is allowed to move freely between countries (ie there are not exchange controls) all countries must have consistent policies on interest rates.

4.5 Floating exchange rates

Key term

> **Floating exchange rates** are exchange rates which are allowed to fluctuate according to demand and supply conditions in the foreign exchange markets.

Floating exchange rates are at the opposite end of the spectrum to fixed rates. At this extreme, exchange rates are completely left to the free play of demand and supply market forces, and there is no official financing at all. The ruling exchange rate is, therefore, at equilibrium by definition.

In practice, many governments seek to combine the advantages of exchange rate stability with flexibility and to avoid the disadvantages of both rigidly fixed exchange rates and free floating. **Managed** (or dirty) **floating** refers to a system whereby exchange rates are allowed to float, but from time to time the authorities will intervene in the foreign exchange market:

- To use their official reserves of foreign currencies to buy their own domestic currency
- To sell their domestic currency to buy more foreign currency for the official reserves

Buying and selling in this way would be intended to influence the exchange rate of the domestic currency. Governments do not have official reserves large enough to dictate exchange rates to the market, and can only try to 'influence' market rates with intervention.

Speculation in the capital markets often has a much bigger impact short-term than changes in supply and demand. While exchange rates remain volatile, international trading companies can do a number of things to reduce their risk of suffering losses on foreign exchange transactions, including the following.

- (a) Many companies buy currencies **'forward'** at a fixed and known price.

- (b) **Dealing in a 'hard' currency** may lessen the risks attached to volatile currencies.

- (c) **Operations can be managed** so that the proportion of sales in one currency are matched by an equal proportion of purchases in that currency.

- (d) **Invoicing can be in the domestic currency**. This means that the customer bears all the foreign exchange risk, however, and, in industries where customers have high bargaining power, this may be an unacceptable arrangement. Furthermore there is the risk that sales will be adversely affected by high prices, reducing demand.

- (e) **Outsource activities** to the local market. Many of the Japanese car firms which have invested in the UK in recent years have made efforts to obtain many of their inputs, subject to quality limits, from local suppliers. Promotional activities can also be sourced locally.

- (f) Firms can aim at **segments** in the market which are not particularly price sensitive. For example, many German car marques such as Mercedes have been marketed in the US on the basis of quality and exclusivity. This is a type of strategy based on differentiation focus.

4.6 Consequences of membership of an exchange rate system

Exchange rate stability within an exchange rate regime may **help dampen inflation** by preventing a government from allowing the currency to drift downwards in value to compensate for price inflation.

At the same time, it means that **interest rate policy** must be **consistent** with keeping the currency stable.

Other possible consequences of stabilisation within an exchange rate system are that there may be effects on **people's expectations** and on the **perceived risk of exchange rate** movements between member currencies. As well as allowing firms to **plan and forecast** with **greater certainty**, exchange rate stability ought to make a currency **less risky** to hold.

4.7 European Economic and Monetary Union

There are three main aspects to the European monetary union.

- (a) **A common currency** (the euro).

- (b) **A European central bank**. The European central bank has several roles.
    - Issuing the common currency
    - Conducting monetary policy on behalf of the central government authorities
    - Acting as lender of last resort to all European banks
    - Managing the exchange rate for the common currency

- (c) A **centralised monetary policy** would apply across all the countries within the union. This would involve the surrender of control over aspects of economic policy and therefore surrender of some political sovereignty by the government of each member state to the central government body of the union.

4.7.1 The EMU timetable

EMU is a topical issue. Italy, France, Ireland, Germany, Belgium, Luxembourg, the Netherlands, Finland, Greece, Spain, Portugal and Austria signed up for EMU and replaced their own currencies with the euro on 1 January 2002. The UK decided to opt out but retains the right to join at a later stage.

4.7.2 For and against EMU

The arguments for and against EMU can be summarised as follows, with particular reference to the UK's position.

For	Against
Economic policy stability • EMU members will be required to keep to strict economic criteria • Politicians in member countries will be less able to pursue short-term economic policies, for example just before an election, to gain political advantage **Facilitation of trade** • Will eliminate risk of currency fluctuations affecting trade and investment between EMU member countries • Will eliminate need to 'hedge' against such risks • Will be savings in foreign exchange transaction costs for companies, as well as tourists • Will enhance ease of trade with non EU countries **Lower interest rates** • Will remove risk of inflation and depreciating currencies, reducing interest rates • Will stabilise interest rates at a level closer to that of Germany, reducing interest costs for businesses and government **Preservation of the City's position** • If the UK opts out of EMU, the City's position as one of the major European financial capitals will be threatened • In turn, the City's role as a leading global financial market would also be jeopardised • Inward investment from the rest of the EU would also be likely to diminish **Seigneurage** • Seigneurage is the benefits accruing from the right to issue currency. If the euro becomes a global reserve currency, non-EU nations will buy it to hold rather than for purposes of trade. This will support the exchange rate and allow interests rate to be lower	**Loss of national control over economic policy** • Under EMU, monetary policy would largely be in the hands of the new European central bank • Individual countries' fiscal policies would also need to stay in line with European policy criteria • The European economic policy framework would put great emphasis on price stability • Restrictive monetary policies could result in disproportionate unemployment and output effects **Compensate for weaker economies** • For the UK, the possible benefits of being economically linked to stronger European economies are reduced and possibly even outweighed by the need to compensate for weaker economies • Stronger economies would be under pressure to 'bail out' member countries which borrow too much in order to hold the system together **Confusion in the transition to EMU** • Introduction of a new currency and coinage would cause confusion to businesses and consumers • Firms might use it as an opportunity to push through price rises **Loss of national pride** • Sterling is a symbol of national cohesion • EMU puts its members on the road to a federal Europe, it is suggested, making the UK parliament into little more than a regional town hall within Europe, with no more power than local government. Such a move might dent national pride and adversely affect economic confidence • The proposal to have national variants of euro coins and notes is merely a cosmetic attempt to preserve national identities

16: MACROECONOMIC POLICY

The ultimate impact of the Euro cannot be assessed until all European Union members are also members of the common currency. However the single currency is already having a number of impacts upon business.

(a) UK companies that have an **overseas parent company** may be asked to issue invoices in Euros. Therefore UK companies may have to make payments in Euros to domestic suppliers and thus face **potential foreign exchange exposure.**

(b) The introduction of the Euro may **increase competition.** Prices from suppliers in all countries that use the Euro will be quoted in the same currency and hence it will be easier for customers to compare prices between different suppliers.

5 Inflation

FAST FORWARD

Inflation is a sustained increase in the general level of prices over time.

Inflation is a problem for individuals and firms, for example **lenders** and those on **fixed incomes.** It could also **affect economic growth, investment, international competitiveness** and the **evaluation of companies' performance.**

5.1 Why is inflation a problem?

An economic policy objective which now has a central place in the policy approaches of the governments of many developed countries is that of stable prices. Why is a high rate of price inflation harmful and undesirable?

5.1.1 Redistribution of income and wealth

Inflation leads to a redistribution of income and wealth in ways which may be undesirable. Redistribution of wealth might take place from creditors to debtors. This is because debts lose real value with inflation. For example, if you owed £1,000, and prices then doubled, you would still owe £1,000, but the **real value of your debt** would have been halved.

In general, in times of inflation those with **economic power** tend to gain at the expense of others, particularly those on fixed incomes.

5.1.2 Balance of payments effects

If a country has a higher rate of inflation than its major trading partners, its exports will become relatively expensive and imports relatively cheap. As a result, the **balance of trade** will **suffer**, affecting employment in exporting industries and in industries producing import-substitutes.

5.1.3 Uncertainty of the value of money and prices

If the rate of inflation is imperfectly anticipated, no one has certain knowledge of the true rate of inflation. As a result, no one has certain knowledge of the **value of money** or of the **real meaning of prices.** As prices convey less information, the process of resource allocation is less efficient and rational decision-making is almost impossible.

5.1.4 Resource costs of changing prices

In times of high inflation **substantial labour time** is spent on planning and implementing price changes. **Customers** may also have to **spend more** time making price comparisons if they seek to buy from the lowest cost source.

5.1.5 Economic growth and investment

It is sometimes claimed that inflation is harmful to a country's economic growth and level of investment. A study by *Robert Barro* (*Bank of England Quarterly Bulletin*, May 1995) examines whether the evidence available supports this view. Barro found from data covering over 100 countries from 1960 to 1990 that, on average, an increase in inflation of ten percentage points per year reduced the growth rate of real GDP per capita by 0.2 to 0.3 percentage points per year, and lowered the ratio of investment to GDP by 0.4 to 0.6 percentage points.

5.2 Measuring inflation

We have already referred to the way in which inflation erodes the real value of money. In order to measure changes in the real value of money as a single figure, we need to group all goods and services into a single price index.

5.2.1 Consumer price indices

A consumer price index is based on a chosen 'basket' of items which consumers purchase. A weighting is decided for each according to the average spending on the item by consumers.

The **UK Retail Prices Index** (RPI) is intended to measure the change from month to month in the cost of goods and services of the sort bought by a typical household. The relative importance attached to each of the various goods and services is revised each year using the latest available results of the Family Expenditure Survey. Unlike the general consumer price indices of many other countries, the UK RPI includes mortgage repayment costs.

An alternative measure of the rate of inflation is the Consumer Price Index (CPI) which is used in inflation targeting by the UK government and the Bank of England Monetary Policy Committee.

5.3 The causes of inflation

The causes of inflation are complex, because there will be several factors operating simultaneously, each having some effect on price levels. The relative strength or influence of each of these factors at any given time may be difficult to assess.

5.3.1 Demand-pull inflation

Demand-pull inflation occurs when the economy is buoyant and there is a high aggregate demand which is **in excess of the economy's ability to supply.**

(a) Because aggregate demand exceeds supply, prices rise.

(b) Since supply needs to be raised to meet the higher demand, there will be an increase in demand for factors of production, and so factor rewards (wages, interest rates, and so on) will also rise.

5.3.2 Cost-push inflation

Cost-push inflation occurs where the costs of factors of production rise regardless of whether or not they are in short supply. This appears to be particularly the case with **wages**: workers anticipate inflation rates and demand wage increases to compensate. Interest rate rises can also add to the rate of inflation, because mortgage costs will rise.

Import cost-push inflation occurs when the cost of essential imports rise regardless of whether or not they are in short supply. This has occurred in the past with the oil price rises of the 1970s. Additionally, a fall in the value of a country's currency will have import cost-push effects since a weakening currency increases the price of imports.

5.3.3 Expectational inflation

A further problem is that once the rate of inflation has begun to increase, a serious danger of **expectational inflation** will occur.

(a) This means, regardless of whether the factors that have caused inflation are still persistent or not, there will arise a generally held view of what inflation is likely to be.

(b) To protect future income, **wages and prices** will be **raised** now by the **expected amount** of future inflation. This can lead to the vicious circle known as the **wage-price spiral**, in which inflation becomes a relatively permanent feature because of people's expectations that it will occur.

Question — Government policies

(a) A government can help to counter demand-pull inflation by reducing interest rates. True or false?

(b) A government can help to counter demand-pull inflation by increasing value added tax. True or false?

(c) A government can help to counter cost-push inflation by increasing income tax rates. True or false?

(d) A government can help to counter cost-push inflation by linking wage increases to productivity improvements. True or false?

Answer

(a) *False*. On the contrary, this would increase consumer borrowing and hence stimulate demand-pull inflation.

(b) *True*. This might increase total spending on goods and services *inclusive* of the tax, but spending *net* of tax will probably fall.

(c) *False*. Increasing direct taxation will reduce consumers' disposable income, and is therefore a measure aimed at countering demand-pull inflation, not cost-push inflation.

(d) *True*. This will reduce the unit costs of production.

PART D THE FRAMEWORK OF FINANCIAL MANAGEMENT

5.4 Control of inflation: various approaches

The best way of controlling inflation will depend on the causes of it. In practice, it may be difficult to know which cause is most significant. The table on the next page sets out various policies designed to control inflation.

ANTI-INFLATION POLICIES	
Perceived cause of inflation	**Policy to control inflation**

• Demand-pull (high consumer demand)	• Take steps to reduce demand in the economy, perhaps by
	  – Higher taxation, to cut consumer spending
	  – Lower government expenditure (and lower government borrowing to finance its expenditure)
	  – Higher interest rates

• Cost-push factors (higher wage costs and other costs working through to higher prices)	• Take steps to reduce production costs and price rises
	  – De-regulate labour markets
	  – Encourage greater productivity in industry
	  – Apply controls over wage and price rises (prices and incomes policy)

• Import cost-push factors	• Take steps to reduce the quantities or the price of imports. Such a policy might involve trying to achieve either an appreciation or depreciation of the domestic currency

• Excessively fast growth in the money supply	• Take steps to try to reduce the rate of money supply growth, perhaps by
	  – Cutting the Public Sector Borrowing Requirement
	  – Funding the PSBR by borrowing from the non-bank private sector
	  – Trying to control or reduce bank lending
	  – Trying to achieve a balance of trade surplus
	  – Maintaining interest rates at a level that might deter money supply growth

• Expectations of inflation	• Pursue clear policies which indicate the government's determination to reduce the rate of inflation

6 The balance of payments

FAST FORWARD

A country can **rectify** a **balance of payments deficit** in three ways.
- Allowing its currency to depreciate or **devalue** in foreign exchange value
- Imposing **protectionist measures** or exchange control regulations
- **Deflationary** economic measures in the domestic economy

6.1 The nature of the balance of payments

The balance of payments is a statistical 'accounting' record of a country's international trade transactions (the purchase and sale of goods and services) and capital transactions (the acquisition and disposal of assets and liabilities) with other countries during a period of time.

Under the current method of presentation of the UK balance of payments statistics, the broad classifications of transactions are as follows.

Current account transactions are sub-divided into:

(a) Trade in goods
(b) Trade in services
(c) Investment income
(d) Transfers

The **capital account** shows changes in the UK's external assets and liabilities, sub-divided into:

(a) **Changes in the UK's external assets.** External assets include:

   (i) Holdings of foreign currency by anyone resident in the UK

   (i) Holdings of shares or other investments in overseas companies by anyone resident in the UK (including UK firms)

   (iii) Loans to anyone overseas by UK banks

(b) **Changes in the UK's external liabilities.** External liabilities include:

   (i) Investments in the UK, for example in UK government stocks or shares of UK firms, by overseas residents (such as overseas firms)

   (ii) Borrowing from abroad by anyone in the UK

6.2 A country's balance of payments position

A country's balance of payments position is perhaps best analysed by a consideration of its long-term surplus or deficit on its current account.

If a country has a **surplus** on its current account year after year, it might invest the surplus abroad or add it to official reserves. The balance of payments position would be strong. There is the problem, however, that if one country which is a major trading nation (eg Japan) has a continual surplus on its balance of payments current account, other countries must be in a continual deficit.

Deficits on the current account must be financed by a run down of official reserves, or borrowing. A country cannot finance deficits in this way indefinitely. Its official reserves will run out completely one day! Clearly, if a country has a long-term deficit, its balance of payments position will be very weak, and it must eventually take action to improve the position.

6.3 Rectifying a balance of payments deficit or surplus

Which solution to a balance of payments problem is best may well depend on the cause of the problem on the balance of payments itself.

(a) **A depreciation (or devaluation) of the currency**

Key term

A decline or **depreciation** in the value of a currency against other currencies is called a **devaluation** when it involves a reduction in a fixed or pegged exchange rate within a managed exchange rate system.

Assuming that changes in exchange rates are translated into changes in the prices of goods and services, **devaluation** of the currency would make **exports relatively cheaper** to foreign buyers, and so the demand for exports would probably rise.

After a time lag, **production of exports and import substitutes** will **rise**, so that the volume of exports will rise, thereby increasing the sterling value of exports (regardless of sterling's lower exchange rate), and the volume of imports will fall further. This will improve the current account balance.

The improvement in the balance of payments will thus have some limit, and the current balance should eventually level off.

(b) **Direct measures**

Direct measures to restrict the volume of imports or to encourage exports might consist of **tariff** and **non-tariff** barriers to trade. **Export subsidies** might also be considered. Another direct measure is to introduce **exchange control regulations** restricting flows of currency in and out of the country. Direct measures such as these may be contrary to World Trade Organisation (WTO) agreements. Such measures may also give rise to counter-measures by other countries.

(c) **Domestic deflation**

The most common method for dealing with balance of payments problems and probably the only successful long term measure is to deflate the economy.

Deflationary measures include cutting government spending, increasing taxation and raising interest rates. The purpose of deflationary measures would be:

- To **reduce** the **demand for goods and services** at home, and so to reduce imports
- To **encourage industry** to switch to export markets, because of the fall in domestic demand
- To **tackle domestic inflation**

6.4 Interest rates and the balance of payments

Comparative interest rates between one country and another, and changes in interest rates, affect the balance of payments both:

(a) **Directly**, by **stimulating** or **discouraging foreign investment**, and so inflows and outflows of capital, and

(b) **Indirectly**, through the **exchange rate** (High interest rates attract foreign investors, thus creating a demand for the currency and keeping the exchange rate at a high level.)

Is a high interest rate policy a good solution to the problem of a deficit on the balance of payments current account?

(a) If a country relies on inflows of capital to finance a continuing balance of trade deficit, the country's **balance of payments** will **never** get into **equilibrium**. High interest rates will keep the exchange rate high for the country's currency, and this will make it more difficult to export (high export prices to foreign buyers) and encourage imports (cheaper prices). The country might therefore be unable to rectify its balance of trade deficit.

(b) If there is a continuing balance of trade deficit, there will always be a threat that the country's currency will eventually **depreciate in value**. This will deter investors.

Investors will only put money into capital investments abroad if they have satisfactory expectations about what the exchange rate for the foreign currency will be. Interest rates alone are not the only factor on which to base an investment decision. After all, what is the value to an investor of high interest rates from investments in a foreign currency when the exchange value of the currency is falling? A depreciation may lead to currency sales, creating pressure for further depreciation.

Chapter Roundup

- Macroeconomic policy involves
    - Policy **objectives** – the ultimate aims of economic policy
    - Policy **targets** – quantified levels or ranges which policy is intended to achieve
    - Policy **instruments** – the tools used to achieve objectives

- Achievement of **economic growth, low inflation, full employment** and a **trade balance** are policy objectives.

- Policy targets might be set for **money supply growth** or the **rate of inflation**, for example.

- **Fiscal policy** seeks to influence the economy by managing the amounts which the government spends and the amounts it collects through taxation. Fiscal policy can be used as an instrument of **demand management**.

- A government may use **monetary policies** to pursue its economic aims. Tools for implementing monetary policy include:
    - Influence over interest rates
    - Fiscal policy
    - Exchange rate policy
    - The regulation of banks and other financial institutions

- Exchange rates are determined by **supply and demand**, even under fixed exchange rate systems.

- Governments can intervene to influence the exchange rate by, for example, **adjusting interest rates**. Government policies on exchange rates might be **fixed or floating exchange rates** as two extreme policies, but 'in-between' schemes have been more common.

- **Inflation** is a sustained increase in the general level of prices over time.

- Inflation is a problem for individuals and firms, for example **lenders** and those on **fixed incomes**. It could also **affect economic growth, investment, international competitiveness** and the **evaluation of companies' performance.**

- A country can **rectify** a **balance of payments deficit** in three ways.
    - Allowing its currency to depreciate or **devalue** in foreign exchange value
    - Imposing **protectionist measures** or exchange control regulations
    - **Deflationary** economic measures in the domestic economy

Quick Quiz

1. What is the difference between fiscal policy and monetary policy?
2. What effect does a high interest rate have on the exchange rate?
3. How do deflationary measures help to eliminate a balance of payments deficit?
4. *Fill in the blank.*

    .... involves the study of the economy at large, in particular the behaviour of aggregates such as national income, money supply and levels of employment.
5. Name five factors that can influence the level of exchange rates.
6. What are likely to be the main aims of a government's economy policy?
7. What is the wage-price spiral?

PART D   THE FRAMEWORK OF FINANCIAL MANAGEMENT

8   What causes inflation?

Match the characteristics with the types.

(i)   Demand – pull
(ii) Cost – push
(iii) Expectational
(iv) Money supply growth

A   It leads to the wage-price spiral
B   The economy is buoyant and there is pressure on its ability to supply
C   Keynesians argue that this is a symptom rather than a cause
D   Factor rewards rise whether or not they are in short supply

Answers to Quick Quiz

1   A government's fiscal policy is concerned with taxation, borrowing and spending and their effects upon the economy. Monetary policy is concerned with money, the money supply, interest rates, inflation and the exchange rate.

2   It attracts foreign investment, thus increasing the demand for the currency. The exchange rate rises as a result.

3   Domestic deflation cuts demand, including demand for imports. Industry is thus encouraged to switch to export markets.

4   Macroeconomics

5   (a)   Comparative inflation rates
    (b)   Comparative interest rates
    (c)   Balance of payments
    (d)   Speculation
    (e)   Government policy

6   Main objectives include:

    (a)   Sustainable growth
    (b)   Control of price inflation
    (c)   Full employment
    (d)   Balance between imports and exports

7   The wage-price spiral is where businesses and employees expect prices to rise and thus seek to increase their prices and wages. The result is that expectations of price rises become self-fulfilling.

8   (i)   B   Aggregate demand exceeds the output capacity of the economy. Keynesians saw this as the main cause of inflation and predicted it could only occur when unemployment was low.

    (ii) D   Particularly by rises in wages.

    (iii) A   The expectation of inflation will cause it to persist even when the underlying causes have been removed, since higher wages will be demanded.

    (iv) C   However, monetarists argue that expansion of the money supply beyond the rate of real growth will be inflationary.

Now try the questions below from the Exam Question Bank

Number	Level	Marks	Time
Q19	Introductory	n/a	35 mins

Government intervention

Topic list	Syllabus reference
1 Competition policy	2(f)
2 Official aid schemes	2(f)
3 Supply side policies	2(f)
4 Environmental ('green') policies	2(f)
5 Corporate governance	2(f)

Introduction

This chapter is the last in the book to deal with the broader economic environment within which organisations operate.

PART D THE FRAMEWORK OF FINANCIAL MANAGEMENT

Study guide

Section 2 – The economic environment II

Aspects of government intervention and regulation

- Explain the requirement for and the role of competition policy
- Explain the requirement for and the role of official aid intervention
- Explain the requirement for and the role of Green policies
- Identify examples of government intervention and regulation

Exam guide

These topics are most likely to be tested as part of a question. If, for example, the company described in the question is considering taking over another company, you may be asked you to discuss the circumstances under which the government might intervene. Corporate governance is quite topical at present, as there has been recent UK guidance.

1 Competition policy

1.1 Regulation and market failure

FAST FORWARD

The government influences markets in various ways, one of which is through direct **regulation** (eg the **Competition Commission**).

Key term

Market failure is said to occur when the market mechanism fails to result in economic efficiency, and therefore the outcome is sub-optimal.

An important role of the government is the regulation of private markets where these fail to bring about an efficient use of resources. In response to the existence of market failure, and as an alternative to taxation and public provision of production, the state often resorts to regulating economic activity in a variety of ways. Of the various forms of market failure, the following are the cases where regulation of markets can often be the most appropriate policy response.

(a) **Imperfect competition**

Where one company's large share or complete domination of the market is leading to **inefficiency** or **excessive profits**, the state may intervene, for example through controls on prices or profits, in order to try to reduce the effects of this power.

(b) **Social costs**

A possible means of dealing with the problem of social costs or **externalities** is *via* some form of regulation. Regulations might include, for example, controls on emissions of pollutants, restrictions on car use in urban areas, the banning of smoking in public buildings, or compulsory car insurance.

(c) **Imperfect information**

Regulation is often the best form of government action whenever informational inadequacies are undermining the efficient operation of private markets. This is particularly so when consumer choice is being distorted.

(d) **Equity**

The government may also resort to regulation to **improve social justice**.

1.2 Types of regulation

Regulation can be defined as any form of state interference with the operation of the free market. This could involve regulating demand, supply, price, profit, quantity, quality, entry, exit, information, technology, or any other aspect of production and consumption in the market.

In many markets the participants (especially the firms) may decide to maintain a system of voluntary **self-regulation**, possibly in order to try to avert the imposition of government controls. Areas where self-regulation often exists include the professions (eg the Law Society, the British Medical Association and other professional bodies).

1.3 Competition policy in the UK

Overall responsibility for the conduct of policy lies with the Secretary of State for Trade and Industry. However, day to day supervision is carried out by the Office of Fair Trading (OFT), headed by its Director General (DG). The OFT may refer companies to the **Competition Commission** (formerly called the Monopolies and Mergers Commission) or the Restrictive Practices Court for investigation.

1.4 Monopolies and mergers   12/03

Key term

> In a pure **monopoly**, there is only one firm, the sole producer of a good, which has no closely competing substitutes.

A monopoly situation can have some advantages.

  (a) In certain industries arguably only by achieving a monopoly will a company be able to benefit from the kinds of **economies of scale** (benefits of conducting operations on a large scale) that can minimise prices.

  (b) Establishing a monopoly may be the best way for a business to **maximise its profits**.

However monopolies often have several adverse consequences.

  (a) Companies can impose **higher prices** on consumers.

  (b) The lack of incentive of competition may mean companies have **no incentive** to **improve their products** or **offer a wider range of products**.

  (c) There is no pressure on the company to **improve the efficiency** of its **use of resources**.

In practice government policy is concerned not just with situations where one firm has a 100% market share, but other situations where an organisation has a significant market share.

The Competition Commission can also be asked to investigate what could be called **'oligopoly situations'** involving explicit or implicit collusion between firms.

The investigation is not automatic. Once the case has been referred, the Commission must decide whether or not the monopoly is acting **'against the public interest'**.

In its report, the Competition Commission will say if a monopoly situation has been found to exist and, if so, will make recommendations to deal with it. These may involve various measures.

- Price cuts
- Price and profit controls
- Removal of entry barriers
- The breaking up of the firm (rarely).

Case Study

In October 2000 the Competition Commission published a report into the supply of groceries by multiple stores, considering whether these stores were making excessive profits. The report concluded that because of industry changes, in particular the entry of Wal-Mart into the industry, that there was sufficient competition, and that excessive prices were not being charged, nor excessive profits being earned.

The Commission did however identify three areas of concern.

(a) The relationship between supermarket chains and their suppliers including farmers. The Commission recommended that a compulsory Code of Practice should be introduced for the largest chains (ASDA, Safeway, Sainsbury, Somerfield and Tesco) including provisions about standard terms, prompt payment and appropriate compensation.

(b) There were some instances of persistent selling below cost, and price flexing (varying prices in different geographical areas in the light of local competition.) The Commission considered a number of remedies including a ban on below cost selling and requiring supermarkets to put their prices on the Internet. However in the end it concluded that no action should be taken because the remedies would themselves have adverse effects.

(c) The Commission expressed concern about the limited choice of supermarkets in certain areas and recommended that consumer choice be increased by new store openings wherever possible.

A prospective **merger** between two or more companies may be referred to the Competition Commission for investigation if either of the following two criteria are satisfied.

(a) The merger will create a firm with **monopoly power**, ie one that has 25% or more market share.

(b) The merger involves the **transfer** of at least **£30 million** of assets.

Again, referral to the Competition Commission is not automatic, and since the legislation was first introduced, only a small proportion of all merger proposals have been referred.

If a potential merger is investigated, the Commission has again to determine whether or not the merger would be against the public interest. As with monopolies, it will assess the relative benefits and costs in order to arrive at a decision.

Exam focus point

Question 4 in December 2003 required candidates to discuss the economic consequences of monopoly.

Question — Competition Commission

Look through newspapers or on the Internet for a report on the activities of the Competition Commission. Why is the investigation being carried out and how was it initiated?

1.5 Restrictive practices

The other strand of competition policy is concerned with preventing the development of anti-competitive practices such as **price-fixing agreements** (cartels). Under the legislation, all agreements between firms must be notified to the OFT and the DG will then decide if the agreement should be examined by the Restrictive Practices Court. The presumption of the Court is that the agreement will be declared illegal, unless it can be shown to satisfy one of the 'gateways' as defined in the Restrictive Practices Act 1976.

These gateways (ie reasons for allowing the agreement) include the following.

- To protect employment in a particular area
- To protect the public against injury
- To protect exports
- To counter measures taken by other firms which restrict competition

1.6 European Union competition policy

As a member of the European Union (EU), the UK is also now subject to EU competition policy. This is enshrined in Articles 81 (dealing with restrictive practices) and 82 (concerned with monopoly) of the Treaty of Rome.

1.7 Deregulation

Deregulation or 'liberalisation' is, in general, the opposite of regulation. Deregulation can be defined as the removal or weakening of any form of statutory (or voluntary) regulation of free **market activity**. Deregulation allows **free market forces** more scope to determine the outcome.

Case Study

Here are some examples of deregulation in the UK over recent years.

(a) Deregulation of road passenger transport – both buses (stage services) and coaches (express services) – was brought about by the Transport Acts of 1980 and 1985. There is now effective free entry into both markets (except in London).

(b) The monopoly position enjoyed by some professions has been removed, for example in opticians' supply of spectacles and solicitors' monopoly over house conveyancing. In addition, the controls on advertising by professionals have been loosened.

Deregulation, whose main aim is to introduce more competition into an industry by removing statutory or other entry barriers, has the following potential benefits.

(a) **Improved incentives for internal/cost efficiency**

Greater competition compels managers to try harder to keep down costs.

(b) **Improved allocative efficiency**

Competition keeps down prices closer to marginal cost, and firms therefore produce closer to the socially optimal output level.

In some industries it could have certain disadvantages, including the following.

(a) **Loss of economies of scale**

If increased competition means that each firm produces less output on a smaller scale, unit costs will be higher.

(b) **Lower quality or quantity of service**

The need to reduce costs may lead firms to reduce quality or eliminate unprofitable but socially valuable services.

(c) **Need to protect competition**

It may be necessary to implement a regulatory regime to protect competition where inherent forces have a tendency to eliminate it, for example if there is a dominant firm already in the industry, as in the case of British Telecom. In this type of situation, effective 'regulation for competition' will be required, ie regulatory measures aimed at maintaining competitive pressures, whether existing or potential.

1.8 Privatisation and denationalisation

> **FAST FORWARD**
>
> **Privatisation** is a policy of introducing private enterprise into industries which were previously stated-owned or state-operated.

Privatisation takes three broad forms.

(a) The **deregulation of industries**, to allow private firms to compete against state-owned businesses where they were not allowed to compete before (for example, deregulation of bus and coach services; deregulation of postal services)

(b) **Contracting out work** to **private firms**, where the work was previously done by government employees – for example, refuse collection or hospital laundry work

(c) **Transferring the ownership** of **assets from** the **state to private shareholders** – for example, the denationalisation of British Gas and British Telecom (now called BT)

Privatisation can improve efficiency, in one of two ways.

(a) If the effect of privatisation is to **increase competition**, the effect might be to reduce or eliminate allocative inefficiency.

(b) The effect of denationalisation might be to make the **industries more cost-conscious**, because they will be directly answerable to shareholders, and under scrutiny from stock market investors.

There are other possible advantages of privatisation.

(a) Denationalisation provides an **immediate source of money** for the government.

(b) Privatisation reduces **bureaucratic and political meddling** in the industries concerned.

(c) It encourages **wider share ownership**. Denationalisation is one method of creating wider share ownership, as the sale of BT, British Gas and some other nationalised industries have shown in the UK.

There are arguments against privatisation too.

(a) State-owned industries are more likely to respond to the **public interest**, ahead of the profit motive. For example, state-owned industries are more likely to cross-subsidise unprofitable operations from profitable ones; for example the Post Office will continue to deliver letters to the isles of Scotland even though the service might be very unprofitable.

(b) Encouraging private competition to state-run industries might be **inadvisable** where significant economies of scale can be achieved by monopoly operations.

2 Official aid schemes

FAST FORWARD

The freedom of European governments to offer cash **grants** and other forms of direct assistance to business is limited by European Union policies designed to prevent the distortion of free market competition.

The government provides finance to companies in cash grants and other forms of official direct assistance, as part of its policy of helping to develop the national economy, especially in high technology industries and in areas of high unemployment.

Government incentives might be offered on:

(a) A **regional basis**, giving help to firms that invest in an economically depressed area of the country

(b) A **selective national basis**, giving help to firms that invest in an industry that the government would like to see developing more quickly, for example robotics or fibre optics

In Europe, such assistance is increasingly limited by European Union policies designed to prevent the distortion of free market competition. The UK government's powers to grant aid for modernisation and development are now severely restricted.

2.1 The Enterprise Initiative

The Enterprise Initiative is a package of measures offered by the Department of Trade and Industry (DTI) to businesses in the UK. It includes regional selective grant assistance. A network of 'Business Links', which are local business advice centres, is also provided.

Regional selective assistance is available for investment projects undertaken by firms in **Assisted Areas**. The project must be commercially viable, create or safeguard employment, demonstrate a need for assistance and offer a distinct regional and national benefit. The amount of grant will be negotiated as the minimum necessary to ensure the project goes ahead.

3 Supply side policies

FAST FORWARD

The **supply side economics** of the monetarists is directed at deregulation of markets and reduction in the role of government.

Supply side economists, focus policy upon the **conditions of aggregate supply**, taking the view that the availability, quality, and cost of resources are the long-term determinants of national income and prices. They argue that by putting resources to work an economy will **automatically** generate the additional income necessary to purchase the higher outputs, ie **supply creates its own demand.**

Supply side economists advise against state involvement in the economy at both the microeconomic and macroeconomic levels.

Microeconomic involvement is disliked for the following reasons.

(a) Price regulation **distorts** the **signalling function** essential for markets to reach optimal equilibrium.

(b) Wage regulation **distorts** the labour market's **ability to ensure full employment**.

(c) Public ownership **blunts** the **incentive effects** of the profit motive and leads to inefficiency.

(d) Government grants and subsidies **encourage inefficient** and lame-duck **industries**.

(e) Public provision of services **may not encourage efficiency** and can **limit** the **discipline** of consumer choice.

(f) Employment legislation, such as employment protection, **limits market flexibility** by discouraging recruitment and encouraging over-manning.

Macroeconomic intervention by government is regarded as harmful for several reasons.

(a) **Demand management** will be **inflationary** in the long run.

(b) **High taxes** will act as a **disincentive**.

(c) The **possibility** of **politically motivated policy changes** will create damaging uncertainty in the economy. This will discourage long-term investment.

4 Environmental ('green') policies

FAST FORWARD

There are a number of policy approaches to **pollution**, such as **polluter pays policies, subsidies** and direct **legislation**.

The environment is increasingly seen as an important issue facing managers in both the public and private sectors. The problems of pollution and the environment appear to call for international co-operation between governments. Pollutants expelled into the atmosphere in the UK are said to cause 'acid rain' to fall in Scandinavia, for example.

4.1 Pollution policy

Key term

Externalities are positive or negative effects on third parties resulting from production and consumption activities.

Pollution, for example from exhaust gas emissions or the dumping of waste, is often discussed in relation to environmental policy. If polluters take little or no account of their actions on others, this generally results in the output of polluting industries being greater than is optimal.

One solution is to levy a tax on polluters equal to the cost of removing the effect of the externality they generate: the **polluter pays principle**. This will encourage firms to cut emissions and provides an incentive for them to research ways of permanently reducing pollution.

Apart from the imposition of a tax, there are a number of other measures open to the government in attempting to reduce pollution. One of the main measures available is the application of **subsidies** which may be used either to persuade polluters to reduce output and hence pollution, or to assist with expenditure on production processes, such as new machinery and air cleaning equipment, which reduce levels of pollution.

Case Study

One subsidy in the UK is that given to householders for loft insulation. This reduces energy consumption, in turn reducing emissions of pollutants.

4.2 Legislation

An alternative approach used in the UK is to impose **legislation** laying down regulations governing waste disposal and atmospheric emissions. Waste may only be disposed of with prior consent and if none is given, or it is exceeded, the polluter is fined. There may also be attempts with this type of approach to specify standards of, for example, air and water quality with appropriate penalties for not conforming to the required standards.

Exam focus point

> The UK Chancellor of the Exchequer, Gordon Brown has asserted that the environment would be put 'at the core of the government's objectives for the tax system'. This statement makes green taxes a topical issue, and therefore perhaps more likely to be examined.

4.3 Advantages of 'environmentally friendly policies' for a firm

There may be various reasons why a firm may gain from adopting a policy of strict compliance with environmental regulations, or of going further and taking voluntary initiatives to protect aspects of the environment.

(a) If potential customers perceive the firm to be environmentally friendly, some may be **more inclined** to **buy its products**.

(b) A corporate image which embraces environmentally friendly policies may **enhance relationships** with the **public in general** or with local communities.

(c) People may prefer to work for an **environmentally friendly firm**.

(d) **'Ethical' investment funds** may be more likely to buy the firm's shares.

5 Corporate governance   12/02

FAST FORWARD

> The **corporate governance** reports aim to encourage better **corporate governance** and practice. The **Cadbury, Greenbury** and **Hampel** reports set down guidelines on **board operations, directors' remuneration, audits** and **company meetings**. The recommendations of these reports are joined in a **Combined Code**.

Key term

> **Corporate governance** is 'the system by which companies are directed and controlled'.

5.1 Cadbury report

The first major development during the 1990s in corporate governance was the Cadbury committee.

5.1.1 Corporate governance

The Cadbury committee reported in December 1992. Its report went beyond purely financial matters and made recommendations about corporate governance in general.

5.1.2 Code of Best Practice

This was aimed at the directors of all UK plcs, but the directors of all companies were encouraged to use the Code for guidance.

5.1.3 Board of directors

The report stressed the importance of the board of directors meeting on a **regular basis**, retaining **full control** over the company and monitoring executive management. Certain matters such as major acquisitions or disposals of assets, should be **referred** automatically to the **board**. There should be a **clear division of responsibilities** at the head of a company. Generally this would mean the posts of chairman and chief executive being held by different people; if they were held by the same person there should be a **strong independent element** on the board.

5.1.4 Accounts

The Cadbury committee stressed the importance of the board presenting a **balanced** and **understandable assessment** of the company's position. The directors should **explain** their **responsibilities** for preparing accounts. Statements should also be made about the company's ability to continue as a **going concern**, and the effectiveness of its **internal controls**.

5.2 Greenbury report

In July 1995 the Greenbury committee's report on directors' remuneration was published. The report developed a number of recommendations of the Cadbury committee. Greenbury stressed the importance of the role of the **remuneration committee**, which the report recommended should consist entirely of non-executive directors.

5.2.1 The remuneration committee

The most important recommendation was that the board should set up a remuneration committee of non-executive directors to **determine** the company's **general policy** on the **remuneration** of **executive directors and** specific remuneration packages for each director.

5.3 The Hampel report

The Hampel committee was set up in 1996 to **conduct a review** of the Cadbury code and its implementation to ensure that the original purpose is being achieved, proposing amendments to and deletions from the code as necessary.

The Hampel committee produced a final report in January 1998. The introduction to the report pointed out that the primary duty of directors is to shareholders, to **enhance** the **value** of **shareholders' investment** over time. Relationships with other stakeholders were important, but making the directors responsible to other stakeholders would mean there was no clear yardstick for judging directors' performance.

5.3.1 Directors

The committee stressed that executive and non-executive directors should continue to have the same duties under the law. The committee stated that the roles of **chairman** and **chief executive** should generally be **separate**, but whether or not the roles of chairman and chief executive are combined, a **senior non-executive director** should be **identified**. The report also stressed the importance of monitoring director performance with all directors submitting themselves for **re-election at least once every three years**, and boards assessing the performance of individual directors and collective board performance.

5.3.2 Directors' remuneration

In common with the Cadbury and Greenbury reports, the Hampel committee saw the remuneration committee as the key mechanism for setting the pay of executive directors. Remuneration committees should develop policy on remuneration and devise reasonable remuneration packages for individual executive directors.

5.4 Stock Exchange requirements

Hampel proposed combining the various best practices, principles and codes of Cadbury, Greenbury and Hampel into one single 'supercode'. The Stock Exchange has issued a **Combined Code** on corporate governance, which was derived from the recommendations of the Cadbury, Greenbury and Hampel reports. In June 1998 the Stock Exchange Listing Rules were amended to make compliance with the new code obligatory for listed companies for accounting periods ending after 31 December 1998.

The Combined Code requires listed companies to include in their accounts:

(a) A narrative statement of how they **applied** the **principles** set out in the Combined Code. This should provide explanations which enable their shareholders to assess how the principles have been applied.

(b) A statement as to whether or not they **complied throughout** the **accounting period** with the provisions set out in the Combined Code. Listed companies that did not comply throughout the accounting period with all the provisions must specify the provisions with which they did not comply, and give **reasons** for **non-compliance**.

> **Exam focus point**
>
> A question in December 2002 asked how good corporate governance could address the problem of differing stakeholder objectives.

5.5 Recent developments

A number of developments have occurred in corporate governance matters in recent years.

5.6 Directors' remuneration

Listed companies in the UK are now required to publish a report on directors' remuneration. The report must include details of individual pay packages and justification for any compensation packages given in the preceding year, also comparing packages with company performance. The report must be voted on by shareholders, although the company is not bound by the shareholders' vote.

Despite these new measures, a number of companies have faced serious criticism from shareholders that director packages were excessive, and did not reflect company performance.

5.7 Non-executive directors

The **Higgs Report**, published in 2003, contained a revised draft of the Combined Code.

The key feature of the revised Code was the importance placed on the role of non-executive directors.

5.8 Independent non-executive directors

The draft revised Code contains a principle that:

> 'The board should include a **balance of executive and non-executive directors** (including independent non-executives) such that no individual or small group of individuals can dominate the board's decision taking.'

The provisions in the revised Code relating to non-executive directors have been **widely perceived to be too difficult for companies to meet**. The independence criteria do appear to restrict companies from seeking non-executive directors from channels they may have used in the past, such as former employees and respected business advisers.

5.9 Audit committees

The **Smith report** on the application of the Combined Code guidance to audit committees was published in the UK in early 2003. The guidance recommends that audit committees should:

- **Recommend** the **appointment** of the internal auditor and **approve** the **remuneration** and **terms of engagement**
- **Monitor** and **review** the external auditors' **independence, objectivity and effectiveness**
- **Develop and implement policy** on what, if any, **non-audit services** should be supplied by the external auditor
- **Monitor** and **review** internal audit, management systems and published financial information.

5.10 American developments

Strengthened statutory rules are being introduced in America as a result of the 2002 Sarbanes-Oxley Act, passed in the wake of corporate scandals, most notably Enron. Under the Act companies will not be able to obtain a listing unless they have an **audit committee**, and auditors are prohibited from offering a variety of **non-audit services** to audit clients. **Disclosure requirements** are expanded. The Act also requires investigations to be undertaken in a number of areas including **compulsory rotation of auditors** and the **areas of reporting** that are most susceptible to fraud.

Chapter Roundup

- The government influences markets in various ways, one of which is through direct **regulation** (eg the **Competition Commission**).
- **Privatisation** is a policy of introducing private enterprise into industries which were previously stated-owned or state-operated.
- The freedom of European governments to offer cash **grants** and other forms of direct assistance to business is limited by European Union policies designed to prevent the distortion of free market competition.
- The **supply side economics** of the monetarists is directed at deregulation of markets and reduction in the role of government.
- There are a number of policy approaches to **pollution**, such as **polluter pays policies, subsidies** and direct **legislation**.
- The **corporate governance** reports aim to encourage better **corporate governance** and practice. The **Cadbury, Greenbury** and **Hampel** reports set down guidelines on **board operations, directors' remuneration, audits** and **company meetings**. The recommendations of these reports are joined in a **Combined Code**.

Quick Quiz

1. Give four reasons for government intervention in markets.

2. *Fill in the blanks.*

   Privatisation has three forms

   .... of industries

   .... to private firms

   Transferring .... from .... to ....

3. According to the theories of supply-side economists, what will happen if the market is freed from government intervention?

4. What is the situation called when there is only one firm, the sole producer of a good, which has no closely competing substitutes?

   A Duopoly
   B Oligopoly
   C Monopoly
   D Totopoly

5. *Fill in the blank.*

   .... are positive or negative effects on third parties resulting from production and consumption activities.

6. What is corporate governance?

7. What according to supply side economists determine national income and prices?

8. Which of the following measures can be used to deal with monopolies?

   A Price controls
   B Profit controls
   C Removal of entry barriers
   D Breaking the firm up

Answers to Quick Quiz

1. (a) Imperfect competition
   (b) Social costs/externalities
   (c) Imperfect information
   (d) Equity

2. Deregulation of industries

   Contracting out to private firms

   Transferring ownership of assets from the state to private shareholders

3. The free market will automatically generate the highest level of national income and employment available to the economy.

4. C   Monopoly

5. Externalities

6. The system by which companies are directed and controlled

7. The availability, quality and cost of resources

8. All of them

Now try the questions below from the Exam Question Bank

Number	Level	Marks	Time
Q20	Examination	25	45 mins

Part E
Working capital management

Management of working capital

Topic list	Syllabus reference
1 Working capital and its management	3
2 Working capital and cash flow	3

Introduction

The framework of **financial management** was described in Chapter 14. In Chapters 15 to 17, we have studied the **macroeconomic environment** within which all organisations and their financial managers must work. In this chapter, we return to consider functions of the financial manager relating to the **management of working capital** in general terms.

In Chapters 19 to 20, we shall be looking at specific aspects of the management of **cash**, **stocks** (inventories), **debtors** and **creditors**.

PART E WORKING CAPITAL MANAGEMENT

Study guide

Section 5 – Management of working capital I

General issues

- Explain the nature and scope of working capital management
- Distinguish between cash flow and profits
- Explain the requirement for effective working capital management
- Explain the relationship between working capital management and business solvency
- Distinguish the working capital needs of different types of business

Exam guide

Working capital is a key topic in this paper so the next four chapters are very important. The 50 mark compulsory question may be mainly about working capital.

You need to be able to discuss the elements of working capital, assess the significance of different levels of working capital, explain how working capital might be financed and show how poor working capital management can lead to over-capitalisation, or overtrading (and possibly insolvency). The Oxford Brookes degree Research and Analysis Project Topic 15 requires you to analyse the role of working capital on the profitability and/or efficiency of an organisation of your choice.

1 Working capital and its management   12/02, 6/03, 6/04

1.1 Importance of working capital management

FAST FORWARD

The amount tied up in **working capital** is equal to the value of raw materials, work-in-progress, finished stocks and debtors less creditors. The size of this net figure has a direct effect on the **liquidity** of an organisation.

Key term

Net working capital of a business is its current assets less its current liabilities.

KEY CURRENT ASSETS AND LIABILITIES	
Current assets	**Current liabilities**
Cash	Trade creditors
Stock of raw materials	Taxation payable
Work in progress	Dividend payments due
Finished goods	Short-term loans
Amounts receivable from debtors	Long-term loans maturing within one year
Marketable securities	

Every business needs adequate **liquid resources** to maintain day-to-day cash flow. It needs enough to pay wages, salaries and creditors if it is to keep its workforce and ensure its supplies.

Maintaining adequate working capital is **not just important** in the **short term**. Adequate liquidity is needed to ensure the survival of the business in the long term. Even a profitable company may fail without adequate cash flow to meet its liabilities.

On the other hand, an excessively conservative approach to working capital management resulting in high levels of cash holdings will harm profits because the opportunity to make a return on the assets tied up as cash will have been missed.

18: MANAGEMENT OF WORKING CAPITAL

Exam focus point

> Some aspect of working capital management is likely to be included in every paper.

Key term

> **Working capital cycle** is the period of time which elapses between the point at which cash begins to be expended on the production of a product and the collection of cash from a purchaser.

The connection between investment in working capital and cash flow may be illustrated by means of the **working capital cycle** (also called the **cash cycle, operating cycle** or **trading cycle**).

The working capital cycle in a manufacturing business equals:

> The average time that raw materials remain in stock
> *Less* the period of credit taken from suppliers
> *Plus* the time taken to produce the goods
> *Plus* the time taken by customers to pay for the goods

If the turnover periods for stocks and debtors lengthen, or the payment period to creditors shortens, then the operating cycle will lengthen and the investment in working capital will increase.

1.2 Example: Cash operating cycle

Wines Ltd buys raw materials from suppliers that allow Wines 2.5 months credit. The raw materials remain in stock for one month, and it takes Wines 2 months to produce the goods. The goods are sold within a couple of days of production being completed and customers take on average 1.5 months to pay.

Required

Calculate Wines's working capital cycle.

Solution

We can ignore the time finished goods are in stock as it is no more than a couple of days.

	Months
The average time that raw materials remain in stock	1.0
Less: The time taken to pay suppliers	(2.5)
The time taken to produce the goods	2.0
The time taken by customers to pay for the goods	1.5
	2.0

The company's working capital cycle is 2 months. This can be illustrated diagrammatically as follows.

```
    0                    2.5   3              4.5
    |----------------------|---|----------------|
    ↓                      ↓   ↓                ↓
  Goods               Goods sold
 purchased            to customers
                          ↓                    ↓
                      Suppliers           Cash received
                        paid              from customers

                          ←———————————————→
                          Working capital cycle
                              two months
```

The working capital cycle is the period between the suppliers being paid and the cash being received from the customers.

PART E WORKING CAPITAL MANAGEMENT

1.3 Working capital (liquidity) ratios

FAST FORWARD

> **Liquidity ratios** may help to indicate whether a company is **over-capitalised**, with excessive working capital, or if a business is likely to fail. A business which is trying to do too much too quickly with too little long-term capital is **overtrading**.

1.3.1 The current ratio and the quick ratio

The **current ratio** is the standard test of liquidity.

Key term

$$\text{Current ratio} = \frac{\text{Current assets}}{\text{Current liabilities}}$$

A company should have enough current assets that give a promise of 'cash to come' to meet its commitments to pay its current liabilities. Obviously, a ratio in **excess of 1** should be expected. In practice, a ratio comfortably in excess of 1 should be expected, but what is 'comfortable' varies between different types of businesses.

1.3.2 The quick ratio

Key term

$$\text{Quick ratio or acid test ratio} = \frac{\text{Current assets less stocks}}{\text{Current liabilities}}$$

Companies are not able to convert all their current assets into cash very quickly. In some businesses, where stock turnover is slow, most stocks are not very liquid assets, because the cash cycle is so long. For these reasons, we calculate an additional liquidity ratio, known as the quick ratio or acid test ratio.

This ratio should ideally be at least 1 for companies with a slow stock turnover. For companies with a fast stock turnover, a quick ratio can be less than 1 without suggesting that the company is in cash flow difficulties.

1.3.3 The debtors' payment period

Key term

$$\text{Debtors' days or debtors' payment period} = \frac{\text{Trade debtors}}{\text{Credit sales turnover}} \times 365 \text{ days}$$

This is a rough measure of the average length of time it takes for a company's debtors to pay what they owe.

The trade debtors are not the *total* figure for debtors in the balance sheet, which includes prepayments and non-trade debtors. The trade debtors figure will be itemised in an analysis of the total debtors, in a note to the accounts.

The estimate of debtor days is only approximate.

(a) The **balance sheet value** of debtors might be **abnormally high** or low compared with the 'normal' level the company usually has. This may apply especially to smaller companies, where the size of year-end debtors may largely depend on whether a few or even a single large debtor pay just before or just after the year-end.

(b) Turnover in the profit and loss account excludes value added tax (VAT), but the debtors' figure in the balance sheet includes VAT. We are not strictly comparing like with like.

1.3.4 The stock turnover period

Key terms

$$\text{Stock turnover} = \frac{\text{Cost of sales}}{\text{Average stock}}$$

The stock turnover period can also be calculated:

$$\text{Stock turnover period (Finished goods)} = \frac{\text{Average stock}}{\text{Cost of sales}} \times 365 \text{ days}$$

$$\text{Raw materials stockholding period} = \frac{\text{Average raw materials stock}}{\text{Annual purchases}} \times 365 \text{ days}$$

$$\text{Average production (work-in-progress) period} = \frac{\text{Average WIP} \times \text{Degree of WIP completion} \times 365 \text{ days}}{\text{Cost of sales}}$$

These indicate the average number of days that items of stock are held for. As with the average debt collection period, these are only approximate figures, but ones which should be reliable enough for finding changes over time. Average stock can be replaced by end-of-year stock in order to compare changes in stock turnover over the year.

A lengthening stock turnover period indicates:

(a) A **slowdown** in **trading**, or

(b) A **build-up** in **stock levels**, perhaps suggesting that the investment in stocks is becoming excessive

If we add together the stock days and the debtor days, this should give us an indication of how soon stock is convertible into cash, thereby giving a further indication of the **company's liquidity**.

1.3.5 The creditors' payment period

Key term

$$\text{Creditors' payment period} = \frac{\text{Average trade creditors}}{\text{Purchases or Cost of sales}} \times 365 \text{ days}$$

or **Creditors' turnover period**

The creditors' payment period often helps to assess a company's liquidity; an increase in creditor days is often a sign of lack of long-term finance or poor management of current assets, resulting in the use of extended credit from suppliers, increased bank overdraft and so on.

All the ratios calculated above will **vary by industry**; hence **comparisons** of ratios calculated with other similar companies in the same industry are important.

You may need to use the periods to calculate the operating cycle.

	Days
Raw materials stockholding period	X
Creditors' payment period	(X)
Average production period	X
Stock turnover period (Finished goods)	X
Debtors' payment period	X
Operating cycle	X

1.4 The need for funds for investment in current assets

These liquidity ratios are a guide to the risk of cash flow problems and insolvency. If a company suddenly finds that it is **unable to renew** its **short-term liabilities** (for example, if the bank suspends its overdraft facilities, there will be a **danger of insolvency** unless the company is able to turn enough of its current assets into cash quickly.

Current liabilities are often a cheap method of finance (trade creditors do not usually carry an interest cost). Companies may therefore consider that, in the interest of higher profits, it is worth accepting some risk of insolvency by increasing current liabilities, taking the maximum credit possible from suppliers.

1.5 Working capital needs of different types of business

Different industries have different optimum working capital profiles, reflecting their methods of doing business and what they are selling.

(a) Businesses with a lot of **cash sales** and few credit sales should have **minimal debtors**.

(b) Businesses that exist solely to trade will only have **finished goods in stock**, whereas **manufacturers** will have **raw materials** and **work in progress** as well. Also some finished goods, notably foodstuffs, have to be sold within a few days because of their perishable nature.

(c) **Large companies** may be able to use their strength as customers to obtain **extended credit periods** from their suppliers. By contrast small companies, particularly those that have recently commenced trading, may be required to pay their suppliers immediately.

(d) Some businesses will be receiving **most of their monies** at **certain times** of the year, whilst incurring expenses throughout the year. Examples include travel agents who will have peaks reflecting demand for holidays during the summer and at Christmas.

1.6 Over-capitalisation and working capital

If there are excessive stocks, debtors and cash, and very few creditors, there will be an over-investment by the company in current assets. Working capital will be excessive and the company will be in this respect over-capitalised.

Indicators of over-capitalisation	
Sales/working capital	Compare with previous years or, similar companies
Liquidity ratios	Current ratio > 2:1 Quick ratio > 1:1 indicate over-investment
Turnover periods	Long turnover periods for stock and debtors or short credit period from suppliers may be unnecessary

1.7 Example: Working capital ratios

Calculate liquidity and working capital ratios from the following accounts of a manufacturer of products for the construction industry, and comment on the ratios.

	20X8 £m	20X7 £m
Turnover	2,065.0	1,788.7
Cost of sales	1,478.6	1,304.0
Gross profit	586.4	484.7
Current assets		
Stocks	119.0	109.0
Debtors (note 1)	400.9	347.4
Short-term investments	4.2	18.8
Cash at bank and in hand	48.2	48.0
	572.3	523.2
Creditors: amounts falling due within one year		
Loans and overdrafts	49.1	35.3
Corporation taxes	62.0	46.7
Dividend	19.2	14.3
Creditors (note 2)	370.7	324.0
	501.0	420.3
Net current assets	71.3	102.9

Notes

		20X8 £m	20X7 £m
1	Trade debtors	329.8	285.4
2	Trade creditors	236.2	210.8

Solution

	20X8		20X7	
Current ratio	$\dfrac{572.3}{501.0}$	= 1.14	$\dfrac{523.2}{420.3}$	= 1.24
Quick ratio	$\dfrac{453.3}{501.0}$	= 0.90	$\dfrac{414.2}{420.3}$	= 0.99
Debtors' payment period	$\dfrac{329.8}{2,065.0}$	× 365 = 58 days	$\dfrac{285.4}{1,788.7}$	× 365 = 58 days
Stock turnover period	$\dfrac{119.0}{1,478.6}$	× 365 = 29 days	$\dfrac{109.0}{1,304.0}$	× 365 = 31 days
Creditors' turnover period	$\dfrac{236.2}{1,478.6}$	× 365 = 58 days	$\dfrac{210.8}{1,304.0}$	× 365 = 59 days

(a) The company is a manufacturing group serving the construction industry, and so would be expected to have a comparatively lengthy debtors' turnover period, because of the relatively poor cash flow in the construction industry.

(b) The company compensates for this by ensuring that they do not pay for raw materials and other costs before they have sold their stocks of finished goods (hence the similarity of debtors' and creditors' turnover periods).

(c) The company's current and quick ratios have fallen but are still reasonable, and the quick ratio is not much less than the current ratio. This suggests that stock levels are strictly controlled, which is reinforced by the low stock turnover period.

It would seem that working capital is tightly managed, to avoid the poor liquidity which could be caused by a high debtors' turnover period and comparatively high creditors.

PART E   WORKING CAPITAL MANAGEMENT

1.8 Overtrading   12/03

In contrast with over-capitalisation, overtrading happens when a business tries to **do too much too quickly** with **too little long-term capital**, so that it is trying to support too large a volume of trade with the capital resources at its disposal.

Even if an overtrading business operates at a profit, it could easily run into serious trouble because it is **short of money**. Such liquidity troubles stem from the fact that it does not have enough capital to provide the cash to pay its debts as they fall due.

Symptoms of overtrading are as follows.

(a) There is a **rapid increase** in **turnover**.

(b) There is a **rapid increase** in the **volume of current assets** and possibly also fixed assets. **Stock turnover** and **debtors turnover** might slow down, in which case the rate of increase in stocks and debtors would be even greater than the rate of increase in sales.

(c) There is only a **small increase** in **proprietors' capital** (perhaps through retained profits). Most of the increase in assets is financed by credit, especially:

   (i) **Trade creditors** - the payment period to creditors is likely to lengthen

   (ii) A **bank overdraft**, which often reaches or even exceeds the limit of the facilities agreed by the bank

(d) Some **debt ratios** and **liquidity ratios** alter dramatically.

   (i) The **proportion** of **total assets** financed by proprietors' capital falls, and the proportion financed by credit rises.

   (ii) The **current ratio** and the **quick ratio** fall.

   (iii) The business might have a **liquid deficit**, that is, an excess of current liabilities over current assets.

   (iv) The rate of turnover to working capital will increase as turnover increases rapidly.

Exam focus point

> This list of signs is important; you must be aware of why businesses run into financial difficulties. In the exam you might be expected to diagnose overtrading from information given about a company.

1.9 Example: Overtrading

Great Ambition Ltd appoints a new managing director who has great plans to expand the company. He wants to increase turnover by 100% within two years, and to do this he employs extra sales staff. He recognises that customers do not want to have to wait for deliveries, and so he decides that the company must build up its stock levels. There is a substantial increase in the company's stocks. These are held in additional warehouse space which is now rented. The company also buys new cars for its extra sales representatives.

The managing director's policies are immediately successful in boosting sales, which double in just over one year. Stock levels are now much higher, but the company takes longer credit from its suppliers, even though some suppliers have expressed their annoyance at the length of time they must wait for payment. Credit terms for debtors are unchanged, and so the volume of debtors, like the volume of sales, rises by 100%.

In spite of taking longer credit, the company still needs to increase its overdraft facilities with the bank, which are raised from a limit of £40,000 to one of £80,000. The company is profitable, and retains some profits in the business, but profit margins have fallen. **Gross profit margins** are lower because some prices have been reduced to obtain extra sales. **Net profit margins** are lower because overhead costs are higher. These include sales representatives' wages, car expenses and depreciation on cars, warehouse rent and additional losses from having to write off out-of-date and slow-moving stock items.

The balance sheet of the company might change over time from (A) to (B).

	Balance sheet (A)			Balance sheet (B)		
	£	£	£	£	£	£
Fixed assets			160,000			210,000
Current assets						
Stock		60,000			150,000	
Debtors		64,000			135,000	
Cash		1,000			–	
		125,000			285,000	
Current liabilities						
Bank	25,000			80,000		
Creditors	50,000			200,000		
		75,000			280,000	
			50,000			5,000
			210,000			215,000
Share capital			10,000			10,000
Profit and loss account			200,000			205,000
			210,000			215,000
Sales			£1,000,000			£2,000,000
Gross profit			£200,000			£300,000
Net profit			£50,000			£20,000

In situation (B), the company has **reached** its **overdraft** limit and has **four times** as many **creditors** as in situation (A) but with only **twice the sales turnover**. **Stock levels** are much **higher**, and **stock turnover** is **lower**.

The company is overtrading. If it had to pay its next trade creditor, or salaries and wages, before it received any income, it could not do so without the bank allowing it to exceed its overdraft limit. The company is profitable, although profit margins have fallen, and it ought to expect a prosperous future. But if it does not sort out its cash flow and liquidity, it will not survive to enjoy future profits.

Suitable solutions to the problem would be measures to reduce the degree of overtrading.

(a) **New capital** from the shareholders could be injected.

(b) **Better control** could be applied to stocks and debtors. The company could **abandon ambitious plans** for increased sales and more fixed asset purchases until the business has had time to consolidate its position, and build up its capital base with retained profits.

A business seeking to increase its turnover too rapidly without an adequate capital base is not the only **cause of overtrading**. **Other causes** are as follows.

(a) When a business repays a loan, it often replaces the old loan with a new one. However a business might **repay a loan without replacing it**, with the consequence that it has **less long-term capital** to finance its current level of operations.

(b) A business might be profitable, but in a period of **inflation**, its **retained profits** might be **insufficient** to pay for **replacement** fixed assets and stocks, which now cost more because of inflation.

1.10 The working capital requirement 12/01

Computing the working capital requirement is a matter of calculating the value of current assets less current liabilities, perhaps by taking averages over a one year period.

The level of investment in working capital may be described as aggressive, conservative or moderate in approach. The approach will reflect the attitude of owners and managers.

1.11 Example: Working capital requirements

The following data relate to Corn Ltd, a manufacturing company.

Turnover for the year	£1,500,000
Costs as percentages of sales	%
Direct materials	30
Direct labour	25
Variable overheads	10
Fixed overheads	15
Selling and distribution	5

On average:

(a) Debtors take 2.5 months before payment

(b) Raw materials are in stock for three months

(c) Work-in-progress represents two months worth of half produced goods

(d) Finished goods represents one month's production

(e) Credit is taken as follows:

(i)	Direct materials	2 months
(ii)	Direct labour	1 week
(iii)	Variable overheads	1 month
(iv)	Fixed overheads	1 month
(v)	Selling and distribution	0.5 months

Work-in-progress and finished goods are valued at material, labour and variable expense cost

Compute the working capital requirement of Corn Ltd assuming the labour force is paid for 50 working weeks a year.

Solution

(a) The annual costs incurred will be as follows.

		£
Direct materials	30% of £1,500,000	450,000
Direct labour	25% of £1,500,000	375,000
Variable overheads	10% of £1,500,000	150,000
Fixed overheads	15% of £1,500,000	225,000
Selling and distribution	5% of £1,500,000	75,000

(b) The average value of current assets will be as follows.

		£	£
Raw materials	3/12 × £450,000		112,500
Work-in-progress			
Materials (50% complete)	1/12 × £450,000	37,500	
Labour (50% complete)	1/12 × £375,000	31,250	
Variable overheads (50% complete)	1/12 × £150,000	12,500	
			81,250
Finished goods			
Materials	1/12 × £450,000	37,500	
Labour	1/12 × £375,000	31,250	
Variable overheads	1/12 × £150,000	12,500	
			81,250
Debtors	2.5/12 × £1,500,000		312,500
			587,500

(c) Average value of current liabilities will be as follows.

		£
Materials	2/12 × £450,000	75,000
Labour	1/50 × £375,000	7,500
Variable overheads	1/12 × £150,000	12,500
Fixed overheads	1/12 × £225,000	18,750
Selling and distribution	0.5/12 × £75,000	3,125
		116,875

(d) Working capital required is (£(587,500 − 116,875)) = 470,625

It has been assumed that all the direct materials are allocated to work-in-progress when production starts.

Exam focus point

In the exam you may be asked to calculate the working capital requirement in £ using the method described above. Alternatively (as was the case in the December 2001 exam) you may be asked to calculate the requirement in terms of time, in which case the answer would be the length of the **working capital cycle** (see earlier in this chapter).

1.12 Predicting business failure

Investors will wish to know whether additional funds could be lent to the company with reasonable safety, and whether the company would fail without additional funds.

One method of predicting business failure is the use of **liquidity ratios** (the current ratio and the quick ratio). A company with a current ratio well below 2:1 or a quick ratio well below 1:1 might be considered illiquid and in danger of failure, although as previously noted the value of these ratios depends upon the nature of the business being considered.

PART E WORKING CAPITAL MANAGEMENT

2 Working capital and cash flow

FAST FORWARD

> Cash budgeting is an important part of short term planning, but there will always be unforeseen changes which can affect the pattern and quantities of cash flows.

2.1 Cash flow planning

Since a company must have adequate cash inflows to survive, management should plan and control cash flows as well as profitability. **Cash budgeting** is an important element in short-term cash flow planning. If a budget reveals that a short-term cash shortage can be expected, steps will be taken to meet the problem (perhaps by arranging a bigger bank overdraft facility).

Cash budgets and cash flow forecasts on their own do not give full protection against a cash shortage and enforced liquidation of the business by creditors. There may be **unexpected changes** in cash flow patterns.

Question — Changes to cash flow

Give examples of unforeseen changes which may affect cash flow patterns.

Answer

Your list probably included some of the following.

(a) A change in the **general economic environment**. An economic recession will cause a slump in trade.
(b) A **new product**, launched by a competitor, which takes business away from a company's traditional and established product lines.
(c) **New cost-saving product technology**, which forces the company to invest in the new technology to remain competitive.
(d) **Moves by competitors** which have to be countered (for example a price reduction or a sales promotion).
(e) **Changes in consumer preferences**, resulting in a fall in demand.
(f) **Government action** against certain trade practices or against trade with a country that a company has dealings with.
(g) **Strikes** or other industrial action.
(h) **Natural disasters**, such as floods or fire damage, which curtail an organisation's activities.

2.2 Strategic fund management

Strategic fund management is an extension of cash flow planning, which takes into consideration the ability of a business to overcome unforeseen problems with cash flows. It recognises that the assets of a business can be divided into three categories.

(a) Assets which are needed to carry out the 'core' activities of the business.
(b) **Assets** which are **not essential** for carrying out the main activities of the business, and which could be **sold off** at **fairly short notice**. These assets will consist mainly of short-term marketable investments.

(c) **Assets** which are **not essential** for carrying out the main activities of the business, and which could be sold off to raise cash, although it would probably take **time to arrange** the sale, and the amount of **cash obtainable** from the sale might be **uncertain**. These assets would include:

   (i) Long-term investments (for example, substantial shareholdings in other companies)

   (ii) Subsidiary companies engaged in 'peripheral' activities, which might be sold off to another company or in a management buyout

   (iii) Land and buildings

If an unexpected event takes place which threatens a company's cash position, the company could meet the threat by:

(a) **Working capital management** to improve cash flows by reducing stocks and debtors, taking more credit, or negotiating a higher bank overdraft facility

(b) **Changes to dividend policy**

(c) Arranging to **sell off non-essential assets**

Exam focus point

Look out when you read through the rest of Part E for ways of improving working capital management, as this is a popular topic in the exam.

Chapter Roundup

- The amount tied up in **working capital** is equal to the value of raw materials, work-in-progress, finished stocks and debtors less creditors. The size of this net figure has a direct effect on the **liquidity** of an organisation.

- **Liquidity ratios** may help to indicate whether a company is **over-capitalised**, with excessive working capital, or if a business is likely to fail. A business which is trying to do too much too quickly with too little long-term capital is **overtrading**.

- Cash budgeting is an important part of short term planning, but there will always be unforeseen changes which can affect the pattern and quantities of cash flows.

PART E   WORKING CAPITAL MANAGEMENT

Quick Quiz

1   Which of the following is the most likely to be a symptom of overtrading?

   A   Static levels of stock turnover
   B   Rapid increase in profits
   C   Increase in the level of the current ratio
   D   Rapid increase in sales

2   The operating cycle is:

   A The time [_____]
   Less   B The time [_____]
   Plus   C The time [_____]
   Plus   D The time [_____]

   Fill in the blanks.

3   Fill in the blanks with the following:

   Current liabilities; current assets; stocks; 2; 1.

   Quick ratio = ... less ....   (This should be at least ....)
   ....

4   Which of the following describes *overcapitalisation* and which describes *overtrading*?

   A   A company with excessive investment in working capital
   B   A company trying to support too large a volume of trade with the capital resources at its disposal

5   Which of the following statements best defines the current ratio?

   A   The ratio of current assets to current liabilities.
       For the majority of businesses it should be at least 2.

   B   The ratio of current assets to current liabilities.
       For the majority of businesses it should be at least 1.

   C   The ratio of current assets excluding stock to current liabilities.
       For the majority of businesses it should be at least 1.

   D   The ratio of current assets excluding stock to current liabilities.
       For the majority of businesses it should be at least 2.

6   The debtors' payment period is a calculation of the time taken to pay by all debtors.

   [ ]   True
   [ ]   False

7   What are the two most likely reasons for a lengthening stock turnover period?

8   What is the working capital requirement of a company with the following average figures over a year?

	£
Stock	3,750
Trade debtors	1,500
Cash and bank balances	500
Trade creditors	1,800

Answers to Quick Quiz

1. D   Rapid increase in sales

2. A   The time raw materials remain in stock
   B   The time period of credit taken from suppliers
   C   The time taken to produce goods
   D   The time taken by customers to pay for goods

3. Quick ratio = $\dfrac{\text{Current assets less stocks}}{\text{Current liabilities}}$ (This should be at least 1)

4. A   Overcapitalisation
   B   Overtrading

5. A   Current assets to current liabilities: 2

6. False; the calculation normally only includes trade debtors.

7. (a) A slowdown in trading
   (b) A build-up of stock levels

8. Working capital requirement = current assets less current liabilities

   = 3,750 + 1,500 + 500 − 1,800
   = £3,950

Now try the questions below from the Exam Question Bank

Number	Level	Marks	Time
Q21	Examination	25	45 mins

19

The management of debtors and creditors

Topic list	Syllabus reference
1 Total credit	3
2 The management of debtors	3
3 Using debtor information	3
4 Foreign trade and debt management	3
5 The management of creditors and short-term finance	3

Introduction

This chapter deals with specific techniques in the management of debtors, creditors and short-term finance. These include overall credit control policies (should the business offer credit – if so how much and to whom), and ensuring amounts owed are not excessive.

Whilst working through this chapter, try not to think of debtors and creditors in isolation; they are part of working capital, each element of which will have knock-on effects when there is a change in another. For example, an increase in the credit period taken by debtors will reduce the amount of cash available to pay creditors and invest in stock.

PART E WORKING CAPITAL MANAGEMENT

Study guide

Section 6 – Management of working capital II

Management of debtors

- Explain the role of debtors in the working capital cycle
- Explain how the credit-worthiness of customers may be assessed
- Evaluate the balance of risks and costs of customer default against the profitability of marginal business
- Explain the role of factoring and invoice discounting
- Explain the role of early settlement discounts
- Discuss the particular problems of managing overseas debtors
- Calculate and interpret debtor ratios
- Apply the tools and techniques of debtor management
- Analyse and evaluate the results of debtor management techniques

Management of creditors

- Explain the role of creditors in the working capital cycle
- Explain the availability of credit and the role of the guarantee
- Identify the risks of taking increased credit and buying under extended credit terms
- Explain how methods of paying suppliers may influence cash flows of both parties
- Discuss the particular problems of managing overseas accounts payable
- Calculate and interpret creditor ratios
- Apply the tools and techniques of creditor management
- Analyse and evaluate the results of creditor management technique

Exam guide

Debtor management is a key aspect of working capital management. You may be asked to calculate the financial effects of different policies or to discuss the benefits and drawbacks of trade credit as a source of finance.

1 Total credit

FAST FORWARD

> Offering credit has a cost: the value of the interest charged on an overdraft to fund the period of credit, or the interest lost on the cash not received and deposited in the bank. An increase in profit from extra sales resulting from offering credit could offset this cost.

Finding a **total level of credit** which can be offered is a matter of finding the least costly balance between enticing customers, whose use of credit entails considerable costs, and refusing opportunities for profitable sales. Firstly it helps to see what debtors, which often account for 30% of the total assets of a business, actually represent.

1.1 Measuring total debtors

Debtors control can be measured using the **debtors turnover** ratio. This can be calculated as an annual figure. It represents the length of the credit period taken by customers.

Key term

$$\text{Debtors turnover} = \frac{\text{Total debtors} \times 365}{\text{Sales in 365 days}}$$

For example, in 20X4 X plc made sales of £700,000 and at 31 December 20X4, debtors stood at £90,000. The comparable figures for 20X3 were £600,000 (annual sales) and £70,000 (debtors at 31.12.X3).

	20X4		20X3	
Debtors turnover	$\dfrac{£90,000 \times 365}{£700,000}$	= 47 days	$\dfrac{£70,000 \times 365}{£600,000}$	= 43 days

In 20X4, the company is taking longer to collect its debts.

1.2 Effect on profit of extending credit

The main cost of offering credit is the interest expense. How can we assess the effect on profit?

Let us assume that the Zygo Company sells widgets for £1,000, which enables it to earn a profit, after all other expenses except interest, of £100 (ie a 10% margin).

(a) Aibee buys a widget for £1,000 on 1 January 20X1, but does not pay until 31 December 20X1. Zygo relies on overdraft finance, which costs it 10% pa. The effect is:

	£
Net profit on sale of widget	100
Overdraft cost £1,000 × 10% pa	(100)
Actual profit after 12 months credit	Nil

In other words, the entire profit margin has been wiped out in 12 months.

(b) If Aibee had paid after six months, the effect would be:

	£
Net profit	100
Overdraft cost £1,000 × 10% pa × $^6/_{12}$ months	(50)
	50

Half the profit has been wiped out. (*Tutorial note.* The interest cost might be worked out in a more complex way to give a more accurate figure.)

(c) If the cost of borrowing had been 18%, then the profit would have been absorbed before seven months had elapsed. If the net profit were 5% and borrowing costs were 15%, the interest expense would exceed the net profit after four months.

A second general point is the relation of **total credit to bad debts**. Burt Edwards argues that there is a law of 10-to-1: 'Experience in different industries shows that the annual interest expense of borrowings to support overdue debts, ie those in excess of agreed payment terms, is at least ten times the total lost in bad debts'. This is not a 'law', but has been observed to be the case over a variety of UK businesses.

Question — Cost of debtors

Winterson Tools Ltd has an average level of debtors of £2m at any time representing 60 days outstanding. (Their terms are thirty days.) The firm borrows money at 10% a year. The managing director is proud of the credit control: 'I only had to write off £10,000 in bad debts last year,' she says proudly. Is she right to be proud?

> **Answer**
>
> At the moment, Winterson Tools Ltd is paying 10% × £1m (ie $^{30}/_{60}$ days × £2m) = £100,000 in interest caused by customers taking the extra month to pay.

The level of total credit can then have a significant effect on **profitability**. That said, if credit considerations are included in pricing calculations, extending credit can, in fact, increase profitability. If offering credit generates extra sales, then those extra sales will have additional repercussions on:

(a) The amount of stock maintained in the warehouse, to ensure that the extra demand must be satisfied

(b) The amount of money the company owes to its creditors (as it will be increasing its supply of raw materials)

2 The management of debtors   12/03

Several factors should be considered by management when a policy for **credit control** is formulated. These include:

(a) The administrative costs of **debt collection**

(b) The procedures for **controlling credit** to individual customers and for debt collection

(c) The amount of **extra capital required** to finance an extension of total credit - there might be an increase in debtors, stocks and creditors, and the net increase in working capital must be financed

(d) The cost of the **additional finance** required for any increase in the volume of debtors (or the savings from a reduction in debtors) - this cost might be bank overdraft interest, or the cost of long-term funds (such as loan stock or equity)

(e) Any **savings or additional expenses** in operating the credit policy (for example the extra work involved in pursuing slow payers)

(f) The **ways** in which the credit policy could be **implemented** - for example:

   (i) Credit could be eased by giving debtors a longer period in which to settle their accounts - the cost would be the resulting increase in debtors

   (ii) A discount could be offered for early payment - the cost would be the amount of the discounts taken

(g) The **effects of easing credit**, which might be to encourage a higher proportion of bad debts, and an increase in sales volume. Provided that the extra gross contribution from the increase in sales exceeds the increase in fixed cost expenses, bad debts, discounts and the finance cost of an increase in working capital, a policy to relax credit terms would be profitable

2.1 Assessing creditworthiness

FAST FORWARD

> In managing **debtors**, the **creditworthiness** of customers needs to be assessed. The risks and costs of a customer defaulting will need to be balanced against the profitability of the business provided by that customer.

Credit control involves the initial investigation of potential credit customers and the continuing control of outstanding accounts. The main points to note are as follows.

(a) New customers should give two **good references**, including one from a bank, before being granted credit.

(b) **Credit ratings** might be **checked** through a credit rating agency.

(c) A **new customer's credit limit** should be **fixed** at a **low level** and only increased if his payment record subsequently warrants it.

(d) For large value customers, a **file** should be **maintained** of any available financial information about the customer. This file should be reviewed regularly. Information is available from:

   (i) An analysis of the company's annual report and accounts

   (ii) Extel cards (sheets of accounting information about public companies in the UK, and also major overseas companies, produced by Extel)

(e) The **Department of Trade and Industry** and the Export Credit Guarantee Department will both be able to advise on overseas companies.

(f) **Press comments** may give information about what a company is currently doing (as opposed to the historical results in Extel cards or published accounts which only show what the company has done in the past).

(g) The company could send a member of staff to **visit** the company concerned, to get a first-hand impression of the company and its prospects. This would be advisable in the case of a prospective major customer.

(h) **Aged lists of debts** should be produced and reviewed at regular intervals. Credit control monitoring should be an integral part of monitoring total working capital.

(i) The **credit limit** for an existing customer should be periodically **reviewed**, but it should only be raised if the customer's credit standing is good.

(j) Procedures should be in place to ensure that **further orders** are **not accepted** from nor goods sent to a customer who is in difficulties. If a customer has exceeded his credit limit, or has not paid debts despite several reminders, or is otherwise known to be in difficulties, sales staff and warehouse staff must be notified immediately (and not, for example, at the end of the week, by which time more goods might have been supplied).

An organisation might devise a **credit-rating system** for new individual customers that is based on characteristics of the customer (such as whether the customer is a home owner, and the customer's age and occupation). Points would be awarded according to the characteristics of the customer, and the amount of credit that is offered would depend on his or her credit score.

2.2 Extension of credit

To determine whether it would be profitable to extend the level of total credit, it is necessary to assess:

- The **extra sales** that a **more generous credit policy** would stimulate
- The **profitability** of the **extra sales**
- The **extra length** of the **average debt collection period**
- The **required rate of return** on the investment in additional debtors

PART E WORKING CAPITAL MANAGEMENT

2.3 Example: Debtor management (1)

Russian Beard Ltd is considering a change of credit policy which will result in an increase in the average collection period from one to two months. The relaxation in credit is expected to produce an increase in sales in each year amounting to 25% of the current sales volume.

Selling price per unit	£10
Variable cost per unit	£8.50
Current annual sales	£2,400,000

The required rate of return on investments is 20%. Assume that the 25% increase in sales would result in additional stocks of £100,000 and additional creditors of £20,000.

Advise the company on whether or not to extend the credit period offered to customers, if:

(a) All customers take the longer credit of two months

(b) Existing customers do not change their payment habits, and only the new customers take a full two months credit

Solution

The change in credit policy is justifiable if the rate of return on the additional investment in working capital would exceed 20%.

Extra profit	
Contribution/sales ratio	15%
Increase in sales revenue	£600,000
Increase in contribution and profit	£90,000

(a) *Extra investment, if all debtors take two months credit*

	£
Average debtors after the sales increase (2/12 × £3,000,000)	500,000
Less current average debtors (1/12 × £2,400,000)	200,000
Increase in debtors	300,000
Increase in stocks	100,000
	400,000
Less increase in creditors	20,000
Net increase in working capital investment	380,000

Return on extra investment $\dfrac{£90,000}{£380,000} = 23.7\%$

(b) *Extra investment, if only the new debtors take two months credit*

	£
Increase in debtors (2/12 of £600,000)	100,000
Increase in stocks	100,000
	200,000
Less increase in creditors	20,000
Net increase in working capital investment	180,000

Return on extra investment $\dfrac{£90,000}{£180,000} = 50\%$

In both case (a) and case (b) the new credit policy appears to be worthwhile.

2.4 Settlement discounts

FAST FORWARD

Settlement discounts may be employed to shorten average credit periods, and to reduce the investment in debtors and therefore **interest costs**. The benefit in interest cost saved should exceed the cost of the discounts allowed.

To see whether the offer of a **settlement discount** (for early payment) is financially worthwhile we must compare the cost of the discount with the benefit of a reduced investment in debtors.

Varying the discount allowed for early payment of debts affects the **average collection period** and affects the **volume of demand** (and possibly, therefore, indirectly affects bad debt losses). We shall begin with examples where the offer of a discount for early payment does not affect the volume of demand.

2.5 Example: Debtor management (2)

Lowe and Price Ltd has annual credit sales of £12,000,000, and three months are allowed for payment. The company decides to offer a 2% discount for payments made within ten days of the invoice being sent, and to reduce the maximum time allowed for payment to two months. It is estimated that 50% of customers will take the discount. If the company requires a 20% return on investments, what will be the effect of the discount? Assume that the volume of sales will be unaffected by the discount.

Solution

Our approach is to calculate:

(a) The profits forgone by offering the discount
(b) The interest charges saved or incurred as a result of the changes in the cash flows of the company

Thus:

(a) The volume of debtors, if the company policy remains unchanged, would be:

3/12 × £12,000,000 = £3,000,000.

(b) If the policy is changed the volume of debtors would be:

$(\frac{10}{365} \times 50\% \times £12{,}000{,}000) + (\frac{2}{12} \times 50\% \times £12{,}000{,}000)$

= £164,384 + £1,000,000 = £1,164,384.

(c) There will be a reduction in debtors of £1,835,616.

(d) Since the company can invest at 20% a year, the value of a reduction in debtors (a source of funds) is 20% of £1,835,616 each year in perpetuity, that is, £367,123 a year.

(e) *Summary*

	£
Value of reduction in debtors each year	367,123
Less discounts allowed each year (2% × 50% × £12,000,000)	120,000
Net benefit of new discount policy each year	247,123

An extension of the payment period allowed to debtors may be introduced in order to increase sales volume.

Question — Extension of credit

Enticement Ltd currently expects sales of £50,000 a month. Variable costs of sales are £40,000 a month (all payable in the month of sale). It is estimated that if the credit period allowed to debtors were to be increased from 30 days to 60 days, sales volume would increase by 20%. All customers would be expected to take advantage of the extended credit. If the cost of capital is 12½% a year (or approximately 1% a month), is the extension of the credit period justifiable in financial terms?

Answer

	£
Current debtors (1 month)	50,000
Debtors after implementing the proposal (2 months)	120,000
Increase in debtors	70,000
Financing cost (× 12½%)	8,750
Annual contribution from additional sales	
(12 months × 20% × £10,000)	24,000
Annual net benefit from extending credit period	15,250

The percentage cost of an early settlement discount to the company giving it can be estimated by the formula:

Formula to learn

$$1 - \left(\frac{100}{100-d}\right)^{\frac{365}{t}} \%$$

where:

d is the discount offered (5% = 5, etc)
t is the reduction in the payment period in days that is necessary to obtain the early payment discount

2.6 Bad debt risk

Different credit policies are likely to have differing levels of bad debt risk. The higher turnover resulting from easier credit terms should be sufficiently profitable to exceed the cost of:

- Bad debts, and
- The additional investment necessary to achieve the higher sales

2.7 Example: Debtor management (3)

Grabbit Quick Ltd achieves current annual sales of £1,800,000. The cost of sales is 80% of this amount, but bad debts average 1% of total sales, and the annual profit is as follows.

	£
Sales	1,800,000
Less cost of sales	1,440,000
	360,000
Less bad debts	18,000
Profit	342,000

The current debt collection period is one month, and the management consider that if credit terms were eased (option A), the effects would be as follows.

	Present policy	Option A
Additional sales (%)	–	25%
Average collection period	1 month	2 months
Bad debts (% of sales)	1%	3%

The company requires a 20% return on its investments. The costs of sales are 75% variable and 25% fixed. Assume there would be no increase in fixed costs from the extra turnover; and that there would be no increase in average stocks or creditors. Which is the preferable policy, Option A or the present one?

Solution

The increase in profit before the cost of additional finance for Option A can be found as follows.

(a) Increase in contribution from additional sales   £
      25% × £1,800,000 × 40%*   180,000
      Less increase in bad debts
      (3% × £2,250,000) − £18,000   49,500
      Increase in annual profit   130,500

* The C/S ratio is 100% − (75% × 80%) = 40%

(b)   £
      Proposed investment in debtors
      £2,250,000 × 1/6   375,000
      Less current investment in debtors
      £1,800,000 × 1/12   150,000
      Additional investment required   225,000

      Cost of additional finance at 20%   £45,000

(c) As the increase in profit exceeds the cost of additional finance, Option A should be adopted.

2.8 Credit insurance

Companies might be able to obtain credit insurance against certain approved debts going bad through a specialist credit insurance firm. A company cannot insure against all its bad debt losses, but may be able to insure against losses above the normal level.

When a company arranges **credit insurance**, it must submit specific proposals for credit to the insurance company, stating the name of each customer to which it wants to give credit and the amount of credit it wants to give. The insurance company will accept, amend or refuse these proposals, depending on its assessment of each of these customers.

2.9 Factoring   12/01, 12/03

FAST FORWARD

> Some companies use **factoring** and **invoice discounting** to help short-term liquidity or to reduce administration costs. **Insurance**, particularly of overseas debts, can also help reduce the risk of bad debts.

A **factor** is defined as 'a doer or transactor of business for another', but a factoring organisation specialises in trade debts, and manages the debts owed to a client (a business customer) on the client's behalf.

Key term

> **Factoring** is an arrangement to have debts collected by a factor company, which advances a proportion of the money it is due to collect.

The main aspects of factoring include the following.

(a) **Administration** of the client's invoicing, sales accounting and debt collection service

(b) **Credit protection** for the client's debts, whereby the factor takes over the risk of loss from bad debts and so 'insures' the client against such losses. This is known as a **non-recourse** service. However, if a **non-recourse** service is provided the factor, not the firm, will decide what action to take against non-payers.

(c) Making **payments** to the client **in advance** of collecting the debts. This is sometimes referred to as 'factor finance' because the factor is providing cash to the client against outstanding debts.)

2.10 Benefits of factoring

The **benefits of factoring** for a business customer include the following.

(a) The business can **pay** its **suppliers promptly**, and so be able to take advantage of any early payment discounts that are available.

(b) **Optimum stock levels** can be **maintained**, because the business will have enough cash to pay for the stocks it needs.

(c) **Growth** can be **financed** through **sales** rather than by injecting fresh external capital.

(d) The business gets **finance linked** to its **volume of sales**. In contrast, overdraft limits tend to be determined by historical balance sheets.

(e) The **managers** of the business **do not** have to **spend** their **time** on the problems of **slow paying debtors**.

(f) The business does **not incur** the **costs** of **running** its own **sales ledger department**, and can use the **expertise** of debtor management that the factor has.

An important **disadvantage** is that debtors will be making payments direct to the factor, which is likely to present a negative picture of the firm's **attitude to customer relations**. It may also indicate that the firm is in need of rapid cash, raising questions about its **financial stability**.

2.11 Example: Factoring

A company makes annual credit sales of £1,500,000. Credit terms are 30 days, but its debt administration has been poor and the average collection period has been 45 days with 0.5% of sales resulting in bad debts which are written off.

A factor would take on the task of debt administration and credit checking, at an annual fee of 2.5% of credit sales. The company would save £30,000 a year in administration costs. The payment period would be 30 days.

The factor would also provide an advance of 80% of invoiced debts at an interest rate of 14% (3% over the current base rate). The company can obtain an overdraft facility to finance its debtors at a rate of 2.5% over base rate.

Should the factor's services be accepted? Assume a constant monthly turnover.

Solution

It is assumed that the factor would advance an amount equal to 80% of the invoiced debts, and the balance 30 days later.

(a) The current situation is as follows, using the company's debt collection staff and a bank overdraft to finance all debts.

Credit sales	£1,500,000 pa
Average credit period	45 days

The annual cost is as follows:

	£
$\frac{45}{365} \times £1,500,000 \times 13.5\%$ (11% + 2.5%)	24,966
Bad debts: 0.5% × £1,500,000	7,500
Administration costs	30,000
Total cost	62,466

(b) *The cost of the factor.* 80% of credit sales financed by the factor would be 80% of £1,500,000 = £1,200,000. For a consistent comparison, we must assume that 20% of credit sales would be financed by a bank overdraft. The average credit period would be only 30 days. The annual cost would be as follows.

			£
Factor's finance	$\frac{30}{365}$	× £1,200,000 × 14%	13,808
Overdraft	$\frac{30}{365}$	× £300,000 × 13.5%	3,329
			17,137
Cost of factor's services: 2.5% × £1,500,000			37,500
Cost of the factor			54,637

(c) *Conclusion.* The factor is cheaper. In this case, the factor's fees exactly equal the savings in bad debts (£7,500) and administration costs (£30,000). The factor is then cheaper overall because it will be more efficient at collecting debts. The advance of 80% of debts is not needed, however, if the company has sufficient overdraft facility because the factor's finance charge of 14% is higher than the company's overdraft rate of 13.5%.

An **alternative way** of carrying out the calculation is to consider the changes in costs that using a factor will mean.

			£
Effect of reduction in collection period	$\frac{45-30}{365}$	× £1,500,000 × 13.5%	8,322
Extra interest cost of factor finance	$\frac{30}{365}$	× £1,200,000 × (14 – 13.5)%	(493)
Cost of factor's services: 2.5% × £1,500,000			(37,500)
Savings in bad debts 0.5% × £1,500,000			7,500
Savings in company's administration costs			30,000
Net benefit of using factor			7,829

Check: £62,466 – £54,637 = £7,829

Exam focus point

Points to look out for in questions about factoring are who bears the risk of bad debts, and company administration costs that may be saved by using a factor. The examiner has commented that calculations of the cost of factoring have often been poor.

2.12 Invoice discounting

Key term

Invoice discounting is the purchase (by the provider of the discounting service) of trade debts at a discount. Invoice discounting enables the company from which the debts are purchased to raise working capital.

Invoice discounting is related to factoring and many factors will provide an invoice discounting service. It is the purchase of a selection of invoices, at a discount. The invoice discounter does not take over the administration of the client's sales ledger.

A client should only want to have some invoices discounted when he has a temporary cash shortage, and so invoice discounting tends to consist of one-off deals. **Confidential invoice discounting** is an arrangement whereby a debt is confidentially assigned to the factor, and the client's customer will only become aware of the arrangement if he does not pay his debt to the client.

If a client needs to generate cash, he can approach a factor or invoice discounter, who will offer to purchase selected invoices and advance up to 75% of their value. At the end of each month, the factor will pay over the balance of the purchase price, less charges, on the invoices that have been settled in the month.

The overall **debt collection policy** of the firm should be such that the administrative costs and other costs incurred in debt collection do not exceed the benefits from incurring those costs. Beyond a certain level of spending, however, additional expenditure on debt collection would not have enough effect on bad debts or on the average collection period to justify the extra administrative costs.

Collecting debts is a two-stage process.

(a) Having agreed credit terms with a customer, a business should issue an invoice and expect to receive payment when it is due. **Issuing invoices** and **receiving payments** is the task of sales ledger staff. They should ensure that:

- The **customer is fully aware** of the terms.
- The **invoice is correctly drawn up** and issued promptly.
- They are aware of any **potential quirks** in the customer's system.
- **Queries are resolved quickly**.
- **Monthly statements** are **issued promptly**.

(b) If payments become overdue, they should be 'chased'. Procedures for pursuing overdue debts must be established, for example:

(i) **Instituting reminders or final demands**

These should be sent to a named individual, asking for repayment by return of post. A second or third letter may be required, followed by a final demand stating clearly the action that will be taken. The aim is to goad customers into action, perhaps by threatening not to sell any more goods on credit until the debt is cleared.

(ii) **Chasing payment by telephone**

The telephone is of greater nuisance value than a letter, and the greater immediacy can encourage a response. It can however be time-consuming, in particular because of problems in getting through to the right person.

(iii) **Making a personal approach**

Personal visits can be very time-consuming and tend only to be made to important customers who are worth the effort.

(iv) **Notifying debt collection section**

This means not giving further credit to the customer until he has paid the due amounts.

(v) **Handing over debt collection to specialist debt collection section**

Certain, generally larger, organisations may have a section to collect debts under the supervision of the credit manager.

(vi) **Instituting legal action to recover the debt**

Premature legal action may unnecessarily antagonise important customers.

(vii) **Hiring external debt collection agency to recover debt**

Again this may upset customers.

3 Using debtor information

> **FAST FORWARD**
>
> Regular monitoring of debtors is very important. Individual debtors can be assessed using a **customer history analysis** and a **credit rating system**. The overall level of debtors can be monitored using an **aged debtors listing** and **credit utilisation report**, as well as reports on the level of bad debts.

3.1 Payment record of individual debtors

Debtors' payment records must be **monitored** continually. This depends on successful sales ledger administration.

(a) **Invoices** must be posted at the right time.

(b) **Receipts** should be posted when they arrive, and allocated specifically to the invoices to which they relate.

(c) Any **queries** (eg customers debiting their own credit balance with a debit note as 'notification' to the supplier) need to be dealt with quickly.

(d) Orders should *always* be **vetted against credit limits**: this indicates the importance of prompt updating, as above.

(e) A **customer history analysis** can be prepared: this is like a statement, but with:

    (i) Total annual sales, on a rolling twelve month basis
    (ii) Outstanding amounts owed
    (iii) Days sales outstanding at each month end

The advantage of this is that trends in the account can be monitored, as can also the ageing of the debtor balance.

Account Name:

Number:

Credit Limit:

Month	Total debt at month end	Current	1 - 30 days	31 - 60 days	61 - 90 days	91 days and over	Sales in past 12 months	Days sales outstanding
January								
February								
March								

With this information it should be possible to develop in-house credit ratings.

3.2 In-house credit ratings

Credit monitoring can be simplified by a system of **in-house credit ratings**. For example, a company could have five credit-risk categories for its customers. These credit categories or ratings could be used to decide either individual credit limits for customers within that category or the frequency of the credit review. Guidelines could be provided to help credit controllers decide into which category a customer belongs.

Over time, the payment habits of a customer can be assessed, and the customer's credit rating (and credit limits) can be set accordingly. Any deterioration in a customer's payment record could raise concerns about the customer's creditworthiness.

3.3 Example: Categorisation of credit customers

A company categorises its credit customers into the following four groups.

1. Prompt payers
2. Those who pay within 30 days of the due date
3. Those who pay between 40 and 60 days of the due date
4. Those who pay over 60 days late

The recent payment record of a regular customer, Victor, is as follows.

Invoice number	Date of invoice	Date payable	Payment received	Days overdue
3257	7 March	7 April	28 April	21
3816	26 June	26 July	1 September	37
3942	19 July	19 August	1 September	13
4185	3 September	3 October	5 November	33
				104

Average days overdue = 26 days (104 ÷ 4)

Victor would be rated in credit category 2 by the company. A review of the payment record suggests that Victor delays payment until around the end of the month following the due date. This is quite typical business practice, and although Victor is not a good payer, there is a discernible payment pattern that could persuade the company to treat Victor as an average credit risk.

A **credit taken ratio** can be used to monitor the credit limits of customers. This compares the amount currently owed by a customer with the annual sales turnover in his account.

3.4 Example: Credit taken ratio

A company has two debtors, Able and Baker. Each customer owes £20,000. Annual sales to Able are about £200,000, and annual sales to Baker are about £100,000.

The credit taken ratio is 10% for Able (20,000 ÷ 200,000 × 100%) and 20% for Baker. Baker could be regarded as a higher credit risk. The company might wish to keep the credit-taken ratio for customers below a certain limit. If this limit were 20%, a request from Baker for further credit would be refused until the outstanding debts are settled. The company would be willing, however, to consider a request from Able for more credit.

3.5 Credit reviews

A **customer's payment record** and the **debtors aged analysis** should be examined regularly, as a matter of course. Breaches of the credit limit, or attempted breaches of it, should be brought immediately to the attention of the credit controller.

Otherwise, the credit controller will not have the time to examine *each* customer's account thoroughly every month. The credit controller's efforts will be expended on customers thought to be higher risk, or where there are other special factors (a debt that has gone bad). The credit situation will be reviewed more frequently, and a decision taken as to whether the credit should be extended. Illustrative internal weightings, review periods and credit offered are indicated below.

Rating	Payment record	Financial indicators	Frequency of credit reviews	Credit limit (as % of customer's annual purchases)
A Very high risk	Accounts over-due by 60 + days	Low profits Poor liquidity Highly indebted		Cash only (payment with order)
B High risk	Accounts over-due by 30 - 60 days	Deteriorating profitability, liquidity, or gearing High credit taken ratio	Monthly	Reduce to 10% of annual purchases
C Average risk	Accounts over-due up to 30 days	Stable position	Quarterly	15% of annual purchases
D Below average risk	Accounts paid on time	Stable or improving position	Six-monthly	25% of annual purchases
E Low risk	Accounts paid early Public sector customers	Strong financial position, or public sector ownership	Annually	For negotiation with the customer

3.6 Debtors age analysis

An **aged debtors listing** will probably look very much like the schedule illustrated below. The analysis splits up the total balance on the account of each customer across different columns according to the dates of the transactions which make up the total balance. Thus, the amount of an invoice which was raised 14 days ago will form part of the figure in the column headed 'up to 30 days', while an invoice which was raised 36 days ago will form part of the figure in the column headed 'up to 60 days'. (In the schedule below, 'up to 60 days' is used as shorthand for 'more than 30 days but less than 60 days'.)

```
HEATH LIMITED
AGE ANALYSIS OF DEBTORS AS AT 31.1.X2
Account                                    Up to     Up to    Up to      Over
number     Customer name      Balance    30 days   60 days  90 days   90 days
B004       Brilliant Ltd        804.95    649.90    121.00     0.00     34.05
E008       Easimat Ltd          272.10    192.90     72.40     6.80      0.00
H002       Hampstead Ltd      1,818.42      0.00      0.00   724.24  1,094.18
M024       Martlesham Ltd       284.45    192.21     92.24     0.00      0.00
N030       Nyfen Ltd          1,217.54  1,008.24    124.50     0.00     84.80
T002       Todmorden College    914.50    842.00      0.00    72.50      0.00
T004       Tricorn Ltd           94.80      0.00      0.00     0.00     94.80
V010       Volux Ltd            997.06    413.66    342.15   241.25      0.00
Y020       Yardsley Smith & Co  341.77    321.17     20.60     0.00      0.00
Totals                        6,745.59  3,620.08    772.89 1,044.79  1,307.83
Percentage                       100%     53.6%     11.5%    15.5%     19.4%
```

The age analysis of debtors may be used to help decide what action to take about older debts. Going down each column in turn starting from the column furthest to the right and working across, we can see that there are some rather old debts which ought to be investigated.

PART E WORKING CAPITAL MANAGEMENT

A number of **refinements** can be suggested to the aged debtors listing to make it easier to use.

(a) A report can be printed in which **overdue accounts** are seen first: this highlights attention on these items.

(b) It can help to aggregate data by **class of customer**. In this case, a report would be printed containing, for debtors aggregated into regions, type of customer, industry sectors etc:

   (i) Sales revenue
   (ii) Outstanding amount owed, broken down into age
   (iii) Days' sales outstanding

(c) There is no reason why this should not apply to individual debtor accounts as below. You could also include the date of the last transaction on the account (eg last invoice, last payment).

Account number	Customer name	Balance	Up to 30 days	Up to 60 days	Up to 90 days	Over 90 days	Sales revenue in last 12 months	Days sales outstanding
B004	Brilliant Ltd	804.95	649.90	121.00	0.00	34.05	6,789.00	43

We can see from the age analysis of Heath Ltd's debtors given earlier that the relatively high proportion of debts over 90 days (19.4%) is largely due to the debts of Hampstead Ltd. Other customers with debts of this age are Brilliant Ltd, Nyfen Ltd and Tricorn Ltd.

3.7 Debtors' ageing and liquidity

Also of interest to the credit controller is the *total* percentage figure calculated at the bottom of each column. In practice the credit controller will be concerned to look at this figure first of all, in order to keep the ageing figures consistent. Why might a credit controller be worried by an increase in the ageing? If the credit controller knows the customers are going to pay, should it matter?

The answer is that any reduction in the inflow caused by an overall increase in the debtors period affects the company's ability to pay its debts and increases its use of overdraft finance: unauthorised overdrafts carry a hefty fee as well as interest.

Additional ratios which might be useful in debtor management, in addition to day's sales outstanding, are as follows.

(a) **Overdues as a percentage of total debt**. For example, assume that if Heath Limited (Paragraph 1.2) offers credit on 30 day terms. Brilliant Ltd's debt could be analysed as:

$$\frac{£121.00 + £34.05}{£804.95} = 19.3\% \text{ overdue}$$

(b) **If debts are disputed**, it is helpful to see what a proportion these are of the total debtors and the total overdue. If, of Heath's total debtors of £6,745.59, an amount of £973.06 related to disputed items, the ratio of disputed debts to total outstanding would be:

$$\frac{£973.06}{£6,745.59} = 14.4\%$$

As a percentage of total items *over* 30 days old:

$$\frac{£973.06}{£6,745.59 - £3,620.08} = 31\%$$

An increasing disputes ratio can indicate:

(i) Invoicing problems
(ii) Operational problems

3.8 Debtor quality and liquidity

The **quality** of debtors has an important impact on a firm's overall liquidity. Debtor quality is determined by their age and risk.

Some **industries** have a higher level of risk than others, in other words, there is a higher probability that customers will fail to pay. Some markets are riskier than others, which is why export credit insurance premiums are higher for some countries than others. Selling goods to a country with possible payment difficulties is riskier than selling them in the home market.

3.8.1 Policing total credit

The total amount of credit offered, as well as individual accounts, should be policed to ensure that the senior management policy with regard to the total credit limits is maintained. A **credit utilisation report** can indicate the extent to which total limits are being utilised. An example is given below.

Customer	Limit £'000	Utilisation £'000	%
Alpha	100	90	90
Beta	50	35	70
Gamma	35	21	60
Delta	250	125	50
	435	271	
		62.2%	

This might also contain other information, such as days sales outstanding and so on.

Reviewed in aggregate, this can reveal the following.

(a) The **number of customers** who might **want more credit**

(b) The **extent** to which the **company is exposed to debtors**

(c) The **'tightness'** of the policy (It might be possible to increase profitable sales by offering credit. On the other hand, perhaps the firm offers credit too easily.)

It is possible to design credit utilisation reports to highlight other trends.

(a) The **degree of exposure** to **different countries**

(b) The **degree of exposure** to **different industries** (Some countries or industries may be worthy of more credit; others may be too risky.)

Credit utilisation can also be analysed by industry within country or by country within industry. It is also useful to relate credit utilisation to total sales.

PART E WORKING CAPITAL MANAGEMENT

4 Foreign trade and debt management

FAST FORWARD

Exporters have to address the problems of larger stocks and debtors, and an increased risk of bad debts due to the transportation time and additional paperwork involved in sending goods abroad.

Foreign debts raise the following special problems.

(a) When goods are sold abroad, the customer might ask for credit. Exports take time to arrange, and there might be complex paperwork. Transporting the goods can be slow, if they are sent by sea. These **delays** in **foreign trade** mean that exporters often build up large investments in stocks and debtors. These working capital investments have to be financed somehow.

(b) The **risk of bad debts** can be **greater** with foreign trade than with domestic trade. If a foreign debtor refuses to pay a debt, the exporter must pursue the debt in the debtor's own country, where procedures will be subject to the laws of that country.

There are several measures available to exporters to overcome these problems.

4.1 Reducing the investment in foreign debtors

A company can reduce its investment in foreign debtors by insisting on **earlier payment** for goods. Another approach is for an exporter to arrange for a bank to give **cash for a foreign debt**, sooner than the exporter would receive payment in the normal course of events. There are several ways in which this might be done.

(a) **Advances against collections**. Where the exporter asks his bank to handle the collection of payment (of a bill of exchange or a cheque) on his behalf, the bank may be prepared to make an advance to the exporter against the collection. The amount of the advance might be 80% to 90% of the value of the collection.

(b) **Negotiation of bills or cheques**. This is similar to an advance against collection, but would be used where the bill or cheque is payable outside the exporter's country (for example in the foreign buyer's country).

(c) **Documentary credits**. These are described below.

4.2 Reducing the bad debt risk

Methods of minimising bad debt risks are broadly similar to those for domestic trade. An exporting company should vet the creditworthiness of each customer, and grant credit terms accordingly.

4.3 Export factoring

The functions performed by an **overseas factor** or **export factor** are essentially the same as with the factoring of domestic trade debts, which was described earlier in this chapter.

The charges levied by an overseas factor may turn out to be cheaper than using alternative methods such as letters of credit, which are discussed below.

4.4 Documentary credits

Documentary credits provide a method of payment in international trade, which gives the exporter a secure risk-free method of obtaining payment.

The buyer (a foreign buyer, or a UK importer) and the seller (a UK exporter or a foreign supplier) first of all agree a contract for the sale of the goods, which provides for payment through a documentary credit. The *buyer* then requests a bank in his country to issue a **letter of credit** in favour of the exporter. The issuing bank, by issuing its letter of credit, guarantees payment to the beneficiary.

A documentary credit arrangement must be made between the exporter, the buyer and participating banks **before the export sale takes place**. Documentary credits are slow to arrange, and administratively cumbersome; however, they might be considered essential where the risk of non-payment is high.

One form of trade credit is Bills of Exchange which are dealt with more fully in Section 5.4 below.

4.5 Export credit insurance

Key term

> **Export credit insurance** is insurance against the risk of non-payment by foreign customers for export debts.

You might be wondering why export credit insurance should be necessary, when exporters can pursue **non-paying customers** through the courts in order to obtain payment. The answer is that:

(a) If a credit customer defaults on payment, the task of pursuing the case through the courts will be lengthy, and it might be a long time before payment is eventually obtained.

(b) There are various reasons why non-payment might happen (Export credit insurance provides insurance against non-payment for a variety of risks in addition to the buyer's failure to pay on time.)

Not all exporters take out export credit insurance because premiums are very high and the benefits are sometimes not fully appreciated. If they do, they will obtain an insurance policy from a private insurance company that deals in export credit insurance.

4.6 Overseas debtors; general policies

There are also a number of general credit control policies that can be particularly important when dealing with overseas customers.

(a) Prior to the sale, the customer's **credit rating** should be **checked**, and the terms of the contract specified. One key term may be demanding the use of an **irrevocable letter of credit** as a term of release of goods. The terms of the **remittance** and the bank to be used should be specified.

(b) The **paperwork** relating to the sales should be carefully completed and checked, in particular the shipping and delivery documentation.

(c) Goods should only be released if payment has been made, or is sufficiently certain, either because of the customer's **previous record** or because the customer has issued a **promissory note**.

(d) Receipts should be **rapidly processed** and late **payments chased**.

5 The management of creditors and short-term finance

FAST FORWARD

> Effective management of **trade creditors** involves seeking satisfactory credit terms from supplier, getting credit extended during periods of cash shortage, and maintaining good relations with suppliers.

Exam focus point

> It may seem an obvious point, but take care not to confuse debtors and creditors, as many students do under exam pressure.

PART E   WORKING CAPITAL MANAGEMENT

5.1 Management of trade creditors

The management of trade creditors involves:

- Attempting to obtain **satisfactory credit** from suppliers
- Attempting to **extend credit** during periods of cash shortage
- Maintaining **good relations** with regular and important suppliers

If a supplier offers a discount for the early payment of debts, the evaluation of the decision whether or not to **accept the discount** is similar to the **evaluation of the decision** whether or not to **offer a discount**. One problem is the mirror image of the other. The methods of evaluating the offer of a discount to customers were described earlier.

5.2 Sources of short-term finance

Taking trade credit from suppliers is one way in which a company can obtain some **short-term finance**, in addition to its longer term sources. Short-term finance can also be obtained:

(a) With a **bank overdraft**

(b) By **raising finance** from a bank or other organisation against the **security of trade debtors**, for example through factoring or invoice discounting (both described earlier in this chapter)

(c) For larger companies, by issuing **short-term debt instruments**, such as 'commercial paper'

5.2.1 Trade credit

Taking credit from suppliers is a normal feature of business. Nearly every company has some trade creditors waiting for payment. Trade credit is a source of short-term finance because it helps to keep working capital down. It is usually a cheap source of finance, since suppliers rarely charge interest. However, trade credit *will* have a cost, whenever a company is offered a discount for early payment, but opts instead to take longer credit.

5.2.2 Trade credit and the cost of lost early payment discounts

Trade credit from suppliers is a major source of finance. It is particularly important to small and fast growing firms. The costs of making maximum use of trade credit include the loss of suppliers' goodwill, and the loss of any available cash discounts for the early payment of debts.

The cost of lost cash discounts can be estimated by the formula:

$$1 - \left(\frac{100}{100-d}\right)^{\frac{365}{t}} \%$$

where d   is the % discount, d = 5 for 5%.

   t   is the reduction in the payment period in days which would be necessary to obtain the early payment discount, final date to obtain discount – final date for payment

This is the same formula that was used for debtors.

5.3 Example: Trade credit

X Ltd has been offered credit terms from its major supplier of 2/10, net 45. That is, a cash discount of 2% will be given if payment is made within ten days of the invoice, and payments must be made within 45 days of the invoice. The company has the choice of paying 98p per £1 on day 10 (to pay before day 10 would be unnecessary), or to invest the 98p for an additional 35 days and eventually pay the supplier £1 per £1. The decision as to whether the discount should be accepted depends on the opportunity cost of investing 98p for 35 days. What should the company do?

Solution

If the company refuses the cash discount, and pays in full after 45 days, the implied cost in interest per annum would be approximately:

$$\left(\frac{100}{100-2}\right)^{\frac{365}{35}} = 23.5\%$$

Suppose that X Ltd can invest cash to obtain an annual return of 25%, and that there is an invoice from the supplier for £1,000. The two alternatives are as follows.

	Refuse discount £	Accept discount £
Payment to supplier	1,000.0	980
Return from investing £980 between day 10 and day 45: $£980 \times \frac{35}{365} \times 25\%$	23.5	
Net cost	976.5	980

It is cheaper to refuse the discount because the investment rate of return on cash retained, in this example, exceeds the saving from the discount.

Although a company may delay payment beyond the final due date, thereby obtaining even longer credit from its suppliers, such a policy would generally be inadvisable. Unacceptable delays in payment will **worsen the company's credit rating**, and additional credit may become difficult to obtain.

5.4 Bills of exchange   06/05

Bills of exchange are a form of trade credit. When A sells goods to B, the settlement of the debt might be arranged by means of a **bill of exchange** (called a **trade bill** as B is a trader).

Step 1 A draws bill on B

> B will pay certain sum of money on certain date

Step 2 B accepts the bill by signing it, acknowledging B's debt to A and giving a promise to pay

> B will pay certain sum of money on certain date.
> Signed: B

Step 3 After term of bill expired, B pays A.

B =£££⇒ A

5.4.1 Trade bills and obtaining finance against the security of debtors

When a company obtains payment from its customers through **trade bills**, it can arrange to obtain finance from its bank against the security of the bill.

If A Ltd sells goods to B Ltd for £50,000, the terms of payment might be agreed so that A Ltd draws a 90 day bill of exchange on B Ltd for £50,000, which B Ltd 'accepts'. A Ltd can then ask its bank to discount the bill, and A Ltd will receive payment (less discount) now from the bank instead of in 90 days from B Ltd. After 90 days, B Ltd must pay the bank or other holder of the bill.

The rate of discount on the bill, which is the cost to A Ltd of discounting, will depend on the **'quality'** of the bill. A **higher discount** applies to **trade bills** (bills drawn on and accepted by companies such as B Ltd) than to **bank bills** (bills drawn on and accepted by a bank). A lower discount is called a 'finer' discount.

5.4.2 Acceptance credits

Acceptance credits (also known as **bank bills**) are a source of finance from banks for large companies, which are an alternative to bank overdrafts. Acceptance credits have much in common with bills of exchange, but they are different.

(a) A bank and a large corporate customer **agree a facility** which allows the customer to **draw bills** on the bank, which the bank will accept. The bills are normally payable after 60 or 90 days, but might have a term as long as 180 days. They can be denominated in sterling or in a foreign currency.

(b) The **accepted bills** are then **sold** (discounted) by the bank in the discount market on behalf of the customer, and the money obtained from the sale, minus the bank's acceptance commission, is made available to the customer. Because of the bank's standing and reputation, bills accepted by it can be sold in the market at a low rate of discount.

(c) When a bill matures, the **company** will **pay the bank** the **value** of the bill and the bank will use the money in turn to pay the bill holder.

Acceptance credits are attractive to customers for the following reasons.

(a) They provide companies with **alternative finance** to a bank overdraft, with the money being obtained from a source outside the bank (the purchaser of the discounted bills).

(b) The amount of credit is promised to the customer for a **stated period of time**.

(c) There may be a **cost advantage** to the customer, because the rate of discount on bank bills in the discount market might be lower than the interest rate on a bank loan, or overdraft, which is related to the bank base rate or LIBOR. The reason for this is mainly that the interest rate on a discounted bill is fixed for the life of the bill (typically 90 days). Overdraft rates are going up, it would be more costly to maintain an overdraft than to have an acceptance credit facility.

(d) The company can **assess** the **cost of its credit facility** with **more certainty**, because costs are fixed over the life of a bill.

5.5 Assessment of creditors

How long a company takes to pay its trade creditors is measured by the creditors' turnover.

Key term

> **Creditors' turnover or Creditors' payment period**
>
> $= \dfrac{\text{Average creditors}}{\text{Purchases}} \times 365 \text{ days}$
>
> Cost of sales may be used as an alternative to purchases.

The creditors' turnover ratio often helps to assess a company's liquidity. An increase in creditors days is often a sign of **lack** of **long-term finance** or **poor management** of **current assets**.

Chapter Roundup

- Offering credit has a cost: the value of the interest charged on an overdraft to fund the period of credit, or the interest lost on the cash not received and deposited in the bank. An increase in profit from extra sales resulting from offering credit could offset this cost.

- In managing **debtors**, the **creditworthiness** of customers needs to be assessed. The risks and costs of a customer defaulting will need to be balanced against the profitability of the business provided by that customer.

- **Settlement discounts** may be employed to shorten average credit periods, and to reduce the investment in debtors and therefore **interest costs**. The benefit in interest cost saved should exceed the cost of the discounts allowed.

- Some companies use **factoring** and **invoice discounting** to help short-term liquidity or to reduce administration costs. **Insurance**, particularly of overseas debts, can also help reduce the risk of bad debts.

- Regular monitoring of debtors is very important. Individual debtors can be assessed using a **customer history analysis** and a **credit rating system**. The overall level of debtors can be monitored using an **aged debtors listing** and **credit utilisation report**, as well as reports on the level of bad debts.

- Exporters have to address the problems of larger stocks and debtors, and an increased risk of bad debts due to the transportation time and additional paperwork involved in sending goods abroad.

- Effective management of **trade creditors** involves seeking satisfactory credit terms from supplier, getting credit extended during periods of cash shortage, and maintaining good relations with suppliers.

Quick Quiz

1. How can we calculate the number of days sales represented by debtors?

2. List typical column headings that you would expect to see in an aged analysis of debtors.

3. What service involves collecting debts of a business, advancing a proportion of the money it is due to collect?

4. What service involves advancing a proportion of a selection of invoices, without administration of the sales ledger of the business?

5. Cost of lost discount = $1 - \left(\dfrac{100}{(100-d)}\right)^{\frac{365}{t}}$ %. What do d and t represent?

6. Which of the following does not determine the amount of credit offered by a supplier?

    A   The credit terms the supplier obtains from its own suppliers
    B   The ease with which the buyer can go elsewhere
    C   The supplier's total risk exposure
    D   The number of purchases made by the buyer each year

7. If a customer decided to pass up the chance of a cash discount of 1% in return for reducing her average payment period from 70 to 30 days, what would be the implied cost in interest per annum?

    A   9.13%
    B   9.6%
    C   12.17%
    D   12.29%

PART E WORKING CAPITAL MANAGEMENT

8   Which of the following is a **disadvantage** to a company of using a factor for its debtors?

   A   It is easier to finance growth through sales
   B   Managers spend less time on slow paying debtors
   C   Debtors pay direct to the factor
   D   It is easier to pay suppliers promptly to obtain discounts

Answers to Quick Quiz

1   $\dfrac{\text{Total debtors}}{\text{Annual sales}} \times 365 = $ Days sales

2
   - Account number
   - Customer name
   - Total balance
   - Up to 30 days
   - Up to 60 days
   - Up to 90 days
   - Over 90 days

3   Factoring.

4   Invoice discounting.

5   d is the percentage discount given, t is the reduction in payment to obtain the discount (in days).

6   D   The number of purchases. (Although the amount of annual purchases may well be a factor)

7   B   Cost $= 1 - \left(\dfrac{100}{100-d}\right)^{\frac{365}{t}}$ %

   $= 1 - \left(\dfrac{100}{100-1}\right)^{\frac{365}{40}}$

   $= 9.6\%$

8   C   This may present a negative picture of the company to customers.

Now try the questions below from the Exam Question Bank

Number	Level	Marks	Time
Q22	Introductory	n/a	30 mins

The management of stocks and cash

Topic list	Syllabus reference
1 The management of stocks	3
2 The management of cash	3
3 Foreign exchange risk	3
4 Treasury management	3

Introduction

This chapter concludes our study of working capital management methods by considering how stock and cash are managed. We also cover in outline how some companies can reduce risks from fluctuating exchange rates, a topic that will be very important when you come to study Paper 3.7.

PART E   WORKING CAPITAL MANAGEMENT

Study guide

Section 5 – Management of working capital I

Management of stock

- Calculate and interpret stock ratios
- Explain the role of stock in the working capital cycle
- Apply the tools and techniques of stock management including the EOQ model
- Analyse and evaluate the results of stock management techniques

Section 7 – Management of working capital II

Management of cash

- Explain the role of cash in the working capital cycle
- Calculate optimal cash balances
- Describe the functions of and evaluate the benefits from centralised cash control and Treasury Management
- Calculate and interpret cash ratios
- Apply the tools and techniques of cash management including the Baumol model and the Miller-Orr model
- Analyse and evaluate the results of cash management techniques

Exam guide

You may be asked to make calculations of economic order quantities, or discuss different management policies (for example different ways of managing the treasury function).

1 The management of stocks   12/02, 6/05

FAST FORWARD

> An **economic order quantity** can be calculated as a guide to minimising costs in managing stock levels. **Bulk discounts** can however mean that a different order quantity minimises stock costs.

Almost every company carries stocks of some sort, even if they are only stocks of consumables such as stationery. For a manufacturing business, stocks (sometimes called inventories), in the form of **raw materials**, **work in progress** and **finished goods**, may amount to a substantial proportion of the total assets of the business.

Some businesses attempt to control stocks on a scientific basis by balancing the costs of stock shortages against those of stock holding. The 'scientific' control of stocks may be analysed into three parts.

(a) The **economic order quantity (EOQ) model** can be used to decide the optimum order size for stocks which will minimise the costs of ordering stocks plus stockholding costs.

(b) If **discounts for bulk purchases** are available, it may be cheaper to buy stocks in large order sizes so as to obtain the discounts.

(c) Uncertainty in the demand for stocks and/or the supply lead time may lead a company to decide to hold **buffer stocks** in order to reduce or eliminate the risk of 'stock-outs' (running out of stock).

20: THE MANAGEMENT OF STOCKS AND CASH

STOCK COSTS	
Holding costs	The cost of capital
	Warehousing and handling costs
	Deterioration
	Obsolescence
	Insurance
	Pilferage
Procuring costs	Ordering costs
	Delivery costs
Shortage costs	Contribution from lost sales
	Extra cost of emergency stock
	Cost of lost production and sales in a stock-out
Cost of stock	Relevant particularly when calculating discounts

1.1 The basic EOQ formula

Key term

The **economic order quantity (EOQ)** is the optimal ordering quantity for an item of stock which will minimise costs.

Let D = usage in units for one period (the demand)

P = purchase price per item
C_o = cost of placing one order
C_H = holding cost per unit of stock for one period
Q = reorder quantity

} relevant costs only

Assume that demand is constant, the lead time is constant or zero and purchase costs per unit are constant (ie no bulk discounts).

The total annual cost of having stock is:

(a) Holding costs + ordering costs

$$\frac{Q \times C_H}{2} + \frac{C_o \times D}{Q}$$

The more orders are made each year the higher the ordering costs, but the lower the holding costs (as less stock is held).

(b) The objective is to minimise $T = \frac{Q \times C_H}{2} + \frac{C_o \times D}{Q}$

The order quantity, EOQ, which will minimise these total costs is:

Exam formula

$$EOQ = \sqrt{\frac{2C_oD}{C_H}}$$

Exam focus point

The EOQ formula will be given on the exam formulae sheet but you do need to be confident in using it.

1.2 Example: Economic order quantity

The demand for a commodity is 40,000 units a year, at a steady rate. It costs £20 to place an order, and 40p to hold a unit for a year. Find the order size to minimise stock costs, the number of orders placed each year, and the length of the stock cycle.

Solution

$$Q = \sqrt{\frac{2C_oD}{C_H}} = \sqrt{\frac{2 \times 20 \times 40,000}{0.4}} = 2,000 \text{ units.}$$

This means that there will be

$$\frac{40,000}{2,000} = 20 \text{ orders placed each year.}$$

The stock cycle is therefore

$$\frac{52 \text{ weeks}}{20 \text{ orders}} = 2.6 \text{ weeks.}$$

Total costs will be $(20 \times £20) + (\frac{2,000}{2} \times 40p) = £800$ a year.

1.3 Uncertainties in demand and lead times: a re-order level system

FAST FORWARD

Uncertainties in demand and lead times taken to fulfil orders mean that stock will be ordered once it reaches a re-order level (maximum usage × maximum lead time).

Key term

Reorder level = maximum usage × maximum lead time.

The re-order level is the measure of stock at which a replenishment order should be made.

(a) If an order is placed **too late**, the organisation may run out of stock, **a stock-out**, resulting in a loss of sales and/or a loss of production.

(b) If an order is placed **too soon**, the organisation will hold too much stock, and stock holding costs will be excessive.

Use of a re-order level builds in a measure of safety stock and minimises the risk of the organisation running out of stock, a **stock-out**. This is particularly important when the volume of demand or the supply lead time are uncertain.

The **average annual** cost of such a safety stock would be:

Quantity of safety stock × Stock holding cost
(in units)   per unit per annum

The diagram below shows how the stock levels might fluctuate with this system. Points marked 'X' show the re-order level at which a new order is placed. The number of units ordered each time is the EOQ. Actual stock levels sometimes fall below the safety stock level, and sometimes the re-supply arrives before stocks have fallen to the safety level. On average, however, extra stock holding will approximate the safety stock. The size of the safety stock will depend on whether stock-outs (running out of stock) are allowed.

1.4 Maximum and minimum stock levels

Key term

Maximum **stock level** = reorder level + reorder quantity – (minimum usage × minimum lead time)

The maximum level acts as a warning signal to management that stocks are reaching a potentially wasteful level.

Key term

Minimum **stock level** or **buffer safety stock** = reorder level – (average usage × average lead time)

The minimum level acts as a warning to management that stocks are approaching a dangerously low level and that stockouts are possible.

Key term

Average stock = Minimum level + $\dfrac{\text{reorder level}}{2}$

This formula assumes that stock levels fluctuate evenly between the minimum (or safety) stock level and the highest possible stock level (the amount of stock immediately after an order is received, safety stock and reorder quantity).

This approach assumes that a business wants to minimise the risk of stock-outs at all costs. In the modern manufacturing environment stock-outs can have a disastrous effect on the production process.

PART E WORKING CAPITAL MANAGEMENT

If, however, you are given a question where the risk of stock-outs is assumed to be worth taking, and the costs of stock-outs are quantified, the re-order level may not be calculated in the way described above. For **each possible re-order level**, and therefore each **possible level** of buffer stock, **calculate**:

- The **costs of holding buffer stock** per annum
- The **costs of stock-outs** (Cost of one stock-out × expected number of stock-outs per order × number of orders per year)

The expected number of stock-outs per order reflects the various levels by which demand during the lead time could exceed the re-order level.

1.5 Example: Possibility of stock-outs (1)

If re-order level is 4 units, but there was a probability of 0.2 that demand during the lead time would be 5 units, and 0.05 that demand during the lead time would be 6 units, then Expected number of stock-outs = $((5 - 4) \times 0.2) + ((6 - 4) \times 0.05) = 0.3$.

1.5.1 Demand normally distributed

Alternatively you may be told that demand is normally distributed. If this is the case you need to know:

- Average weekly demand
- Standard deviation of demand
- Lead time
- Acceptable risk levels

Re-order level = (Average weekly demand × lead time) + $x\sigma$

Where $x =$ number of standard deviations that correspond to the chance business wishes to have of avoiding stock-outs

$\sigma =$ standard deviation of demand

1.6 Example: Possibility of stock-outs (2)

Average weekly demand is 200 units, the standard deviation of demand (σ) is 40 units and demand is normally distributed. Lead time for orders is one week. What re-order levels should the business set if it wishes to have

(a) A 90% chance
(b) A 95% chance
(c) A 99% chance

of avoiding running out of stock. The relevant values from normal distribution tables are respectively:

(a) 1.28
(b) 1.65
(c) 2.33

Solution

Re-order level = (Average weekly demand × lead time) + xσ

(a) Re-order level = (200 × 1) + (1.28 × 40)
= 251.2 units

(b) Re-order level = 200 + (1.65 × 40)
= 266 units

(c) Re-order level = 200 + (2.33 × 40)
= 293.2 units

1.7 The effect of discounts

The solution obtained from using the simple EOQ formula may need to be modified if bulk discounts (also called quantity discounts) are available. To decide mathematically whether it would be worthwhile taking a discount and ordering larger quantities, it is necessary to minimise:

Total purchasing costs + Ordering costs + Stockholding costs.

The total cost will be minimised:

- At the pre-discount EOQ level, so that a discount is not worthwhile, or
- At the minimum order size necessary to earn the discount

1.8 Example: Bulk discounts

The annual demand for an item of stock is 45 units. The item costs £200 a unit to purchase, the holding cost for one unit for one year is 15% of the unit cost and ordering costs are £300 an order. The supplier offers a 3% discount for orders of 60 units or more, and a discount of 5% for orders of 90 units or more. What is the cost-minimising order size?

Solution

(a) The EOQ ignoring discounts is:

$$\sqrt{\frac{2 \times 300 \times 45}{15\% \text{ of } 200}} = 30 \text{ units}$$

	£
Purchases (no discount) 45 × £200	9,000
Holding costs ($^{30}/_2$) 15 units × £30	450
Ordering costs 1.5 orders × £300	450
Total annual costs	9,900

(b) With a discount of 3% and an order quantity of 60 units costs are as follows.

	£
Purchases £9,000 × 97%	8,730
Holding costs 30 units × 15% of 97% of £200	873
Ordering costs 0.75 orders × £300	225
Total annual costs	9,828

(c) With a discount of 5% and an order quantity of 90 units costs are as follows.

	£
Purchases £9,000 × 95%	8,550.0
Holding costs 45 units × 15% of 95% of £200	1,282.5
Ordering costs 0.5 orders × £300	150.0
Total annual costs	9,982.5

The cheapest option is to order 60 units at a time.

PART E WORKING CAPITAL MANAGEMENT

Question — Bulk orders

Question: Bulk orders

A company uses an item of stock as follows.

Purchase price:	£96 per unit
Annual demand:	4,000 units
Ordering cost:	£300
Annual holding cost:	10% of purchase price
Economic order quantity:	500 units

Should the company order 1,000 units at a time in order to secure an 8% discount?

Answer

The total annual cost at the economic order quantity of 500 units is as follows.

	£
Purchases 4,000 × £96	384,000
Ordering costs £300 × (4,000/500)	2,400
Holding costs £96 × 10% × (500/2)	2,400
	388,800

The total annual cost at an order quantity of 1,000 units would be as follows.

	£
Purchases £384,000 × 92%	353,280
Ordering costs £300 × (4,000/1,000)	1,200
Holding costs £96 × 92% × 10% × (1,000/2)	4,416
	358,896

The company should order the item 1,000 units at a time, saving £(388,800 − 358,896) = £29,904 a year.

1.9 Just-in-time (JIT) procurement   12/02, 6/05

Some manufacturing companies have sought to reduce their inventories of raw materials and components to as low a level as possible. **Just-in-time procurement** and **stockless production** are terms which describe a policy of obtaining goods from suppliers at the latest possible time (ie when they are needed) and so avoiding the need to carry any materials or components stock.

Introducing JIT might bring the following potential benefits.

- Reduction in stock holding costs
- Reduced manufacturing lead times
- Improved labour productivity
- Reduced scrap/rework/warranty cost

Reduced stock levels mean that a lower level of investment in working capital will be required.

JIT will not be appropriate in some cases. For example, a restaurant might find it preferable to use the traditional economic order quantity approach for staple non-perishable food stocks but adopt JIT for perishable and 'exotic' items. In a hospital, a stock-out could quite literally be fatal and so JIT would be quite unsuitable.

Exam focus point

You may be required to evaluate the benefits of introducing a JIT arrangement, given certain assumptions about the costs and benefits.

1.10 Stock ratios

Key terms

$$\text{Stock days} = \frac{\text{Average stock}}{\text{Cost of sales}} \times 365 \text{ days}$$

$$\text{Stock turnover} = \frac{\text{Cost of sales}}{\text{Average stock}}$$

The optimum period of **stock days** will vary industry by industry, and may vary for different lines held by the same firm.

A high stock days or low stock turnover figure may arise for various reasons. It may be that the firm is being excessively **prudent** in its stockholding policies, or it may be due to **obsolete** or **slow-moving** stock.

An excessively low figure for **stock days** or **high turnover** figure may also give cause for concern. It may indicate **supply difficulties**, and that there is a significant chance that the company will run out of stock and hence lose sales.

2 The management of cash

2.1 Why organisations hold cash

The economist John Maynard Keynes identified three reasons for holding cash.

(a) Firstly, a business needs cash to meet its **regular commitments** of paying its creditors, its employees' wages, its taxes, its annual dividends to shareholders and so on. This reason for holding cash is what Keynes called the **transactions motive**.

(b) Keynes identified the **precautionary motive** as a second motive for holding cash. This means that there is a need to maintain a 'buffer' of cash for **unforeseen contingencies**. In the context of a business, this buffer may be provided by an **overdraft facility**, which has the advantage that it will cost nothing until it is actually used.

(c) Keynes identified a third motive for holding cash - the **speculative motive**. Some businesses hold surplus cash as a speculative asset in the hope that interest rates will rise. However many businesses would regard large long-term holdings of cash as not prudent.

How much cash should a company keep on hand or 'on short call' at a bank? The more cash which is on hand, the easier it will be for the company to meet its bills as they fall due and to take advantage of discounts.

However, holding cash or near equivalents to cash has a cost - the **loss of earning** which would otherwise have been obtained by using the funds in another way. The financial manager must try to balance liquidity with profitability.

2.2 Cash flow problems

Cash flow problems can arise in various ways.

(a) **Making losses**

If a business is continually making losses, it will eventually have cash flow problems. If the loss is due to a large depreciation charge, the cash flow troubles might only begin when the business needs to replace fixed assets.

(b) **Inflation**

In a period of inflation, a business needs **ever-increasing amounts** of cash just to replace used-up and worn-out assets. A business can be making a profit in historical cost accounting terms, but still not be receiving enough cash to buy the replacement assets it needs.

(c) **Growth**

When a business is growing, it needs to **acquire more fixed assets**, and to **support higher amounts of stocks and debtors**. These additional assets must be paid for somehow (or financed by creditors).

(d) **Seasonal business**

When a business has seasonal or cyclical sales, it may have cash flow difficulties at certain times of the year, when

(i) Cash inflows are low, but

(ii) Cash outflows are high, perhaps because the business is building up its stocks for the next period of high sales

(e) **One-off items of expenditure**

A single non-recurring item of expenditure may create a cash flow problem. Examples include the repayment of loan capital on maturity of the debt or the purchase of an exceptionally expensive item, such as a freehold property.

2.3 Methods of easing cash shortages

FAST FORWARD

Cash shortages can be eased by postponing capital expenditure, selling assets, taking longer to pay creditors and pressing debtors for earlier payment.

The steps that are usually taken by a company when a need for cash arises, and when it cannot obtain resources from any other source such as a loan or an increased overdraft, are as follows.

(a) **Postponing capital expenditure**

Some new fixed assets might be needed for the **development and growth of the business**, but some capital expenditures might be postponable without serious consequences. If a company's policy is to replace company cars every two years, but the company is facing a cash shortage, it might decide to replace cars every three years.

(b) **Accelerating cash inflows which would otherwise be expected in a later period**

One way would be to press debtors for earlier payment. Often, this policy will result in a **loss of goodwill** and problems with customers. It might be possible to encourage debtors to pay more quickly by offering discounts for earlier payment.

(c) **Reversing past investment decisions by selling assets previously acquired**

Some assets are less crucial to a business than others. If cash flow problems are severe, the option of selling investments or property might have to be considered.

(d) **Negotiating a reduction in cash outflows, to postpone or reduce payments**

There are several ways in which this could be done.

(i) **Longer credit** might be taken from suppliers. Such an extension of credit would have to be negotiated carefully: there would be a risk of having further supplies refused.

(ii) **Loan repayments** could be rescheduled by agreement with a bank.

(iii) A **deferral** of the payment of **corporation tax** might be agreed with the Inland Revenue. The Inland Revenue will charge interest on the outstanding amount of tax.

(iv) **Dividend payments** could be **reduced**. Dividend payments are discretionary cash outflows, although a company's directors might be constrained by shareholders' expectations, so that they feel obliged to pay dividends even when there is a cash shortage.

2.4 Deviations from expected cash flows

Cash budgets, whether prepared on an annual, monthly, weekly or even a daily basis, can only be estimates of cash flows. Even the best estimates will not be exactly correct, so deviations from the cash budget are inevitable.

A cash budget model could be constructed, using a PC and a spreadsheet package, and the **sensitivity** of cash flow forecasts to changes in estimates of sales, costs and so on could be analysed. By planning for different eventualities, management should be able to prepare **contingency measures** in advance and also **appreciate** the **key factors** in the cash budget.

A knowledge of the **probability distribution** of possible outcomes for the cash position will allow a **more accurate estimate** to be made of the minimum cash balances, or the borrowing power necessary, to provide a satisfactory margin of safety. Unforeseen deficits can be hard to finance at short notice, and advance planning is desirable.

2.5 Float

The term **float** is sometimes used to describe the amount of money tied up between **the time when a payment is initiated** (for example when a debtor sends a cheque in payment, probably by post), and **the time when the funds become available for use** in the recipient's bank account.

There are three reasons why there might be a lengthy float.

(a) **Transmission delay**

When payment is sent through the post, it will take a day or longer for the payment to reach the payee.

(b) **Delay in banking the payments received**

The payee, on receipt of a cheque or cash, might **delay presenting** the **cheque** or the cash to his bank. The length of this (lodgement) delay will depend on administrative procedures in the payee's organisation.

(c) **The time needed for a bank to clear a cheque**

A payment is not available for use in the payee's bank account until the **cheque** has been **cleared**. This will usually take two or three days for cheques payable in the UK. For cheques payable abroad, the delay is much longer.

There are several measures that could be taken to reduce the float.

(a) The payee should ensure that the lodgement delay is kept to a minimum. **Cheques** received should be presented to the bank on the day of receipt.

(b) The payee might, in some local cases, arrange to **collect cheques** from the payer's premises.

(c) The payer might be asked to pay through his own branch of a bank, using the **bank giro system.**

(d) **BACS** (Bankers' Automated Clearing Services Ltd) is a banking system which provides for the computerised transfer of funds between banks. In addition, BACS is available to **corporate customers** of banks for **making payments**.

(e) For regular payments, **standing orders** or **direct debits** might be used.

(f) **CHAPS** (Clearing House Automated Payments System) is a computerised system for banks to make **same-day clearances** (that is, immediate payment) between each other.

PART E WORKING CAPITAL MANAGEMENT

2.6 Inefficient cash management

A lengthy float suggests inefficient cash management. But there are other types of delay in receiving payment from debtors, which might also suggest inefficient cash management.

(a) There is the delay created by the **length of credit** given to customers. There is often a 'normal' credit period for an industry, and companies might be unable to grant less time for payment than this.

(b) There are avoidable delays caused by **poor administration** (in addition to lodgement delay), such as:

  (i) **Failure to notify** the **invoicing department** that goods have been despatched, so that invoices are not sent promptly

  (ii) **Cheques from debtors** being **made out incorrectly**, to the wrong company perhaps, because invoices do not contain clear instructions

2.7 Example: Cash management

Ryan Coates owns a chain of seven clothes shops in the London area. Takings at each shop are remitted once a week on Thursday evening to the head office, and are then banked at the start of business on Friday morning. As business is expanding, Ryan Coates has hired an accountant to help him. The accountant gave him the following advice.

'Turnover at the seven shops totalled £1,950,000 last year, at a constant daily rate, but you were paying bank overdraft charges at a rate of 11%. You could have reduced your overdraft costs by banking the shop takings each day, except for Saturday's takings. Saturday takings could have been banked on Mondays.'

Comment on the significance of this statement, stating your assumptions. The shops are closed on Sundays.

Solution

(a) A bank overdraft rate of 11% a year is approximately 11/365 = 0.03% a day.

(b) Annual takings of £1,950,000 would be an average of £1,950,000/312 = £6,250 a day for the seven shops in total, on the assumption that they opened for a 52 week year of six days a week (312 days).

(c) Using the approximate overdraft cost of 0.03% a day, the cost of holding £6,250 for one day instead of banking it is 0.03% × £6,250 = £1.875.

(d) Banking all takings up to Thursday evening of each week on Friday morning involves an unnecessary delay in paying cash into the bank. The cost of this delay would be **either** the opportunity cost of investment capital for the business **or** the cost of avoidable bank overdraft charges.

It is assumed here that the overdraft cost is higher and is therefore more appropriate to use. It is also assumed that, for interest purposes, funds are credited when banked.

Takings on	Could be banked on	Number of days delay incurred by Friday banking
Monday	Tuesday	3
Tuesday	Wednesday	2
Wednesday	Thursday	1
Thursday	Friday	0
Friday	Saturday	6
Saturday	Monday	4
		16

In one week, the total number of days delay incurred by Friday banking is 16. At a cost of £1.875 a day, the weekly cost of Friday banking was £1.875 × 16 = £30.00, and the annual cost of Friday banking was £30.00 × 52 = £1,560.

(e) *Conclusion.* The company could have saved about £1,560 a year in bank overdraft charges last year. If the overdraft rate remains at 11% and turnover continues to increase, the saving from daily banking would be even higher next year.

2.8 Baumol model approach to cash management   12/05

FAST FORWARD

Optimal **cash** holding levels can be calculated from formal models, such as the **Baumol model** and the **Miller-Orr model**.

A number of different cash management models indicate the **optimum amount of cash** that a company should hold. One such model is based on the idea that deciding on optimum cash balances is like deciding on optimum stock levels. This is known as either the Baumol model or inventory approach.

We can distinguish two types of cost which are involved in obtaining cash:

(a) The **fixed cost** represented, for example, by the issue cost of equity finance or the cost of negotiating an overdraft

(b) The **variable cost** (opportunity cost) of keeping the money in the form of cash

The inventory approach uses an equation of the same form as the EOQ formula for stock management which we looked at earlier. The average total cost incurred for period in holding a certain average level of cash (C) is:

$$\frac{Qi}{2} + \frac{FS}{Q}$$

Where S = the amount of cash to be used in each time period
       F = the fixed cost of obtaining new funds
       i = the interest cost of holding cash or near cash equivalents
       Q = the total amount to be raised to provide for S

Similarly to the EOQ, C is minimised when:

$$Q = \sqrt{\frac{2FS}{i}}$$

2.8.1 Example: Baumol approach to cash management

Finder Limited faces a fixed cost of £4,000 to obtain new funds. There is a requirement for £24,000 of cash over each period of one year for the foreseeable future. The interest cost of new funds is 12% per annum; the interest rate earned on short-term securities is 9% per annum. How much finance should Finder Limited raise at a time?

Solution

The cost of holding cash is 12% − 9% = 3%

The optimum level of Q (the 'reorder quantity') is:

$$\sqrt{\frac{2 \times 4,000 \times 24,000}{0.03}} = £80,000$$

The optimum amount of new funds to raise is £80,000. This amount is raised every 80,000 ÷ 24,000 = 3⅓ years.

2.9 Drawbacks of the Baumol approach

The inventory approach illustrated above has the following drawbacks.

(a) In reality, it is unlikely to be **possible** to **predict amounts required** over future periods with much certainty.

(b) No **buffer stock** of cash is allowed for. There may be costs associated with running out of cash.

(c) There may be other **normal costs** of holding cash which increase with the average amount held.

> **Exam focus point**
>
> Question 5 in December 2005's exam required an explanation of the Baumol model and its usefulness to the company in question.

2.10 The Miller-Orr model

In an attempt to produce a more realistic approach to cash management, various models more complicated than the inventory approach have been developed. One of these, the **Miller-Orr model**, manages to achieve a reasonable degree of realism while not being too elaborate.

We can begin looking at the Miller-Orr model by asking what will happen if there is no attempt to manage cash balances. Clearly, the cash balance is likely to 'meander' upwards or downwards. The Miller-Orr model imposes limits to this meandering.

If the cash balance reaches an **upper limit** (point A in Figure 2) the firm **buys sufficient securities** to return the cash balance to a normal level (called the 'return point'). When the cash balance reaches a lower limit (point B in Figure 2), the firm sells securities to bring the balance back to the return point.

Figure 2 Miller-Orr model

How are the upper and lower limits and the return point set? Miller and Orr showed that the answer to this question depends on the **variance of cash flows**, **transaction costs** and **interest rates**. If the day-to-day variability of cash flows is high or the transaction cost in buying or selling securities is high, then wider limits should be set. If interest rates are high, the limits should be closer together.

To keep the interest costs of holding cash down, the return point is set at one-third of the distance (or 'spread') between the lower and the upper limit.

Return point = Lower limit + $\frac{1}{3}$ × spread

The formula for the spread is:

$$\text{Spread} = 3\left(\frac{3}{4} \times \frac{\text{transaction cost} \times \text{variance of cashflows}}{\text{interest rate}}\right)^{\frac{1}{3}}$$

Exam focus point

The Miller-Orr formulae for return point and spread are included in the formulae sheet provided with the examination paper.

To use the Miller-Orr model, it is necessary to follow the steps below.

Step 1 Set the **lower limit** for the **cash balance**. This may be zero, or it may be set at some minimum safety margin above zero.

Step 2 **Estimate** the **variance** of **cash flows**, for example from sample observations over a 100-day period.

Step 3 **Note the interest rate** and the **transaction cost** for each sale or purchase of securities (the latter is assumed to be fixed).

Step 4 **Compute the upper limit** and the **return point** from the model and implement the limits strategy.

You may be given the information to help you through the early steps, as in the question below.

Question — Miller-Orr model

The following data applies to a company.

Step 1 The minimum cash balance is £8,000.

Step 2 The variance of daily cash flows is 4,000,000, equivalent to a standard deviation of £2,000 per day.

Step 3 The transaction cost for buying or selling securities is £50. The interest rate is 0.025 per cent per day.

You are required to formulate a decision rule using the Miller-Orr model.

Answer

Step 4 The spread between the upper and the lower cash balance limits is calculated as follows.

$$\text{Spread} = 3\left(\frac{3}{4} \times \frac{\text{transaction cost} \times \text{variance of cash flows}}{\text{interest rate}}\right)^{\frac{1}{3}}$$

$$= 3\left(\frac{3}{4} \times \frac{50 \times 4,000,000}{0.00025}\right)^{\frac{1}{3}} = 3(6 \times 10)^{\frac{1}{3}} = 3 \times 8434.33$$

= £25,303, say £25,300

The upper limit and return point are now calculated.

Upper limit = Lower limit + £25,300 = £8,000 + £25,300 = £33,300
Return point = lower limit + $\frac{1}{3}$ × spread = £8,000 + $\frac{1}{3}$ × £25,300 = £16,433, say £16,400

The decision rule is as follows. If the cash balance reaches £33,300, buy £16,900 (= 33,300 − 16,400) in marketable securities. If the cash balance falls to £8,000, sell £8,400 of marketable securities for cash.

The **usefulness of the Miller-Orr model** is limited by the assumptions on which it is based. In practice, cash inflows and outflows are unlikely to be entirely **unpredictable** as the model assumes: for example, for a retailer, seasonal factors are likely to affect cash inflows.

However, the Miller-Orr model may save management time which might otherwise be spent in responding to those cash inflows and outflows which cannot be predicted.

2.11 Applying probabilities in cash management problems

Probabilities can be applied to cash management problems.

2.12 Example: Probabilities in cash management

Sinkos Wim Ltd has an overdraft facility of £100,000, and currently has an overdraft balance at the bank of £34,000. The company maintains a cash float of £10,000 for transactions and precautionary purposes. It is unclear whether a long awaited economic recovery will take place, and the company has prepared cash budgets as set out below for the next three months using two different assumptions about economic events. The cash flow in months 2 and 3 depend on the cash flows in the previous month.

Estimated net cash flows

Month 1		Month 2		Month 3	
Probability	Cash flow £'000	Probability	Cash flow £'000	Probability	Cash flow £'000
		0.8	25	0.5	30
0.7	(40)			0.5	20
		0.2	10	0.5	10
				0.5	0
		0.8	0	0.5	(10)
0.3	(60)			0.5	(20)
		0.2	(10)	0.5	(40)
				0.5	(50)

If the company intends to maintain a cash float of £10,000 at the end of each month, what is the probability that this will be possible at the end of each of months 1, 2 and 3 given the current overdraft limit?

Solution

The opening balance at the beginning of month 1 is £10,000.

Month 1				Month 2				Month 3			
Prob.	Cash flow £'000	Clos. bal. £'000	Over-draft £'000	Prob.	Cash flow £'000	Clos. bal. £'000	Over-draft £'000	Prob.	Cash flow £'000	Clos. bal. £'000	Over-draft £'000
								0.28	30	10	19
				0.56	25	10	49	0.28	20	10	29
0.7	(40)	10	74								
								0.07	10	10	54
				0.14	10	10	64	0.07	0	10	64
								0.12	(10)	6	100
				0.24	0	10	94	0.12	(20)	(4)	100

0.3	(60)	10	94			0.03	(40)	(34)	100
				0.06	(10)	6	100	0.03	(50)	(44)	100

The probabilities that the cash float of £10,000 can be maintained at the end of each month are as follows.

Month 1:   0.7 + 0.3 = 1.0
Month 2:   0.56 + 0.14 + 0.24 = 0.94
Month 3:   0.28 + 0.28 + 0.07 + 0.07 = 0.7

Question — Cash shortage

Using the figures in the above example, state the probabilities that the company completely runs out of cash at the end of each month.

Answer

Under none of the projected outcomes for months 1 and 2 does the company run out of cash.

For month 3, the probability of the company running out of cash is:

0.12 + 0.03 + 0.03 = 0.18

2.13 Investing surplus cash

FAST FORWARD

Temporary surpluses of cash can be invested in a variety of financial instruments. Longer-term surpluses should be returned to shareholders if there is a lack of investment opportunities.

Companies and other organisations sometimes have a **surplus of cash** and become 'cash rich'. A cash surplus is likely to be **temporary**, but while it exists the company should invest or deposit the cash bearing the following considerations in mind:

(a) **Liquidity** – money should be available to take advantage of favourable short-term interest rates on bank deposits, or to grasp a strategic opportunity, for example paying cash to take over another company

(b) **Profitability** – the company should seek to obtain a **good return** for the **risk** incurred

(c) **Safety** – the company should **avoid** the risk of a **capital loss**

Other factors that organisations need to consider include:

(a) Whether to invest at **fixed or floating rates.** Floating rate investments are likely to be chosen if interest rates are expected to rise.

(b) **Term to maturity.** The terms chosen will be affected by the business's desire for **liquidity** and **expectations** about future rates of interest; if there are major uncertainties about future interest rate levels it will be better to choose short-term investments. There may also be **penalties** for **early liquidation**.

(c) How easy it will be to **realise** the investment.

(d) Whether a **minimum amount** has to be invested in certain investments.

(e) Whether to invest on **international markets**.

If a company has no plans to grow or to invest, then surplus cash not required for transactions or precautionary purposes should normally be **returned** to **shareholders**.

Surplus cash may be returned to shareholders by:

(a) Increasing the usual level of the annual **dividends** which are paid

(b) Making a one-off **special dividend payment** (For example, National Power plc and BT plc have made such payments in recent years.)

(c) Using the money to **buy back its own shares** from some of its shareholders. This will reduce the total number of shares in issue, and should therefore raise the level of **earnings per share**

If surplus cash is to be invested on a regular basis, organisations should have investment guidelines in place covering the following issues:

(a) Surplus funds can only be invested in **specified types of investment** (eg no equity shares).

(b) All investments must be **convertible into cash** within a set number of days.

(c) Investments should be **ranked**: surplus funds to be invested in higher risk instruments only when a sufficiency has been invested in lower risk items (so that there is always a cushion of safety).

(d) If a firm invests in certain financial instruments, a **credit rating** should be obtained. Credit rating agencies, discussed in a later chapter, issue gradings according to risk.

2.13.1 Short-term investments

Temporary cash surpluses are likely to be:

(a) **Deposited** with a **bank** or similar financial institution

(b) Invested in **short-term debt instruments** (Debt instruments are debt securities which can be traded.)

(c) Invested in **longer term debt instruments**, which can be sold on the stock market when the company eventually needs the cash

(d) Invested in **shares of listed companies**, which can be sold on the stock market when the company eventually needs the cash

2.13.2 Short-term deposits

Cash can of course be put into a **bank deposit** to **earn interest**. The rate of interest obtainable depends on the size of the deposit, and varies from bank to bank.

There are other types of deposit.

(a) **Money market lending**

There is a very large money market in the UK for inter-bank lending. The interest rates in the market are related to the London Interbank Offer Rate (LIBOR) and the London Interbank Bid Rate (LIBID).

(b) **Local authority deposits**

Local authorities often need **short-term cash**, and investors can deposit funds with them for periods ranging from overnight up to one year or more.

(c) **Finance house deposits**

These are **time deposits** with finance houses (usually subsidiaries of banks).

2.13.3 Short-term debt instruments

There are a number of **short-term debt instruments** which an investor can re-sell before the debt matures and is repaid. These debt instruments include **certificates of deposit** (CDs) and **Treasury bills**.

2.13.4 Certificates of deposit (CDs)

A **CD** is a security that is issued by a bank, acknowledging that a certain amount of money has been deposited with it for a certain period of time (usually, a short term). The CD is issued to the **depositor**, and attracts a **stated amount of interest**. The **depositor** will be another bank or a large commercial organisation.

CDs are negotiable and traded on the CD market (a money market), so if a CD holder wishes to obtain immediate cash, he can sell the CD on the market at any time. This second-hand market in CDs makes them attractive, flexible investments for organisations with excess cash.

2.13.5 Treasury bills

Treasury bills are issued weekly by the government to finance short-term cash deficiencies in the government's expenditure programme. They are **IOUs** issued by the government, giving a promise to pay a certain amount to their holder on maturity. Treasury bills have a term of **91 days to maturity**, after which the holder is paid the full value of the bill.

3 Foreign exchange risk 06/05

FAST FORWARD

The use of **forward exchange contracts** in which a future rate of exchange is fixed in advance, is one of the most important ways in reducing foreign exchange risk. Other means include **matching receipts and payments**, **leads and lags**, **invoicing in the domestic currency** and **money market hedging**.

Exam focus point

If any calculations are required relating to exchange rate risk in Paper 2.4, they will only be simple calculations.

A company may become exposed to risk from movements in exchange rates in a number of ways, as an exporter of goods or services or through being a member of an international group.

Perhaps the most important aspect of **managing overseas debtors** is the problem that **exchange rates** may **change** before payment is received. Hedging involves measures to reduce exposure to such **foreign exchange risk**.

3.1 Transaction exposure

Much international trade involves credit. An importer will take credit often for **several months** and **sometimes longer**, and an exporter will **grant credit**. One consequence of taking and granting credit is that international traders will know in advance about the receipts and payments arising from their trade.

Importers and exporters alike will be concerned about the profit they can expect to make from trade.

The great danger to profit margins is the movement in exchange rates. The risk faces:

- Exporters who invoice in a foreign currency, and
- Importers who pay in a foreign currency

3.2 Matching receipts and payments

A company can reduce or eliminate its foreign exchange transaction exposure by matching receipts and payments. Wherever possible, a company that expects to make payments and have receipts in the same foreign currency should plan to **offset** its **payments** against its **receipts** in the currency.

Since the company will be setting off foreign currency receipts against foreign currency payments, it does not matter whether the currency strengthens or weakens against the company's 'domestic' currency because there will be no purchase or sale of the currency.

The process of matching is made simpler by having **foreign currency accounts** with a bank. UK residents are allowed to have bank accounts in any foreign currency. Receipts of foreign currency can be credited to the account pending subsequent payments in the currency.

Since a company is unlikely to have exactly the same amount of receipts in a currency as it makes payments, it will still be exposed to the extent of the surplus of income, and so the company may wish to avoid exposure on this surplus by arranging forward exchange cover.

Offsetting (matching payments against receipts) will be cheaper than arranging a forward contract to buy currency and another forward contract to sell the currency, provided that:

- **Receipts occur before payments**, and
- The **time difference** between receipts and payments in the currency is **not too long**

3.3 Leads and lags

Companies might try to use:

- **Lead payments**: payments in advance, or
- **Lagged payments**: delaying payments beyond their due date

in order to take advantage of foreign exchange rate movements.

With a lead payment, paying in advance of the due date, there is a finance cost to consider. This is the interest cost on the money used to make the payment.

3.4 Currency of invoice

One way of avoiding exchange rate risk is for an exporter to **invoice** his foreign customer in his **domestic currency**, or for an importer to **arrange** with his **foreign supplier** to be **invoiced** in his **domestic currency**. However, although either the exporter or the importer can avoid any exchange risk in this way, only one of them can deal in his domestic currency. The other must accept the exchange risk, since there will be a period of time elapsing between agreeing a contract and paying for the goods (unless payment is made with the order).

3.5 Forward exchange contracts

Forward exchange contracts allow a trader who knows that he will have to buy or sell foreign currency at a date in the future, to make the purchase or sale at a predetermined rate of exchange. The trader will therefore know in advance either how much **local currency** he will **receive** (if he is selling foreign currency to the bank) or how much local currency he must **pay** (if he is buying foreign currency from the bank).

Key term

A **forward exchange contract** is:

(a) An immediately firm and binding contract between a bank and its customer
(b) For the purchase or sale of a specified quantity of a stated foreign currency
(c) At a rate of exchange fixed at the time the contract is made

(d) For performance (delivery of the currency and payment for it) at a future time which is agreed upon when making the contract. This future time will be either a specified date, or any time between two specified dates.

3.6 Forward rates and future exchange rate movements

A forward price is the **spot price** ruling on the day a forward exchange contract is made plus or minus the **interest differential** for the period of the contract.

The forward rate is not a forecast of what the spot rate will be on a given date in the future; it will be a coincidence if the forward rate turns out to be the same as the spot rate on that future date.

It is however likely that the spot rate will move in the direction **indicated** by the **forward** rate. Currencies with **high interest rates** are likely to **depreciate in value** against currencies with **lower interest rates**. The attraction of higher interest persuades investors to hold amounts of a currency that is expected to depreciate.

3.7 Example: Movement of spot rates

For example, suppose that a spot rate on 1 June is US$1.7430 - 1.7440 to £1, and the three months forward rate (for 1 September) is US$1.7380 - 1.7395 to £1. It is likely that between 1 June and 1 September, sterling will weaken slightly against the dollar. In this example, interest rates in the UK on 1 June would be higher than interest rates in the USA, which accounts for the forward rates for dollars against sterling being lower than the spot rates on 1 June.

3.8 Fixed and option contracts

A forward exchange contract may be either **fixed** or **option**.

(a) '**Fixed**' means that **performance** of the contract will **take place** on a **specified date** in the **future**. For example, a two months forward fixed contract taken out on 1 September will require performance on 1 November.

(b) '**Option**' means that performance of the contract may take place, at the **option** of the **customer**:

(i) **At any date** from the contract being made up to and including a specified final date for performance

(ii) **At any date** between **two specified dates**.

The contract must be performed at some time; the customer cannot avoid performance altogether.

3.9 Premiums and discounts: quoting a forward rate

A forward exchange rate might be higher or lower than the spot rate. If it is higher, the quoted currency will be cheaper forward than spot. For example, if in the case of Swiss francs against sterling (i) the spot rate is 2.156 – 2.166 and (ii) the three months forward rate is 2.207 – 2.222:

(a) A bank would sell 2,000 francs:

(i) At the spot rate, now, for £927.64

$$\left(\frac{2,000}{2.156}\right)$$

	(ii)	In three months time, under a forward contract, for	£906.21 $\left(\dfrac{2,000}{2.207}\right)$
(b)	A bank would buy 2,000 francs:		
	(i)	At the spot rate, now, for	£923.36 $\left(\dfrac{2,000}{2.166}\right)$
	(ii)	In three months time, under a forward contract, for	£900.09 $\left(\dfrac{2,000}{2.222}\right)$

In both cases, the quoted currency (Francs) would be worth less against sterling in a forward contract than at the current spot rate. This is because it is quoted **forward cheaper**, or 'at a discount', against sterling.

If the **forward exchange rate** is **lower** than the spot rate, the **quoted currency** will be **more expensive forward** than spot. For example, if the spot rate for Euros against sterling is 1.60 - 1.61, and the one month forward rate is 1.57 – 1.58, then Euros are more expensive (quoted 'at a premium') forward than spot.

(a) If the **forward rate** for a currency is **cheaper** than the spot rate, it is at a **forward discount** to the spot rate. The **forward rate** will be **higher** than the **spot rate** by the **amount** of the **discount**.

(b) If the **forward rate** for a currency is **more expensive** than the spot rate, it is at a **forward premium** to the spot rate. The forward rate will be lower than the spot rate by the amount of the premium.

A **discount** is therefore **added** to the spot rate, and a **premium** is therefore **subtracted** from the spot rate. It might help you to think of the mnemonic 'ADDIS'. This may help you to remember that we ADD DIScounts and so subtract premiums.

3.10 Example: Forward exchange contracts

A UK importer knows on 1 April that he must pay a foreign seller 26,500 Swiss francs in one month's time, on 1 May. He can arrange a forward exchange contract with his bank on 1 April, whereby the bank undertakes to sell the importer 26,500 Swiss francs on 1 May, at a fixed rate of say 2.64.

The UK importer can be certain that whatever the spot rate is between Swiss francs and sterling on 1 May, he will have to pay on that date, at this forward rate:

$$\dfrac{26,500}{2.64} = £10,037.88.$$

(a) If the spot rate is lower than 2.64, the importer would have **successfully protected himself** against a weakening of sterling, and would have avoided paying more sterling to obtain the Swiss francs.

(b) If the spot rate is higher than 2.64, sterling's value against the Swiss franc would mean that the **importer** would **pay more** under the forward exchange contract than he would have had to pay if he had obtained the francs at the spot rate on 1 May. He cannot avoid this extra cost, because a forward contract is binding.

3.11 Option forward exchange contracts

Option contracts are normally used to cover whole months straddling the likely payment date, where the customer is not sure of the exact date on which he will want to buy or sell currency.

Option contracts can also be used bit by bit. For example, if a customer makes an option forward contract to sell 100,000 Euros at any time between 3 July and 3 August, he might sell €20,000 on 5 July, €50,000 on 15 July and €30,000 on 1 August.

When a customer makes an option forward exchange contract with his bank, the bank will quote the rate which is **most favourable to itself** out of the forward rates for all dates within the option period. The customer has the option to call for performance of the contract on any date within the period, and the bank will try to ensure that the customer does not obtain a favourable rate at the bank's expense.

3.12 Money market hedges

An exporter who invoices foreign customers in a foreign currency can hedge against the exchange risk by:

- **Borrowing** an amount in the foreign currency **immediately**
- **Converting** the **foreign currency** into **domestic currency** at the **spot rate**
- **Repaying the loan** with **interest** out of the eventual foreign currency receipts

Similarly, if a company has to make a foreign currency payment in the future, it can **buy the currency now** at the spot rate and **put it on deposit**, using the principal and the interest earned to make the foreign currency payment when it falls due.

3.13 Choosing between the forward exchange market and the money market

When a company expects to receive or pay a sum of foreign currency in the next few months, it can choose between using the forward exchange market and the money market to hedge against the foreign exchange risk.

3.14 Example: Choosing the cheapest method

Trumpton plc has bought goods from a US supplier, and must pay $4,000,000 for them in three months time. The company's finance director wishes to hedge against the foreign exchange risk, and the company wishes to consider either using forward exchange contracts or using money market borrowing or lending.

The following annual interest rates and exchange rates are currently available.

	US dollar		Sterling	
	Deposit rate %	Borrowing rate %	Deposit rate %	Borrowing rate %
1 month	7	10.25	10.75	14.00
3 months	7	10.75	11.00	14.25

	$/£ exchange rate ($ = £1)
Spot	1.8625 – 1.8635
1 month forward	0.60c – 0.58c pm
3 months forward	1.80c – 1.75c pm

Which is the cheapest method for Trumpton plc? Ignore commission costs (the bank charges for arranging a forward contract or a loan).

PART E   WORKING CAPITAL MANAGEMENT

Solution

The two methods must be compared on a similar basis, which means working out the cost of each to Trumpton either now or in three months time. Here the cost to Trumpton now will be determined.

Choice 1: the forward exchange market

Trumpton must buy dollars in order to pay the US supplier. The exchange rate in a forward exchange contract to buy $4,000,000 in three months time (bank sells) is:

	$
Spot rate	1.8625
Less 3 months premium	0.0180
Forward rate	1.8445

The cost of the $4,000,000 to Trumpton in three months time will be:

$$\frac{\$4,000,000}{\$1.8445} = £2,168,609.38$$

This is the cost in three months. To work out the cost now, we could say that by deferring payment for three months, the company is:

(a) Saving having to borrow money now at 14.25% a year to make the payment now, or
(b) Avoiding the loss of interest on cash on deposit, earning 11% a year

The choice between (a) and (b) depends on whether Trumpton plc needs to borrow to make any current payment (a) or is cash rich (b). Here, assumption (a) is selected, but (b) might in fact apply.

At an annual interest rate of 14.25% the rate for three months is approximately 14.25/4 = 3.5625%. The 'present cost' of £2,168,609.38 in three months time is:

$$\frac{£2,168,609.38}{1.035625} = £2,094,010.27$$

Choice 2: the money markets

Using the money markets involves **borrowing in the foreign currency**, if the company will eventually receive the currency, or **lending in the foreign currency**, if the company will eventually pay the currency.

Here, Trumpton will pay $4,000,000 and so it would lend US dollars. It would lend enough US dollars for three months, so that the principal repaid in three months time plus interest will amount to the payment due of $4,000,000.

(a) Since the US dollar deposit rate is 7%, the rate for three months is approximately 7/4 = 1.75%.
(b) To earn $4,000,000 in three months time at 1.75% interest, Trumpton would have to lend now:

$$\frac{\$4,000,000}{1.0175} = \$3,931,203.93$$

These dollars would have to be purchased now at the spot rate of (bank sells) $1.8625. The cost would be:

$$\frac{\$3,931,203.93}{\$1.8625} = £2,110,713.52$$

By lending US dollars for three months, Trumpton is matching eventual receipts and payments in US dollars, and so has hedged against foreign exchange risk.

4 Treasury management

FAST FORWARD

A large organisation will have a **treasury department** to manage liquidity, short-term investment, borrowings, foreign exchange risk and other, specialised, areas such as forward contracts and futures etc.

Key term

Treasury management can be defined as: 'The corporate handing of all financial matters, the generation of external and internal funds for business, the management of currencies and cash flows, and the complex strategies, policies and procedures of corporate finance.' (Association of Corporate Treasurers)

Large companies rely heavily on the financial and currency markets. These markets are volatile, with interest rates and foreign exchange rates changing continually and by significant amounts. To manage cash (funds) and currency efficiently, many large companies have set up a separate treasury department.

A treasury department, even in a large organisation, is likely to be quite small, with perhaps a staff of three to six qualified accountants, bankers or corporate treasurers working under the treasurer.

4.1 Centralisation of the treasury department

The following are advantages of having a specialist **centralised treasury department**.

(a) **Centralised liquidity management**

   (i) Avoids having a mix of cash surpluses and overdrafts in different localised bank accounts

   (ii) Facilitates bulk cash flows, so that lower bank charges can be negotiated

(b) Larger volumes of cash are available to invest, giving better **short-term investment opportunities** (for example money markets, high-interest accounts and CDs).

(c) Any **borrowing** can be **arranged in bulk**, at lower interest rates than for smaller borrowings, and perhaps on the eurocurrency or eurobond markets.

(d) **Foreign exchange risk management** is likely to be improved in a group of companies. A central treasury department can **match foreign currency income** earned by one subsidiary with **expenditure** in the same currency by another subsidiary. In this way, the risk of losses on adverse exchange rate movements can be avoided with out the expense of forward exchange contracts or other hedging methods.

(e) A specialist treasury department can employ **experts** with knowledge of dealing in forward contracts, futures, options, eurocurrency markets, swaps and so on. Localised departments could not have such expertise.

(f) The centralised pool of **funds required for precautionary purposes** will be **smaller** than the sum of separate precautionary balances which would need to be held under decentralised treasury arrangements.

(g) Through having a separate **profit centre**, attention will be focused on the contribution to group profit performance that can be achieved by good cash, funding, investment and foreign currency management.

Possible advantages of **decentralised** cash management are as follows.

(a) Sources of finance can be **diversified** and can match **local assets**.

(b) **Greater autonomy** can be given to **subsidiaries** and divisions because of the closer relationships they will have with the decentralised cash management function.

PART E WORKING CAPITAL MANAGEMENT

(c) A decentralised treasury function may be **more responsive** to the needs of individual operating units.

(d) Since cash balances will not be aggregated at group level, there will be **more limited opportunities** to invest such balances on a short-term basis.

Chapter Roundup

- An **economic order quantity** can be calculated as a guide to minimising costs in managing **stock** levels. **Bulk discounts** can however mean that a different order quantity minimises stock costs.

- Optimal **cash** holding levels can be calculated from formal models, such as the **inventory approach** and the **Miller-Orr model**.

- **Uncertainties** in demand and lead times taken to fulfil orders mean that stock will be ordered once it reaches a re-order level (maximum usage x maximum lead time).

- **Cash shortages** can be eased by postponing capital expenditure, selling assets, taking longer to pay creditors and pressing debtors for earlier payment.

- **Temporary surpluses** of cash can be invested in a variety of financial instruments. Longer-term surpluses should be returned to shareholders if there is a lack of investment opportunities.

- The use of **forward exchange contracts** in which a future rate of exchange is fixed in advance, is one of the most important ways in reducing foreign exchange risk. Other means include **matching receipts and payments**, **leads and lags**, **invoicing in the domestic currency** and **money market hedging**.

- A large organisation will have a **treasury department** to manage liquidity, short-term investment, borrowings, foreign exchange risk and other, specialised, areas such as forward contracts and futures etc.

Quick Quiz

1. The basic EOQ formula for stock indicates whether bulk discounts should be taken advantage of

   ☐ True

   ☐ False

2. Identify the potential benefits of JIT manufacturing.

3. Possible reasons for a lengthy float are:

   (a) .... delay

   (b) .... delay

   (c) .... delay

4. In the Miller-Orr cash management model

   Return point = Lower limit + ... × spread

5. Why might a treasurer choose *not* to 'hedge' against the risk of a foreign exchange movement?

6. PB Ltd uses 2,500 units of component X per year. The company has calculated that the cost of placing and processing a purchase order for component X is £185, and the cost of holding one unit of component X for a year is £25.

   What is the economic order quantity (EOQ) for component X, and assuming a 52-week year, what is the average frequency at which purchase orders should be placed?

7. The economic order quantity model can be used to determine:

Order quantity	Buffer stock	Re-order level
Yes/No	Yes/No	Yes/No

8. Which of the following is most likely to reduce a firm's working capital?

   A   Adopting the Miller-Orr model of cash management
   B   Lengthening the period of credit given to debtors
   C   Buying new machinery
   D   Adopting just-in-time procurement and lean manufacturing

PART E   WORKING CAPITAL MANAGEMENT

Answers to Quick Quiz

1   False. It may be necessary to modify the formula to take account of bulk discounts.

2   (a) Reduction in stock holding costs
    (b) Reduced manufacturing lead times
    (c) Improved labour productivity
    (d) Reduced scrap/warranty/rework/costs
    (e) Price reductions on purchased materials
    (f) Reduction in the number of accounting transactions

3   (a) Transmission delay
    (b) Lodgement delay
    (c) Clearance delay

4   One third

5   Because she thinks it likely that a profit will be made in refraining from hedging the risk.

6   C $EOQ = \sqrt{\dfrac{2C_o D}{C_h}}$

    Economic order quantity $= \sqrt{\dfrac{2 \times 185 \times 2{,}500}{25}}$

    $= 192$ units

    Frequency of ordering $= \dfrac{192}{2{,}500}$

    $= 4$ weeks

7   The EOQ model finds order quantity only, not buffer stock and re-order level.

8   D   The aim of using these methods is to minimise stockholdings. The impact of using the Miller-Orr model will depend on how the firm was managing cash before (A). Giving more credit to debtors will increase working capital (B). New machinery is not part of working capital (C); the impact, if any, on working capital will depend on how the purchase is financed.

Now try the questions below from the Exam Question Bank

Number	Level	Marks	Time
Q23	Examination	25	45 mins

Part F
Sources of finance

Equity financing

Topic list	Syllabus reference
1 Sources of equity funds	4
2 Equity shares and markets	4
3 Rights issues and vendor placings	4
4 Scrip dividends, scrip issues and stock splits	4
5 Preference shares	4
6 Stock market ratios	4(d)
7 Dividend policy	4

Introduction

In the case of long-term finance (covered in this chapter and Chapter 22), the main choice is between **equity** and **debt** finance.

If a company decides to raise new equity finance, it needs to consider which method would be best for its circumstances. An important distinction is made between share issues that bring in new funds (**new share issues** and **rights issues**), and those which do not (**scrip dividends**, **scrip or bonus issues** and **stock splits**).

Dividend policy plays a big part in a company's relations with its equity shareholders, and a company must consider how the stock market will view its results. Investors will analyse the performance of the company by means of various stock market ratios to which we referred in Chapter 14; now is the time to look at these in more detail.

PART F SOURCES OF FINANCE

Study guide

Section 9 – Sources of finance II: Equity financing

- Describe ways in which a company may obtain a stock market listing
- Describe how stock markets operate, including AIM
- Explain the requirements of stock market investors in terms of returns of investment
- Calculate, analyse and evaluate appropriate financial ratios (eg EPS, PE, yield, etc.)
- Outline and apply the dividend valuation model, including the growth adjustment
- Explain the importance of internally generated funds
- Describe the advantages and disadvantages of rights issues
- Calculate the price of rights
- Explain the purpose and impact of a bonus issue, scrip dividends and stock splits

Section 10 – Sources of finance III: Debt financing

- Explain the features of different types of preference shares and the reasons for their issue

Exam guide

Sources of finance are a major topic. You may be asked to describe appropriate sources of finance for a particular company, and also discuss in general terms when different sources of finance should be utilised and when they are likely to be available. Dividend policy is also important for all types of company.

1 Sources of equity funds   12/03

FAST FORWARD

> Equity finance is raised by a **new issue** of equity shares or a **rights issue**. Cash generated by the use of **retained earnings** is another source of equity funds.

A company might raise equity funds from the following sources.

(a) Cash from retained earnings

(b) The capital markets:
 (i) New share issues
 (ii) Rights issues

1.1 Retained earnings

Retained cash earnings are the most important form of equity finance in practice, offering a low cost source of finance. The company may have cash or short-term investments that are needed to finance existing operations, and could therefore be used as a source of finance for expansion.

Retained earnings may not be enough however if a company is trying to **grow**. A company may also have trouble retaining sufficient earnings if shareholders require dividend levels to be maintained or increased.

Exam focus point

> Make sure you understand what equity finance is and isn't. To quote from the examiner's report on the December 2003 exams, discussing a question that required candidates to identify how an unlisted company might raise equity finance:
>
> 'No credit was given to those answers that suggested leasing, hire purchase, sale and leaseback, factoring, bonus issue, conversion of capital reserves, convertible debentures, loans and bank loans, since these are not ways of receiving cash in exchange for the issue of new ordinary shares.'

21: EQUITY FINANCING

2 Equity shares and markets

2.1 Ordinary (equity) shares

FAST FORWARD

> A company can obtain a **stock market listing** for its shares through an offer for sale, a prospectus issue, a placing or an introduction.

Ordinary shares are issued to the owners of a company. The ordinary shares of UK companies have a nominal or 'face' value, typically £1 or 50p, but shares with a nominal value of 1p, 2p or 25p are not uncommon.

You should understand that the **market value** of a quoted company's shares bears **no relationship** to their nominal value, except that when ordinary shares are issued for cash, the issue price must be equal to or (more usually) more than the nominal value of the shares. Outside the UK it is not uncommon for a company's shares to have no nominal value.

Deferred ordinary (equity) shares are a form of ordinary shares, which are entitled to a dividend only after a certain date or only if profits rise above a certain amount. Voting rights might also differ from those attached to other ordinary shares.

A new issue of shares might be made in a variety of different circumstances.

(a) The company might want to raise more cash, for example for expansion of its operations. If, for example, a company with 200,000 ordinary shares in issue decides to issue 50,000 new shares to raise cash, should it offer the **new shares** to **existing shareholders**, or should it **sell them** to **new shareholders** instead?

   (i) If a company sells the new shares to existing shareholders in proportion to their existing shareholding in the company, we have a **rights issue**.

   (ii) If the **number** of **new shares** is **small** compared to the number of shares already in issue, it might be decided instead to sell them to **new shareholders**, since ownership of the company would only be minimally affected.

(b) The company might want to issue new shares partly to raise cash but more importantly to **'float' its shares** on a stock market. When a UK company is floated, it must make available a **minimum proportion** of its shares to the general investing public.

(c) The company might issue **new shares** to the shareholders of another company, in order to take it over.

A public company that wishes to obtain additional equity funds may do so by obtaining a listing either on:

(a) The **Alternative Investment Market**, or

(b) **Recognised Investment Exchanges**. The most important of these is the London **Stock Exchange**.

2.2 Reason for seeking a stock market listing

The following are reasons why a company may seek a stock market listing.

(a) **Access to a wider pool of finance**

   A stock market listing widens the number of potential investors. It may also improve the company's credit rating, making debt finance easier and cheaper to obtain.

(b) **Improved marketability of shares**

Shares that are traded on the stock market can be bought and sold in relatively small quantities at any time. Existing investors can easily realise a part of their holding.

(c) **Transfer of capital to other uses**

Founder owners may wish to liquidate the major part of their holding either for personal reasons or for investment in other new business opportunities.

(d) **Enhancement of the company image**

Quoted companies are commonly believed to be more financially stable. Listing may improve the image of the company with its customers and suppliers, allowing it to gain additional business and to improve its buying power.

(e) **Facilitation of growth by acquisition**

A listed company is in a better position to make a paper offer for a target company than an unlisted one.

However, the owners of a private company which becomes a listed 'plc' (public company) must accept that the change is likely to involve a significant **loss of control** to a wider circle of investors. The **risk** of the company being **taken over** will also **increase** following listing.

In order to issue shares on a recognised investment exchange, a company has to obtain:

- Admission to listing from the Financial Services Authority
- Admission to trading from the recognised investment exchange

2.3 Issues of shares

Shares can be issued on the London Stock Exchange by means of an **offer for sale**, a **prospectus issue**, a **placing** or an **introduction**. Of these an offer for sale or a placing are the most common.

2.4 Offers for sale

An **offer for sale** is a means of selling the shares of a company to the public at large.

(a) When companies 'go public' for the first time, a **large issue** will probably take the form of an offer for sale. A smaller issue is more likely to be a placing, since the amount to be raised can be obtained more cheaply if the issuing house or other sponsoring firm approaches selected institutional investors privately.

(b) A new issue by an already quoted company is likely to be a placing or a rights issue, which are described later.

2.4.1 The issue price and offers for sale

The offer price must be advertised a short time in advance, so it is fixed **without certain knowledge** of the condition of the market at the time applications are invited. To ensure the success of an issue share prices are often set at a low level. An issuing house normally tries to ensure that a share price rises to a premium above its issue price soon after trading begins. A target premium of 20% above the issue price would be fairly typical.

Companies will be keen to avoid over-pricing an issue, so that the issue is **undersubscribed**, leaving underwriters with the unwelcome task of having to buy up the unsold shares. On the other hand, if the issue price is too low then the issue will be **oversubscribed** and the company would have been able to raise the required capital by issuing fewer shares.

The share price of an issue is usually advertised as being based on a certain **P/E ratio**, the ratio of the price to the company's most recent earnings per share figure in its audited accounts. The issue's P/E ratio can then be compared by investors with the P/E ratios of similar quoted companies.

2.4.2 Offers for sale by tender

One way of trying to ensure that the issue price reflects the value of the shares as perceived by the market is to make an **offer for sale by tender.** A **minimum price** will be fixed and subscribers will be invited to tender for shares at prices equal to or above the minimum. The shares will be **allotted at the highest price** at which they will **all be taken up**. This is known as the **striking price**.

Offers by tender are less common than offers for sale for the following reasons.

(a) The decision to make an **offer by tender reflects** badly on the **issuing house's ability** to determine the issue price.

(b) The use of tenders may leave the **determination of prices** to the **public** rather than the City 'experts'. However, in practice the major influence on the striking price will be the tenders of the institutional investors.

(c) An offer for sale is **more certain** in the amount of finance that will be raised.

(d) Some potential investors may be deterred from applying for shares as they do **not wish** to **have to decide** on a price.

An increase in the use of offers for sale by tender might follow a **general increase** in **share values**. The striking price in an offer for sale by tender is likely to be higher than the issue price set by the issuing company itself, since the issue price would have to be sufficiently low to make reasonably certain that the issue would be fully subscribed by investors.

2.5 A placing

A **placing** is an arrangement whereby the shares are not all offered to the public. Instead, the sponsoring market maker arranges for most of the issue to be bought by a **small number of investors**, usually institutional investors such as pension funds and insurance companies.

2.5.1 The choice between an offer for sale and a placing

When a company is planning a flotation on to the AIM, or a full Stock Exchange listing, is it likely to prefer an offer for sale of its shares, or a placing? **Placings are much cheaper**, although most of the shares will be placed with a relatively small number of (institutional) shareholders, which means that most of the shares are unlikely to be available for trading after the flotation. This is a particular problem for smaller companies.

2.5.2 A prospectus issue

In a **prospectus issue**, or public issue, a company offers its **own shares** to the general public. An issuing house or merchant bank may act as an agent, but not as an underwriter. This type of issue is therefore risky, and is rare. Well known companies making a large new issue may use this method, and the company would almost certainly already have a quotation on the Stock Exchange.

2.5.3 A Stock Exchange introduction

By this method of obtaining a quotation, no shares are made available to the market, neither existing nor newly created shares; nevertheless, the Stock Exchange grants a quotation. This will only happen where shares in a large company are already widely held, so that a market can be seen to exist. A company might want an **introduction** to obtain:

- Greater marketability for the shares
- A known share valuation for inheritance tax purposes
- Easier access in the future to additional capital

2.5.4 Intermediaries offer

An intermediaries offer is an issue of shares where intermediaries such as brokers and investment banks apply for shares on behalf of their own client base. It is a method of issuing shares used by companies which are obtaining a listing of their shares for the first time.

2.5.5 Underwriting

A company about to issue new securities in order to raise finance might decide to have the issue underwritten. **Underwriters** are financial institutions which agree (in exchange for a fixed fee, perhaps 2% of the finance to be raised) to **buy** at the **issue price** any securities which are not subscribed for by the investing public.

Underwriters **remove the** risk of a share issue's being **under-subscribed**, but at a cost to the company issuing the shares. It is not compulsory to have an issue underwritten.

As an alternative to underwriting an issue, a company could choose to issue its share at a **deep discount**, that is, at a price well below the current market price, to ensure the success of the issue. A major disadvantage of issuing shares at a deep discount is that, the total amount required for dividends in future years will be that **much higher**, since more shares would have to be issued at the low price to raise the amount of finance required.

Because of the costs of underwriting, many companies now use a **'bought deal'**, whereby an investment bank buys the whole of a new issue at a small discount to the market.

2.6 Pricing shares for a stock market launch

The following factors will be taken into account.

(a) Are there **similar companies already quoted**, whose P/E ratios can be used for comparison? The chosen P/E ratio can be multiplied by the company's most recent EPS, as shown in the prospectus, to arrive at a draft share price. This price can be negotiated with the company's current owners.

A company which is coming to the AIM will obtain a lower P/E ratio than a similar company on the main market.

(b) What are **current market conditions**?

(c) With what **accuracy** can the company's **future trading prospects** be forecast?

(d) Companies normally set a price which gives an **immediate premium** when the launch takes place. A sponsor will usually try to ensure that the market price rises to a premium of about 20% over the launch price on the day that the launch takes place.

(e) A **steady growth** in the share price year by year should be achievable.

2.7 The timing and costs of new equity issues

New equity issues in general will be more common when share prices are high than when share prices are low.

(a) When **share price are high**, investors' confidence will probably be high, and investors will be more willing to put money into companies with the potential for growth.

(b) By issuing shares at a high price, a company will **reduce** the **number of shares** it **needs** to issue to raise the amount of capital it wants. This will **reduce** the **dilution of earnings** for existing shareholders.

(c) Following on from (b), the company's **total dividend commitment** on the new shares, to meet shareholders' expectations, will be **lower**.

(d) If **share prices are low**, **business confidence** is likely to be **low** too. Companies may not want to raise capital for new investments until expectations begin to improve.

Typical **costs** of a share issue include:

- Underwriting costs
- The Stock Exchange listing fee (the initial charge) for the new securities
- Fees of the issuing house, solicitors, auditors, and public relations consultants
- Charges for printing and distributing the prospectus
- Advertising, which must be done in national newspapers

3 Rights issues and vendor placings 12/04

FAST FORWARD

A **rights issue** is an offer to existing shareholders enabling them to buy more shares, usually at a price lower than the current market price.

Existing shareholders have **pre-emption rights** when new shares are issued. So that existing shareholders' wealth is not diluted by the issue of new shares, section 89 of Companies Act 1985 requires that before any equity shares are allotted for cash they must first be offered to existing shareholders.

A **rights issue** provides a way of raising new share capital by means of an offer to existing shareholders, inviting them to subscribe cash for new shares in proportion to their existing holdings.

For example, a rights issue on a one for four basis at 280p per share would mean that a company is inviting its existing shareholders to subscribe for one new share for every four shares they hold, at a price of 280p per new share. A rights issue may be made by any type of company. The analysis below, however, applies primarily to listed companies.

The major advantages of a rights issue are as follows.

(a) Rights issues are **cheaper** than **offers for sale** to the general public. This is partly because **no prospectus** is not normally required, partly because the administration is simpler and partly because the cost of underwriting will be less.

(b) Rights issues are **more beneficial** to **existing shareholders** than issues to the general public. New shares are issued at a discount to the current market price, to make them attractive to investors. A rights issue **secures** the **discount** on the market price for existing shareholders, who may either keep the shares or sell them if they wish.

(c) **Relative voting** rights are **unaffected** if shareholders all take up their rights.

(d) The finance raised may be used to **reduce gearing** in book value terms by increasing share capital and/or to pay off long-term debt which will reduce gearing in market value terms.

3.1 Deciding the issue price for a rights issue

The **offer price** in a rights issue will be lower than the current market price of existing shares. This is a way of protecting against a fall in market price prior to a rights issue. The size of the discount will vary, and will be larger for difficult issues. The offer price must however be at or above the **nominal value** of the shares, so as not to contravene company law.

PART F SOURCES OF FINANCE

A company making a rights issue must set a price which is **low enough** to **secure** the **acceptance** of shareholders, who are being asked to provide extra funds, but not too low, so as to avoid excessive dilution of the earnings per share.

Exam focus point

A question could ask for discussion on the effect of a rights issue, as well as calculations, eg of the effect on EPS.

3.2 Example: Rights issue (1)

Seagull plc can achieve a profit after tax of 20% on the capital employed. At present its capital structure is as follows.

	£
200,000 ordinary shares of £1 each	200,000
Retained earnings	100,000
	300,000

The directors propose to raise an additional £126,000 from a rights issue. The current market price is £1.80.

Required

(a) Calculate the number of shares that must be issued if the rights price is:
£1.60; £1.50; £1.40; £1.20.

(b) Calculate the dilution in earnings per share in each case.

Solution

The earnings at present are 20% of £300,000 = £60,000. This gives earnings per share of 30p. The earnings after the rights issue will be 20% of £426,000 = £85,200.

Rights price £	No of new share (£126,000 ÷ rights price)	EPS (£85,200 ÷ total no of shares) Pence	Dilution Pence
1.60	78,750	30.6	+ 0.6
1.50	84,000	30.0	–
1.40	90,000	29.4	– 0.6
1.20	105,000	27.9	– 2.1

Note that at a high rights price the earnings per share are increased, not diluted. The breakeven point (zero dilution) occurs when the rights price is equal to the capital employed per share: £300,000 ÷ 200,000 = £1.50.

3.2.1 The market price of shares after a rights issue: the theoretical ex rights price

When a rights issue is announced, all existing shareholders have the right to subscribe for new shares, and so there are rights attached to the existing shares. The shares are therefore described as being **'cum rights'** (with rights attached) and are traded cum rights. On the first day of dealings in the newly issued shares, the rights no longer exist and the old shares are now **'ex rights'** (without rights attached).

After the announcement of a rights issue, share prices normally **fall**. The extent and duration of the fall may depend on the number of shareholders and the size of their holdings. This temporary fall is due to **uncertainty** in the market about the consequences of the issue, with respect to future profits, earnings and dividends.

After the issue has actually been made, the market price per share will normally fall, because there are more shares in issue and the new shares were issued at a discount price.

21: EQUITY FINANCING

In theory, the new market price will be the consequence of an adjustment to allow for the discount price of the new issue, and a theoretical ex rights price can be calculated.

Formula to learn

> **Theoretical ex-rights price** = $\frac{1}{N+1}((N \times \text{cum rights price}) + \text{issue price})$
>
> where N = number of shares required to buy one new share.

3.2.2 Example: Rights issue (2)

Fundraiser plc has 1,000,000 ordinary shares of £1 in issue, which have a market price on 1 September of £2.10 per share. The company decides to make a rights issue, and offers its shareholders the right to subscribe for one new share at £1.50 each for every four shares already held. After the announcement of the issue, the share price fell to £1.95, but by the time just prior to the issue being made, it had recovered to £2 per share. This market value just before the issue is known as the cum rights price. What is the theoretical ex rights price?

Solution

The theoretical ex rights price = $\frac{1}{4+1}((4 \times £2) + £1.50) = \frac{£9.50}{5}$ = £1.90

An alternative method, not using the formula, would be to say:

Value of the portfolio for a shareholder with 4 shares before the rights issue:

	£
4 shares @ £2.00	8.00
1 share @ £1.50	1.50
	9.50

so the value per share after the rights issue (or TERP) is 9.50/5 = £1.90.

3.2.3 The value of rights

The value of rights is the theoretical gain a shareholder would make by exercising his rights.

(a) Using the above example, if the price offered in the rights issue is £1.50 per share, and the market price after the issue is expected to be £1.90, the value attaching to a right is £1.90 − £1.50 = £0.40. A shareholder would therefore be expected to gain 40 pence for each new share he buys.

If he does not have enough money to buy the share himself, he could sell the right to subscribe for a new share to another investor, and receive 40 pence from the sale. This other investor would then buy the new share for £1.50, so that his total outlay to acquire the share would be £0.40 + £1.50 = £1.90, the theoretical ex rights price.

(b) The value of rights attaching to existing shares is calculated in the same way. If the value of rights on a new share is 40 pence, and there is a one for four rights issue, the value of the rights attaching to each existing share is 40 ÷ 4 = 10 pence.

3.2.4 The theoretical gain or loss to shareholders

The possible courses of action open to shareholders are:

(a) To **'take up' or 'exercise' the rights**, that is, to buy the new shares at the rights price. Shareholders who do this will maintain their percentage holdings in the company by subscribing for the new shares.

(b) To **'renounce' the rights** and sell them on the market. Shareholders who do this will have lower percentage holdings of the company's equity after the issue than before the issue, and the total value of their shares will be less.

(c) To **renounce part of the rights and take up the remainder**. For example, a shareholder may sell enough of his rights to enable him to buy the remaining rights shares he is entitled to with the sale proceeds, and so keep the total market value of his shareholding in the company unchanged.

(d) To **do nothing**. Shareholders may be protected from the consequences of their inaction because rights not taken up are sold on a shareholder's behalf by the company. The Stock Exchange rules state that if new securities are not taken up, they should be sold by the company to new subscribers for the benefit of the shareholders who were entitled to the rights.

Question — Rights issue

Gopher plc has issued 3,000,000 ordinary shares of £1 each, which are at present selling for £4 per share. The company plans to issue rights to purchase one new equity share at a price of £3.20 per share for every three shares held. A shareholder who owns 900 shares thinks that he will suffer a loss in his personal wealth because the new shares are being offered at a price lower than market value. On the assumption that the actual market value of shares will be equal to the theoretical ex rights price, what would be the effect on the shareholder's wealth if:

(a) He sells all the rights
(b) He exercises half of the rights and sells the other half
(c) He does nothing at all?

Answer

The theoretical ex rights price $= \dfrac{1}{3+1}((3 \times 4) + 3.20)$

$= £3.80$

Alternative solution

Value of the portfolio for a shareholder with 3 shares before the rights issue

	£
3 shares @ £4.00	12.00
1 share @ £3.20	3.20
4	15.20

so the value per share after the rights issue (or TERP) is 15.20/4 = 3.80.

	£
Theoretical ex rights price	3.80
Price per new share	3.20
Value of rights per new share	0.60

The value of the rights attached to each existing share is $\dfrac{£0.60}{3} = £0.20$.

We will assume that a shareholder is able to sell his rights for £0.20 per existing share held.

(a) If the shareholder sells all his rights:

	£
Sale value of rights (900 × £0.20)	180
Market value of his 900 shares, ex rights × £3.80)	3,420
Total wealth	3,600
Total value of 900 shares cum rights (× £4)	£3,600

The shareholder would neither gain nor lose wealth. He would not be required to provide any additional funds to the company, but his shareholding as a proportion of the total equity of the company will be lower.

(b) If the shareholder exercises half of the rights (buys 450/3 = 150 shares at £3.20) and sells the other half:

	£
Sale value of rights (450 × £0.20)	90
Market value of his 1,050 shares, ex rights (× £3.80)	3,990
	4,080
Total value of 900 shares cum rights (× £4)	3,600
Additional investment (150 × £3.20)	480
	4,080

The shareholder would neither gain nor lose wealth, although he will have increased his investment in the company by £480.

(c) If the shareholder does nothing, but all other shareholders either exercise their rights or sell them, he would lose wealth as follows.

	£
Market value of 900 shares cum rights (× £4)	3,600
Market value of 900 shares ex rights (× £3.80)	3,420
Loss in wealth	180

It follows that the shareholder, to protect his existing investment, should either exercise his rights or sell them to another investor. If he does not exercise his rights, the new securities he was entitled to subscribe for might be sold for his benefit by the company, and this would protect him from losing wealth.

3.3 The actual market price after a rights issue

The actual market price of a share after a rights issue may differ from the theoretical ex rights price. This will occur when:

3.4 Expected yield from new funds raised ≠ Earnings yield from existing funds

The market will take a view of how profitably the new funds will be invested, and will value the shares accordingly. An example will illustrate this point.

3.5 Example: Rights issue (3)

Musk plc currently has 4,000,000 ordinary shares in issue, valued at £2 each, and the company has annual earnings equal to 20% of the market value of the shares. A one for four rights issue is proposed, at an issue price of £1.50. If the market continues to value the shares on a price/earnings ratio of 5, what would be the value per share if the new funds are expected to earn, as a percentage of the money raised:

PART F SOURCES OF FINANCE

(a) 15%?
(b) 20%?
(c) 25%?

How do these values in (a), (b) and (c) compare with the theoretical ex rights price? Ignore issue costs.

Solution

The theoretical ex rights price will be calculated first.

	£
Four shares have a current value (× £2) of	8.00
One new share will be issued for	1.50
Five shares would have a theoretical value of	9.50

Theoretical ex rights price $= \dfrac{1}{4+1}((4 \times 2) + 1.50)$

$= £1.90$

The new funds will raise $1,000,000 \times £1.50 = £1,500,000$.

Earnings as a % of Money raised	Additional earnings £	Current earnings £	Total earnings after the issue £
15%	225,000	1,600,000	1,825,000
20%	300,000	1,600,000	1,900,000
25%	375,000	1,600,000	1,975,000

If the market values shares on a P/E ratio of 5, the total market value of equity and the market price per share would be as follows.

Total earnings £	Market value £	Price per share (5,000,000 shares) £
1,825,000	9,125,000	1.825
1,900,000	9,500,000	1.900
1,975,000	9,875,000	1.975

(a) If the additional funds raised are expected to generate earnings at the **same rate** as existing funds, the **actual market value** will probably be the **same** as the theoretical ex rights price.

(b) If the new funds are expected to generate earnings at a **lower rate**, the **market value** will **fall** below the theoretical ex rights price. If this happens, **shareholders** will **lose**.

(c) If the new funds are expected to earn at a **higher rate** than current funds, the **market value** should **rise** above the theoretical ex rights price. If this happens, shareholders will profit by taking up their rights.

The decision by individual shareholders as to whether they take up the offer will therefore depend on:

- The **expected rate of return** on the investment (and the risk associated with it)
- The **return obtainable from other investments** (allowing for the associated risk)

3.5.1 Rights issues or issuing shares for cash to new investors?

When shares are issued for cash to outside buyers, existing shareholders forfeit their **pre-emption rights** to shares. Companies can issue shares for cash without obtaining prior approval from shareholders for each such share issue, provided that they have obtained approval from shareholders within the past 12 months to make new issues of shares for cash which are not rights issues. (This shareholder approval could be obtained at the company's AGM.)

Companies can thus issue shares for cash without having to bear the high costs of a rights issue, for example by placing shares for cash at a higher price than they might have been able to obtain from a rights issue.

3.6 Vendor placings

A vendor placing occurs when there is an issue of shares by one company to take over another. The shares are then sold in a placing to raise cash to pay to the shareholders in the target company, who are selling their shares in the takeover.

3.7 Other instances of issuing shares

There are some other methods of issuing shares on the Stock Exchange. These are as follows.

(a) **Open offer**

This is an offer to existing shareholders to subscribe for new shares in the company but, unlike a rights issue:

(i) The offer is **not** necessarily **pro rata** to existing shareholdings

(ii) The offer is not allotted on **renounceable documents** (With rights issues the offer to subscribe for new shares must be given on a renounceable letter, so that the shareholder can sell his rights if he so wishes)

(b) **Capitalisation issue**

This is a **'scrip issue'** of shares which does not raise any new funds (see later in this chapter). It is made to 'capitalise' reserves of the company: in effect, to change some reserves into share capital. Shareholders receive new shares **pro rata** to their existing shareholdings.

(c) **Vendor consideration issue**

This is an issue of shares whereby one company acquires the shares of another in a takeover or merger. For example, if A plc wishes to take over B plc, A might make a 'paper' offer to B's shareholders, try to buy the shares of B by offering B's shareholders newly issued shares of A. This is now a common form of share issue, because mergers and takeovers are fairly frequent events.

(d) **Employee share option schemes**

These are schemes for awarding shares to employees. A company awards its employees share options, which are rights to subscribe for new shares at a later date at a **predetermined price** (commonly, the market price of the shares when the options are awarded, or the market price less a discount). When and if the options are eventually exercised, the employees will receive the newly issued shares at a price that ought by then to be below the market price.

4 Scrip dividends, scrip issues and stock splits

FAST FORWARD

> **Scrip dividend schemes** involve shareholders being issued with new shares in lieu of a cash dividend.
>
> **Bonus** or **scrip issues**, and **stock splits**, are ways of increasing the *number* of shares without raising any extra capital.

Scrip dividends, scrip issues and stock splits are not methods of raising new equity funds, but they

- Alter the share capital structure of a company
- Increase the issued share capital of the company (scrip dividends and scrip issues)

4.1 Scrip dividends

Key term

> A **scrip dividend** is a dividend payment which takes the form of new shares instead of cash.

Effectively, it converts profit and loss reserves into issued share capital. When the directors of a company would prefer to retain funds within the business but consider that they must pay at least a certain amount of dividend, they might offer equity shareholders the choice of a **cash dividend** or a **scrip dividend**. Each shareholder would decide separately which to take.

Recently **enhanced scrip dividends** have been offered by a number of companies. With enhanced scrip dividends, the value of the shares offered is much greater than the cash alternative, giving investors an incentive to choose the shares.

4.2 Scrip issues

Key term

> A **scrip issue** (or **bonus issue**) is an issue of new shares to existing shareholders, by converting equity reserves into issued share capital.

For example, if a company with issued share capital of 100,000 ordinary shares of £1 each made a one for five scrip issue, 20,000 new shares would be issued to existing shareholders, one new share for every five old shares held. Issued share capital would be increased by £20,000, and reserves (probably share premium account, if there is one) reduced by this amount.

By creating more shares in this way, a scrip issue does not raise new funds, but does have the advantage of making **shares cheaper** and therefore (perhaps) more easily marketable on the Stock Exchange.

4.3 Stock splits

The advantage of a scrip issue mentioned above is also the reason for a **stock split**. A stock split occurs where, for example, each ordinary share of £1 each is split into two shares of 50p each, thus creating cheaper shares with greater marketability. Investors also normally should expect a company which splits its shares in this way to be planning for substantial earnings growth and dividend growth in the future. As a consequence, the market price of shares may benefit.

The difference between a stock split and a scrip issue is that a scrip issue converts equity reserves into share capital, whereas a stock split leaves reserves unaffected.

5 Preference shares

FAST FORWARD

Preference shares carry priority over ordinary equity shares with regard to dividend payments. They do not carry voting rights. They may be attractive to corporate investors, as (unlike interest receipts) dividends received are not subject to corporation tax. However, for the issuing company, dividend payments (unlike interest payments) are not tax-deductible.

Key term

Preference shares are shares which have a fixed percentage dividend, payable in priority to any dividend paid to the ordinary shareholders.

As with ordinary shares a preference dividend can only be paid if **sufficient distributable profits are available**, although with **cumulative preference shares** the right to an unpaid dividend is carried forward to later years. The arrears of dividend on cumulative preference shares must be paid before any dividend is paid to the ordinary shareholders. The stated dividend (such as 7%) on preference shares is the cash dividend, not grossed up.

5.1 Why issue preference shares?

From the company's point of view, preference shares have some positive features.

(a) **Dividends** do **not** have to be **paid** in a year in which **profits** are **poor**, while this is not the case with interest payments on long-term debt (loans or debentures).

(b) Since they do not normally carry voting rights, preference shares **avoid diluting** the **control** of existing shareholders while an issue of equity shares would not.

(c) Unless they are redeemable, issuing preference shares will **lower** the company's **gearing**. Redeemable preference shares are normally treated as debt when gearing is calculated.

(d) The issue of preference shares does **not restrict** the company's **borrowing power**, at least in the sense that preference share capital is not secured against assets of the business.

(e) The non-payment of dividend does not give the preference shareholders the right to appoint a receiver, a right which is normally given to debenture holders.

However, **dividend payments on preference shares are not tax deductible** in the way that interest payments on debt are. Furthermore, for preference shares to be attractive to investors, the level of payment needs to be higher than for interest on debt to compensate for the additional risks.

From the point of view of the investor, preference shares are less attractive than loan stock.

(a) They **cannot be secured** on the company's assets.

(b) The **dividend yield traditionally** offered on preference dividends has been **much too low** to provide an attractive investment compared with the interest yields on loan stock in view of the additional risk involved.

In recent years preference shares have formed a very small proportion only of new capital issues.

PART F SOURCES OF FINANCE

6 Stock market ratios
6/04, 12/04, 6/05

FAST FORWARD

Indicators such as **dividend yield**, **EPS**, **PE ratio** and **dividend cover** can be used to assess investor returns.

A company will only be able to raise finance if investors think that the returns they can expect are satisfactory in view of the risks they are taking. We must therefore consider how investors appraise companies. We will concentrate on quoted companies.

Information that is relevant to market prices and returns is available from published stock market information, and in particular from certain **stock market ratios**.

6.1 The dividend yield

Key term

$$\text{Dividend yield} = \frac{\text{Gross dividend per share}}{\text{Market price per share}} \times 100\%$$

The gross dividend is the dividend paid plus the appropriate tax credit. The gross dividend yield is used in preference to a net dividend yield, so that investors can make a direct comparison with (gross) interest yields from loan stock and gilts.

6.2 Example: Dividend yield

A company pays a dividend of 15p (net) per share. The market price is 240p. What is the dividend yield if the rate of tax credit is 10%?

$$\text{Gross dividend per share} = 15p \times \frac{100}{(100-10)} = 16.67p$$

$$\text{Dividend yield} = \frac{16.67p}{240p} = 6.95\%$$

6.3 Interest yield

Key term

$$\text{Interest yield} = \frac{\text{Gross interest}}{\text{Market value of loan stock}} \times 100\%$$

6.4 Example: Interest yield

An investment buys £1,000 (nominal value) of a bond with a coupon of 8% for the current market value of £750.

$$\text{Interest yield} = \frac{1,000 \times 8\%}{750} \times 100\% = 10.67\%$$

Exam focus point

The interest yield, which is the investor's rate of return, is different from the coupon rate of 8%. Many students confuse these in their exam answers.

6.5 Dividend yield and interest yield

In practice, the dividend yield on shares of quoted companies is less than the interest yield on debentures and loan stock. The share price often rises each year, giving shareholders capital gains. In the long run, shareholders will want the **return** on their **shares**, in terms of dividends received plus capital gains, to **exceed** the **return** that investors get from **fixed interest securities**.

6.6 Earnings per share (EPS)

Key term

> **Earnings per share** is calculated by dividing the net profit or loss attributable to ordinary shareholders (the numerator) with the weighted average number of ordinary shares outstanding (the denominator) during the period. For the purpose of calculating basic earnings per share, the amounts attributable to ordinary equity holders should be the net profit or loss for the period after deducting dividends and other appropriations in respect of non-equity shares. (Summarised from *Financial Reporting Standard 22*)

Earnings per share (EPS) is widely used as a measure of a company's performance and is of particular importance in comparing results over a period of several years. A company must be able to sustain its earnings in order to pay dividends and re-invest in the business so as to achieve future growth. Investors also look for **growth** in the EPS from one year to the next.

EPS on its own does not tell us anything. It must be seen in the context of several other matters.

(a) EPS is used for **comparing results** of a company over time. Is its EPS growing? What is the rate of growth? Is the rate of growth increasing or decreasing?

(b) Is there likely to be a **significant dilution** of EPS in the future, perhaps due to the exercise of share options or warrants, or the conversion of convertible loan stock into equity?

(c) EPS should **not** be **used blindly** to compare the earnings of one company with another. For example, if A plc has an EPS of 12p for its 10,000,000 10p shares and B plc has an EPS of 24p for its 50,000,000 25p shares, we must take account of the numbers of shares. When earnings are used to compare one company's shares with another, this is done using the P/E ratio or perhaps the earnings yield.

(d) If EPS is to be a reliable basis for comparing results, it must be **calculated consistently**.

Question — Earnings per share

Walter Wall Carpets plc made profits before tax in 20X8 of £9,320,000. Tax amounted to £2,800,000. The company's share capital is as follows.

	£
Ordinary shares (10,000,000 shares of £1)	10,000,000
8% preference shares	2,000,000
	12,000,000

Calculate the EPS for 20X8.

Answer

	£
Profits before tax	9,320,000
Less tax	2,800,000
Profits after tax	6,520,000
Less preference dividend (8% of £2,000,000)	160,000
Earnings	6,360,000
Number of ordinary shares	10,000,000
EPS	63.6p

Note that:

(a) EPS is a figure based on **past data**, and
(b) It is **easily manipulated** by changes in accounting policies and by mergers or acquisitions

The use of the measure in calculating management bonuses makes it particularly liable to manipulation. The attention given to EPS as a performance measure by City analysts is arguably disproportionate to its true worth. Investors should be more concerned with future earnings, but of course estimates of these are more difficult to reach than the readily available figure.

A **fully diluted EPS** (FDEPS) can be measured where the company has issued securities that might be converted into ordinary shares at some future date, such as convertible loan stock, share warrants or share options.

Key term

> The **fully diluted earnings per share** measures a hypothetical EPS, based on earnings in the period under review, if the company's ordinary shares were increased to their maximum number by the exercise of all existing share options and warrants, and the conversion of existing convertible loan stock etc. The FDEPS gives investors an appreciation of by how much EPS might be affected if and when the options, warrants or conversion rights are exercised.

Total earnings are increased by:

(a) The **savings in interest** (net of tax) from the conversion of loan stock into shares

(b) In the case of share options or warrants, the **addition to profits** (net of tax) from investing the cash obtained from their exercise (estimated on the assumption that the cash is invested in $2\frac{1}{2}\%$ Consolidated Stock at their market price on the first) day of the period)

6.7 Example: Fully diluted earning per share

Suppose that Walter Wall Carpets plc (see Question 2 above) has in issue £4,000,000 8% convertible unsecured loan stock, convertible in three years' time, with a conversion ratio of 5 shares per £100 of loan stock. The company pays tax at 30%. What is the fully diluted EPS?

Solution

Undiluted EPS is 63.6 pence, as shown in Question 2.

If all holders of the convertible stock convert their holding to ordinary shares, an additional 200,000 (= 4,000,000/100 × 5) shares will be issued in three years' time.

The interest saving on conversion is:

£4,000,000 × 8% × 0.70 = £224,000.

Therefore:

$$\text{FDEPS} = \frac{6,360,000 + 224,000}{10,000,000 + 200,000} = \frac{6,584,000}{10,200,000} = 64.5 \text{ pence}$$

6.8 The price earnings ratio

Key term

> Price earnings ratio = $\dfrac{\text{Market price of share in pence}}{\text{EPS in pence}}$

The **price earnings (P/E) ratio** is the most important yardstick for assessing the relative worth of a share.

This is the same as:

$$\frac{\text{Total market value of equity}}{\text{Total earnings}}$$

The **value of the P/E ratio** reflects the **market's appraisal** of the share's **future prospects**. It is an important ratio because it relates two key considerations for investors, the market price of a share and its earnings capacity.

6.9 Example: Price earnings ratio

A company has recently declared a dividend of 12p per share. The share price is £3.72 cum div and earnings for the most recent year were 30p per share. Calculate the P/E ratio.

Solution

$$\text{P/E ratio} = \frac{\text{MV ex div}}{\text{EPS}} = \frac{£3.60}{30p} = 12$$

6.10 Changes in EPS: the P/E ratio and the share price

The **dividend valuation** model or fundamental theory of share values is the theory that **share prices** are **related** to **expected future dividends** on the shares.

Another approach to assessing what share prices ought to be, which is often used in practice, is a P/E ratio approach.

(a) The relationship between the **EPS** and the **share price** is measured by the **P/E ratio**

(b) The **P/E ratio** does **not vary much** over time

(c) So if the **EPS goes up** or **down**, the **share price** should be expected to **move up or down** too, and the new share price will be the new EPS multiplied by the constant P/E ratio

For example, if a company had an EPS last year of 30p and a share price of £3.60, its P/E ratio would have been 12. If the current year's EPS is 33p, we might expect that the P/E ratio would remain the same, 12, and so the share price ought to go up to 12 × 33p = £3.96.

6.11 Example: Effects of a rights issue

Annette Cord Sports Goods plc has 6,000,000 ordinary shares in issue, and the company has been making regular annual profits after tax of £3,000,000 for some years. The share price is £5. A proposal has been made to issue 2,000,000 new shares in a rights issue, at an issue price of £4.50 per share. The funds would be used to redeem £9,000,000 of 12% debenture stock. The rate of corporation tax is 30%.

What would be the predicted effect of the rights issue on the share price, and would you recommend that the issue should take place?

Solution

If the stock market shows semi-strong form efficiency, the share price will change on announcement of the rights issue, in anticipation of the change in EPS. The current EPS is 50p per share, and so the current P/E ratio is 10.

	£	£
Current annual earnings		3,000,000
Increase in earnings after rights issue		
Interest saved (12% × £9,000,000)	1,080,000	
Less tax on extra profits (30%)	324,000	
		756,000
Anticipated annual earnings		3,756,000

PART F   SOURCES OF FINANCE

Number of shares (6,000,000 + 2,000,000)	8,000,000
EPS	46.95 pence
Current P/E ratio	10

The anticipated P/E ratio is assumed to be the same.

Anticipated share price   469.5 pence

The proposed share issue is a one for three rights issue, and we can estimate the theoretical ex rights price.

Theoretical ex rights price $= \dfrac{1}{3+1}((3 \times 5) + 4.50) = £4.875$

The anticipated share price after redeeming the debentures would be 469.5 pence per share, which is less than the theoretical ex rights price. If the rights issue goes ahead and the P/E ratio remains at 10, shareholders should expect a fall in share price below the theoretical ex rights price, which indicates that there would be a **capital loss** on their investment. The rights issue is for this reason not recommended.

6.11.1 Changes in the P/E ratio over time

Changes in the P/E ratios of companies over time will depend on several factors.

(a) If **interest rates go up**, investors will be attracted away from shares and into debt capital. Share prices will fall, and so P/E ratios will fall. Similarly, if interest rates go down, shares will become relatively more attractive to invest in, so share prices and P/E ratios will go up.

(b) If **prospects** for company **profits improve**, share prices will go up, and P/E ratios will rise.

(c) **Investors' confidence** might be **changed by** a variety of circumstances, such as:
- The prospect of a change in government
- The prospects for greater exchange rate stability between currencies

6.12 Dividend cover

Key term

> **Dividend cover** $= \dfrac{\text{Maximum possible equity dividend that could be paid out of current profits}}{\text{Actual dividend for ordinary shareholders}}$

The **dividend cover** is the number of times the actual dividend could be paid out of current profits.

The figures for the maximum dividend and the actual dividend may be either **both gross** or **both net**.

The dividend cover indicates the **proportion** of **distributable profits** for the year that is being **retained** by the company, and the level of risk that the company will not be able to maintain the same dividend payments in future years, should earnings fall. A high dividend cover means that a high proportion of profits are being retained, which might indicate that the company is investing to achieve earnings growth in the future.

6.13 Dividend payout ratio

Key term

> **Dividend payout ratio** $= \dfrac{\text{Dividends for the year} \times 100\%}{\text{Profits after interest and taxation}} = \dfrac{\text{Dividends per share} \times 100\%}{\text{Earnings per share}}$

The **dividend payout ratio** is closely related to the dividend cover, as it calculates the percentage of post-tax earnings that are distributed as dividends.

6.14 Example: Dividend cover and dividend payout ratio

The EPS of York plc is 20p. The dividend was 20% on the 25p ordinary shares. Calculate the dividend cover and the dividend payout ratio.

Solution

Dividend cover = $\dfrac{20p}{20\% \text{ of } 25p} = 4$

A dividend cover of 4 means that the company is retaining 75% of its earnings for reinvestment.

Dividend payout ratio = $\dfrac{20\% \text{ of } 25p}{20p} \times 100\% = 25\%$

7 Dividend policy

FAST FORWARD

Practical considerations of **dividend policy** suggest that both **dividends** and **earnings** may be important in determining share price.

For any company, the amount of earnings retained within the business has a direct impact on the amount of dividends. Profit re-invested as retained earnings is profit that could have been paid as a **dividend**. The major **reasons for using funds from retained earnings** to finance new investments, rather than to pay higher dividends and then raise new equity funds for the new investments, are as follows.

(a) The use of **retained earnings** as a **source of funds** does **not lead** to a **payment** of cash to new providers of finance.

(b) The dividend policy of a company is in practice determined by the directors. From their standpoint, retained earnings are an attractive source of finance because **investment projects** can be undertaken **without involving** either the **shareholders** or any **outsiders**.

(c) The use of retained earnings as opposed to new shares or debentures **avoids issue** costs.

(d) The use of retained earnings **avoids** the possibility of a **change in control** resulting from an issue of new shares.

Another factor that may be of importance is the **financial and taxation position** of the company's shareholders. If, for example, because of taxation considerations, they would rather make a capital profit (which will only be taxed when the shares are sold) than receive current income, then finance through retained earnings would be preferred to other methods.

A company must restrict its self-financing through retained profits because shareholders should be paid a **reasonable dividend**, in line with realistic expectations, even if the directors would rather keep the funds for re-investing. At the same time, a company that is looking for extra funds will not be expected by investors (such as banks) to pay generous dividends, nor over-generous salaries to owner-directors.

7.1 Signalling effects

The signalling effect of a company's dividend policy may be used by the management of a company which faces a possible takeover. The dividend level might be increased as a defence against the takeover; investors may take the increased dividend as a signal of improved future prospects, thus **driving** the **share price higher** and making the company more expensive for a potential bidder to take over.

Investors usually expect a **consistent dividend policy** from the company, with stable dividends each year or, even better, steady dividend growth. Stable dividends or steady dividend growth are usually needed for share price stability. A cut in dividends may be treated by investors as signalling that the future prospects of the company are weak.

7.2 Dividends and market values

What affects the market value of a company's shares? It seems reasonable to suppose that share values will depend upon:

- The **amount in dividends** that a **company pays**
- The **rate of growth** of **dividends**
- The **rate of return** which shareholders require

The purpose of a company's dividend policy should be to **maximise shareholders' wealth**, which depends on both current dividends and capital gains. Capital gains can be achieved by retaining some earnings for reinvestment and dividend growth in the future.

The **rate of growth in dividends** is sometimes expressed, theoretically, as:

$$g = bR$$

where g   is the annual growth rate in dividends
       b   is the proportion of profits that are retained
       R   is the rate of return on new investments

7.3 Example: Dividend growth

(a) If a company has a payout ratio of 40%, and retains the rest for investing in projects which yield 15%, the annual rate of growth in dividends could be estimated as 15% × 60% = 9%.

(b) If a company pays out 80% of its profits as dividends, and retains the rest for reinvestment at 15%, the current dividend would be twice as big as in (a), but annual dividend growth would be only 15% × 20% = 3%.

7.4 An approach to dividend and retentions policy

FAST FORWARD

> The **dividend valuation model** can be applied with or without dividend growth. The model assumes that a stock market value depends upon the future flow of dividends which can be expected.

A well established theory of share values is that an equilibrium price for any share (or bond) on a stock market is:

- The **future expected stream of income** from the security
- **Discounted** at a suitable **cost of capital**

Equilibrium market price is thus a **present value** of a **future expected income stream**. The annual income stream for a share is the expected dividend every year in perpetuity.

The basic dividend-based formula for the market value of shares is expressed in the **dividend valuation model** as follows:

$$\text{MV (ex div)} = \frac{D}{1+r} + \frac{D}{(1+r)^2} + \frac{D}{(1+r)^3} + \ldots = \frac{D}{r}$$

where   MV = ex dividend market value of the shares
        D   = constant annual dividend
        r   = shareholders' required rate of return

Using the **dividend growth model**, we have:

$$P_0 = \frac{D_0(1+g)}{(1+r)} + \frac{D_0(1+g)^2}{(1+r)} + \ldots = \frac{D_0(1+g)}{(r-g)}$$

where D_0 = Current year's dividend
       g = Growth rate in earnings and dividends
       $D_0(1+g)$ = Expected dividend in one year's time
       P_0 = Market value excluding any dividend currently payable

7.5 Example: Dividend growth model

Tantrum plc has achieved earnings of £800,000 this year. The company intends to pursue a policy of financing all its investment opportunities out of retained earnings. There are considerable investment opportunities, which are expected to be available indefinitely. However, if Tantrum plc does not exploit any of the available opportunities, its annual earnings will remain at £800,000 in perpetuity. The following figures are available.

Proportion of earnings retained %	Growth rate in Earnings %	Required return on all investments by shareholders %
0	0	14
25	5	15
40	7	16

The rate of return required by shareholders would rise if earnings are retained, because of the risk associated with the new investments. What is the optimum retentions policy for Tantrum plc? The full dividend payment for this year will be paid in the near future in any case.

Solution

Since P_0 (MV ex div) = $\dfrac{D(1+g)}{(r-g)}$

MV cum div = $\dfrac{D(1+g)}{(r-g)} + D$

We are trying to maximise the value of shareholder wealth, which is currently represented by the cum div market value, since a dividend will soon be paid.

(a) If retentions are 0%

   MV cum div = $\dfrac{800{,}000}{0.14} + 800{,}000 = £6{,}514{,}286$

(b) If retentions are 25%, the current dividend will be £600,000 and:

   MV cum div = $\dfrac{600{,}000(1.05)}{(0.15-0.05)} + 600{,}000 = £6{,}900{,}000$

(c) If retentions are 40%, the current dividend will be £480,000 and:

   MV cum div = $\dfrac{480{,}000(1.07)}{(0.16-0.07)} + 480{,}000 = £6{,}186{,}667$

The best policy (out of the three for which figures are provided) would be to retain 25% of earnings.

7.6 Assumption of dividend models

(a) Investors act **rationally**.

(b) The **estimates** of future dividends and prices used are **reasonable**.

(c) Investors' attitudes to receiving different cash flows at different times can be modelled using **discounted cashflow arithmetic**.

(d) Directors use dividends to **signal** the strength of the company's position (however companies that pay zero dividends do not have zero share values).

(e) Dividends either show **no growth** or **constant growth**.

(f) **Other influences** on share prices are **ignored**.

(g) The company's **earnings** will **increase** sufficiently to maintain dividend growth levels.

(h) The **discount rate** used **exceeds** the **dividend growth rate.**

7.7 Dividend policy and shareholders' personal taxation

Presumably, a company should choose between **dividend payout** and **earnings retention** so as to maximise the wealth of its shareholders. However, if not all shareholders have the same tax rates and after tax cost of capital, there might **not** be an **optimum policy** which satisfies all shareholders.

A further problem occurs when **income from dividends** might be **taxed** either **more or less** heavily than **capital gains**. In the UK, individuals have an annual capital gains exemption which is not available against income, and companies are taxed on capital gains but not on dividend income.

7.8 Practical aspects of dividend policy

So far, we have concentrated on a theoretical approach to establishing an optimal dividend and retentions policy. A practical approach to dividends and retentions should take the following extra factors into consideration.

(a) The need to **remain profitable**. Dividends are paid out of profits, and an unprofitable company cannot for ever go on paying dividends out of retained profits made in the past.

(b) The **law on distributable** profits imposes restrictions.

(c) **Dividend restraints** might be imposed by loan agreements.

(d) The effect of inflation, and the need to retain some profit within the business just to maintain its operating capability unchanged.

(e) The company's **gearing level**. If the company wants extra finance, the sources of funds used should strike a balance between equity and debt finance. Cash from retained earnings is the most readily available source of growth in equity finance.

(f) The company's **liquidity position**. Dividends are a cash payment, and a company must have enough cash to pay the dividends it declares.

(g) Investors usually expect a **consistent dividend policy** from the company, with stable dividends each year or, even better, steady dividend growth.

(h) A large rise or fall in dividends in any year will have a marked effect on the **company's share price**. Stable dividends or steady dividend growth are usually needed for share price stability.

(i) The ease with which the company **could raise extra finance** from sources other than cash from retained earnings. Small companies which find it hard to raise finance might have to rely more heavily on cash generated from retained earnings than large companies.

(j) If a company wants extra finance to invest, cash might be generated through **retention of earnings** can be obtained without incurring transaction costs. Costs of raising new share capital can be high, and even bank borrowings can be quite expensive.

In practical terms, it is unclear how far dividends play a predominant role in determining share values. At some times, dividends seem to be more important to the market, while at other times, earning figures seem to become predominant.

Question — Dividend policy

Ochre plc is a company that is still managed by the two individuals who set it up 12 years ago. In the current year, the company acquired plc status and was launched on the Alternative Investment Market (AIM). Previously, all of the shares had been owned by its two founders and certain employees. Now, 40% of the shares are in the hands of the investing public. The company's profit growth and dividend policy are set out below. Will a continuation of the same dividend policy as in the past be suitable now that the company is quoted on the AIM?

	Profits £'000	Dividend £'000	Shares in issue
4 years ago	176	88	800,000
3 years ago	200	104	800,000
2 years ago	240	120	1,000,000
1 year ago	290	150	1,000,000
Current year	444	222 (proposed)	1,500,000

Answer

	Dividend per share p	Dividend as % of profit
4 years ago	11.0	50%
3 years ago	13.0	52%
2 years ago	12.0	50%
1 year ago	15.0	52%
Current year	14.8	50%

The company appears to have pursued a dividend policy of paying out half of after-tax profits in dividend.

This policy is only suitable when a company achieves a stable EPS or steady EPS growth. Investors do not like a fall in dividend from one year to the next, and the fall in dividend per share in the current year is likely to be unpopular, and to result in a fall in the share price.

The company would probably serve its shareholders better by paying a dividend of at least 15p per share, possibly more, in the current year, even though the dividend as a percentage of profit would then be higher.

Exam focus point

Take care not to write in the exam that new investment can be financed by reserves or retained earnings. It is the **cash generated** from retention of earnings which can be used for financing purposes.

PART F   SOURCES OF FINANCE

Chapter Roundup

- Equity finance is raised by a **new issue** of equity shares or a **rights issue**. Cash generated by the use of **retained earnings** is another source of equity funds.

- A company can obtain a **stock market listing** for its shares through an offer for sale, a prospectus issue, a placing or an introduction.

- A **rights issue** is an offer to existing shareholders for them to buy more shares, usually at lower than the current share price.

- **Scrip dividend schemes** involve shareholders being issued with new shares in lieu of a cash dividend.

- **Bonus** or **scrip issues**, and **stock splits**, are ways of increasing the *number* of shares without raising any extra capital.

- **Preference shares** carry priority over ordinary equity shares with regard to dividend payments. They do not carry voting rights. They may be attractive to corporate investors, as (unlike interest receipts) dividends received are not subject to corporation tax. However, for the issuing company, dividend payments (unlike interest payments) are not tax-deductible.

- Indicators such as **dividend yield**, **EPS**, **PE ratio** and **dividend cover** can be used to assess investor returns.

- The **dividend valuation model** can be applied with or without dividend growth. The model assumes that a stock market value depends upon the future flow of dividends which can be expected.

- Practical considerations of **dividend policy** suggest that both **dividends** and **earnings** may be important in determining share price.

Quick Quiz

1   Identify four reasons why a company may seek a stock market listing.

2   A company's shares have a nominal value of £1 and a market value of £3. In a rights issue, one new share would be issued for every three shares at a price of £2.60. What is the theoretical ex-rights price?

3   A company offers to pay a dividend in the form of new shares which are worth more than the cash alternative which is also offered. What is this dividend in the form of shares called?

4   Match A/B to (i)/(ii), to express the difference between a stock split and a scrip issue.

    A   A scrip issue ....   (i)   .... converts equity reserves into share capital
    B   A stock split ....   (ii)   .... leaves reserves unaffected

5   Which of the following sources of finance to companies is the most widely used in practice?

    A   Bank borrowings
    B   Rights issues
    C   New share issues
    D   Retained earnings

6   Which of the following is least likely to be a reason for seeking a stock market flotation?

    A   Improving the existing owners' control over the business
    B   Access to a wider pool of finance
    C   Enhancement of the company's image
    D   Transfer of capital to other uses

7   A scrip dividend is

    A   A dividend paid at a fixed percentage rate on the nominal value of the shares

    B   A dividend paid at a fixed percentage rate on the market value of the shares on the date that the dividend is declared

    C   A dividend payment that takes the form of new shares instead of cash

    D   An issue of new shares to existing shareholders by converting equity reserves into issued share capital

8   Which of the following is not true of a rights issue by a listed company?

    A   Rights issues do not require a prospectus
    B   The rights issues price can be at a discount to market price
    C   If shareholders do not take up the rights, the rights lapse
    D   Relative voting rights are unaffected if shareholders exercise their rights

Answers to Quick Quiz

1   **Four** of the following **five**: access to a wider pool of finance; improved marketability of shares; transfer of capital to other uses (eg founder members liquidating holdings); enhancement of company image; making growth by acquisition possible.

2   $\frac{1}{3+1}$ ((£3 × 3) + £2.60) = £2.90.

3   An enhanced scrip dividend.

4   A(i); B(ii).

5   D   Retained earnings

6   A   Flotation is likely to involve a significant loss of control to a wider circle of investors.

7   C   A would most commonly be a preference dividend. D is a definition of a scrip issue, not a scrip dividend.

8   C   Shareholders have the option of renouncing the rights and selling them on the market.

Now try the questions below from the Exam Question Bank			
Number	**Level**	**Marks**	**Time**
Q24	Examination	25	45 mins

Debt financing

Topic list	Syllabus reference
1 Sources of debt finance	4
2 Loan stock	4
3 Convertibles and warrants	4

Introduction

In this chapter, we continue with the coverage of the sources of long-term finance begun in Chapter 21, looking at long-term debt finance including **loan stock, convertibles** and **warrants**.

When sources of **long-term finance** are used, large sums are usually involved, and so the financial manager needs to consider all the options available with care, looking to the possible effects on the company in the long term.

Study guide

Section 10 – Sources of finance III: Debt and near-debt financing

- Explain the features of different types of long-term straight debt and the reasons for their issue
- Explain the features of convertible debt and warrants and the reasons for their issue
- Broadly describe the reasons for the choice of financing between preference shares, debt and near-debt instruments in terms of the risk/return trade-off
- Assess the effect on EPS of conversion and option rights
- Broadly describe international debt markets and the financing of foreign trade
- Calculate and interpret appropriate ratios

Exam guide

As with equity financing, you should be able to discuss when a company should seek debt finance.

The distinction between equity and debt finance is important, but surprisingly students often confuse the two in the exam.

1 Sources of debt finance
12/03, 6/04

FAST FORWARD

The choice of debt finance that a company can make depends upon:

- The size of the business (a public issue of loan stock is only available to a large company)
- The duration of the loan
- Whether a fixed or floating interest rate is preferred (fixed rates are more expensive, but floating rates are riskier)
- The security that can be offered

1.1 Reasons for seeking debt finance

Sometimes businesses may need long-term funds, but may not wish to issue equity capital. Perhaps the current shareholders will be unwilling to **contribute additional capital**; possibly the company does not wish to involve outside shareholders who will have more onerous requirements than current members.

Other reasons for choosing debt finance may include **lesser cost** and **easier availability**, particularly if the company has little or no existing debt finance.

1.2 Sources of debt finance

If a company does wish to raise debt finance, it will need to consider what **type** of finance will be available. If it is seeking medium-term bank finance, it ought to be in the form of a **loan**, although an overdraft is a virtually permanent feature of many companies' balance sheets. Bank finance is a most important source of debt for small companies, and we shall consider it in greater detail in Chapter 24. **Leasing arrangements**, which we shall consider in Chapter 30, are also an alternative, particularly for smaller companies once again.

If a company is seeking to issue loan stock, it must decide whether the loan stock will be **repaid (redeemed)**, whether there will be **conversion rights** into shares, and whether **warrants** will be attached.

1.3 Factors influencing choice of debt finance

In Chapter 23, we shall look in detail at the factors that determine the mix of debt and equity finance that a company chooses. For now, you need to bear in mind when reading this chapter the following considerations influencing what type of debt finance is sought.

(a) **Availability**

Only listed companies will be able to make a public issue of loan stock on a stock exchange; smaller companies may only be able to obtain significant amounts of debt finance from their bank.

(b) **Duration**

If loan finance is sought to buy a particular asset to generate revenues for the business, the length of the loan should **match** the length of time that the asset will be generating revenues.

(c) **Fixed or floating rate**

Expectations of interest rate movements will determine whether a company chooses to borrow at a fixed or floating rate. Fixed rate finance may be more expensive, but the business runs the risk of adverse upward rate movements if it chooses floating rate finance.

(d) **Security and covenants**

The choice of finance may be determined by the assets that the business is willing or able to offer as **security**, also on the restrictions in **covenants** that the lenders wish to impose.

2 Loan stock   6/03, 6/05

> **FAST FORWARD**
>
> The term **bonds** describes various forms of long-term debt a company may issue, such as **loan stock** or **debentures**, which may be:
>
> - **Redeemable**
> - **Irredeemable**
>
> Bonds or loans come in various forms, including:
>
> - **Floating rate debentures**
> - **Zero coupon bonds**
> - **Convertible loan stock**

Key term

> **Loan stock** is long-term debt capital raised by a company for which interest is paid, usually half yearly and at a fixed rate. Holders of loan stock are therefore long-term creditors of the company.

Exam focus point

> The examiner has asked relatively straightforward questions on the applicability of loan stock when raising finance.

Loan stock has a nominal value, which is the debt owed by the company, and interest is paid at a stated **'coupon'** on this amount. For example, if a company issues 10% loan stock, the coupon will be 10% of the nominal value of the stock, so that £100 of stock will receive £10 interest each year. The rate quoted is the gross rate, before tax.

Unlike shares, debt is often issued **at par**, ie with £100 payable per £100 nominal value. Where the coupon rate is fixed at the time of issue, it will be set according to **prevailing market conditions** given the **credit**

PART F   SOURCES OF FINANCE

rating of the company issuing the debt. Subsequent changes in market (and company) conditions will cause the **market value** of the bond to fluctuate, although the coupon will stay at the fixed percentage of the nominal value.

> **Key term**
>
> **Debentures** are a form of loan stock, the written acknowledgement of a debt incurred by a company, normally containing provisions about the payment of interest and the eventual repayment of capital.

A **debenture trust deed** would empower a trustee (such as an insurance company or a bank) to intervene on behalf of debenture holders if the conditions of borrowing under which the debentures were issued are not being fulfilled. This might involve:

(a) **Failure to pay interest** on the due dates

(b) An attempt by the company to **sell off important assets** contrary to the terms of the loan

(c) A company taking out **additional loans** and thereby exceeding previously agreed borrowing limits established either by the articles or by the terms of the debenture trust deed

2.0.1 Advantages of debentures over preference shares

(a) Debentures are a **cheaper form of finance** than preference shares because, unlike preference shares, debenture interest is tax-deductible.

(b) Debentures should be **more attractive** to investors because they will be **secured** on the assets of the company.

(c) Debentureholders **rank above preference shareholders** in the event of a liquidation.

(d) **Issue costs** should be **lower** for debentures than for preference shares.

2.1 Debentures with a floating rate of interest

With these, the issuer can charge the **coupon rate of interest**, in accordance with changes in **market rates of interest**. They may be attractive to both lenders and borrowers when interest rates are volatile, and preferable to fixed interest loan stock or debentures.

For example, suppose that a company issues 6% fixed rate debentures at par when the market rate of interest is 6%. If interest rates suddenly rise to 12%, the market value of the debentures would fall by half to £50 per cent (£100 nominal value). However, if the debentures had carried a floating rate of interest, the interest rate would have been raised to 12% and the debentures would have retained their market value at par (£100 per cent).

2.2 Deep discount bonds

> **Key term**
>
> **Deep discount bonds** are loan stock issued at a price which is at a large discount to the nominal value of the stock, and which will be redeemable at par (or above par) when they eventually mature.

For example a company might issue £1,000,000 of loan stock in 20X1, at a price of £50 per £100 of stock, and redeemable at par in the year 20X9. For a company with specific cash flow requirements, the low servicing costs during the currency of the bond may be an attraction, coupled with a high cost of redemption at maturity.

Investors might be attracted by the **large capital gain** offered by the bonds, which is the difference between the **issue price** and the **redemption value**. However, deep discount bonds will carry a much **lower rate of interest** than other types of loan stock. The only tax advantage is that the gain gets taxed (as **income**) in one lump on maturity or sale, not as amounts of interest each year. The borrower can, however, **deduct notional interest** each year in computing profits.

2.3 Zero coupon bonds

Key term

> **Zero coupon bonds** are bonds that are issued at a discount to their redemption value, but no interest is paid on them.

The investor gains from the difference between the issue price and the redemption value. There is an implied interest rate in the amount of discount at which the bonds are issued (or subsequently re-sold on the market).

(a) The advantage for borrowers is that zero coupon bonds can be used to **raise cash immediately**, and there is **no cash repayment** until redemption date. The cost of redemption is known at the time of issue. The borrower can plan to have funds available to redeem the bonds at maturity.

(b) The **advantage for lenders** is **restricted**, unless the rate of discount on the bonds offers a high yield. The only way of obtaining cash from the bonds before maturity is to sell them. Their **market value** will depend on the **remaining term** to maturity and **current market interest rates**.

The tax advantage of zero coupon bonds is the same as that for deep discount bonds (see 2.2 above).

2.4 Security

Loan stock and debentures will often be secured. **Security** may take the form of either a **fixed charge** or a **floating charge**.

Fixed charge	Floating charge
Security relates to specific asset/group of assets (land and buildings)	Security in event of default is whatever assets of the class secured (stock/debtors) company then owns
Company can't dispose of assets without providing substitute/consent of lender	Company can dispose of assets until default takes place
	In event of default lenders appoint receiver rather than lay claim to asset

Not all loan stock is secured. Investors are likely to expect a higher yield with **unsecured loan stock** to compensate them for the extra risk.

2.5 The redemption of loan stock

Key term

> **Redemption** is repayment of preference shares and debentures.

Loan stock and debentures are usually redeemable. They are issued for a term of ten years or more, and perhaps 25 to 30 years. At the end of this period, they will 'mature' and become redeemable (at par or possibly at a value above par).

Most redeemable stocks have an earliest and a latest redemption date. For example, 12% Debenture Stock 20X7/X9 is redeemable, at any time between the earliest specified date (in 20X7) and the latest date (in 20X9). The **issuing company** can choose the date.

Some loan stock does not have a redemption date, and is **'irredeemable'** or 'undated'. Undated loan stock might be redeemed by a company that wishes to pay off the debt, but there is no obligation on the company to do so.

PART F   SOURCES OF FINANCE

2.5.1 How will a company finance the redemption of long-term debt?

There is no guarantee that a company will be able to raise a new loan to pay off a maturing debt. One item you should look for in a company's balance sheet is the **redemption date** of current loans, to establish how much new finance is likely to be needed by the company, and when.

Occasionally, perhaps because the secured assets have fallen in value and would not realise much in a forced sale, or perhaps out of a belief that the company can improve its position soon, unpaid debenture holders might be persuaded to surrender their debentures. In exchange they may get an **equity interest** in the company or **convertible debentures**, paying a lower rate of interest, but carrying the option to convert the debentures into shares at a specified time in the future.

2.6 Tax relief on loan interest

As far as companies are concerned, debt capital is a potentially attractive source of finance because interest charges **reduce the profits** chargeable to corporation tax.

(a)   A new issue of loan stock is likely to be preferable to a new issue of preference shares.

(b)   Companies might wish to **avoid dilution of shareholdings** and **increase gearing** (the ratio of fixed interest capital to equity capital) in order to improve their earnings per share by benefiting from tax relief on interest payments.

2.7 Mortgages

Mortgages are a specific type of secured loan. Companies place the title deeds of freehold or long leasehold property as security with a lender and receive cash on loan, usually repayable over a specified period, with interest payable at a fixed or floating rate. Most organisations owning property which is unencumbered by any charge should be able to obtain a mortgage up to two thirds of the value of the property.

3 Convertibles and warrants   6/02

FAST FORWARD

> **Convertible securities** give investors the opportunity to turn their stock into shares at a later date if they wish and, because of this, they usually carry a lower rate of interest than a similar non-convertible security. For the companies issuing them, convertibles may be viewed as a delayed form of equity which does not immediately affect EPS.
>
> **Warrants** allow shareholders to subscribe for new shares at a **fixed, pre-determined** price in the future.

3.1 Convertible loan stock

Key term

> **Convertible securities** are fixed return securities that may be converted, on pre-determined dates and at the option of the holder, into ordinary shares of the company at a predetermined rate.

Conversion terms often vary over time. For example, the conversion terms of convertible stock might be that on 1 April 20X2, £2 of stock can be converted into one ordinary share, whereas on 1 April 20X3, the conversion price will be £2.20 of stock for one ordinary share. Once converted, convertible securities cannot be converted back into the original fixed return security.

3.1.1 The conversion value and the conversion premium

The current market value of ordinary shares into which a unit of stock may be converted is known as the conversion value.

(a) The **conversion value** will be below the value of the stock at the date of issue. It will though be expected to increase as the date for conversion approaches on the assumption that a company's shares ought to increase in market value over time.

(b) The difference between the market value of the stock and the conversion value as at the date of issue is the implicit **conversion premium**.

Question — Convertible loan stock

The 10% convertible loan stock of Starchwhite plc is quoted at £142 per £100 nominal. The earliest date for conversion is in four years time, at the rate of 30 ordinary shares per £100 nominal loan stock. The share price is currently £4.15. Annual interest on the stock has just been paid.

Required

(a) What is the average annual growth rate in the share price that is required for the stockholders to achieve an overall rate of return of 12% a year compound over the next four years, including the proceeds of conversion?

(b) What is the implicit conversion premium on the stock?

Answer

(a)

Year	Investment £	Interest £	Discount factor 12%	Terminal value £
0	(142)		1.000	(142.00)
1		10	0.893	8.93
2		10	0.797	7.97
3		10	0.712	7.12
4		10	0.636	6.36
				(111.62)

The value of 30 shares on conversion at the end of year 4 must have a present value of at least £111.62, to provide investors with a 12% return.

The money value at the end of year 4 needs to be £111.62 ÷ 0.636 = £175.50.

The current market value of 30 shares is (× £4.15) £124.50.

The growth factor in the share price over four years needs to be:

$$\frac{175.50}{124.50} = 1.4096$$

If the annual rate of growth in the share price, expressed as a proportion, is g, then:

$(1 + g)^4$ = 1.4096
$1 + g$ = 1.0896
g = 0.0896, say 0.09

Conclusion. The rate of growth in the share price needs to be 9% a year (compound).

(b) The conversion premium can be expressed as an amount per share or as a percentage of the current conversion value.

(i) As an amount per share $\dfrac{£142 - £(30 \times 4.15)}{30} = £0.583$ per share

(ii) As a % of conversion value $\dfrac{£0.583}{£4.15} \times 100\% = 14\%$

3.1.2 The issue price and the market price of convertible loan stock

A company will aim to issue loan stock with the **greatest possible conversion premium**. This will mean that, for the amount of capital raised, it will, on conversion, have to issue the **lowest number** of new ordinary shares. The premium that will be accepted by potential investors will depend on the company's **growth potential** and so on prospects for a sizeable increase in the share price.

Convertible loan stock issued at par normally has a **lower coupon rate of interest** than straight debentures. This lower yield is the price the investor has to pay for the conversion rights. It is, of course, also one of the reasons why the issue of convertible stock is attractive to a company.

When convertible loan stock is traded on a stock market, its **minimum market price** will be the **price of straight debentures** with the same coupon rate of interest. If the market value falls to this minimum, it follows that the market attaches no value to the conversion rights.

The actual market price of convertible stock will depend on:

- The **price of straight debt**
- The **current conversion value**
- The **length of time** before conversion may take place
- The **market's expectation** as to future equity returns and the associated risk

If the conversion value rises above the straight debt value then the price of convertible stock will normally reflect this increase.

Most companies issuing convertible stocks expect them to be converted. They view the stock as **delayed equity**. They are often used either because the company's ordinary share price is considered to be particularly **depressed** at the time of issue or because the issue of equity shares would result in an immediate and significant **drop in earnings per share**. There is no certainty, however, that the security holders will exercise their option to convert; therefore the stock may run its full term and need to be redeemed.

3.2 Example: Convertible debentures

CD plc has issued 50,000 units of convertible debentures, each with a nominal value of £100 and a coupon rate of interest of 10% payable yearly. Each £100 of convertible debentures may be converted into 40 ordinary shares of CD plc in three years time. Any stock not converted will be redeemed at 110 (that is, at £110 per £100 nominal value of stock).

Estimate the likely current market price for £100 of the debentures, if investors in the debentures now require a pre-tax return of only 8%, and the expected value of CD plc ordinary shares on the conversion day is:

(a) £2.50 per share
(b) £3.00 per share

Solution

(a) **Shares are valued at £2.50 each**

If shares are only expected to be worth £2.50 each on conversion day, the value of 40 shares will be £100, and investors in the debentures will presumably therefore redeem their debentures at 110 instead of converting them into shares.

The market value of £100 of the convertible debentures will be the discounted present value of the expected future income stream.

Year		Cash flow £	Discount factor 8%	Present value £
1	Interest	10	0.926	9.26
2	Interest	10	0.857	8.57
3	Interest	10	0.794	7.94
3	Redemption value	110	0.794	87.34
				113.11

The estimated market value is £113.11 per £100 of debentures.

(b) **Shares are valued at £3 each**

If shares are expected to be worth £3 each, the debenture holders will convert their debentures into shares (value per £100 of stock = 40 shares × £3 = £120) rather than redeem their debentures at 110.

Year		Cash flow/value £	Discount factor 8%	Present value £
1	Interest	10	0.926	9.26
2	Interest	10	0.857	8.57
3	Interest	10	0.794	7.94
3	Value of 40 shares	120	0.794	95.28
				121.05

The estimated market value is £121.05 per £100 of debentures.

Question — Conversion of debentures

Downon Howett plc is unable to pay the interest on its debt capital, which consists of £5,000,000 of 10% debenture stock. The debenture holders are entitled, under the terms of their trust deed, to appoint a receiver, but the current financial position of Downon Howett plc is so poor that the enforced liquidation of the company would not realise more than a small fraction of the amount owed to the debenture holders. The debenture holders are therefore willing to consider alternatives.

Downon Howett has suggested that either of two options might satisfy them. The debenture holders would surrender their debentures, in exchange for:

(a) 15,000,000 ordinary shares under option 1

(b) £5,000,000 of non-interest-bearing convertible debentures under option 2. The debentures would be convertible into ordinary shares in two years time at the rate of 200 shares per £100 of stock. Alternatively, the debentures (which would not be secured) would be repayable at par after two years.

PART F SOURCES OF FINANCE

Estimates of the net realisable value of Downon Howett's assets in two years time are as follows.

Probability	Net realisable value
	£m
0.2	2
0.4	4
0.3	6
0.1	8

If Downon Howett does not go into liquidation, its value as a going concern after two years is estimated to be 150% of the net realisable value of its assets, and the share price will reflect this value. Downon Howett would not be allowed to issue any additional shares, nor pay any dividend, for the next two years. There are currently 10,000,000 shares in issue.

Which option would the debenture holders prefer, on the assumption that they choose the one that maximises the expected value of their wealth?

Answer

(a) If option 1 is selected, the debenture holders would own:

$$\frac{15}{10+15} = 60\% \text{ of the shares.}$$

After two years, the EV of these shares would be as follows.

Break up value £m	Market value (going concern) 150% £m	Ex debenture holder's share 60% £m	Probability	EV £m
2	3	1.8	0.2	0.36
4	6	3.6	0.4	1.44
6	9	5.4	0.3	1.62
8	12	7.2	0.1	0.72
				4.14

(b) If option 2 is selected, the debenture holders could choose to demand repayment of the debentures, out of the proceeds of sale of the assets of the company, or to convert the debentures into shares.

They would own $\frac{10}{10+10} = 50\%$ of the total number of shares.

Break-up value £m	Going concern value £m	Value of convertibles as equity £m	Value of convertibles as debt £m	Convert? *yes or no	Value of debenture holders' securities £m	Probability	EV £m
2	3	1.5	2.0	No	2	0.2	0.4
4	6	3.0	4.0	No	4	0.4	1.6
6	9	4.5	5.0	No	5	0.3	1.5
8	12	6.0	5.0	Yes	6	0.1	0.6
							4.1

* The answer is 'no' if the break-up value or the total debt of £5,000,000, whichever is lower, exceeds the value of 50% of the equity of the going concern. The debenture holders will compare the value of their convertibles as debt and as shares, and opt to use them in the form that gives the greater value.

The debenture holders would prefer option 1 to option 2, but only marginally so (with a difference in expected value of only £40,000).

3.3 Warrants

Key term

> A **warrant** is a right given by a company to an investor, allowing him to subscribe for new shares at a future date at a fixed, pre-determined price (the **exercise price**).

Warrants are usually issued as part of a package with unsecured loan stock: an investor who buys stock will also acquire a certain number of warrants. The purpose of warrants is to make the loan stock more attractive.

Once issued, warrants are detachable from the stock and can be sold and bought separately before or during the 'exercise period' (the period during which the right to use the warrants to subscribe for shares is allowed). The market value of warrants will depend on expectations of actual share prices in the future.

During the exercise period, the price of a warrant should not fall below the higher of:

- **Nil**
- The **'theoretical value'**, which equals:

(Current share price – Exercise price) × Number of shares obtainable from each warrant

If, for example, a warrant entitles the holder to purchase two ordinary shares at a price of £3 each, when the current market price of the shares is £3.40.

Minimum market value ('theoretical value') of a warrant = (£3.40 – £3) × 2 = 80p.

For a company with good growth prospects, the warrant will usually be quoted at a premium above the minimum prior to the exercise period. This premium is known as the **warrant conversion premium.** It is sometimes expressed as a percentage of the current share price.

3.4 Example: Warrant conversion premium

An investor holds some warrants which can be used to subscribe for ordinary shares on a one for one basis at an exercise price of £2.50 during a specified future period. The current share price is £2.25 and the warrants are quoted at 50p. What is the warrant conversion premium?

Solution

The easiest way of finding the premium is to deduct the current share price from the cost of acquiring a share using the warrant, treating the warrant as if it were currently exercisable:

	£
Cost of warrant	0.50
Exercise price	2.50
	3.00
Current share price	2.25
Premium	0.75

In the short run the warrant price and share price normally move fairly closely in line with each other. In the longer term the price of the warrant and hence the premium will depend on:

- The **length of time** before the warrants may be exercised
- The **current price** of the shares compared with the exercise price, and
- The **future prospects** of the company

As the exercise period approaches, the premium will reduce. Towards the end of the exercise period the premium will disappear because, if there were a premium, it would be cheaper to buy the shares directly rather than via the warrant.

You may be wondering why an investor would prefer to buy warrants at 50p when this means that it will cost him more to get the ordinary shares than if he bought them directly. The attractions of warrants to the investor are:

(a) **Low initial outlay**

The investor only has to spend 50p per share as opposed to £2.25. The investor will be able to buy 4½ times as many warrants as shares or, alternatively, invest the remaining £1.75 in other, less risky investments.

(b) **Lower downside potential**

The maximum loss per share is 50p instead of £2.25. Of course the risk of the loss of 50p is much greater than the risk of losing £2.25. The share price of £2.25 is below the exercise price. If it remained at this level until the beginning of the exercise period, the warrants would become worthless as it would not be worthwhile exercising them.

(c) **High potential returns**

Warrants offer the investor the possibility of making a high profit as a percentage of initial cost, as the price of the warrants will tend to move in line with the price of the shares. Thus, if the share price rises by 50p the increase in the value of the warrant will be similar. Using the previous prices, a 50p increase in share price is about 22% but a 50p increase in the warrant price is 100%.

(d) **Capital gains**

As warrants provide no income all profits are in the **form of capital gains** which will be attractive to higher-rate taxpayers who have not used up their annual tax-free allowance.

The advantages of warrants to the company are as follows.

(a) Warrants themselves do **not involve** the payment of any **interest** or **dividends**. Furthermore, when they are initially attached to loan stock, the interest rate on the loan stock will be lower than for a comparable straight debt.

(b) Warrants make a **loan stock issue more attractive** and may make an issue of unsecured loan stock possible where adequate security is lacking.

(c) Warrants provide a means of **generating additional equity funds** in the future without any immediate dilution in earnings per share.

22: DEBT FINANCING

Chapter Roundup

- The choice of debt finance that a company can make depends upon:
    - The size of the business (a public issue of loan stock is only available to a large company)
    - The duration of the loan
    - Whether a fixed or floating interest rate is preferred (fixed rates are more expensive, but floating rates are riskier)
    - The security that can be offered
- The term **bonds** describes various forms of long-term debt a company may issue, such as **loan stock** or **debentures**, which may be:
    - **Redeemable**
    - **Irredeemable**
- Bonds or loans come in various forms, including:
    - **Floating rate debentures**
    - **Zero coupon bonds**
    - **Convertible loan stock**
- **Convertible securities** give investors the opportunity to turn their stock into shares at a later date if they wish and, because of this, they usually carry a lower rate of interest than a similar non-convertible security. For the companies issuing them, convertibles may be viewed as a delayed form of equity which does not immediately affect EPS.
- **Warrants** allow shareholders to subscribe for new shares at a **fixed, pre-determined** price in the future.

Quick Quiz

1. Debentures are more similar to equity than preference shares.

    ☐ True

    ☐ False

2. Holders of loan stock are long-term debtors of the company.

    ☐ True

    ☐ False

3. A company has 12% debentures in issue, which have a market value of £135 per £100 nominal value. What is:

    (a) The coupon rate?
    (b) The amount of interest payable per annum per £100 (nominal) of stock?

4. Does an investor have the option of redeeming a company's 11% Debenture Stock 2006/2008 at any date between 1 January 2006 and 31 December 2008 inclusive?

5. Convertible securities are fixed return securities that may be converted into zero coupon bonds/ordinary shares/warrants. (Delete as appropriate.)

PART F SOURCES OF FINANCE

6   Which of the following statements about convertible securities is false?

    A   They are fixed return securities.
    B   They must be converted into shares before the redemption date.
    C   The price at which they will be converted into shares is predetermined.
    D   Issue costs are lower than for equity.

7   Do borrowers benefit from floating rate debentures when interest rates are rising or falling?

8   What is the value of £100 12% debt redeemable in 3 years time at a premium of 20p per £ if the loanholder's required return is 10%?

Answers to Quick Quiz

1   False. Debentures are a form of loan stock

2   False. They are long-term creditors of the company.

3   (a) 12%   (b) £12

4   No. The company will be able to choose the date of redemption.

5   Ordinary shares.

6   B   The holder has the option to convert, but he will only convert if it is advantageous for him to do so. If the share price falls, the stock may run its full term and need to be redeemed.

7   Falling

8

Years		£	Discount factor 10%	Present value £
1-3	Interest	12	2.487	29.84
3	Redemption premium	120	0.751	90.12
Value of debt				119.96

Now try the questions below from the Exam Question Bank

Number	Level	Marks	Time
Q25	Examination	25	45 mins

The capital structure decision

23

Topic list	Syllabus reference
1 Factors influencing capital structure	4(c), (e)
2 Restrictions on capital structure	4(c), (e)
3 Gearing	4(d), (e)
4 Short-term financing and capital structure	4(c), (e)

Introduction

In Chapters 21 and 22, we described different methods by which a company can obtain long-term finance, both in the form of **equity** and in the form of **debt**.

This chapter follows on from Chapters 21 and 22, looking now at the question of what a company's **financial structure** should be. A central question here is: What are the implications of using different proportions of equity and debt finance?

The answer to this has to take account the attitudes of investors to the financial risk associated with increasing levels of debt finance, and the trade-off between risk and return.

We also look at various gearing ratios which give us a measure of the extent to which a company is financed by debt.

PART F   SOURCES OF FINANCE

Study guide

Section II – Sources of finance IV: The capital structure decision

- Explain and calculate the level of financial gearing
- Distinguish between operational and financial gearing, and business risk and financial risk
- Outline the effects of gearing on the value of shares, company risk and required return
- Explain how a company may determine its capital structure in terms of interest charges, dividends, risk and redemption requirements
- Explain the role of short term financing in the capital structure decision
- Explain the relationship between the management of working capital and the long term capital structure decision
- Calculate and interpret appropriate ratios

Exam guide

You may be asked to explain the implications of different financing decisions on investment opportunities and the company's continued health. Capital structure, particularly of smaller companies, is a significant topic in this exam. Understanding the **principles** involved, also that capital structure may be determined by what finance is **available**, is important.

The examiner has emphasised that it is not enough just to know about the variety of possible sources; evaluation of the choice between different sources is a core skill.

1 Factors influencing capital structure   12/03, 6/04

FAST FORWARD

> Debt finance tends to be relatively low risk for the debtholder as it is interest-bearing and can be secured. The cost of debt to the company is therefore relatively low.
>
> The greater the level of debt, the more **financial risk** (of reduced dividends after the payment of debt interest) to the shareholder of the company, so the higher is their required return.

1.1 Principles of capital structure

Key term

> **Capital structure** refers to the way in which an organisation is financed, by a combination of long-term capital (ordinary shares and reserves, preference shares, debentures, bank loans, convertible loan stock and so on) and short-term liabilities, such as a bank overdraft and trade creditors. The mix of finance can be measured by gearing ratios (covered in Section 3).

The assets of a business must be financed somehow, and when a business is growing, the additional assets must be financed by additional capital.

However a high level of debt creates financial risk. **Financial risk** can be seen from different points of view.

(a) **The company as a whole**

If a company builds up debts that it cannot pay when they fall due, it will be forced into liquidation.

(b) **Creditors**

If a company cannot pay its debts, the company will go into liquidation owing creditors money that they are unlikely to recover in full. Lenders will thus want a **higher interest yield** to compensate them for higher financial risk and gearing.

(c) **Ordinary shareholders**

A company will not make any distributable profits unless it is able to earn enough profit before interest and tax to pay all its interest charges, and then tax. The lower the profits or the higher the interest-bearing debts, the less there will be, if there is anything at all, for shareholders. Ordinary shareholders will probably want a **bigger expected return** from their shares to compensate them for a **higher financial risk**. The market value of shares will therefore depend on gearing, because of this premium for financial risk that shareholders will want to earn.

In this section we shall examine how a business can decide what a suitable capital structure might be.

1.2 Company circumstances

One determinant of the suitability of the gearing mix is the **stability** of the company. It may seem obvious, but it is worth stressing that debt financing will be more appropriate when:

- The company is in a **healthy competitive position**.
- **Cash flows** and **earnings** are stable.
- **Profit margins** are **reasonable**.
- **Operating gearing** is **low** (ie the fixed costs that have to be covered by profits from trading activities are low).
- The **bulk of the company's assets** are **tangible**.
- The **liquidity** and **cash flow position** is **strong**.
- The **debt-equity ratio** is **low**.
- **Share prices** are **low**.

1.3 Matching assets with funds

As a general rule, **assets that yield profits over a long period of time should be financed** by **long-term funds**.

In this way, the returns made by the asset will be sufficient to pay either the interest cost of the loans raised to buy it, or dividends on its equity funding.

If, however a long-term asset is financed by short-term funds, the company cannot be certain that when the loan becomes repayable, it will have enough cash (from profits) to repay it.

A company would not normally finance all of its short-term assets with short-term liabilities, but instead finance **short-term assets partly with short-term funding** and **partly with long-term funding**.

1.4 Long-term capital requirements for replacement and growth

A distinction can be made between long-term capital that is needed to finance the replacement of worn-out assets, and capital that is needed to finance growth.

Aims	Main funding sources
Maintenance of current level of operations	Internal sources
Growth	External finance

1.5 Signalling

Some investors may see the issue of debt capital as a sign that the directors are confident enough of the future cash flows of the business to be prepared to commit the company to making **regular interest payments** to **lenders**. However this depends on the view that market efficiency is not very high. A strongly efficient market should have sufficient information to be able to make its own mind up about the debt issue, without needing to take the directors' views into account.

1.6 Clientele effect

When considering whether to change gearing significantly, directors may take into account changes in the profile of shareholders. If gearing does change significantly, the company may adjust to a **new risk-return trade-off** that is unsuitable for many shareholders. These shareholders will look to sell their shares, whilst other shareholders, who are attracted by the new gearing levels, will look to buy shares in the company.

1.7 Domestic and international borrowing

If the company is receiving income in a foreign currency or has a long-term investment overseas can try to limit the **risk of adverse exchange rate movements** by matching. It can take out a long-term loan and use the foreign currency receipts to repay the loan. Similarly it can try to **match its foreign assets** (property, plant etc) by a **long-term loan** in the foreign currency.

1.7.1 Cost and flexibility

The **cost of debt** is likely to be lower than the cost of equity, because debt is **less risky** from the debtholders' viewpoint. As we have seen, interest has to be paid no matter what the level of profits, and debt capital can be secured by **fixed** and **floating charges**.

Interest rates on longer-term debt may be higher than interest rates on shorter-term debt, because many lenders believe longer-term lending to be riskier. However **issue costs** or **arrangement fees** will be **higher** for shorter-term debt as it has to be renewed more frequently.

A business may also find itself locked into **longer-term debt**, with adverse interest rates and large penalties if it repays the debt early. Both **inflation** and **uncertainty** about future interest rate changes are reasons why companies are unwilling to borrow long-term at high rates of interest and investors are unwilling to lend long-term when they think that interest yields might go even higher.

1.8 Optimal capital structure and the cost of capital

When we consider the capital structure decision, the question arises of whether there is an optimal mix of capital and debt which a company should try to achieve.

One view is that there is an optimal capital mix at which the **average cost of capital**, weighted according to the different forms of capital employed, is **minimised**. As gearing rises, so the return demanded by the ordinary shareholders begins to rise in order to compensate them for the risk resulting from a larger share of profits going to the providers of debt. At very high levels of gearing the holders of debt too will begin to require higher returns as they become exposed to the risk of inadequate profits.

Briefly, the alternative view of **Modigliani and Miller** is that the firm's overall **weighted average cost of capital** is **not influenced** by changes in its **capital structure**. Their argument is that the issue of debt causes the cost of equity to rise in such a way that the benefits of debt on returns are exactly offset. Investors themselves adjust their level of personal gearing and thus the level of corporate gearing becomes irrelevant.

The Modigliani-Miller view however does contain some debatable assumptions. It assumes that investors operate in a **perfect market** where **full information** is **equally available** to all players, and that **transaction costs** are **irrelevant**. Further, **companies** can often borrow on better terms than private investors, and importantly the **effects of taxation** are **ignored** in the original Modigliani-Miller theory.

2 Restrictions on capital structure

> **FAST FORWARD**
>
> Factors which affect the capital structure include
>
> - the attitudes of the shareholders and directors to risk and return
> - the loss of control brought about by additional capital
> - shareholders' willingness to contribute further funds
> - availability of capital in a depressed market
> - conditions in existing loan agreements restricting further loans

2.1 Attitudes to risk and return

The choice of capital structure will not only depend on company circumstances, but the **attitudes** that directors and owners have towards the **principal risks**. This will include not the risks that are specific to the business and more general economic risks, but also the risks of raising finance. It could for example adversely affect the company's reputation if it made a rights issue that was not fully subscribed.

Owner-director attitudes to risk may also differ. Owners will be concerned about the combination of **risk and return**, but may in fact prefer higher risk levels than the directors deem desirable, provided returns are high enough to compensate for these risks. Directors may be concerned with the **risk** to their **income** and **job security**, but on the other hand if there are significant profit incentives in their remuneration packages, they may take more risks than the owners deem desirable.

A large issue of equity may also run the risk of **diluting unacceptably** present shareholders' earnings, unless the investments financed by the equity issue produce rapid returns.

2.2 Loss of control

The directors and shareholders may be unwilling to accept the **conditions** and the **loss of control** that obtaining extra finance will bring. Control may be diminished whether equity or loan funding is sought:

(a) **Issuing shares** to outsiders may **dilute** the **control** of the existing shareholders and directors, and the company will be subject to **greater regulatory control** if it obtains a stock market listing.

(b) The price of additional debt finance may be **security** restricting disposal of the assets secured and **covenants** that may limit the company's rights to **dispose of assets** in general or to pay dividends.

2.3 Costs

The directors may consider that the **extra interest costs** the company is committed to are too high.

2.4 Commitments

The interest and repayment schedules that the company is required to meet may be felt to be **too tight**. The collateral loan providers require may also be too much, particularly if the directors are themselves required to provide **personal guarantees.**

2.5 Present sources of finance

Perhaps it's easy to find reasons why new sources of finance may not be desirable, but equally they may be considered more acceptable than drawing on current sources. For example shareholders may be **unwilling to contribute further funds** in a rights issue; the business may wish to improve its relations with its suppliers, and one condition may be lessening its reliance on trade credit.

2.6 Availability of capital

If the **stock market** is **depressed**, it may be difficult to raise cash through share issues. Even if shares can be issued, it may be at a low price that dilutes the value of current shareholdings. Current shareholders may be unwilling to contribute to a rights issue because of lack of financial resources. On the other hand debt capital may not be available if the company is in **financial difficulties** or has a poor **credit rating**.

2.7 Future trends

Likely **future trends** of **fund availability** will be significant if an organisation's current strategy will mean that it requires a number of injections of funds over the next few years.

2.8 Restrictions in loan agreements

Restrictions written into agreements on current loans may prohibit a business from taking out **further loans**, or may require that its gearing does **not exceed specified limits**.

2.9 Maturity dates

If a business already has significant debt repayable in a few years' time, because of likely **cash flow limitations** it may not be able to take out further debt repayable around the same time.

Position of small and medium-sized enterprises

The options open to small and medium-sized enterprises (SMEs) may be particularly limited. They face **competition** for funds, as investors have opportunities to invest in all sizes of organisation, also overseas and in government debt. In this competition they are handicapped by the problem of **uncertainty**. We shall discuss their problems further in the next chapter.

3 Gearing

FAST FORWARD

> **Gearing** must be considered when deciding how to finance a business.
>
> **Financial gearing** and **operating** or **operational gearing** need to be distinguished.
>
> - **Financial gearing** measures the relationship between **shareholders' funds** and **prior charge capital.**
> - **Operating gearing** measures the relationship between **contribution** and **profit before interest and tax.**
>
> If a company can generate returns on capital in excess of the interest payable on debt, financial gearing will raise the EPS. Gearing will, however, also increase **the variability of returns** for shareholders and increase the chance of corporate **failure**.
>
> **Gearing** is also limited by the reluctance of lenders to lend to a company which does not have an adequate equity base.

3.1 Gearing ratios 6/03, 6/04, 12/04

Exam focus point

You need to be able to explain *and calculate* the level of financial gearing using alternative measures.

Financial gearing measures the relationship between shareholders' capital plus reserves, and either prior charge capital or borrowings or both.

Commonly used measures of financial gearing are based on the balance sheet values of the fixed interest and equity capital. They include:

Formula to learn

$$\text{Financial gearing} = \frac{\text{Prior charge capital}}{\text{Equity capital (including reserves)}}$$

$$\text{and} = \frac{\text{Prior charge capital}}{\text{Total capital employed}^*}$$

* Either including or excluding minority interests, deferred tax and deferred income.

With the first definition above, a company is low geared if the gearing ratio is less than 100%, highly geared if the ratio is over 100% and neutrally geared if it is exactly 100%. With the second definition, a company is neutrally geared if the ratio is 50%, low geared below that, and highly geared above that.

With both financial gearing ratios, a sector gearing ratio can be a guide to what is considered safe or acceptable by companies and investors.

Exam focus point

If the question specifies a gearing formula, you must use that formula.

Question — Gearing

From the following balance sheet, compute the company's financial gearing ratio.

	£'000	£'000	£'000
Fixed assets			12,400
Current assets		1,000	
Creditors: amounts falling due within one year			
Loans	120		
Bank overdraft	260		
Trade creditors	430		
Bills of exchange	70		
		880	
Net current assets			120
Total assets less current liabilities			12,520
Creditors: amounts falling due after more than one year			
Debentures		4,700	
Bank loans		500	
			(5,200)
Provisions for liabilities and charges: deferred taxation			(300)
Deferred income			(250)
			6,770

PART F SOURCES OF FINANCE

	£'000
Capital and reserves	
Called up share capital	
Ordinary shares	1,500
Preference shares	500
	2,000
Share premium account	760
Revaluation reserve	1,200
Profit and loss account	2,810
	6,770

Answer

	£'000
Prior charge capital	
Preference shares	500
Debentures	4,700
Long-term bank loans	500
Prior charge capital, ignoring short-term debt	5,700
Short-term loans	120
Overdraft	260
Prior charge capital, including short-term interest bearing debt	6,080

Either figure, £6,080,000 or £5,700,000, could be used. If gearing is calculated with capital employed in the denominator, and capital employed is net fixed assets plus **net** current assets, it would seem more reasonable to exclude short-term interest bearing debt from prior charge capital. This is because short-term debt is set off against current assets in arriving at the figure for net current assets.

Equity = 1,500 + 760 + 1,200 + 2,810 = £6,270,000

The gearing ratio can be calculated in any of the following ways.

(a) $\dfrac{\text{Prior charge capital}}{\text{Equity}} \times 100\% = \dfrac{6,080}{6,270} \times 100\% = 97\%$

(b) $\dfrac{\text{Prior charge capital}}{\text{Equity plus prior charge capital}} \times 100\% = \dfrac{6,080}{(6,080 + 6,270)} \times 100\% = 49.2\%$

(c) $\dfrac{\text{Prior charge capital}}{\text{Total capital employed}} \times 100\% = \dfrac{5,700}{12,520} \times 100\% = 45.5\%$

3.1.1 Gearing ratios based on market values

An alternative method of calculating a gearing ratio is one based on **market values**:

Formula to learn

$$\text{Financial gearing} = \dfrac{\text{Market value of debt (including redeemable preference shares)}}{\text{Market value of equity} + \text{Market value of debt}}$$

The advantage of this method is that potential investors in a company are able to judge the further debt capacity of the company more clearly by **reference** to **market values** than they could by looking at balance sheet values.

23: THE CAPITAL STRUCTURE DECISION

The disadvantage of a gearing ratio based on market values is that it **disregards** the **value** of the company's **assets**, which might be used to secure further loans. A gearing ratio based on balance sheet values arguably gives a better indication of the security for lenders of fixed interest capital.

3.1.2 The effect of gearing on earnings

A highly geared company must earn enough profits to **cover** its **interest** charges before anything is available for equity. On the other hand, if borrowed funds are invested in projects which provide returns in excess of the cost of debt capital, then shareholders will enjoy increased returns on their equity.

Provided that a company can generate returns on capital in excess of the interest payable on debt, introducing financial gearing into the capital structure will enable **earnings per share** to be raised. If the company fails to generate such returns, earnings per share will be reduced, and so gearing increases the **variability of shareholders' earnings**.

Gearing, however, also **increases** the **probability** of **financial failure** occurring through a company's inability to meet interest payments in poor trading circumstances.

3.1.3 Example: Gearing

Suppose that two companies are identical in every respect except for their gearing. Both have assets of £20,000 and both make the same operating profits (profit before interest and tax: PBIT). The only difference between the two companies is that Nonlever Ltd is all-equity financed and Lever Ltd is partly financed by debt capital, as follows.

	Nonlever Ltd £	Lever Ltd £
Assets	20,000	20,000
10% Loan stock	0	(10,000)
	20,000	10,000
Ordinary shares of £1	20,000	10,000

Because Lever Ltd has £10,000 of 10% loan stock it must make a profit before interest of at least £1,000 in order to pay the interest charges. Nonlever Ltd, on the other hand, does not have any minimum PBIT requirement because it has no debt capital. A company which is lower geared is considered less risky than a higher geared company because of the greater likelihood that its PBIT will be high enough to cover interest charges and make a profit for equity shareholders.

3.1.4 Operating gearing

Financial risk, as we have seen, can be measured by financial gearing. **Business risk** refers to the risk of making only low profits, or even losses, due to the nature of the business that the company is involved in. One way of measuring business risk is by calculating a company's **operating gearing** or 'operational gearing'.

Formula to learn

$$\text{Operating gearing} = \frac{\text{Contribution}}{\text{Profit before interest and tax (PBIT)}}$$

Contribution is sales minus variable cost of sales.

The significance of operating gearing is as follows.

(a) **If contribution is high but PBIT is low**, fixed costs will be high, and only just covered by contribution. Business risk, as measured by operating gearing, will be high.

(b) **If contribution is not much bigger than PBIT**, fixed costs will be low, and fairly easily covered. Business risk, as measured by operating gearing, will be low.

3.1.5 Total gearing

Total gearing is the sum of operational gearing and financial gearing, that is business risk plus financial risk.

3.2 Interest cover

Interest cover is a measure of financial risk which is designed to show the risks in terms of profit rather than in terms of capital values.

Formula to learn

$$\text{Interest cover} = \frac{\text{Profit before interest and tax}}{\text{Interest}}$$

The reciprocal of this, the interest to profit ratio, is also sometimes used. As a general guide, an interest cover of **less than three times** is considered low, indicating that profitability is too low given the gearing of the company.

3.3 The debt ratio (debt/equity ratio)

Another measure of financial risk is the **debt ratio**.

Debt ratio = Total debts : Total assets
Debt/equity ratio = Debt : Equity

Debt does not include long-term provisions and liabilities such as deferred taxation.

There is no firm rule on the maximum safe debt ratio, but as a general guide, you might regard 50% as a safe limit to debt.

Question — Timothy plc

Timothy plc is planning to invest in new machinery costing £10 million. The revenues and costs arising from the investment are as follows:

	£'000
Sales	2,500
Variable cost of sales	1,100
Other variable operating expenses	200
Other fixed operating expenses including tax allowable depreciation	120

The purchase of the machinery will be financed solely by an issue of 7% debentures, repayable in 20X9.

Timothy's budgeted profit and loss account for the year ended, and balance sheet at, 31 December 20X4 before taking into account the effects of the new investment are set out below.

Profit and loss account

	20X4	
	£000	£000
Sales		16,000
Cost of sales (100% variable)		9,600
Gross profit		6,400
Other operating expenses (50% variable)		2,800
Profit before interest and tax		3,600
Interest		800
Profit before tax		2,800
Tax (30%)		840
Profit after tax		1,960
Dividends (Dividend cover is constant 2:1)		980
Retained earnings		980

23: THE CAPITAL STRUCTURE DECISION

Balance sheet	£000	£000
Fixed assets		25,000
Current assets	10,000	
Current liabilities	3,000	
		7,000
10% Debentures 20X8		8,000
		24,000
Equity share capital and reserves		24,000

Required

Demonstrate the effects of the new investment on:

(a) Operating gearing
(b) Interest cover
(c) Financial gearing $(= \dfrac{\text{Prior charge capital}}{\text{Total capital employed}})$

Answer

The best approach is firstly to calculate the impact on the budgeted profit and loss account and the finance section of the balance sheet.

Profit and loss account

	20X4
	£000
Sales (16,000 + 2,500)	18,500
Cost of sales (9,600 + 1,100)	10,700
Gross profit	7,800
Other variable operating expenses (50% × 2,800) + 200	1,600
Other fixed operating expenses (50% × 2,800) + 120	1,520
Profit before interest and tax	4,680
Interest (800 + (7% × 10,000))	1,500
Profit before tax	3,180
Tax (840 + (30% × (2,500 – 1,100 – 200 – 120 – 700)))	954
Profit after tax	2,226
Dividends (50% × 2,226)	1,113
Retained earnings	1,113

Balance sheet

7% Debentures 20X9	10,000
10% Debentures 20X8	8,000
	18,000
Equity share capital and reserves (24,000 + (1,113 – 980))	24,133

(a) Operating gearing $= \dfrac{\text{Contribution}}{\text{Profit before interest and tax (PBIT)}}$

Before the investment

Operating gearing $= \dfrac{16,000 - 9,600 - (50\% \times 2,800)}{3,600} = 1.39$

After the investment

Operating gearing $= \dfrac{18,500 - 10,700 - 1,600}{4,680} = 1.32$

(b) Interest cover $= \dfrac{\text{Profit before interest and tax}}{\text{Interest}}$

Before the investment

Interest cover $= \dfrac{3,600}{800} = 4.5$

After the investment

Interest cover $= \dfrac{4,680}{1,500} = 3.12$

(c) Financial gearing $= \dfrac{\text{Prior charge capital}}{\text{Total capital employed}}$

Before investment

Financial gearing $= \dfrac{8,000}{8,000 + 24,000} = 25\%$

After investment

Financial gearing $= \dfrac{8,000 + 10,000}{8,000 + 10,000 + 24,133} = 42.7\%$

4 Short-term financing and capital structure 12/01, 6/04

FAST FORWARD

The way in which a company funds its current and permanent assets through either short-term or long-term finance may be **conservative** at on extreme or **aggressive** at the other.

Current and fixed assets can be funded in different ways by employing different capital structures with different proportions of long and short-term sources of funding.

A distinction is often drawn, when funding of current assets is being discussed, between permanent current assets (many businesses will always have certain minimum levels of stock, debtors, and cash) and fluctuating current assets (the excess of assets held over minimum levels).

The diagram below illustrates three alternative types of policy A, B and C. The dotted lines A, B and C are the cut-off levels between short-term and long-term financing for each of the policies A, B and C respectively. Assets above the relevant dotted line are financed by short-term funding while assets below the dotted line are financed by long-term funding.

Fluctuating current assets together with permanent current assets form part of the working capital of the business. This may be financed by either long-term funding (including equity capital) or by current liabilities (short-term funding). This can be seen in terms of policies A, B and C.

(a) Policy A can be characterised as **conservative**. All fixed assets and permanent current assets, as well as part of fluctuating current assets, are financed by long-term funding. The company will only call upon short-term financing at times when fluctuations in current assets push total assets above the level of dotted line A. At times when fluctuating current assets are low and total assets fall below line A, there will be surplus cash which the company will be able to invest in marketable securities.

(b) Policy B is more **aggressive** in its approach to financing working capital. Not only are fluctuating current assets all financed out of short-term sources, but also a part of the permanent current assets. This policy presents an increased risk of liquidity and cash flow problems, although potential returns will be increased if short-term financing can be obtained more cheaply than long-term finance.

(c) A **balance** between risk and return might be best achieved by policy C, in which long-term funds finance permanent assets while short-term funds finance non-permanent assets.

[Diagram: Assets vs Time showing a fluctuating curve above a horizontal line A (dashed), with line C (dashed) below, then line B (dashed); regions labelled "Fluctuating current assets" (between A and C), "Permanent current assets" (between C and the fixed assets line), and "Fixed assets" at the bottom.]

Exam focus point

The examiner commented in his report on the June 2003 paper that candidates confused the financing of working capital with the management of working capital.

This topic has tended to be examined from the perspective of working capital management (see Chapter 18).

Chapter Roundup

- Debt finance tends to be relatively low risk for the debtholder as it is interest-bearing and can be secured. The cost of debt to the company is therefore relatively low.

  The greater the level of debt, the more **financial risk** (of reduced dividends after the payment of debt interest) to the shareholder of the company, so the higher is their required return.

- Factors which affect the capital structure include
    - the attitudes of the shareholders and directors to risk and return
    - the loss of control brought about by additional capital
    - shareholders' willingness to contribute further funds
    - availability of capital in a depressed market
    - conditions in existing loan agreements restricting further loans

- **Gearing** must be considered when deciding how to finance a business.

- **Financial gearing** and **operating** or **operational gearing** need to be distinguished.
    - **Financial gearing** measures the relationship between **shareholders' funds** and **prior charge capital.**
    - **Operating gearing** measures the relationship between **contribution** and **profit before interest and tax.**

- If a company can generate returns on capital in excess of the interest payable on debt, financial gearing will raise the EPS. Gearing will, however, also increase **the variability of returns** for shareholders and increase the chance of corporate **failure**.

- **Gearing** is also limited by the reluctance of lenders to lend to a company which does not have an adequate equity base.

- The way in which a company funds its current and permanent assets through either short-term or long-term finance may be **conservative** at on extreme or **aggressive** at the other.

Quick Quiz

1. Fill in the blank.

    .... gearing = $\dfrac{\text{Prior charge capital}}{\text{Total capital employed}}$

2. Fill in the blank.

    .... gearing = $\dfrac{\text{Contribution}}{\text{Profit before interest and tax}}$

3. Fill in the blank.

    Interest cover = ...

4. What type of policy is characterised by all fixed assets and permanent current assets being financed by long-term funding?

5. Puppy plc has decided to calculate its gearing ratio according to the formula:

    prior charge capital: equity capital (incl reserves)

    At what level would it be neutrally geared?

6. Why should a long-term asset not be financed by short-term loans?

7. What condition has to be fulfilled for increased financial gearing to result in increased earnings per share?

8. What is the debt ratio?

PART F SOURCES OF FINANCE

Answers to Quick Quiz

1. Financial gearing = $\dfrac{\text{Prior charge capital}}{\text{Total capital employed}}$

2. Operating gearing = $\dfrac{\text{Contribution}}{\text{Profit before interest and tax}}$

3. Interest cover = $\dfrac{\text{Profit before interest and tax}}{\text{Interest}}$

4. Conservative

5. Gearing is neutral where Debt = Equity, 100% on the basis of this calculation

6. When the loan becomes repayable, the company cannot be certain that it will have generated enough profits to repay the loan.

7. The returns on capital investment must exceed the interest payable on the extra debt used to finance the investment.

8. Total debt: Total assets

Now try the questions below from the Exam Question Bank

Number	Level	Marks	Time
Q26	Examination	25	45 mins

Financing of small and medium-sized enterprises

24

Topic list	Syllabus reference
1 Small and medium-sized enterprises	4
2 The problems of financing SMEs	4
3 Sources of finance for SMEs	4
4 Government aid for SMEs	4

Introduction

In this chapter we shall be concentrating on how small and medium-sized enterprises (SMEs) obtain finance. The sources of finance are important but this chapter also discusses why SMEs have difficulty raising finance and how they can tackle the obstacles that exist to obtaining finance.

PART F   SOURCES OF FINANCE

Study guide

Section 8 – Sources of finance I: Small and medium-sized enterprises

- Explain financing in terms of the risk/return trade-off
- Describe the requirements for finance of SMEs (purpose, how much, how long)
- Describe the nature of the financing problem for small businesses in terms of the funding gap, the maturity gap and inadequate security
- Identify the role of risk and the lack of information on small companies to help explain the problems of SME financing
- Explain the role of information provision provided by financial statements
- Describe the particular financing problems of low-earning/high growth companies
- Describe the response of government agencies and financial institutions to the SME financing problem
- Explain what other measures may be taken to ease the financial problems of SMEs such as trade creditors, factoring, leasing, hire purchase, AIM listing, business angels and venture capital
- Describe how capital structure decisions in SMEs may differ from larger organisations
- Describe appropriate sources of finance for SMEs
- Calculate and interpret appropriate ratios

Exam guide

Financing of small enterprises is an important topic. You must be able to show in the exam you appreciate the special circumstances of small companies, for example that capital structure may depend solely upon whether funds are available rather than what is optimal in a given situation. The financing of small enterprises was included in the pilot paper *and* the December 2001 exam.

1 Small and medium-sized enterprises (SMEs)

FAST FORWARD

SMEs are generally:
- Unquoted
- Owned by a small number of individuals
- Not micro-businesses

Key terms

Small and medium-sized enterprises (SMEs) can be defined as having three characteristics

(a) Firms are likely to be unquoted

(b) Ownership of the business is restricted to a few individuals, typically a family group

(c) They are not micro businesses that are normally regarded as those very small businesses that act as a medium for self-employment of the owners.

Laney

The characteristics may alter over time, with the enterprise perhaps looking for a listing on the Alternative Investment Market as it expands.

24: FINANCING OF SMALL AND MEDIUM-SIZED ENTERPRISES

The SME sector accounts for between a third and a half of sales and employment. The sector is likely to grow over the next few years with the need for businesses to serve niche markets and the shift from the manufacturing to the service sector. If market conditions do change, small businesses may be **more adaptable**.

There is, however, a significant failure rate amongst small firms. According to a Bank of England survey in 1998, only 47% of new firms still survive five years after commencing trading.

2 The problems of financing SMEs 12/01

FAST FORWARD

SMEs may **not know about** the sources of finance available.

Finance may be difficult to obtain because of the **risks** faced by SMEs.

The money for investment that SMEs can obtain comes from the savings individuals make in the economy. Government policy will have a major influence on the level of funds available.

(a) **Tax policy** including concessions given to businesses to invest (capital allowances) and taxes on distributions (higher taxes on dividends mean less income for investors)

(b) **Interest rate policy** with high interest rates working in different ways – borrowing for SMEs becomes more expensive, but the supply of funds is also greater as higher rates give greater incentives to investors to save

SMEs however also face **competition** for funds. Investors have opportunities to invest in all sizes of organisation, also overseas and in government debt.

The main handicap that SMEs face in accessing funds is the problem of **uncertainty.**

(a) Whatever the details provided to potential investors, SMEs have **neither** the **business history nor larger track record** that larger organisations possess.

(b) Larger enterprises are subject by law to **more public scrutiny**; their accounts have to contain more detail and be audited, they receive more press coverage and so on.

(c) Because of the uncertainties involved, banks often use **credit scoring** systems to **control exposure.**

Because the information is not available in other ways, SMEs will have to provide it when they seek finance. They will need to give a business plan, list of the firm's assets, details of the experience of directors and managers and show how they intend to provide security for sums advanced.

Prospective lenders, often banks, will then make a decision based on the information provided. The terms of the loan (interest rate, term, security, repayment details) will depend on the **risk** involved, and the lender will also want to monitor their investment.

A common problem is often that the banks will be **unwilling** to increase **loan funding** without an increase in **security given** (which the owners may be unwilling or unable to give), or an increase in **equity funding** (which may be difficult to obtain). We shall see in the next two sections how mechanisms and policies have been designed to give small firms easier access to equity funding.

PART F SOURCES OF FINANCE

2.1 Problems of low asset companies

The problems of uncertainty apply in particular to companies with few tangible assets such as high-technology companies.

> **Case Study**
>
> Jim Melton, a significant investor in Internet stocks, has commented that the main three criteria he uses when deciding whether to invest are:
>
> (a) An intuitive factor
>
> (b) The track record of the management
>
> (c) Assessment of the overall market place and whether the business model is actually sustainable in terms of making a profit.

3 Sources of finance for SMEs   12/01, 12/05

FAST FORWARD

Potential sources of financing for small and medium-sized companies include the following.

- Owner financing
- Overdraft financing
- Bank loans
- Trade credit
- Equity finance
- Business angel financing
- Venture capital
- Leasing (see Chapter 30)
- Factoring (see Chapter 19)

Key sources of finance are discussed in more detail below.

Surveys have suggested that small firms have problems accessing different sources of finance because managers are insufficiently informed about what is available. However the increased amount of literature and government agencies designed to help small businesses have resulted in a reduction in this difficulty.

3.1 Owner financing

Finance from the owner(s)' personal resources or those of family connections is generally the initial source of finance. At this stage because many assets are intangible, external funding may be difficult to obtain.

3.2 Overdraft financing

Remember this is where payments from a current account exceed income to the account for a temporary period, the bank finances the deficit by means of an **overdraft**. It is very much a form of **short-term lending**, available to both personal and business customers.

Factors associated with an overdraft are as follows.

(a) **Amount**

The debit amount should not exceed a certain limit agreed between the bank and the borrower, usually with reference to known income.

(b) **Margin**

Interest is charged on the amount overdrawn, usually as a margin over base rate. Interest is calculated on the daily amount overdrawn and is charged to the account quarterly. A fee may also be levied where the bank has agreed a large facility with the customer, even where this facility is not fully used.

(c) **Purpose**

Overdrafts are usually required to cover short-term deficits: for instance, many people run short at the end of each month before their salaries are paid in.

(d) **Repayment**

Overdrafts are technically repayable on demand and it is usual in the facility letter to make this plain to the customer.

(e) **Security**

Depending on the size of the facility open to the customer, security may be required by the bank.

(f) **Benefits**

The customer has a flexible means of short term borrowing; the bank has to accept the fluctuation in the account.

3.3 Overdrafts and the operating cycle

Many SMEs require their bank to provide financial assistance for normal trading over the **operating cycle**. To some extent, a business can – and should – put up finance to cover the needs of the operating cycle – ie the need to invest in stocks and debtors; and to some extent, trade creditors will provide financial support by granting credit. However, a bank might also provide financial support by allowing the business an overdraft facility.

A feature of bank lending to support normal trading finance is that the amount of the overdraft required at any time will depend on the **cash flows of the business**: the timing of receipts and payments, seasonal variations in trade patterns and so on. An overdraft will increase in size if the customer writes more cheques, but will reduce in size when money is paid into the account. There should be times when there will be no overdraft at all, and the account is in credit for a while.

If the hard core element of the overdraft appears to be becoming a long-term feature of the business, the bank might wish, after discussions with the customer, to convert the hard core of the overdraft into a **medium-term loan**, thus giving formal recognition to its more permanent nature. Otherwise **annual reductions** in the hard core of an overdraft would typically be a requirement of the bank.

3.4 Overdrafts and loans compared

A customer might ask the bank for an overdraft facility when the bank would wish to suggest a loan instead; alternatively, a customer might ask for a loan when an overdraft would be more appropriate.

(a) In most cases, when a customer wants finance to help with **'day to day' trading** and cash flow needs, an overdraft would be the appropriate method of financing. The customer should not be short of cash all the time, and should expect to be in credit in some days, but in need of an overdraft on others.

(b) When a customer wants to borrow from a bank for only a short period of time, even for the purchase of a major fixed asset such as an item of plant or machinery, an overdraft facility might be **more suitable** than a loan, because the customer will stop paying interest as soon as his account goes into credit.

(c) When a customer wants to borrow from a bank, but cannot see his way to repaying the bank except over the course of a few years, the medium-term nature of the financing is best catered for by the provision of a loan rather than an overdraft facility.

3.4.1 Advantages of an overdraft over a loan

(a) The customer only pays interest when he is overdrawn.

(b) The bank has the flexibility to review the customer's overdraft facility periodically, and perhaps agree to additional facilities, or insist on a reduction in the facility.

(c) An overdraft can do the same job as a medium-term loan: a facility can simply be renewed every time it comes up for review.

(d) Being short-term debt, an overdraft will not affect the calculation of a company's gearing.

Bear in mind, however, that overdrafts are normally repayable on demand.

3.4.2 Advantages of a medium-term loan

(a) Both the customer and the bank **know exactly** what the repayments of the loan will be and how much interest is payable, and when. This makes planning (budgeting) simpler.

(b) The customer does not have to worry about the bank deciding to reduce or **withdraw** an overdraft facility before he is in a position to repay what is owed. There is an element of 'security' or 'peace of mind' in being able to arrange a loan for an agreed term.

(c) Medium-term loans normally carry a **facility letter** setting out the precise terms of the agreement.

For purchases of a fixed asset it is important, however, that the term of the loan **should not exceed the economic or useful life** of the asset purchased with the money from the loan. A businessman will often expect to use the revenues earned by the asset to repay the loan, and obviously, an asset can only do this as long as it is in operational use.

However, a **mix** of overdrafts and loans might be suggested in some cases. Consider a case where a business asks for a loan, perhaps to purchase a shop with stock. The banker **might** wish to suggest a loan to help with the purchase of the shop, but that stock ought to be financed by an overdraft facility. The offer of part-loan part-overdraft is an option that might be well worth considering.

In practice, although an increasing amount of bank lending is on a fixed-term basis, the time scale may not be all that long. Because of the risk involved, banks are often lending for a period significantly shorter than the life of the investment.

3.5 Trade credit

The use of trade credit finance is discussed in Chapter 19. Undoubtedly trade credit can be a useful source of finance early in a SME's life. Its principal problem is that taking extended credit will mean the **loss of early payment discounts**, and the amounts involved may be significant.

3.6 Equity finance

Other than investment by owners or business angels, businesses with few tangible assets will probably have difficulty obtaining equity finance when they are formed (a problem known as the **equity gap**).

However, once small firms have become established, they do not necessarily need to seek a market listing to obtain equity financing; shares can be **placed privately**. Letting external shareholders invest does not necessarily mean that the original owners have to cede control, particularly if the shares are held by a number of small investors. However, small companies may find it difficult to obtain large sums by this means.

As noted above, owners will need to invest a certain amount of capital when the business starts up. However, subsequently owners can choose whether they withdraw profits from the business or re-invest them.

Surveys have suggested that the amount of equity invested by owners in a business after startup and retained earnings are relatively low compared with other sources of finance. However the failure of owners to invest limits the assets that can be acquired, and hence the amount of security that can be given for debt capital.

A major problem with obtaining equity finance can be the inability of the small firm to offer an easy **exit route** for any investors who wish to sell their stake.

(a) The **firm** can **purchase its own shares** back from the shareholders, but this involves the use of cash that could be better employed elsewhere.

(b) The **firm** can obtain a **market listing** but not all small firms do.

3.7 Business angel financing

Business angel financing can be an important initial source of business finance. Business angels are wealthy individuals or groups of individuals who invest directly in small businesses.

The main problem with business angel financing is that it is informal in terms of a market and can be difficult to set up. However informality can be a strength. There may be less need to provide business angels with detailed information about the company, since business angels generally have prior knowledge of the industry.

Surveys suggest that business angels are often more patient than providers of other sources of finance. However the money available from individual business angels may be limited, and large sums may only be available from a consortium of business angels.

3.8 Venture capital organisations

Key term

> **Venture capital** is risk capital, normally provided in return for an equity stake.

Venture capital organisations have been operating for many years. There are now quite a large number of such organisations.

(a) The British Venture Capital Association is a regulatory body for all the institutions that have joined it as members.

(b) **Investors in Industry plc**, or the **3i group** as it is more commonly known, is the biggest and oldest of the venture capital organisations. It is involved in many venture capital schemes in Europe, Singapore, Japan and the US.

The supply of venture capital in the UK has grown in recent years, as governments have helped to create an environment which supports entrepreneurial business.

Like other venture capitalists, the 3i group wants to invest in companies that will be successful. The group's publicity material states that successful investments have certain common characteristics.

- Highly motivated individuals with a strong management team in place
- A well defined strategy
- A clearly defined target market
- Current turnover between £1m and £100m
- A proven ability to outperform your competitors
- Innovation

The types of venture that the 3i group might invest in include the following.

(a) **Business start-ups**. When a business has been set up by someone who has already put time and money into getting it started, the group may be willing to **provide finance** to enable it to get off the ground.

(b) **Business development**. The group may be willing to **provide development capital** for a company which wants to invest in new products or new markets or to make a business acquisition, and so which needs a major capital injection.

(c) **Management buyouts**. A management buyout is the **purchase** of all or parts of a **business** from its owners by its managers.

(d) Helping a company where one of its owners wants to **realise all or part of his investment**. The 3i group may be prepared to buy some of the company's equity.

3.8.1 Venture capital funds

Some other organisations are engaged in the creation of **venture capital funds.** In these the organisation raises venture capital funds from investors and invests in management buyouts or expanding companies. The venture capital fund managers usually reward themselves by taking a percentage of the portfolio of the fund's investments.

Venture capital trusts are a special type of fund giving investors tax reliefs.

3.8.2 Finding venture capital

When a company's directors look for help from a venture capital institution, they must recognise that:

(a) The institution will want an **equity stake** in the company

(b) It will need convincing that the company can be successful (management buyouts of companies which already have a record of **successful trading** have been increasingly favoured by venture capitalists in recent years)

(c) It may want to have a **representative** appointed to the company's board, to look after its interests, or an **independent director** (the 3i group runs an Independent Director Scheme)

The directors of the company must then contact venture capital organisations, to try to find one or more which would be willing to offer finance. Typically, a venture capitalist will consider offering finance of £500,000 upwards. A venture capital organisation will only give funds to a company that it believes can succeed.

A survey has indicated that around 75% of requests for venture capital are rejected on an initial screening, and only about 3% of all requests survive both this screening and further investigation and result in actual investments.

The venture capital organisation ('VC' below) will take account of various factors in deciding whether to not to invest.

Factors in investment decisions	
The nature of the company's **product**	Viability of production and selling potential
Expertise in **production**	Technical ability to produce efficiently
Expertise in **management**	Commitment, skills and experience
The **market and competition**	Threat from rival producers or future new entrants
Future profits	Detailed business plan showing profit prospects that compensate for risks
Board membership	To take account of VC's interests and ensure VC has say in future strategy
Risk borne by existing owners	Owners bear significant risk and invest significant part of their overall wealth

3.9 Capital structure

Significant influences on the capital structure of small firms are:

- The **lack of separation** between **ownership** and **management**
- The **lack of equity finance**

Studies have suggested that the owners' preference and market considerations are also significant. Small firms tend not to have target debt ratios.

Other studies suggest that the life-cycle of the firm is important. Debt finance is an important early source, its availability depending upon the security available. Longer-term loans may in fact be easier to obtain because they can be secured by mortgages against property.

As firms mature, however, the reliance on debt declines. There seems to be little evidence of a relationship between gearing, and profitability and risk levels.

4 Government aid for SMEs

> **FAST FORWARD**
>
> **Government aid** for SMEs includes the Loan Guarantee Scheme, Enterprise Initiatives and development agencies.

> **Exam focus point**
>
> Availability of government assistance is country-specific. For the exam, at a minimum, you should be aware of the possibilities of such assistance and the major schemes operating in at least one country.

The UK government has introduced a number of assistance schemes to help businesses, and several of these are designed to encourage lenders and investors to make finance available to small and unquoted businesses. They include the Loan Guarantee Scheme, the Enterprise Initiative, development agencies, the Enterprise Investment Scheme and venture capital trusts.

4.1 The Loan Guarantee Scheme

The **Loan Guarantee Scheme** was introduced by the government in 1981. It is intended to help small businesses to get a loan from the bank, when a bank would otherwise be unwilling to lend because the business cannot offer the security that the bank would want. The borrower's annual turnover must not exceed a limit which depends on the type of business.

Under the scheme, which was revised in 1993, the bank can lend up to £250,000 without security over **personal** assets or a personal guarantee being required of the borrower. However, all available **business** assets must be used as security if required. The government will guarantee the bulk of the loan, while the borrower must pay an annual premium on the guaranteed part of the loan.

4.2 The Enterprise Initiative

The Enterprise Initiative is a package of measures offered by the Department of Trade and Industry (DTI) to businesses in the UK, including some regional selective grant assistance. Also provided is a network of 'Business Links', which are local business advice centres.

Regional selective assistance is available for investment projects undertaken by firms in **Assisted Areas**. The project must be commercially viable, create or safeguard employment, demonstrate a need for assistance and offer a distinct regional and national benefit. The amount of grant will be negotiated as the minimum necessary to ensure the project goes ahead.

The **Regional Enterprise Grants** scheme is specially geared to help small firms employing fewer than 25 in one of the Development Areas to expand and diversify. Regional enterprise grants can help finance viable projects for:

(a) Investment – grants of 15% of the cost of fixed assets up to a maximum of £15,000 are available

(b) Innovation – grants of 50% of the agreed project cost up to a maximum grant of £25,000 are available

4.3 Development agencies

The UK government has set up the **Scottish and Welsh Development Agencies** which have been given the task of trying to encourage the development of trade and industry in their areas. The strategy of the agencies has been mainly to encourage the **start-up** and **development of small companies,** although they will also give help to larger companies too.

The assistance that a development agency might give to a firm could include:

(a) Free factory accommodation, or factory accommodation at a low rent

(b) Financial assistance, in the form of

(i) An interest relief grant for a bank loan (A company developing its business in an area might obtain a bank loan, and the development agency will agree to compensate the bank for providing the loan at a low rate of interest.)

(ii) Direct financial assistance in the form of equity finance or loans

4.4 The Enterprise Investment Scheme

The **Enterprise Investment Scheme (EIS)** is intended to encourage investment in the ordinary shares of unquoted companies. When a qualifying individual subscribes for eligible shares in a qualifying company, the individual saves tax at 20% on the amount subscribed (including any share premium). A **qualifying individual** is one who is not connected with the company at any time in the period from two years before the issue (or from incorporation if later) to five years after the issue. The maximum total investment that can qualify in a tax year is £150,000 per individual. Capital gains generated by individual investors in the EIS are tax-free provided the investment is held for five years.

4.5 Venture capital trusts

Venture capital providers have been around for many years, but in 1993, the UK Government introduced a second measure to encourage equity investment in the form of a new kind of investment trust called a **venture capital trust (VCT)** which came into being in 1995. This followed criticism from banks and small business groups that small companies were too dependent on short-term finance.

The investment trust must be approved by the Inland Revenue, under rules which require it to invest a large proportion of assets in unquoted companies. Investors gain 20% income tax relief on dividends, provided shares are held in the VCT for three years, and capital gains rollover relief if the gain is invested in a VCT. There is an investment ceiling per person of £100,000.

24: FINANCING OF SMALL AND MEDIUM-SIZED ENTERPRISES

Question — Debt finance

Ella Ltd, a small company, is currently considering a major capital investment project for which additional finance will be required. It is not currently feasible to raise additional equity finance, consequently debt finance is being considered. The decision has not yet been finalised whether this debt finance will be short or long term and if it is to be at fixed or variable rates. The financial controller has asked you for your assistance in the preparation of a report for a forthcoming meeting of the board of directors.

Required

Prepare a draft report to the board of directors which identifies and briefly explains:

(a) The main factors to be considered when deciding on the appropriate mix of short, medium or long-term debt finance for Ella Ltd.

(b) The practical considerations which could be factors in restricting the amount of debt which Ella Ltd could raise.

Answer

(a) To: Board
From: Accountant
Date: 8 January 20X2
Re: Debt finance

The term of the finance

The term should be appropriate to the **asset** being acquired. As a general rule, long-term **assets** should be **financed** from **long-term finance** sources. Cheaper short-term funds should be used to finance short-term requirements, such as fluctuations in the level of working capital.

Flexibility

Short-term debt is a **more flexible** source of finance; there may be penalties for repaying long-term debt early. If the company takes out long-term debt and interest rates fall, it will find itself locked into unfavourable terms.

Repayment terms

The company must have **sufficient funds** to be able to **meet repayment schedules** laid down in loan agreements, and to cover interest costs. Although there may be no specific terms of repayment laid down for short-term debt, it may possibly be **repayable on demand**, so it may be risky to finance long-term capital investments in this way.

Costs

Interest on short-term debt is usually **less** than on long-term debt. However, if short-term debt has to be renewed frequently, issue expenses may raise its cost significantly.

Availability

It may be **difficult to renew short-term finance** in the future if the company's position or economic conditions change adversely.

Effect on gearing

Certain types of short-term debt (bank overdrafts, increased credit from suppliers) will not be included in gearing calculations. If a company is seen as **too highly geared**, lenders may be **unwilling to lend money**, or judge that the high risk of default must be compensated by higher interest rates or restrictive covenants.

PART F SOURCES OF FINANCE

(b) **Previous record of company**

If the company (or possibly its directors or even shareholders) has a **low credit rating** with credit reference agencies, investors may be unwilling to subscribe for debentures. Banks may be influenced by this, and also by their own experiences of the company as customer (has the company exceeded overdraft limits in the past on a regular basis).

Restrictions in memorandum and articles

The company should examine the legal documents carefully to see if they place any restrictions on what the company can borrow, and for what purposes.

Restrictions of current borrowing

The **terms** of any **loans** to the company that are **currently outstanding** may contain restrictions about further borrowing that can be taken out.

Uncertainty over project

The project is a significant one, and presumably the **interest and ultimately repayment** that lenders obtain may be very dependent on the success of the project. If the results are uncertain, lenders may not be willing to take the risk.

Security

The company may be **unwilling to provide the security** that lenders require, particularly if it is faced **with restrictions** on what it can do with the **assets secured**.

Alternatively it may have **insufficient assets** to provide the necessary security.

Chapter Roundup

- **SMEs** are generally:
    - Unquoted
    - Owned by a small number of individuals
    - Not micro-businesses

- SMEs may **not know about** the sources of finance available.

- Finance may be difficult to obtain because of the **risks** faced by SMEs.

- The availability of certain sources of finance will often be conditioned by the **security** that SMEs can offer.

- Possible sources of finance for SMEs include:
    - Owner financing
    - Overdraft financing
    - Bank loans
    - Trade credit
    - Equity finance
    - Business angel financing
    - Venture capital
    - Leasing
    - Factoring

- **Government aid** for SMEs includes the Loan Guarantee Scheme, Enterprise Initiatives and development agencies.

Quick Quiz

1. What are the main characteristics of small and medium-sized enterprises defined by Laney?
2. What is business angel financing?
3. What are the key factors involved in the granting of an overdraft?
4. What is the main incentive offered by the Enterprise Investment Scheme?
5. List four factors that a venture capitalist would consider when deciding whether to invest in a company.
6. Which of the following statements about venture capital is correct?

    A   Venture capital would not be appropriate to finance a management buyout

    B   Venture capital organisations may provide loan finance as well as equity finance to a company

    C   Secured medium-term bank loans are a form of venture capital

    D   Companies with a stock market quotation would have no difficulty raising finance from a venture capital organisation

7. Which of the following business opportunities would be the most attractive to a venture capitalist?

    A   A consultancy specialising in sustainable development currently employing four consultants that wishes to expand its workforce by 25%

    B   A manufacturing business that is facing liquidity problems and needs an injection of capital

    C   A management buyout of a medium sized electrical engineering company

    D   A carpet manufacturing company that wants to renovate one of its production lines

8. Which of the following sources of funds for business is not commonly offered by commercial banks?

    A   Overdraft facilities
    B   Short-term loans
    C   Medium-term loans
    D   Long-term loans

PART F SOURCES OF FINANCE

Answers to Quick Quiz

1. (a) Firms are likely to be unquoted.
   (b) Ownership of the business is restricted to a few individuals, typically a family group.
   (c) They are not micro businesses that offer a medium for self-employment of their owners.

2. Direct investment in SMEs by individuals or small groups of investors.

3. (a) Amount
   (b) Margin
   (c) Purpose
   (d) Repayment
   (e) Security
   (f) Benefits

4. When a qualifying individual subscribers for eligible shares in a qualifying company, the individual saves tax at 20% on the amounts subscribed.

5. (a) Nature of company's product
   (b) Production expertise
   (c) Management expertise
   (d) Future prospects
   (e) Board membership
   (f) Risk borne by existing owners

6. B Loan finance may be provided.

7. C Venture capital is appropriate for new business ventures or business expansions. It is not appropriate for the day-to-day financing of existing operations, as in B and D. Option A is likely to be too small to attract a venture capital investment.

8. D This is the correct answer. Long-term loans are rarely negotiated with the commercial banks, unless in the form of a mortgage on property.

   A Overdraft facilities are funds that are drawn down as required, up to a pre-determined maximum limit agreed with the bank. They are repayable on demand and are the traditional form of bank finance.

   B Short-term loans with a fixed period of up to three years are another traditional form of bank finance. They carry less risk than the overdraft, but interest will be payable on the full amount, not just the amount in use at any one time.

   C Medium-term loans are for a period of three to ten years. This is a growing form of bank lending, which used to be restricted mainly to short-term financing.

Now try the questions below from the Exam Question Bank

Number	Level	Marks	Time
Q27	Examination	25	45 mins

Part G
Investment appraisal

Investment decisions

Topic list	Syllabus reference
1 Investment	5(b)
2 Identification of investment opportunities	5(b)
3 The payback period	5(b)(iii)
4 The return on capital employed method	5(b)(ii)

Introduction

This chapter introduces **investment appraisal** and covers the manner in which investment opportunities are identified. It also introduces two relatively straightforward, but widely used, investment appraisal methods: **payback period** and **return on capital employed**. Chapter 26 will look at investment appraisal using the more sophisticated **Discounted cash flow (DCF)** methods, which address some of the weaknesses of the traditional approaches covered in this chapter (make sure you know what these are!).

PART G   INVESTMENT APPRAISAL

Study guide

Section 12 – Investment decisions

- Define and distinguish between capital and revenue expenditure
- Compare and contrast fixed asset investment and working capital investment
- Describe the impact of investment projects on financial statements
- Calculate payback and assess its usefulness as a measure of investment worth
- Calculate ROCE and assess its usefulness as a measure of investment worth

Exam guide

As well as using the techniques to assess projects, you may be asked to discuss their drawbacks. The Oxford Brookes degree Research and Analysis Project Topic 14 requires you to investigate recent project decisions by an organisation of your choice.

1 Investment

FAST FORWARD

> Investment can be divided into **capital expenditure** and **revenue expenditure** and can be made in **fixed assets** or **working capital**.

Investment is any expenditure in the expectation of future benefits. We can divide such expenditure into two categories: **capital expenditure**, and **revenue expenditure**.

Suppose that a business purchases a building for £30,000. It then adds an extension to the building at a cost of £10,000. The building needs to have a few broken windows mended, its floors polished and some missing roof tiles replaced. These cleaning and maintenance jobs cost £900.

The original purchase (£30,000) and the cost of the extension (£10,000) are **capital expenditure** because they are incurred to **acquire** and then **improve** a fixed asset. The other costs of £900 are **revenue expenditure** because they merely maintain the building and thus the earning capacity of the building.

Key terms

> **Capital expenditure** is expenditure which results in the **acquisition** of fixed assets or an **improvement** in their earning capacity. It is not charged as an expense in the profit and loss account; the expenditure appears as a fixed asset in the balance sheet.
>
> **Revenue expenditure** is charged to the profit and loss account and is expenditure which is incurred:
>
> (a) For the purpose of the trade of the business - this includes expenditure classified as selling and distribution expenses, administration expenses and finance charges
>
> (b) To maintain the existing earning capacity of fixed assets

1.1 Fixed asset investment and working capital investment

Investment can be made in **fixed assets** or **working capital**.

(a) **Investment in fixed assets** involves a significant elapse of time between commitment of funds and recoupment of the investment. Money is paid out to acquire resources which are going to be used on a continuing basis within the organisation.

(b) **Investment in working capital** arises from the need to pay out money for resources (such as raw materials) before it can be recovered from sales of the finished product or service. The funds are therefore only committed for a short period of time.

1.2 Investment by the commercial sector

Investment by commercial organisations might include investment in:

- Plant and machinery
- Research and development
- Advertising
- Warehouse facilities

The overriding feature of a commercial sector investment is that it is generally **based on financial considerations alone.** The various capital expenditure appraisal techniques that we will be looking at assess the financial aspects of capital investment.

1.3 Investment by not-for-profit organisations

Investment by not-for-profit organisations differs from investment by commercial organisations for several reasons.

(a) Relatively few not-for-profit organisations' capital investments are made with the **intention** of earning a **financial return**.

(b) When there are two or more ways of achieving the same objective (mutually exclusive investment opportunities), a commercial organisation might prefer the option with the **lowest present value of cost**.

Not-for-profit organisations, however, rather than just considering financial cost and financial benefits, will often have regard to the **social costs** and **social benefits** of investments.

(c) The **cost of capital** that is applied to project cash flows by the public sector will not be a 'commercial' rate of return, but one that is **determined** by the **government**. Any targets that a public sector investment has to meet before being accepted will therefore not be based on the same criteria as those in the commercial sector.

2 Identification of investment opportunities

FAST FORWARD

Strategic analysis aids the identification of investment opportunities and involves **environmental analysis** and **internal appraisal**, which are combined in **SWOT analysis**.

A company can be offered a number of possible investment projects, each of which might appear attractive in the return it offers as assessed by investment appraisal techniques such as discounted cash flow.

Igor Ansoff argues, however, that capital investment appraisal is concerned with only the last two steps of a more complex process of strategic decision making. This process has four stages.

- Perception of the need for an investment, or awareness of a potential opportunity
- Formulation of alternative courses of action
- Evaluation of the alternatives
- Choice of one of these alternatives for implementation

2.1 Corporate appraisal: SWOT analysis

Environmental analysis and internal assessment are combined, in a process of corporate appraisal known as **SWOT** analysis. This involves a critical assessment of the strengths and weaknesses, opportunities and threats in relation to the internal and environmental factors affecting the organisation.

A cruciform chart is a table listing the significant strengths and weaknesses and opportunities and threats. It can be used to summarise the major conclusions of a SWOT analysis. In the example below, the development of potential strategies from the analysis is illustrated.

Strengths	Weaknesses
£10 million of capital available. Production expertise and appropriate marketing skills	Heavy reliance on a small number of customers. Limited product range, with no new products and expected market decline. Small marketing organisation.
Threats	**Opportunities**
Major competitor has already entered the new market.	Government tax incentives for new investment. Growing demand in a new market, although customers so far relatively small in number.

In this simple example, you can see that the company is in imminent danger of losing its existing markets and must **diversify** its products, or its products and markets. The new market opportunity exists to be exploited. Since the number of customers is currently few, the relatively small size of the existing marketing force would not be an immediate hindrance.

You can get used to the basic thinking that underlies planning if you try the following short question in SWOT analysis.

Question — SWOT analysis

Hall Faull Downes Ltd has been in business for 25 years, during which time profits have risen by an average of 3% per annum, although there have been peaks and troughs in profitability due to the ups and downs of trade in the customers' industry. The increase in profits until five years ago was the result of increasing sales in a buoyant market, but more recently, the total market has become somewhat smaller and Hall Faull Downes has only increased sales and profits as a result of improving its market share.

The company produces components for manufacturers in the engineering industry. In recent years, the company has developed many new products and currently has 40 items in its range compared to 24 only five years ago. Over the same five-year period, the number of customers has fallen from 20 to nine, two of whom together account for 60% of the company's sales.

Give your appraisal of the company's future, and suggest what it is probably doing wrong.

Answer

A general interpretation of the facts as given might be sketched as follows.

(a) **Objectives.** The company has no declared objectives. Profits have risen by 3% per annum in the past, therefore failing to keep pace with inflation but this may have been a satisfactory rate of increase in the current conditions of the industry. Even so, stronger growth is indicated in the future.

(b)

Strengths	Weaknesses
Many new products developed.	Products may be reaching the end of their life and entering decline.
Marketing success in increasing market share.	New product life cycles may be shorter.
	Reduction in customers.
	Excessive reliance on a few customers.
	Doubtful whether profit record is satisfactory.
Threats	**Opportunities**
Possible decline in the end-product. Smaller end-product market will restrict future sales prospects for Hall Faull Downes.	None identified.

(c) **Strengths.** The growth in company sales in the last five years has been as a result of increasing the market share in a declining market. This success may be the result of the following.

   (i) Research and development spending
   (ii) Good product development programmes
   (iii) Extending the product range to suit changing customer needs
   (iv) Marketing skills
   (v) Long-term supply contracts with customers
   (vi) Cheap pricing policy
   (vii) Product quality and reliable service

(d) **Weaknesses**

   (i) The products may be custom-made for customers so that they provide little or no opportunity for market development.

   (ii) Products might have a shorter life cycle than in the past, in view of the declining total market demand.

   (iii) Excessive reliance on two major customers leaves the company exposed to the dangers of losing their custom.

(e) **Threats**. There may be a decline in the end-market for the customers' product so that the customer demands for the company's own products will also fall.

(f) **Opportunities**. No opportunities have been identified, but in view of the situation as described, new strategies for the longer term would appear to be essential.

(g) **Conclusions**. The company does not appear to be planning beyond the short term, or is reacting to the business environment in a piecemeal fashion. A strategic planning programme should be introduced.

(h) **Recommendation**. The company must look for new opportunities in the longer term.

   (i) In the short term, current strengths must be exploited to continue to increase market share in existing markets and product development programmes should also continue.

   (ii) In the longer term, the company must diversify into new markets or into new products and new markets. Diversification opportunities should be sought with a view to exploiting any competitive advantage or synergy that might be achievable.

   (iii) The company should use its strengths (whether in R & D, production skills or marketing expertise) in exploiting any identifiable opportunities.

   (iv) Objectives need to be quantified in order to assess the extent to which new long-term strategies are required.

2.2 Product-market mix

A firm may be faced with a bewildering variety of options, in relation both to product development and its possible markets. Igor Ansoff developed a tool for analysing these opportunities as follows.

Market penetration	Sell more existing products in existing markets
Market development	Sell existing products in new markets
Product development	Sell new products in existing markets
Diversification	Sell new products in new markets

In practice, this tool is an oversimplification. New products are often not unrelated to existing ones. They may be a logical development from them (such as a cheesemaker making and selling butter). The new market may have similarities with the existing ones.

2.3 Organic growth or acquisition?

A company which is planning to grow must decide on whether to pursue a policy of 'organic' internal growth or a policy of taking over other established businesses, or a mix of the two.

Organic growth requires funding in cash, whereas acquisitions can be made by means of share exchange transactions. A company pursuing a policy of organic growth would need to take account of the following.

(a) The company must make the **finance available**, possibly out of retained profits. However, the company should then know how much it can afford, and with careful management, should not over-extend itself by trying to achieve too much growth too quickly.

(b) The company can use its **existing staff and systems** to create the growth projects, and this will open up career opportunities for the staff. In contrast, when expansion is achieved by taking over other businesses, the company usually acquires and assimilates the staff of those businesses.

25: INVESMENT DECISIONS

(c) Overall expansion can be **planned more efficiently**. For example, if a company wishes to open a new factory or depot, it can site the new development in a place that helps operational efficiency (eg close to other factories, to reduce transport costs). With acquisitions, the company must take on existing sites no matter where they happen to be.

(d) **Economies of scale** can be achieved from more efficient use of central head office functions such as finance, purchasing, personnel and management services. With acquisitions, a company buys the head office functions of other companies and there will either be fewer economies of scale, or more redundancies.

Acquisitions can be made to **enter new product areas**, or to **expand in existing markets**, much **more quickly**. Organic growth takes time. With acquisitions, entire existing operations are assimilated into the company at one fell swoop. Acquisitions can be made without cash, if share exchange transactions are acceptable to both the buyers and sellers of any company which is to be taken over.

When an acquisition is made to diversify into new product areas, the company will be buying technical expertise, goodwill and customer contracts and so on, which it might take years to develop if it tried to enter the market by growing organically.

> **Exam focus point**
>
> For the exam, you will be expected to have an appreciation of the advantages and disadvantages of internal *versus* external growth.

3 The payback period   12/04

> **FAST FORWARD**
>
> The **payback method** of investment appraisal and the **ROCE/ARR/ROI** methods of investment appraisal are popular appraisal techniques despite their limitations (of which you should be aware).
>
> - **Payback** is the amount of time it takes for cash inflows = cash outflows

There are a number of ways of evaluating capital projects, two of which we will be examining in this chapter. We will look first at the payback method.

> **Exam focus point**
>
> Exam questions often ask about the pros and cons of the payback method.

> **Key term**
>
> **Payback** is the time it takes the cash inflows from a capital investment project to equal the cash outflows, usually expressed in years.

Payback is often used as a 'first screening method'. By this, we mean that when a capital investment project is being considered, the first question to ask is: 'How long will it take to pay back its cost?' The organisation might have a **target payback**, and so it would reject a capital project unless its payback period were less than a certain number of years.

However, a project should not be evaluated on the basis of payback alone. If a project gets through the payback test, it ought then to be evaluated with a more sophisticated investment appraisal technique.

3.1 Why is payback alone an inadequate investment appraisal technique?

The reason why payback should not be used on its own to evaluate capital investments should seem fairly obvious if you look at the figures below for two mutually exclusive projects (this means that only one of them can be undertaken).

	Project P	Project Q
Capital asset	£60,000	£60,000
Profits before depreciation (a rough approximation of cash flows)		
Year 1	£20,000	£50,000
Year 2	£30,000	£20,000
Year 3	£40,000	£5,000
Year 4	£50,000	£5,000
Year 5	£60,000	£5,000

Project P pays back in year 3 (about one quarter of the way through year 3). Project Q pays back half way through year 2. Using payback alone to judge capital investments, project Q would be preferred.

However the returns from project P over its life are much higher than the returns from project Q. **Project P** will earn total profits before depreciation of £140,000 on an investment of £60,000. **Project Q** will earn total profits before depreciation of only £25,000 on an investment of £60,000.

3.2 Disadvantages of the payback method

There are a number of serious drawbacks to the payback method.

(a) It **ignores** the **timing** of cash flows within the payback period, the cash flows after the end of payback period and therefore the total project return.

(b) It **ignores the time value of money** (a concept incorporated into more sophisticated appraisal methods). This means that it does not take account of the fact that £1 today is worth more than £1 in one year's time. An investor who has £1 today can either consume it immediately or alternatively can invest it at the prevailing interest rate, say 10%, to get a return of £1.10 in a year's time.

(c) Payback is **unable to distinguish between projects** with the same payback period.

(d) The choice of any **cut-off** payback period by an organisation is **arbitrary**.

(e) It may lead to **excessive investment** in **short-term projects**.

(f) It takes account of the risk of the timing of cash flows but not the **variability** of those cash flows.

3.3 Advantages of the payback method

In spite of its limitations, the payback method continues to be popular, and the following points can be made in its favour.

(a) It is **simple to calculate** and **simple to understand**. This may be important when management resources are limited. It is similarly helpful in communicating information about minimum requirements to managers responsible for submitting projects

(b) It uses **cash flows** rather than accounting profits.

(c) It can be used as a **screening device** as a first stage in eliminating obviously inappropriate projects prior to more detailed evaluation.

(d) The fact that it tends to **bias** in favour of **short-term projects** means that it tends to minimise both financial and business risk.

(e) It can be used when there is a **capital rationing situation** to identify those projects which generate additional cash for investment quickly.

4 The return on capital employed method 6/04, 12/04

FAST FORWARD

$$ROCE = \frac{\text{Estimated average/total profits}}{\text{Estimated average/initial investment}} \times 100\%$$

The **return on capital employed** method (ROCE) (also called the **accounting rate of return** method or the **return on investment** ROI method) of appraising a capital project is to estimate the accounting rate of return that the project should yield. If it exceeds a target rate of return, the project will be undertaken. In Chapter 14 we discussed how return on capital employed is measured for financial accounting purposes. Here the measure is calculated in relation to investments.

Unfortunately, there are several different definitions of 'return on investment'. One of the most popular is as follows.

$$ROCE = \frac{\text{Estimated average profits}}{\text{Estimated average investment}} \times 100\%$$

The others include:

$$ROCE = \frac{\text{Estimated total profits}}{\text{Estimated initial investment}} \times 100\%$$

$$ROCE = \frac{\text{Estimated average profits}}{\text{Estimated initial investment}} \times 100\%$$

There are arguments in favour of each of these definitions. The most important point is, however, that the method selected should be used consistently. For examination purposes we recommend the first definition unless the question clearly indicates that some other one is to be used.

4.1 Example: The return on capital employed

A company has a target return on capital employed of 20% (using the first definition in Paragraph 4.1 above), and is now considering the following project.

Capital cost of asset	£80,000
Estimated life	4 years
Estimated profit before depreciation	
Year 1	£20,000
Year 2	£25,000
Year 3	£35,000
Year 4	£25,000

The capital asset would be depreciated by 25% of its cost each year, and will have no residual value. You are required to assess whether the project should be undertaken.

4.2 Solution

The annual profits after depreciation, and the mid-year net book value of the asset, would be as follows.

Year	Profit after depreciation £	Mid-year net book value £	ROCE in the year %
1	0	70,000	0
2	5,000	50,000	10
3	15,000	30,000	50
4	5,000	10,000	50

As the table shows, the ROCE is low in the early stages of the project, partly because of low profits in Year 1 but mainly because the net book value of the asset is much higher early on in its life.

The project does not achieve the target ROCE of 20% in its first two years, but exceeds it in years 3 and 4. So should it be undertaken?

When the ROCE from a project varies from year to year, it makes sense to take an overall or 'average' view of the project's return. In this case, we should look at the return as a whole over the four-year period.

	£
Total profit before depreciation over four years	105,000
Total profit after depreciation over four years	25,000
Average annual profit after depreciation	6,250
Original cost of investment	80,000
Average net book value over the four year period $\frac{(80,000 + 0)}{2}$	40,000

ROCE = 6,250/40,000 = 15.6%

The project would not be undertaken because it would fail to yield the target return of 20%.

4.3 The ROCE and the comparison of mutually exclusive projects

The ROCE method of capital investment appraisal can also be used to compare two or more projects which are mutually exclusive. The project with the highest ROCE would be selected (provided that the expected ROCE is higher than the company's target ROCE).

4.4 Example: The ROCE and mutually exclusive projects

Arrow Ltd wants to buy a new item of equipment which will be used to provide a service to customers of the company. Two models of equipment are available, one with a slightly higher capacity and greater reliability than the other. The expected costs and profits of each item are as follows.

	Equipment item X	Equipment item Y
Capital cost	£80,000	£150,000
Life	5 years	5 years
Profits before depreciation	£	£
Year 1	50,000	50,000
Year 2	50,000	50,000
Year 3	30,000	60,000
Year 4	20,000	60,000
Year 5	10,000	60,000
Disposal value	0	0

ROCE is measured as the average annual profit after depreciation, divided by the average net book value of the asset. You are required to decide which item of equipment should be selected, if any, if the company's target ROCE is 30%.

Solution

	Item X £	Item Y £
Total profit over life of equipment		
Before depreciation	160,000	280,000
After depreciation	80,000	130,000
Average annual profit after depreciation	16,000	26,000
(Capital cost + disposal value)/2	40,000	75,000
ROCE	40%	34.7%

Both projects would earn a return in excess of 30%, but since item X would earn a bigger ROCE, it would be preferred to item Y, even though the profits from Y would be higher by an average of £10,000 a year.

4.5 The drawbacks to the ROCE method of capital investment appraisal

The ROCE method of capital investment appraisal has the serious drawback that it does not take account of the **timing** of the **profits from an investment**. Whenever capital is invested in a project, money is tied up until the project begins to earn profits which pay back the investment. Money tied up in one project cannot be invested anywhere else until the profits come in. Management should be aware of the benefits of early repayments from an investment, which will provide the money for other investments.

There are a number of other disadvantages.

(a) It is based on **accounting profits** and not cash flows. Accounting profits are subject to a number of different accounting treatments.

(b) It is a **relative measure** rather than an absolute measure and hence takes no account of the size of the investment.

(c) It takes no account of the length of the project.

(d) Like the payback method, it ignores the time value of money.

There are, however, advantages to the ROCE method.

(a) It is a quick and simple calculation.
(b) It involves a familiar concept of a percentage return.
(c) It looks at the entire project life.

Chapter Roundup

- Investment can be divided into **capital expenditure** and **revenue expenditure** and can be made in **fixed assets** or **working capital**.

- **Strategic analysis** aids the identification of investment opportunities and involves **environmental analysis** and **internal appraisal**, which are combined in **SWOT analysis**.

- The **payback method** of investment appraisal and the **ROCE/ARR/ROI** methods of investment appraisal are popular appraisal techniques despite their limitations (of which you should be aware).

    - **Payback** is the amount of time it takes for cash inflows = cash outflows

    - $\text{ROCE} = \dfrac{\text{Estimated average/total profits}}{\text{Estimated average/initial investment}} \times 100\%$

PART G INVESTMENT APPRAISAL

Quick Quiz

1   S
    W
    O
    T
    stands for?

2
	Markets	Products
Market penetration		
Market development		
Product development		
Diversification		

    Complete the grid using the words 'New' or 'Existing'.

3   *Fill in the blank.*

    .... is the time it takes the cash inflows from a capital investment project to equal the cash outflows.

4   Which of the following can be used to calculate the accounting rate of return?

    (a) $\dfrac{\text{Estimated average profits}}{\text{Estimated average investment}} \times 100\%$

    (b) $\dfrac{\text{Estimated total profits}}{\text{Estimated initial investment}} \times 100\%$

    (c) $\dfrac{\text{Estimated average profits}}{\text{Estimated initial investment}} \times 100\%$

5   *Fill in the blanks in these statements about the advantages of the payback method.*

    (a) Focus on early payback can enhance ....

    (b) Investment risk is .... if payback is longer.

    (c) .... term forecasts are likely to be more reliable.

6   The accounting rate of return method of investment appraisal uses accounting profits before depreciation charges.

    ☐ True

    ☐ False

7   One reason that capital expenditure may be incurred is to maintain the earning capacity of existing fixed assets.

    ☐ True

    ☐ False

8   Name the four stages of strategic decision making identified by Ansoff.

Answers to Quick Quiz

1. **S**trengths
   Weaknesses
   Opportunities
   Threats

2.
	Markets	Products
Market penetration	Existing	Existing
Market development	New	Existing
Product development	Existing	New
Diversification	New	New

3. Payback

4. All three could be used, although (a) $\dfrac{\text{Estimated average profits}}{\text{Estimated average investment}} \times 100\%$ is generally best.

5. (a) liquidity
   (b) increased
   (c) shorter

6. False

7. False. This is a reason for incurring **revenue** expenditure.

8.
   - Perception of the need for investment/awareness of potential opportunity
   - Formulation of alternative courses of action
   - Evaluation of alternatives
   - Choice of alternatives

Now try the questions below from the Exam Question Bank

Number	Level	Marks	Time
Q28	Examination	25	45 mins

Investment appraisal using DCF methods

Topic list	Syllabus reference
1 Discounted cash flow and the cost of capital	5(a)
2 The net present value method	5(a), 5(b)(v)
3 The internal rate of return method	5(a), 5(b)(iv)
4 NPV and IRR compared	5(a), 5(b)(iv), (v)
5 Assessment of DCF methods of project appraisal	5(a), 5(b)(ii), (iii), (iv), (v)
6 Asset replacement decisions	5(a), 5(b)(viii)

Introduction

The **payback** and **ROCE** methods of investment appraisal were considered in the previous chapter. This chapter will look at **discounted cash flow (DCF) methods** of investment appraisal which take into account changes in the value of money over time. These two methods, **Net Present Value (NPV)** and **Internal Rate of Return (IRR)**, use the technique of **discounting** to bring all cash flows resulting from the investment to a present day value by eliminating the **interest** that would have been earned on that cash flow had it happened now rather than later.

The interest rate (referred to as **discount rate** in this context) used in this calculation is specific to each organisation, and depends on the relative levels of debt and equity funding of the organisation. This links in with our previous studies of capital structure. We also return to relevant costs, as NPV and IRR consider only relevant cash flows in their calculation.

Chapter 27 will look at how **inflation** and **taxation** can be incorporated into appraisal techniques.

PART G INVESTMENT APPRAISAL

Study guide

Section 13 – Interest and discounting

- Explain the difference between simple and compound interest
- Explain what is meant by future values and calculate future values, including application of the annuity formula
- Explain what is meant by discounting and calculate present values, including the application of annuity and perpetuity formulae, and the use of present value and annuity tables
- Explain the importance of the time value of money

Section 14 – Investment appraisal using DCF methods

- Explain the role of the cost of capital in appraising investments
- Identify and evaluate relevant cash flows of potential investments
- Calculate present values to derive the NPV and IRR measures of investment worth
- Explain the superiority of DCF methods over payback and ROCE
- Assess the merits of IRR and NPV
- Apply DCF methods to asset replacement decisions

Exam guide

You may be asked to discuss the relative merits of the various investment appraisal techniques as well as demonstrate your ability to apply the techniques themselves. Investment appraisal using the NPV method was part of the compulsory question in June 2004. This is a regular topic in both sections of the paper, and is particularly likely to be a substantial part of the compulsory 50 mark question in Section A.

1 Discounted cash flow and the cost of capital

FAST FORWARD

There are two methods of using DCF to evaluate capital investments, the **NPV method** and the **IRR/DCF yield method**.

The **weighted average cost of capital (WACC)** is the best **discount rate** to use when discounting cash flows to their **present value** if the funds raised to finance the investment are in proportion to the company's current capital structure. Otherwise, the **marginal cost of capital** may be a better rate.

Discounted cash flow, or **DCF** for short, is an investment appraisal technique which takes into account both the timings of cash flows and also total profitability over a project's life.

Two important points about DCF are as follows.

(a) DCF looks at the **cash flows** of a project, not the accounting profits. Cash flows are considered because they show the costs and benefits of a project when they actually occur and ignore notional costs such as depreciation.

(b) The **timing** of cash flows is taken into account by **discounting them**. The effect of discounting is to give a bigger value per £1 for cash flows that occur earlier: £1 earned after one year will be worth more than £1 earned after two years, which in turn will be worth more than £1 earned after five years, and so on.

1.1 Compounding

Suppose that a company has £10,000 to invest, and wants to earn a return of 10% (compound interest) on its investments. This means that if the £10,000 could be invested at 10%, the value of the investment with interest would build up as follows.

(a) After 1 year   £10,000 × (1.10)   = £11,000
(b) After 2 years   £10,000 × (1.10)^2 = £12,100
(c) After 3 years   £10,000 × (1.10)^3 = £13,310 and so on.

This is **compounding**. The formula for the future value of an investment plus accumulated interest after n time periods is:

$$FV = PV(1+r)^n$$

where   FV is the future value of the investment with interest
PV is the initial or 'present' value of the investment
r is the compound rate of return per time period, expressed as a proportion
(so 10% = 0.10, 5% = 0.05 and so on)
n is the number of time periods.

1.1.1 Simple and compound interest

The example above illustrates compound interest where the interest rate is applied to the original principal **and** any accumulated interest.

Simple interest is a method of computing interest on a principal sum where the interest rate is applied **only** to the original principal amount.

1.2 Discounting

Key term

> **Present value** is the cash equivalent now of a sum of money receivable or payable at a stated future date, discounted at a specified rate of return.

Discounting starts with the future value, and converts a future value to a present value. For example, if a company expects to earn a (compound) rate of return of 10% on its investments, how much would it need to invest now to have the following investments?

(a) £11,000 after 1 year
(b) £12,100 after 2 years
(c) £13,310 after 3 years

The answer is £10,000 in each case, and we can calculate it by discounting. The discounting formula to calculate the present value of a future sum of money at the end of n time periods is:

$$PV = FV \frac{1}{(1+r)^n}$$

Exam formula

> **Present value** of 1 = $(1+r)^{-n}$ or $\frac{1}{(1+r)^n}$

(a) After 1 year, £11,000 × $\frac{1}{1.10}$ = £10,000

(b) After 2 years, £12,100 × $\frac{1}{1.10^2}$ = £10,000

PART G INVESTMENT APPRAISAL

(c) After 3 years, £13,310 × $\frac{1}{1.10^3}$ = £10,000

Discounting can be applied to both money receivable and also to money payable at a future date. By discounting all payments and receipts from a capital investment to a present value, they can be compared on a common basis at a value which takes account of when the various cash flows will take place.

Question — Present value

Spender Ltd expects the cash inflow from an investment to be £40,000 after 2 years and another £30,000 after 3 years. Its target rate of return is 12%. Calculate the present value of these future returns, and explain what this present value signifies.

Answer

(a)

Year	Cash flow £	Discount factor 12%	Present value £
2	40,000	$\frac{1}{(1.12)^2}$ = 0.797	31,880
3	30,000	$\frac{1}{(1.12)^3}$ = 0.712	21,360
			Total PV 53,240

(b) The present value of the future returns, discounted at 12%, is £53,240. This means that if Spender Ltd can invest now to earn a return of 12% on its investments, it would have to invest £53,240 now to earn £40,000 after 2 years plus £30,000 after 3 years.

1.3 The cost of capital

The **cost of capital** has two aspects to it.

(a) It is the **cost of funds** that a company raises and uses.

(b) The return that investors expect to be paid for putting funds into the company. It is therefore the **minimum return** that a company should make from its own investments, to earn the cash flows out of which investors can be paid their return.

The cost of capital can therefore be measured by studying the returns required by investors, and used to derive a discount rate for DCF analysis and investment appraisal.

1.4 The cost of ordinary share capital

New funds from equity shareholders are obtained from **new issues of shares**, or as the cash or other funds generated from **retained earnings**.

Both of these sources of funds have a cost. Shareholders will not be prepared to provide funds for a new issue of shares unless the **return on their investment** is sufficiently attractive. **Retained earnings** also have a cost. This is an **opportunity cost**, the **dividend forgone** by shareholders.

If we begin by ignoring share issue costs, the cost of equity, both for new issues and retained earnings, can be estimated on the assumption that the **market value** of shares is **directly related** to expected **future dividends** on the shares. Different assumptions can be made about whether dividends are expected to grow in the future.

1.5 The cost of debt capital and fixed dividend capital

The cost of debt capital already issued is, briefly, the **rate of interest** (the internal rate of return) which **equates** the **current market price** with the **discounted future cash receipts** from the security.

1.6 Computing a discount rate

It is possible to compute the costs of individual sources of capital for a company, for example in the form of debt or share capital. But how will this help us to work out the **cost of capital** as a whole, or the **discount rate** to apply in DCF investment appraisals?

In many cases it will be difficult to associate a particular project with a particular form of finance. A company's funds may be viewed as a pool of resources. Under these circumstances it might seem appropriate to use an average cost of capital as the discount rate. The correct cost of capital to use in investment appraisal is the **marginal cost of the funds raised (or earnings retained)** to finance the investment.

Key term

> The **weighted average cost of capital** is the average cost of the company's finance, weighted according to the relative size of each element compared with total capital.

The **weighted average cost of capital (WACC)** might be considered the most reliable guide to the marginal cost of capital, but only on the assumptions that the company continues to invest:

- In the future
- In projects of a standard level of business risk
- By raising funds in the same proportions as its existing capital structure

Exam focus point

> For the Paper 2.4 exam, you will not be required to produce computations of, or to comment on, a WACC: these more advanced skills form part of the Paper 3.7 syllabus. In this paper an exam question will give a discount rate as and where appropriate.

1.7 Example: Weighted average cost of capital

Prudence plc is financed partly by equity and partly by debentures. The equity proportion is always kept at two thirds of the total. The cost of equity is 18% and that of debt 12%. A new project is under consideration which will cost £100,000 and will yield a return before interest of £17,500 a year in perpetuity. Should the project be accepted? Ignore taxation.

Solution

Since the company will maintain its gearing ratio unchanged, it is reasonable to assume that its marginal cost of funds equals its WACC. The weighted average cost of capital is as follows.

	Proportion	Cost	Cost × proportion
Equity	$\frac{2}{3}$	18%	12%
Debt	$\frac{1}{3}$	12%	4%
		WACC	16%

The present value of the future returns in perpetuity can be found using the WACC as the discount rate, as follows.

Present value of future cash flows = $\dfrac{\text{Annual cash flow}}{\text{Discount rate}} = \dfrac{£17,500}{0.16} = £109,375$

The NPV of the investment is £109,375 – £100,000 = £9,375.

1.7.1 Weighting

In the last example, we simplified the problem of weighting the different costs of capital by giving the proportions of capital. Weights could be based on **market values** (by this method, the cost of retained earnings is implied in the market value of equity). Alternatively, weights could be based on **book values**.

Although the latter are often easier to obtain they are of doubtful economic significance. It is, therefore, more meaningful to use market values when reliable data is available (which it should be for quoted companies).

When using market values it is not possible to split the equity value between share capital and reserves and only one **cost of equity** can be **used**. This removes the need to estimate a separate cost of retained earnings.

1.8 Arguments for and against using the WACC

The weighted average cost of capital is **recommended for use in investment appraisal** on the following assumptions.

(a) New investments must be **financed** by **new sources of funds**; retained earnings, new share issues, new loans and so on.

(b) The cost of capital to be applied to project evaluation must reflect the **marginal cost** of new capital.

(c) The weighted average cost of capital reflects the company's **long-term future capital structure**, and capital costs. If this were not so, the current weighted average cost would become irrelevant because eventually it would not relate to any actual cost of capital.

Thus the **current weighted average cost of capital** should be used to evaluate projects, because a company's capital structure changes only very slowly over time; the marginal cost of new capital should be roughly equal to the weighted average cost of current capital.

If this view is correct, then by undertaking investments which offer a return in excess of the WACC, a company will increase the market value of its ordinary shares in the long run. This is because the excess returns would provide surplus profits and dividends for the shareholders.

The following **arguments against using the WACC** as the cost of capital for investment appraisal are based on criticisms of the assumptions that are used to justify use of the WACC.

(a) New investments undertaken by a company might have different **business risk** characteristics from the company's existing operations. As a consequence, the **return required by investors** might go up (or down) if the investments are undertaken, because their business risk is perceived to be higher (or lower).

(b) The finance that is raised to fund a new investment might substantially **change the capital structure** and the perceived **financial risk** of investing in the company. Depending on whether the project is financed by equity or by debt capital, the perceived financial risk of the entire company might change. This must be taken into account when appraising investments.

(c) Many companies raise **floating rate debt capital** as well as fixed interest debt capital. With floating rate debt capital, the interest rate is variable, and is altered every three or six months or so in line with changes in current market interest rates. The cost of debt capital will therefore fluctuate as market conditions vary. Floating rate debt is difficult to incorporate into a WACC computation, and the best that can be done is to substitute an 'equivalent' fixed interest debt capital cost in place of the floating rate debt cost

1.9 Required returns in the public sector

For private sector projects, the objective in setting required returns will normally be to match or exceed the returns obtainable from comparable investments by those who subscribe capital. In the public sector, the authorities may choose to take account of externalities and the wider social costs and benefits of projects, some of which will not be priced by the market.

The **social opportunity cost return approach** focuses on the opportunity cost to society of undertaking the project. The discount rate chosen reflects the **rate of return** obtainable from the **next best alternative** use of public funds, including all externalities.

The **social rate of time preference approach** to adopting a discount rate for public sector projects is based on the argument that society has a longer time horizon than private individuals. To reflect this, a **lower discount rate** is used than would be used for a private sector project.

1.10 Effective and nominal rates of interest   12/05

1.10.1 Effective annual rate of interest

Interest may be compounded daily, weekly, monthly, quarterly or annually.

The **equivalent annual rate of interest**, when interest is compounded at shorter intervals than annually, may be calculated as follows. This is known as an **effective annual rate of interest**.

Effective Annual Rate = $[(1 + i)^{\frac{12}{n}} - 1]$ or $[(1 + i)^{\frac{365}{x}} - 1)]$

Where i is the rate of interest for each time period
            n is the number of months in the time period
            x is the number of days in the time period.

1.10.2 Example: the effective annual rate of interest

You are required to calculate the effective annual rate of interest of:

(a)   1.5% per month, compound
(b)   4.5% per quarter, compound
(c)   9% per half year, compound

Solution

(a) $(1.015)^{12} - 1 = 0.1956 = 19.56\%$
(b) $(1.045)^{4} - 1 = 0.1925 = 19.25\%$
(c) $(1.09)^{2} - 1 = 0.1881 = 18.81\%$

1.10.3 Nominal rates of interest and the annual percentage rate

Most interest rates are expressed as **per annum figures** even when the interest is compounded over periods of less than one year. In such cases, the given interest rate is called a **nominal rate**. We can, however, work out the **effective rate**. It is this effective rate (shortened to one decimal place) which is quoted in advertisements as the **annual percentage rate (APR)**.

Depending on whether the compounding is done daily, weekly, monthly, quarterly or six monthly, the APR will vary by differing amounts from the nominal rate.

PART G INVESTMENT APPRAISAL

1.10.4 Example: nominal and effective rates of interest (APR)

(a) A building society may offer investors 10% per annum interest payable half-yearly. If the 10% is a nominal rate of interest, the building society would in fact pay 5% every six months, compounded so that the effective annual rate of interest (APR) would be

$$[(1.05)^2 - 1] = 0.1025 = 10.25\% \text{ per annum.}$$

(b) Similarly, if a bank offers depositors a nominal 12% per annum, with interest payable quarterly, the effective rate of interest (APR) would be 3% compound every three months, which is

$$[(1.03)^4 - 1] = 0.1255 = 12.55\% \text{ per annum.}$$

2 The net present value method

12/01, 6/02, 6/03, 6/04, 6/05, 12/05

> **FAST FORWARD**
>
> The **NPV method** of investment appraisal is to accept projects with a positive NPV. Ensure that you are aware of the three conventions concerning the timings of cash flows.
>
> An **annuity** is a constant cash flow for a number of years. A **perpetuity** is a constant cash flow forever.

There are two methods of using DCF to evaluate capital investments.

- The net present value **(NPV)** method
- The internal rate of return **(IRR)** method, or DCF yield method

Key terms

Net present value or **NPV** is the value obtained by discounting all cash outflows and inflows of a capital investment project by a chosen target rate of return or **cost of capital.**

The NPV method compares the **present value** of all the **cash inflows** from an investment with the **present value** of all the **cash outflows** from an investment. The NPV is thus calculated as the PV of **cash inflows** minus the PV of **cash outflows**.

NPV	
NPV positive	Return from investment's cash inflows in excess of cost of capital $\Rightarrow$ undertake project
NPV negative	Return from investment's cash inflows below cost of capital $\Rightarrow$ don't undertake project
NPV 0	Return from investment's cash inflows same as cost of capital

Note. We assume that the cost of capital is the organisation's target rate of return.

2.1 Example: NPV

Slogger Ltd is considering a capital investment, where the estimated cash flows are as follows.

Year	Cash flow £
0 (ie now)	(100,000)
1	60,000
2	80,000
3	40,000
4	30,000

The company's cost of capital is 15%. You are required to calculate the NPV of the project and to assess whether it should be undertaken.

Solution

Year	Cash flow £	Discount factor 15%	Present value £
0	(100,000)	1.000	(100,000)
1	60,000	$\frac{1}{(1.15)} = 0.870$	52,200
2	80,000	$\frac{1}{(1.15)^2} = 0.756$	60,480
3	40,000	$\frac{1}{(1.15)^3} = 0.658$	26,320
4	30,000	$\frac{1}{(1.15)^4} = 0.572$	17,160
		NPV =	56,160

(**Note**. The discount factor for any cash flow 'now' (year 0) is always = 1, regardless of what the cost of capital is.) The PV of cash inflows exceeds the PV of cash outflows by £56,160, which means that the project will earn a DCF yield in excess of 15%. It should therefore be undertaken.

2.2 Timing of cash flows: conventions used in DCF

Discounted cash flow applies discounting arithmetic to the relevant costs and benefits of an investment project. Discounting, which reduces the value of future cash flows to a present value equivalent, is clearly concerned with the timing of the cash flows. As a general rule, the following guidelines may be applied.

(a) A cash outlay to be incurred at the beginning of an investment project (**'now'**) occurs in **year 0**. The present value of £1 now, in year 0, is £1 regardless of the value of r.

(b) A cash outlay, saving or inflow which occurs **during the course of a time period** (say, one year) is assumed to occur all at once **at the end of the time period** (at the end of the year). Receipts of £10,000 during year 1 are therefore taken to occur at the end of year 1.

(c) A cash outlay or receipt which occurs **at the beginning of a time period** (say at the beginning of one year) is taken to occur **at the end of the previous year**. Therefore a cash outlay of £5,000 at the beginning of year 2 is taken to occur at the end of year 1.

Exam focus point

Examiners' reports suggest that candidates often get the timing of cash flows wrong, particularly initial investment, working capital and tax.

2.3 Discount tables for the PV of £1

The discount factor that we use in discounting is $\frac{1}{(1+r)^n} = (1+r)^{-n}$

Instead of having to calculate this factor every time we can use tables. Discount tables for the present value of £1, for different values of r and n, are shown in the Appendix to this Study Text. Use these tables to work out your own solution to the following question.

Exam focus point

Remember that interest should *not* be included in the calculation; it is allowed for in the discount rate.

PART G INVESTMENT APPRAISAL

Question
Net present value

LCH Limited manufactures product X which it sells for £5 per unit. Variable costs of production are currently £3 per unit, and fixed costs 50p per unit. A new machine is available which would cost £90,000 but which could be used to make product X for a variable cost of only £2.50 per unit. Fixed costs, however, would increase by £7,500 per annum as a direct result of purchasing the machine. The machine would have an expected life of 4 years and a resale value after that time of £10,000. Sales of product X are estimated to be 75,000 units per annum. LCH Limited expects to earn at least 12% per annum from its investments. Ignore taxation.

You are required to decide whether LCH Limited should purchase the machine.

Answer

Savings are 75,000 × (£3 − £2.50) = £37,500 per annum.

Additional costs are £7,500 per annum.

Net cash savings are therefore £30,000 per annum. (Remember, depreciation is not a cash flow and must be ignored as a 'cost'.)

The first step in calculating an NPV is to establish the relevant costs year by year. All future cash flows arising as a direct consequence of the decision should be taken into account. It is assumed that the machine will be sold for £10,000 at the end of year 4.

Year	Cash flow £	PV factor 12%	PV of cash flow £
0	(90,000)	1.000	(90,000)
1	30,000	0.893	26,790
2	30,000	0.797	23,910
3	30,000	0.712	21,360
4	40,000	0.636	25,440
		NPV =	+7,500

The NPV is positive and so the project is expected to earn more than 12% per annum and is therefore acceptable.

2.4 Annuity tables

In the previous exercise, the calculations could have been simplified for years 1-3 as follows.

$$
\begin{aligned}
& 30,000 \times 0.893 \\
+\ & 30,000 \times 0.797 \\
+\ & 30,000 \times 0.712 \\
=\ & 30,000 \times 2.402
\end{aligned}
$$

Where there is a constant cash flow from year to year, we can calculate the present value by adding together the discount factors for the individual years.

These total factors could be described as 'same cash flow per annum' factors, 'cumulative present value' factors or **'annuity' factors**. They are shown in the table for cumulative PV of £1 factors which is shown in the Appendix to this Study Text (2.402, for example, is in the column for 12% per annum and the row for year 3.)

26: INVESTMENT APPRAISAL USING DCF METHODS

Exam formula

Present value of an annuity of $1 = \dfrac{1-(1+r)^{-n}}{r}$

Where r = Discount rate
n = Number of periods

Question — Annuities

If you have not used them before, check that you can understand annuity tables by trying the following exercise.

(a) What is the present value of £1,000 in contribution earned each year from years 1-10, when the required return on investment is 11%?

(b) What is the present value of £2,000 costs incurred each year from years 3-6 when the cost of capital is 5%?

Answer

(a) The PV of £1,000 earned each year from year 1-10 when the required earning rate of money is 11% is calculated as follows.

£1,000 × 5.889 = £5,889

(b) The PV of £2,000 in costs each year from years 3-6 when the cost of capital is 5% per annum is calculated as follows.

PV of £1 per annum for years 1 – 6 at 5% =	5.076
Less PV of £1 per annum for years 1 – 2 at 5% =	1.859
PV of £1 per annum for years 3 – 6 =	3.217

PV = £2,000 × 3.217 = £6,434

2.5 Sinking funds   12/05

Key term

A **sinking fund** is an investment into which equal annual instalments are paid in order to earn interest, so that by the end of a given number of years, the investment is large enough to pay off a known commitment at that time.

If an individual needs £5,000 in three years time, he could make an annual payment into a sinking fund, so that after three years, the total investment (payments into the fund plus interest earned) equals £5,000.

Sinking funds are commonly used for the **repayment of debt**. Another common known future commitment is the need to replace an asset a the end of its life. To ensure that the money is available to buy a replacement, a company might decide to invest cash in a sinking fund during the course of the life of the existing asset.

2.5.1 Example: sinking funds

A company has just bought an asset with a life of four years. At the end of four years, a replacement asset will cost £12,000, and the company has decided to provide for this future commitment by setting up a sinking fund into which equal annual investments will be made, starting at year 1 (one year from now). The fund is expected to earn interest at the rate of 12% per annum.

Solution

The total value of an investment (fund) at the end of n years is given by the formula:

$$= A \left[\frac{(1+r)^n - 1}{r} \right] \text{ (given in exam)}$$

where A is the annual investment and r is the rate of interest earned, expressed as a decimal.

Let us go back to our example. Since the fund must equal £12,000 by year 4,

$$12,000 = \frac{A \times (1.12^4 - 1)}{1.12 - 1}$$

$$12,000 = \frac{0.573519A}{0.12}$$

$$A = £2,510.81$$

Four investments, each of £2,510.81, should therefore be enough to allow the company to replace the asset.

2.5.2 Example: a sinking fund to repay a loan

Submerged Ltd intends to purchase a new equipment costing £30,000. The funds to buy the equipment are being provided as a loan by the managing director. The agreed rate of interest is 12%, and the loan will be repayable in full with interest at the end of the four-year term.

To provide for this eventual repayment, the board of directors of Submerged ltd decide to put an equal annual amount at the end of each year into a sinking fund, which will earn 15% per annum interest.

Calculate the annual payment into the sinking fund which will repay the loan after four years.

Solution

Let the annual payments into the sinking fund be £S.

The cash flows are as follows:

Year		Cash flow
1	Payment into sinking fund	S
2	Payment into sinking fund	S
3	Payment into sinking fund	S
4	Payment into sinking fund	S
4	Repay loan	$30,000 \times 1.12^4$

By year 4, the value of the sinking fund must have risen to £30,000 x 1.12^4 = £47,205.58 to enable the company to repay the loan in full with interest at 12%.

$$S \left[\frac{(1.15)^4 - 1}{0.15} \right] \text{ has to equal } £30,000 \times (1.12)^4$$

$$\therefore 4.993375S = £47,3205.58$$

$$S = £9,453.64$$

Annual payments into a sinking fund of £9,453.58 at the end of each year will therefore create a fund large enough, earning 15% per annum, to repay the loan at the end of four years, where the original loan is £30,000 and interest on the loan is at 12%.

2.5.3 Sinking funds and mortgages

Repayments against a **repayment mortgage** can also be seen as payments into a sinking fund. The total of the constant annual payments (which are usually paid in equal monthly instalments) plus the interest they earn over the term of the mortgage must be sufficient to pay off the initial loan plus accrued interest, interest being added to the loan retrospectively at the end of each year.

2.5.4 Example: mortgage

Sam has taken out at £30,000 mortgage over 25 years. Interest is to be charged at 10% per annum. Calculate the monthly repayment assuming that the repayments will earn interest at 13% per annum.

Solution

$S = £30,000 \times (1.10)^{25} = £325,041$

$\therefore £325,041 = \dfrac{A((1.13)^{25} - 1)}{0.13}$

Annual repayment = £2,089

$\therefore$ Monthly repayment = £174.08

2.5.5 Example: Sinking funds and debt

Suppose a company borrows £40,000, which is compounded at 10%. The debt will be discharged at the end of four years with regular annual payments into a sinking fund which pays 8%. Calculate the annual payment into the fund and construct a schedule, assuming the first payment into the fund is made a year from now.

Solution

In four year's time the debt $= £30,000 \times (1.1)^4$
$= £58,564$

$£58,564 = \dfrac{A(1.08)^4 - 1)}{0.08}$

$\therefore A = £12,996.57$

Sinking fund schedule

Year	Debt at start of year £	Interest £	Debt at end of year £	Amount in fund at start of year £	Interest earned £	Payments into fund £	Amount in fund at year end £
1	40,000	4,000	44,000	-	-	12,996.57	12,996.57
2	44,000	4,400	48,400	12,996.57	1,039.73	12,996.57	27,032.87
3	48,400	4,840	53,240	27,032.87	2,162.63	12,996.57	42,192.07
4	53,240	5,324	58,564	42,192.07	3,375.36	12,996.57	58,564.00

PART G   INVESTMENT APPRAISAL

2.6 Annual cash flows in perpetuity   12/01

You need to know how to calculate the cumulative present value of £1 per annum for every year in perpetuity (that is, forever).

Formula to learn

> When the cost of capital is r, the cumulative PV of £1 per annum in perpetuity is **£1/r**.

For example, the PV of £1 per annum in perpetuity at a discount rate of 10% would be £1/0.10 = £10.

Similarly, the PV of £1 per annum in perpetuity at a discount rate of 15% would be £1/0.15 = £6.67 and at a discount rate of 20% it would be £1/0.20 = £5.

Question   Perpetuities

An organisation with a cost of capital of 14% is considering investing in a project costing £500,000 that would yield cash inflows of £100,000 pa in perpetuity.

Required

Assess whether the project should be undertaken.

Answer

Year	Cash flow £	Discount factor 14%	Present value £
0	(500,000)	1.000	(500,000)
1 – ∞	100,000	1/0.14 = 7.143	714,300
		Net present value	214,300

The NPV is positive and so the project should be undertaken.

2.7 Relevant costs in NPV calculations

The cash flows that should be considered in NPV calculations are those which arise as a **consequence** of the investment decision under evaluation.

Cash flows that are not relevant include:

- Any costs incurred in the **past**
- Any **committed costs** which will be **incurred regardless** of whether or not an investment is undertaken
- **Centrally-allocated overheads** that are not a consequence of undertaking the project

The **annual profits** from a project can be calculated as:

Incremental contribution earned **minus any incremental fixed costs** which are additional cash items of expenditure (that is, ignoring depreciation and so on).

There are, however, other cash flows to consider. These might include the following.

(a)   **Opportunity costs**

As we saw in Chapter 3 these are the costs incurred or revenues lost from diverting existing resources from their best use. For example if a salesman, who is paid an annual salary of £30,000, is diverted to work on a new project and as a result existing sales of £50,000 are lost, the opportunity cost to the new project will be the £50,000 of lost sales. The salesman's salary of £30,000 is **not** an opportunity cost since it will be incurred however the salesman's time is spent.

(b) **Taxation**

The extra **taxation** that will be payable on extra profits, or the reductions in tax arising from capital allowances or operating losses in any year.

(c) **Disposal proceeds**

The **residual value or disposal value of equipment at the end of its life, or its disposal costs** should be included.

(d) **Working capital**

If a company invests £20,000 in working capital and earns cash profits of £50,000, the net cash receipts will be £30,000. Working capital will be released again at the end of a project's life, and so there will be a cash inflow arising out of the eventual realisation into cash of the project's stocks and debtors in the final year of the project.

Finance-related cash flows, on the other hand, are normally **excluded** from project appraisal exercises because the **discounting process takes account** of the time value of money, that is the opportunity cost of investing the money in the project.

(a) If you included the cash inflow from, say, a loan, then the cash outflows of the interest payments and the loan repayment would also have to be included.

(b) These flows would all be **discounted at the cost of capital**, (which we assume is the same as the cost of the loan) and they would reduce to a zero net present value. They would therefore have had no effect on the NPV and are thus deemed irrelevant to the appraisal.

Finance-related cash flows are **only relevant if they incur a different rate of interest from that which is being used as the discount rate**. For example, a company may be offered a loan at a preferential rate below that which it uses for its discount rate and so the inclusion and discounting of the loan's cash flows produces a differential NPV.

Dividend payments should also be **ignored** as they represent a distribution of the benefits of the project, rather than a **cash flow** influencing its appraisal.

2.8 Example: NPV

Elsie Limited is considering the manufacture of a new product which would involve the use of both a new machine (costing £150,000) and an existing machine, which cost £80,000 two years ago and has a current net book value of £60,000. There is sufficient capacity on this machine, which has so far been under-utilised. Annual sales of the product would be 5,000 units, selling at £32 per unit. Unit costs would be as follows.

	£
Direct labour (4 hours at £2 per hour)	8
Direct materials	7
Fixed costs including depreciation	9
	24

The project would have a five-year life, after which the new machine would have a net residual value of £10,000. Because direct labour is continually in short supply, labour resources would have to be diverted from other work which currently earns a contribution of £1.50 per direct labour hour. The fixed overhead absorption rate would be £2.25 per hour (£9 per unit) but actual expenditure on fixed overhead would not alter.

PART G INVESTMENT APPRAISAL

Working capital requirements would be £10,000 in the first year, rising to £15,000 in the second year and remaining at this level until the end of the project, when it will all be recovered. The company's cost of capital is 20%. Ignore taxation.

You are required to assess whether the project is worthwhile.

Solution

The relevant cash flows are as follows.

(a)	Year 0	Purchase of new machine	£150,000
(b)	Years 1-5	Contribution from new product	£
		(5,000 units × £(32 – 15))	85,000
		Less contribution foregone	
		(5,000 × (4 × £1.50))	30,000
			55,000

(c) The project requires £10,000 of working capital at the end of year 1 and a further £5,000 at the start of year 2. **Increases** in working capital **reduce** the **net cash flow** for the period to which they relate. When the working capital tied up in the project is 'recovered' at the end of the project, it will provide an extra cash inflow (for example debtors will eventually pay up).

(d) All other costs, which are past costs, notional accounting costs or costs which would be incurred anyway without the project, are not relevant to the investment decision.

(e) The NPV is calculated as follows.

Year	Equipment £	Working capital £	Contribution £	Net cash flow £	Discount factor 20%	PV of net cash flow £
0	(150,000)	(10,000)		(160,000)	1.000	(160,000)
1		(5,000)		(5,000)	0.833	(4,165)
1-5			55,000	55,000	2.991	164,505
5	10,000	15,000		25,000	0.402	10,050
					NPV =	10,390

The NPV is positive and the project is worthwhile, although there is not much margin for error. Some risk analysis of the project is recommended.

3 The internal rate of return method   6/04

FAST FORWARD

The **IRR method** of investment appraisal is to accept projects whose IRR (the rate at which the NPV is zero) exceeds a target rate of return. The IRR is calculated using interpolation.

Using the **NPV method of discounted cash flow**, present values are calculated by discounting at a target rate of return, or cost of capital, and the difference between the PV of costs and the PV of benefits is the NPV. In contrast, the **internal rate of return (IRR)** method is to calculate the **exact DCF rate of return** which the project is expected to achieve, in other words the rate at which the **NPV is zero**. If the expected rate of return (the IRR or DCF yield) **exceeds** a **target rate** of return, the project would be worth undertaking (ignoring risk and uncertainty factors).

Without a computer or calculator program, the calculation of the internal rate of return is made using a hit-and-miss technique known as the interpolation method.

Step 1 Calculate a net present value using a rate for the cost of capital that

(a) Is a **whole number**

(b) May give an NPV **close to zero**. As a rough guide try a rate that is about two thirds or three quarters of the accounting return on investment, or accounting rate of return.

Step 2 Having calculated the NPV using the first rate,

(a) If the NPV is **positive**, use a second rate that is **greater** than the first rate
(b) If the NPV is **negative**, use a second rate that is **less** than the first rate

Step 3 Use the two NPV values to **estimate the IRR**. The formula to apply is as follows.

$$IRR \approx a + \left[\left(\frac{A}{A-B}\right)(b-a)\right]\%$$

where a = the lower of the two rates of return used
b = the higher of the two rates of return used
A = the NPV obtained using rate a
B = the NPV obtained using rate b

Note. Ideally A will be a positive value and B will be negative. (If B is negative, then in the equation above you will be subtracting a negative, ie treating it as an added positive).

However, do not worry if you have two positive or two negative values, provided they are fairly close to zero. In the exam you will not have time to calculate NPVs using more than two rates.

3.1 Example: the IRR method

A company is trying to decide whether to buy a machine for £80,000 which will save costs of £20,000 per annum for 5 years and which will have a resale value of £10,000 at the end of year 5. If it is the company's policy to undertake projects only if they are expected to yield a DCF return of 10% or more, ascertain whether this project be undertaken.

Solution

Annual depreciation would be £(80,000 – 10,000)/5 = £14,000.

Step 1 Calculate the first NPV, using a rate that is three quarters of the return on investment.

The return on investment would be:

$$\frac{20,000 - \text{depreciation of } 14,000}{\frac{1}{2} \text{ of } (80,000 + 10,000)} = \frac{6,000}{45,000} = 13.3\%$$

Two thirds of this is 8.9% and so we can start by trying 9%.

The IRR is the rate for the cost of capital at which the NPV = 0.

Year	Cash flow £	PV factor 9%	PV of cash flow £
0	(80,000)	1.000	(80,000)
1-5	20,000	3.890	77,800
5	10,000	0.650	6,500
		NPV	4,300

This is fairly close to zero. It is also **positive**, which means that the actual **rate of return** is **more than 9%**. We can use 9% as one of our two NPVs close to zero.

Step 2 Calculate the second NPV, using a rate that is **greater** than the first rate, as the first rate gave a positive answer.

Suppose we try 12%.

Year	Cash flow £	PV factor 12%	PV of cash flow £
0	(80,000)	1.000	(80,000)
1-5	20,000	3.605	72,100
5	10,000	0.567	5,670
		NPV	(2,230)

This is fairly close to zero and **negative**. The real rate of return is therefore greater than 9% (positive NPV of £4,300) but less than 12% (negative NPV of £2,230).

Step 3 Use the two NPV values to estimate the IRR.

The interpolation method assumes that the NPV rises in linear fashion between the two NPVs close to 0. The real rate of return is therefore assumed to be on a straight line between NPV = £4,300 at 9% and NPV = –£2,230 at 12%.

Using the formula

$$IRR \approx a + \left(\left(\frac{A}{A-B}\right)(b-a)\right)\%$$

$$IRR \approx 9 + \left[\frac{4,300}{4,300+2,230} \times (12-9)\right]\% = 10.98\%, \text{ say } 11\%$$

If it is company policy to undertake investments which are expected to yield 10% or more, this project would be undertaken.

If we were to draw a graph of a 'typical' capital project, with a negative cash flow at the start of the project, and positive net cash flows afterwards up to the end of the project, we could draw a graph of the project's NPV at different costs of capital. It would look like Figure 1.

Figure 1

If we use a cost of capital where the NPV is slightly positive, and use another cost of capital where it is slightly negative, we can estimate the IRR – where the NPV is zero – by drawing a straight line between the two points on the graph that we have calculated.

Figure 2

Consider Figure 2.

(a) If we establish the NPVs at the two points P, we would estimate the IRR to be at point A.
(b) If we establish the NPVs at the two points Q, we would estimate the IRR to be at point B.

The closer our NPVs are to zero, the closer our estimate will be to the true IRR.

Question
IRR

Find the IRR of the project given below and state whether the project should be accepted if the company requires a minimum return of 17%.

Time		£
0	Investment	(4,000)
1	Receipts	1,200
2	"	1,410
3	"	1,875
4	"	1,150

Answer

The total receipts are £5,635 giving a total profit of £1,635 and average profits of £409. The average investment is £2,000. The ARR is £409 ÷ £2,000 = 20%. Two thirds of the ARR is approximately 14%. The initial estimate of the IRR that we shall try is therefore 14%.

		Try 14% Discount		Try 16% Discount	
Time	Cash flow	factor	PV	factor	PV
	£		£		£
0	(4,000)	1.000	(4,000)	1.000	(4,000)
1	1,200	0.877	1,052	0.862	1,034
2	1,410	0.769	1,084	0.743	1,048
3	1,875	0.675	1,266	0.641	1,202
4	1,150	0.592	681	0.552	635
		NPV	83	NPV	(81)

The IRR must be less than 16%, but higher than 14%. The NPVs at these two costs of capital will be used to estimate the IRR.

Using the interpolation formula:

$$\text{IRR} = 14\% + \left[\frac{83}{83 + 81} \times (16\% - 14\%)\right] = 15.01\%$$

The IRR is, in fact, exactly 15%. The project should be rejected as the IRR is less than the minimum return demanded.

4 NPV and IRR compared

FAST FORWARD

There are advantages and disadvantages to each appraisal method. Make sure that you can discuss them.

Given that there are two methods of using DCF, the NPV method and the IRR method, the relative merits of each method have to be considered.

4.1 Advantages and disadvantages of IRR method

The main advantage of the IRR method is that the information it provides is **more easily understood** by managers, especially non-financial managers. For example, it is fairly easy to understand the meaning of the following statement.

> 'The project will be expected to have an initial capital outlay of £100,000, and to earn a yield of 25%. This is in excess of the target yield of 15% for investments.'

It is not so easy to understand the meaning of this statement.

> 'The project will cost £100,000 and have an NPV of £30,000 when discounted at the minimum required rate of 15%.'

However managers may **confuse IRR** and accounting return on capital employed, **ROCE**.

The IRR method **ignores** the **relative size** of investments. Both the following projects have an IRR of 18%.

	Project A £	Project B £
Cost, year 0	350,000	35,000
Annual savings, years 1-6	100,000	10,000

Clearly, project A is bigger (ten times as big) and so more 'profitable' but if the only information on which the projects were judged were to be their IRR of 18%, project B would be made to seem just as beneficial as project A, which is not the case.

4.2 Non-conventional cash flows

The projects we have considered so far have had conventional cash flows (an initial cash outflow followed by a series of inflows). When flows vary from this they are termed non-conventional. The following project has **non-conventional cash flows**.

Year	Project X £'000
0	(1,900)
1	4,590
2	(2,735)

Project X would have two IRRs as shown by Figure 3.

Figure 3

The NPV rule suggests that the project is acceptable between costs of capital of 7% and 35%.

Suppose that the required rate on project X is 10% and that the IRR of 7% is used in deciding whether to accept or reject the project. The project would be rejected since it appears that it can only yield 7%.

The diagram shows, however, that between rates of 7% and 35% the project should be accepted. Using the IRR of 35% would produce the correct decision to accept the project. **Lack of knowledge** of **multiple IRRs** could therefore lead to serious errors in the decision of whether to accept or reject a project.

In general, if the sign of the net cash flow changes in successive periods, the calculations may produce as many IRRs as there are sign changes. IRR should not normally be used when there are non-conventional cash flows.

Exam focus point

> You need to be aware of the possibility of multiple IRRs, but the area is not examinable at a computational level.

4.3 Mutually exclusive projects

Mutually exclusive projects are two or more projects from which only one can be chosen. Examples include the choice of a factory location or the choice of just one of a number of machines. The IRR and NPV methods can, however, give conflicting rankings as to which project should be given priority.

Let us suppose that a company is considering two mutually exclusive options, option A and option B. The cash flows for each would be as follows.

Year		Option A £	Option B £
0	Capital outlay	(10,200)	(35,250)
1	Net cash inflow	6,000	18,000
2	Net cash inflow	5,000	15,000
3	Net cash inflow	3,000	15,000

The company's cost of capital is 16%.

The NPV of each project is calculated below.

		Option A		Option B	
Year	Discount factor	Cash flow	Present value	Cash flow	Present value
		£	£	£	£
0	1.000	(10,200)	(10,200)	(35,250)	(35,250)
1	0.862	6,000	5,172	18,000	15,516
2	0.743	5,000	3,715	15,000	11,145
3	0.641	3,000	1,923	15,000	9,615
			NPV = +610		NPV = +1,026

The DCF yield (IRR) of option A is 20% and the yield of option B is only 18% (workings not shown.) On a comparison of NPVs, option B would be preferred, but on a comparison of IRRs, option A would be preferred.

If the projects were independent this would be irrelevant since under the NPV rule both would be accepted. With mutually exclusive projects, however, only one project can be accepted. Therefore the ranking is crucial and we cannot be indifferent to the outcomes of the NPV and IRR appraisal methods. The NPV method is preferable.

4.4 Reinvestment assumptions

An assumption underlying the NPV method is that any net cash inflows generated during the life of the project will be reinvested at the cost of capital (that is, the **discount rate**). The IRR method, on the other hand, assumes these cash flows can be reinvested to earn a return equal to the IRR of the original project.

In the example above, the NPV method assumes that the cash inflows of £6,000, £5,000 and £3,000 for option A will be reinvested at the cost of capital of 16% whereas the IRR method assumes they will be reinvested at 20%. In theory, a firm will have accepted all projects which provide a return in excess of the cost of capital. Any other funds which become available can only be reinvested at the cost of capital. This is the assumption implied in the NPV rule.

4.5 Summary of NPV and IRR comparison

(a) When cash flow patterns are conventional both methods gives the **same accept or reject decision**.

(b) The IRR method is **more easily understood**.

(c) NPV is **technically superior** to IRR and simpler to calculate.

(d) **IRR** and **accounting ROCE** can be **confused**.

(e) **IRR ignores** the **relative sizes** of investments.

(f) Where cash flow patterns are non-conventional, there may be **several IRRs** which decision makers must be aware of to avoid making the wrong decision.

(g) The **NPV method** is superior for **ranking mutually exclusive projects** in order of attractiveness.

(h) The **reinvestment assumption** underlying the **IRR** method cannot be **substantiated**.

(i) When **discount rates** are **expected to differ** over the life of the project, such **variations** can be incorporated easily into **NPV** calculations, but not into IRR calculations.

(j) Despite the advantages of the NPV method over the IRR method, the **IRR method** is **widely used** in practice.

5 Assessment of DCF methods of project appraisal

FAST FORWARD

DCF methods of appraisal have a number of advantages over other appraisal methods.

- The time value of money is taken into account.
- The method takes account of all of a project's cash flows.
- It allows for the timing of cash flows.
- There are universally accepted methods of calculating the NPV and IRR.

5.1 Advantages of DCF methods

DCF is a capital appraisal technique that is based on a concept known as the time value of money: the concept that £1 received today is not equal to £1 received in the future. Given the choice between receiving £100 today, and £100 in one year's time, most people would opt to receive £100 today because they could spend it or invest it to earn interest. If the interest rate was 10%, you could invest £100 today and it would be worth (£100 × 1.10) = £110 in one year's time.

There are, however, other reasons why a present £1 is worth more than a future £1.

(a) **Uncertainty.** Although there might be a promise of money to come in the future, it can never be certain that the money will be received until it has actually been paid.

(b) **Inflation** also means £1 now is worth more than £1 in the future because of inflation. The time value of money concept applies even if there is zero inflation but inflation obviously increases the discrepancy in value between monies received at different times.

Taking account of the time value of money (by discounting) is one of the principal advantages of the DCF appraisal method. Other advantages are as follows.

- The method uses **all relevant cash flows** relating to the project.
- It allows for the **timing** of the cash flows.
- There are **universally accepted methods** of calculating the NPV and the IRR.

5.2 Problems with DCF methods

Although DCF methods are theoretically the best methods of investment appraisal, you should be aware of their limitations.

(a) DCF methods use **future cash flows** that may be difficult to forecast. Although other methods use these as well, arguably the problem is greater with DCF methods that take cash flows into the longer-term.

(b) The basic decision rule, accept all projects with a positive NPV, will not apply when the capital available for investment is **rationed**.

(c) The **cost of capital** used in DCF calculations may be **difficult to estimate**.

(d) The **cost of capital** may **change** over the life of the investment.

5.3 The use of appraisal methods in practice

One reason for the failure of many businesses to use NPV is that its (sometimes long-term) nature may conflict with judgements on a business that are concerned with its (short-term) profits. **Manager's remuneration** may depend upon the level of annual profits, and they may thus be unwilling to risk large initial expenditure on a project that only offers good returns in the significantly uncertain long-term.

PART G INVESTMENT APPRAISAL

In addition the NPV method is based on the assumption that businesses seek to **maximise the wealth of their shareholders**. As discussed previously, this may conflict with the interests of other stakeholders. Public sector organisations will be concerned with the **social opportunity costs.**

Even when **wealth maximisation** is the key objective, there may be factors that help maximise wealth, but cannot be quantified for NPV purposes, for example investment in a loss-making project for strategic reasons such as obtaining an initial share in an important market.

6 Asset replacement decisions   12/04

FAST FORWARD

> DCF techniques can assist **asset replacement decisions**. When an asset is being replaced with an identical asset, the **equivalent annual cost method** can be used to calculate an **optimum replacement cycle**.

As well as assisting with decisions between particular assets, DCF techniques can be used in **asset replacement decisions**, to assess **when** and **how frequently** an asset should be replaced. When an asset is to be replaced by an 'identical' asset, the problem is to decide the optimum interval between replacements. As the asset gets older, it may cost more to maintain and operate, its residual value will decrease, and it may lose some productivity/operating capability.

There are three basic methods of deciding the optimum replacement cycle.

- The **lowest common multiple method**
- The **finite horizon method**
- The **equivalent annual cost method**

Each method will give the same recommendation.

All three methods are concerned with the problem that a replacement asset will eventually be replaced itself by an asset which will also in its turn be replaced. Replacements are continuous, and are assumed to occur into the indefinite future.

Exam focus point

The only method you will be asked to use in the exam is the equivalent annual cost method.

6.1 Equivalent annual cost method

The equivalent annual cost method is the quickest method to use in a period of no inflation.

Step 1 Calculate the **present value of costs** for each **replacement cycle** over **one cycle only**.

These costs are not comparable because they refer to different time periods, whereas replacement is continuous.

Step 2 **Turn the present value** of costs for each replacement cycle into an **equivalent annual cost** (an annuity).

The equivalent annual costs is calculated as follows.

$$\frac{\text{The PV of cost over one replacement cycle}}{\text{The cumulative present value factor for the number of years in the cycle}}$$

For example if there are three years in the cycle, the denominator will be the present value of an annuity for three years at 10% (2.487).

Example: replacement of an identical asset

James Ltd operates a machine which has the following costs and resale values over its four year life.

Purchase cost: £25,000

	Year 1 £	Year 2 £	Year 3 £	Year 4 £
Running costs (cash expenses)	7,500	10,000	12,500	15,000
Resale value (end of year)	15,000	10,000	7,500	2,500

The organisation's cost of capital is 10%. You are required to assess how frequently the asset should be replaced.

Solution

In our example:

Step 1 Calculate the present value of costs for each replacement cycle over one cycle.

	Replace every year		Replace every 2 years		Replace every 3 years		Replace every 4 years	
Year	Cash flow £	PV at 10% £	Cash flow £	PV at 10% £	Cash flow £	PV at 10% £	Cash flow £	PV at 10% £
0	(25,000)	(25,000)	(25,000)	(25,000)	(25,000)	(25,000)	(25,000)	(25,000)
1	7,500	6,818	(7,500)	(6,818)	(7,500)	(6,818)	(7,500)	(6,818)
2			0	0	(10,000)	(8,260)	(10,000)	(8,260)
3					(5,000)	(3,755)	(12,500)	(9,388)
4							(12,500)	(8,538)
PV of cost over one replacement cycle		(18,182)		(31,818)		(43,833)		(58,004)

Step 2 Calculate the equivalent annual cost.

We use a discount rate of 10%.

(a) Replacement every year:

$$\text{Equivalent annual cost} = \frac{£(18,182)}{0.909} = £(20,002)$$

(b) Replacement every two years:

$$\text{Equivalent annual cost} = \frac{£(31,818)}{1.736} = £(18,328)$$

(c) Replacement every three years:

$$\text{Equivalent annual cost} = \frac{£(43,833)}{2.487} = £(17,625)$$

(d) Replacement every four years:

$$\text{Equivalent annual cost} = \frac{£(58,004)}{3.170} = £(18,298)$$

6.2 Conclusion

The optimum replacement policy is the one with the lowest equivalent annual cost, every three years. This is the same conclusion reached by the earlier lowest common multiple method.

PART G INVESTMENT APPRAISAL

Chapter Roundup

- There are two methods of using DCF to evaluate capital investments, the **NPV method** and the **IRR/DCF yield method.**
- The **weighted average cost of capital (WACC)** is the best **discount rate** to use when discounting cash flows to their **present value** if the funds raised to finance the investment are in proportion to the company's current capital structure. Otherwise, the **marginal cost of capital** may be a better rate.
- The **NPV method** of investment appraisal is to accept projects with a positive NPV. Ensure that you are aware of the three conventions concerning the timings of cash flows.
- An **annuity** is a constant cash flow for a number of years. A **perpetuity** is a constant cash flow forever.
- The **IRR method** of investment appraisal is to accept projects whose IRR (the rate at which the NPV is zero) exceeds a target rate of return. The IRR is calculated using interpolation.
- There are advantages and disadvantages to each appraisal method. Make sure that you can discuss them.
- **DCF methods of appraisal** have a number of **advantages** over other appraisal methods.
    - The time value of money is taken into account.
    - The method takes account of all of a project's cash flows.
    - It allows for the timing of cash flows.
    - There are universally accepted methods of calculating the NPV and IRR.
- DCF techniques can assist **asset replacement decisions**. When an asset is being replaced with an identical asset, the **equivalent annual cost method** can be used to calculate an **optimum replacement cycle**.

Quick Quiz

1   What is the formula for calculating the future value of an investment plus accumulated interest after n time periods?

2   What is the formula for calculating the present value of a future sum of money out the end of n time periods?

3   List three cash flow timing conventions used in DCF.

4   What is the perpetuity formula?

5   List three advantages of the DCF method of project appraisal over other appraisal methods.

6   For a certain project, the net present value at a discount rate of 15% is £3,670, and at a rate of 18% the net present value is negative at (£1,390). What is the internal rate of return of the project?

    A   15.7%
    B   16.5%
    C   16.6%
    D   17.2%

7   Tick the correct box to indicate whether or not the following items are included in the cash flows when determining the net present value of a project.

		Included	Not included
(a)	The disposal value of equipment at the end of its life	☐	☐
(b)	Depreciation charges for the equipment	☐	☐
(c)	Research costs incurred prior to the appraisal	☐	☐
(d)	Interest payments on the loan to finance the investment	☐	☐

8   The net present value of the costs of operating a machine for the next three years is £10,724 at a cost of capital of 15%. What is the equivalent annual cost of operating the machine?

    A   £4,697
    B   £3,575
    C   £4,111
    D   £3,109

PART G   INVESTMENT APPRAISAL

Answers to Quick Quiz

1. $FV = PV(1+r)^n$

2. $PV = FV \dfrac{1}{(1+r)^n}$

3. (a) A cash outlay to be incurred at the beginning of an investment project occurs in year 0.
   (b) A cash outlay, saving or inflow which occurs during the course of a time period is assumed to occur all at once at the end of the time period.
   (c) A cash outlay or receipt that occurs at the beginning of a time period is taken to occur at the end of the previous year.

4. Annual cash flow/discount rate.

5. (a) It takes account of the time value of money.
   (b) It uses all cash flows relating to a project.
   (c) It allows for the timing of cash flows.

6. D $15\% + \{(3{,}670/[3{,}670 + 1{,}390]) \times 3\%\} = 17.2\%$

7. (a) Included
   (b) Not included (non-cash)
   (c) Not included (past cost)
   (d) Not usually included, unless the loan incurs a different rate of interest from that which is being used as the discount rate

8. A   £10,724/2.283 = £4,697

Now try the questions below from the Exam Question Bank

Number	Level	Marks	Time
Q29	Introductory	n/a	45 mins

Allowing for inflation and taxation

Topic list	Syllabus reference
1 Allowing for inflation	5(b)
2 Allowing for taxation	5(b)

Introduction

Having covered the more sophisticated of the investment appraisal techniques which are available in Chapter 26, we will be looking in this chapter at how to incorporate **inflation** and **taxation** into investment decisions. A key concept in this chapter which you must grasp is the difference between **money rates of return** and **real rates of return**, and when each is to be used as the discount rate.

The next chapter will consider how the **risk** associated with a project can be assessed and taken into account.

PART G INVESTMENT APPRAISAL

Study guide

Section 13 – Interest and discounting

- Explain the relationship between inflation and interest rates, distinguishing between real and nominal rates and calculate nominal interest rates

Section 15 – Project appraisal allowing for inflation and taxation

Inflation

- Distinguish general inflation from specific price increases and assess their impact on cash flows
- Evaluate capital investment projects on a real terms basis
- Evaluate capital investment projects on a nominal terms basis

Taxation

- Calculate the effect of capital allowances and corporation tax on project cash flows
- Evaluate the profitability of capital investment projects on a post-tax basis

Exam guide

As well as bringing inflation into your DCF calculations, you may be asked to explain the differences between real and nominal rates. There were 12 marks in the compulsory question in the June 2004 exam for IRR calculations involving taxation, and 18 marks in December 2004 for an NPV calculation with tax and inflation.

1 Allowing for inflation   12/04

FAST FORWARD

Inflation is a feature of all economies, and it must be accommodated in financial planning.

(1+ money rate of return) = (1 + real rate of return) × (1 + rate of inflation)

Real cash flows (ie adjusted for inflation) should be discounted at a **real discount rate**.

Money cash flows should be discounted at a money discount rate.

So far we have not considered the effect of **inflation** on the appraisal of capital investment proposals. As the inflation rate increases so will the minimum return required by an investor. For example, you might be happy with a return of 5% in an inflation-free world, but if inflation was running at 15% you would expect a considerably greater yield.

1.1 Example: Inflation (1)

A company is considering investing in a project with the following cash flows.

Time	Actual cash flows
	£
0	(15,000)
1	9,000
2	8,000
3	7,000

The company requires a minimum return of 20% under the present and anticipated conditions. Inflation is currently running at 10% a year, and this rate of inflation is expected to continue indefinitely. Should the company go ahead with the project?

Let us first look at the company's required rate of return. Suppose that it invested £1,000 for one year on 1 January, then on 31 December it would require a minimum return of £200. With the initial investment of £1,000, the total value of the investment by 31 December must therefore increase to £1,200. During the course of the year the purchasing value of the pound would fall due to inflation. We can restate the amount received on 31 December in terms of the purchasing power of the pound at 1 January as follows.

Amount received on 31 December in terms of the value of the pound at 1 January = $\dfrac{£1,200}{(1.10)^1}$ = £1,091

In terms of the value of the pound at 1 January, the company would make a profit of £91 which represents a rate of return of 9.1% in 'today's money' terms. This is **the real rate of return**. The required rate of 20% is a **money rate of return** (sometimes called a **nominal rate of return**). The **money rate** measures the return in terms of the **pound** which is, of course, falling in value. The **real rate** measures the return in **constant price level** terms.

The two rates of return and the inflation rate are linked by the equation

Formula to learn

> **(1 + money rate) = (1 + real rate) × (1 + inflation rate)**
>
> where all the rates are expressed as proportions.

In our example,

$(1 + 0.20) = (1 + 0.091) \times (1 + 0.10) = 1.20$

Exam focus point

> You may be asked in the exam to explain the difference between a real and money terms analysis.

1.2 Do we use the real rate or the money rate?

The rule is as follows.

(a) If the cash flows are expressed in terms of the **actual number of pounds** that will be **received** or **paid** on the **various future dates**, we use the **money rate** for discounting.

(b) If the cash flows are expressed in terms of the **value of the pound at time 0** (that is, in constant price level terms), we use the **real rate**.

The cash flows given above are expressed in terms of the **actual number** of **pounds** that will be received or paid at the relevant dates. We should, therefore, discount them using the **money rate of return**.

Time	Cash flow	Discount factor	PV
	£	20%	£
0	(15,000)	1.000	(15,000)
1	9,000	0.833	7,497
2	8,000	0.694	5,552
3	7,000	0.579	4,053
			2,102

The project has a positive net present value of £2,102.

The future cash flows can be re-expressed in terms of the value of the pound at time 0 as follows, given inflation at 10% a year.

Time	Actual cash flow		Cash flow at time 0 price level
	£		£
0	(15,000)		(15,000)
1	9,000	$9{,}000 \times \dfrac{1}{1.10}$ =	8,182
2	8,000	$8{,}000 \times \dfrac{1}{(1.10)^2}$ =	6,612
3	7,000	$7{,}000 \times \dfrac{1}{(1.10)^3}$ =	5,259

The cash flows expressed in terms of the value of the pound at time 0 can now be discounted using the real rate of 9.1%.

Time	Cash flow	Discount factor	PV
	£	9.1%	£
0	(15,000)	1.00	(15,000)
1	8,182	$\dfrac{1}{1.091}$	7,500
2	6,612	$\dfrac{1}{(1.091)^2}$	5,555
3	5,259	$\dfrac{1}{(1.091)^3}$	4,050
		NPV	2,105

The NPV is the same as before (and the present value of the cash flow in each year is the same as before) apart from rounding errors.

1.3 The advantages and misuses of real values and a real rate of return

Although generally companies should discount money values at the money cost of capital, there are some advantages of using real values discounted at a real cost of capital.

(a) When all costs and benefits rise at the same rate of price inflation, **real values** are the **same as current day values**, so that no **further adjustments** need be made to cash flows before discounting. In contrast, when money values are discounted at the money cost of capital, the **prices** in **future years** must be **calculated** before discounting can begin.

(b) The government might prefer to set a **real return** as a target for investments, as being more suitable than a commercial money rate of return.

1.3.1 Costs and benefits which inflate at different rates

Not all costs and benefits will rise in line with the general level of inflation. In such cases, we can apply the **money rate** to **inflated values** to determine a project's NPV.

1.4 Example: Inflation (2)

Rice Ltd is considering a project which would cost £5,000 now. The annual benefits, for four years, would be a fixed income of £2,500 a year, plus other savings of £500 a year in year 1, rising by 5% each year because of inflation. Running costs will be £1,000 in the first year, but would increase at 10% each year because of inflating labour costs. The general rate of inflation is expected to be 7½% and the company's required money rate of return is 16%. Is the project worthwhile? Ignore taxation.

Solution

The cash flows at inflated values are as follows.

Year	Fixed income £	Other savings £	Running costs £	Net cash flow £
1	2,500	500	1,000	2,000
2	2,500	525	1,100	1,925
3	2,500	551	1,210	1,841
4	2,500	579	1,331	1,748

The NPV of the project is as follows.

Year	Cash flow £	Discount factor 16%	PV £
0	(5,000)	1.000	(5,000)
1	2,000	0.862	1,724
2	1,925	0.743	1,430
3	1,841	0.641	1,180
4	1,748	0.552	965
			+ 299

The NPV is positive and the project would seem therefore to be worthwhile.

1.4.1 Variations in the expected rate of inflation

If the rate of inflation is expected to change, the calculation of the money cost of capital is slightly more complicated.

1.5 Example: Inflation (3)

Mr Gable has just received a dividend of £1,000 on his shareholding in Gonwithy Windmills plc. The market value of the shares is £8,000 ex div. What is the (money) cost of the equity capital, if dividends are expected to rise because of inflation by 10% in years 1, 2 and 3, before levelling off at this year 3 amount?

Solution

The money cost of capital is the internal rate of return of the following cash flows.

Year	Cash flow £	PV factor 15%	PV at 15% £	PV factor 20%	PV at 20% £
0	(8,000)	1.000	(8,000)	1.000	(8,000)
1	1,100	0.870	957	0.833	916
2	1,210	0.756	915	0.694	840
3 – ∞ *	1,331 pa	5.041	6,709	3.472	4,621
			581		(1,623)

The IRR is approximately $15\% + \left[\frac{581}{581 - -1,623} \times (20-15) \right] \% = 16.3\%$, say 16%

* The present value factor = Factor 1 – ∞ – Factor yrs 1-2.

For 15%

FV factor $= \frac{1}{0.15} - 1.626 = 5.041$

For 20%

FV factor $= \frac{1}{0.2} - 1.528 = 3.472$

1.6 Expectations of inflation and the effects of inflation

When managers evaluate a particular project, or when shareholders evaluate their investments, they can only guess at what the rate of inflation is going to be. Their expectations will probably be inaccurate, because it is extremely difficult to forecast the rate of inflation correctly. The only way in which uncertainty about inflation can be allowed for in project evaluation is by **risk** and **uncertainty analysis**. Plans should be made to obtain **'contingency funds'**, for example a higher bank overdraft facility if the rate of inflation exceeds expectations.

Inflation may be **general**, affecting prices of all kinds, or **specific** to particular prices. Generalised inflation has the following effects.

(a) Since fixed assets and stocks will increase in money value, the same quantities of assets must be financed by **increasing amounts** of capital.

(b) Inflation means higher costs and **higher selling prices**. The effect of higher prices on demand may **not** be **easy to predict**. A company that raises its prices by 10% because the general rate of inflation is running at 10% might suffer a serious fall in demand.

(c) Inflation, because it affects financing needs, is also likely to affect **gearing**, and so the **cost of capital**.

1.7 Mid-year and end of year money values

You might wonder why, in all the examples so far, the cash flows have been inflated to the end of year money prices. Inflation does not usually run at a steady rate.

In DCF calculations it is more appropriate to use **end of year money values**. This is because by convention, all **cash flows** are assumed to **occur** at the **end of the year**, and a discount factor appropriate to the end of the year is applied.

In an examination question which introduces inflation into the calculation where **DCF** is **not required** to reach a solution, it may be better to use mid-year prices rather than end of year prices in your figures.

2 Allowing for taxation   6/04, 12/04, 12/05

FAST FORWARD

Taxation is a major practical consideration for businesses. It is vital to take it into account in making decisions.

In investment appraisal, tax is often assumed to be payable **one year in arrears**.

Capital allowances details should be checked in any question you attempt.

So far, in looking at project appraisal, we have ignored **taxation**. However, payments of tax, or reductions of tax payments, are cash flows and ought to be considered in DCF analysis. Assumptions which may be stated in questions are as follows.

(a) Corporation tax is payable in the year following the one in which the taxable profits are made. Thus, if a project increases taxable profits by £10,000 in year 2, there will be a tax payment, assuming tax at 30%, of £3,000 in year 3.

(b) Net cash flows from a project should be considered as the **taxable profits** (not just the taxable revenues) arising from the project (unless an indication is given to the contrary).

Exam focus point

Check any question involving tax carefully to see what assumptions about tax rates are made. Also look out for questions which state that tax is payable in the same year as that in which the profits arise.

2.1 Capital allowances

Capital allowances are used to reduce taxable profits, and the consequent reduction in a tax payment should be treated as a **cash saving** arising from the acceptance of a project. Writing down allowances are generally allowed on the cost of **plant and machinery** at the rate of 25% on a **reducing balance** basis.

Thus if a company purchases plant costing £80,000, the subsequent writing down allowances would be as follows.

Year		Capital allowance £	Reducing balance £
1	(25% of cost)	20,000	60,000
2	(25% of RB)	15,000	45,000
3	(25% of RB)	11,250	33,750
4	(25% of RB)	8,438	25,312

When the plant is eventually sold, the difference between the sale price and the reducing balance amount at the time of sale will be treated as a **taxable profit** if the **sale price exceeds** the **reducing balance**, and as a **tax allowable loss** if the **reducing balance exceeds** the **sale price**.

Examination questions often assume that this loss will be available immediately, though in practice the balance less the sale price continues to be written off at 25% a year as part of a pool balance unless the asset has been de-pooled.

The cash saving on the capital allowances (or the cash payment for the charge) is calculated by

Allowance charge × Corporation tax rate.

Assumptions about capital allowances could be **simplified** in an **exam question**.

(a) You might be told that capital allowances can be claimed at the rate of 25% of cost on a straight line basis (that is, over four years)

(b) A question might refer to 'tax allowable depreciation', so that the capital allowances equal the depreciation charge.

There are two possible assumptions about the time when capital allowances start to be claimed.

(a) It can be assumed that the first claim for capital allowances occurs at the **start** of the **project** (at year 0) and so the first tax saving occurs one year later (at year 1).

(b) Alternatively it can be assumed that the **first claim** for **capital allowances** occurs **later** in the **first year**, so the first tax saving occurs one year later, that is, **year 2**.

Examination questions generally will indicate which of the two assumptions is required but you should state your assumptions clearly if you have to make assumptions.

Exam focus point

A common mistake in exams is to include the writing down allowance itself in the NPV calculation; it is the **tax affect** of the allowance that should be included.

2.2 Example: Taxation

A company is considering whether or not to purchase an item of machinery costing £40,000 in 20X5. It would have a life of four years, after which it would be sold for £5,000. The machinery would create annual cost savings of £14,000.

The machinery would attract writing down allowances of 25% on the reducing balance basis which could be claimed against taxable profits of the current year, which is soon to end. A balancing allowance or charge would arise on disposal. The rate of corporation tax is 30%. Tax is payable one year in arrears. The after-tax cost of capital is 8%. Assume that tax payments occur in the year following the transactions.

Should the machinery be purchased?

PART G INVESTMENT APPRAISAL

Solution

The first capital allowance is claimed against year 0 profits.

Cost: £40,000

Year	Allowance £		Reducing balance (RB) £
(0) 20X5 (25% of cost)	10,000	30,000	(40,000 – 10,000)
(1) 20X6 (25% of RB)	7,500	22,500	(30,000 – 7,500)
(2) 20X7 (25% of RB)	5,625	16,875	(22,500 – 5,625)
(3) 20X8 (25% of RB)	4,219	12,656	(16,875 – 4,219)
(4) 20X9 (25% of RB)	3,164	9,492	(12,656 – 3,164)

	£
Sale proceeds, end of fourth year	5,000
Less reducing balance, end of fourth year	9,492
Balancing allowance	4,492

Having calculated the allowances each year, the tax savings can be computed. The year of the cash flow is one year after the year for which the allowance is claimed.

Year of claim	Allowance £	Tax saved £	Year of tax payment/saving
0	10,000	3,000	1
1	7,500	2,250	2
2	5,625	1,688	3
3	4,219	1,266	4
4	7,656	2,297	5
	35,000 *		

* Net cost £(40,000 – 5,000) = £35,000

These tax savings relate to capital allowances. We must also calculate the extra tax payments on annual savings of £14,000.

The net cash flows and the NPV are now calculated as follows.

Year	Equipment £	Savings £	Tax on savings £	Tax saved on capital allowances £	Net cash flow £	Discount factor 8%	Present value of cash flow £
0	(40,000)				(40,000)	1.000	(40,000)
1		14,000		3,000	17,000	0.926	15,742
2		14,000	(4,200)	2,250	12,050	0.857	10,327
3		14,000	(4,200)	1,688	11,488	0.794	9,121
4	5,000	14,000	(4,200)	1,266	16,066	0.735	11,809
5			(4,200)	2,297	(1,903)	0.681	(1,296)
							5,703

The NPV is positive and so the purchase appears to be worthwhile.

2.2.1 An alternative and quicker method of calculating tax payments or savings

In the above example, the tax computations could have been combined, as follows.

Year	0	1	2	3	4
	£	£	£	£	£
Cost savings	0	14,000	14,000	14,000	14,000
Capital allowance	10,000	7,500	5,625	4,219	7,656
Taxable profits	(10,000)	6,500	8,375	9,781	6,344
Tax at 30%	3,000	(1,950)	(2,512)	(2,934)	(1,903)

The net cash flows would then be as follows.

Year	Equipment	Savings	Tax	Net cash flow
	£	£	£	£
0	(40,000)			(40,000)
1		14,000	3,000	17,000
2		14,000	(1,950)	12,050
3		14,000	(2,512)	11,488
4	5,000	14,000	(2,934)	16,066
5			(1,903)	(1,903)

The net cash flows are exactly the same as calculated previously.

2.3 Taxation and DCF

The effect of taxation on capital budgeting is theoretically quite simple. Organisations must pay tax, and the effect of undertaking a project will be to increase or decrease tax payments each year. These incremental tax cash flows should be included in the cash flows of the project for discounting to arrive at the project's NPV.

When **taxation is ignored** in the DCF calculations, the discount rate will reflect the **pre-tax rate of return** required on capital investments. When **taxation is included** in the cash flows, a **post-tax required rate of return** should be used.

Question — DCF and taxation

A company is considering the purchase of an item of equipment, which would earn profits before tax of £25,000 a year. Depreciation charges would be £20,000 a year for six years. Capital allowances would be £30,000 a year for the first four years. Corporation tax is at 30%.

What would be the annual net cash inflows of the project:

(a) For the first four years
(b) For the fifth and sixth years

assuming that tax payments occur in the same year as the profits giving rise to them, and there is no balancing charge or allowance when the machine is scrapped at the end of the sixth year?

Answer

(a)
	Years 1-4 £	Years 5-6 £
Profit before tax	25,000	25,000
Add back depreciation	20,000	20,000
Net cash inflow before tax	45,000	45,000
Less capital allowance	30,000	0
	15,000	45,000
Tax at 30%	4,500	13,500

Years 1 – 4 Net cash inflow after tax £45,000 – £4,500 = £40,500

(b) Years 5 – 6 Net cash inflow after tax = £45,000 – £13,500 = £31,500

Question
Tax implications

A company is considering the purchase of a machine for £150,000. It would be sold after four years for an estimated realisable value of £50,000. By this time capital allowances of £120,000 would have been claimed. The rate of corporation tax is 30%.

What are the tax implications of the sale of the machine at the end of four years?

Answer

There will be a balancing charge on the sale of the machine of £(50,000 – (150,000 – 120,000)) = £20,000. This will give rise to a tax payment of 30% × £20,000 = £6,000.

2.4 Quarterly accounting for corporation tax

Under the new UK system, corporation tax is **payable** by companies **quarterly**.

- In the seventh and tenth months of the year in which the profit is earned
- In the first and fourth months of the following year

This simply means that **half the tax is payable in the year in which the profits are earned** and **half in the following year**.

Exam focus point

This payment timetable is not difficult to remember but details will be given in the exam question anyway.

2.5 Example: Payment of corporation tax

If a project increases taxable profits by £10,000 in year 2, there will be tax payments of £10,000 × 30% × 50% = £1,500 in both year 2 and in year 3 (assuming a tax rate of 30%). It is these tax payments (that are a direct result of the project) that need to be included in a DCF analysis.

As half the tax on profit is paid in the year to which the profits relate, and half in the following year, the **benefit of the capital or writing down allowance** is also felt **half in the year to which it relates** and **half in the following year**.

27: ALLOWING FOR INFLATION AND TAXATION

2.6 Example: Taxation

A company is considering whether or not to purchase an item of machinery costing £40,000. It would have a life of four years, after which it would be sold for £5,000. The machinery would create annual cost savings of £14,000.

The machinery would attract writing down allowances of 25% on the reducing balance basis. A balancing allowance or charge would arise on disposal. The rate of corporation tax is 30%. Tax is payable quarterly in the seventh and tenth months of the year in which the profit is earned and in the first and fourth months of the following year. The after-tax cost of capital is 8%.

Should the machinery be purchased?

Solution

Step 1   WDAs and balancing charges / allowances

We begin by calculating the WDAs and balancing charge / allowance.

Year		Reducing balance £
0	Purchase	40,000
1	WDA	(10,000)
	Value at start of year 2	30,000
2	WDA	(7,500)
	Value at start of year 3	22,500
3	WDA	(5,625)
	Value at start of year 4	16,878
4	Sale	(5,000)
	Balancing allowance	11,875

Step 2   Calculate tax savings / payments

Having calculated the allowances each year, the tax savings can be computed. The tax savings effect two years, the year for which the allowance is claimed and the following year.

					Tax saving		
Year of claim	Allowance £	Tax saved £	Yr 1 £	Yr 2 £	Yr 3 £	Yr 4 £	Yr 5 £
1	10,000	3,000	1,500	1,500			
2	7,500	2,250		1,125	1,125		
3	5,625	1,688			844	844	
4	11,875	3,562	–	–	–	1,781	1,781
	35,000 *		1,500	2,625	1,969	2,625	1,781

* Net cost £(40,000 – 5,000) = £35,000

These tax savings relate to capital allowances. We must also take **the tax effects of the annual savings** of £14,000 into account.

The savings increase taxable profit (costs are lower) and so extra tax must be paid. Each saving of £14,000 will lead to extra tax of £14,000 × 30% × 50% = £2,100 in the year in question and the same amount in the following year.

Step 3   Calculate NPV

The **net cash flows and the NPV** are now calculated as follows.

PART G INVESTMENT APPRAISAL

Year	Equipment £	Savings £	Tax on savings £	Tax saved on capital allowances £	Net cash flow £	Discount factor 8%	Present value of cash flow £
0	(40,000)				(40,000)	1.000	(40,000)
1		14,000	(2,100)	1,500	13,400	0.926	12,408
2		14,000	(4,200)	2,625	12,425	0.857	10,648
3		14,000	(4,200)	1,969	11,769	0.794	9,345
4	5,000	14,000	(4,200)	2,625	17,425	0.735	12,807
5			(2,100)	1,781	(319)	0.681	(217)
							4,991

The NPV is positive and so the purchase appears to be worthwhile.

2.6.1 An alternative and quicker method of calculating tax payments or savings

In the above example, the tax computations could have been combined, as follows.

Year	1 £	2 £	3 £	4 £	5 £
Cost savings	14,000	14,000	14,000	14,000	
Capital allowance	10,000	7,500	5,625	11,875	
Taxable profits	4,000	6,500	8,375	2,125	
Tax (paid)/received at 30%	(1,200)	(1,950)	(2,512)	(638)	
Yr of (payment)/saving	(600)	(600)			
		(975)	(975)		
			(1,256)	(1,256)	
				(319)	(319)
(Payment)/saving	(600)	(1,575)	(2,231)	(1,575)	(319)

The net cash flows would then be as follows.

Year	Equipment £	Savings £	Tax £	Net cash flow £
0	(40,000)			(40,000)
1		14,000	(600)	13,400
2		14,000	(1,575)	12,425
3		14,000	(2,231)	11,769
4	5,000	14,000	(1,575)	17,425
5			(319)	(319)

The net cash flows are exactly the same as calculated previously.

> **Exam focus point**
> Remember it is the **tax benefit** of the capital allowance that is included in the NPV calculation, not the capital allowance itself.

Chapter Roundup

- **Inflation** is a feature of all economies, and it must be accommodated in financial planning.
- (1+ money rate of return) = (1 + real rate of return) × (1 + rate of inflation)
- **Real cash flows** (ie adjusted for inflation) should be discounted at a **real discount rate**.
- **Money cash flows** should be discounted at a money discount rate.
- **Taxation** is a major practical consideration for businesses. It is vital to take it into account in making decisions.
- In investment appraisal, tax is often assumed to be payable **one year in arrears.**
- **Capital allowances** details should be checked in any question you attempt.

Quick Quiz

1. What is the relationship between the money rate of return, the real rate of return and the rate of inflation?

2. The money cost of capital is 11%. The expected annual rate of inflation is 5%. What is the real cost of capital? (See below)

3. A company wants a minimum real return of 3% a year on its investments. Inflation is expected to be 8% a year. What is the company's minimum money cost of capital? (See below)

4. Summarise briefly how taxation is taken into consideration in capital budgeting.

5. A company is appraising an investment that will save electricity costs. Electricity prices are expected to rise at a rate of 15% per annum in future, although the general inflation rate will be 10% per annum. The money cost of capital for the company is 20%. What is the appropriate discount rate to apply to the forecast actual money cash flows for electricity?

    A   20.0%
    B   22.0%
    C   26.5%
    D   32.0%

6. *Choose the correct words from those highlighted.*

    Capital allowances are used to (1) **increase/reduce** taxable profits, and the consequent reduction in a tax payment should be treated as a (2) **cash saving/cash payment** arising from the acceptance of a project.

    Writing down allowances are generally allowed on the cost of (3) **materials and labour/plant and machinery** at the rate of (4) **25%/30%** on a (5) **straight line/reducing balance** basis.

    When the plant is eventually sold, the difference between the sales price and the reducing balance amount will be treated as a (6) **taxable profit/tax allowable loss** if the sales price exceeds the reducing balance, and as a (7) **taxable profit/tax allowable loss** if the reducing balance exceeds the sales price.

PART G INVESTMENT APPRAISAL

7   If cash flows are expressed in terms of the actual number of pounds that will be received or paid on various future dates, should the money rate or real rate be used for discounting?

8   Red Ltd is considering the purchase of a machine for £2,190,000. It would be sold after four years for an estimated realisable value of £790,000. By this time capital allowances of £1,450,000 would have been claimed. The rate of corporation tax is 30%.

What is the cash flow arising as a result of tax implications on the sale of the machine at the end of four years?

A   Inflow of £15,000
B   Outflow of £50,000
C   Outflow of £459,000
D   Outflow of £15,000

Answers to Quick Quiz

1   (1 + money rate) = (1 + real rate) × (1 + inflation rate)

2   $\frac{1.11}{1.05}$ = 1.057. The real cost of capital is 5.7%.

3   1.03 × 1.08 = 1.1124. The money cost of capital is 11.24%.

4   If tax is included in the cash flows, the post-tax rate of required return on capital investments should be used. If tax is ignored, the discount rate should reflect the pre-tax rate of return.

5   A   The money rate of 20% is applied to the money cash flows.

6   (1) reduce
    (2) cash saving
    (3) plant and machinery
    (4) 25%
    (5) reducing balance
    (6) taxable profit
    (7) tax allowable loss

7   The money rate

8   D   There will be a balancing charge on the sale of the machine of £(790,000 − (2,190,000 − 1,450,000)) = £50,000. This will give rise to a tax payment of 30% × £50,000 = £15,000.

Now try the questions below from the Exam Question Bank

Number	Level	Marks	Time
Q30	Examination	25	45 mins

Project appraisal and risk

28

Topic list	Syllabus reference
1 What is risk and why does it arise?	5(b)
2 Sensitivity analysis. Certainty-equivalents	5(b)
3 Probability analysis	5(b)
4 Simulation models	5(b)
5 Ways of reducing risk	5(b)

Introduction

This chapter will show some of the different methods of assessing and taking account of the **risk** associated with a project. The last two chapters of this Study Text will consider two further project appraisal topics - **capital rationing** and **leasing**.

PART G INVESTMENT APPRAISAL

Study guide

Section 16 – Project appraisal allowing for risk

- Distinguish between risk and uncertainty
- Identify the sources of risk affecting project profitability
- Evaluate the sensitivity of project NPV to changes in key variables
- Apply the probability approach to calculating expected NPV of a project and the associated standard deviation
- Explain the role of simulation in generating a probability distribution for the NPV of a project
- Identify risk reduction strategies for projects
- Evaluate the usefulness of risk assessment methods

Exam guide

Sensitivity calculations are important for exam purposes. In the December 2001 compulsory question 12 marks were available for sensitivity calculations. In June 2004 there were 8 marks in a compulsory question for discussion of risk and uncertainty. The Oxford Brookes degree Research and Analysis Project Topic 14 requires knowledge of how use of different methods of risk and uncertainty analysis might affect investment decisions.

1 What is risk and why does it arise? 6/04, 12/04

FAST FORWARD

Risk can be applied to a situation where there are several possible outcomes and, on the basis of past relevant experience, probabilities can be assigned to the various outcomes that could prevail.

Uncertainty can be applied to a situation where there are several possible outcomes but there is little past relevant experience to enable the probability of the possible outcomes to be predicted.

There are a wide range of techniques for incorporating risk into project appraisal.

A distinction should be made between the terms risk and uncertainty.

Risk	• Several possible outcomes • On basis of past relevant experience, assign probabilities to outcomes
Uncertainty	• Several possible outcomes • Little past experience, thus difficult to assign probabilities to outcomes

A risky situation is one where we can say that there is a 70% probability that returns from a project will be in excess of £100,000 but a 30% probability that returns will be less than £100,000. If, however, no information can be provided on the returns from the project, we are faced with an uncertain situation.

In general, risky projects are those whose future cash flows, and hence the project returns, are likely to be variable. The greater the variability is, the greater the risk. The problem of risk is more acute with capital investment decisions than other decisions for the following reasons.

(a) **Estimates** of capital expenditure might be for **several years ahead**, such as for major construction projects. Actual costs may escalate well above budget as the work progresses.

(b) Estimates of **benefits** will be for **several years ahead**, sometimes 10, 15 or 20 years ahead or even longer, and such long-term estimates can at best be approximations.

2 Sensitivity analysis. Certainty-equivalents   12/04

FAST FORWARD

Sensitivity analysis assesses how responsive the project's NPV is to changes in the variables used to calculate that NPV. One particular approach to sensitivity analysis, the certainty – equivalent approach, involves the conversion of the expected cash flows of the project to riskless equivalent amounts.

Key term

Sensitivity analysis is one method of analysing the risk surrounding a capital expenditure project and enables an assessment to be made of how responsive the project's NPV is to changes in the variables that are used to calculate that NPV.

The NPV could depend on a number of uncertain independent variables.

- Selling price
- Sales volume
- Cost of capital
- Initial cost
- Operating costs
- Benefits

The basic approach of sensitivity analysis is to **calculate the project's NPV** under **alternative assumptions** to determine how sensitive it is to changing conditions. An indication is thus provided of those variables to which the NPV is most sensitive (**critical variables**) and the **extent** to which those variables **may change** before the investment results in a negative NPV.

Sensitivity analysis therefore provides an indication of why a project might fail. Management should review critical variables to assess whether or not there is a strong possibility of events occurring which will lead to a negative NPV. Management should also pay particular attention to controlling those variables to which the NPV is particularly sensitive, once the decision has been taken to accept the investment.

When carrying out sensitivity analysis, you may need to use your knowledge of **breakeven analysis** (cost-volume-profit analysis) from your earlier studies.

Knowledge brought forward from earlier studies

Cost-volume-profit (breakeven) analysis

- Contribution per unit = unit selling price – unit variable costs
- Profit = (sales volume × contribution per unit) – fixed costs
- Breakeven point = activity level at which there is neither profit nor loss

$$= \frac{\text{total fixed costs}}{\text{contribution per unit}} = \frac{\text{contribution requ'd to breakeven}}{\text{contribution per unit}}$$

- Contribution/sales (C/S) ratio = profit/volume (P/V) ratio = (contribution/sales) × 100%

- Sales revenue at breakeven point = $\dfrac{\text{fixed costs}}{\text{C/S ratio}}$

PART G INVESTMENT APPRAISAL

> **Knowledge brought forward from earlier studies (continued)**
>
> - Margin of safety (in units) = budgeted sales units – breakeven sales units
>
>   Margin of safety (as %)
>
> $= \dfrac{\text{budgeted sales} - \text{breakeven sales}}{\text{budgeted sales}} \times 100\%$
>
> - Sales volume to achieve a target profit
>
> $= \dfrac{\text{fixed cost} + \text{target profit}}{\text{contribution per unit}}$
>
> **Example**
>
> Selling price = £15 per unit
>
> Variable cost = £12 per unit
>
> Fixed costs = £5,400 per annum
>
> Budgeted annual sales = 3,000 units
>
> Breakeven point in units = $\dfrac{£5,400}{£(15-12)}$ = 1,800 units
>
> C/S ratio = (3/15) × 100% = 20%
>
> Breakeven point in revenue = $\dfrac{£5,400}{0.2}$ = £27,000
>
> Sales volume to achieve profit of £3,300 = $\dfrac{£(5,400+3,300)}{£3}$ = 2,900 units
>
> Margin of safety (as a %) = $\dfrac{3,000-1,800}{3,000}$ × 100% = 40%

2.1 Example: Sensitivity analysis

Kenney Ltd is considering a project with the following cash flows.

	Initial investment £'000	Variable costs £'000	Cash inflows £'000	Net cash flows £'000
0	7,000			
1		(2,000)	6,500	4,500
2		(2,000)	6,500	4,500

Cash flows arise from selling 650,000 units at £10 per unit. Kenney Ltd has a cost of capital of 8%.

Required

Measure the sensitivity of the project to changes in variables.

Solution

The PVs of the cash flow are as follows.

Year	Discount factor 8%	PV of initial investment £'000	PV of variable costs £'000	PV of cash inflows £'000	PV of net cash flow £'000
0	1.000	(7,000)			(7,000)
1	0.926		(1,852)	6,019	4,167
2	0.857		(1,714)	5,571	3,857
		(7,000)	(3,566)	11,590	1,024

The project has a positive NPV and would appear to be worthwhile. The changes in cash flows which would need to occur for the project to breakeven (and hence be on the point of being unacceptable) are as follows.

(a) **Initial investment.** The initial investment can rise by £1,024,000 before the investment breaks even. The initial investment may therefore increase by 1,024/7,000 = 15%.

(b) **Sales volume.** The present value of the cash inflows less the present value of the variable costs will have to fall to £7,000,000 for the NPV to be zero.

We need to find the net cash flows in actual values. As the cash flows are equal each year, cumulative discount tables can be used.

   (i) The discount factor for 8% and year 2 is 1.783.

   (ii) If the discount factor is divided into the required present value of £7,000,000 we get an annual cash flow of £3,925,968.

   (iii) Given that the most likely net cash flow is £4,500,000, the net cash flow may decline by approximately £574,032 (4,500,000 – 3,925,968) each year before the NPV becomes zero.

   (iv) Total sales revenue may therefore decline by £831,930 (assuming net cash flow is 69% (4,500/6,500) of sales) (therefore sales = 574,032 × 6,500/4,500). At a selling price of £10 per unit this represents 83,193 units.

   (v) Alternatively we may state that sales volume may decline by 13% before the NPV becomes negative.

(c) **Selling price.** When sales volume is 650,000 units per annum, total sales revenue can fall to £5,925,968 (£(6,500,000 – 574,032) per annum before the NPV becomes negative. This represents a selling price of £9.12 per unit, which represents a 8.8% reduction in the selling price.

(d) **Variable costs.** The total variable cost can increase by £574,032, or £0.88 per unit. This represents an increase of 28.7%.

(e) **Cost of capital.** We need to calculate the IRR of the project. Let us try discount rates of 15% and 20%.

Year	Net cash flow £'000	Discount factor 15%	PV £'000	Discount factor 20%	PV £'000
0	(7,000)	0.870	(6,090)	0.833	(5,831)
1	4,500	0.756	3,402	0.694	3,123
2	4,500	0.658	2,961	0.579	2,606
			NPV = 273		NPV = (102)

$$\text{IRR} = 0.15 + \left[\frac{273}{273+102} \times (0.20-0.15)\right] = 18.64\%$$

The cost of capital can therefore increase by 133% before the NPV becomes negative.

The elements to which the NPV appears to be most sensitive are the selling price followed by the sales volume. Management should thus pay particular attention to these factors so that they can be carefully monitored.

PART G INVESTMENT APPRAISAL

2.2 Weaknesses of this approach to sensitivity analysis

These are as follows.

(a) The method requires that **changes** in each key variable are **isolated**. However management is more interested in the combination of the effects of changes in two or more key variables.

(b) Looking at factors in isolation is unrealistic since they are often **interdependent**.

(c) Sensitivity analysis does not examine the **probability** that any particular variation in costs or revenues might occur.

(d) **Critical factors** may be those over which managers have no control.

(e) In itself it does not provide a decision rule. Parameters defining **acceptability** must be laid down by managers.

Question — Sensitivity analysis

Nevers Ure Ltd has a cost of capital of 8% and is considering a project with the following 'most-likely' cash flows.

Year	Purchase of plant £	Running costs £	Savings £
0	(7,000)		
1		2,000	6,000
2		2,500	7,000

Required

Measure the sensitivity (in percentages) of the project to changes in the levels of expected costs and savings.

Answer

The PVs of the cash flows are as follows.

Year	Discount factor 8%	PV of plant cost £	PV of running costs £	PV of savings £	PV of net cash flow £
0	1.000	(7,000)			(7,000)
1	0.926		(1,852)	5,556	3,704
2	0.857		(2,143)	5,999	3,856
		(7,000)	(3,995)	11,555	560

The project has a positive NPV and would appear to be worthwhile. The changes in cash flows which would need to occur for the project to break even (NPV = 0) are as follows.

(a) Plant costs would need to increase by a PV of £560, that is by (560/7,000) × 100% = 8%
(b) Running costs would need to increase by a PV of £560, that is by (560/3,995) × 100% = 14%
(c) Savings would need to fall by a PV of £560, that is by (560/11,555) × 100% = 4.8%

Exam focus point

The examiner has commented that sensitivity analysis is often confused with the internal rate or return.

2.3 The certainty-equivalent approach

Another method is the **certainty-equivalent approach**. By this method, the expected cash flows of the project are converted to riskless equivalent amounts. The greater the risk of an expected cash flow, the smaller the 'certainty-equivalent' value (for receipts) or the larger the certainty equivalent value (for payments).

2.4 Example: Certainty-equivalent approach

Dark Ages Ltd, whose cost of capital is 10%, is considering a project with the following expected cash flows.

Year	Cash flow £	Discount factor 10%	Present value £
0	(9,000)	1.000	(9,000)
1	7,000	0.909	6,363
2	5,000	0.826	4,130
3	5,000	0.751	3,755
		NPV	+5,248

The project seems to be clearly worthwhile. However, because of the uncertainty about the future cash receipts, the management decides to reduce them to 'certainty-equivalents' by taking only 70%, 60% and 50% of the years 1, 2 and 3 cash flows respectively. (Note that this method of risk adjustment allows for different risk factors in each year of the project.)

On the basis of the information set out above, assess whether the project is worthwhile.

Solution

The risk-adjusted NPV of the project is as follows.

Year	Cash flow £	Discount factor 10%	Present value £
0	(9,000)	1.000	(9,000)
1	4,900	0.909	4,454
2	3,000	0.826	2,478
3	2,500	0.751	1,878
		NPV =	– 190

The project is too risky and should be rejected.

The disadvantage of the 'certainty-equivalent' approach is that the amount of the adjustment to each cash flow is decided **subjectively**.

3 Probability analysis 12/04

FAST FORWARD

A **probability analysis** of expected cash flows can often be estimated and used both to calculate an expected NPV and to measure risk. The standard deviation of the NPV can be calculated to assess risk when the construction of probability distributions is complicated.

A **probability distribution** of '**expected cash flows**' can often be estimated, recognising there are several possible outcomes, not just one. This may be used to do the following.

Step 1 Calculate an expected value of the NPV

Step 2 Measure risk, for example in the following ways.

(a) By calculating the worst possible outcome and its probability
(b) By calculating the probability that the project will fail to achieve a positive NPV
(c) By calculating the standard deviation of the NPV

PART G INVESTMENT APPRAISAL

3.1 Example: Probability estimates of cash flows

A company is considering a project involving the outlay of £300,000 which it estimates will generate cash flows over its two year life at the probabilities shown in the following table.

Cash flows for project

Year 1

Cash flow	Probability
£	
100,000	0.25
200,000	0.50
300,000	0.25
	1.00

Year 2

If cash flow in Year 1 is:	there is a probability of:	that the cash flow in Year 2 will be:
£		£
100,000	0.25	Nil
	0.50	100,000
	0.25	200,000
	1.00	
200,000	0.25	100,000
	0.50	200,000
	0.25	300,000
	1.00	
300,000	0.25	200,000
	0.50	300,000
	0.25	350,000
	1.00	

The company's investment criterion for this type of project is 10% DCF.

You are required to calculate the expected value (EV) of the project's NPV and the probability that the NPV will be negative.

Solution

Step 1   Calculate expected value of the NPV.

First we need to draw up a probability distribution of the expected cash flows. We begin by calculating the present values of the cash flows.

Year	Cash flow	Discount factor	Present value
	£'000	10%	£'000
1	100	0.909	90.9
1	200	0.909	181.8
1	300	0.909	272.7
2	100	0.826	82.6
2	200	0.826	165.2
2	300	0.826	247.8
2	350	0.826	289.1

Year 1 PV of cash flow £'000 (a)	Probability (b)	Year 2 PV of cash flow £'000 (c)	Probability (d)	Joint probability (b) × (d)	Total PV of cash inflows £'000 (a) + (c)	EV of PV of cash inflows £'000
90.9	0.25	0.0	0.25	0.0625	90.9	5.681
90.9	0.25	82.6	0.50	0.1250	173.5	21.688
90.9	0.25	165.2	0.25	0.0625	256.1	16.006
181.8	0.50	82.6	0.25	0.1250	264.4	33.050
181.8	0.50	165.2	0.50	0.2500	347.0	86.750
181.8	0.50	247.8	0.25	0.1250	429.6	53.700
272.7	0.25	165.2	0.25	0.0625	437.9	27.369
272.7	0.25	247.8	0.50	0.1250	520.5	65.063
272.7	0.25	289.1	0.25	0.0625	561.8	35.113
						344.420

	£
EV of PV of cash inflows	344,420
Less project cost	300,000
EV of NPV	44,420

Step 2 Measure risk.

Since the EV of the NPV is positive, the project should go ahead unless the risk is unacceptably high. The probability that the project will have a negative NPV is the probability that the total PV of cash inflows is less than £300,000. From the column headed 'Total PV of cash inflows', we can establish that this probability is 0.0625 + 0.125 + 0.0625 + 0.125 = 0.375 or 37.5%. This might be considered an unacceptably high risk.

3.2 The standard deviation of the NPV

The disadvantage of using the EV of NPV approach to assess the risk of the project is that the **construction** of the **probability distribution** can become **very complicated**. If we were considering a project over 4 years, each year having five different forecasted cash flows, there would be 625 (5^4) NPVs to calculate. To avoid all of these calculations, an indication of the risk may be obtained by calculating the **standard deviation** of the NPV.

3.3 Example: Standard deviation of the net present value

Frame plc is considering which of two mutually exclusive projects, A or B, to undertake. There is some uncertainty about the running costs with each project, and a probability distribution of the NPV for each project has been estimated, as follows.

Project A NPV £'000	Probability	Project B NPV £'000	Probability
– 20	0.15	+ 5	0.2
+ 10	0.20	+ 15	0.3
+ 20	0.35	+ 20	0.4
+ 40	0.30	+ 25	0.1

You are required to decide which project should the company choose, if either.

PART G INVESTMENT APPRAISAL

Solution

We can begin by calculating the EV of the NPV for each project.

Project A			Project B		
NPV	Prob	EV	NPV	Prob	EV
£'000		£'000	£'000		£'000
–20	0.15	(3.0)	5	0.2	1.0
10	0.20	2.0	15	0.3	4.5
20	0.35	7.0	20	0.4	8.0
40	0.30	12.0	25	0.1	2.5
		18.0			16.0

Project A has a higher EV of NPV, but what about the risk of variation in the NPV above or below the EV? This can be measured by the standard deviation of the NPV.

The standard deviation of a project's NPV, s, can be calculated as:

$$s = \sqrt{\Sigma p(x - \bar{x})^2}$$

where $\bar{x}$ is the EV of the NPV.

Project A, $\bar{x}$ = 18				Project B, $\bar{x}$ = 16			
x	p	x – $\bar{x}$	$p(x-\bar{x})^2$	x	p	x – $\bar{x}$	$p(x-\bar{x})^2$
£'000		£'000		£'000		£'000	
–20	0.15	–38	216.6	5	0.2	–11	24.2
10	0.20	–8	12.8	15	0.3	–1	0.3
20	0.35	+2	1.4	20	0.4	+4	6.4
40	0.30	+22	145.2	25	0.1	+9	8.1
			376.0				39.0

	Project A			Project B	
Standard deviation s =		√376	Standard deviation s =		√39.0
	=	19.391		=	6.245
	=	£19,391		=	£6,245

Although Project A has a higher EV of NPV, it also has a higher standard deviation of NPV, and so has greater risk associated with it.

Which project should be selected? Clearly it depends on the attitude of the company's management to risk.

(a) If management are prepared to take the risk of a **low NPV** in the hope of a high NPV they will opt for project A.

(b) If management are **risk-averse**, they will opt for the less risky project B.

3.4 Problems with expected values

There are the following problems with using expected values in making investment decisions.

- An investment may be **one-off**, and 'expected' NPV may never actually occur.
- **Assigning probabilities** to events is highly **subjective**.
- Expected values **do not evaluate the range** of possible NPV outcomes.

4 Simulation models

FAST FORWARD

Simulation models can be used to assess products which have a large number of possible outcomes, or projects which have correlated cash flows.

Simulation will overcome problems of having a very large number of possible outcomes, also the correlation of cash flows (a project which is successful in its early years is more likely to be successful in its later years).

4.1 Example: Simulation model

The following probability estimates have been prepared for a proposed project.

	Year	Probability	£
Cost of equipment	0	1.00	(40,000)
Revenue each year	1-5	0.15	40,000
		0.40	50,000
		0.30	55,000
		0.15	60,000
Running costs each year	1-5	0.10	25,000
		0.25	30,000
		0.35	35,000
		0.30	40,000

The cost of capital is 12%. Assess how a simulation model might be used to assess the project's NPV.

Solution

A simulation model could be constructed by assigning a range of random number digits to each possible value for each of the uncertain variables. The random numbers must exactly match their respective probabilities. This is achieved by working upwards cumulatively from the lowest to the highest cash flow values and assigning numbers that will correspond to probability groupings as follows.

Revenue				Running costs		
£	Prob	Random numbers		£	Prob	Random numbers
40,000	0.15	00 – 14	*	25,000	0.10	00 – 09
50,000	0.40	15 – 54	**	30,000	0.25	10 – 34
55,000	0.30	55 – 84	***	40,000	0.35	35 – 69
60,000	0.15	85 – 99		40,000	0.30	70 – 99

*   Probability is 0.15 (15%). Random numbers are 15% of range 00 – 99.

** Probability is 0.40 (40%). Random numbers are 40% of range 00 – 99 but starting at 15.

*** Probability is 0.30 (30%). Random numbers are 30% of range 00 – 99 but starting at 55.

For revenue, the selection of a random number in the range 00 and 14 has a probability of 0.15. This probability represents revenue of £40,000. Numbers have been assigned to cash flows so that when numbers are selected at random, the cash flows have exactly the same probability of being selected as is indicated in their respective probability distribution above.

Random numbers would be generated, for example by a computer program, and these would be used to assign values to each of the uncertain variables.

For example, if random numbers 378420015689 were generated, the values assigned to the variables would be as follows.

	Revenue		Costs	
Calculation	Random number	Value £	Random number	Value £
1	37	50,000	84	40,000
2	20	50,000	01	25,000
3	56	55,000	89	40,000

A computer would calculate the NPV may times over using the values established in this way with more random numbers, and the results would be analysed to provide the following.

(a) An **expected NPV** for the project

(b) A **statistical distribution** pattern for the possible variation in the NPV above or below this average

The decision whether to go ahead with the project would then be made on the basis of **expected return** and **risk**.

5 Ways of reducing risk   12/01

Only if management know for certainty what is going to happen in the future can they appraise a project in the knowledge that there is no risk. However the future is uncertain by nature. There are, nevertheless, steps that management can take to reduce the riskiness of a project.

(a) A **maximum payback period** can be set to reflect the fact that risk increases the longer the time period under consideration.

(b) A **high discounting rate** can be used so that a cash flow which occurs quite some time in the future will have less effect on the decision.

(c) Projects with **low standard deviations** and **acceptable average predicted outcomes** can be selected. If a business is undertaking a range of projects, it should ensure that some are **low-risk (diversification)**.

(d) **Sensitivity analysis** can be used to determine the critical factors within the decision-making process. Management effort can then be directed to those factors which are critical to the success of a particular decision.

(e) To ensure that future events are no worse than predicted, **prudence**, **slack** and **overly pessimistic estimates** can be applied.

Chapter Roundup

- **Risk** can be applied to a situation where there are several possible outcomes and, on the basis of past relevant experience, probabilities can be assigned to the various outcomes that could prevail.

- **Uncertainty** can be applied to a situation where there are several possible outcomes but there is little past relevant experience to enable the probability of the possible outcomes to be predicted.

- There are a wide range of techniques for incorporating risk into project appraisal.

- **Sensitivity analysis** assesses how responsive the project's NPV is to changes in the variables used to calculate that NPV. One particular approach to sensitivity analysis, the certainty – equivalent approach, involves the conversion of the expected cash flows of the project to riskless equivalent amounts.

- A **probability analysis** of expected cash flows can often be estimated and used both to calculate an expected NPV and to measure risk. The standard deviation of the NPV can be calculated to assess risk when the construction of probability distributions is complicated.

- Simulation models can be used to assess products which have a large number of possible outcomes, or projects which have correlated cash flows.

Quick Quiz

1. Give three examples of uncertain independent variables upon which the NPV of a project may depend.

2. How are simulation models constructed?

3. Describe in a sentence each three ways in which managers can reduce risk.

4. Sensitivity analysis allows for uncertainty in project appraisal by assessing the probability of changes in the decision variables.

    ☐ True

    ☐ False

5. *Fill in the blanks.*

    The .... is where expected cashflows are converted to riskless equivalent amounts.

6. Give three examples of ways that risk can be measured in probability analysis.

7. Expected values can help an accountant evaluate the range of possible Net Present Value outcomes.

    ☐ True

    ☐ False

8. $s = \sqrt{\Sigma p(x - \bar{x})^2}$

    where $\bar{x} = ?$

PART G INVESTMENT APPRAISAL

Answers to Quick Quiz

1. (a) Selling price
   (b) Sales volume
   (c) Cost of capital
   (d) Initial cost
   (e) Operating costs
   (f) Benefits

2. By assigning a range of random number digits to each possible value of each of the uncertain variables.

3. (a) Set maximum payback period.
   (b) Use high discounting rate.
   (c) Select projects with low standard deviations and acceptable average predicted outcomes.
   (d) Use sensitivity analysis to determine the critical factors within the decision-making process.
   (e) Use pessimistic estimates.

4. False. Sensitivity analysis does not assess probability.

5. Certainty equivalent approach

6. Calculating the worst possible outcome and its probability
   Calculating the probability that the project will fail to achieve a positive NPV
   Calculating the standard deviation of the NPV

7. False

8. The expected value of the NPV.

Now try the questions below from the Exam Question Bank

Number	Level	Marks	Time
Q31	Introductory	n/a	30 mins

Capital rationing

Topic list	Syllabus reference
1 Causes of a shortage of capital	5(b)(vi)
2 Single period capital rationing	5(b)(vi)
3 Multi-period capital rationing	5(b)(vi)

Introduction

Having looked in Chapters 24 to 28 at the methods available for appraising projects when funds are available, we will now be considering the procedure for assessing projects when capital is a **scarce** resource.

We will use two different techniques for finding the best way to use our limited funds. If there is **single period capital rationing** we rank our projects in order of their **profitability index**, which measures the PV of the future cash flows per pound invested. For **multi-period capital rationing** we use **linear programming**.

PART G INVESTMENT APPRAISAL

Study guide

Section 17 – Capital rationing

- Distinguish hard and soft capital rationing
- Apply profitability index techniques for single period divisible projects
- Evaluate projects involving single and multi-period capital rationing

Exam guide

The examiner has stated that questions on single period capital rationing will contain numbers (and often prove difficult for students). Questions on multi-period capital rationing will probably be discussion-based.

Research and Analysis Project Topic 16 in the Oxford Brookes degree requires you to consider the effect of capital rationing on the investment decision.

1 Causes of a shortage of capital

FAST FORWARD

Capital rationing may occur due to internal factors (soft capital rationing) or external factors (hard capital rationing).

Key terms

Capital rationing: a situation in which a company has a limited amount of capital to invest in potential projects, such that the different possible investments need to be compared with one another in order to allocate the capital available most effectively.

Soft capital rationing is brought about by internal factors; **hard capital rationing** is brought about by external factors.

If an organisation is in a **capital rationing** situation it will not be able to enter into all projects with positive NPVs because there is not enough capital for all of the investments.

1.1 Soft and hard capital rationing

Soft capital rationing may arise for one of the following reasons.

- (a) Management may be **reluctant** to **issue additional share capital** because of concern that this may lead to **outsiders** gaining control of the business.
- (b) **Management** may be **unwilling** to **issue additional share capital** if it will lead to a **dilution of earnings** per share.
- (c) Management may **not want to raise additional debt capital** because they do not wish to be committed to **large fixed interest payments**.
- (d) Management may wish to **limit investment** to a level that can be financed solely from **retained earnings**.
- (e) **Capital expenditure budgets** may restrict spending.

Hard capital rationing may arise for one of the following reasons.

- (a) Raising money through the stock market may not be possible if **share prices** are **depressed**.
- (b) There may be **restrictions** on **bank lending** due to government control.

(c) Lending institutions may consider an organisation to be **too risky** to be granted further loan facilities.

(d) The **costs** associated with making small **issues** of capital may be too great.

1.2 Relaxation of capital constraints

If an organisation adopts a policy that restricts funds available for investment (soft capital rationing), the policy may be less than optimal. The organisation may reject projects with a positive net present value and forgo opportunities that would have enhanced the market value of the organisation.

A company may be able to limit the effects of hard capital rationing and exploit new opportunities.

(a) It might **seek joint venture partners** with which to share projects.

(b) As an alternative to direct investment in a project, the company may be able to consider a **licensing** or **franchising agreement** with another enterprise, under which the licensor/franchisor company would receive royalties.

(c) It may be possible to **contract** out parts of a project to reduce the initial capital outlay required.

(d) The company may seek **new** alternative **sources of capital** (subject to any restrictions which apply to it) for example:

- Venture capital
- Debt finance secured on the assets of the project
- Sale and leaseback of property or equipment (see the next chapter)
- Grant aid
- More effective capital management

2 Single period capital rationing 12/02, 12/03

FAST FORWARD

When capital rationing occurs in a **single period**, projects are ranked in terms of **profitability index**.

We shall begin our analysis by assuming that capital rationing occurs in a single period, and that capital is freely available at all other times.

The following further assumptions will be made.

(a) If a company does not accept and undertake a project during the period of capital rationing, the **opportunity** to undertake it is **lost**. The project cannot be postponed until a subsequent period when no capital rationing exists.

(b) There is **complete certainty** about the outcome of each project, so that the choice between projects is not affected by considerations of risk.

(c) **Projects** are **divisible**, so that it is possible to undertake, say, half of Project X in order to earn half of the net present value (NPV) of the whole project.

The basic approach is to rank all investment opportunities so that the NPVs can be maximised from the use of the available funds.

Ranking in terms of absolute NPVs will normally give incorrect results. This method leads to the **selection** of **large projects**, each of which has a high individual NPV but which have, in total, a lower NPV than a large number of smaller projects with lower individual NPVs. Ranking is therefore in terms of what is called the **profitability index.**

This profitability index is a ratio that measures the PV of future cash flows per £1 of investment, and so indicates which investments make the best use of the limited resources available.

PART G INVESTMENT APPRAISAL

Key term

> **Profitability index** is the ratio of the present value of the project's future cash flows (not including the capital investment) divided by the present value of the total capital investment.

2.1 Example: Capital rationing

Suppose that Hard Times Ltd is considering four projects, W, X, Y and Z. Relevant details are as follows.

Project	Investment required £	Present value of cash inflows £	NPV £	Profitability index (PI)	Ranking as per NPV	Ranking as per PI
W	(10,000)	11,240	1,240	1.12	3	1
X	(20,000)	20,991	991	1.05	4	4
Y	(30,000)	32,230	2,230	1.07	2	3
Z	(40,000)	43,801	3,801	1.10	1	2

Without capital rationing all four projects would be viable investments. Suppose, however, that only £60,000 was available for capital investment. Let us look at the resulting NPV if we select projects in the order of ranking per NPV.

Project	Priority	Outlay £	NPV £	
Z	1st	40,000	3,801	
Y (balance)*	2nd	20,000	1,487	(2/3 of £2,230)
		60,000	5,288	

* Projects are divisible. By spending the balancing £20,000 on project Y, two thirds of the full investment would be made to earn two thirds of the NPV.

Suppose, on the other hand, that we adopt the profitability index approach. The selection of projects will be as follows.

Project	Priority	Outlay £	NPV £	
W	1st	10,000	1,240	
Z	2nd	40,000	3,801	
Y (balance)	3rd	10,000	743	((1/3 of £2,230)
		60,000	5,784	

By choosing projects according to the PI, the resulting NPV if only £60,000 is available is increased by £496.

2.1.1 Problems with the Profitability Index method

(a) The approach can only be used if **projects** are **divisible**. If the projects are not divisible a decision has to be made by examining the **absolute NPVs** of all possible combinations of complete projects that can be undertaken within the constraints of the capital available. The combination of projects which remains at or under the limit of available capital without any of them being divided, and which maximises the total NPV, should be chosen.

(b) The **selection criterion** is fairly **simplistic**, taking no account of the possible strategic value of individual investments in the context of the overall objectives of the organisation.

(c) The method is of limited use when projects have **differing cash flow patterns**. These patterns may be important to the company since they will affect the timing and availability of funds. With multi-period capital rationing, it is possible that the project with the highest Profitability Index is the slowest in generating returns.

(d) The Profitability Index **ignores** the **absolute size** of individual projects. A project with a high index might be very small and therefore only generate a small NPV.

Question — Capital rationing

Bleak House Ltd is experiencing capital rationing in year 0, when only £60,000 of investment finance will be available. No capital rationing is expected in future periods, but none of the three projects under consideration by the company can be postponed. The expected cash flows of the three projects are as follows.

Project	Year 0 £	Year 1 £	Year 2 £	Year 3 £	Year 4 £
A	(50,000)	(20,000)	20,000	40,000	40,000
B	(28,000)	(50,000)	40,000	40,000	20,000
C	(30,000)	(30,000)	30,000	40,000	10,000

The cost of capital is 10%. You are required to decide which projects should be undertaken in year 0, in view of the capital rationing, given that projects are divisible.

Answer

The ratio of NPV at 10% to outlay in year 0 (the year of capital rationing) is as follows.

Project	Outlay in Year 0 £	PV £	NPV £	Ratio	Ranking
A	50,000	55,700	5,700	1.114	3rd
B	28,000	31,290	3,290	1.118	2nd
C	30,000	34,380	4,380	1.146	1st

Working

Present value A

Year		£	Discount factor 10%	Present value £
1	Cash flow	(20,000)	0.909	(18,180)
2	Cash flow	20,000	0.826	16,520
3	Cash flow	40,000	0.751	30,040
4	Cash flow	40,000	0.683	27,320
				55,700

Present value B

Year		£	Discount factor 10%	Present value £
1	Cash flow	(50,000)	0.909	(45,450)
2	Cash flow	40,000	0.826	33,040
3	Cash flow	40,000	0.751	30,040
4	Cash flow	20,000	0.683	13,660
				31,290

PART G INVESTMENT APPRAISAL

Present value C

Year		£	Discount factor 10%	Present value £
1	Cash flow	(30,000)	0.909	(27,270)
2	Cash flow	30,000	0.826	24,780
3	Cash flow	40,000	0.751	30,040
4	Cash flow	10,000	0.683	6,830
				34,380

The optimal investment policy is as follows.

Ranking	Project	Year 0 outlay £	NPV £
1st	C	30,000	4,380
2nd	B	28,000	3,290
3rd	A (balance)	2,000 (4% of 5,700)	228
NPV from total investment			7,898

2.2 Postponing projects

We have so far assumed that projects cannot be postponed until year 1. If this assumption is removed, the choice of projects in year 0 would be made by reference to the loss of NPV from **postponement**

2.3 Example: Postponing projects

The figures in the previous exercise will be used to illustrate the method. If any project, A, B or C, were delayed by one year, the 'NPV' would now relate to year 1 values, so that in year 0 terms, the NPVs would be as follows.

		NPV in Year 1 £			NPV in Year 0 Value £	Loss in NPV £
(a)	Project A	5,700 ×	$\frac{1}{1.10}$	=	5,182	518
(b)	Project B	3,290 ×	$\frac{1}{1.10}$	=	2,991	299
(c)	Project C	4,380 ×	$\frac{1}{1.10}$	=	3,982	398

An index of postponability would be calculated as follows.

Project	Loss in NPV from one-year postponement £	Outlay deferred from year 0 £	Postponability index (loss/outlay)
A	518	50,000	0.0104
B	299	28,000	0.0107
C	398	30,000	0.0133

The loss in NPV by deferring investment would be greatest for Project C, and least for Project A. It is therefore more profitable to postpone A, rather than B or C, as follows.

Investment in year 0:

Project	Outlay		NPV
	£		£
C	30,000		4,380
B	28,000		3,290
A (balance)	2,000	(4% of 5,700)	228
	60,000		7,898

Investment in year 1 (balance):

Project A	£48,000 (96% of 5,182)	4,975

Total NPV (as at year 0) of investments in years 0 and 1   12,873

3 Multi-period capital rationing

FAST FORWARD

When capital rationing occurs in a **number of periods** and two projects are under consideration, the graphical approach to **linear programming** is used to arrive at an NPV - maximising mix of products.

Although the graphical approach is a useful technique to use for arriving at optimum project mixes, you should be aware of its limitations.

When capital is expected to be in short supply for more than one period, the selection of an optimal investment programme cannot be made by ranking projects according to a profitability index. Other techniques, notably linear programming, should be used.

3.1 Solution by graphical linear programming

You will have already covered the **graphical approach to linear programming** in your earlier studies. You will be aware that the technique can only be used if there are two variables. The variables in this instance are the **individual investment projects.** This method is confined to dealing with those scenarios concerned with a choice between just two investment projects. We will illustrate this particular approach to multi-period capital rationing with an example. In the exam you won't be expected to draw graphs, but you may be asked to discuss this approach.

3.2 Example: Graphical linear programming approach

Finch Ltd has the chance to invest in two projects, A and B, details of which are set out below.

Investment project	Present value of outlay in period 1 £'000	Present value of outlay in period 2 £'000	Present value of outlay in period 3 £'000	Net present value of investment at time 0 £'000
A	30	10	10	56
B	20	4	2	8

Capital investment limits, as set by Finch Ltd's parent company, are as follows.

	£'000
Period 1	36
Period 2	8
Period 3	6

It is assumed that the capital investment limits are absolute and cannot be expanded by project generated cash inflows. Projects are divisible but cannot be repeated more than once. You are required to formulate and solve the linear programming model which will maximise net present value.

PART G INVESTMENT APPRAISAL

Solution

Step 1 **Define variables**

Let x = the proportion of project A accepted. Let y = the proportion of project B accepted.

Step 2 Establish constraints

$30x + 20y \leq 36$ (period 1 investment)
$10x + 4y \leq 8$ (period 2 investment)
$10x + 2y \leq 6$ (period 3 investment)
$x, y \leq 1$ (proportion must be less than or equal to 1)
$x, y \geq 0$ (proportion must be greater than or equal to 0)

The last two constraints ensure that a project cannot be undertaken more than once but allows for a project to be partially accepted.

Step 3 **Establish objective function**

The objective is to maximise the NPV from the total investment in periods 1, 2 and 3.

Maximise $56x + 8y$.

Step 4 **Graph the model**

The feasible region is represented by OABC.

Step 5 **Find the best solution**

Using the 'iso-NPV line' plotted on the graph, the optimal solution can be established as at point C (0.6, 0). The optimal solution is therefore to invest in 0.6 of project A and to make no investment in project B.

The total NPV available is therefore 0.6 × £56,000 = £33,600.

More than two investments under consideration

> **Exam focus point**
>
> The graphical approach to linear programming cannot deal with situations where there are more than two investments under consideration. A method for solving such linear programming problems is called the simplex method. This is outside the scope of your syllabus. However, you may be asked to formulate the constraints and objective functions.

3.3 Limitations of the linear programming approach to capital rationing

When two constraints apply, the graphical approach to linear programming may be a useful method of selecting projects but there are a number of assumptions and limitations which must be kept in mind if the use of the technique is to be considered.

(a) It assumes that variables are **linearly related**.

(b) It assumes that projects are **divisible** or that scalar multiples of projects are possible.

(c) It assumes that the **returns** of the projects are in **proportion** to the amount invested in each project.

(d) **Uncertainty** is **ignored**. It assumes that all future cash flows and available resources are known with certainty.

(e) It assumes that **all projects** and **constraints** are **independent**.

(f) It is possible that **other investment opportunities** not included in the linear programming model could realise a higher NPV.

(g) Linear programming cannot be used when projects are **mutually exclusive** in multi-period capital rationing situations. Instead integer programming (not part of your syllabus) has to be used.

(h) No account of **risk** attached to the projects or the company's attitude to risk is taken.

Chapter Roundup

- **Capital rationing** may occur due to internal factors (soft capital rationing) or external factors (hard capital rationing).

- When capital rationing occurs in a **single period**, projects are ranked in terms of **profitability index**.

- When capital rationing occurs in a **number of periods** and two projects are under consideration, the graphical approach to **linear programming** is used to arrive at an NPV - maximising mix of products.

- Although the graphical approach is a useful technique to use for arriving at optimum project mixes, you should be aware of its limitations.

PART G INVESTMENT APPRAISAL

Quick Quiz

1 Profitability index = ... ?
2 Give three assumptions of single period capital rationing.
3 What are the five steps of the graphical linear programming approach to multi-period capital rationing?
4 *Fill in the blanks.*

   (1) .... capital rationing is brought about by external factors; (2) .... capital rationing by internal factors.

5 The profitability index method takes into account the absolute size of individual projects.

   ☐ True
   ☐ False

6 How many possible investment choices can the graphical linear programming method assess?
7 What is the problem with ranking possible investment projects by size of absolute NPV in a single period capital rationing situation?
8 The profitability index method cannot be used if capital rationing is expected to last for more than one period.

   ☐ True
   ☐ False

Answers to Quick Quiz

1 Profitability index = $\dfrac{\text{PV of project's future cash flows (excluding original capital investment)}}{\text{PV of total capital outlays}}$

2 (a) If a project is not accepted and undertaken during the period, the opportunity to undertake it is lost.
   (b) There is complete certainty about the outcome of each project.
   (c) Projects are divisible.

3 (1) Define variables
   (2) Establish constraints
   (3) Establish objective function
   (4) Graph the model
   (5) Find the best solution

4 (1) Hard
   (2) Soft

5 False

6 Two

7 This method leads to the selection of large projects, each of which has a high individual NPV, but which have in total lower NPVs than a large number of smaller projects with lower individual NPVs.

8 True

Now try the questions below from the Exam Question Bank

Number	Level	Marks	Time
Q32	Examination	25	45 mins

Leasing decisions

30

Topic list	Syllabus reference
1 Leasing as a source of finance	5(b)(vii)
2 Lease or buy decisions	5(b)(vii)

Introduction

In this chapter, we consider the option of **leasing** an asset.

As well as looking at the advantages and disadvantages of different types of lease compared with **other forms of credit finance**, we shall be discussing the tax and cash flow implications of leasing.

PART G INVESTMENT APPRAISAL

Study guide

Section 18 – Leasing decisions

- Distinguish between operating and finance leases
- Apply DCF methods to projects involving buy or lease problems
- Assess the relative advantages and disadvantages of different types of lease
- Describe the impact of leasing on company gearing

Exam guide

You may be asked to calculate the results of different options, and also discuss implications such as differing cash flow patterns.

1 Leasing as a source of finance   12/05

FAST FORWARD

Leasing is a commonly used source of finance.

We distinguish three types of leasing:

- **Operating leases** (**lessor** responsible for maintaining asset)
- **Finance leases** (**lessee** responsible for maintenance)
- **Sale and leaseback** arrangements

1.1 The nature of leasing

Rather than buying an asset outright, using either available cash resources or borrowed funds, a business may lease an asset.

Key terms

Leasing is a contract between a lessor and a lessee for hire of a specific asset selected from a manufacturer or vendor of such assets by the lessee.

The **lessor** has ownership of the asset.

The **lessee** has possession and use of the asset on payment of specified rentals over a period.

1.1.1 Examples of lessors

- Banks
- Insurance companies

1.1.2 Types of asset leased

- Office equipment
- Computers
- Cars
- Commercial vehicles
- Aircraft
- Ships
- Buildings

30: LEASING DECISIONS

```
            TYPES OF
             LEASES
           /    |    \
    Finance  Operating  Sale and
    leases    leases   leaseback
```

1.2 Operating leases 12/02

Key term

> **Operating lease** is a lease where the lessor retains most of the risks and rewards of ownership.

Operating leases are rental agreements between a lessor and a lessee.

(a) The lessor **supplies** the equipment to the **lessee**.

(b) The **lessor** is **responsible** for **servicing and maintaining** the leased equipment

(c) The **period** of the lease is fairly **short**, **less** than the expected **economic life** of the asset. At the end of one lease agreement, the lessor can either lease the same equipment to someone else, and obtain a good rent for it, or sell the equipment second-hand

Much of the growth in the UK leasing business in recent years has been in operating leases.

1.3 Finance leases 12/02

> A **finance lease** is a lease that transfers substantially all of the risks and rewards of ownership of an asset to the lessee. It is an agreement between the lessee and the lessor for most or all of the asset's expected useful life.

There are other important characteristics of a finance lease.

(a) The lessee is responsible for the **upkeep**, **servicing** and **maintenance** of the asset.

(b) The lease has a **primary period** covering all or most of the useful economic life of the asset. At the end of this period, the lessor would not be able to lease the asset to someone else, because the asset would be worn out. The lessor must therefore ensure that the lease payments during the primary period pay for the **full cost** of the asset as well as providing the lessor with a **suitable return** on his investment.

(c) At the end of the primary period the lessee can normally continue to lease the asset for an indefinite secondary period, in return for a very low nominal rent, sometimes called a 'peppercorn rent'. Alternatively, the lessee might be allowed to sell the asset on a lessor's behalf (since the lessor is the owner) and perhaps to keep most of the sale proceeds.

1.4 Example: A motor lease

The primary period of the lease might be three years, with an agreement by the lessee to make three annual payments of £6,000 each. The lessee will be responsible for repairs and servicing, road tax, insurance and garaging. At the end of the primary period of the lease, the lessee may have the option either to continue leasing the car at a nominal rent (perhaps £250 a year) or to sell the car and pay the lessor 10% of the proceeds.

1.5 Sale and leaseback

Key term

> **Sale and leaseback** is when a business that owns an asset agrees to sell the asset to a financial institution and lease it back on terms specified in the sale and leaseback agreement.

The business retains **use** of the asset but has the **funds** from the sale, whilst having to pay rent.

1.6 Attractions of leasing

Attractions include the following.

(a) The supplier of the equipment is **paid** in **full** at the beginning. The equipment is sold to the lessor, and other than guarantees, the supplier has no further financial concern about the asset.

(b) The lessor **invests finance** by purchasing assets from suppliers and makes a **return** out of the lease payments from the lessee. The lessor will also get capital allowances on his purchase of the equipment.

(c) Leasing may have advantages for the lessee:

   (i) The lessee may not have enough cash to pay for the asset, and would have difficulty obtaining a bank loan to buy it. If so the lessee has to rent the asset to obtain use of it at all.

   (ii) Finance leasing may be cheaper than a bank loan.

   (iii) The lessee may find the tax relief available advantageous.

Operating leases have further advantages.

(a) The leased equipment does not have to be shown in the **lessee's** published **balance sheet**, and so the lessee's balance sheet shows no increase in its gearing ratio.

(b) The equipment is leased for a **shorter period** than its expected useful life. In the case of high-technology equipment, if the equipment becomes out of date before the end of its expected life, the lessee does not have to keep on using it. The lessor will bear the risk of having to sell obsolete equipment secondhand.

A major growth area in operating leasing in the UK has been in computers and office equipment (such as photocopiers and fax machines) where technology is continually improving.

1.7 Hire purchase

Another form of credit finance with which leasing can be contrasted is **hire purchase**, which is a form of **instalment credit**. There are two basic forms of instalment credit, where an individual or business purchases goods and pays for them by instalments.

(a) **Lender credit** occurs when the buyer borrows money and uses the money to purchase goods outright.

(b) **Vendor credit** occurs when the buyer obtains goods on credit and agrees to pay the vendor by instalments. Hire purchase is an example of vendor credit.

Hire purchase is similar to leasing, with the exception that ownership of the goods passes to the hire purchase customer on payment of the final credit instalment, whereas a lessee never becomes the owner of the goods.

Hire purchase agreements nowadays usually involve a finance house.

- The supplier sells the goods to the finance house.
- The supplier delivers the goods to the customer who will eventually purchase them.
- The hire purchase arrangement exists between the finance house and the customer.

The finance house will nearly always insist that the hirer should pay a **deposit** towards the purchase price, perhaps as low as 10%, or as high as 33%. This is in contrast to a finance lease, where the lessee might not be required to make any large initial payment.

An industrial or commercial business can use hire purchase as a source of finance. With **industrial hire purchase**, a business customer obtains hire purchase finance from a finance house in order to purchase a fixed asset. Goods bought by businesses on hire purchase include company vehicles, plant and machinery, office equipment and farming machinery. Hire purchase arrangements for fleets of motor cars are quite common.

When faced with an investment opportunity, an organisation may have to decide whether to

- Purchase the equipment
- Acquire it under a finance lease arrangement
- Acquire it under a hire purchase arrangement

When a company acquires a capital asset under a hire purchase agreement, it will eventually obtain full legal title to the asset. The HP payments consist of

- 'Capital' payments towards the purchase of the asset
- Interest charges

For example, if a company buys a car costing £10,000 under an HP agreement, the car supplier might provide HP finance over a three year period at an interest cost of 10%, and the HP payments might be, say, as follows.

	Capital element £	Interest element £	Total HP payment £
Year 0: down payment	2,540	0	2,540
Year 1	2,254	746	3,000
Year 2	2,479	521	3,000
Year 3	2,727	273	3,000
Total	10,000	1,540	11,540

The tax position on a hire purchase arrangement is as follows.

(a) The buyer obtains whatever capital allowances are available, based on the capital element of the cost.

(b) In addition, **interest payments** within the HP payments are an **allowable** expense against tax, spread over the term of the HP agreement.

(c) **Capital payments** within the HP payments, however, are **not allowable** against tax.

2 Lease or buy decisions   12/02, 12/03, 12/05

FAST FORWARD

The decision whether to **lease or buy** an asset involves two steps.

- The **acquisition decision**: is the asset worth having? Test by discounting project cash flows at a suitable cost of capital.
- The **financing decision**: if the asset should be acquired, compare the cash flows of purchasing and leasing or HP arrangements. The cash flows can be discounted at an after-tax cost of borrowing.

PART G INVESTMENT APPRAISAL

There are several ways of evaluating a decision whether to lease an asset, or to purchase it by another means of finance. The **traditional method** is in two stages.

Step 1 An **acquisition decision** is made on whether the asset is worth having. The present values of operational costs and benefits from using the asset are found to derive a net present value (NPV).

Step 2 A **financing decision** is then made if the acquisition is justified by a positive NPV. This is the decision on whether to **lease or buy**.

The traditional method is complicated by the need to choose a discount rate for each stage of the decision. In the case of a **non-taxpaying organisation**, the method is applied as follows.

Step 1 The cost of capital that should be applied to the cash flows for the acquisition decision is the cost of capital that the organisation would normally apply to its **project evaluations**.

Step 2 The cost of capital that should be applied to the (differential) cash flows for the financing decision is the **cost of borrowing**.

(i) We assume that if the organisation decided to purchase the equipment, it would finance the purchase by **borrowing funds.**

(ii) We therefore **compare** the **cost of borrowing** with the **cost of leasing** (or hire purchase) by applying this cost of borrowing to the financing cash flows.

In the case of a tax-paying organisation, taxation should be allowed for in the cash flows, so that the traditional method would recommend:

Step 1 **Discount** the cash flows of the acquisition decision at the firm's **after-tax cost of capital**

Step 2 **Discount** the cash flows of the financing decision at the **after-tax cost of borrowing**

The tax treatment of finance leases in the UK under Finance Act 1991 rules is:

(a) To allow **depreciation** as an expense

(b) To allow the **interest element** of the finance charge as an expense over the period of the lease

This treatment leads to some complex calculations. The result may not be materially different from that obtained if we assume that the lease payments are allowable for tax in full.

Exam focus point

In the exam, it should be acceptable to make this latter assumption provided that you state it in your answer and provided that the question does not direct otherwise.

2.1 Example: Lease or buy decisions (1)

Mallen and Mullins Ltd has decided to install a new milling machine. The machine costs £20,000 and it would have a useful life of five years with a trade-in value of £4,000 at the end of the fifth year. Additional cash profits from the machine would be £8,000 a year for five years. A decision has now to be taken on the method of financing the project. Three methods of finance are being considered.

(a) The company could purchase the machine for cash, using bank loan facilities on which the current rate of interest is 13% before tax.

(b) The company could lease the machine under an agreement which would entail payment of £4,800 at the end of each year for the next five years.

(c) The company could purchase the machine under a hire purchase agreement. This would require an initial deposit of £6,500 and payments of £4,400 per annum at the end of each of the next five years. The interest part of the payments, for tax purposes, would be £2,100 at the end of year 1 and £1,800, £1,400, £1,000 and £700 at the end of each of years 2, 3, 4 and 5 respectively.

The company's weighted average cost of capital, normally used for project evaluating, is 12% after tax. The rate of corporation tax is 30%. If the machine is purchased, the company will be able to claim an annual writing down allowance of 25% of the reducing balance.

Advise the management on whether to acquire the machine, on the most economical method of finance, and on any other matter which should be considered before finally deciding which method of finance should be adopted.

Solution

The traditional method begins with the **acquisition decision**. The cash flows of the project should be discounted at 12%. The first writing down allowance is assumed to be claimed in the first year resulting in a saving of tax at year 2.

Capital allowances

Year	Allowance	£
1	25% of £20,000	5,000
2	25% of £(20,000 – 5,000)	3,750
3	25% of £(15,000 – 3,750)	2,813
4	25% of £(11,250 – 2,813)	2,109
		13,672
5	£(20,000 – 13,672 – 4,000)	2,328
		16,000

Taxable profits and tax liability

Year	Cash profits £	Capital allowance £	Taxable profits £	Tax at 30% £
1	8,000	5,000	3,000	900
2	8,000	3,750	4,250	1,275
3	8,000	2,813	5,187	1,556
4	8,000	2,109	5,891	1,767
5	8,000	2,328	5,672	1,702

NPV calculation for the acquisition decision

Year	Equipment £	Cash profits £	Tax £	Net cash flow £	Discount factor £	Present value £
0	(20,000)			(20,000)	1.000	(20,000)
1		8,000		8,000	0.893	7,144
2		8,000	(900)	7,100	0.797	5,659
3		8,000	(1,275)	6,725	0.712	4,788
4		8,000	(1,556)	6,444	0.636	4,098
5	4,000	8,000	(1,767)	10,233	0.567	5,802
6			(1,702)	(1,702)	0.507	(863)
					NPV	6,628

Conclusion

The net present value (NPV) is positive, and the machine should be acquired, regardless of the method used to finance the acquisition.

The second stage is the **financing decision**, and cash flows are discounted at the after-tax cost of borrowing, which is at 13% × 70% = 9.1%, say 9%. The only cash flows that we need to consider are those which will be affected by the choice of the method of financing. The operating savings of £8,000 a year, and the tax on these savings, can be ignored.

PART G INVESTMENT APPRAISAL

(a) **The present value (PV) of purchase costs**

Year	Item		Cash flow £	Discount factor 9%	PV £
0	Equipment cost		(20,000)	1.000	(20,000)
5	Trade-in value:	Tax savings, from allowances	4,000	0.650	2,600
2	30% × £5,000		1,500	0.842	1,263
3	30% × £3,750		1,125	0.772	869
4	30% × £2,813		844	0.708	598
5	30% × £2,109		633	0.650	411
6	30% × £2,328		698	0.596	416
				NPV of purchase	(13,843)

(b) **The PV of leasing costs**

It is assumed that the tax payments are fully tax-allowable.

Year	Lease payment £	Savings in tax (30%) £	Discount factor 9%	PV £
1-5	(4,800) pa		3.890	(18,672)
2-6		1,440 pa	3.569	5,139
			NPV of leasing	(13,533)

(c) **The PV of hire purchase**

Year	HP payments £	Capital allowances – tax saved £	Tax saved due to interest on HP payments at 30%	Net cash flow £	Discount factor at 9%	PV £
0	(6,500)			(6,500)	1.000	(6,500)
1	(4,400)			(4,400)	0.917	(4,035)
2	(4,400)	1,500	630	(2,270)	0.842	(1,911)
3	(4,400)	1,125	540	(2,735)	0.772	(2,111)
4	(4,400)	844	420	(3,136)	0.708	(2,220)
5	(400)*	633	300	533	0.650	346
6		698	210	908	0.596	541
				NPV of hire purchase		(15,890)

* £4,400 less £4,000 trade-in value

The cheapest option would be to lease the machine. However, other matters should be considered.

(a) **Running expenses**

The calculations assume that the running costs are the same under each alternative. However expenses like maintenance, consumable stores, insurance and so on may differ between the alternatives.

(b) **The effect on cash flow**

Purchasing requires an immediate outflow of £20,000 compared to nothing for leasing. This effect should be considered in relation to the company's liquidity position, which in turn will affect its ability to discharge its debts and to pay dividends.

(c) **Alternative uses of funds**

The proposed outlay of £20,000 for purchase should be considered in relation to alternative investments.

(d) **The trade-in value**

The net present value of purchase is materially affected by the trade-in value of £4,000 in the fifth year. This figure could be very inaccurate.

> **Exam focus point**
>
> Once a company has made the decision to acquire an asset, the comparison of lease vs buy only needs to include the costs that differ; the costs that are common to each option needn't be included.

A disadvantage of the traditional approach to making a lease or buy decision is that if there is a negative NPV when the operational cash flows of the project are discounted at the firm's cost of capital, the investment will be rejected out of hand. However, the costs of leasing might be so low that the project would be worthwhile provided the leasing option were selected. This suggests that an investment opportunity should not be rejected without first giving some thought to its financing costs.

Other methods of making lease or buy decisions are as follows.

(a) **Make the financing decision first.** Compare the cost of leasing with the cost of purchase, and select the cheaper method of financing; then calculate the NPV of the project on the assumption that the cheaper method of financing is used.

(b) **Combine the acquisition and financing decisions together into a single-stage decision.** Calculate an NPV for the project if the machine is **purchased**, and secondly if the machine is **leased**. Select the method of financing which gives the higher NPV, provided that the project has a positive NPV.

2.2 Example: Lease or buy decisions (2)

In the case of Mallen and Mullins Ltd, the NPV with purchase would be + £6,548. This was calculated above. The NPV with leasing would be as follows. A discount rate of 12% is used here.

Year	Profit less leasing cost £	Tax at 30% £	Net cash flow £	Discount factor 12%	PV £
1	3,200		3,200	0.893	2,858
2	3,200	(960)	2,240	0.797	1,785
3	3,200	(960)	2,240	0.712	1,595
4	3,200	(960)	2,240	0.636	1,425
5	3,200	(960)	2,240	0.567	1,270
6		(960)	(960)	0.507	(487)
				NPV	8,446

Using this method, leasing is preferable, because the NPV is £1,898 higher.

Since **operating leases** are a form of renting, the only cash flows to consider for this type of leasing are the **lease payments** and the **tax saved**. Operating lease payments are allowable expenses for tax purposes.

> **Exam focus point**
>
> Remember that the decisions made by companies are not solely made according to the results of calculations like these. Other factors (short-term cash flow advantages, flexibility, use of different costs of capital) may be significant.

PART G INVESTMENT APPRAISAL

2.3 The position of the lessor

Exam focus point

So far, we have looked at examples of leasing decisions from the viewpoint of the lessee. You may be asked to evaluate a leasing arrangement from the position of the lessor. This is rather like a mirror image of the lessee's position.

The lessor will receive capital allowances on the expenditure, and the lease payments will be taxable income.

2.4 Example: Lessor's position

Continuing the same case of Mallen and Mullins Ltd, suppose that the lessor's required rate of return is 12% after tax. The lessor's cash flows will be as follows.

	Cash flow £	Discount factor 12%	PV £
Purchase costs (see paragraph 2.7)			
Year 0	(20,000)	1.000	(20,000)
Year 5 trade-in	4,000	0.567	2,268
Tax savings			
Year 2	1,500	0.797	1,196
Year 3	1,125	0.712	801
Year 4	844	0.636	537
Year 5	633	0.567	359
Year 6	698	0.507	354
Lease payments: years 1-5	4,800	3.605	17,304
Tax on lease payments: years 2-6	(1,440)	3.218	(4,634)
NPV			(1,315)

Conclusion

The proposed level of leasing payments are not justifiable for the lessor if it seeks a required rate of return of 12%, since the resulting NPV is negative.

Question
Lease or buy

The management of a company has decided to acquire Machine X which costs £63,000 and has an operational life of four years. The expected scrap value would be zero. Tax is payable at 30% on operating cash flows one year in arrears. Capital allowances are available at 25% a year on a reducing balance basis.

Suppose that the company has the opportunity either to purchase the machine or to lease it under a finance lease arrangement, at an annual rent of £20,000 for four years, payable at the end of each year. The company can borrow to finance the acquisition at 10%. Should the company lease or buy the machine?

30: LEASING DECISIONS

Answer

Working

Capital allowances

Year		£
1	(25% of £63,000)	15,750
2	(75% of £15,750)	11,813
3	(75% of £11,813)	8,859
		36,422
4	(£63,000 – £36,422)	26,578

The financing decision will be appraised by discounting the relevant cash flows at the after-tax cost of borrowing, which is 10% × 70% = 7%.

(a) *Purchase option*

Year	Item	Cash flow £	Discount factor 7%	Present value £
0	Cost of machine	(63,000)	1.000	(63,000)
	Tax saved from capital allowances			
2	30% × £15,750	4,725	0.873	4,125
3	30% × £11,813	3,544	0.816	2,892
4	30% × £8,859	2,658	0.763	2,028
5	30% × £26,578	7,973	0.713	5,685
				(48,270)

(b) *Leasing option*

It is assumed that the lease payments are tax-allowable in full.

Year	Item	Cash Flow £	Discount factor 7%	Present value £
1-4	Lease costs	(20,000)	3.387	(67,740)
2-5	Tax savings on lease costs (× 30%)	6,000	3.165	18,990
				(48,750)

The purchase option is cheaper, using a cost of capital based on the after-tax cost of borrowing. On the assumption that investors would regard borrowing and leasing as equally risky finance options, the purchase option is recommended.

Chapter Roundup

- **Leasing** is a commonly used source of finance.
- We distinguish three types of leasing:
    - **Operating leases** (**lessor** responsible for maintaining asset)
    - **Finance leases** (**lessee** responsible for maintenance)
    - **Sale and leaseback** arrangements
- The decision whether to **lease or buy** an asset involves two steps.
    - The **acquisition decision:** is the asset worth having? Test by discounting project cash flows at a suitable cost of capital.
    - The **financing decision:** if the asset should be acquired, compare the cash flows of purchasing and leasing or HP arrangements. The cash flows can be discounted at an after-tax cost of borrowing.

Quick Quiz

1 Operating leases and finance leases are distinguished for accounting purposes. Which of the following statements is not true of an operating lease?

   A The lessor supplies the equipment to the lessee.
   B The period of the lease is less than the expected economic life of the asset.
   C The lessee is normally responsible for maintaining the leased equipment.
   D The lessor retains most of the risks and rewards of ownership.

2 Who is responsible for the servicing of a leased asset in the case of:

   (a) An operating lease?

   (b) A finance lease?

   | The lessee | or | The lessor |

3 What two steps in a lease or buy decision evaluation may be distinguished?

4 Which discount rate should be used at each stage (delete as applicable)?

	(a)	Discount rate (b)
Step 1		Pre-tax/after-tax cost of capital/cost of borrowing
Step 2		Pre-tax/after-tax cost of capital/ cost of borrowing

5 Why should operating leases be popular for users of high technology equipment?

6 Cemstone Plc has decided to acquire a new grinding machine. It cannot afford to purchase the machine outright, and has therefore arranged to pay for it in regular instalments using a finance house. What type of arrangement is this?

   A Finance lease
   B Operating lease
   C Lender credit
   D Vendor credit

7 A hire purchase contract is a contract for the hire of an asset that contains a provision giving the hirer an option to acquire legal title to the asset upon the fulfilment of certain conditions stated in the contract.

   ☐ True
   ☐ False

8 *Fill in the blank.*

   .... credit occurs when the buyer borrows money and uses it to purchase goods outright.

PART G INVESTMENT APPRAISAL

Answers to Quick Quiz

1. C   The lessor is normally responsible for maintaining the equipment.
2. (a) The lessor
   (b) The lessee
3/4. **Step 1** The acquisition decision – discount at the firm's after-tax cost of capital
   Step 2 The financing decision – discount at the after-tax cost of borrowing
5. Because such equipment may soon become obsolete.
6. D   Vendor credit. This is also known as hire purchase.
7. True
8. Lender credit

Now try the questions below from the Exam Question Bank

Number	Level	Marks	Time
Q33	Examination	25	45 mins

Appendix
Mathematical tables

Present value table

Present value of 1 ie $(1+r)^{-n}$

where r = discount rate

  n = number of periods until payment

Periods (n)	\multicolumn{10}{c}{Discount rates (r)}									
	1%	2%	3%	4%	5%	6%	7%	8%	9%	10%
1	0.990	0.980	0.971	0.962	0.952	0.943	0.935	0.926	0.917	0.909
2	0.980	0.961	0.943	0.925	0.907	0.890	0.873	0.857	0.842	0.826
3	0.971	0.942	0.915	0.889	0.864	0.840	0.816	0.794	0.772	0.751
4	0.961	0.924	0.888	0.855	0.823	0.792	0.763	0.735	0.708	0.683
5	0.951	0.906	0.863	0.822	0.784	0.747	0.713	0.681	0.650	0.621
6	0.942	0.888	0.837	0.790	0.746	0.705	0.666	0.630	0.596	0.564
7	0.933	0.871	0.813	0.760	0.711	0.665	0.623	0.583	0.547	0.513
8	0.923	0.853	0.789	0.731	0.677	0.627	0.582	0.540	0.502	0.467
9	0.914	0.837	0.766	0.703	0.645	0.592	0.544	0.500	0.460	0.424
10	0.905	0.820	0.744	0.676	0.614	0.558	0.508	0.463	0.422	0.386
11	0.896	0.804	0.722	0.650	0.585	0.527	0.475	0.429	0.388	0.350
12	0.887	0.788	0.701	0.625	0.557	0.497	0.444	0.397	0.356	0.319
13	0.879	0.773	0.681	0.601	0.530	0.469	0.415	0.368	0.326	0.290
14	0.870	0.758	0.661	0.577	0.505	0.442	0.388	0.340	0.299	0.263
15	0.861	0.743	0.642	0.555	0.481	0.417	0.362	0.315	0.275	0.239

Periods (n)	11%	12%	13%	14%	15%	16%	17%	18%	19%	20%
1	0.901	0.893	0.885	0.877	0.870	0.862	0.855	0.847	0.840	0.833
2	0.812	0.797	0.783	0.769	0.756	0.743	0.731	0.718	0.706	0.694
3	0.731	0.712	0.693	0.675	0.658	0.641	0.624	0.609	0.593	0.579
4	0.659	0.636	0.613	0.592	0.572	0.552	0.534	0.516	0.499	0.482
5	0.593	0.567	0.543	0.519	0.497	0.476	0.456	0.437	0.419	0.402
6	0.535	0.507	0.480	0.456	0.432	0.410	0.390	0.370	0.352	0.335
7	0.482	0.452	0.425	0.400	0.376	0.354	0.333	0.314	0.296	0.279
8	0.434	0.404	0.376	0.351	0.327	0.305	0.285	0.266	0.249	0.233
9	0.391	0.361	0.333	0.308	0.284	0.263	0.243	0.225	0.209	0.194
10	0.352	0.322	0.295	0.270	0.247	0.227	0.208	0.191	0.176	0.162
11	0.317	0.287	0.261	0.237	0.215	0.195	0.178	0.162	0.148	0.135
12	0.286	0.257	0.231	0.208	0.187	0.168	0.152	0.137	0.124	0.112
13	0.258	0.229	0.204	0.182	0.163	0.145	0.130	0.116	0.104	0.093
14	0.232	0.205	0.181	0.160	0.141	0.125	0.111	0.099	0.088	0.078
15	0.209	0.183	0.160	0.140	0.123	0.108	0.095	0.084	0.074	0.065

MATHEMATICAL TABLES

Annuity table

Present value of annuity of 1, ie present value of £1 per annum, receivable or payable at the end of each year for n years $\dfrac{1-(1+r)^{-n}}{r}$

where r = discount rate

n = number of periods.

Periods (n)	\	\	\	\	Discount rates (r)	\	\	\	\	\
	1%	2%	3%	4%	5%	6%	7%	8%	9%	10%
1	0.990	0.980	0.971	0.962	0.952	0.943	0.935	0.926	0.917	0.909
2	1.970	1.942	1.913	1.886	1.859	1.833	1.808	1.783	1.759	1.736
3	2.941	2.884	2.829	2.775	2.723	2.673	2.624	2.577	2.531	2.487
4	3.902	3.808	3.717	3.630	3.546	3.465	3.387	3.312	3.240	3.170
5	4.853	4.713	4.580	4.452	4.329	4.212	4.100	3.993	3.890	3.791
6	5.795	5.601	5.417	5.242	5.076	4.917	4.767	4.623	4.486	4.355
7	6.728	6.472	6.230	6.002	5.786	5.582	5.389	5.206	5.033	4.868
8	7.652	7.325	7.020	6.733	6.463	6.210	5.971	5.747	5.535	5.335
9	8.566	8.162	7.786	7.435	7.108	6.802	6.515	6.247	5.995	5.759
10	9.471	8.983	8.530	8.111	7.722	7.360	7.024	6.710	6.418	6.145
11	10.368	9.787	9.253	8.760	8.306	7.887	7.499	7.139	6.805	6.495
12	11.255	10.575	9.954	9.385	8.863	8.384	7.943	7.536	7.161	6.814
13	12.134	11.348	10.635	9.986	9.394	8.853	8.358	7.904	7.487	7.103
14	13.004	12.106	11.296	10.563	9.899	9.295	8.745	8.244	7.786	7.367
15	13.865	12.849	11.938	11.118	10.380	9.712	9.108	8.559	8.061	7.606

Periods (n)	11%	12%	13%	14%	15%	16%	17%	18%	19%	20%
1	0.901	0.893	0.885	0.877	0.870	0.862	0.855	0.847	0.840	0.833
2	1.713	1.690	1.668	1.647	1.626	1.605	1.585	1.566	1.547	1.528
3	2.444	2.402	2.361	2.322	2.283	2.246	2.210	2.174	2.140	2.106
4	3.102	3.037	2.974	2.914	2.855	2.798	2.743	2.690	2.639	2.589
5	3.696	3.605	3.517	3.433	3.352	3.274	3.199	3.127	3.058	2.991
6	4.231	4.111	3.998	3.889	3.784	3.685	3.589	3.498	3.410	3.326
7	4.712	4.564	4.423	4.288	4.160	4.039	3.922	3.812	3.706	3.605
8	5.146	4.968	4.799	4.639	4.487	4.344	4.207	4.078	3.954	3.837
9	5.537	5.328	5.132	4.946	4.772	4.607	4.451	4.303	4.163	4.031
10	5.889	5.650	5.426	5.216	5.019	4.833	4.659	4.494	4.339	4.192
11	6.207	5.938	5.687	5.453	5.234	5.029	4.836	4.656	4.486	4.327
12	6.492	6.194	5.918	5.660	5.421	5.197	4.988	4.793	4.611	4.439
13	6.750	6.424	6.122	5.842	5.583	5.342	5.118	4.910	4.715	4.533
14	6.982	6.628	6.302	6.002	5.724	5.468	5.229	5.008	4.802	4.611
15	7.191	6.811	6.462	6.142	5.847	5.575	5.324	5.092	4.876	4.675

Formulae

Economic order quantity = $\sqrt{\dfrac{2C_0 D}{C_H}}$

Discount factor = $\dfrac{1}{(1+r)^n}$

Annuities

Future value = $A\left(\dfrac{(1+r)^n - 1}{r}\right)$

Present value = $\dfrac{A}{r}\left(1 - \dfrac{1}{(1+r)^n}\right)$

Dividend growth model

$P_0 = \dfrac{D_0(1+g)}{(r-g)}$

Miller-Orr Model

Return point = Lower limit + ($\dfrac{1}{3}$ x spread)

Spread = $3\left(\dfrac{\tfrac{3}{4} \times \text{transaction cost} \times \text{variance of cashflows}}{\text{interest rate}}\right)^{\tfrac{1}{3}}$

Linear regression

$y = a + bx$

$b = \dfrac{n\sum xy - \sum x \sum y}{n \sum x^2 - (\sum x)^2}$

$a = \dfrac{\sum y}{n} - \dfrac{b \sum x}{n}$

$r = \dfrac{n \sum xy - \sum x \sum y}{\sqrt{n \sum x^2 - (\sum x)^2)(n \sum y^2 - (\sum y)^2)}}$

Indices

Laspeyre price index = $\dfrac{\sum(p_1 \times q_0)}{\sum(p_0 \times q_0)}$ x 100

Paasche price index = $\dfrac{\sum(p_1 \times q_1)}{\sum(p_0 \times q_1)}$ x 100

Laspeyre quantity index = $\dfrac{\sum(q_1 \times p_0)}{\sum(q_0 \times p_0)}$ x 100

Paasche quantity index = $\dfrac{\sum(q_1 \times p_1)}{\sum(q_0 \times p_1)}$ x 100

Exam question bank

EXAM QUESTION BANK

1 Over emphasis   45 mins

A significant proportion of the management accounting activity within most organisations is concerned with the production and reporting of information for control purposes.

Some commentators have asserted that the control aspect of management accounting is over emphasised. This over emphasis is, they believe, to the detriment of the prime functions of management accounting which are to produce information to assist planning and decision making.

Required

Discuss the above assertion and give your view of its validity.   **(25 marks)**

2 Ryman Couplets   45 mins

Ryman Couplets Ltd is a newly established company which plans to start operations from the beginning of 20X2. During the first two years, it is considered that there will be some build-up of stocks, so that production volumes will normally exceed demand in the year. Budgeted production and sales for the first two years are as follows.

	20X2			20X3		
Product	X	Y	Z	X	Y	Z
Production (000's of units)	20	20	10	20	20	10
Sales (000's of units)	14	16	3	14	12	14

From 20X4 onwards, it is expected that annual production levels will be about the same, but that sales demand will rise to these same levels. The unit sales price and variable costs during 20X2 and 20X3 are expected to be as follows.

Product	Unit sales price	Unit variable costs
	£	£
X	30	16
Y	35	18
Z	25	12

Fixed production costs will be £560,000 per annum in total.

The products are all manufactured by machine, but some additional direct labour effort is required to finish them. The time required per unit has been measured, by work study techniques, is as follows.

Product	Machine hours per unit	Labour hours per unit
X	3	2
Y	1	4
Z	2	2

The company's managing director wished to ascertain the expected profitability of each product and the total company profits for 20X2 and 20X3. (You may ignore administration, selling and distribution costs.) His management accountant produced three sets of figures, one using marginal costing and the other two using absorption costing, but each with a different basis of overhead recovery. The managing director was somewhat irate, because each set of figures gave differing results, and he demanded to know which figures were right and which were wrong.

Required

(a) Prepare the three standards of total profit in each of the two years, and the profitability of each product individually.   **(10 marks)**

(b) Compare the resulting figures, and comment on how the absorption costing figures might be improved. Advise the managing director which set of figures is 'correct' and which are 'wrong'.
                                                                (7 marks)

EXAM QUESTION BANK

(c) It is decided to increase production quantities in the first year only by a further 25% in order to build up stocks to a higher level. Calculate the following.

(i) The annual cost to Ryman Couplets Ltd of the stock increase, if the financial cost of holding stocks is 14% per annum

(ii) The effect this increase would have on reported profits during 20X2 (only) using each of the three costing methods described **(8 marks)**

(Total = 25 marks)

3 Southcott   30 mins

Southcott Ltd is a firm of financial consultants which offers short revision courses on taxation and auditing for professional examinations. The firm has budgeted annual overheads totalling £152,625. Until recently the firm has applied overheads on a volume basis, based on the number of course days offered. The firm has no variable costs and the only direct costs are the consultants' own time which they divide equally between their two courses. The firm is considering the possibility of adopting an activity based costing (ABC) system and has identified the overhead costs as shown below.

Details of overheads

	£
Centre hire	62,500
Enquiries administration	27,125
Brochures	63,000
Total	152,625

The following information relates to the past year and is expected to remain the same for the coming year.

Course	No of courses sold	Duration of course	No of enquiries per course	No of brochures printed per course
Auditing	50	2 days	175	300
Taxation	30	3 days	70	200

All courses run with a maximum number of students (30), as it is deemed that beyond this number the learning experience is severely diminished, and the same centre is hired for all courses at a standard daily rate. The firm has the human resources to run only one course at any one time.

Required

(a) Calculate the overhead cost per course for both auditing and taxation using traditional volume based absorption costing.

(b) Recalculate the overhead costs per course using activity based costing and explain your choice of cost driver in your answer.

4 Broadly the same   45 mins

(a) T Ltd makes three main products, using broadly the same production methods and equipment for each. A conventional product costing system is used at present, although an activity based costing (ABC) system is being considered. Details of the three products for a typical period are as follows.

	Hours per unit		Materials per unit	Volumes
	Labour hours	Machine hours	£	Units
Product X	1/2	1 1/2	20	750
Product Y	1 1/2	1	12	1,250
Product Z	1	3	25	7,000

Direct labour costs £6 per hour and production overheads are absorbed on a machine hour basis. The rate for the period is £28 per machine hour.

Required

Calculate the cost per unit for each product using conventional methods. **(5 marks)**

(b) Further analysis shows that the total of production overheads can be divided as follows.

	%
Costs relating to set-ups	35
Costs relating to machinery	20
Costs relating to materials handling	15
Costs relating to inspection	30
Total production overhead	100

The following activity volumes are associated with the product line for the period as a whole.

Total activities for the period

	Number of set-ups	Number of movements of materials	Number of inspections
Product X	75	12	150
Product Y	115	21	180
Product Z	480	87	670
	670	120	1,000

Required

Calculate the cost per unit for each product using ABC principles. **(16 marks)**

(c) Comment on the reasons for any differences in the costs in your answers to (a) and (b). **(4 marks)**

(Total = 25 marks)

5 Standard costing system 45 mins

(a) As a member of your organisation's management accounting team, you are asked to plan the installation and operation of a standard costing system. Describe how you would install this system. Indicate what problems are likely to be encountered and how they could be overcome.

(17 marks)

(b) A member of your management accounting team believes that past performance is the best guide to ascertaining standard costs. Discuss this point of view. **(8 marks)**

(Total = 25 marks)

6 Pan Co 45 mins

Pan Co Ltd, a manufacturing firm, operates a standard marginal costing system. It makes a number of products including product ZX, which uses a single raw material VW. Standard costs relating to ZX have been calculated as follows.

Standard cost schedule – ZX

	£ per unit
Direct material VW, 10 kg @ £15 per kg	150
Direct labour, 5 hours @ £9 per hour	45
	195
Variable production overhead, 5 hours @ £3 per hour	15
	210

During the week ending 9 November 20X1, 1,000 units of ZX were produced, the relevant information regarding actual performance being as follows.

4,000 kgs of direct material VW were in opening stock, 10,000 kgs were purchased during the week (actual cost being £144,000), and 3,000 kgs were in closing stock. Stocks of the direct material VW are valued at the standard price of £15 per kg. 5,200 direct labour hours were worked during the week, total wages being £48,360. The actual cost of variable production overhead for the week was £16,800.

Required

(a) Compute the cost variances which arose in the week ending 9 November 20X1 under the following headings.

    (i) Variable production cost variance

    (ii) Direct wages cost variance, and analyse into rate and efficiency

    (iii) Direct material cost variance, and analyse into price and usage

    (iv) Variable production overhead variance   **(11 marks)**

(b) Prepare a report providing a commentary on the variances for the production manager, indicating any additional information which might prove useful in explaining them.   **(8 marks)**

(c) Answer a criticism by the production manager that, given time and usage standards in hours and kgs respectively, he could control the company satisfactorily without the use of any cost standards.
    (6 marks)
    (Total = 25 marks)

7 Reconciliation statement   45 mins

The following profit reconciliation statement summarises the performance of one of CL Ltd's products for March 20X7. CL uses a standard absorption costing system.

	Adverse £	Favourable £	£	
Budgeted profit			4,250	
Sales volume variance			850	A
Standard profit on actual sales			3,400	
Selling price variance			4,000	A
			(600)	
Cost variances				
Direct material price		1,000		
Direct material usage	150			
Direct labour rate	200			
Direct labour efficiency	150			
Variable overhead expenditure	600			
Variable overhead efficiency	75			
Fixed overhead expenditure		2,500		
Fixed overhead volume		150		
	1,175	3,650	2,475	F
Actual profit			1,875	

The budget for the same period contained the following data.

Sales volume		1,500 units
Sales revenue	£20,000	
Production volume		1,500 units
Direct materials purchased		750 kgs
Direct materials used		750 kgs
Direct material cost	£4,500	
Direct labour hours		1,125
Direct labour cost	£4,500	
Variable overhead cost	£2,250	
Fixed overhead cost	£4,500	

Additional information

(a) Stocks of raw materials and finished goods are valued at standard cost.
(b) During the month the actual number of units produced was 1,550.
(c) The actual sales revenue was £12,000.
(d) The direct materials purchased were 1,000 kgs.

Required

(a) Calculate the following.

　(i) The actual sales volume
　(ii) The actual quantity of materials used
　(iii) The actual direct material cost
　(iv) The actual direct labour hours
　(v) The actual direct labour cost
　(vi) The actual variable overhead cost
　(vii) The actual fixed overhead cost **(14 marks)**

(b) Explain the possible causes of the direct materials usage variance, direct labour rate variance, and sales volume variance. **(6 marks)**

(c) Explain why different variances are calculated depending upon the choice of marginal or absorption costing. **(5 marks)**

(Total = 25 marks)

8 M   45 mins

(a) M Ltd operates a standard absorption costing system in respect of its only product. The standard cost card of this product for the budget year ending 31 December 20X0 is as follows.

	£	£
Selling price		120.00
Direct material A (5 kgs)	12.50	
Direct material B (10 kgs)	40.00	
Direct wages (3 hours)	18.00	
Variable overhead (3 hours)	9.00	
Fixed overhead* (3 hours)	15.00	
		94.50
Profit/unit		25.50

*Fixed overhead is absorbed on the basis of direct labour hours. Budgeted fixed overhead costs are £180,000 for the year. Cost and activity levels are budgeted to be constant each month.

During January 20X0, when budgeted sales and production were 1,000 units, the following actual results were achieved.

	£
Sales (900 units)	118,800
Production costs (1,050 units)	
Direct material A (5,670 kg)	14,742
Direct material B (10,460 kg)	38,179
Direct wages (3,215 hours)	19,933
Variable overhead	10,288
Fixed overhead	15,432

Direct material and direct labour variances have already been calculated as follows.

		£
Direct material A	price variance	567 (A)
	usage variance	1,050 (A)
Direct material B	price variance	3,661 (F)
	usage variance	160 (F)
Direct labour	rate variance	643 (A)
	efficiency variance	390 (A)

You have confirmed with the production manager that the nature of the production method is such that direct materials A and B are mixed together to produce the final product.

All materials were purchased and used during January.

Required

Prepare for the production manager a statement that reconciles the budgeted and actual profits for January 20X0 using the following variances.

(i) Sales volume profit
(ii) Sales price
(iii) Direct material price
(iv) Total direct material mix (valued using standard prices)
(v) Total direct material yield
(vi) Direct labour rate
(vii) Direct labour efficiency
(viii) Variable production overhead expenditure
(ix) Variable production overhead efficiency
(x) Fixed production overhead expenditure
(xi) Fixed production overhead capacity
(xii) Fixed production overhead efficiency

Variances should be calculated so as to provide useful information to the production manager.

(15 marks)

(b) Variance analysis involves the separation of individual cost variances into component parts. The benefit that may be derived from variance analysis depends on the interpretation and investigation of the component variances.

Required

Explain, with the aid of a simple numeric example, the logic, purpose and limitation of the separation of the fixed overhead volume variance into capacity, utilisation and efficiency components, and describe how the management accountant should go about investigating the component variances disclosed.

(10 marks)
(Total = 25 marks)

9 TF

45 mins

TF plc is considering introducing a computerised responsibility accounting system. You are responsible for the design and implementation of the system, and have shown the managing director a typical report that the system will generate. The managing director has asked the following questions.

- Why does the report highlight controllable cost and profit?
- How does one determine which costs are controllable?
- What is the difference between a cost centre, profit centre and investment centre?
- What benefits are to be gained from a system of responsibility accounting?

Required

Draft a report to the managing director addressing the specific issues he has raised. **(25 marks)**

10 Freewheel

45 mins

Freewheel is in the process of preparing its master budget for the six months ending December 20X2. The balance sheet for the year ended 30 June 20X2 is estimated to be as follows.

	Cost £	Deprec prov £	NBV £
Fixed assets	140,000	14,000	126,000
Current assets			
Stock	25,000		
Trade debtors	24,600		
Bank	3,000		
Net current liabilities			
		52,600	
Creditors: Amounts falling due within one year			
Trade creditors	25,000		
Other creditors	9,000		
		34,000	
Net current assets			18,600
Total assets less current liabilities			144,600
Capital and reserves			
Share capital			100,000
Profit and loss account			44,600
			144,600

The budget committee have derived the following trading forecasts for the six months ended 31 December 20X2.

	Sales in units	Purchases £	Wages And Salaries £	Overheads excl. deprec £	Purchase of fixed assets £	Issue of 20,000 £1 shares £	Dividends £
May	4,000	12,000	8,000	7,000			
June	4,200	13,000	8,000	7,000			
July	4,500	14,000	8,000	7,000			
August	4,600	18,000	10,000	7,000			
September	4,800	16,000	10,000	7,000		20,000	
October	5,000	14,000	10,000	8,000			10,000
November	3,800	12,000	12,000	8,000	30,000		
December	3,000	12,000	12,000	8,000			

You are given the following information.

(a) The selling price in May 20X2 was £6 per unit and this is to be increased to £8 per unit in October. 50% of sales are for cash and 50% on credit to be paid two months later.

(b) Purchases are to be paid for two months after purchase.

(c) Wages and salaries are to be paid 75% in the month incurred and 25% in the following month.

(d) Overheads are to be paid in the month after they are incurred.

(e) The fixed assets are to be paid for in three equal instalments in the three months following purchase.

(f) Dividends are to be paid three months after they are declared and the receipts from the share issue are budgeted to be received in the month of issue.

(g) Fixed assets are depreciated 10% per annum on a straight line basis on those assets owned at 31 December 20X2.

(h) Closing stock at the beginning of the period under review was equal to the previous two months purchases. At 31 December 20X2 it was equal to three months purchases.

Required

(a) Prepare the following budgets for the six months ended 31 December 20X2.

(i) Cash budget **(9 marks)**
(ii) Budgeted profit and loss account **(5 marks)**
(iii) Budgeted balance sheet **(6 marks)**

(b) Comment upon the results, highlighting those areas that you wish to draw to the attention of the budget committee. **(5 marks)**

(Total = 25 marks)

11 Presentation 45 mins

The following statement has been produced for presentation to the general manager of Department X.

	Month ended 31 October 20Y0		
	Original budget £	Actual result £	Variance £
Sales	600,000	550,000	(50,000)
Direct materials	150,000	130,000	20,000
Direct labour	200,000	189,000	11,000
Production overhead			
Variable with direct labour	50,000	46,000	4,000
Fixed	25,000	29,000	(4,000)
Variable selling overhead	75,000	72,000	3,000
Fixed selling overhead	50,000	46,000	4,000
Total costs	550,000	512,000	38,000
Profit	50,000	38,000	(12,000)
Direct labour hours	50,000	47,500	
Sales and production units	5,000	4,500	

Note. There are no opening and closing stocks.

The general manager says that this type of statement does not provide much relevant information for him. He also thought that the profit for the month would be well up to budget and was surprised to see a large adverse profit variance.

Required

(a) Re-draft the above statement in a form which would be more relevant for the general manager.

(7 marks)

(b) Calculate all sales, material, labour and overhead variances and reconcile to the statement produced in (a). **(10 marks)**

(c) Produce a short report explaining the principles upon which your re-drafted statement is based and what information it provides. **(8 marks)**

(Total = 25 marks)

12 Budgets and people 45 mins

In his study of *The Impact of Budgets on People* Argyris reported inter alia the following comment by a financial controller on the practice of participation in the setting of budgets in his company.

'We bring in the supervisors of budget areas, we tell them that we want their frank opinion but most of them just sit there and nod their heads. We know they're not coming out with exactly how they feel. I guess budgets scare them.'

Required

Suggest reasons why managers may be reluctant to participate fully in setting budgets, and suggest also unwanted side effects which may arise from the imposition of budgets by senior management. **(25 marks)**

13 Rolling 20 mins

The managing director of B Ltd believes that the existing annual budget system is costly to operate and produces unsatisfactory results for a number of reasons.

- Long preparation period
- Business decisions being made throughout the year
- Unpredictable changes in the rate of general inflation
- Sudden changes in the availability and price of raw materials

He has read about rolling budgets and wonders whether these might be more useful for his decision making.

Required

Provide the following.

(a) A brief explanation of rolling budgets
(b) A description of how a rolling budget system would operate
(c) Three significant advantages of a rolling budget system
(d) Three problems likely to be encountered in using a rolling budget system

14 Domestic appliance 35 mins

A domestic electrical appliance was introduced on the market in 20X2. At the point of sale customers are offered the chance to purchase an insurance policy to cover repairs and parts for the first five years of operation; these policies cannot be purchased later on, only when the appliance is bought. The table below shows the total industry sales of this appliance for the years 20X2 to 20X8 together with the number of insurance policies sold.

EXAM QUESTION BANK

Year	Sales of appliance £m	Policy sales (number)
20X2	3	400
20X3	5	300
20X4	7	600
20X5	10	1,200
20X6	15	1,700
20X7	18	2,200
20X8	26	2,100

Required

(a) Calculate the coefficient of determination between the appliance sales figures and the insurance policy sales, and interpret your value.

(b) Calculate the least squares regression equation to predict insurance policy sales from deflated appliance sales.

(c) The total sales of the electrical appliance in 20X9 are estimated at £51,000,000. Use the least squares regression equation to obtain a forecast of insurance policy sales for 20X9.

(d) Comment on why using this type of approach for predicting insurance policy sales in 20X9 may be problematic.

15 Weighted index   15 mins

The following information relates to three products sold by a company over a five-year period.

	Year 1		Year 5	
	'000 units sold	Selling price per unit £	'000 units sold	Selling price per unit £
Product A	76	0.60	72	0.78
Product B	52	0.75	60	1.00
Product C	28	1.10	40	1.32

Required

(a) Calculate the percentage increase in total sales revenue over the period.

(b) Calculate the Laspeyre price index for Year 5 based on Year 1.

(c) Provide an explanation of the change in sales over the period, using the answers to (a) and (b) above.

16 CM   22 mins

CM Limited was formed ten years ago to provide business equipment solutions to local businesses. It has separate divisions for research, marketing, product design, technology and communication services, and now manufactures and supplies a wide range of business equipment (copiers, scanners, printers, fax machines and similar items).

To date it has evaluated its performance using monthly financial reports that analyse profitability by type of equipment.

While on the course, the managing director of CM Limited overheard someone mention how the performance of their company had improved after they introduced 'benchmarking'.

Required

Explain 'benchmarking' and how it could be used to improve the performance of CM Limited. **(12 marks)**

EXAM QUESTION BANK

17 Corporate objectives
20 mins

Discuss whether a quoted company's directors should seek only the maximisation of the company's profit.

18 Market efficiency
30 mins

Describe the various forms of market efficiency and explain whether it is possible for institutions to out-perform the market.

19 Mixed economy
35 mins

In a mixed economy, two of the objectives of a government could be:

(a) To minimise its borrowing requirements, and
(b) To reduce the taxation of incomes.

Required

(a) Identify the general economic effects of these policies on private sector businesses.

(b) Identify the effects that might result from attempts to achieve these objectives by *each* of:

    (i) Reductions in public expenditure
    (ii) Increases in charges made for the products or services of nationalised industries
    (iii) Selling nationalised assets

20 Midsouth Electric
45 mins

(a) Among the industries which have been privatised by the UK government in recent years is the electricity supply industry.

Required

Outline the likely objectives of an electricity supply company:

(i) Operating in the public (government-run) sector   **(4 marks)**
(ii) Operating in the private sector (following privatisation)   **(4 marks)**

The information below relates to parts (b) and (c) of the question

Midsouth Electric plc (MSE) is an electricity supply company which was privatised six years ago, in 20X0, having formerly been an authority under government control. On privatisation, the newly issued shares in the company went to an immediate 40% premium on the share market. As a privatised electricity supply company, MSE is now subject to regulatory controls over prices.

The data given below is available. The 20X0 *proforma* figures reflect the company's performance during its last year under government control adjusted to reflect the accounting conventions applying in the private sector.

Midsouth Electric plc

Summarised financial and operational information

	20X0 Proforma £m	20X1 £m	20X2 £m	20X3 £m	20X4 £m	20X5 £m	20X6 £m
Turnover	760	800	850	880	920	955	995
Profit before taxation	37	49	62	74	88	94	99
Profit after taxation	30	47	52	62	74	77	80
Wages and salaries	110	109	108	108	107	106	106
Directors' emoluments	1.2	1.6	1.8	2.4	3.1	3.4	3.6
Dividends	10*	11	12	14	17	20	24
Net assets	120	126	130	150	165	180	205
Capital spending	25	30	35	50	75	82	90
Price earnings ratio	–	7.4	7.5	8.1	8.5	8.7	9.0
Number of employees	14,500	14,200	14,000	13,700	13,600	13,400	13,200
Output of electricity supplied**	100	102.5	105	107.5	110	113	116

* Notional dividend which would be paid under post-privatisation dividend policy.

** 20X0 = 100

The Retail Prices Index for the years shown is set out below.

	RPI
20X0	100
20X1	102
20X2	103
20X3	105
20X4	106
20X5	107
20X6	109

(b) *Required*

Evaluate whether the privatisation of Midsouth Electric has been a positive step from the point of view of:

   (i)   Ordinary shareholders **(5 marks)**

   (ii)   Employees of the company **(4 marks)**

   (iii)   Customers **(4 marks)**

(c) You read a letter in the press which suggests that electricity supply privatisation has, along with other privatisations, been of great benefit to the economy.

Required

Assess whether Midsouth Electric's privatisation appears to have:

   (i)   Assisted with attainment of the government's anti-inflation objective **(2 marks)**

   (ii)   Been beneficial to growth in the national economy **(2 marks)**

(Total = 25 marks)

21 Gustaffson   45 mins

(a) Define what is meant by the term 'overtrading' and describe some of the typical symptoms.

(8 marks)

(b) Gustaffson plc is a toy manufacturing company. It manufactures Polly Playtime, the latest doll craze amongst young girls. The company is now at full production of the doll. The final accounts for 20X9 have just been published and are as follows. 20X8's accounts are also shown for comparison purposes.

PROFIT AND LOSS ACCOUNT Y/E 31 DECEMBER

	20X9	20X8
	£'000	£'000
Sales	30,000	20,000
Cost of sales	20,000	11,000
Operating profit	10,000	9,000
Interest	450	400
Profit before tax	9,550	8,600
Tax	2,000	1,200
Profit after tax	7,550	7,400
Dividends	2,500	2,500
Retained profit	5,050	4,900

BALANCE SHEET AS AT 31 DECEMBER

	20X9					20X8
	£'000	£'000	£'000	£'000	£'000	£'000
Fixed assets			1,500			1,400
Current assets						
Stock	7,350			3,000		
Debtors	10,000			6,000		
Cash	2,500			4,500		
		19,850			13,500	
Current liabilities						
Overdraft	2,000			–		
Dividends owing	2,500			2,500		
Trade creditors	4,200			2,500		
		(8,700)			(5,000)	
Net current assets			11,150			8,500
8% debentures			(1,200)			(3,500)
Net assets			11,450			6,400
Ordinary shares (25p)			5,000			5,000
Profit and loss a/c			6,450			1,400
			11,450			6,400

(i) By studying the above accounts and using ratio analysis, identify the main problems facing Gustaffson. **(13 marks)**

(ii) Provide possible solutions to the problems identified in (i). **(4 marks)**

(Total = 25 marks)

22 H Finance   30 mins

H Finance plc is prepared to advance 80% of D Ltd's sales invoicing, provided its specialist collection services are used by D Ltd. H Finance plc would charge an additional 0.5% of D Ltd's turnover for this service. D Ltd would avoid administration costs it currently incurs amounting to £80,000 per annum.

The history of D Ltd's debtors' ledgers may be summarised as follows:

	20X8	20X9	20Y0
Turnover (£'000)	78,147	81,941	98,714
% debtors at year end	17	20	22
% debtors of 90+ days (of turnover)	1.5	2	2.5
Bad debts (£'000)	340	497	615

EXAM QUESTION BANK

D Ltd estimates that the aggressive collection procedures adopted by the finance company are likely to result in lost turnover of some 10% of otherwise expected levels.

Currently, each £1 of turnover generates 18 pence additional profit before taxation. D Ltd turns its capital over, on average, three times each year. On receipt by H Finance plc of amounts due from D Ltd's customers, a further 15% of the amounts are to be remitted to D Ltd. The cheapest alternative form of finance would cost 20% per annum.

Required

(a) Calculate whether the factoring of D Ltd's debtors ledger would be worthwhile.
(b) Explain how the factoring of sales invoicing may assist a firm's financial performance.

23 SF   45 mins

SF Ltd is a family-owned private company with five main shareholders.

SF Ltd has just prepared its cash budget for the year ahead, details of which are shown below. The current overdraft facility is £50,000 and the bank has stated that it would not be willing to increase the facility at present, without a substantial increase in the interest rate charged, due to the lack of assets to offer as security.

The shareholders are concerned by the cash projections, and have sought advice from external consultants.

All figures, £'000

	J	F	M	A	M	J	J	A	S	O	N	D
Collections from customers	55	60	30	10	15	20	20	25	30	40	55	80
Dividend on investment						10						
Total inflows	55	60	30	10	15	30	20	25	30	40	55	80
Payments to suppliers		20		20		25		28		27		25
Wages and salaries	15	15	15	15	15	20	20	15	15	15	15	15
Payments for fixed assets			2		5	10		15				
Dividend payable				25								
Corporation tax									30			
Other operating expenses	5	5	5	5	7	7	7	7	7	7	8	8
Total outflows	20	40	22	65	27	62	27	65	52	49	23	48
Net in or (out)	35	20	8	(55)	(12)	(32)	(7)	(40)	(22)	(9)	32	32
Bank balance (overdraft)												
Opening	20	55	75	83	28	16	(16)	(23)	(63)	(85)	(94)	(62)
Closing	55	75	83	28	16	(16)	(23)	(63)	(85)	(94)	(62)	(30)

The following additional information relating to the cash budget has been provided by SF Ltd.

(i) All sales are on credit. Two months' credit on average is granted to customers.

(ii) Production is scheduled evenly throughout the year. Year-end stocks of finished goods are forecast to be £30,000 higher than at the beginning of the year.

(iii) Purchases of raw materials are made at two-monthly intervals. SF Ltd typically takes up to 90 days to pay for goods supplied. Other expenses are paid in the month in which they arise.

(iv) The capital expenditure budget comprises:
Office furniture	March	£2,000
Progress payments on building extensions	May	£5,000
Car	June	£10,000
New equipment	August	£15,000

Required

Assume you are an external consultant employed by SF Ltd. Prepare a report for the board advising on the possible actions it might take to improve its budgeted cash flow for the year, and consider the possible impact of these actions on the company's business. Your report should also identify possible short-term investment opportunities for the cash surpluses identified in the first part of the budget year. **(25 marks)**

24 Headwater   45 mins

It is now August 20X6. In 20X0, the current management team of Headwater plc, a manufacturer of car and motorcycle parts, bought the company from its conglomerate parent company in a management buyout deal. Six years on, the managers are considering the possibility of obtaining a listing for the company's shares on the stock market. The following information is available.

HEADWATER PLC
PROFIT AND LOSS ACCOUNT FOR THE YEAR ENDED 30 JUNE 20X6

	£ million
Turnover	36.5
Cost of sales	(31.6)
Profit before interest and taxation	4.9
Interest	(1.3)
Profit before taxation	3.6
Taxation	(0.5)
Profit attributable to ordinary shareholders	3.1
Dividends	(0.3)
Retained profit	2.8

BALANCE SHEET AS AT 30 JUNE 20X6

	£ million	£ million
Fixed assets (at cost less accumulated depreciation)		
Land and buildings		3.6
Plant and machinery		9.9
		13.5
Current assets		
Stocks	4.4	
Debtors	4.7	
Cash at bank	1.0	
	10.1	
Current liabilities		
Trade creditors	7.0	
Bank overdraft	2.0	
	9.0	
Net current assets		1.1
Total assets less current liabilities		14.6
Creditors due after more than one year: 12% Debenture 20X8		(2.2)
Net assets		12.4
Financed by		
Ordinary £1 shares		
Voting		1.8
'A' shares (non-voting)		0.9
Reserves		9.7
Shareholders' funds		12.4

Average performance ratios for the industry sector in which Headwater operates are given below.

Industry sector ratios

Return before interest and tax on long-term capital employed	24%
Return after tax on equity	16%
Operating profit as percentage of sales	11%
Current ratio	1.6:1
Quick (acid test) ratio	1.0:1
Total debt: equity (gearing)	24%
Dividend cover	4.0
Interest cover	4.5
Price/earnings ratio	10.0

Required

(a) Evaluate the financial state and performance of Headwater by comparing it with that of its industry sector. **(10 marks)**

(b) Discuss the probable reasons why the management of Headwater is considering a Stock Exchange listing. **(5 marks)**

(c) Explain how you think Headwater should restructure its balance sheet before becoming a listed company. **(6 marks)**

(d) Discuss changes in financial policy which the company would be advised to adopt once it has been floated on the Stock Exchange. **(4 marks)**

(Total = 25 marks)

25 KB   45 mins

(a) KB plc has a paid-up ordinary share capital of £1,500,000 represented by 6 million shares of 25p each. It has no loan capital. Earnings after tax in the most recent year were £1,200,000. The P/E ratio of the company is 12.

The company is planning to make a large new investment which will cost £5,040,000 and is considering raising the necessary finance through a rights issue at 192p.

Required

(i) Calculate the current market price of KB plc's ordinary shares. **(2 marks)**

(ii) Calculate the theoretical ex-rights price, and state what factors in practice might invalidate your calculation. **(8 marks)**

(iii) Briefly explain what is meant by a deep-discounted rights issue, identifying the main reasons why a company might raise finance by this method and also the drawbacks of using it. **(5 marks)**

(b) As an alternative to a rights issue, KB plc might raise the £5,040,000 required by means of an issue of convertible loan stock at par, with a coupon rate of 6%. The loan stock would be redeemable in seven years' time. Prior to redemption, the loan stock may be converted at a rate of 35 ordinary shares per £100 nominal loan stock.

Required

(i) Explain the term *conversion premium* and calculate the conversion premium at the date of issue implicit in the data given. **(5 marks)**

(ii) Identify the advantages to KB plc of issuing convertible loan stock instead of the rights issue to raise the necessary finance. **(5 marks)**

(Total = 25 marks)

26 Rump   45 mins

Rump Ltd is an all equity financed, listed company which operates in the food processing industry. The Rump family owns 40% of the ordinary shares; the remainder are held by large financial institutions. There are 10 million £1 ordinary shares currently in issue.

The company has just finalised a long-term contract to supply a large chain of restaurants with a variety of food products. The contract requires investment in new machinery costing £24 million. This machinery would become operational on 1 January 20X2, and payment would be made on the same date. Sales would commence immediately thereafter.

Company policy is to pay out all profits as dividends and, if Rump plc continues to be all equity financed, there will be an annual dividend of £9 million in perpetuity commencing 31 December 20X2.

There are two alternatives being considered to finance the required investment of £24 million:

(1) A 2-for-5 rights issue, in which case the annual dividend would be £9 million. The cum rights price per share would be £6.60.

(2) Issuing 7.5% irredeemable debentures at par with interest payable annually in arrears. For this alternative, interest would be paid out of the £9 million otherwise available to pay dividends.

For either alternative, the directors expect the cost of equity to remain at its present annual level of 10%.

Required

(a) Calculate the issue and ex rights share prices of Rump plc assuming a 2-for-5 rights issue is used to finance the new project at 1 January 20X2. Ignore taxation. **(5 marks)**

(b) Calculate the value per ordinary share in Rump plc at 1 January 20X2 if 7.5% irredeemable debentures are issued to finance the new project. Assume that the cost of equity remains at 10% each year. Ignore taxation. **(4 marks)**

(c) Write a report to the directors of Rump plc which:

    (i) Compares and contrasts the rights issue and the debenture issue methods of raising finance – you may refer to the calculations in your answer to requirements (a) and (b) and to any assumptions made.

    (ii) Explains and evaluates the appropriateness of the following alternative methods of issuing equity finance *in the specific circumstances* of Rump plc:

        (1) A placing
        (2) An offer for sale
        (3) A public offer for subscription **(16 marks)**

(Total = 25 marks)

27 DF   45 mins

DF Ltd is a manufacturer of sports equipment. All of the shares of DF are held by the Wong family.

The company has recently won a major 3-year contract to supply FF plc with a range of sports equipment. FF plc is a large company with over 100 sports shops. The contract may be renewed after 3 years.

The new contract is expected to double DF Ltd's existing total annual sales, but demand from FF plc will vary considerably from month to month.

The contract will, however, mean a significant additional investment in both fixed and current assets. A loan from the bank is to be used to finance the additional fixed assets, as the Wong family is currently unable to supply any further share capital. Also, the Wong family does not wish to raise new capital by issuing shares to non-family members.

The financing of the additional current assets is yet to be decided. In particular, the contract with FF plc will require orders to be delivered within two days. This delivery period gives DF Ltd insufficient time to manufacture items, thus significant stocks need to be held at all times. Also, FF plc requires 90 days' credit from its suppliers. This will result in a significant additional investment in debtors by DF Ltd.

If the company borrows from the bank to finance current assets, either using a loan or an overdraft, it expects to be charged annual interest at 12%. Consequently, DF Ltd is considering alternative methods of financing current assets. These include debt factoring, invoice discounting and offering a 3% cash discount to FF plc for settlement within 10 days rather than the normal 90 days.

Required

(a) Calculate the annual equivalent rate of interest implicit in offering a 3% discount to FF plc for settlement of debts within 10 days rather than 90 days.

Briefly explain the factors, other than the rate of interest, that DF Ltd would need to consider before deciding on whether to offer a cash discount. **(6 marks)**

(b) Write a report to the Wong family shareholders explaining the various methods of financing available to DF Ltd to finance the additional current assets arising from the new FF plc contract. The report should include the following headings:

- Bank loan
- Overdraft
- Debt factoring
- Invoice discounting **(14 marks)**

(c) Discuss the factors that a venture capital organisation will take into account when deciding whether to invest in DF Ltd. **(5 marks)**

(Total = 25 marks)

28 Project appraisal 45 mins

(a) A company is considering two capital expenditure proposals. Both proposals are for similar products and both are expected to operate for four years. Only one proposal can be accepted.

The following information is available.

	Profit/(loss) Proposal A £	Proposal B £
Initial investment	46,000	46,000
Year 1	6,500	4,500
Year 2	3,500	2,500
Year 3	13,500	4,500
Year 4	(1,500)	14,500
Estimated scrap value at the end of year 4	4,000	4,000

Depreciation is charged on the straight line basis.

The company estimates its cost of capital at 20% pa.

	Discount factor
Year 1	0.833
Year 2	0.694
Year 3	0.579
Year 4	0.482

Required

(i) Calculate the following for both proposals.

    (1) The payback period to one decimal place **(5 marks)**
    (2) The return on capital employed on initial investment, to one decimal place **(2 marks)**

(ii) Give two advantages for each of the methods of appraisal used in (i) above. **(5 marks)**

(b) D'Arcy Toby Wise Ltd is a private family business of aluminium founders, incorporated in 1949. It makes castings by three processes of pressure die-casting, gravity die-casting and sand casting and serves a variety of customers and trades, though 40% of its output goes to one particular customer who makes do-it-yourself tools.

Profits have always been low, but liquidity has remained high, due to careful cash management. The company has invested its surplus cash in stocks and shares of quoted companies.

A new professional managing director was appointed two years ago after the retirement of the firm's founder. He has proposed to the Board that since the stocks and shares do not provide a satisfactory return and have shown little capital growth, they should be sold to provide funds to exploit other business opportunities. In particular, he has recommended either of the following.

(i) The purchase of a small aluminium foundry
(ii) Diversification into new products and new markets

Required

Describe the main factors to consider in deciding the strategy to be adopted by D'Arcy Toby Wise Ltd. **(13 marks)**

(Total = 25 marks)

29 Knuckle Down   45 mins

The management of Knuckle Down Ltd are reviewing the company's capital investment options for the coming year, and are considering six projects.

Project A would cost £29,000 now, and would earn the following cash profits.

1st year	£8,000	3rd year	£10,000
2nd year	£12,000	4th year	£ 6,000

The capital equipment purchased at the start of the project could be resold for £5,000 at the start of the fifth year.

Project B would involve a current outlay of £44,000 on capital equipment and £20,000 on working capital. The profits from the project would be as follows.

Year	Sales	Variable costs	Contribution	Fixed costs	Profit
	£	£	£	£	£
1	75,000	50,000	25,000	10,000	15,000
2	90,000	60,000	30,000	10,000	20,000
3	42,000	28,000	14,000	8,000	6,000

Fixed costs include an annual charge of £4,000 for depreciation. At the end of the third year the working capital investment would be recovered and the equipment would be sold for £5,000.

Project C would involve a current outlay of £50,000 on equipment and £15,000 on working capital. The investment in working capital would be increased to £21,000 at the end of the first year. Annual cash profits would be £18,000 for five years, at the end of which the investment in working capital would be recovered.

EXAM QUESTION BANK

Project D would involve an outlay of £20,000 now and a further outlay of £20,000 after one year. Cash profits thereafter would be as follows.

2nd year £15,000   3rd year £12,000   4th to 8th years £8,000 pa

Project E is a long-term project, involving an immediate outlay of £32,000 and annual cash profits of £4,500 in perpetuity.

Project F is another long-term project, involving an immediate outlay of £20,000 and annual cash profits as follows.

1st to 5th years £5,000   6th to 10th years £4,000   11th year onwards for ever £3,000

The company discounts all projects of ten years duration or less at a cost of capital of 12%, and all other projects at a cost of 15%.

Ignore taxation.

Required

(a) Calculate the NPV of each project, and determine which should be undertaken by the company on financial grounds.

(b) Calculate the IRR of projects A, C and E.

30 Dinard   45 mins

(a) Explain the difference between real rates of return and money rates of return and outline the circumstances in which the use of each would be appropriate when appraising capital projects under inflationary conditions. **(8 marks)**

(b) Dinard plc has just developed a new product to be called Rance and is now considering whether to put it into production. The following information is available.

(i) Costs incurred in the development of Rance amount to £480,000.

(ii) Production of Rance will require the purchase of new machinery at a cost of £2,400,000 payable immediately. This machinery is specific to the production of Rance and will be obsolete and valueless when that production ceases. The machinery has a production life of four years and a production capacity of 30,000 units per annum.

(iii) Production costs of Rance (at year 1 prices) are estimated as follows.

	£
Variable materials	8.00
Variable labour	12.00
Variable overheads	12.00

In addition, fixed production costs (at year 1 prices), including straight line depreciation on plant and machinery, will amount to £800,000 per annum.

(iv) The selling price of Rance will be £80.00 per unit (at year 1 prices). Demand is expected to be 25,000 units per annum for the next four years.

(v) The retail price index is expected to increase at 5% per annum for the next four years and the selling price of Rance is expected to increase at the same rate. Annual inflation rates for production costs are expected to be as follows.

	%
Variable materials	4
Variable labour	10
Variable overheads	4
Fixed costs	5

(vi) The company's weighted average cost of capital in money terms is expected to be 15%.

Required

Advise the directors of Dinard plc whether it should produce Rance on the basis of the information above. **(17 marks)**

(Total = 25 marks)

Notes

Unless otherwise specified all costs and revenues should be assumed to rise at the end of each year. Ignore taxation.

31 Muggins   30 mins

Muggins plc is evaluating a project to produce a new product. The product has an expected life of four years. Costs associated with the product are expected to be as follows.

Variable costs per unit
Labour: £30
Materials:
  6 kg of material X at £1.64 per kg
  3 units of component Y at £4.20 per unit
Other variable costs: £4.40

Indirect cost each year
Apportionment of head office salaries £118,000
Apportionment of general building occupancy £168,000
Other overheads £80,000, of which £60,000 represent additional cash expenditures (including rent of machinery)

To manufacture the product, a product manager will have to be recruited at an annual gross cost of £34,000, and one assistant manager, whose current annual salary is £30,000, will be transferred from another department, where he will be replaced by a new appointee at a cost of £27,000 a year.

The necessary machinery will be rented. It will be installed in the company's factory. This will take up space that would otherwise be rented to another local company for £135,000 a year. This rent (for the factory space) is not subject to any uncertainty, as a binding four-year lease would be created.

60,000 kg of material X are already in stock, at a purchase value of £98,400. They have no use other than the manufacture of the new product. Their disposal value is £50,000.

Expected sales volumes of the product, at the proposed selling price of £125 a unit, are as follows.

Year	Expected sales Units
1	10,000
2	18,000
3	18,000
4	19,000

All sales and costs will be on a cash basis and should be assumed to occur at the end of the year. Ignore taxation.

The company requires that certainty-equivalent cash flows have a positive NPV at a discount rate of 14%. Adjustment factors to arrive at certainty-equivalent amounts are as follows.

Year	Costs	Benefits
1	1.1	0.9
2	1.3	0.8
3	1.4	0.7
4	1.5	0.6

Required

Assess on financial grounds whether the project is acceptable.

32 Banden   45 mins

Banden Ltd is a highly geared company that wishes to expand its operations. Six possible capital investments have been identified, but the company only has access to a total of £620,000. The projects are not divisible and may not be postponed until a future period. After the project's end it is unlikely that similar investment opportunities will occur.

Expected net cash inflows (including salvage value)

Project	Year 1 £	2 £	3 £	4 £	5 £	Initial outlay £
A	70,000	70,000	70,000	70,000	70,000	246,000
B	75,000	87,000	64,000			180,000
C	48,000	48,000	63,000	73,000		175,000
D	62,000	62,000	62,000	62,000		180,000
E	40,000	50,000	60,000	70,000	40,000	180,000
F	35,000	82,000	82,000			150,000

Projects A and E are mutually exclusive. All projects are believed to be of similar risk to the company's existing capital investments.

Any surplus funds may be invested in the money market to earn a return of 9% per year. The money market may be assumed to be an efficient market.

Banden's cost of capital is 12% a year.

Required

(a) (i) Calculate the expected net present value for each of the six projects.

    (ii) Calculate the expected profitability index associated with each of the six projects.

    (iii) Rank the projects according to both of these investment appraisal methods. Explain briefly why these rankings differ. **(10 marks)**

(b) Give reasoned advice to Banden Ltd recommending which projects should be selected. **(6 marks)**

(c) A director of the company has suggested that using the company's normal cost of capital might not be appropriate in a capital rationing situation. Explain whether you agree with the director.
(5 marks)

(d) The director has also suggested the use of linear programming to assist with the selection of projects. Discuss the advantages and disadvantages of this mathematical programming method to Banden Ltd. **(4 marks)**

(Total = 25 marks)

33 Flocks   45 mins

The management of Flocks Ltd is trying to decide which of two machines to purchase, to help with production. Only one of the two machines will be purchased.

Machine X costs £63,000 and machine Y costs £110,000. Both machines would require a working capital investment of £12,500 throughout their operational life, which is four years for machine X and six years for machine Y. The expected scrap value of either machine would be zero.

The estimated pre-tax operating net cash inflows with each machine are as follows.

Year	Machine X £	Machine Y £
1	25,900	40,300
2	28,800	32,900
3	30,500	32,000
4	29,500	32,700
5	–	48,500
6	–	44,200

With machine Y, there is some doubt about its design features, and consequently there is some risk that it might prove unsuitable. Because of the higher business risk with machine Y, the machine Y project cash flows should be discounted at 15%, whereas machine X cash flows should be discounted at only 13%.

Flocks Ltd intends to finance the machine it eventually selects, X or Y, by borrowing at 10%.

Tax is payable at 30% on operating cash flows one year in arrears. Capital allowances are available at 25% a year on a reducing balance basis.

Required

(a) For both machine X and machine Y, calculate:

    (i) The (undiscounted) payback period
    (ii) The net present value

    and recommend which of the two machines Flocks Ltd should purchase. **(16 marks)**

(b) Suppose that Flocks Ltd has the opportunity to lease machine X under a finance lease arrangement, at an annual rent of £20,000 for four years, payable at the end of each year. Recommend whether the company should lease or buy the machine, assuming it chooses machine X. **(9 marks)**

(Total = 25 marks)

34 Milbao   45 mins

Milbao plc make and sell three types of electronic game for which the following budget/standard information and actual information is available for a four-week period.

Model	Budget sales Units	Standard unit data Selling price £	Variable cost £	Actual sales Units
Superb	30,000	100	40	36,000
Excellent	50,000	80	25	42,000
Good	20,000	70	22	18,000

Required

(a) Calculate the *individual* sales quantity and sales mix variances for Milbao plc for the four-week period, using contribution as the valuation base. **(5 marks)**

EXAM QUESTION BANK

(b) The following additional information is available for the four-week period.

The actual selling prices and variable costs of Milbao plc are 10% and 5% lower respectively than the original budget/standard.

General market prices have fallen by 6% from the original standard. Short-term strategy by Milbao plc accounts for the residual fall in selling price.

3% of the variable cost reduction from the original budget/standard is due to an over-estimation of a wage award, the remainder (ie 2%) is due to short-term operational improvements.

Prepare a summary for a four-week period for models 'Superb' and 'Good' *only*, which reconciles original budget contribution with actual contribution where planning and operational variances are taken into consideration. **(15 marks)**

(c) Comment on the usefulness to management of planning and operational variance analysis in feedback and feedforward control. **(5 marks)**
(Total = 25 marks)

Approaching the answer

You should read through the requirement before working through and annotating the question as we have done so that you are aware of what things you are looking for.

[Note the time frame]

Milbao plc make and sell three types of electronic game for which the following budget/standard information and actual information is available for a four-week period.

[This is in units, not £]

Model	Budget sales Units	Standard unit data Selling price £	Variable cost £	Actual sales Units
Superb	30,000	100	40	36,000
Excellent	50,000	80	25	42,000
Good	20,000	70	22	18,000

[This is standard unit data in £]

[This is actual data]

Required

[Not total variance] [Three models]

(a) Calculate the *individual* sales quantity and sales mix variances for Milbao plc for the four-week period, using contribution as the valuation base. **(5 marks)**

[Same time frame as above] [Very important] [It's that time frame again]

(b) The following additional information is available for the four-week period.

[Differences between original and actual]

The actual selling prices and variable costs of Milbao plc are 10% and 5% lower respectively than the original budget/standard.

[Differences between original standard and revised standard?]

General market prices have fallen by 6% from the original standard. Short-term strategy by Milbao plc accounts for the residual fall in selling price.

[Differences between revised standard and actual?]

3% of the variable cost reduction from the original budget/standard is due to an over-estimation of a wage award, the remainder (ie 2%) is due to short-term operational improvements.

[Difference between revised standard and actual]

[Annotations on question:]
- This is the reconciliation required
- Not detail
- Time frame
- So not Excellent
- Don't forget to include them
- Not detailed analysis
- So not normal variance analysis
- Do you know what these are?

Prepare a summary for a four-week period for models 'Superb' and 'Good' *only*, which reconciles original budget contribution with actual contribution where planning and operational variances are taken into consideration.

(15 marks)

(c) Comment on the usefulness to management of planning and operational variance analysis in feedback and feedforward control.

(5 marks)

(Total = 25 marks)

Framework for your answer

Part (a)

The **sales quantity variance** is calculated as the difference between the total actual sales quantity (given) in the budgeted proportions (you need to work out these proportions) and the budgeted sales quantities (given). You then need to value these differences at the standard contribution per unit (easy to calculate!)

The **sales mix variance** is calculated as the difference between the total actual sales quantity in the budgeted proportions (which you will have calculated already for the quantity variance) and the actual sales (given). You then need to value the difference at the standard contribution per unit (as above).

Part (b)

First reconcile **original budget contribution** (easy to calculate from information given in the question) to **revised budget contribution** via **planning variances**.

- The **selling price planning variance** is the difference between the original budget revenue and the revised budget revenue (based on original budget volumes).

- The **variable cost planning variance** is the difference between the original budget variable cost and the revised budget variable cost (based on original volumes).

Then take account of the **sales volume variance** (valued at the revised standard margin) to give the **revised standard contribution** (ie the contribution that should have been achieved for the actual activity level).

Lastly, calculate the **operational variances** (calculated using revised standards) to reconcile to actual contribution.

Part (c)

Useful for **feedback control** as operational variances can be controlled by management.

Useful for **feedforward control** as revised standards can be used when budgets next prepared.

35 Swansea   90 mins

(a) Swansea plc has entered into a long-term contract under which it will be required to make a number of cash payments (S) of £1 million each at a steady rate over the following twelve months. The company holds only a very small amount of cash at the present time.

Required

(i) Evaluate the following two alternative methods of providing for the payment of these amounts. (Ignore taxation and the time value of money.)

(1) *Sale of securities*. Swansea expects to make an average rate of return (i) of 10% on its holdings of securities over the next year. A sale of securities gives rise to a transaction cost (F) of £20, and following the sale the company will earn 4.5% per annum interest on the amount deposited. The optimal amount of cash raised by a sale of securities is given by the following formula.

$$Q = \sqrt{\frac{2FS}{i}}$$

(2) *Loan*. It would be possible for Swansea to borrow the £1 million required for payments at an interest rate of 13% of the amount loaned per annum. The arrangement fee of £6,000 for such a loan could be paid from existing cash resources. The amount borrowed would be placed as a term deposit at an interest rate of 8%, for drawing down when needed. **(9 marks)**

(ii) What are the possible limitations of the cash management model which Swansea plc is using in part (a)(i). **(5 marks)**

(b) Mumbles Ltd, a subsidiary of Swansea, wishes to install computerised equipment with a four year life which would involve an outlay of £5 million (residual value: nil). The Financial Director has carried out a study which shows that the project has a positive net present value when this is calculated using the shareholders' required rate of return as a discount rate.

Mumbles has asked Castles Leasing Limited ('Castles'), a subsidiary of a major bank, for a quotation for the acquisition of the equipment on a leasing contract under which maintenance of the equipment would be provided by Castles.

Castles has quoted an annual rental of £1,800,000. The maintenance services would cost Mumbles £190,000 annually if it had to obtain them from another source.

Mumbles pays corporate tax at a rate of 33%, and the tax becomes payable 12 months after the relevant cash flow. A writing down allowance can be claimed on a 25% reducing balance basis. A pre-tax borrowing rate of 18% applies to Mumbles.

Required

(i) Describe the key aspects of:

(1) Finance leases **(2 marks)**
(2) Hire purchase **(2 marks)**
(3) Sale and leaseback **(2 marks)**

(ii) Disregarding the savings in maintenance costs, evaluate whether Mumbles Ltd should lease the equipment from Castles or borrow money to purchase the equipment itself. **(6 marks)**

(iii) Calculate whether a different evaluation should be made if the savings in maintenance costs for Mumbles Ltd are accounted for. **(2 marks)**

(c) Gower Ltd is another subsidiary of Swansea plc and is required to make a rate of return on capital employed of at least 10% pa. For this purpose, capital employed is defined as fixed assets and investment in stocks. This rate of return is also applied as a hurdle rate for new investment projects. Gower has limited borrowing powers and all capital projects are centrally funded.

The following is an extract from Gower's accounts.

Profit and loss account for the year ended 31 December 20X4

	£m
Turnover	120
Cost of sales	(100)
Operating profit	20

Assets employed as at 31 December 20X4

	£m	£m
Fixed (net)		75
Current assets (including stocks £25m)	45	
Current liabilities	(32)	
		13
Net capital employed		88

Gower's production engineers wish to invest in a new computer-controlled press. The equipment cost is £14m. The residual value is expected to be £2m after four years operation, when the equipment will be shipped to a customer in South America.

The new machine is capable of improving the quality of the existing product and also of producing a higher volume. The firm's marketing team is confident of selling the increased volume by extending the credit period. The expected additional sales are:

Year 1	2,000,000 units
Year 2	1,800,000 units
Year 3	1,600,000 units
Year 4	1,600,000 units

Sales volume is expected to fall over time due to emerging competitive pressures. Competition will also necessitate a reduction in price by £0.5 each year from the £5 per unit proposed in the first year. Operating costs are expected to be steady at £1 per unit, and allocation of overheads (none of which are affected by the new project) by the central finance department is set at £0.75 per unit.

Higher production levels will require additional investment in stocks of £0.5m, which would be held at this level until the final stages of operation of the project. Customers at present settle accounts after 90 days on average, but some of the company's customers have recently been pressing for an extension to their credit period.

Required

(i) Determine whether the proposed capital investment is attractive to Gower, using the return on capital employed method, defined as average profit to average capital employed, ignoring debtors and creditors.

(*Note*. Ignore taxes.) **(8 marks)**

(ii) (1) Suggest *three* problems which arise with the use of the return on capital employed method for appraising new investments. **(3 marks)**

(2) In view of the problems associated with this method, explain why companies continue to use it in project appraisal. **(3 marks)**

(iii) Briefly discuss the dangers of offering more generous credit, and suggest ways of assessing customers' creditworthiness. **(8 marks)**

(Total = 50 marks)

EXAM QUESTION BANK

Approaching the answer

You should read through the requirement before working through and annotating the question as we have done so that you are aware of what things you are looking for.

(a) Swansea plc has entered into a long-term contract under which it will be required to make a number of cash payments (S) of £1 million each at a **steady rate** over the following twelve months. The company **holds only a very small amount of cash** at the present time.

[Annotation: Can't use surplus cash holdings]
[Annotation: This information will be significant]

Required

(i) **Evaluate** the following two alternative methods of providing for the payment of these amounts. (Ignore taxation and the time value of money.)

[Annotation: Need to discuss other factors as well as calculation]

(1) *Sale of securities*. Swansea expects to make an average rate of return (i) of 10% on its holdings of securities over the next year. A sale of securities gives rise to a **transaction cost** (F) of £20, and following the sale the company will **earn 4.5%** per annum interest on the amount deposited. The optimal amount of cash raised by a sale of securities is given by the following formula.

$$Q = \sqrt{\frac{2FS}{i}}$$

[Annotation: What costs are involved? Is any income gained or lost?]

(2) *Loan*. It would be possible for Swansea to borrow the £1 million required for **payments at an interest rate of 13%** of the amount loaned per annum. The **arrangement fee** of £6,000 for such a loan could be paid from existing cash resources. The amount borrowed would be placed as a term deposit at an **interest rate of 8%**, for drawing down when needed. **(9 marks)**

[Annotation: What is wrong with its assumptions?]

(ii) What are the possible **limitations** of the cash management model which Swansea plc is using in part (a)(i). **(5 marks)**

(b) Mumbles Ltd, a subsidiary of Swansea, wishes to install computerised equipment with a four year life which would involve an outlay of £5 million (residual value: nil). The Financial Director has carried out a study which shows that the project has a **positive net present value** when this is calculated using the shareholders' required rate of return as a discount rate.

[Annotation: Investing decision been made]

Mumbles has asked Castles Leasing Limited ('Castles'), a subsidiary of a major bank, for a quotation for the acquisition of the equipment on a leasing contract under which maintenance of the equipment would be provided by Castles.

Castles has quoted an annual rental of £1,800,000. The maintenance services **would cost Mumbles £190,000 annually** if it had to obtain them from another source.

[Annotation: Should this be brought into calculation?]

Mumbles pays corporate tax at a rate of 33%, and the tax becomes payable 12 months after the relevant cash flow. A **writing down allowance** can be claimed on a 25% reducing balance basis. A **pre-tax borrowing rate** of 18% applies to Mumbles.

[Annotation: Cash effect]
[Annotation: Need to include tax cash flows]

Required

(i) Describe the **key aspects** of:

[Annotation: Lengthy discussion not required. Few quick points each]

(1) Finance leases **(2 marks)**
(2) Hire purchase **(2 marks)**
(3) Sale and leaseback **(2 marks)**

EXAM QUESTION BANK

Effect (iii) — (ii) Disregarding the savings in maintenance costs, evaluate whether Mumbles Ltd should lease the equipment from Castles or borrow money to purchase the equipment itself. **(6 marks)**

Finance decision

(iii) Calculate whether a different evaluation should be made if the savings in maintenance costs for Mumbles Ltd are accounted for. **(2 marks)**

Unusual definition but must use

(c) Gower Ltd is another subsidiary of Swansea plc and is required to make a rate of return on capital employed of at least 10% pa. For this purpose, capital employed is defined as fixed assets and investment in stocks. This rate of return is also applied as a hurdle rate for new investment projects. Gower has limited borrowing powers and all capital projects are centrally funded.

The following is an extract from Gower's accounts.

Profit and loss account for the year ended 31 December 20X4

	£m
Turnover	120
Cost of sales	(100)
Operating profit	20

Assets employed as at 31 December 20X4

	£m	£m
Fixed (net)		75
Current assets (including stocks £25m)	45	
Current liabilities	(32)	
		13
Net capital employed		88

Gower's production engineers wish to invest in a new computer-controlled press. The equipment cost is £14m. The residual value is expected to be £2m after four years operation, when the equipment will be shipped to a customer in South America.

The new machine is capable of improving the quality of the existing product and also of producing a higher volume. The firm's marketing team is confident of selling the increased volume by extending the credit period. The expected additional sales are:

Year 1	2,000,000 units
Year 2	1,800,000 units
Year 3	1,600,000 units
Year 4	1,600,000 units

Be careful to calculate the correct effect — Sales volume is expected to fall over time due to emerging competitive pressures. Competition will

Should these be brought in? — also necessitate a reduction in price by £0.5 each year from the £5 per unit proposed in the first year. Operating costs are expected to be steady at £1 per unit, and allocation of overheads (none of which are affected by the new project) by the central finance department is set at £0.75 per unit.

Affects capital employed

A long time — Higher production levels will require additional investment in stocks of £0.5m, which would be held at this level until the final stages of operation of the project. Customers at present settle accounts after 90 days on average, but some of the company's customers have recently been pressing for an extension to their credit period.

EXAM QUESTION BANK

Required

> [annotation: What is current ROCE? Do we need to consider it?]

(i) Determine whether the proposed capital investment is attractive to Gower, using the return on capital employed method, defined as average profit to average capital employed, ignoring debtors and creditors.

(*Note.* Ignore taxes.) **(8 marks)**

> [annotation: Methods of calculations. Impact of cash]

(ii) (1) Suggest *three* problems which arise with the use of the return on capital employed method for appraising new investments. **(3 marks)**

(2) In view of the problems associated with this method, explain why companies continue to use it in project appraisal. **(3 marks)**

(iii) Briefly discuss the dangers of offering more generous credit, and suggest ways of assessing customers' creditworthiness. **(8 marks)**

(Total = 50 marks)

Framework for your answer

Part (a)(i)

The net costs of selling the securities are:

- Transaction costs (you need to calculate number of transactions using the formula)
- Less interest received on cash balances held (calculated on average balances)
- Plus interest foregone on securities (again calculated on average balance)

Answer also brings out problems of selling securities – the evaluation required is more than just financial calculations.

The net costs of using the loan finance are:

- Interest paid (on full loan balance)
- Less interest received on cash balance held (calculated on average balance)
- Plus arrangement fee

Again the answer mentions wider issues, in this case repayment problems.

Part (a)(ii)

The answer takes each element of the formula in turn, discusses the assumptions made and then considers whether the model misses anything out.

Part (b)(i)

Certain key considerations need to be discussed with all three methods:

- Who has ownership
- Responsibilities
- Taxation
- Effect on accounts

Part (b)(ii) and (iii)

It is easier to show the payments for each year in a single column. Bringing tax in means that you have to use an after tax discount rate and consider the tax implications of all revenues and payments. Don't assume that the sole tax implication is the ability to claim capital allowances. Your answer will be incomplete if you do not calculate the total net present value **and** make appropriate comparisons.

Part (c)(i)

You need first to calculate the current ROCE – all the information is used. A summary calculation, plus workings for each element, is the best way to show the impact of the press. Remember that you are after one average figure for the lifetime of the press. A conclusion comparing the ROCE of the press with the target rate and the current rate is essential.

Part (c)(ii)

The answer covers the elements contained in the calculation and discusses their nature (easy to manipulate) and how they are used. It also considers what the calculation does not contain (the cash movements). Different criteria apply though in practice – is it easy to do the calculation? Is its result easily understandable?

Part (c)(iii)

The first part involves assessment of the current position, and what will happen if the period is extended. The second part brings out the different types of evidence that can be obtained on prospective credit customers.

Exam answer bank

1 Over emphasis

> **Top tips.** You might think we're being a bit mean but we've given you an exam-standard question straight away. But don't panic! You could have probably made a fair attempt at this question before you had even opened this Study Text.
>
> As well as using information from Chapter 1, you could **have introduced material from Paper 1.2** (such as on information, on the differences between financial accounting and management accounting and on non-financial indicators). It is important to remember that your studies are **cumulative**: knowledge from lower levels needs to be brought forward and applied as you progress through your ACCA exams.
>
> Answers to this question would have been wide and varied so don't worry if yours is not too similar to ours! It would have been perfectly acceptable to draw upon your **own experience** where relevant.
>
> Take note of the **layout** of our answer. The basic principles adopted here have been used throughout this answer bank where relevant and you should endeavour to use them too. They will make your answer much easier to mark than an uninterrupted flow of words covering two sheets of paper.
>
> - **Short paragraphs**
> - **Headings**
> - **Emboldening** (you can underline) of key words and phrases
> - Reference in headings to key words/phrases in the question

The identification, generation, presentation, interpretation and use of information for planning, control and decision making are all important aspects of management accounting, along with providing information for formulating strategy, safeguarding assets, optimising the use of resources and so on.

Planning

Planning involves **establishing objectives** and **selecting appropriate strategies** to achieve those objectives. It forces management to **think ahead** systematically in both the short term (via the setting of budgets) and the long term (via strategic planning).

Decision making

Decision making is carried out at all levels of an organisation. At the **strategic** level, a decision might be taken to close down a division, at the **tactical** level to terminate a member of staff's employment and at the **operational** level to reduce a customer's credit limit.

Control

Control involves two stages. The performance of an organisation as set out in detailed operational plans is **compared** with actual performance on a regular and continuous basis. Any **deviations** from the plans are **identified** (variance analysis) and **corrective action** is taken by the manager responsible for the area in question as part of a system of responsibility accounting. The plans are then **reviewed** in the light of the first stage of control and modified to take account of any changes to the parameters upon which the plans were based.

Information required

Planning, control and decision making all require different types of information. **Planning information** must be essentially **forward looking** and must include **non-financial information** relating to personnel, markets and so on. The most important requirements of **decision-making information** are that it is **relevant, timely, accurate** and **appropriate**. **Control information**, on the other hand, is mostly **historic**.

The impact of the financial accounting system

As mentioned earlier, management accounting is concerned with the provision of information for planning, control and decision making. **In the past the most comprehensive information system was the financial accounting system.** As the **control** function relies on **historic** information, the **financial accounting system** provides a ready **source** of suitable information. Moreover, its suitability has only been reinforced in the past by the **concentration on the financial results** of an organisation.

Such information is entirely **unsuitable for planning and decision making**, however. The use of absorption costing to comply with the requirements of SSAP 9, for example, produces information which is totally misleading for product and output decisions.

It is because accounting information is so readily available from the financial accounting system that organisations have tended to **concentrate their efforts on control**, either disregarding the planning and decision making functions because of a lack of suitable information *or* using totally inappropriate information for planning and decision-making purposes.

The value of non-financial indicators

Financial results are no longer seen as the only way of assessing an organisation's performance, however, and it has recently become evident that **effective control** is possible using both **financial and non-financial information**. For example, there has been an increase in the use of non-financial indicators which are based on information more suited to planning and decision making. Moreover, the increase in the use of **activity based costing** and other activity based techniques means that information more relevant to planning and decision making is now available.

The impact of the nature of the organisation

The nature of an organisation may of course have an **impact on the relative importance of the control activity**. For example, public sector organisations may place more emphasis on control. This may be due to the need for greater accountability and is not necessarily to the detriment of the other functions of management accounting.

Other factors to consider

Other factors which may influence the relative importance of planning and decision– making activities compared with control activities include the following.

(a) The **nature of the environment in which the organisation operates**. Dynamic environments may require more emphasis on planning.

(b) The **management accounting resources** and the **sophistication of the information system** available. Some organisations may wish to spend more effort on planning but they may not have the resources available.

(c) The **complexity of the organisation**. More complex organisations may need to expend more effort on the control activity.

Conclusion

It is therefore **not necessarily detrimental** for an organisation to emphasise the control function in its management accounting activity.

However, it may be that organisations have **concentrated too much** on the control aspect of management accounting simply because of a **lack of suitable information** for planning and decision-making purposes. It is possible that as the importance of **non-financial results increases** and more **sophisticated management accounting techniques** are employed, the provision of information for planning, control and decision making will all become equally important for the management accountant.

2 Ryman Couplets

> **Top tips.** Although you need to do lots of calculations in the answer to this exam-standard question, you have already covered absorption costing and marginal costing in your earlier studies so you should have had no problem with the techniques and processes required.
>
> When drawing up the marginal costing statement in (a)(i), don't forget that only variable costs are included in cost of production and sales, and stocks are valued at variable production cost. As well as the direct costs of production included in (a)(i), you also need to include the overheads absorbed (overhead cost per unit × number of units produced) in the absorption costing statement in (a)(ii). Closing stock is valued at full cost.
>
> Because budget figures are being considered in **(a)(ii), over and under absorption does not occur**. There would be no under– or over-absorbed overhead if actual production volumes turned out to be the same as budgeted production volumes.
>
> In part (a)(iii), you can use the same direct costs as in (a)(ii) but the overheads absorbed have changed.
>
> Part (b) (the **comparison of absorption costing and marginal costing results**) is likely to be **examined fairly regularly** so if you made mistakes you must work through our answer carefully so that you can find out where you went wrong. There are three distinct parts to part (b), so make sure that you answer all of them.
>
> Part (c)(i) of the question tests your understanding of a particular aspect of cost behaviour (that only variable costs increase if production increases within the relevant range). In part (c)(ii), total variable production costs will change (× 125%) because of the increase in production. Because sales levels have not increased, closing stock will increase by the additional production volumes (25% of the original production volumes).
>
> In the 'real' exam, you may run out of time before you get to part (c)(ii), but it would have only have been worth about 5 marks.

(a) We begin by calculating the overhead cost per unit of the three products using the two different absorption bases.

Product		*Machine hours per annum* Hours	*Labour hours per annum* Hours
X		60,000	40,000
Y		20,000	80,000
Z		20,000	20,000
		100,000	140,000
Budgeted annual overhead costs		£560,000	£560,000
Absorption rate		£5.60 per machine hour	£4 per direct labour hour
Overhead cost per unit	X	£16.80 per unit	£8 per unit
	Y	£5.60 per unit	£16 per unit
	Z	£11.20 per unit	£8 per unit

(i) **Marginal costing**

	20X2				20X3			
	X	Y	Z	Total	X	Y	Z	Total
	£'000	£'000	£'000	£'000	£'000	£'000	£'000	£'000
Opening stocks	0	0	0	0	96	72	84	252
Direct prod costs	320	360	120	800	320	360	120	800
	320	360	120	800	416	432	204	1,052
Closing stocks	96	72	84	252	192	216	36	444
Variable cost of production and sales	224	288	36	548	224	216	168	608
Sales	420	560	75	1,055	420	420	350	1,190
Contribution	196	272	39	507	196	204	182	582
Overheads				560				560
Profit/(loss)				(53)				22

(ii) **Absorption costing, using a machine hour rate of recovery**

	20X2				20X3			
	X	Y	Z	Total	X	Y	Z	Total
	£'000	£'000	£'000	£'000	£'000	£'000	£'000	£'000
Opening stock	0	0	0	0	196.8	94.4	162.4	453.6
Direct costs of production	320.0	360.0	120.0	800.0	320.0	360.0	120.0	800.0
O/hds absorbed	336.0	112.0	112.0	560.0	336.0	112.0	112.0	560.0
	656.0	472.0	232.0	1,360.0	852.8	566.4	394.4	1,813.6
Closing stock (W)	196.8	94.4	162.4	453.6	393.6	283.2	69.6	746.4
Full cost of sales	459.2	377.6	69.6	906.4	459.2	283.2	324.8	1,067.2
Sales	420.0	560.0	75.0	1,055.0	420.0	420.0	350.0	1,190.0
Profit	(39.2)	182.4	5.4	148.6	(39.2)	136.8	25.2	122.8

Working

Per unit: X £(16 + 16.8) = £32.80; Y £23.60; Z £23.20

(iii) **Absorption costing, using a direct labour hour rate of recovery**

	20X2				20X3			
	X	Y	Z	Total	X	Y	Z	Total
	£'000	£'000	£'000	£'000	£'000	£'000	£'000	£'000
Opening stock	0	0	0	0	144	136	140	420
Direct costs of prod	320	360	120	800	320	360	120	800
Overheads absorbed	160	320	80	560	160	320	80	560
	480	680	200	1,360	624	816	340	1,780
Closing stock (W)	144	136	140	420	288	408	60	756
Full cost of sales	336	544	60	940	336	408	280	1,024
Sales	420	560	75	1,055	420	420	350	1,190
Profit	84	16	15	115	84	12	70	166

Working

Per unit: X (£16 + £8) = £24; Y £34; Z £20

(b) The **figures differ because of the overhead content in stock carried forward or stock brought forward in each period, and thus in the valuation of opening and closing stocks.**

(i) **20X2**

	Stock b/f	Stock c/f	Stock change	Profit/(loss)
	£'000	£'000	£'000	£'000
Marginal costing	0	252.0	+ 252.0	(53.0)
Full costing – machine hr method	0	453.6	+ 453.6	148.6
Full costing – labour hr method	0	420.0	+ 420.0	115.0

The difference in the stock change between each method explains the difference in profit; for example the difference in the stock change with a machine hour recovery rate is (in £'000s)

453.6 − 252 = 201.6. The difference in profit is 148.6 − (−53) = 201.6.

(ii) **20X3**

	Stock b/f £'000	Stock c/f £'000	Stock change £'000	Profit/(loss) £'000
Direct costing	252.0	444.0	+ 192.0	22.0
Full costing − machine hr method	453.6	746.4	+ 292.8	122.8
Full costing − labour hr method	420.0	756.0	+ 336.0	166.0

Once again, the difference in profit is explained by the difference in the value of stock changes; for example, the difference in profit between the two methods of absorption costing ((166 − 122.8) = £43,200) is the same as the difference in stock changes (336 − 292.8).

How to improve the absorption costing figures

The absorption costing method of stock valuations might be improved if separate departmental overhead absorption rates could be used for machining work (for which a machine hour rate would be applied) and for finishing work (for which a direct labour hour rate would be applied). Total overheads would need to be apportioned fairly between the two departments, so that the more equitable method of recovering fixed costs in product costs would be possible. This system of separate departmental rates is fairer because it would make allowance for both the machine hours and the labour hours worked on each product.

Which is correct?

Of the three costing systems, **none is more 'correct' than the other**. Each is equally 'right' or 'wrong'. Different costing principles have been applied to stock valuations, therefore different (short-term) period profits will be reported.

(c) (i) If production in 20X2 is increased by 25% the **extra costs** incurred in producing the additional stock would be the **variable costs** of production.

Total direct costs in original budget for 20X2	£800,000
A 25% increase in costs would be	£200,000
Interest rate per annum	14%
Annual interest cost of extra stocks	£28,000

(ii) If the increase in production is budgeted and fixed costs remain unaffected by the higher output, the **overhead recovery rates would be reduced**, as follows.

	Machine hours	Labour hours
Budget	(125% of 100,000) = 125,000	(125% of 140,000) = 175,000
Budgeted overheads	£560,000	£560,000
Recovery rate	£4.48 per machine hour	£3.20 per labour hour
Unit costs: X	£(16 + 13.44) = £29.44	£(16 + 6.40) = £22.40
Y	£(18 + 4.48) = £22.48	£(18 +12.80) = £30.80
Z	£(12 + 8.96) = £20.96	£(12 + 6.40) = £18.40

EXAM ANSWER BANK

	Marginal costing £'000	£'000	Absorption costing Machine hr method £'000	£'000	Absorption costing Labour hr method £'000	£'000
20X2						
Opening stock		0		0		0
Production costs:						
Direct (800 × 125%)		1,000		1,000		1,000
Fixed		560		560		560
		1,560		1,560		1,560
Closing stocks						
X (6K + (20K × 25%))	176		324		246	
Y (4K + (20K × 25%))	162		202		277	
Z (7K + (10K × 25%))	114		199		175	
		452		725		698
Cost of sales		1,108		835		862
Sales		1,055		1,055		1,055
Profit		(53)		220		193

The loss in marginal costing would be unaffected, but with absorption costing a larger proportion of fixed costs would be carried forward in closing stock values, so that total profits in 20X2 would increase.

3 Southcott

> **Top tips.** Because ABC is new to you, this first ABC question in the bank is **not exam standard**. Nevertheless, you need to be able to provide a good answer as it tests the key skills you need for the topic.
>
> Part (a) should have caused you no problems. The original absorption basis was course days and so you simply needed to calculate the number of course days (number of courses × duration of course) for each course and total the results. Dividing total overheads by this figure gives an overhead cost per course day. Overheads are included in the cost of a course on the basis of the course duration.
>
> Part (b) provides an example of the application of ABC to a **service organisation.** The **principles** to apply are the **same** as those you would apply when dealing with a manufacturing organisation.
>
> Step 1. Determine the cost driver for each category of overhead.
> Step 2. Calculate a cost per cost driver (cost/number of cost drivers)
> Step 3. Include overhead in the cost of a course on the basis of the number of cost drivers generated by a course.
>
> Don't forget to provide **reasons** for your choice of cost drivers. A 'tag-on' requirement like this might be worth the three marks that can make the difference between a pass and a fail.

(a)

	Auditing	Taxation	Total
No of courses sold	50	30	
Duration of course (days)	2	3	
No of course days	100	90	190

Overhead cost per course day = $\dfrac{£152,625}{190}$ = £803.29

Overhead cost per course

Auditing   £803.29 × 2 days = £1,606.58
Taxation   £803.29 × 3 days = £2,409.87

(b) **Overhead costs per course using activity based costing**

		Auditing £ per course		Taxation £ per course
Centre hire at £328.95 per day	(× 2)	657.90	(× 3)	986.85
Enquiries administration at £2.50 per enquiry	(× 175)	437.50	(× 70)	175.00
Brochures at £3 per brochure	(× 300)	900.00	(× 200)	600.00
Overhead cost per course		1,995.40		1,761.85

Workings

1 Centre hire cost per course day = $\dfrac{£62,500}{190}$ = £328.95

2 Enquiries administration cost per enquiry = $\dfrac{£27,125}{(50 \times 175) + (30 \times 70)}$ = £2.50

3 Brochure cost per brochure printed = $\dfrac{£63,000}{(50 \times 300) + (30 \times 200)}$ = £3 per brochure

Reasons for the choice of cost drivers

(i) The cost driver for centre hire costs is the number of course days, since the centre is hired at a standard daily rate.

(ii) The cost driver for enquiries administration is the number of enquiries, since more enquiries would result in an increase in the cost of enquiries administration.

(iii) The cost driver for brochure costs is the number of brochures printed, since an increase in the number of brochures printed would lead to a higher cost.

4 Broadly the same

> **Top tips.** The ABC calculations in part (b) are fairly straightforward but remember to show clear workings so that the examiner can award marks for your method, even if you make an error. If you feel that there is more than one potential cost driver, select the one which seems most appropriate and state the reasons for your choice.

(a) **Cost per unit for each product**

	Product X £ per unit	Product Y £ per unit	Product Z £ per unit
Materials	20	12	25
Direct labour	3	9	6
Production overhead	42	28	84
	65	49	115

(b) **Calculation of total production overhead for the period**

Product	Volumes units	Production overhead £ per unit	£
X	750	42	31,500
Y	1,250	28	35,000
Z	7,000	84	588,000
			654,500

Analysis of total production overhead

Costs relating to	%	Overhead cost £	Cost driver	Cost driver rate
Set-ups	35	229,075	670 set-ups	£341.90 per set-up
Machinery	20	130,900	23,375* machine hours	£5.60 per machine hour
Materials handling	15	98,175	120 movements	£818.13 per movement
Inspection	30	196,350	1,000 inspections	£196.35 per inspection
	100	654,500		

* Total number of machine hours.

Product	Units	Machine hours per unit	Total machine hours
X	750	1.5	1,125
Y	1,250	1.0	1,250
Z	7,000	3.0	21,000
			23,375

Calculation of production overhead per unit, applying the calculated cost driver rates

	Product X		Product Y		Product Z	
Costs relating to:	Number of cost drivers	Overhead £	Number of cost drivers	Overhead £	Number of cost drivers	Overhead £
Machinery	1,125	6,300	1,250	7,000	21,000	117,600
Materials handling	12	9,817	21	17,181	87	71,177
Inspection	150	29,453	180	35,343	670	131,554
Total production overhead		71,213		98,843		484,444
Number of units		750		1,250		7,000
Production overhead cost per unit		£95		£79		£69

Summary

Cost per unit using ABC principles

	Product		
	X £ per unit	Y £ per unit	Z £ per unit
Materials	20	12	25
Direct labour	3	9	6
Production overhead	95	79	69
	118	100	100

(c) Products X and Y both have a higher unit cost using ABC principles whereas the unit cost is lower for product Z.

The conventional basis

Using machine hours as an absorption base, this **assumes that overheads are volume and time related**. Hence product **Z**, which has the **greatest output volume** in the period and which **takes the longest to manufacture**, has **absorbed most** of the overheads.

However, the analysis of the overheads shows that **many of them are not volume or time related**. They are driven by other factors or activities such as the number of set-ups and movements of materials.

ABC

The analysis of activities shows that **product Z has fewer set-ups, fewer materials movements** and **fewer inspections** per unit than products X and Y. Therefore when overheads are allocated according to each products' usage of these activities, products X and Y absorb proportionally more of the overhead compared with the use of conventional absorption methods.

5 Standard costing system

> **Top tips.** Part (a) of this question highlights the importance of reading the question carefully. You are told that you are a **member of your organisation's management accounting team**. So, when asked to describe how you would install a standard costing system you are not, as a management accountant, going to be too concerned with the specific computer hardware required. This would be the remit of the systems manager, say. Instead you need to consider issues such as how the standards will be set, the type of performance standard that will be used and the way in which costs will be collected. In all of these areas, the management accountant would be concerned with the **behavioural impact** of the standard costing system.
>
> This part of the question could have resulted in wide variety of answers, however, so don't be too despondent if yours wasn't exactly the same as ours.
>
> Again, in part (b), **behavioural issues** need to be mentioned, underlining the importance of the workforce to the successful implementation of a standard costing system. Other issues to consider here include inflation and changes in working practices.

(a) Before attempting to install a standard costing system it would be **essential to be familiar with a number of aspects of the organisation and its products.** In particular the following aspects would be important.

(i) A full understanding of the **structure of the organisation**: the cost centres in operation, the identity and ability of each cost centre manager, the reports and feedback information already available.

(ii) The **manufacturing processes** in use: how operations are carried out, the extent to which they can be standardised and monitored, and so on.

(iii) **How other operations are carried out**: the ordering and storage procedures for materials, any bonus schemes in operation for the payment of labour and so on.

Performance standards

Establishing a standard costing system involves calculating predetermined units costs for each cost element of each product. A decision must be taken as to **which type of performance standard** is to be used. For example an **ideal standard would not include any allowances for inefficiencies, breakdowns, losses and so on**. An **attainable standard** would allow an efficient level of breakdowns, losses and so on and this type of standard is **likely to have a more favourable motivational impact**. Motivation problems could arise if an ideal standard is used, since such a standard almost always results in adverse variances which can be demotivating.

Setting standards

(i) **Direct material costs**

It will be necessary to **establish a standard for material usage and for material price**. Standard material usage would take account of any allowances for breakages and losses and would be based on careful monitoring and observation of the production processes used. Standard material price would take account of a number of factors including desired quality, the availability of bulk discounts and any anticipated price inflation.

    (ii) **Direct labour costs**

Standards must be established for labour times and for hourly rates of pay. The former would require the assistance of a work study specialist, who would investigate the method used and establish an efficient standard time. Employees may be suspicious of the reasons for which they are being observed and timed as they are doing their work. This problem can be overcome by involving them fully in the task of establishing standard times. They should understand that the standard times are to be used for cost control purposes and not as a device to reduce or affect their remuneration or job security. The personnel department would assist in establishing standard rates of pay, taking account of the skill levels required and the likely results of any future negotiations with trade unions.

    (iii) **Production overhead**

The cost centre structure would be used to **allocate and apportion overheads to obtain cost centre totals for forecast overheads**. There may be a problem in identifying the most **appropriate basis for overhead absorption** but it is likely to be some form of time based method. An hourly rate could be determined for production overhead and this rate would be applied to the standard times identified in the work study exercise.

Collecting information

Once the standards have been established it will be necessary to install a **system for collecting the actual costs** for the purposes of monitoring and controlling costs. Once again there may be **resistance** from employees if they do not understand the reasons for the monitoring. For example they may not be willing to co-operate in completing the necessary documentation for the analysis of labour times. It will be important to **educate** and **communicate** with all employees involved in the monitoring of actual costs, to ensure the smooth and efficient installation and operation of the system.

(b) **Past performance** is **one possible guide to the ascertainment of standard costs but it is not necessarily the best guide**. For example, if it is known at the time when standards are being set that a new labour rate has been agreed, that new more efficient working methods are to be introduced, that materials prices are going to rise or that the materials specification of products is going to change then the standard should be revised accordingly. There is no point in measuring performance against out-of-date standards.

The point should also be made that **standards can be used as a psychological incentive** by giving employees a realistic but challenging target of efficiency. Standards based on past performance will not have any motivational impact.

The most that can be said, therefore, is that past performance may offer a starting point for ascertaining standard costs, but only in the absence of change will it provide the best available basis for doing so.

EXAM ANSWER BANK

6 Pan Co

> **Top tips.** As this is the first question on variance analysis in this bank, we have decided to start you off gently, as **parts (a) and (b)** of this question are possibly **slightly easier than potential variance analysis questions in the exam**. Part (c), however, is certainly exam standard.
>
> You may have been confused by the requirement in **(a)(i)** to compute a variable production cost variance, but this simply means calculating a variance based on the **total variable cost made up of labour, materials and overhead**. The expected cost is easy to calculate (actual output × standard cost per unit of £210) but the calculation of the actual cost requires a little thought in terms of the direct materials cost. You need information about the **materials used in production**, not the materials purchased, as the variance is based on production levels and so you need to use opening stock + purchases – closing stock = materials used in production. (The material price variance, on the other hand will be based on materials purchased.)
>
> Part (a)(ii) was straightforward. How did you do in part (a)(iii)? As we said above, the **material price variance** needs to be based on the quantity **purchased** while the **material usage variance** needs to be based on the quantity **used**. Variable production overhead variance is simply the difference between what the actual output should have cost in terms of overhead and what it did cost.
>
> Once you have completed part (a)(iv) you can **compare** the **sum of the variances calculated in (a)(ii), (a)(iii) and (a)(iv)** with your answer to **(a)(i)** – they **should be the same**!
>
> In the exam it is vital to present information in the **format requested**. **In part (b)** you were asked to use a report so make sure that you used appropriate headings (to, from and so on) as there will always be **marks for presentation**. Make sure you **take note of the recipient** of the information (the production manager in this case), and tailor your answer appropriately. A finance manager would be interested in monetary implications, whereas the production manager will want to know about resource implications too. You commentary should cover issues such as why the variances might have occurred and any possible interrelationships between them. Don't forget that you were also asked to indicate any **additional information** that you might require.
>
> **Part (c)** is the trickiest part of the question and the key to a successful answer hinges on an issue we mentioned above, that of taking note of the recipient of the information. This is not to say that a production manager is only concerned with resource usage. The cost of the resource has an impact too. You also needed to mention the need for **comparability** across the organisation of various variances, achieved by converting quantity variances into monetary variances.

			£
(a)	(i)	Variable production cost should be (1,000 × £210)	210,000
		but was (W1)	224,160
		Variable production cost variance	14,160 (A)
		Check	£
		Wages (from (ii))	3,360 (A)
		Materials (from (iii))	9,000 (A)
		Overhead (from (iv))	1,800 (A)
			14,160 (A)

EXAM ANSWER BANK

(ii)	5,200 hours should cost (× £9)		£ 46,800
	but did cost		48,360
	Direct wages rate variance		1,560 (A)

1,000 units should take (× 5 hours)		5,000 hrs
but did take		5,200 hrs
Direct wages efficiency variance		200 hrs (A)
× standard rate		× £9
Direct wages efficiency variance		1,800 (A)

Summary
	£
Direct wages rate variance	1,560 (A)
Direct wages efficiency variance	1,800 (A)
Direct wages variance	3,360 (A)

(iii)		£
	10,000 kg should cost (× £15)	150,000
	but did cost	144,000
	Direct materials price variance	6,000 (F)

1,000 units should use (× 10 kg)	10,000 kg
but did use (W)	11,000 kg
Usage variance	1,000 kg (A)
	× £15
× standard cost	
Direct materials usage variance	£15,000 (A)

Summary
Direct materials price variance	6,000 (F)
Direct materials usage variance	15,000 (A)
Direct materials variance	9,000 (A)

(iv)		£
	Variable production overhead should cost (1,000 × £15)	15,000
	but did cost	16,800
	Variable production overhead variance	1,800 (A)

Workings

1   *Variable production cost*

	£
Total wages	48,360
Variable production overhead	16,800
Direct materials (W2)	159,000
	224,160

2   *Direct materials*

		Standard cost	
	kg	£	£
Opening stock	4,000	15	60,000
Purchases	10,000		144,000
	14,000		204,000
Closing stock	(3,000)	15	(45,000)
Production	11,000		159,000

(b) **REPORT**

To: Production manager
From: Management accountant
Date: 21 November 20X1
Subject: **Commentary on variances arising in the week ending 9 November 20X1**

Variable production cost variance.

The total variance is an adverse one of £14,160. This represents 6% of total standard production cost. Investigation is clearly warranted to identify what control action is required to bring costs back into line with budget. The total variance may be analysed into its different components to give a clearer idea of where problems are arising, as follows.

Direct wages rate variance

An adverse variance arises because the labour force were paid an average of (£48,360/5,200) = £9.30 per hour instead of the standard cost of £9 per hour. If this is a new agreed rate the standard should be revised. It may, however, be due to a short-term need to recruit temporary labour at rates more expensive than standard or to overtime working or bonus payments. The production manager and/or the personnel department should be contracted for further information.

Direct wages efficiency variance

An adverse variance of £1,800 has arisen because the labour force took 200 hours more to produce 1,000 units than the standard allowance. The production manager should be asked to explain the variance. Possible causes are lack of training or machine breakdown, but the material variances may also offer a clue as to the explanation.

Materials price variance

Materials were purchased for £14.40 per kg in the week, a price £0.60 less than standard giving rise to a favourable price variance of £6,000. However this appears to have been at the expense of quality, to judge from the usage variance.

Materials usage variance

1,000 kg more than standard were used to make 1,000 units. This seems most likely to be because cheaper, poor quality materials were purchased, probably resulting in excessive waste. It is possible that the need for rectification work due to poor materials also explains why the labour force was less efficient than standard.

Variable production overhead variance

An adverse variance of £1,800 has arisen. Variable overhead appears to vary in line with labour costs and thus 200 hours × £3 = £600 of the variance is explicable by reference to the extra labour hours worked. The remainder is due to an increase in variable overhead costs: the actual rate per hour was £16,800/5,200 hours = £3.23, as opposed to the standard rate of £3. For further explanation we need to know what the overhead comprises and who is responsible for the expenditure.

(c) The advantage of putting **money prices** to efficiency and usage variances is that they **indicate** the **effect on profit of that inefficiency**, provided that the standard prices for materials or labour are realistic. For example, an adverse usage variance of 2,000 units of material may appear more serious than an adverse efficiency variance of 500 hours. If the material only costs 30p per unit, and labour costs £6 per hour, however, the effect on costs and profits of each variance would be £600(A) and £3,000(A) respectively. The labour variance would be more significant.

Variances in production should also be **viewed in the context of the organisation as a whole**. A **comparison** must be possible between an adverse usage of 4,000 kg of material A in department A, an adverse usage of 3,000 kg of material B in department B, a shortfall in achieving the sales quota in sales department C and excess mileage travelled by lorries in distribution department D. The obvious basis for comparison is achieved by **converting all variances into a monetary value**.

On the other hand **many control measures** can be reported, at least in the **first instance**, in a non-financial **form as stated** by the production manager. Such information is **quicker** to produce for control purposes and may be **more easily understood** by the personnel responsible for day to day operational control.

7 Reconciliation statement

> **Top tips.** This question in **unusual** because instead of being asked to calculate variances on the basis of budget and actual data provided in the question, you are given the variances and budget data and have to '**work backwards**' to determine the actual data. This type of question did come up once in an exam under the old syllabus version of Paper 2.4 so it is worth making sure that you can 'work backwards'.
>
> We think the easiest approach is to **lay out a variance calculation as normal** but to **use X, say, for the missing piece of actual data** and to insert the variance given in the question data as the final line of the calculation. You can then use algebra (don't panic at the mention of this word) to find the value of X by **equating the difference between the expected or standard data and actual data (which will contain X) with the variance**. It is important to **take account** of whether you are dealing with **favourable or adverse variances**. If the variance is adverse, the difference between the expected figure and the actual figure (say 300 kgs – X) will be negative because the actual figure is greater than the expected figure.
>
> Part (b) was a gift and you should have been able to earn full marks. It is vital that you check that the reasons you **provide make sense in the context of the question**. There is very little point in giving the activities of competitors as the reason for an adverse sales volume variance if you know that the organisation is a monopolist!
>
> You should also have been able to score full marks for part (c) by mentioning the **implications** on **sales volume and fixed overhead volume variances**.

(a) Budgeted profit = £4,250

∴ Budgeted profit per unit = £4,250 ÷ 1,500 = £17/6

(i)
Budgeted sales volume	1,500 units
Actual sales volume	X units
Sales volume variance in units (£850 ÷ £17/6)	300 units (A)

Note that the variance is adverse so actual volume must be less than budget volume.

∴ 1,500 – X = 300
∴ 1,500 – 300 = X = 1,200

∴ Actual sales volume = 1,200 units

(ii)
1,550 units should have used (× (750 ÷ 1,500) kgs)	775 kgs
but did use	X kgs
Material usage variance in kgs	(775 – X) kgs (A)
× standard cost per kg (£4,500 ÷ 750 kgs)	× £6
Material usage variances in £	£150 (A)

Because the variance is **adverse**, X must be greater than 775 and hence 775 – X is **negative**.

∴ – (775 – X) × £6	=	150
– 775 + X	=	25
X	=	800

∴ Actual material usage = 800 kgs

(iii)
	£
1,000 kgs should have cost (× £6)	6,000
but did cost	X
Material price variance	1,000 (F)

∴ (6,000 – X) = £1,000
∴ 5,000 = X

∴ Actual direct material cost = £5,000

(iv)
1,550 units should have taken (× (1,125 ÷ 1,500) hours)	1,162.5	hrs
but did take	X	hrs
Labour efficiency variance in hrs	(1,162.5 – X)	hrs (A)
× standard rate per hour (4,500 ÷ 1,125)	× £4	
Labour efficiency variance	£150	(A)

Because the variance is **adverse**, 1,162.5 is less than X and so (1,162.5 – X) is **negative**.

∴ – (1,162.5 – X) × 4 = 150
– (1,162.5 – X) = 37.5
X = 37.5 + 1,162.5 = 1,200

∴ Actual direct labour hours = 1,200

(v)
	£
1,200 hours should have cost (× £4)	4,800
but did cost	X
Direct labour rate variance	200 (A)

∴ – (4,800 – X) = 200
X = 200 + 4,800 = £5,000

Actual direct labour cost = £5,000

(vi)
	£
1,200 hrs should have cost (× £(2,250 ÷ 1,125))	2,400
but did cost	X
Variable overhead expenditure variance	600 (A)

∴ – (2,400 – X) = 600
X = 600 + 2,400 = 3,000

Actual variable overhead cost = £3,000

(vii)
	£
Budgeted fixed overhead expenditure	4,500
Actual fixed overhead expenditure	X
Fixed overhead expenditure variance	2,500 (F)

∴ 4,500 – X = 2,500
X = 2,000

Actual fixed overhead cost = £2,000

(b) The **adverse direct materials usage variance** may have been caused by any of the following.

- Defective material
- Excessive waste
- Theft of material

- Stricter quality control (so that units had to be reworked)
- Errors in allocating material to jobs

The **adverse direct labour rate variance** may have been caused by any of the following.

- A wage rate increase
- The use of a higher grade labour than expected

The **adverse sales volume variance** may have been used by any of the following.

- The activities of competitors
- A general downturn in consumer spending
- Adverse reports about the product

(c) In absorption costing fixed overheads are absorbed into the cost of products. Variances will arise not only if actual fixed cost expenditure differs from budgeted fixed cost expenditure, (the expenditure variance), but also if actual activity levels differ from those expected. If there is a difference between actual and budgeted activity level, there will be over or under absorption of overheads as a result, and hence a volume variance.

By contrast **fixed overheads** are **not absorbed** into the cost of products under **marginal costing**. Hence no volume variance can arise, and the **only variance** that is therefore relevant will be the **fixed overhead expenditure variance**. This will be the **same** as the **expenditure variance** arising in **absorption costing**.

The other significant variance where differences arise is the **sales volume variance**. Under both marginal and absorption costing the variance will be calculated on the basis of the difference between expected sales and actual sales. However the difference in units will be **priced differently** under the two costing methods. Under marginal costing the difference in units will be priced at contribution per unit. Under absorption costing the difference in units will be priced at standard profit per unit. The standard profit figure will equal contribution less fixed overhead absorbed per unit.

8 M

> **Top tips.** The only complication in (a) is the calculation of the mix and yield variances.
>
> Part (b) specified the use of a **simple** generic example. But it would have been all to easy to get caught up in an extremely complicated example, wasting time and obscuring the issues you were meant to be explaining.
>
> You would have lost marks if you had ignored the requirement to provide an example and had instead provided a wholly discursive answer.

(a) Workings

(i)
Budgeted sales volume	1,000 units
Actual sales volume	900 units
Variance in units	100 units (A)
× standard profit per unit	× £25.50
Sales volume variance	£2,550 (A)

(ii)
	£
900 units should have sold for (× £120)	108,000
but did sell for	118,800
Sales price variance	10,800 (F)

(iii) Material A – provided in question – £567 (A)
Material B – provided in question – £3,661 (F)

(iv) Actual input = (5,670 + 10,460) kgs = 16,130 kgs

Standard mix of actual input

A = 16,130 × 5/15 = 5,376.67 kgs
B = 16,130 × 10/15 = 10,753.33 kgs
                     16,130.00 kgs

	Actual input Kgs	Standard mix of actual input Kgs	Variance Kgs	× standard price £	Variance £
A	5,670	5,376.67	293.33 (A)	2.50	733.33 (A)
B	10,460	10,753.33	293.33 (F)	4.00	1,173.33 (F)
	16,130	16,130.00	–		440.00 (F)

Alternative approach

Standard weighted average cost = standard cost/standard quantity
= £(40 + 12.50)/(5 + 10) kgs
= £3.50 per kg

	Actual input Kgs	Standard mix of actual input Kgs	Difference Kgs	× difference between w. av. price and standard price £	Variance £
A	5,670	5,376.67	293.33	£(3.50 – 2.50) 1.00	293.33 (F)
B	10,460	10,753.33	(293.33)	£(3.50 – 4.00) (0.50)	146.67 (F)
	16,130	16,130.00	–		440.00 (F)

(v) Yield variance = (actual total quantity used – quantity that should have been used for actual output) × standard weighted average cost per unit input.

= ((5,670 + 10,460) – (1,050 × 15)) × £3.50 = £1,330 (A)

(vi)
	£
3,215 hours should have cost (× £6)	19,290
but did cost	19,933
Labour rate variance	643 (A)

(vii)
1,050 units should have taken (× 3hrs)	3,150 hrs
but did take	3,215 hrs
Variance in hrs	65 hrs (A)
× standard rate per hr (× £6)	× £6
Labour efficiency variance	£390 (A)

(viii)
	£
3,215 hours of variable overhead should have cost (× £3)	9,645
but did cost	10,288
Variable production overhead expenditure variance	643 (A)

(ix)

1,050 units should have taken (× 3hrs)	3,150 hrs
but did take	3,215 hrs
Variance in hrs	65 hrs (A)
× standard rate per hr	× £3
Variable production overhead efficiency variance	£195 (A)

(x)

	£
Budgeted expenditure (£180,000/12)	15,000
Actual expenditure	15,432
Fixed production overhead expenditure variance	432 (A)

(xi)

Budgeted labour hours	3,000 hrs
Actual labour hours	3,215 hrs
Variance in hrs	215 hrs (F)
× standard absorption rate per hr	× £5
Fixed production overhead capacity variance	£1,075 (F)

(xii)

Variable overhead efficiency variance in hrs	65 hrs (A)
× standard absorption rate per hr	× £5
Fixed production overhead efficiency variance	£325 (A)

PROFIT RECONCILIATION STATEMENT (BUDGET TO ACTUAL) JANUARY 20X0

	£ (F)	£ (A)	£
Budgeted profit (1,000 units × £25.50)			25,500
Sales volume variance			2,550 (A)
Standard profit from sales achieved			22,950
Operating variances			
Sales price	10,800.00		
Material price – A		567	
– B	3,661.00		
Material mix	440.00		
Material yield		1,330	
Labour rate		643	
Labour efficiency		390	
Variance production overhead expenditure		643	
Variable production overhead efficiency		195	
Fixed production overhead expenditure		432	
Fixed production overhead capacity	1,075.00		
Fixed production overhead efficiency		325	
	15,976.00	4,525	11,451 (F)
Actual profit			34,401

We can do a check on the actual profit figure in the reconciliation statement by calculating actual profit based on the figures given in the question.

Top tips. Only do this if you have time in the exam – perhaps at the very end if you have a few minutes to spare.

Check	£	£
Sales		118,800
Costs incurred	98,574	
Closing stock (150 × £94.50)	(14,175)	
		84,399
Actual profit		34,401

(b) Logic, purpose and limitations of fixed overhead variances

(i) **Volume variance**

The **fixed production overhead volume variance** generated in an absorption costing system is a measure of over- or under-absorption of overhead cost caused by actual production volume differing from that budgeted. It is calculated as the **difference between the budgeted and actual production levels, valued at the standard absorption rate per unit**.

(ii) **Capacity utilisation variation**

The **fixed production overhead capacity utilisation variance** measures the over- or under-absorption of fixed production overhead costs caused by the actual hours worked differing from the hours originally budgeted to be worked. It is calculated as the **difference between actual hours of work and budgeted hours of work, valued at the standard absorption rate per hour**.

(iii) **Efficiency variance**

The **fixed production overhead efficiency variance** measures the over- or under-absorption of fixed production overhead costs caused by actual labour efficiency differing from the standard level of labour efficiency. It is calculated as the **difference between the number of hours that actual production should have taken and the number of hours taken, valued at the standard absorption cost per hour**.

Example

Let's consider a simple **example**. Suppose that the budgeted fixed overhead for a month is £500,000 and the budgeted output is 2,000 units, each unit requiring 10 labour hours. The overhead absorption rate is therefore £250 per unit or £25 per hour. If the actual output in a month is 1,600 units and the actual hours worked are 16,400 then the variances are calculated as follows.

Fixed production overhead volume variance = (2,000 – 1,600) units × £250 = £100,000 (A)

Fixed production overhead capacity utilisation variance = (20,000 – 16,400) hours × £25 = £90,000 (A)

Fixed production overhead efficiency variance = (16,000 – 16,400) hours × £25 = £10,000 (A)

Dividing the volume variance

The fixed overhead variance is divided into capacity and efficiency variances because the actual production volume used to calculate the fixed production overhead **volume variance** is a **function of the labour hours worked (i.e. capacity) and the efficiency with which the labour hours are used**. The two sub-variances are meant to **highlight** variations from budget in terms of both the **availability** and the **efficiency** of direct labour.

Limitations of dividing the volume variance

The volume variances can only be calculated in an absorption costing system and the **limitations** of dividing it into the sub-variances are those which are inherent in absorption costing.

(i) Fixed overhead costs **are treated** as if they **are variable** (in relation to labour hours).

EXAM ANSWER BANK

(ii) The analysis concentrates on the effect of **only one input** (labour) when others, such as machine hours, may have a significant impact.

(iii) The measures may **encourage managers** to **over-produce** in order to achieve favourable volume variances. For example, labour may be used to produce output for stock (which may never be required) rather than being left idle. This could waste both materials and power.

Investigating the component variances

(i) **Capacity variance**

The management accountant, when investigating **capacity variances**, needs to find out **why more (or less) labour was available than budgeted**. Was it due to budgeting error, to non-standard sickness or absence or labour turnover, to under- or over-recruitment, to excessive overtime, to a fall or increase in demand or perhaps to a strike? Hence, investigation of both the payroll and production records is required, along with discussions with the HR department and production supervisors.

(ii) **Efficiency variance**

If the organisation operates in a jobbing or batch production environment, the **efficiency variance** may be isolated on a job-by-job basis. Jobs which have a significantly higher or lower efficiency variance can be investigated in collaboration with **production supervisors**. **Production records** can also be used to identify whether **idle time** levels were significantly different from standard. The management accountant should check whether the **mix of labour** (between experienced and less experienced staff) differs from standard. S/he should also check with production supervisors whether factors such as poor quality material, machine failures or excessive reworking may have contributed to the efficiency variance.

9 TF

> **Top tips.** Even though there is not reams of information to absorb from this question, it required **careful reading**. The system under consideration is a **responsibility accounting system** rather than a budgetary control or standard costing system more frequently included in examination question scenarios. It would therefore be **inappropriate to refer to nothing but standards and/or variances** (although you could explain that only variances over which a manager has control should be included in any responsibility accounting system report). A responsibility accounting report could show divisional profit, for example, or the actual controllable costs incurred by a cost centre. Note, however, that budgetary control and standard costing systems can be part of a responsibility accounting system.
>
> And did you use a **report format**? If this were the exam you would have thrown away a vital mark or two if you had simply produced an essay.
>
> It's a good idea to use the questions raised by the managing director as the framework for your report, covering each question in turn. The second question is probably the most difficult to answer; you will probably need to provide simple **examples** to get your points across.

REPORT

To: The managing director
From: The management accountant
Date: xx.xx.xx
Subject: **Responsibility accounting system**

This report addresses the issues you have raised in respect of the proposed computerised responsibility accounting system.

Why does the report highlight controllable cost and profit?

A **responsibility centre** is a part of the organisation, the performance of which is the responsibility of a specific manager. **Controllable costs** are those which can be **influenced by the manager of the responsibility centre**. If the manager is also able to influence the centre's revenues then the resulting profits are referred to as controllable profits.

There are two main **reasons why such controllable items are highlighted.**

(a) **Busy managers' attention should be drawn to the areas over which it is possible to exercise control.** If managers cannot influence certain items, the report should not give prominence to these uncontrollable items. The result is that managers can quickly focus their attention on the most important information in the report.

(b) The report could have a negative motivational impact if managers feel that their performance is being judged based on factors which are outside their control. Highlighting controllable items and monitoring performance based on these factors will improve the motivational impact of the report.

How does one determine which costs are controllable?

Each cost should be considered separately in order to decide whether or not a responsibility centre manager is able to influence it and hence control it. A few examples should help to illustrate the considerations involved.

(a) Most **variable costs** within a division are usually controllable in the short term because managers can influence the efficiency with which resources are used.

(b) **Fixed costs** such as depreciation, rent and salaries are controllable if the divisional manager has influence over the factors which cause them to be incurred. For example, if the manager has the authority to decide whether or not to invest in a fixed asset then depreciation is a controllable cost. If the manager decides which premises to occupy and which staff to hire, then rent and salaries are controllable costs, and so on.

(c) **Discretionary fixed costs** such as advertising, training costs and consultancy fees may initially be authorised as a result of top management decisions, but the actual incurring of the expenditure may be within the control of the responsibility centre manager.

(d) **Apportioned costs of the central sales department** would have to be considered individually. The general rule is that any cost over which the manager has some influence is controllable. For example, it may be the responsibility of the sales department manager to control sales costs within budget allowances, but the sales costs in total will be partly fixed and partly variable, and the variable cost element will depend on the volume of demand for the sales department's services. If a particular division has some very demanding customers who require a great deal of sales effort we might expect higher sales costs, and the relevant divisional manager should therefore be made accountable for the extra sales costs that the central sales department incurs on the division's behalf.

What are cost centres, profit centres and investment centres?

Cost centres, profit centres and investment centres are all types of **responsibility centre**. The main difference between them lies in the amount of responsibility given to the manager of the centre.

A **cost centre** is a responsibility centre where the manager is responsible only for the costs incurred by the centre. Cost centres form the basis for building up cost records for cost measurement, budgeting and control.

A **profit centre** is a responsibility centre to which it is possible to assign revenues as well as costs, so that the profitability of the centre's activities can be determined. The revenues might come from external sales or from internal sales to other profit centres, or from work done for them, for which a notional selling price (a transfer price) can be charged.

Where a divisional manager is allowed some discretion about the amount of investment undertaken by the division, for example in working capital and fixed assets, the profit earned by the division can be related to the amount of capital invested. This type of centre is known as an **investment centre** and its performance can be measured by its return on investment (ROI).

What benefits are to be gained from a system of responsibility accounting?

The benefits to be gained from a system of responsibility accounting include the following.

(a) Each responsibility centre manager receives information on the performance of the centre so that they are aware of what is happening to all of the items within their area of authority.

(b) Management attention can be focused where action is needed by highlighting controllable items within the report.

(c) Senior managers have a basis for monitoring and rewarding the performance of the divisional managers.

(d) The authority to act to improve performance, combined with a well-designed reward structure linked to the system of responsibility accounting, can act as a valuable motivator to responsibility centre managers.

If you would like to discuss any of these items in more detail please do not hesitate to contact me.

10 Freewheel

> **Top tips.** It's a good idea to draw up **proformas** to begin with, into which you can insert figures either directly from the information in the question straight away or from each working as you complete it. The balance sheet will have the same format as the one in the question. Take care with the cash budget and budgeted profit and loss account and leave spaces until you are sure what the various expenses, payments and so on will be.
>
> Careful layout of **workings** is of paramount importance. Never try to insert figures directly into the budgets without careful working, as you run the risk of missing things out.
>
> Take the receipts from sales working, for example. By noting the total sales each month to begin with, you can then work on a month-by-month basis inserting the cash figure and credit figure under the appropriate month. For example, the receipts from the £27,600 of sales made in August are received half in August as cash (£13,800) and half in October when the debtors pay two months after the sales are made. If you had read through the question in advance you would know that a debtors figure is required (for the balance sheet) and this can also be noted on the same working (50% of November's and December's sales).
>
> Remember that when you have **receipts or payments in different time periods to when the sales are made or the goods received/the labour cost incurred**, there will be **debtors and creditors**. Creditors are also incurred on the purchase of fixed assets (as in this question), not just on purchases for production.
>
> One of the reasons for asking you to prepare both a cash budget and a budgeted profit and loss account is to see whether you appreciate the fact that the **cash budget** is prepared on a **receipts/payments basis, the profit and loss account** on an **accruals basis**. So don't make the mistake of adding up the receipts/payments in the cash budget and including the totals as the sales/purchases/expenses figures in the profit and loss account. The other reason is to determine whether you know not to include **certain non-cash items** like depreciation in the cash budget.
>
> You are unlikely not to be asked to provide some sort of **analysis** of the budgets you have prepared, as in (b) here. Budgets are a form of **feedforward control**, giving management the opportunity to take control action now in an attempt to ensure actual results turn out as planned.

EXAM ANSWER BANK

(a) (i) **CASH BUDGET JULY TO DECEMBER 20X2**

	July £	Aug £	Sept £	Oct £	Nov £	Dec £
Receipts						
From sales (W1)	25,500	26,400	27,900	33,800	29,600	32,000
Share issue	–	–	20,000	–	–	–
	25,500	26,400	47,900	33,800	29,600	32,000
Payments						
Purchases (W2)	12,000	13,000	14,000	18,000	16,000	14,000
Wages/salaries (W3)	8,000	9,500	10,000	10,000	11,500	12,000
Overheads	7,000	7,000	7,000	7,000	8,000	8,000
Fixed assets (W5)	–	–	–	–	–	10,000
	27,000	29,500	31,000	35,000	35,500	44,000
Excess of receipts over payments	(1,500)	(3,100)	16,900	(1,200)	(5,900)	(12,000)
Balance b/f	3,000	1,500	(1,600)	15,300	14,100	8,200
Balance c/f	1,500	(1,600)	15,300	14,100	8,200	(3,800)

(ii) **BUDGETED PROFIT AND LOSS ACCOUNT JULY TO DECEMBER 20X2**

	£	£
Sales (W7)		177,800
Less cost of sales		
Opening stock	25,000	
Purchases	86,000	
Closing stock	(38,000)	
		(73,000)
Gross profit		104,800
Less expenses		
Wages and salaries	62,000	
Overheads	45,000	
Depreciation (W8)	8,500	
		(115,500)
Net loss		(10,700)
Profit and loss account balance b/f		44,600
Profits available for appropriation		33,900
Less dividends		(10,000)
Profit and loss account balance c/f		23,900

(iii) **BUDGETED BALANCE SHEET AS AT 31 DECEMBER 20X2**

	Cost £	Provision for depreciation £	Net book value £
Fixed assets	170,000	22,500	147,500
Current assets			
Stock	38,000		
Trade debtors (W1)	27,200		
		65,200	
Current liabilities			
Bank overdraft	3,800		
Trade creditors (W2)	24,000		
Other creditors (W9)	41,000		
		(68,800)	
Net current assets			(3,600)
Total assets less current liabilities			143,900

Capital and reserves
  Share capital   120,000
  Profit and loss account   23,900
    143,900

Workings

1. **Receipts from sales**

	May £'000	June £'000	July £'000	Aug £'000	Sept £'000	Oct £'000	Nov £'000	Dec £'000	Debtors £'000
Total	24.0	25.2	27.0	27.6	28.8	40.0	30.4	24.0	NA
Cash	12.0	12.6	13.5	13.8	14.4	20.0	15.2	12.0	NA
Credit	NA	NA	12.0	12.6	13.5	13.8	14.4	20.0	*27.2
Receipts	NA	NA	25.5	26.4	27.9	33.8	29.6	32.0	

*(£15,200 + £12,000)

2. **Purchases**

	May £'000	June £'000	July £'000	Aug £'000	Sept £'000	Oct £'000	Nov £'000	Dec £'000	Creditors £'000
Purchases	12	13	14	18	16	14	12	12	NA
Payment	NA	NA	12	13	14	18	16	14	*24

*(£12,000 + £12,000)

3. **Wages and salaries**

	June £'000	July £'000	Aug £'000	Sept £'000	Oct £'000	Nov £'000	Dec £'000	Creditors £'000
Total incurred	8	8	10	10	10	12	12	NA
75%	NA	6	7.5	7.5	7.5	9.0	9	NA
25%	NA	2	2.0	2.5	2.5	2.5	3	3
		8	9.5	10.0	10.0	11.5	12	

4. **Overheads**

Creditor at December of £8,000

5. **Fixed assets**

	November £'000	December £'000	Creditor £'000
Purchase	30		
Payment		10	
Creditor			20

6. **Dividends**

Declared October and therefore paid in January and to creditor at December of £10,000

7. **Sales**

    £
(4,500 + 4,600 + 4,800) × £6 =   83,400
(5,000 + 3,800 + 3,000) × £8 =   94,400
    177,800

8. **Depreciation**

    £
Assets owned at 30 June 20X2   140,000
Additions   30,000
    170,000

Depreciation = £170,000 × 10% × 0.5 =   £8,500

	9	**Other creditors**	
			£'000
		Wages and salaries (W3)	3
		Overheads (W4)	8
		Fixed assets (W5)	20
		Dividend (W6)	10
			41

(b) (i) The cash budget shows that there will be an overdraft at the end of August and at the end of December, despite the share issue in September. Payments in January and February 20X2 for the fixed asset and the payment of the dividend in January will only increase the overdraft. **Sufficient overdraft facilities must therefore be arranged or other action**, such as a reversal of the decision to purchase the fixed asset, should be considered.

(ii) A **reduction in sales quantities** in November and December results in a net loss of £10,700. If such a reduction is not part of a plan then ways of either cutting costs or increasing sales must be considered.

(iii) **Stock** at the end of the period represents three months' purchases whereas stock at the beginning of the period represents two months' purchases. If this is due to the reduction in sales quantities then it may be advisable to reduce purchases if the drop in sales is unavoidable.

11 Presentation

> **Top tips.** The comparison of the actual results for 4,500 units with the budget data for 5,000 units is not particularly useful for the general manager. It is not possible to tell whether cost and revenue differences are caused by changes in activity or by changes in expenditure. So in part (a), a flexible budget presentation would be more relevant, presented **in marginal costing format** (showing variable costs, contribution and fixed costs) to highlight the more easily controlled variable costs. **Variable costs are flexed** by a ratio of 4,500/5,000. **Fixed costs do not change**.
>
> The variances required in part (b) are calculated on marginal costing principles given that marginal costing was used in part (a). This means that there will be **no fixed overhead volume capacity and efficiency variances** as these two variances explain the reasons for under– or over-absorbed fixed production overhead, which cannot arise with marginal costing. The other main difference compared with absorption costing is that **the sales volume variance is valued at standard contribution per unit** (a figure that you need to calculate!).
>
> To **reconcile actual results against the flexed budget does not require** the inclusion of the **sales volume variance** as the very process of flexing has removed any differences in volume (both the flexed budget and actual results being based on the actual volume). Once the sales volume variance is included, however, a reconciliation between actual results and the original budget is possible.
>
> You might have been thrown by the fact that it was not possible to analyse the direct material cost variance into price and usage components but you simply did not have the appropriate information.
>
> The key points for part (c) are that the use of **marginal costing** principles **highlights contribution**, which is a **more-easily controllable** performance measure, and that the use of a **flexible budget** provides more **realistic targets**.

(a)

	Original budget for 5,000 units £'000	Flexed budget for 4,500 units £'000	Actual result £'000	Variance against flexed budget £'000
Sales	600	540.0	550	10
less variable costs				
Direct materials	150	135.0	130	5.0
Direct labour	200	180.0	189	(9.0)
Production overhead	50	45.0	46	(1.0)
Selling overhead	75	67.5	72	(4.5)
Total variable cost	475	427.5	437	(9.5)
Contribution	125	112.5	113	0.5
less fixed overhead:				
Production	25	25.0	29	(4.0)
Selling	50	50.0	46	4.0
Profit	50	37.5	38	0.5

(Direct materials, Direct labour, Production overhead, Selling overhead in original budget column bracketed together with $\times \dfrac{4,500}{5,000}$)

Note. Variances in brackets are adverse.

(b) *Workings*

1 **Standard contribution per unit**

	For 5,000 units	£ per unit
Sales price	£600,000	120
Direct materials	£150,000	30
Direct labour	£200,000	40
Variable production overhead	£50,000	10
Variable selling overhead	£75,000	15
Standard contrib'n per unit		25

2 Standard labour rate per hour = £200,000/50,000 = £4 per hour

3 Standard variable production overhead per hour = £50,000/50,000 = £1 per hour

Variances (*Note.* Variances in brackets are adverse)

Variance against flexed budget

(i) **Selling price variance**

	£	£
Margin on 4,500 units should have been	112,500	
but was (£(550,000 – 427,500))	122,500	
		10,000

(ii) **Direct material cost variance**

No further analysis than that in (a) possible — 5,000

(iii) **Direct labour rate variance**

	£
47,500 hrs should cost (× £4)	190,000
but did cost	189,000
	1,000

Direct labour efficiency variance

4,500 units should have taken (× 10 hrs)	45,000 hrs	
but did take	47,500 hrs	
Variance in hours	2,500 hrs	
× standard rate per hour	× £4	
		(10,000)

(iv) **Variable production overhead efficiency variance**

2,500 hrs × standard rate per hour (× £1)   (2,500)

Variable production overhead expenditure variance

	£	
47,500 hrs should cost (× £1)	47,500	
but did cost	46,000	
		1,500

(v) **Variable selling overhead expenditure variance**

	£	
4,500 units should cost (× £15)	67,500	
but did cost	72,000	
		(4,500)

Total contribution variance   500

(vi) Fixed production overhead expenditure variance

= budget expenditure − actual expenditure
= £(25,000 − 29,000)   (4,000)

(vii) Fixed selling overhead expenditure variance

= budget expenditure − actual expenditure
= £(50,000 − 46,000)   4,000

Profit variance against flexed budget   500

(viii) Sales volume variance

= [actual units − budget units] × std contribution/unit
= (4,500 − 5,000) × £25   (12,500)

Variance against original budget   (12,000)

REPORT

(c) To: General manager
From: Management accountant
Date: 1 January 20Y1
Subject: **The principles upon which the redrafted statement is based**

As requested, I outline below the principles upon which the redrafted statement is based and the information it provides.

(i) **Marginal costing principles**

The report has been prepared using marginal costing principles. Marginal costing highlights the **variable costs**, which may be **more controllable than the fixed costs**.

The report concentrates management attention on **contribution**, which is often the more easily controlled performance measure. The contribution is so called because it contributes towards fixed costs and profits.

(ii) **Flexible budget principles**

The report has also used flexible budget principles. Flexible budgets use the available knowledge about **cost behaviour patterns** to 'flex' the budget. The resulting flexed budget contains **more realistic targets** for costs and revenues at the actual activity level for the period.

The report thus enables managers to **compare like with like**. There is little to be gained by comparing the actual costs and revenues for 4,500 units with the budget figures for 5,000 units. It would not be possible to tell which differences were caused by the volume change, and which were caused by over– and under-spending.

The most important piece of information in the re-drafted budget statement is the **large variance caused by the volume shortfall**. The net profit from sales was only £500 different from the flexed budget, but the large volume shortfall caused a major reduction of £12,500 in the profit result when compared with the original budget.

If I can provide any further information, please do not hesitate to contact me.

12 Budgets and people

> **Top tips.** You are **unlikely to get a full question on the behavioural aspects of budgeting**. The issue is more likely to be examined in the context of a wider question on budgeting. Under the old syllabus equivalent to Paper 2.4, the topic tended to appear in requirements worth five marks.
>
> It is well worth attempting this 25-mark question, however, as it covers a wide range of the possible issues that you could encounter. Make sure that you **deal with both parts** of the question (the reasons for reluctance and the side effects of imposed budgets). Beware, however, of writing down everything you can possibly think of which is remotely related to the behavioural aspects of management accounting.

There is one major **reason why managers may be reluctant to participate** fully in setting up budgets and that is a **lack of education in the purposes of the budgeting process**. The budget's major role is to communicate the various motivations that exist among management so that everybody sees, understands and co-ordinates the goals of the organisation.

Specific reasons for the reluctance of managers to participate are as follows.

(a) Managers view budgets as **too rigid a constraint on their decision making.** For example, a manager may be unable to sanction an item of expenditure if it has not been budgeted for. The natural reaction to this supposed restriction of their autonomy is resistance and self defence.

(b) Managers feel that the top management **goals expressed by the budget will interfere with their personal goals** (for example their desire to 'build an empire' with substantial resources under their control, large personal income and so on). A successful budgetary system will harmonise the budget goals with the managers' personal goals, but it is by no means easy to achieve a successful system.

(c) Managers imagine that the purpose of budgets is to provide senior management with a **rod** with which to chastise those who do not stay within budget. They will be unwilling to help in the construction of such a rod.

(d) Managers view the budgeting process as one in which they must **fight for a fair share** of the organisation's **resources** in competition with colleagues with other responsibilities.

(e) Managers misinterpret the **control function** of the budgeting system to be a method whereby **blame** can be **attached**. By not participating in the budget setting process, they are able to blame an 'unattainable' or 'unrealistic' budget for any poor results they may have.

As a reaction to these uneducated notions, the behaviour of managers involved in budget preparation can conflict with the desires of senior management. Such behaviour is often described as **dysfunctional**; it is counter-productive because it is **not goal congruent.**

The **unwanted side effects** which may arise from the **imposition of budgets** by senior management (for example under an authoritative rather than a participative budgetary system) are examples of **dysfunctional behaviour** and include the following.

(a) There may be a **reluctance to reduce costs** for fear that future budget allowances may be reduced as a consequence of successful cost cutting.

(b) Managers may **spend up to their budget** in order to justify levels of expenditure. This is particularly the case in local government circles where there is a tendency to spend any available cash at the end of a financial year.

(c) There may be **padding**, whereby managers request inflated allowances. In turn senior management may cut budgets where they suspect padding exists. Padding is sometimes called slack and represents the difference between the budget allowance requested and the realistic costs necessary to accomplish the objective.

(d) In extreme cases of authoritative budgeting, the **'emotional' responses** of managers can be highly detrimental to the goals of the organisation, for example non-cooperation.

13 Rolling

> **Top tips.** The alternative approaches to budgeting are likely to be **examined as part of a wider question on budgeting**. For that reason we have not included a full question.
>
> Such parts of questions on non-core topics and techniques are often **'stand alone'**, in that they are not totally integrated within the main questions. They are therefore very important, as they provide you with the opportunity to **pick up marks** on questions even if you have struggled with the main requirement such as the preparation of a flexible or cash budget.
>
> You should have had little trouble with this question as it basically required you to regurgitate book knowledge. You are unlikely to be able to do this in the exam as you will probably have to apply your knowledge of, say, rolling budgets, to a particular scenario.
>
> In an exam **never provide more examples**/advantages/problems **than the number requested.** You are simply wasting your time as only the specified number will earn you marks, the additional ones will be ignored.

(a) A **rolling budget** is a budget which is **continuously updated** by adding a further accounting period (a month or quarter) when the earlier accounting period has expired. They are particularly **beneficial** when **future costs and/or activities cannot be forecast** with any degree of accuracy.

(b) The **system** operates as follows.

  (i) A budget is prepared for the year ahead, broken down into suitable control periods (months or quarters).

  (ii) At the end of the first control period, a comparison is made between that period's results and budget. The conclusions drawn are used to amend the budgets for the remaining control periods and to add a budget for a further period, so that the company once again has budgets available for a year ahead.

  (iii) The process is repeated at the end of each control period.

(c) **Advantages** of a rolling budget system (three required)

    (i) Budgets can be more realistic since they are continuously updated in the light of changing circumstances.

    (ii) The arbitrary and artificial distinction between one financial year and the next is avoided, since budgets are always available for a year ahead.

    (iii) The periodic disruption associated with annual budgeting is avoided.

    (iv) Management feels more accountable because of the frequent review of budgets and the fact that budgets are more realistic.

(d) **Problems** likely to be encountered (three required)

    (i) Greater work-load: will adequate staff be available; will management devote sufficient attention to preparing budgets which they know will shortly be revised?

    (ii) If a standard costing system is in operation in conjunction with the budgetary control system, frequent changes of standard are necessitated.

    (iii) Advantage (iii) above is only partly true as longer-term plans are still required.

    (iv) What time period should be chosen as the control period? Monthly comparison of actual/budget will provide greater management control but can such frequent updating of budgets be justified in terms of the extra work involved?

14 Domestic appliance

Top tips. We think it unlikely that you will get a 25-mark question on forecasting. In the old syllabus version of Paper 2.4, forecasting was always examined as part of a wider question on budgeting usually for about five marks. There is no guarantee that this pattern will continue, however, so you are well advised to attempt this forecasting question.

You are provided with the formula for r in the exam, so in part (a) you simply need to calculate r and square it. It **does not matter which variable you choose for x and which you choose for y when calculating r**, as you are simply determining the strength of the correlation between them. You choice does matter when it comes to **working out the values of a and b in a regression line**, however. The **independent variable must be x, the dependent variable y**. The question requires a regression equation that predicts insurance policy sales from deflated appliance sales, so the **dependent variable is policy sales as it depends on the level of appliance sales for its value**.

Take note of the units you are working in. We worked in £ millions and hundreds of policies, which means that we inserted a figure of 51 in the regression equation to represent sales of £51 million. Our prediction of 28.613 means 28.613 × 100 = 2,861 policies.

(a)

Appliance sales	Policy sales			
x	y	x^2	y^2	xy
£m	Hundreds			
3	4	9	16	12
5	3	25	9	15
7	6	49	36	42
10	12	100	144	120
15	17	225	289	255
18	22	324	484	396
26	21	676	441	546
84	85	1,408	1,419	1,386

The formula for r is provided in the exam.

$$r = \frac{n\Sigma xy - \Sigma x \Sigma y}{\sqrt{[n\Sigma x^2 - (\Sigma x)^2][n\Sigma y^2 - (\Sigma y)^2]}}$$

$$r^2 = \frac{(7 \times 1{,}386 - 84 \times 85)^2}{(7 \times 1{,}408 - 84^2)(7 \times 1{,}419 - 85^2)} = 0.87$$

This shows that **87% of the variation in policy sales is explained by variation in appliance sales**.

(b) For a regression line y = a + bx

$$b = \frac{n\Sigma xy - \Sigma x \Sigma y}{n\Sigma x^2 - (\Sigma x)^2} \text{ and } a = \frac{\Sigma y}{n} - \frac{b\Sigma x}{n}$$

$$\therefore b = \frac{7 \times 1{,}386 - 84 \times 85}{7 \times 1{,}408 - 84^2} = 0.915$$

$$\therefore a = \frac{85}{7} - 0.915 \times \frac{84}{7} = 1.163$$

y = 1.163 + 0.915x

Note that y is in hundreds of policies and x in millions of pounds.

(c) Predicted policy sales

= 1.163 + 0.915 × 51 = 47.828 = 4,783 policies

(d) This prediction is based on the **assumption** that there is a **linear relationship** between appliance sales and policy sales. In fact, a non-linear relationship may exist, and there could well be other influences on policy sales.

15 Weighted index

Top tips. You are unlikely to get a full 25 mark question on this area but indexes may be worth 6 – 7 marks in a part question.

(a)

Product	Year 1 '000 units sold	Year 1 Selling price per unit £	Year 1 Total revenue £'000	Year 2 '000 units sold	Year 2 Selling price per unit £	Year 2 Total revenue £'000
A	76	0.60	45.6	72	0.78	56.16
B	52	0.75	39.0	60	1.00	60.00
C	28	1.10	30.8	40	1.32	52.80
			115.4			168.96

% increase = $\frac{168.96 - 115.4}{115.4} \times 100\% = 46.41\%$

(b) Laspeyre price index for Year 5 based on Year 1

$$= \frac{\Sigma p_n q_0}{\Sigma p_0 q_0} \times 100$$

where p_0, q_0 = prices/quantities in Year 1 and p_n = prices in Year 5.
$\Sigma p_0 q_0$ = total revenue for Year 1 = £115,400 (from (i) above)
$\Sigma p_n q_0$ = (£0.78 × 76,000) + (£1.00 × 52,000) + (£1.32 × 28,000) = £148,240

∴ Laspeyre price index for Year 5 based on Year 1

$$= \frac{148,240}{115,400} \times 100 = 128.46$$

(Alternatively your answer could be given as 1.2846)

(c) Price increases in the five-year period caused total sales revenue to increase by 28.46%. The remaining increase (46.41% − 28.46% = 17.95%) is due to changes in sales volume and sales mix. The volume of total units sold increased by 10.26% (((172,000 − 156,000)/156,000) × 100) and the proportion of the mix comprising the two highest priced products increased (the proportion comprising the lowest priced product obviously decreasing).

16 CM

Top tips. A relatively straightforward question provided you were able to relate your answers to CM Limited.

Benchmarking

Benchmarking can be described as a technique whereby an organisation tries to **emulate or exceed the standards achieved or processes adopted by another organisation**, generally a very successful one. Benchmarking exercises usually reveal improvements and benefits for both sides.

The 'model' organisation could be a direct competitor — ideally one that is acknowledged to be 'best in class' (**competitive benchmarking**). But this is not always the case. Indeed it might be difficult to persuade a direct competitor to part with any information which is useful for comparison purposes.

Functional benchmarking, whereby internal functions are compared with those of the **best external practitioners of those functions, regardless of the industry** they are in, does not always involve direct competitors. For instance a railway company may be identified as the 'best' in terms of on-board catering, and an airline company that operates on different routes could seek opportunities to improve by sharing information and comparing their own operations with those of the railway company.

CM Limited and benchmarking

CM Limited manufactures and sells business equipment and so could consider **benchmarking** its goods inwards, stores, production, stock holding, order taking and delivery **processes** with a **similar organisation** operating in a **different geographical market**. **Alternatively** it could benchmark against a manufacturer of **electrical white goods** operating in the same geographical market.

The benchmarking process should lead **to improved and more efficient processes** and **challenging but achievable** (because they have been already, by another organisation) **targets**. Improvements in internal processes would affect **the internal perspective** of the balanced scorecard; benchmarks which assess how well CM Limited is satisfying customers would impact on the **customer perspective**; any necessary staff training highlighted by the exercise would result in changes to the measures in the **innovation and learning perspective**.

In the **short term**, there may be an **adverse impact** on the **financial perspective** in terms of cash flow but, in the **medium to long term**, the effect of improvements will cause CM Limited's **financial position to improve**.

17 Corporate objectives

> **Top tips.** You may well get a part question on objectives in your exam, and the topic may need to be brought into discussions in other areas, for example how well does an investment that you have appraised fit in with the company's objectives.
>
> The question is answered with a clear structure:
>
> (a) The **extent** to which profit maximisation is the primary corporate objective
> (b) The **problems** with the objective
> (c) Other **financial** objectives
> (d) Other **non-financial** objectives
>
> The question is confined to what the directors of the company should seek. In practice they may pursue other objectives that are in their own, but not necessarily the company's best interests, for example maximisation of their own rewards.
>
> You were only allocated twenty minutes to answer the question, which is typical of the sort of timescale that you would get in the exam. The scope of the question is quite wide for the length of time available, so you must make sure your answer has sufficient breadth, and you do not spend all your time discussing profit maximisation.

As a general rule, increases in a company's profits will be in the interests of the shareholders. However, the maximisation of profits should not be the only goal, and it may be beneficial to aim for profits below the maximum possible.

The limitations of profit as a measure of performance

The profits shown in a company's accounts are not a wholly objective measure of the company's performance. The final figure depends on policies chosen on, for example, depreciation and the writing off of development expenditure. In the short term, profits can be increased by capitalising development expenditure, but such policies do not really increase the company's worth.

It is very hard to work out what profit could have been attained. **Comparisons** with an **industry average** may be useful, but comparisons with exceptional performers **in the industry** may be inappropriate. Profits need to be adjusted to reflect the **resources** used to earn them. A company which doubles its capital and increases its profits by 50% has probably done badly, not well.

Profits are computed annually, with half-yearly interim results. Investments which are highly profitable in the long term but are loss-makers initially could be rejected if management is concerned only with next year's profits.

Alternative financial objectives

A company must ensure its **financial stability** both in the short term and in the long term. Targets for the **reduction of gearing** or the **retention of profits** may therefore be appropriate. Of key importance is the solvency of the company. Profitable investments must be rejected if the expenditure required would leave the company unable to pay its debts.

Non-financial objectives

A company's directors may legitimately take into account a range of **non-financial objectives**, including the welfare of employees and of society, the provision of a service to the public and environmental goals. In some cases the pursuit of such objectives may lead to increased profits, for example when an environmentally responsible company attracts customers who share such concerns.

18 Market efficiency

> **Top tips.** The efficient market hypothesis may be the subject of a part question in 2.4. An answer focusing on a technical concept should always start with a clear definition of that concept, including as appropriate the key assumptions. Here the answer goes on to discuss the various forms of the efficient market hypothesis, concentrating on the differences between them (the amount of information available).
>
> It is also important when discussing a theory that attempts to model actual behaviour to bring in evidence of how much it applies in practice. Here that is a key distinction between the strong form and other forms.
>
> If a theory does not appear to work in practice, you need to indicate why this might be so, or at least that there is no obvious explanation why the theory does not work. Here the strong form hypothesis does not work, so you consider why when discussing the hypothesis. In addition there is the general point that some financial institutions do perform better than expected. Because this applies to all forms of the efficient market hypothesis, and because the subject is highlighted in the question you need a separate paragraph covering why performance of financial institutions might deviate from what is anticipated.
>
> Generally written questions will benefit from a conclusion that sums up the answer and is supported by the preceding discussion.

The **efficient market hypothesis** contends that some capital markets (in the UK and US for instance) are 'efficient markets' in which the prices at which securities are traded reflect all the **relevant information** available. In other words, this information is freely available to all participants in the market and is fully reflected in share prices. Further, it is assumed that **transaction costs** are **insignificant** and do not discourage trading in shares, and that no single individual or group of individuals dominates the market.

The theory exists in three forms: weak form, semi-strong form and strong form.

Weak form efficiency

Weak form efficiency contends that prices only change when new factual information becomes available. Information about past prices is in the public domain and equally available to all players in the market, and thus if this form of the hypothesis is correct, no one player should be able to outperform the market consistently. Thus the fact that financial institutions rarely outperform the market on a regular basis lends weight to this form of the theory.

Semi strong efficiency

The semi-strong form of the theory holds that in addition to responding to information that is publicly available, the market also reflects all other knowledge that is publicly available and relevant to the share valuation. Thus to take the example used above, the share prices of companies involved in a takeover bid will change in **advance of the bid** being **formally announced** as the market anticipates the bid. Once again, this form of the theory is based upon the assumption that all the knowledge upon which share price movements are based is in **the public domain** and **freely available**. Thus no single player or group of players should be able consistently to outperform the market. This form of the theory is supported by empirical research which suggests that share price movements do anticipate merger announcements. The fact that the neither the financial institutions nor any other group of investors regularly beat the market also supports this version of the hypothesis.

Strong form efficiency

The strong form of the theory holds that the market price of securities reflects **all information** that is **available**. This includes knowledge of past performance and anticipated events as in the semi-strong form, and also **'insider' knowledge** not publicly available. This form can be tested by investigating the effect on the share price of the effect of releasing a piece of information previously confidential to the firm; if the strong form of the hypothesis is valid, then this should already be factored into the share value and a significant price movement should not result. The implication is that this sort of information is only available to specialists who are in regular contact with the company, such as investment trust managers, and that as a result they could use their privileged position to outperform other investors. Empirical work suggests that this form of the hypothesis is not valid, and this is what one would expect since insider dealing is illegal in the UK.

Why institutions may perform well

If an institution **does consistently perform well**, it is probably more related to the fund managers' understanding of the structure of the industries and markets in which they invest, and their ability to hold a more widely diversified portfolio than the small investor. This means that they are in a better position to avoid the risk of large losses. The fact that they are in daily contact with the markets also means that they are in practice able to react more quickly to new information that becomes available than is the small investor.

Conclusion

Thus the fact that the financial institutions in general do **not consistently outperform** the **market supports** both the weak and semi-strong forms of the efficient market hypothesis.

19 Mixed economy

> **Top tips.** The question asks for an **identification** of general effects. This means that you have to mention a range of effects. This does not mean single line answers, but you should avoid spending too much time discussing individual effects. The fact that you are just asked to identify rather than carry out deeper analysis (discussion or evaluation) indicates the limits of the question-setter's expectations. Your answer should consist of short paragraphs saying just enough to make clear to the reader how the effects described will impact on businesses.
>
> If you are asked about the general impact of government policy, consider the following areas:
>
> - **Effect on profits**. This means effects on income (sales and also government grants). The impact on costs (especially wage and raw material costs) is critical.
>
> - **Taxation implications**. These will affect the level of profits directly (through the taxing of those profits) and may also impact through the effects on consumer and investor behaviour.
>
> - **Effect on capital structure**. This not only includes effects on the cost of capital, but also the impact upon the supply of funds (a favourite topic of the examiner).
>
> - **Business environment effects**. This includes wider effects such as impact upon competitive environment or company ownership.
>
> You will not get a full question on this subject area but the last part of a question may ask you to discuss the effects of a change in government policy on a specific firm. This will imply a more specific answer than we have given here, because the information you are given in the question should tell you that certain considerations will not apply. (For example a company that deals only with the private sector will not be directly affected by a reduction in government expenditure, as the government does not buy any of its goods.)

(a) **Minimising government borrowing requirements**

   (i) A lower public sector borrowing requirement (PSBR) will **reduce the total market demand** for **long term funds**, since the government's demand for funds will be lower. This could result (through supply and demand) in lower long-term interest rates, and so make it cheaper for businesses to raise long-term debt capital.

   (ii) In theory, if long-term debt capital is cheaper, a company's **overall cost of capital** should **fall**, and so companies might be encouraged to invest in more marginal capital expenditure projects.

(iii) Since investors, particularly institutional investors, might be **unable to invest** as much as before in gilts, **more investment capital** might be **diverted into shares**, thus pushing share prices up.

(iv) The purpose of reducing the PSBR *might* be to **control the growth in the money supply**, as a means towards keeping inflation under control. If such a policy is successful, lower inflation would affect **companies' costs and prices**, as well as the general state of the economy.

(v) If the PSBR is reduced to zero, and if the country has a balance of payments deficit on current account, the deficit would have to be financed by **private sector borrowing** from abroad, or by the sale of assets by the private sector. This would have implications for the ownership of some firms in the country and for divestments of foreign subsidiaries.

Reducing tax on incomes

(i) Lower income tax is thought by some economists to provide **greater incentives** to entrepreneurs and employees to **work harder**. If so, the consequences of lower taxes would include more new businesses, greater productivity and stronger industrial growth.

(ii) Lower income taxes would leave consumers with more income after tax. This could be saved, or invested in the stock market. Alternatively, the **extra income** might be **spent**, leading to a growth in consumer spending. Higher consumer spending will increase market demand for firms' goods and services. If a consumer spending boom is too fast, the rate of inflation will increase.

(iii) It is possible that if employees have more after-tax income because of lower taxation, **annual wage settlements** will be **lower** than they otherwise would be, because employees are already better off.

(iv) Lower taxes on the profits of companies will leave companies with **bigger after-tax profits** which they can either **re-invest** or pay out as **dividends**.

(b) **Reductions in public expenditure**

(i) If the government spends less, the firms that supply the government will suffer **a loss of business**; for example, a firm of defence equipment manufacturers might suffer a loss of orders. Firms suffering a loss of business will need to look to other markets for sales growth, perhaps by exporting more. If they fail to do this, their sales turnover and profits will fall.

(ii) A consequence of lower public expenditure is likely to be a **reduction of government assistance** for industry. Grants and subsidies might be cut, and government offices that provide specialist advice to industries might be closed.

(iii) It is conceivable that the cuts in public expenditure might persuade firms to **pay for services or benefits** that have been **lost**. This would increase firms' costs. (For example, a cut in public health services might persuade a firm to spend more on in-house medical services for its employees.)

(iv) Lower government spending will probably create **new competitive opportunities** for firms in the private sector. For example, lower government spending on schools and hospitals will create more market opportunities for private schools, private hospitals, private education funding schemes, medical insurance schemes and so on.

Increases in nationalised industries' prices

(i) While government finances will benefit from the increased revenue, for companies that buy the goods and services of nationalised industries, **higher prices** will **result in higher** production costs. Higher costs in turn mean lower profits, unless they put their own prices up.

(ii) Employees are likely to suffer from the **higher prices** of the **nationalised industries**, and there will be higher annual wage demands.

(iii) If demand for the goods and services of the nationalised industries falls, because of higher prices, **suppliers of materials** and services to the nationalised industries will **suffer a loss of business**. However, they might be able to raise their own unit prices.

(iv) Higher prices from nationalised industries will, in industries where there is private sector competition, make the **goods** of the **private sector firms more competitive**.

Selling nationalised assets

(i) The sale of nationalised assets could result in the creation of a **competitive private sector** market, such as in public transport in parts of the UK in recent years.

(ii) The opportunity might arise for firms to **purchase** some of the **assets** that are being **sold off**, or to **buy shares** in the **privatised business**.

(iii) The government will **benefit** from the **revenue generated** by asset sales. With large privatisations, there might be an effect on the general level of share prices, since the stock market will be flooded with new shares for sale.

(iv) One consequence of privatisation might be **higher prices** for customers. The nationalised industry, just before or just after privatisation, is likely to put up its prices, in order to become more profitable and so be more attractive to investors. This would result in higher costs for firms that buy goods and services from these industries.

(v) A further consequence of privatisation might be a **change in buying policy** by the privatised company, to a more commercial footing. There might, for example, be a greater willingness to buy from abroad. This would have implications for supplier firms.

20 Midsouth Electric

Top tips. In (a) you need to mention the key differences between the two regimes. These are not just differences in **objectives** but also differences in **responsibility** (to shareholders and the regulator rather than the government). At the same time it is important not to give the impression that the public sector will not be concerned with financial targets – a target rate of return will need to be achieved. Therefore also as well as discussing differing objectives, you need to show that some objectives will stay the same – but be more or less important.

(b) signposts the **stakeholders** whose position you need to discuss. If you are asked for a general discussion on stakeholders, those mentioned in (b) will be important, but you would also need to consider other stakeholders whose connections with the organisation are less direct, for example pressure groups or local communities. (c) in fact highlights relationships with the government which itself is a stakeholder.

(b) also indicates key measures that will interest shareholders. It also shows how you need to bring together the various pieces of information you are given in the question. The sales per employee ratio's significant rise, together with the much smaller rise in average wage indicate the possibility of changes in the composition of the labour force.

(b) also brings out the importance of considering a range of plausible explanations. The increase in prices may be explained by reasons other than tougher pricing policies on core activities. It is valid to speculate on other possibilities and go on to say that more information will be required.

EXAM ANSWER BANK

(a) (i) The primary objective prior to privatisation is likely to be to serve the public interest in the best possible way. Associated objectives are likely to include:

(1) Providing a **safe and reliable source of supply** to domestic and industrial consumers

(2) Keeping **supply and distribution costs as low as possible**

(3) Keeping **prices to consumers low**, often in response to political pressures

(4) Achieving the **target rate of return** on investment set for public sector organisations

(5) **Keeping capital expenditure within limits**, particularly during times of restraint on public sector capital investment

(ii) Following transfer to the private sector, the primary financial objective is likely to be the **maximisation** of the **wealth** of the **ordinary shareholders**. Although some of the objectives such as providing a safe and reliable supply of electricity are likely to remain the same after privatisation, the relative importance of the aims is likely to change, and further objectives will be introduced. These are likely to include:

(1) Establishing and maintaining a **good and reliable stream** of **dividends**

(2) Ensuring that the **use of available funds** is **maximised** in order to provide a good return to shareholders and to protect the company against hostile takeover bids

(3) Fulfilling the **requirements** of the **industry regulator**

The demands of the market may mean that there is a greater concern with short-term results to the detriment of long-term investment.

(b) (i) **Shareholders**

It is assumed that shareholders will demand that the company should operate so as to maximise their wealth accruing from the company. This can be measured in terms of the flow of dividends and the movement in the share price. The figures allow the market capitalisation (in £m) to be calculated. For analytical purposes, we use below the figures for alternate years.

	20X2	20X4	20X6
Profit after tax (£m)	52	74	80
P/E ratio	7.5	8.5	9.0
Market capitalisation (£m)	390	629	720
Dividends (£m)	12	17	24

The shareholders have seen a **rise of 84.6%** in the market capitalisation over the last four years together with a doubling in the level of dividends. If it is assumed that this has not involved the raising of additional equity, then this, together with the premium achieved on the first day of trading suggest that the shareholders have done very well out of the issue.

(ii) **Employees**

Sales per employee have risen from £60,700 in 20X2 to £75,400 in 20X6. However, the average salary has risen from £7,714 to £8,030, an increase of 4.1% compared with an increase of 5.8% in the RPI. Over the same period the number employed has fallen by 800, a reduction of 6.9%. The apparently poor rate of increase in remuneration, particularly when compared with the increase in the level of sales per employee, could partly reflect a move to a **less skilled workforce**, or perhaps a **greater proportion of part-time employees.**

The **directors' emoluments** have trebled since before the privatisation, and have doubled since 20X2. It is not known whether the number of directors has increased, or whether this increase has been solely in order to bring their remuneration into line with that in the private sector in order to retain quality management. It is also not known whether they also hold share options which could be a further valuable benefit.

(iii) **Customers**

Customers, as consumers, are primarily concerned with the quality and consistency of supply and the price that they have to pay for it. Information is not available to assess the service quality performance over the period, but the price levels can be evaluated, given that the output of electricity appears to have increased by an average of 2½% per annum.

Figures for alternate years are shown below.

	20X0	20X2	20X4	20X6
Turnover (£m)	760	850	920	995
Projected turnover (£m) taking into account solely the increase in demand (2½% pa)	760	798	839	881
Increase due to price (£m)		52	29	28
Average annual increase in price (%)		3.4	1.8	2.0
Average annual RPI increase (%)		1.5	1.5	1.4

Thus the component of the growth in turnover due to price has been **rising** at an **increasing rate** over the period and at a **rate** in **excess of the rate of inflation**. At first sight this might appear to be due to weak regulation giving a bad deal to consumers, but there could be two other factors at work, as follows.

(1) The company could be **expanding** into **other unregulated areas** which are accounting for the growth in turnover, for example developing its laboratory facilities into a commercial business.

(2) The increase in price could be **needed to fund investment** in improved service quality and reliability of supply. There is no information available on this area.

(c) (i) The figures above suggest that prices have risen above the rate of inflation, although it is not known whether some of this increase is due to expansion into unregulated businesses. If this is the case then the **company** could have been **attempting to cooperate** with the government's desire for low inflation. At the same time, the **price of labour** as calculated above has been **kept very low** with increases below the rate of inflation, although the same has not been true for the directors. The effect of this is to transfer value to the directors and the shareholders rather than to society at large.

(ii) The company has **demonstrated** a **rapid rate of growth** in both turnover and operating profit over the period. The amount of revenue accruing to the government in the form of corporation tax has almost doubled since 20X2 to £19m in 20X6. Capital investment has increased by 2.57 times compared with 20X2 to £90m in 20X6. This will not only benefit the industry, but also the wider economy through the multiplier effect. (It is assumed that the money has not been spent outside the UK.)

21 Gustaffson

Top tips. The eight marks available for (a) is a lot for a definition part question so your description in (a) needs to be fairly full. Although you are directed to describe the symptoms of overtrading, you would have mentioned them even if you had not been asked.

(b) should be approached by using your calculations to determine whether overtrading exists rather than just calculating random ratios. This means examining the short-term ratios in company finance, as well as sales growth, profit margins, liquidity ratios and working capital ratios. Do not be surprised however if not all the ratios show the same results; here the company is keeping up its payment schedule to creditors despite its other problems.

> (b) concludes by highlighting the most important indicators of overtrading. It is important to do this in an answer where you have given a lot of detail, as you need to pick out where the greatest threats to the business lie. In this question the threats highlighted at the end of part (b) will be those for which remedies are identified in (c).

(a) **Overtrading**

'**Overtrading**' refers to the situation where a company is **over-reliant** on **short-term finance** to support its operations. This is risky because short-term finance may be withdrawn relatively quickly if creditors **lose confidence** in the business, or if there is a general tightening of credit in the economy, and this may result in a liquidity crisis and even bankruptcy, even though the firm is profitable. The fundamental solution to overtrading is to replace short term finance with longer term finance such as term loans or equity funds.

Problems of rapid expansion

The term overtrading is used because the condition commonly arises when a company is expanding rapidly. In this situation, because of increasing volumes, **more cash** is frequently **needed to pay input costs** such as wages or purchases than is currently being collected from debtors. The result is that the company runs up its overdraft to the limit and sometimes there is **insufficient time** to arrange an **increase in facilities** to pay other creditors on the due dates.

Lack of control

These problems are often compounded by a general lack of attention to **cost control** and **working capital management**, such as debt collection, because most management time is spent **organising selling or production**. The result is an unnecessary **drop in profit margins**.

Under-capitalisation

When the overdraft limit is reached the company frequently raises funds from other **expensive short term sources**, such as debt factoring or debtor's prompt payment discounts, and delays payment to creditors, instead of underpinning its financial position with equity funds or a longer term loan. The consequent under-capitalisation **delays investment in fixed assets and staff** and can further harm the quality of the firm's operations.

(b) (i) The company has become significantly more reliant on short term liabilities to finance its operations as shown by the following analysis:

	20X9 £'000		20X8 £'000	
Total assets	21,350		14,900	
Short-term liabilities	8,700	40.7%	5,000	33.6%
Long term funds (equity and debt)	12,650	59.3%	9,900	66.4%
	21,350		14,900	

Overtrading

A major reason for this is classic overtrading: sales increased by 50% in one year, but the operating profit margin fell from 9,000/20,000 = 45% in 20X8 to 10,000/30,000 = 33% in 20X9.

Refinancing

However, the effect is **compounded** by the **repayment** of £2.3 million (66%) of the 8% debentures and replacement with a £2 million bank overdraft and increased trade creditor finance. Although this may be because the interest rate on the overdraft is cheaper than on the debentures, it is generally not advisable in the context of the risk of short term debt.

However, if it is felt that the current sales volume is abnormal and that, when the Polly Playtime doll reaches the end of its product life cycle, sales will stabilise at a lower level, the use of shorter term debt is justified.

Liquidity ratios

As a result of overtrading, the company's **current ratio** has deteriorated from 13,500/5000 = 2.7 in 20X8 to 19,850/8700 = 2.28 in 20X9. The **quick assets ratio** (or 'acid test') has deteriorated from 10,500/5,000 = 2.1 to 12,500/8,700 = 1.44. However these figures are acceptable and only if they continue to deteriorate is there likely to be a liquidity problem. In the 20X9 accounts the company continues to have a healthy bank balance, although this has been achieved partly by halting dividend growth.

Investment in fixed assets

The company has **not maintained an investment in fixed assets** to match its sales growth. Sales/fixed assets has increased from 20,000/1,400 = 14.3 times to 30,000/1,500 = 20 times. This may be putting the quality of production at risk, but may be justified, however, if sales are expected to decline when the doll loses popularity.

Working capital ratios

An investigation of working capital ratios shows that:

(1) **Stock turnover** has **decreased** from 20,000/3,000 = 6.67 times to 30,000/7,350 = 4.08 times. This indicates that there has been a large investment in stock. The question of whether this is justified again depends on expected future sales, but the strategy appears to be the opposite of that adopted for fixed assets.

(2) The **average debtors payment period has increased** from 6,000/20,000 × 365 = 110 days to 10,000/30,000 × 365 = 122 days, indicating a lack of credit control. This has contributed to a weakening of the cash position. There appears to be no evidence of prompt payment discounts to debtors.

(3) The **payment period to creditors** (roughly estimated) has **decreased** from 2,500/11,000 × 365 = 83 days to 4,200/20,000 × 365 = 77 days. This result is unexpected, indicating that there has been no increase in delaying payment to creditors over the year. Creditors are being paid in a significantly shorter period than the period of credit taken by customers.

Conclusion

In summary, the main problem facing Gustaffson is its increasing overdependence on short term finance, caused in the main by:

(1) A major investment in stock to satisfy a rapid increase in sales volumes
(2) Deteriorating profit margins
(3) Poor credit control of debtors
(4) Repayment of debenture capital

(ii) **Future sales**

Possible solutions to the above problems depend on **future sales** and **product projections**. If the rapid increase in sales has been a one-product phenomenon, there is little point in over-capitalising by borrowing long term and investing in a major expansion of fixed assets. If, however, sales of this and future products are expected to continue increasing, and further investment is needed, the company's growth should be underpinned by an injection of equity capital and an issue of longer term debt.

Better working capital management

Regardless of the above, various working capital strategies could be improved. **Debtors** should be encouraged to **pay more promptly**. This is best done by instituting **proper credit control procedures**. **Longer credit periods** could probably be negotiated with creditors and quantity discounts should be investigated.

22 H Finance

> **Top tips.** In the exam you probably would not get a complete question on factoring. The arrangement would most likely be examined in combination with other methods such as invoice discounting or credit insurance.
>
> However the question is typical of the sort of things that might be asked about factoring, combining calculation with discussion of the general issues involved. When comparing the costs of two possibilities, sometimes as here you would calculate the total costs of each arrangement. On other occasions you would use the differences between each method in your calculation. (a) shows where the differences are likely to lie.
>
> To answer (b) well you needed to bring out benefits in different areas (factoring as a source of finance, use of factors as means of improving working capital management and decreasing administration time and costs.) As far as the effect on the accounts is concerned, the gearing point is significant but note the uncertain effect on return on capital employed.

(a) Assuming that the historical data presented is a reasonable guide to what will happen in the future, we can calculate whether the factoring of the debts on the debtors' ledger of D Ltd would be worthwhile as follows. The 20Y0 figures are assumed below to be typical.

Cost of finance

The cost of the finance provided by the factor is 5% of sales, since 80% and then a further 15% is remitted by the factor. This is equivalent to around 23% of debtors (5 ÷ 0.22) based on the 20Y0 year end debtors' figure. However, it should be borne in mind that 15% of the finance is only received when the amounts due are received by the finance company: this delay of course makes the finance less attractive than if 95% were received straight away.

Administration costs

In addition, there would be administration costs of 0.5% × 98.7m = £0.5 million which amounts to considerably more than the amount of £80,000 saved in D Ltd's own administration costs.

Bad debts

There may be some saving through a reduction in bad debts, which in 20Y0 amounted to 0.6% of turnover (£0.6m). However there is against this a loss of contribution amounting to 18% × 10% × £98.7m ≈ £1.8m as a result of the factor's aggressive collection procedures. This will outweigh any savings in the cost of bad debts.

Considering:

(i) The **cost** of the **finance** provided
(ii) The higher administration costs, and
(iii) The loss in contribution from lost turnover

it would appear that factoring is not justified on the basis of any of these three elements.

(b) **Aspects of factoring**

The three main aspects of factoring are as follows.

(i) **Administration** of the client's invoicing, sales accounting and debt collection service.

(ii) **Credit protection** for the client's debts, whereby the factor takes over the risk of loss from bad debts and so 'insures' the client against such losses. This service is also referred to as 'debt underwriting' or the 'purchase of a client's debts'. The factor usually purchases these debts 'without recourse' to the client, which means that in the event that the client's debtors are unable to pay what they owe, the factor will not ask for his money back from the client.

(iii) **Making payments** to the client in **advance** of collecting the debts. This might be referred to as 'factor finance' because the factor is providing cash to the client against outstanding debts.

Benefits of factoring

The benefits of factoring for a business customer include the following.

(i) The business can **pay** its **suppliers promptly**, and so can take advantage of any early payment discounts that are available.

(ii) **Optimum stock** levels can be **maintained**, because the business will have enough cash to pay for the stocks it needs.

(iii) **Growth** can be **financed** through sales rather than by injecting fresh external capital.

(iv) The business gets **finance linked** to its **volume of sales**. In contrast, overdraft limits tend to be determined by historical balance sheets.

(v) The managers of the business do **not have to spend their time** on the **problems** of slow-paying debtors.

(vi) The business does **not incur the costs** of **running its own sales ledger department**.

Effect on accounts

Factoring of sales invoicing leads to a **reduction of debtors** and therefore of assets employed in the business, accompanied by a reduction in profit as a result of the costs involved. Part of these 'costs' are generally reflected in the fact that less than 100% of the debt is paid to the company by the factor. The effect on the **return on capital employed** will depend upon the cost of factoring and the level of profits without factoring relative to assets employed.

Since they reduce assets, the funds advanced by the factor do not show up as **borrowings** in the balance sheet. The apparent gearing will therefore improve. Factoring is attractive to some companies as a method of avoiding borrowing limits or covenants being breached. It provides a means of financing debtors, which are otherwise unsuitable for secured lending because of their volatility.

Disadvantages of factoring

The main disadvantage of factoring is that it is a **relatively expensive form** of finance compared to loan finance. Some businesses will also find it undesirable for customer relations if the administration of debt collection is passed to a third party.

23 SF

Top tips. The first thing to pick up when you read part (a) of this question is that the company is a **small family owned private** company and not a large plc listed on the Stock Exchange. Your suggestions should reflect this and be ones that such a company might reasonably be expected to adopt.

You need to approach this question by making an assessment of the **underlying profitability** of the business, and trying to understand the key reasons for the cash flow problems before proposing possible solutions.

The solution works down the balance sheet suggesting possible ways of improving each element of working capital and obtaining further finance. The suggestions you put forward should make as much use as possible of the data given in the question, for example highlighting the implications of the seasonal nature of sales. At

> the same time there are also other general suggestions that can be made; a company in financial difficulties can almost always think about tightening its credit control procedures for example. Note that the answer includes assessment of how effective the various ways of improving the situation could be.
>
> The conclusion highlights the most urgent action required as well as commenting on the company's overall state of health.

To: Board of Directors, SF Ltd
From: External consultant
Date: 12 November 20X1
Subject: Cash flow budget

Introduction

The budget shows that the company will experience a **positive cash position** for the first quarter of the year, there being a net inflow of cash during this time as well as no use of the overdraft facility. However, thereafter the position deteriorates, with the company being forecast to exceed its overdraft limit from August to November. By the end of the year, the company's cash reserves will be £50,000 lower than at the start of the period.

Possible remedial actions

1 **Production scheduling**

   Sales show a cyclical movement, with receipts from customers being highest during the winter months. However, production is scheduled evenly throughout the year. If production could be **scheduled** to **match the pattern of demand**, the cash balance would remain more even throughout the year. Any resulting increase in the overall level of production costs could be quantified and compared with the savings in interest costs to assess the viability of such a proposal.

2 **Reduce the stockholding period**

   At present it is forecast that stocks will be £30,000 higher by the end of the year. This represents three months' worth of purchases from suppliers. It is not clear to what extent this increase is predicated upon **increasing sales**, although since the building is being extended it is assumed that there will be some increase in the level of production and sales in the near future. However, the size of the increase seems excessive.

3 **Reducing the debt collection period**

   SF Ltd currently allows its customers two months' credit. It is not known how this compares with the industry norms, but it is unlikely to be excessive. However, there may be some scope for **reducing the credit period** for at least some of the customers, and thereby reducing the average for the business as a whole.

4 **Tightening the credit control procedures**

   It is not known what level of bad debts is incurred by SF Ltd, but even if it is low, **tightening up** the **credit control** and **debt collection procedures** could improve the speed with which money is collected.

5 **Factoring the sales ledger**

   The use of a factor to administer the sales ledger might **reduce the collection period** and **save administration costs**. An **evaluation** of the **relevant costs and benefits** could be undertaken to see whether it is worth pursuing this option.

6 **Increase the credit period taken**

   Since SF Ltd already takes 90 days credit, it is unlikely that it will be able to increase this further without **jeopardising** the **relationship** with its suppliers.

7 Defer payment for fixed assets

(a) Presumably the **purchase** of the **office furniture** could be deferred, although the sums involved are relatively insignificant.

(b) The **progress payment** on the **building extension** is likely to be a contractual commitment that cannot be deferred.

(c) The **purchase of the car** could reasonably be **deferred** until the cash position improves. If it is essential to the needs of the business, the company could consider spreading the cost through some form of leasing or hire purchase agreement.

(d) It is not clear why the new **equipment** is being **purchased**. Presumably some form of investment appraisal has been undertaken to establish the financial benefits of the acquisition. However, if it is being purchased in advance of an increase in production then it may be possible to defer it slightly. The company could also look at alternative methods of financing it, as have been suggested in the case of the car.

8 Dividend

SF Ltd is a private company, and therefore the shareholders could agree to **forego** or **defer the dividend**. The practicality of this will depend on the personal situation of the five shareholders.

9 Defer the corporation tax payment

This might be possible by **agreement with the Inland Revenue**. The company should consider the relative **costs of the interest** that would be charged if this were done, and the **cost of financing** the payment through some form of debt.

10 Realise the investment

The dividend from this is £10,000, and therefore assuming an interest rate of, say, 5%, it could be worth in the region of £200,000. It is not clear **what form** this takes or for **what purpose** it is being held, but it may be possible to dispose of a part of it without jeopardising the long-term strategic future of the business.

11 Inject additional long-term capital

The budget assumes that both fixed and working capital will increase by £30,000 during the year, and the directors should therefore consider seeking **additional long term capital** to finance at least the fixed asset acquisitions. Possible sources of capital include:

- Injection of funds from the existing shareholders
- The use of venture capital
- Long-term bank loan, debenture or mortgage

Conclusions

1. It can be seen that there are a number of avenues that SF could explore. It appears that the company is **fundamentally profitable**, given the size of the corporation tax bill, and the fact that were it not for the fixed asset additions and the investment in stock the cash balance would increase by £10,000 during the year. However, the liquidity issues must be addressed now to avoid exceeding the overdraft limit.

2. The company should also consider **investing its cash surpluses** during the first quarter of the year to earn at **least some interest**, although this will be restricted by the short periods for which funds are likely to be available. Possible investments include:

   - Bank deposits
   - Short-term gilts
   - Bills of exchange

EXAM ANSWER BANK

24 Headwater

> **Top tips.** The bulk of the marks in (a) would be available for the written comparisons with the rest of the industry, particularly as you are told which ratios to calculate rather than having to select them yourself. You need to provide sensible explanations for differences with the industry and highlight areas for concern, in particular here the problems over sources of finance.
>
> In (b) you need to show that the company can gain more funds not only because more investors can put money in, but also that listed status provides more reasons for investors to buy a stake (improved marketability of shares being probably the most important).
>
> When answering (c) you should examine the balance sheet and consider how different elements might be made more attractive to investors. This includes looking at share capital and considering whether the issue price of each share is likely to be too high.
>
> (d) brings out the primary pressure that will face the company after floating, to maintain or improve dividend levels. The market will also be sensitive to attempts to massage the balance sheet artificially, for example by using share proceeds to pay off debentures.

(a) The performance and financial health of Headwater in relation to that of the industry sector as a whole can be evaluated by comparing its financial ratios with the industry averages, as follows.

	Headwater plc	Industry average
Return on (long-term) capital employed Operating profit (PBIT): Equity + long-term debt £4.9m: (£12.4m + £2.2m) = 33.6%		24%
Return on equity Profit attributable to ordinary shareholders: Equity £3.1m: £12.4m = 25%		16%
Operating profit margin Operating profit : Sales £4.9m: £36.5m = 13.4%		11%
Current ratio Current assets: Current liabilities £10.1m: £9.0m = 1.12:1		1.6:1
Acid test Current assets excluding stock: Current liabilities £5.7m: £9.0m = 0.63:1		1.0:1
Gearing Debt: Equity (£2m + £2.2m): £12.4m = 33.9%		24%
Dividend cover Profit attributable to equity: Dividends £3.1m: £0.3m = 10.3 times		4.0
Interest cover Profit before interest and tax (PBIT): Interest £4.9m: £1.3m = 3.77 times		4.5

These ratios can be used to evaluate performance in terms of profitability, liquidity and financial security.

Profitability

Headwater's return on capital employed, return on equity and operating profit margin are all significantly above the industry averages. Although the first two measures could be inflated due to assets being shown at low book values, the profit margin indicates that Headwater is managing to make good profits, which could be due to successful marketing, a low cost base or to its occupation of a particularly profitable niche in the market.

Liquidity

Both the current and the quick (acid test) ratios are well below the industry averages. This suggests that Headwater is either short of liquid resources or is managing its working capital poorly. However, the three key working capital ratios modify this impression.

Debtor days:	$365 \times 4.7/36.5$	= 47 days
Stock turnover:	$365 \times 4.4/31.6$	= 51 days
Payment period:	$365 \times 7.0/31.6$	= 81 days

Although the industry averages are not known, these ratios appear to be very good by general standards. It therefore appears that Headwater has become under-capitalised, perhaps through the use of working capital to finance growth.

Financial security

Gearing is **high** in comparison with the rest of the industry, and 48% of the debt is in the form of overdraft which is generally repayable on demand. This is therefore a risky form of debt to use in large amounts. The debenture is repayable in two years and will need to be refinanced since Headwater cannot redeem it out of existing resources. Interest cover is also poor, and this together with the poor liquidity probably account for the low payout ratio (the inverse of the dividend cover).

In summary, profit performance is strong, but there are significant weaknesses in both the liquidity and the financial structure. These problems need to be addressed if Headwater is to be able to maintain its record of strong and consistent growth.

(b) A company such as Headwater may seek a stock market listing for the following reasons.

(i) To **allow access** to a **wider pool of finance:** companies that are growing fast may need to raise larger sums than is possible privately. Obtaining a listing widens the potential number of equity investors, and may also result in an improved credit rating, thus reducing the cost of additional debt finance.

(ii) To **improve the marketability of the shares:** shares that are traded on the stock market can be bought and sold in relatively small quantities at any time. This means that it is easier for existing investors to realise a part of their holding.

(iii) To **allow capital to be transferred** to other ventures: founder owners may wish to liquidate the major part of their holding either for personal reasons or for investment in other new business opportunities.

(iv) To **improve the company image:** quoted companies are commonly believed to be more financially stable, and this may improve the image of the company with its customers and suppliers, allowing it to gain additional business and to improve its buying power.

(v) **Growth by acquisition** is easier: a listed company is in a better position to make a paper offer for a target company than an unlisted one.

(c) Restructuring its balance sheet prior to flotation will help to make Headwater appear a sounder prospect to potential investors who know little about its past performance. Methods available include the following.

Disposal of surplus assets. This will improve both gearing and liquidity.

Fixed asset revaluation. Land and buildings may well be shown in the accounts at values that are significantly below the current market valuation. Adjustment to market values will improve the gearing ratio and the value of shareholders' funds, although the effect of this will be to depress the reported return on capital employed and return on equity. However, since these are currently well above industry averages this should not present too much of a problem.

Liquidity improvement. Although there does not appear to be much scope for tightening the control of working capital, Headwater may be able to improve its cash flow by other means, for example by reducing overheads and delaying the purchase of additional fixed assets.

Sale and leaseback. If Headwater owns valuable freehold premises it may be able to release cash by selling them and exchanging the freehold for an operating lease. This would improve both the liquidity position and the reported return on capital employed although the gearing would be little affected.

Elimination of non-voting 'A' shares. These are not permitted by the Stock Exchange for companies newly entering the market.

Share split. On the basis of the industry average P/E of 10, the shares would be priced at £11.48 (= $10 \times 3.1m/(1.8m + 0.9m)$). A highly priced new issue is likely to deter potential small investors. This problem could be overcome by reducing the nominal value of the shares by means of a share split.

(d) Following the flotation Headwater is likely to come under pressure to **improve** the **payout ratio** and **dividend performance** of the shares. If it wishes to maintain a good share price and the ability to raise further finance in the future then it would be well advised to consider this seriously. It could also work towards **lowering the gearing ratio**, perhaps by using a part of the issue proceeds to **redeem some** or all of the **debentures**. However this should not appear to be the prime reason for the float or the attractiveness of the issue will be diminished.

25 KB

> **Top tips.** Don't forget in (a) (ii) that you need to use the issue price to calculate how many shares should be issued and not the current market price. The answer to (a) (i) is a red herring. The discussion in (a) (ii) takes into account external market factors as well as the performance of the company. Focus on the assumptions made. What are the costs (assumed to be none)? What else might influence the share price? Will the rights issue itself change investors' views of the company?
>
> The key feature that your answer to (a) (iii) should bring out is that issuing shares at a large discount provides **security** that all the shares will be taken up.
>
> Your answer to (b) (ii) should show clearly what an issue of convertible loan stock will achieve that a rights issue will not.

(a) (i) The **current market price** can be found by multiplying the earnings per share (EPS) by the price/earnings (P/E) ratio.

EPS is £1.2m/6m = 20 pence per share
P/E ratio is 12
Market price of shares is $12 \times 20p$ = **£2.40 per share**

(ii) In order to raise £5,040,000 at a price of 192 pence, the company will need to issue an additional 2,625,000 (£5,040,000/£1.92) shares.

Following the investment, the total number of shares in issue will be 8,625,000 (6,000,000 + 2,625,000).

At this point, the total value of the company will be:

(6m × £2.40) + £5,040,000 = £19,440,000

The **theoretical ex-rights price** will therefore be £19.44m/8.625m = **£2.25**.

Problems with calculations

(1) The **costs of arranging the issue** have not been included in the calculations.

(2) The **market view** of the **quality of the new investment** will affect the actual price of the company's shares.

(3) If the **issue** is **not fully subscribed** and a significant number of shares remain with the underwriters, this will **depress the share price**.

(4) The effect of the new investment on the **risk profile** of the company and the expected **future dividend stream** could also cause the share price to differ from that predicted.

(5) The price of the shares depends not only on the financial performance of the company, but also on the **overall level of demand** in the stock market. If the market moves significantly following the announcement of the issue, this will affect the actual price at which the shares are traded.

(iii) **Features of deep discounted rights issue**

In a **deep-discounted** rights issue, the new shares are priced at a **large discount** to the current market price of the shares. The purpose of this is to ensure that the issue is **well subscribed** and that shares are not left with the underwriters, and thus this form of issue pricing is attractive when the stock market is particularly **volatile**. However, the shares cannot be issued at a price which is below their nominal value.

Disadvantage of deep discounted rights issue

The main drawback to this approach is that a **larger number of shares** will need to be **issued** in order to raise the required amount of finance, and this will lead to a larger dilution of earnings per share and dividends per share.

(b) (i) **Conversion premium**

The **conversion premium** is the **difference** between the **issue value** of the **stock** and the **market value** as at the date of issue. In other words it is the measure of the additional expense involved in buying shares via the convertible stock as compared with buying the shares on the open market immediately.

In this case, £100 loan stock can be converted into 35 ordinary shares. The **effective price** of these shares is therefore £2.86 (£100/35) per share.

The **current market price** of the shares is £2.40. The **conversion premium** is therefore £2.86 − £2.40 = **46 pence**. This can also be expressed in percentage terms as **19%** (0.46/2.40).

(ii) **Advantages of issuing convertible loan stock**

(1) **Convertibles** should be **cheaper than equity** because they offer greater security to the investor. This may make them particularly attractive in fast growing but high-risk companies.

(2) **Issue costs** are **lower** for loan stock than for equity.

(3) **Interest** on the **loan stock** is **tax deductible**, unlike dividends on ordinary shares.

(4) There is **no immediate change** in the **existing structure** of control, although this will change over time as conversion rights are exercised.

(5) There is no immediate dilution in earnings and dividends per share.

EXAM ANSWER BANK

26 Rump

> **Top tips.** Note the step by step approach in (a).
>
> **Step 1.** Calculate number of shares
> **Step 2.** Calculate issue price
> **Step 3.** Calculate ex-rights price
>
> In part (c) you need to do more than describe the various alternatives. You must compare and contrast the merits of the rights issue and the debenture, and ensure that all your discussions are related to the circumstances of Rump plc. Your answer needs to bring out the potential difficulties with whatever choice the directors make. Note how the change in financing can have quite wide implications (the impact on strategy of restrictive covenants and a change in the ownership structure). The issue of change in control is also important when we consider the alternative methods of issuing shares.
>
> The conclusion here brings out that the other methods suggested are unlikely to be used and in practice the choice would be between a rights issue and a debenture issue.

(a) There are currently 10m shares in issue. A 2 for 5 rights issue would mean that **4m additional shares** would have to be issued (10m × 2/5).

The rights issue must raise £24m. Therefore the new shares must be issued at a price of **£6 per share** (£24m/4m).

Using the formula

$$\text{Theoretical ex rights price} = \frac{1}{N+1} ((N \times \text{rights price}) + \text{issue price})$$

$$= \frac{1}{2.5+1} ((2.5 \times 6.60) + 6.00)$$

$$= 6.43$$

(b) If the debenture issue is made, the number of equity shares in issue will be unchanged at 10m.

The **profit available** for **dividend** will be reduced by the amount of the debenture interest, which is £1.8m per year (£24m × 7.5%), giving an annual dividend of £7.2 million.

The theoretical share price can be found using the dividend valuation model:

k_e = d/p_0
10% = £0.72/p_0
p_0 = **£7.20**

(c) To: Chairman
From: Finance Director
Date: 20 November 20X1
Subject: Financing alternatives for the new investment

Introduction

The new contract is large in relation to the size of the company, and therefore the new external source of finance could have a **significant effect** on the existing **capital structure** of the business, and on its **ownership and control**. There are two main sources of finance that are being considered, namely a rights issue and a debenture issue, and these will be considered in more detail below. The final section of the report will consider some further methods of raising equity finance that are available to Rump plc.

Rights issue versus debenture issue

Ownership

The rights issue is large in relation to the existing equity in issue, and requires a significant additional investment on the part of the shareholders. If shareholders are likely to be unwilling or unable to exercise their rights, the company should consider underwriting the issue. The underwriters will then take up any shares that remain unsold, but this could result in a **change** in the **balance of control**. A debenture issue by contrast would result in no change in control.

Problems with all equity financing

The company is currently 100% equity financed, and this would continue to be the case in the event of a rights issue. This means that the **level of financial risk** faced by the shareholders is **low**. However, it also means that they cannot take advantage of the **lower cost and tax benefits** of debt finance, and that therefore the potential returns to equity are lower than they might be if some debt were to be used.

Introduction of gearing

A **debenture issue** of this size would introduce a significant element of **gearing** into the company. The value of debt in the company structure would be £24m, and the value of equity would be £72m (10m × £7.20). This gives a gearing ratio of 25% (ratio of prior charge capital to total capital). This represents a significant change in the **level of financial risk** faced by shareholders, and their attitude to this must be taken into account in making the financing decision.

Issue costs

The calculations ignore issue costs. These may be **significant** for a **rights issue,** amounting on average to 4% of the finance raised, although this percentage rises for small issues. The issue costs of debentures would be less than for a rights issue.

Flexibility

Debenture issues are commonly linked to **restrictive covenants** that limit the company's further ability to borrow. The effect of such covenants on the future needs of the company must be taken into account. Equity funding would impose no such restriction.

(ii) **Further methods of raising equity finance**

A placing

This is an arrangement whereby the shares are not all offered to the public, but instead, the sponsoring market maker arranges for **most of the issue** to be **bought by a small number of investors**, usually institutional investors such as pension funds and insurance companies. The **issuing costs** would be **lower** than for a **rights issue**, but the position with regard to **pre-emption rights** of the existing shareholders may have to be resolved. There could be a significant effect on the **control** of the business if the new shares are concentrated in the hands of a small number of institutional investors.

Offer for sale

This means that Rump plc would **allot new shares** to an **issuing house**. The issuing house would then offer the **shares for sale** on the basis of a prospectus, either at a **fixed price** or by **tender**. The **issuing costs** would be significantly **higher** than for a rights issue. This is particularly true for fixed price offers where there is a higher risk that not all the shares will be subscribed. However, the **effect** on the **control of the company** is likely to be less than for a placing.

Public offer for subscription

This is the **direct offer** of shares to the **public** by the company using a **prospectus**. **Issuing costs**, **underwriting** and **publicity costs** are **high**. It is only appropriate for **large issues** of shares.

Conclusion

Although alternative routes are available for raising equity, in this case the choice is really between a rights issue and a debenture issue. The key factors influencing the decision have been summarised above, but probably the major consideration will be the company's attitude to financial risk. This will be significantly increased if the debenture is used, but on the other hand, the cost of this will be less than if more equity is issued, and the potential returns to equity are greater.

27 DF

> **Top tips.** The nature of the calculation in (a) should have suggested to you that the majority of marks would be available for the discussion. The answer looks well beyond the relationship with FF plc, considering the effect on relations with other customers, the effect on DF itself, and whether there are alternative sources of finance for DF.
>
> (b) goes on to cover those alternative sources of finance. Various criteria can be used to consider them:
>
> - **Costs** (including costs saved)
> - **Flexibility** (a company knows when and how much interest and principal it has to pay on a loan but still has to pay it; by contrast an overdraft facility only has interest charged on it if it is used, but it is repayable on demand.)
> - **Commitment** (security that has to be given, how much the company is tied into the arrangement)
> - **Appearances** (effect on gearing, effect on debtors if factor organisation is employed)
>
> Although the question directs you towards discussing certain sources of finance, it does not confine you to those sources. Therefore, although the bulk of your answer to (b) should discuss the sources listed, a section briefly mentioning other sources should also be included.
>
> Don't forget also in (b) to bear in mind the likely level of financial knowledge of the recipients of your report; don't assume a high level of understanding.
>
> (c) is a summary list of the key factors venture capitalists will take into account. As well as the company's market prospects, venture capitalists are also interested in the involvement of management (level of commitment and expertise).

(a) **Cost of discount**

The **percentage cost** of an **early settlement discount** to the company giving it can be estimated by the formula:

$$1 - \left[\frac{100}{100-d}\right]^{\frac{365}{t}}$$

Where d is the size of discount (%)
       t is the reduction in payment period in days necessary to achieve discount

d = 3%
t = 90 − 10 = 80

$$\% \text{ cost} = 1 - \left[\frac{100}{100-3}\right]^{\frac{365}{80}} = 14.9\%$$

The **annual equivalent rate of interest** in offering a 3% cash discount is therefore 14.9%.

Offer of discount

Other factors that DF should take into account before deciding on whether to offer a discount include:

(i) The **attractiveness** of the **discount** to FF plc, and the probability that it will be taken up

(ii) Whether the **discount** will encourage FF plc to **purchase larger volumes** than it would if the discount was not available

(iii) The **relative effect** of the **different financing alternatives** on the administration costs of DF plc

(iv) The **ease** with which DF plc will be **able to raise alternative sources of finance,** the effect on **gearing** of these sources and the need for **security**

(v) The interest **other customers** might show in taking a discount

(vi) The possibility of **withdrawing** from the discount arrangement without loss of FF's goodwill in the future

(b) To: Shareholders in DF Ltd
From: Management Accountant
Date: 11 December 20X1
Subject: Alternative methods of financing current assets

Introduction

The contract to supply FF plc means that DF Ltd will need to make a **significant additional permanent investment** in **current assets** (in the form of additional stocks and higher debtors). There will also be an additional temporary element which **fluctuates** with the level of sales. This will increase the amount of money needed by the company to finance these assets. There are a number of different sources of finance that could be considered.

Bank loan

A bank loan would normally be for a **fixed amount of money** for a fixed term and at a fixed rate of interest. It is not clear whether or not the company has any existing debt finance. However, it has already been decided to use a bank loan to fund the purchase of the additional fixed assets. The **size of this loan** and the **quality of security** available will be key factors in determining whether the bank is willing to make a further advance to cover the investment in current assets. Assuming that a further loan is forthcoming, the company will need to evaluate the effect of this in terms of **cost** and the **effect on the capital structure**.

Advantages of bank loan

(i) **Bank finance** is **cheaper** than the cost of allowing a 3% **settlement discount**, and is also likely to be cheaper than using debt factoring or invoice discounting.

(ii) The **loan** can be **negotiated** for a **fixed term** and a **fixed amount**, and this is less risky than for example using an overdraft, which is repayable on demand.

Disadvantages of bank loan

(i) The company will have to **pay interest** on the **full amount of the loan** for the entire period. This could make it more expensive in absolute terms than using an alternative source of finance where interest is only payable on the amount outstanding.

(ii) The loan will **increase the level** of the company's **financial gearing**. This means that there could be greater volatility in the returns attributable to the ordinary shareholders.

(iii) The bank is likely to **require security**. If there are questions as to the quality of the asset base, the bank may also require personal guarantees or additional security from the directors or shareholders.

Overdraft

An overdraft is a form of lending that is **repayable on demand**. The bank grants the customer a **facility** up to a certain limit, and the customer can take advantage of this as necessary. Overdrafts are essentially short-term finance, but are renewable and may become a near-permanent source.

Advantages of overdraft

The attraction of using an overdraft to finance current assets is that **interest** is only **payable** on the **amount of the facility actually in use** at any one time. This means that the **effective cost of the overdraft** will be **lower** than that of the **bank loan**. This is particularly attractive for a company such as DF Ltd, where demand is expected to fluctuate significantly from month to month, and consequently there are likely to be large variations in the level of working capital. It is also likely to be cheaper than the other alternatives being considered.

Disadvantages of overdraft

The main drawback to using an overdraft is that it will be **repayable on demand**, and therefore the company is in a more vulnerable position than it would be if a bank loan were used instead. A long-term overdraft may be included in the **gearing** calculations, and the bank may require **security.**

Debt factoring

Factoring is an arrangement to have **debts collected** by a **factor company**, which advances a proportion of the money it is due to collect. Services offered by the factor would normally include the following:

(i) **Administration** of the client's invoicing, sales accounting and debt collection service.

(ii) **Credit protection** for the client's debts, whereby the factor takes over the risk of loss from bad debts and so 'insures' the client against such losses.

(iii) **Making advance payments** to the client before the debts are collected.

Benefits of factoring

(i) **Growth** is **effectively financed through sales**, which provide the security to the factor. DF would not have to provide the additional security that might be required by the bank.

(ii) The **managers** of the business will **not** have to **spend time** on the problem of **slow paying debtors**.

(iii) **Administration costs** will be **reduced** since the company will not have to run its own sales ledger department.

Disadvantages of factoring

(i) The **level of finance** is **geared** to the **level of sales**; in other words, finance lags sales. In practice, DF will need finance ahead of sales in order to build up sufficient stocks to meet demand.

(ii) Factoring may be **more expensive** than bank finance. Service charges are generally around 2% of total invoice value, in addition to finance charges at levels comparable to bank overdraft rates.

(iii) The fact that debtors will be making payments direct to the factor may present a **negative picture** of the firm.

Invoice discounting

Invoice discounting is related to factoring and many factors will provide an invoice discounting service. Invoice discounting is the **purchase of a selection of invoices**, at a discount. The discounter does **not take over** the **administration** of the client's sales ledger, and the arrangement is purely for the advance of cash.

Advantages of discounting

The arrangement is thus a **purely financial transaction** that can be used to release working capital, and therefore shares some of the benefits of factoring in that **further security** is **not required**. The discounter will make an assessment of the risk involved, and only good quality invoices will be purchased, but this should not be a problem to DF since FF plc is a large well established company.

Disadvantages of discounting

The main disadvantage is that **invoice discounting** is likely to be **more expensive** than any of the other alternatives. It is normally only used to cover a temporary cash shortage, and not for the routine provision of working capital.

Other options

(i) Finance can be obtained by **delaying payment to creditors.** In theory this is potentially a **cheap source of finance.** The main disadvantage may be a **loss of supplier goodwill,** at a time when the company needs supplier co-operation to fulfil the new order.

(ii) Other methods of loan finance, notably debenture issue, are not appropriate as they are essentially **long-term,** and the **debentureholders** may require **security** that the company is unable to give.

(iii) Although we are told that **increased stock levels** will be needed to **fulfil FF's requirements,** there may be scope for **reducing the stock levels** necessary to fulfil other customers' requirements.

Conclusions

Of the options considered, factoring or some form of bank finance is likely to be the most appropriate. The final decision must take into account the full cost implications, and not just the relative rates of interest on the finance. DF Ltd must also consider the effect of the type of finance selected on the balance sheet, and the type of security that will be required. This could also impact on the ability of the company to raise further finance in the future.

(c) A **venture capital organisation** (below, 'VC') is likely to take the following factors into account when deciding whether or not to invest in Fashions Ltd.

The nature of the company's product

The VC will consider whether the good or service can be produced viably and has potential to sell, in the light of any market research which the company has carried out.

Expertise in production

The VC will want to be sure that the company has the necessary technical ability to implement production plans with efficiency.

Expertise in management

Venture capitalists pay much attention to the quality of management, since they believe that this is crucial to the success of the enterprise. Not only should the management team be committed to the enterprise; they should also have appropriate skills and experience.

The market and competition

The nature of the market for the product will be considered, including the threat which rival producers or future new entrants to the market may present.

Future prospects

The VC will want to be sure that the possible prospects of profits in the future compensate for the risks involved in the enterprise. The VC will expect the company to have prepared a detailed business plan detailing its future strategy.

Board membership

The VC is likely to require a place on the Board of Directors. Board representation will ensure that the VC's interests will be taken account of, and that the VC has a say in matters relating to the future strategy of the business.

Risk borne by the existing owners

The VC is likely to wish to ensure that the existing owners of the business bear a significant part of the investment risk relating to the expansion. If they are owner-managers, bearing part of the risk will provide an incentive for them to ensure the success of the venture. Although the VC may be providing most of the investment, the amounts provided by the owners should be significant in relation to their overall personal wealth.

Exit routes

The means by which the VC can eventually realise its investment are called 'exit routes'. Ideally, the VC will try to ensure that there are a number of exit routes.

28 Project appraisal

> **Top tips.** (a) would be a typical part question on these methods of investment appraisal; the rest of the question might well go on to cover net present value and internal rate of return (covered in the next chapter).
>
> It is unlikely that you would get a question on SWOT analysis for as many marks as part (b) gives. However the technique can be used to help you decide **quickly** what strategy a company should follow in a given set of circumstances. As previous questions have demonstrated, you need to do more than just decide which solution has the lowest cost when making decisions. SWOT analysis helps you focus on all relevant aspects of a business (production, sales/marketing, research and development, management), and how external factors impact upon a business (not just impact upon markets, but also impact upon internal costs).
>
> Note in (b) how the financial position of the company has a significant impact upon the means used to purchase the foundry.
>
> The conclusion in (b) highlights the key decisions that need to be made. You can legitimately say that the absence of strategic objectives means that no long-term decision can be made. What the conclusion does is highlight the principal appeal of each option.

EXAM ANSWER BANK

(a) (i) Depreciation must first be **added back** to the **annual profit figures**, to arrive at the annual cash flows.

Depreciation $= \dfrac{\text{Initial investment £46,000} - \text{scrap value £4,000}}{4 \text{ years}}$

$= £10,500$

Adding £10,500 per annum to the profit figures produces the cash flows for each proposal.

	Proposal A		Proposal B	
Year	Annual cash flow £	Cumulative cash flow £	Annual cash flow £	Cumulative cash flow £
0	(46,000)	(46,000)	(46,000)	(46,000)
1	17,000	(29,000)	15,000	31,000
2	14,000	(15,000)	13,000	(18,000)
3	24,000	9,000	15,000	(3,000)
4	9,000	18,000	25,000	22,000
4	4,000	22,000	4,000	26,000

Proposal A   Proposal B

(1) Payback period =   Payback period =

$2 + \left(\dfrac{15,000}{24,000} \times 1 \text{ year}\right)$ $3 + \left(\dfrac{3,000}{25,000} \times 1 \text{ year}\right)$

= 2.6 years   = 3.1 years

(2) The return on capital employed (ROCE) is calculated using the accounting profits given in the question.

Proposal A   Average profit $= \dfrac{£(6,500 + 3,500 + 13,500 - 1,500)}{4}$

$= \dfrac{£22,000}{4}$

$= £5,500$

ROCE $= \dfrac{£5,500}{£46,000} \times 100\%$

$= 12.0\%$

Proposal B   Average profit $= \dfrac{£(4,500 + 2,500 + 4,500 + 14,500)}{4}$

$= \dfrac{£26,000}{4}$

$= £6,500$

ROCE on initial investment $= \dfrac{£6,500}{£46,000} \times 100\%$

$= 14.1\%$

EXAM ANSWER BANK

(ii) Two advantages of each of the methods of appraisal can be selected from the following.

Payback period

(1) It is **simple** to **calculate**.
(2) It **preserves liquidity** by preferring early cash flows.
(3) It **uses cash flows** instead of more arbitrary accounting profits.
(4) It **reduces risk** by preferring early cash flows.

Return on capital employed

(1) It uses readily available **accounting profits**.
(2) It is **understood** by **non-financial managers**.
(3) It is a measure used by **external analysts** which should therefore be monitored by the company.

(b) A general interpretation might be as follows.

(i) **Objectives**. The company does not have any stated objectives. In view of the probable high (100%) shareholding by the family, it may be that a high level of **liquidity** is required to meet future dividend expectations. There is a clear necessity to agree stated objectives with regard to earnings and dividend payments.

(ii)

Strengths	Weaknesses
High liquidity.	Low profits due to poor returns from investments and possibly high unit costs, low sales or low prices.
A wide range of products and markets.	Family business, therefore possibly weak management.
	Heavy reliance on one customer.
	Poor growth due to limited markets or poor R & D.
Threats	Opportunities
Unknown future for the market for aluminium products.	Investment in stocks and shares. Purchase of a small foundry. Product-market diversification. Major customer involved in the do-it-yourself industry, which still has buoyant markets.

(iii) **Strengths**. The high liquidity is the clearest source of strength. Although the company offers a wide range of products to a variety of customers, growth is poor.

(iv) **Weaknesses**. **Low growth** and **profitability** in current markets and with current products should be a matter of some concern. The reasons for poor performance might range from high variable costs, low output (therefore high unit fixed costs), sluggish demand, weak marketing, high prices, inadequate R & D, ageing machinery and out-of-date technology, poor management, inefficient purchasing and so on. Weaknesses need to be identified more specifically.

(v) **Threats**. None are known, and the future for the aluminium products market may be reasonable if the managing director is correct in his assessment that the purchase of a new foundry would be a viable proposition.

(vi) Opportunities

(1) **Stocks and shares**. The **return** from **existing stocks** and shares has been **poor**, which might be the result of **poor investment management** which should be dealt with. There should be a **prospect of improvement** in the **future**, especially if professional advice is taken to sell parts of the existing portfolio and to re-invest in securities offering a higher return or better capital growth. If high liquidity remains a top priority, this strategy has clear merits.

(2) **Purchase of an aluminium foundry**. This policy of market penetration through the acquisition of a competitor offers several advantages:

- Increased market share (and new customers)
- Perhaps improved technology
- Joint fixed costs of administration and marketing, therefore lower unit costs of output
- Rationalisation of production and distribution
- Possibly, management expertise will be acquired

The **purchase consideration** might be for **cash only**, although it might be possible to obtain agreement to a share exchange deal, or a shares plus cash deal. Because the company is a private company, a share exchange arrangement is unlikely to be attractive (and the poor profit record of the company makes a launch on to the Alternative Investment Market an unlikely prospect).

Although the company already has knowledge of the aluminium industry, a **close investigation** of the **past performance and history** (and the future prospects) of the new foundry would be required.

(3) **Diversification into new products and markets.** This would be a difficult step into the unknown, especially in view of the lack of management experience in the company. It is **not recommended strategy**, unless clear opportunities for profits and growth present themselves since the company has **no obvious strengths** to exploit apart from its cash. However, there is a possibility of vertical integration, by attempting the acquisition of the do-it-yourself tools manufacturer. Leisure industries are prospective growth markets and a closer investigation of this possibility may be worthwhile.

(vii) **Conclusion**. No recommendation is possible, except that a strategic planning exercise should be carried out to recommend a long-term strategy. It is perhaps significant that in a comparison of the three opportunities mentioned the following conclusions can be drawn.

(1) The **continued investment in stocks and shares** promises high liquidity and returns in the long and short term.

(2) The **acquisition** of the **aluminium foundry** offers the prospect of a timescale for achieving profits which might be relatively short.

(3) **Diversification offers** no clear prospects, and the timescale required to earn profits might be long. Carefully chosen acquisitions, however, might yield the greatest long-term profits.

EXAM ANSWER BANK

29 Knuckle down

> **Top tips.** Although this question should take you 45 minutes (the amount of time a question in the exam will take you), an exam question would not consist purely of calculations; it would also most likely include discussion of the benefits and drawbacks of the NPV and IRR methods.
>
> The question nevertheless does give you lots of practice in the techniques and highlights common traps. Depreciation is not a cash flow and should be eliminated. If you have to deal with working capital you need to read the question very carefully. In C the increase in working capital from £15,000 to £21,000 at the end of year 1 is an increase of the **difference** between the figures (£6,000) at the end of year 1. The question also tells you that the working capital investment will be recovered, so that figure ultimately has to be included as a receipt.
>
> The question also requires you to calculate annuities and perpetuities, and deal with cash flows that are constant over a number of years but do not start at year 1. The treatment of the discount rate may have caught you out if you didn't read the question carefully. The discount rate of 15% should be used throughout the duration of all projects lasting more than ten years, and not just from year 10 onwards.
>
> You can use the NPV calculations for A and C as the first rates in the IRR estimation process. The fact that the NPV for C was rather larger than A indicates that you should try a different second rate. The main thing is to pick two higher rates as the NPVs were positive; you would get equal credit if you had chosen any rate in the 15 – 20% band for your second IRR calculation. (Below 15% would probably be a bit too near to the 12%, but you would be unlikely to be penalised very heavily for using 13% or 14%).

(a) (i) Project A

Year	Cash flow £	Discount factor 12%	Present value £
0	(29,000)	1.000	(29,000)
1	8,000	0.893	7,144
2	12,000	0.797	9,566
3	10,000	0.712	7,120
4	11,000	0.636	6,996
		Net present value	1,826

(ii) Project B

Year	Equipment £	Working capital £	Cash profit £	Net cash flow £	Discount factor 12%	Present value £
0	(44,000)	(20,000)		(64,000)	1.000	(64,000)
1			19,000	19,000	0.893	16,967
2			24,000	24,000	0.797	19,128
3	5,000	20,000	10,000	35,000	0.712	24,920
				Net present value		(2,985)

(iii) Project C

Year	Equipment £	Working capital £	Cash profit £	Net cash flow £	Discount factor 12%	Present value £
0	(50,000)	(15,000)		(65,000)	1.000	(65,000)
1		(6,000)		(6,000)	0.893	(5,353)
1-5			18,000	18,000	3.605	64,890
5		21,000		21,000	0.567	11,907
				Net present value		6,439

(iv) Project D

Year	Cash flow £	Discount factor 12%	Present value £
0	(20,000)	1.000	(20,000)
1	(20,000)	0.893	(17,860)
2	15,000	0.797	11,958
3	12,000	0.712	8,544
4-8	8,000	2.566	20,528
		Net present value	3,170

Discount factor at 12%, years 1 to 8	4.968
Less discount factor at 12%, years 1 to 3	2.402
Discount factor at 12%, years 4 to 8	2.566

(v) Project E

The cumulative discount factor for a perpetuity at 15% is 1/0.15 = 6.667.

Year	Cash flow £	Discount factor 15%	Present value £
0	(32,000)	1.000	(32,000)
1-∞	4,500	6.667	30,000
		Net present value	(2,000)

(vi) Project F

1.
	£
Present value (at 15%) of £3,000 a year from year 1 in perpetuity	20,000
Less present value of £3,000 a year for years 1 to 10 (× 5.019)	15,057
Present value of £3,000 a year from year 11 in perpetuity	4,943

2.
Discount factor at 15%, years 1 to 10	5.019
Less discount factor at 15%, years 1 to 5	3.352
Discount factor at 15%, years 6 to 10	1.667

3.
Year	Net cash flow £	Discount factor 15%	Present value £
0	(20,000)	1.000	(20,000)
1-5	5,000	3.352	16,760
6-10	4,000	1.667	6,668
11-∞	3,000	See above	4,943
		Net present value	8,371

(vii) Projects A, C, D and F have positive net present values and should be undertaken. Projects B and E should not be undertaken.

(b) (i) The IRR of project A is above 12% (where the NPV is £1,826). We will calculate the NPV at 15%.

Year	Cash flow £	Discount factor 15%	Present value £
0	(29,000)	1.000	(29,000)
1	8,000	0.870	6,960
2	12,000	0.756	9,072
3	10,000	0.658	6,580
4	11,000	0.572	6,292
		Net present value	(96)

The IRR is between 12% and 15%. By interpolation, we can estimate the IRR as about

$$12\% + \left[\frac{1,826}{(1,826 - -96)} \times (15 - 12) \right] \%$$

= 14.85%

(ii) The IRR of project C is above 12%, where the NPV is £6,439. Try 20%.

Year	Net cash flow £	Discount factor 20%	Present value £
0	(65,000)	1.000	(65,000)
1	(6,000)	0.833	(4,998)
1-5	18,000	2.991	53,838
5	21,000	0.402	8,442
		Net present value	(7,718)

The IRR is approximately $12\% + \left[\frac{6,439}{(6,439 - -7,718)} \times (20 - 12) \right] \% = 15.6\%$

(iii) The IRR, r, of project E is found as follows.

PV of cost = PV of benefits

$(32,000) = \dfrac{4,500}{r}$

$r = \dfrac{4,500}{32,000} = 0.140625$

IRR = 14.0625%

30 Dinard

> **Top tips.** (a) allows you to demonstrate that you understand the topic of real and money returns by explaining the difference between them.
>
> (b) introduces the complication of what you should do if you are told what current (or year 1) prices are but are also given information about price increases over the period of investment. Because the costs are increasing at different rates, the money rate (which you are given) has to be used, and the revenues and costs inflated each year. If the rate of increase for everything had been the same, you could either have used the money rate (and inflated costs and revenues), or calculated the real rate (and used uninflated costs and revenues). Since calculating the real rate only involves one calculation, you should really have chosen that option.
>
> Again don't forget to exclude depreciation as it is not a cash flow. Development costs of £480,000 are sunk costs and should also be excluded from the calculation. Because you are told to confine your answer to the information given, you should not discuss any wider issues that might be involved in the investment.

(a) The **real rate of return** is the rate of return which an investment would show in the **absence of inflation**. For example, if a company invests £100, inflation is 0%, and the investment at the end of the year is worth £110, then the real rate of return is 10%.

In reality however, there is likely to be an element of inflation in the returns due to the change in the purchasing power of money over the period. In the example above, if inflation was running at 5%, then to show a real rate of return of 10%, the investment would need to be worth £115.50 at the

EXAM ANSWER BANK

end of the year. In this case the money rate of return is 15.5% which is made up of the real return of 10% and inflation at 5%.

The relationship between the nominal ('money') rate of return and the real rate of return can be expressed as follows:

(1 + nominal rate) = (1 + real rate) × (1 + inflation rate)

The rate to be used in discounting cash flows for capital project appraisal will depend on the **way** in which the **expected cash flows** are calculated. If the cash flows are expressed in terms of the **actual number of pounds** that will be received or paid on the various future dates, then the **nominal rate** must be used. If however they are expressed in **terms** of the **value of the pound at year 0**, then the **real rate must be used**.

(b) *Workings*

	Year 1	Year 2	Year 3	Year 4
Sales volume	25,000	25,000	25,000	25,000
Unit price (£)	80	84	88	93
Variable material cost (£)	8.00	8.32	8.65	9.00
Variable labour cost (£)	12.00	13.20	14.52	15.97
Variable overhead (£)	12.00	12.48	12.98	13.50

Notes

Evaluation of investment

(All figures £'000)

	Year 0	Year 1	Year 2	Year 3	Year 4
Capital outlay	(2,400)				
Sales		2,000	2,100	2,205	2,315
Direct costs					
Materials		(200)	(208)	(216)	(225)
Labour		(300)	(330)	(363)	(399)
Overhead		(300)	(312)	(324)	(337)
Fixed overheads		(200)	(210)	(221)	(232)
Gross cash flow	(2,400)	1,000	1,040	1,081	1,122
Discount at 15%	1.000	0.870	0.756	0.658	0.572
Present value	(2,400)	870	786	711	642
Cumulative PV	(2,400)	(1,530)	(744)	(33)	608

The investment yields a net present value at the end of four years of £608,000. In the absence of other factors such as a capital rationing situation, production of the Rance should be undertaken.

31 Muggins

Top tips. A methodical set of workings is key to answering this question well (also not confusing the adjustment factors for costs and benefits).

Apart from testing your ability to use the certainty-equivalent approach, the question is a good test of your understanding of relevant costs and opportunity costs.

> - Apportioned costs are not incurred by the project and should not be included.
> - Only the additional element of other overheads should be included.
> - The current assistant manager's salary of £30,000 will be incurred anyway and should not be included; the £27,000 salary of the new manager should however be included since it has been incurred because the current assistant manager is needed on the project.
> - The company will not be able to obtain the rental of £135,000 on the factory space if it undertakes the project; thus the rental is an opportunity cost which should be included.
> - The 60,000 kg of material X currently in stock should not be included at purchase price since this is a sunk cost. However by undertaking the project, the company forgoes the opportunity to sell the raw materials in stock, and they should thus be included at selling price.

Certainty-equivalent cash flows

	Year 1 £'000	Year 2 £'000	Year 3 £'000	Year 4 £'000
Sales (W1)	1,125	1,800	1,575	1,425
Material X (W2)	50	230	248	280
Other variable costs (W3)	517	1,100	1,184	1,340
Management salaries (W4)	67	79	85	92
Rental: opportunity cost	135	135	135	135
Other overheads ($\times$ 1.1, 1.3, 1.4, 1.5)	66	78	84	90
	835	1,622	1,736	1,937
Sales less cash costs	290	178	(161)	(512)
Discount factor at 14%	0.877	0.769	0.675	0.592
Present value	254	137	(109)	(303)

The net present value is –£21,000, so the project is not acceptable.

Workings

1 Sales
   - Year 1 $10,000 \times £125 \times 0.9$
   - Year 2 $18,000 \times £125 \times 0.8$
   - Year 3 $18,000 \times £125 \times 0.7$
   - Year 4 $19,000 \times £125 \times 0.6$

2 Material X
   - Year 1   £50,000 opportunity cost
   - Year 2 $18,000 \times 6 \times £1.64 \times 1.3$
   - Year 3 $18,000 \times 6 \times £1.64 \times 1.4$
   - Year 4 $19,000 \times 6 \times £1.64 \times 1.5$

3 Other variable costs
   Per unit: $£30 + (3 \times £4.20) + £4.40 = £47$
   - Year 1 $10,000 \times £47 \times 1.1$
   - Year 2 $18,000 \times £47 \times 1.3$
   - Year 3 $18,000 \times £47 \times 1.4$
   - Year 4 $19,000 \times £47 \times 1.5$

4 Management salaries
   - Year 1   £34,000 + £27,000 = £61,000 $\times$ 1.1
   - Year 2   £61,000 $\times$ 1.3
   - Year 3   £61,000 $\times$ 1.4
   - Year 4   £61,000 $\times$ 1.5

32 Banden

Top tips. This question gives you practice in doing NPV calculations rapidly. Note how the NPV calculations are laid out in a way that enables you to show clearly how the profitability index is calculated. It would be less time consuming to use the proforma we have used than to do the NPV calculations, and then separately to do the profitability index calculations. What this emphasises is the usefulness of taking a few moments to plan the most efficient way of carrying out calculations.

In (b) because of the constraints you have to calculate the combined NPV of various possible combinations. It is obvious looking at the figures that the company will be undertaking some combination of three of the projects. However you would be penalised (and waste time) if you calculated the NPV of all combinations of three of the six. Any combinations including C should be excluded as the project makes a loss. It is also not possible for a combination to include A and E as they are mutually exclusive.

Our answer shows only those possible combinations of projects that cost less than £620,000. It would also be fine if you showed the cost of combinations that cost more than £620,000; however you should have then stated that they could not be undertaken, and should not have calculated their NPV.

(c) demonstrates why the cost of capital is used as an approximation, but you also need to demonstrate your understanding of its theoretical limitations. In (d) you need to show that linear programming is underpinned by significant simplifying assumptions.

(a) The profitability index will be calculated as the ratio of the PV of net cash inflows to the year 0 capital outlay.

	Year	Cash flow £	Discount factor 12%	Present value £	Profitability index
Project A	1-5	70,000	3.605	252,350	252,350
	0	(246,000)	1.000	(246,000)	246,000
				NPV = 6,350	= 1.026
Project B	1	75,000	0.893	66,975	
	2	87,000	0.797	69,339	
	3	64,000	0.712	45,568	
				181,882	181,882
	0	(180,000)	1.000	(180,000)	180,000
				NPV = 1,882	= 1.010
Project C	1	48,000	0.893	42,864	
	2	48,000	0.797	38,256	
	3	63,000	0.712	44,856	
	4	73,000	0.636	46,428	
				172,404	172,404
	0	(175,000)	1.000	(175,000)	175,000
				NPV = (2,596)	= 0.985
Project D	1-4	62,000	3.037	188,294	188,294
	0	(180,000)	1.000	(180,000)	180,000
				NPV = 8,294	= 1.046

Ranking	NPV	Profitability index
1st	D	D
2nd	A	F
3rd	E	E
4th	F	A
5th	B	B
6th	C	C

The rankings differ because the project's capital outlays differ. NPV shows the absolute benefit from a project, while profitability index scales that benefit according to the project's size.

(b) Project C comes sixth and last in the ranking according to both NPV and profitability index. It has a negative NPV and should not be undertaken.

Banden Ltd cannot afford to undertake more than three projects, given the maximum available capital of £620,000. It should not undertake project C, and it cannot undertake A and E simultaneously. The various feasible options are as follows.

Capital outlay

Projects	In total £	NPV in total £
D, F, E	510,000	18,777
D, F, A	576,000	19,637
D, F, B	510,000	15,169
D, E, B	540,000	15,666
D, A, B	606,000	16,526
F, A, B	576,000	13,225
F, E, B	510,000	12,365

Banden Ltd should not invest any funds in the money markets, because the return would only be 9% pa and the cost of capital for Banden is higher, at 12% pa.

It is assumed that the company does not have to use more funds than it needs to, and so there will not be any surplus funds which have to be invested somewhere.

Recommendation. The company should use £576,000 and invest in projects D, F and A.

(c) When there is **capital rationing**, there is **not enough capital to invest** in all the projects which have a positive NPV, when their NPVs are calculated by discounting the estimated cash flows at the company's cost of capital. The financial director is correct in theory to say that the company's cost of capital is inappropriate. The marginal cost of capital, which will be higher than the company's cost of capital, would be more appropriate for calculating project NPVs and deciding which projects would yield the best returns, given the shortage of capital.

However, the marginal cost of capital cannot be calculated easily, and a practical way of making decisions in a capital rationing situation is to **calculate** the **NPV** of **each project** using the company's normal cost of capital, and then to rank the projects in order of desirability, as in parts (a) and (b) of this solution.

(d) **Advantages of linear programming**

Linear programming has the advantages of helping management:

(i) To identify the optimal capital expenditure programme in a capital rationing situation

(ii) To establish the opportunity cost of capital, from the shadow price for capital in the solution to the linear programming problem

Once the model has been set up, it can be used for sensitivity tests, for example by varying the estimated cash flows of any projects.

Disadvantages of linear programming

Linear programming has the very serious drawback, however, that **projects** are assumed to be **divisible**, and so the optimal solution obtained from a model might be to undertake fractions of one or more projects. This is often unrealistic and impractical.

A second disadvantage of linear programming is that although sensitivity analysis is possible, the **data** used in the model are initially treated as being **certain** and the **constraints as fixed**. In reality, neither of these is the case. For example, when capital is a constraint, management will often be able to raise some extra capital from one source or other.

For Banden Ltd, linear programming seems unnecessarily complex, since there are only seven sensible combinations of projects. A simpler mathematical approach, as illustrated in part (b) of this solution, would seem to be suitable for making the investment decision.

33 Flocks

> **Top tips.** This question splits clearly the investment decision ((a)) and the finance decision ((b)).
>
> (a) requires careful planning of layout. Having separate columns for the items of income and expenditure and including a net cash flow column means you only have to do one net present value calculation per year. This is clearer and more economical than listing in one column all the year 0 figures, then all the year 1 figures, and having to do a net present value calculation for each figure.
>
> The layout of the main calculations can also be simplified by just including the net tax payable figure rather than separate figures for tax on profits and tax saved on capital allowances.
>
> The cumulative cash flow column enables you to work out the payback period easily.
>
> You should not have calculated a writing down allowance for the years of disposal (4 and 6), but a balancing allowance.
>
> In (b) the relevant items are the lease/buy costs and the tax savings.
>
> An exam question on this area might well include a written part asking you to discuss other implications of the choice between leasing and buying.

(a) Workings

(i) Capital allowances

Year		Machine X allowance £	Year		Machine Y allowance £
1	(25% of £63,000)	15,750	1	(25% of £110,000)	27,500
2	(75% of £15,750)	11,813	2	(75% of £27,500)	20,625
3	(75% of £11,813)	8,859	3	(75% of £20,625)	15,469
		36,422	4	(75% of £15,469)	11,602
4	(£63,000 – £36,422)	26,578	5	(75% of £11,602)	8,702
					83,898
			6	(£110,000 – £83,898)	26,102

(ii) *Taxable profits and tax liabilities*

Machine X

Year	Cash profits £	Allowance £	Taxable profits £	Tax at 30% (one year later) £
1	25,900	15,750	10,150	3,045
2	28,800	11,813	16,987	5,096
3	30,500	8,859	21,641	6,492
4	29,500	26,578	2,922	877

Machine Y

Year	Cash profits £	Allowance £	Taxable profits £	Tax at 30% (one year later) £
1	40,300	27,500	12,800	3,840
2	32,900	20,625	12,275	3,683
3	32,000	15,469	16,531	4,905
4	32,700	11,602	21,098	6,329
5	48,500	8,702	39,798	11,939
6	44,200	26,102	18,098	5,429

NPV and payback calculations

Machine X

Year	Machine cost £	Working capital £	Cash profits £	Tax £	Net cash flow £	Discount factor 13%	Present value £	Cumulative cash flow £
0	(63,000)	(12,500)			(75,500)	1.000	(75,500)	(75,500)
1			25,900		25,900	0.885	22,922	(49,600)
2			28,800	(3,045)	25,755	0.783	20,166	(23,845)
3			30,500	(5,096)	25,404	0.693	17,605	1,559
4		12,500	29,500	(6,492)	35,508	0.613	21,766	
5				(877)	(877)	0.543	(476)	
							NPV = 6,483	

The NPV for machine X is + £6,483, and the payback period is about three years.

Machine Y

Year	Machine cost £	Working capital £	Cash profits £	Tax £	Net cash flow £	Discount factor 15%	Present value £	Cumulative cash flow £
0	(110,000)	(12,500)			(122,500)	1.000	(122,500)	(122,500)
1			40,300		40,300	0.870	35,061	(82,200)
2			32,900	(3,840)	29,060	0.756	21,969	(53,140)
3			32,000	(3,683)	28,317	0.658	18,633	(24,823)
4			32,700	(4,905)	27,795	0.572	15,899	2,972
5			48,500	(6,329)	42,171	0.497	20,959	
6		12,500	44,200	(11,939)	44,761	0.432	19,337	
7				(5,429)	(5,429)	0.376	(2,041)	
							NPV = 7,317	

The NPV for machine Y is + £7,317 and the payback period is about four years.

Machine X would appear to be the preferable option.

(b) The financing decision will be appraised by discounting the relevant cash flows at the after-tax cost of borrowing, which is 10% × 70% = 7%.

(i) Purchase option

Year	Item	Cash flow £	Discount factor 7%	Present value £
0	Cost of machine	(63,000)	1.000	(63,000)
	Tax saved from capital allowances			
2	30% × £15,750	4,725	0.873	4,125
3	30% × £11,813	3,544	0.816	2,892
4	30% × £8,859	2,658	0.763	2,028
5	30% × £26,578	7,973	0.713	5,685
				(48,270)

(ii) Leasing option

Years	Item	Cash flow £	Discount factor 7%	Present value £
1 – 4	Lease costs	(20,000)	3.387	(67,740)
2 – 5	Tax savings on lease costs (× 30%)	6,000	3.165	18,990
				(48,750)

The purchase option is marginally cheaper, using a cost of capital based on the after-tax cost of borrowing.

On the assumption that investors would regard borrowing and leasing as equally risky finance options, the purchase option is recommended.

34 Milbao

(a)

Model		Actual sales quantity in budgeted proportions Units	Budgeted sales quantity Units	Sales quantity variance Units	Standard contribution £	Sales quantity variance £
Superb	(3/10)	28,800	30,000	1,200 (A)	60	72,000 (A)
Excellent	(1/2)	48,000	50,000	2,000 (A)	55	110,000 (A)
Good	(1/5)	19,200	20,000	800 (A)	48	38,400 (A)
		96,000	100,000	4,000 (A)		220,400 (A)

For example, actual sales quantity in budget proportions for Superb = 3/10 of 96,000 = 28,800

Sales quantity variance in total: 4,000 units (A); £220,400 (A)

Model		Std mix of actual sales Units	Actual mix Units	Sales mix variance Units	Standard contribution £	Sales mix variance £
Superb	(3/10)	28,800	36,000	7,200 (F)	60	432,000 (F)
Excellent	(1/2)	48,000	42,000	6,000 (A)	55	330,000 (A)
Good	(1/5)	19,200	18,000	1,200 (A)	48	57,600 (A)
		96,000	96,000	–		44,400 (F)

The mix variance is always zero in quantity

Sales mix variance in total: 0 units; £44,400 (F)

EXAM ANSWER BANK

(b)

	Superb		Good	
	£	£	£	£
Original budget contribution (W1)		1,800,000		960,000
Planning variances				
Selling price (W2)	180,000 (A)		84,000 (A)	
Variable cost (W3)	36,000 (F)		13,200 (F)	
		144,000 (A)		70,800 (A)
Revised budget contribution		1,656,000		889,200
Sales volume variance (W4)		331,200 (F)		88,920 (A)
Revised std contribution		1,987,200		800,280
Operational variances				
Selling price (W5)	144,000 (A)		50,400 (A)	
Variable cost (W6)	28,800 (F)		7,920 (F)	
		115,200 (A)		42,480 (A)
Actual contribution		1,872,000		757,800

The inclusion of the sales volume variance results in a figure showing what contribution should have been for actual activity level

Workings

1 Superb   30,000 × £60 = £1,800,000
   Good   20,000 × £48 = £960,000

2 The 6% fall in general market prices results in a planning variance as operational managers could not have controlled the fall.

The other 4% was controllable

Superb

	£
Original budget revenue (30,000 × £100)	3,000,000
Revised budget revenue (30,000 × £100 × 94%)	2,820,000
	180,000 (A)

Based on original budget of 30,000 units

Good

	£
Original budget revenue (20,000 × £70)	1,400,000
Revised budget revenue (20,000 × £70 × 94%)	1,316,000
	84,000 (A)

3 The 3% over estimation of the wage award results in a planning variance as this was a poor piece of planning rather than an operational efficiency or inefficiency.

Superb

	£
Original budget variable cost (30,000 × £40)	1,200,000
Revised budget variable cost (30,000 × £40 × 97%)	1,164,000
	36,000 (F)

Again, uses original budgets of 30,000 and 20,000 units

Good

	£
Original budget variable cost (20,000 × £22)	440,000
Revised budget variable cost (20,000 × £22 × 97%)	426,800
	13,200 (F)

4 The sales volume variances are based on the differences between actual and budget sales units.

	Actual units	Budget units	Sales volume variance
Superb	36,000	30,000	6,000 units (F)
Good	18,000	20,000	2,000 units (A)

Note how the revised standard margin is calculated

The variances are then valued at the revised standard margin, with prices reduced by 6% and costs by 3%.

Superb	Variance in units	6,000	units (F)
	× revised standard margin		
	(× £((100 × 94%) – (40 × 97%)))	× £55.20	
		£331,200	(F)
Good	Variance in units	2,000	units (A)
	× revised standard margin		
	(× £((70 × 94%) – (22 × 97%)))	× £44.46	
		£88,920	(A)

5   Superb

[*Actual volumes at revised standard are compared with actual results*]

	£
Sales revenue for actual volume of 36,000 units should have been (using revised standard of £100 × 94%)	3,384,000
but was (£100 × 90% × 36,000)	3,240,000
	144,000 (A)

Good

	£
Sales revenue for actual volume of 18,000 units should have been (using revised standard of £70 × 94%)	1,184,400
but was (£70 × 90% × 18,000)	1,134,000
	50,400 (A)

6   Variances are 2% of original budget costs for actual volume.

Superb
36,000 × £40 × 2% = £28,800 (F)

Good
18,000 × £22 × 2% = £7,920 (F)

Note. You may find it useful to calculate revised budget contribution using the revised standard figures.

	Superb	*Good*
Revised selling price (W1)	£94.0	£65.80
Revised variable cost (W2)	£38.8	£21.34
Revised contribution	£55.2	£44.46
Budgeted sales	× 30,000	× 20,000
Revised budget contribution	£1,656,000	£889,200

Workings

1	Superb	£100 × 94% = £94
	Good	£70 × 94% = £65.80
2	Superb	£40 × 97% = £38.80
	Good	£22 × 97% = £21.34

[*No need to define feedback and feedforward control here*]

(c) By analysing the variances in this way management are able to see how well the business has performed against what should in hindsight have been the standard. Otherwise part of each variance identified would simply reflect the fact that the original budget was wrong, perhaps through factors beyond the control of management. The analysis into planning and operational variances thus provides more useful **feedback** about operational performance, and this can be used to prompt investigation, cost benefit analysis and control action where possible.

This approach is also useful for **feedforward control**. When budgets are next prepared the revised standards can be used. If it is not possible to set right all of the operational problems, the relevant proportion of operational variances can also be taken into account in future plans.

35 Swansea

> Work out best cash management policy

(a) (i) The two alternative policies will be evaluated separately to determine the most beneficial choice in financial terms.

(1) **Selling securities**

The first step is to determine the optimal amount of cash that will be raised in each transaction, and hence the number of transactions and the level of transaction costs.

$$Q = \sqrt{\frac{2FS}{i}}$$

where: i = average % rate of return   10%
S = cash payments   £1m
F = transaction fee   £20

$$Q = \sqrt{\frac{2 \times £20 \times £1m}{10\%}}$$

= £20,000

Sales made	= £1 million / 20,000
	= 50
Transaction costs	= 50 × £20
	= £1,000
Average level of cash balances	= £20,000 / 2
	= £10,000
Interest on cash balances	= £10,000 × 4.5%
	= £450
Average portfolio balances	= £1,000,000 / 2
	= £500,000
Income lost on portfolio securities	= 10% × £500,000
	= £50,000

Total costs

	£
Transaction costs	1,000
Interest received on cash balances	(450)
Income lost on portfolio securities	50,000
	50,550

(2) **Secured loan**

Average value of remaining cash = £1,000,000 / 2

= £500,000

Interest received = £500,000 × 8%
= £40,000

Total costs

	£
Interest paid (£1 million × 13%)	130,000
Interest received	(40,000)
Arrangement fee	6,000
	96,000

The figures suggest that the policy of **selling securities** is to be preferred since this has a net cost of £50,550, which is £45,450 less than the cost of taking out a secured loan for the period.

The company should also take into account the following other factors associated with the policies.

(1) The **value of the short-term securities** is likely to **fluctuate** and Swansea must consider the possibility that the **value** could **fall** to below that required to meet the cash payments.

(2) **Use of the securities** will **eliminate them** as a future source of finance.

[Key point for loan finance]

(3) If Swansea takes out the loan it must have **funds available** with which to repay it at the end of the period.

(ii) **Limitations** of the model include the following.

(1) It assumes that the **level of transaction costs** is **independent** of the size of the transaction. Again this is unlikely to be true in practice.

(2) In reality, **payments** will **not be made continuously** but at regular intervals. The effect of this 'stepped' effect on the operation of the model should be considered.

(3) It **assumes a steady rate of return** from the securities although this may be very uncertain. Swansea should consider the effect of fluctuations in this rate on the model.

(4) It **does not allow** for a **buffer stock of cash** but assumes that further securities will only be sold when the cash balance reduces to zero. This is unlikely to be realistic in practice.

(b) (i) (1) **Finance leases** are **similar** to **hire purchase contracts** in that the asset is sold not to the user but to an intermediary who then leases the asset to the user in return for periodic payments.

The main differences are as follows:

- Unlike the hire purchase contract, **ownership** of the asset **does not transfer** to the user at the end of the lease period, but is retained by the purchaser.

- The **purchaser** and not the user is able to **claim** the **capital allowances**, which may be passed on to the user in the form of a reduction in the periodic payments.

- Although the user does not own the asset, entries appear in the user's **balance sheet** and **profit and loss account** to reflect the **capital element** of the lease, the **interest element** of the payments, and the **remaining lease commitment**. This is to ensure that all forms of long-term debt are fully reflected in the balance sheet.

Many finance leases are structured into a **'primary period'** which covers the major part of the economic life of the asset, and a **'secondary period'** during which the user continues to lease the asset, but at a much lower (often only nominal) rate.

(2) **Hire purchase** is a form of **instalment credit** whereby the business purchases goods on credit and pays for them by instalments. The goods are accounted for when purchased. The periodic payments include both an **interest element** on the initial price and a **capital repayment** element. At the end of the hire purchase period, ownership of the asset passes to the user, who is also able to claim **capital allowances** on the basic purchase cost of the asset. The mechanics of the transaction are as follows.

- The supplier of the asset sells it to a finance house.
- The supplier of the asset delivers it to the customer who will be the user and the eventual owner.
- The hire purchase agreement is made between the finance house and the customer.

(3) **Sale and leaseback** is an arrangement which is similar to **mortgaging**. A business which already owns an asset, for example a building or an item of equipment, agrees to sell the asset to a financial institution and then immediately to lease it back on terms specified in the agreement. The business has the benefit of the **funds from the sale** while retaining use of the asset, in return for regular payments to the financial institution.

The principal benefit is that the **business** gains **immediate access to liquid funds**; however this is at the expense of the **ability to profit** from any capital appreciation (potentially significant in the case of property) and **tax allowances**. The capacity to borrow elsewhere may be reduced since the balance sheet value of assets will fall.

(ii) The approach is to calculate the net of tax present value of the two options available to Mumbles. The discount rate to be used will be the cost of borrowing net of tax. 18% × (1 − 0.33) = 12%.

> *Easier to show each year's payments in single column*

Purchasing outright

Year	0	1	2	3	4	5
	£'000	£'000	£'000	£'000	£'000	£'000
Initial outlay	5,000					
Tax savings on capital allowances (W)		413	310	232	174	522
Net cash flow	(5,000)	413	310	232	174	522
Discount factor at 12%	1.000	0.893	0.797	0.712	0.636	0.567
PV of cash flow	(5,000)	369	247	165	111	296

Working

Year of claim	Allowance	Tax saved	Year of tax payment
0	5,000 (1,250) 3,750	413	1
1	(938) 2,812	309	2
2	(703) 2,109	232	3
3	(527) 1,582	174	4
4	(1,582) –	522	5

Thus the **NPV cost of purchasing** outright is £3,812,000.

Leasing

Year	0	1	2	3	4
	£'000	£'000	£'000	£'000	£'000
Annual rental	(1,800)	(1,800)	(1,800)	(1,800)	–
Tax savings (rental × 33%)	–	594	594	594	594
Net cash flow	(1,800)	(1,206)	(1,206)	(1,206)	594
Discount factor at 12%	1.000	0.893	0.797	0.712	0.636
PV of cash flow	(1,800)	(1,077)	(961)	(859)	378

Thus the **NPV cost of leasing** is **£4,319,000**. This is £506,000 more than the NPV cost of direct purchase over the life of the equipment, and direct purchase therefore appears more attractive on financial grounds.

(iii) The cost of purchase can be re-evaluated to take into account the **additional maintenance costs** of £190,000 per year. These costs are assumed to start in year 1, with the associated tax saving coming through in the subsequent year.

Year	0	1	2	3	4	5
	£'000	£'000	£'000	£'000	£'000	£'000
Initial outlay	(5,000)					
Tax savings on capital allowances (above)		413	310	232	174	522
Maintenance costs		(190)	(190)	(190)	(190)	
Tax saving			63	63	63	63
Net cash flow	(5,000)	223	183	105	47	585
Discount factor at 12%	1.000	0.893	0.797	0.712	0.636	0.567
PV of cash flow	(5,000)	199	146	75	30	332

If the maintenance costs are taken into account, the NPV cost of purchase rises to £4,218,000, which is slightly less (by £100,000) than the cost of leasing. Although the decision is not reversed, the **relative costs** are **marginal**, and other factors should also be considered, for instance the **reliability** and **availability** of the **different maintenance options**.

(c) (i) Current rate of return on capital employed

		£'000
Operating profit		20,000
Fixed assets	(a)	75,000
Stocks	(b)	25,000
Capital employed	(a) + (b)	100,000

EXAM ANSWER BANK

Rate of return   £20m/£100m=   20%

Incremental profits and investments arising from the project

	Year 1 £'000	Year 2 £'000	Year 3 £'000	Year 4 £'000
Sales (W)	10,000	8,100	6,400	5,600
Operating costs (W)	(2,000)	(1,800)	(1,600)	(1,600)
Overheads (W)	(1,500)	(1,350)	(1,200)	(1,200)
Depreciation (W)	(3,000)	(3,000)	(3,000)	(3,000)
Profit	3,500	1,950	600	(200)

Average profit = £1,463,000

Workings

	Year 1	Year 2	Year 3	Year 4
Sales ('000 units)	2,000	1,800	1,600	1,600
Price per unit (£)	5.00	4.50	4.00	3.50
	£'000	£'000	£'000	£'000
Sales value	10,000	8,100	6,400	5,600
Operating costs at £1/unit	2,000	1,800	1,600	1,600
Overheads at £0.75/unit	1,500	1,350	1,200	1,200

[Include allocated overheads]

	Year 1	Year 2	Year 3	Year 4
NBV at start of year	14,000	11,000	8,000	5,000
Depreciation: (£14m – £2m)/4	3,000	3,000	3,000	3,000
NBV at end of year	11,000	8,000	5,000	2,000
Average NBV	12,500	9,500	6,500	3,500

[Residual value]

[Must use average]

Average capital employed

	Year 1	Year 2	Year 3	Year 4
Fixed assets (average NBV)(W)	12,500	9,500	6,500	3,500
Stock	500	500	500	500
Total	13,000	10,000	7,000	4,000

Average capital employed = £8,500,000

Average return = Average profit/Average capital employed during each year

In this case the average return (ROCE) is 17.2%.

The project shows an **ROCE** of 17.2% which is in excess of the hurdle rate of 10%. However, since the current rate of return achieved by Gower is 20%, acceptance of the project would result in a **small depression** of the overall ROCE. It is therefore unlikely that the management of Gower would find the project attractive since its acceptance would mean that their performance would **appear** to have **deteriorated**.

[Comment and conclusion]

(ii)   (1)   The main problems are as follows.

- The ROCE approach can easily be **manipulated** to put project returns in a good light, for example by changing the method of depreciation or the estimate of the terminal value.

- There is an element of **double counting** in that depreciation is deducted from the profit figure in full, but the use of the average assets figure means that part of this is also included in the denominator. The effect of this is to depress the calculated returns.

- It **ignores** the **actual cashflows** associated with the project, and ignores the effect of the timing of those cashflows on the real return of the project.

[Not cash flow base measure]

(2) The ROCE approach remains popular because it is expressed in terms with which **managers are familiar**, namely **profit** and **capital employed**. It is also **easy to calculate the effect** that the project is likely to have on the reported profit and loss account and balance sheet. Since managers are frequently rewarded in relation to performance against these variables they will be concerned to see the effect on them of undertaking a new project.

[annotation: Manager self interest]

(iii) The dangers of extending the credit period include the following.

(1) The **average collection period** at present is 90 days which is already **long** by the standards of most industries. It is questionable whether extending it further will really achieve the anticipated improvement in sales volume.

(2) Any **additional customers** attracted to Gower will be those to whom **extended credit is important**, and these are likely to be firms which are less financially secure. It is therefore likely that there will be an increased risk of both slow payment and bad debts, and such customers may have a greater tendency to demand discounts.

(3) Where the credit period is very long, the **absolute amount** of any **bad debt** will be **larger** than if the collection period is short since there will be a greater number of months of supply outstanding.

[annotation: Very long]

Ways of assessing customers' creditworthiness are as follows.

(1) Offering a cash-only **trial period** could help to establish the **likely volume** of trade, and **demonstrate** that the customer is capable of paying reliably.

(2) An analysis can be made of their published accounts to establish their liquidity and financial security.

(3) **Visits** to the **customers' premises** are useful in gaining a view of the company and its prospects.

(4) Potential new customers should **supply two good references** including one from a bank before credit is granted.

[annotation: Internal sources]

(5) **Credit ratings** can be **checked** using an agency such as Dun and Bradstreet.

(6) For export customers, **advice** may be **obtained** from the **DTI** and the **ECGD**.

(7) Information relevant to the company and the industry may be gained from the **trade press** and from newspapers.

[annotation: External sources]

(8) The **credit limit** should be **low** for an initial period to allow the payment performance to be checked.

Index

INDEX

Note: **Key Terms** and their page references are given in **bold**.

ABC, 45
Absorption, 18
Absorption base, 24
Absorption costing, 17, 18
Absorption rate, 24
Acceptance credits, 418
Accounting rate of return method, 533
Acid rain, 372
Acid test ratio, 384
Acquisition, 530
Activity, 281
Activity based budgeting, 219
Activity based budgets, 220
Activity based costing, 45
    outline of an ABC system, 46
Activity ratio, 284
Additive model, 241
Agency relationship, 310
Aggregate demand, 347, 348
Algebraic method, 21
Allocation, 18
Allocative efficiency, 369
Alternative Investment Market (AIM), 326
Annual percentage rate (APR), 545
Annuity tables, 548
Ansoff, 527
Apportionment, 18
ARR and the comparison of mutually exclusive projects, 534
Aspiration level, 207
Aspirations budget, 207
Asset replacement decisions, 562
Asset turnover, 315
Attainable standard, 86
Attributable fixed costs, 41
Average price relatives index, 262
Average quantity relatives index, 262
Average relatives indices, 262
Average stock, 425

BACS, 431
Bad debt risk, 404
Bad debts, 399
Balance of payments, 357, 360
Balance sheet valuation, 304
Balancing transactions, 47
Bank lending, 324
Bank of England, 333
Base package, 215

Base period, 257
Base year, 257
Basic standard, 86
Baumol model, 433
Behavioural implications of budgeting, 201
Benchmarking, 289
Bills of exchange, 417
Bottleneck resources, 60
Bottom-up budgeting, 204
Bought deal, 456
Break-up basis, 304
Budget, 151, 159, **167**, 169, 181, 182
    sales, 168
Budget centre, 156
Budget committee, 167
Budget constrained style of evaluation, 205
Budget cost allowance, 195, 197
Budget deficit, 348
Budget development, 168
Budget documentation, 166
Budget implementation, 168
Budget manual, 166
Budget period, 166
Budget preparation timetable, 167
Budget review, 170
Budget surplus, 348
Budget variance, 198
Budgetary control, 196
Budgetary planning
    and control systems, 159
Budgetary slack, 206
Budgeted balance sheet, 181, 182, 189
Budgeted capacity, 85
Budgeted profit and loss account, 181, 182, 189
Budgets as targets, 206
Buffer, 429
Bulk discounts, 427
Business angel financing, 515
Business failure, 391
Business risk, 544

Cadbury report, 373
Capacity, *171*
Capacity levels, 84
    budgeted capacity, 85
    full capacity, 85
    idle capacity, 85
    practical capacity, 85
Capacity ratio, 84, 85, 284
Capital allowances, 573

INDEX

Capital expenditure, 526
Capital markets, 325, 452
Capital rationing, 596
Capital structure, 494, 504, 517
Capitalisation issue, 463
Cash budgets, 174, 179, 431
Cash cycle, 383
Cash flow, 383
Cash flow forecasts, 392
Cash flow problems, 429
Centralised treasury department, 445
Certainty-equivalent approach, 587
Certificates of deposit (CDs), 439
Chain base method, 258
Change transactions, 47
Code of Best Practice, 373
Coefficient of correlation, r, 236
Coefficient of determination, r^2, 236
Collecting debts, 408
Combined Code, 375
Commercial banks, 324
Committed cost, 41
Competition Commission, 367
Competition policy, 367
Competitive performance, 64
Composite index numbers, 262
Compounding, 541
Consensus theory, 304
Consumer price indices, 358
Continuous budgets, 218
Contribution, 27
Control, 150
Control chart, 112
Control cycle, 152
Control process, 152
Control ratios, 284
Control reporting, 159
Controllability, 156, 158
Controllable costs, 157
Controlling, 5, 6
Conversion premium, 485
Conversion value, 485
Convertible debentures, 486
Convertible loan stock, 484
Corporate appraisal, 528
Corporate governance, 373
Corporation tax, 576
Correlation, 233
   and causation, 237
   curvilinear, 235
   negative, 235
   non-linear, 235
   partial, 235
   perfect, 234
   positive, 235

Cost accounting, 8
Cost centre, 157, 276
Cost driver, 46, 49
Cost gap, 57
Cost of capital, 496, 542
Cost of debt capital, 543
Cost of preference shares, 543
Cost of share capital, 542
Cost pools, 46
Cost/sales ratios, 280
Costing, 9
Cost-push inflation, 358
Coupon, 466, 481
Credit control, 400
Credit creation, 323
Credit insurance, 405
Credit ratings, 409
Credit reviews, 410
Credit utilisation report, 413
Creditors, 309, 416
Creditors' turnover, 385
Creditworthiness, 400
Currency of invoice, 440
Current ratio, 384
Current standard, 86
Cusum chart, 113
Cyclical variations, 241

DCF yield method, 546
Debentures, 482
Debt collection policy, 408
Debt ratio, 502
Debt ratios, 316
Debtors, 400
Debtors age analysis, 411
Debtors' payment period, 384
Debtors turnover, 398
Decision making, 5, 6
Decision packages, 215
Decisions, 5
Deep discount bonds, 482
Deferred ordinary shares, 453
Deflation, 260, 362
Demand management, 349
Demand-pull inflation, 358
Denationalisation, 370
Departmental budgets, 171
Dependent variable, 227
Deregulation, 369
Devaluation, 361
Direct costs, 16
Directly attributable fixed costs, 41
Directly attributable overhead, 158
Discount rate computation, 543

Discount tables, 547
Discounted cash flow, 540
Discounts, 427
Discretionary fixed costs, 158
Dividend cover, 470
Dividend decision, 301
Dividend growth model, 472
Dividend payout ratio, 470
Dividend policy, 471
Dividend valuation model, 472
Dividend yield, 466
Dividends, 438
Double loop feedback, 154
Du Pont system of ratio analysis, 314
Dual responsibility, 159
Dynamic conditions, 218

Earnings per share, 467
Economic order quantity, 422
Economic policy, 312, 344
Economy, 287
Effectiveness, 287
Efficiency, 287
Efficiency ratio, 85, 284
Efficient market hypothesis, 328
Efficient portfolios, 336
Elimination method, 21
Employee share option schemes, 463
Employees, 309
Enhanced, 464
Enterprise Initiative, 371, 517
Enterprise Investment Scheme, 518
Environmental ('green') policies, 372
Environmental reporting, 317
Environmentally friendly policies, 373
Equity finance, 514
Equity shares, 453
Ethical investment funds, 373
Eurobond, 339
Eurocurrency, 338
Eurocurrency markets, 338
Euro-equity, 339
European Union, 369
Exchange control regulations, 362
Exchange rate, 351, 353
Exchange rate policy, 346
Exchange rate risk, 440
Exchange rate stability, 355
Expectational inflation, 359
Expectations, 332
Expectations budget, 207
Expected cash flows, 431, 587
Export credit insurance, 415
External trade policy, 346

Externality, 372
Extrapolation, 232

Factoring, 405
Feedback, 152
 negative. See
 positive, 154
Feedforward control, 154
Finance house deposits, 438
Financial accounts, 302
Financial control, 301
Financial gearing, 499
Financial intermediary, 322
Financial management, 300
Financial performance, 64, 313
Financial performance measures, 273
Financial planning, 301
Financial risk, 494, 544
Financial targets, 305
Financing decision, 301
Fiscal policy, 346, 348
Fixed and flexible budgets, 194
Fixed asset investment, 526
Fixed base method, 258
Fixed budget, 194
Fixed charge, 483
Fixed contracts, 441
Fixed costs, 41
Fixed exchange rates, 354
Fixed production overhead expenditure variance, 101
Fixed production overhead total variance, 100
Fixed production overhead variances, 100
Fixed production overhead volume capacity variance, 101,
Fixed production overhead volume efficiency variance, 101, 102
Flexed budget, 195
Flexibility, 65
Flexible budgets, 195
 using absorption costing, 200
Float, 431
Floating charge, 483
Floating exchange rates, 354
Floating rate debt capital, 544
Forecasting, 226, 237, 247
Foreign exchange risk, 439
Foreign exchange risk management, 445
Forward discount, 442
Forward exchange contracts, 440
Forward premium, 442
Full capacity, 85
Fully diluted EPS, 468
Functional budgets, 171

INDEX

Gearing, 306
Gearing ratios, 316, 499
Goal congruence, 205
Golden rule, 349
Government, 309, 311
Government aid, 517
Government incentives, 371
Grants, 371
Graphical approach to linear programming, 601
Greenbury report, 374
Gross profit margin, 280
Growth in dividends, 472

Hampel report, 374
Hard capital rationing, 596
Hedging, 439, 445
Hierarchy of costs, 53
Higher level feedback, 154
Hire purchase, 608
Historigram, 239

Ideal standard, 86
Idle capacity, 85
Idle capacity ratio, 85
Idle time variance, 98
Import cost-push inflation, 358
Imputed cost, 41
Imputed interest, 44
Incremental budgeting, 214
Incremental costs, 40
Incremental packages, 215
Independent variable, 227
Index, 256, 268
Index numbers, 256, 268
    Laspeyre, 265
    Paasche, 265
Index points, 256
Index relative, 258, 268
Indices, 281
Indirect costs, 16
Inflation, 586, 357
Information, quantitative and qualitative, 274
In-house credit ratings, 409
Innovation, 65, 286
Institutional investors, 327
Interdependence between, 110
Interest cover, 502
Interest rates, 331
Interest rates and the balance of payments, 362
Interest yield, 466
Intermediaries offer, 456
Internal rate of return (IRR) method, 554
International capital markets, 338

International money markets, 338
Interpolation, 232
Inter-relationships beween variances, 110
Inventories, 422
Investing surplus cash, 437
Investment, 526
Investment by not-for-profit organisations, 527
Investment by the commercial sector, 527
Investment centre, 157
Investment centres, 277
Investment decisions, 301
Invoice discounting, 407
Issue price for a rights issue, 457

Judgement of outsiders, 291
Just-in-time procurement, 428

Key budget factor, 168
Keynes, 429

Labour efficiency variance, 97
Labour rate variance, 97
Labour total variance, 97
Labour variances, 96
Lagged payments, 440
Laspeyre indices, 265
Laspeyre price index, 265
Laspeyre quantity index, 265
Lead payments, 440
Lease or buy decisions, 609
Leasing, 606
Least squares technique, 230
Legislation, 312
Lessee, 606
Life cycle costing, 54
Life cycle costs, 54
Limiting budget factor, 168
Line of best fit, 230, 233
Linear programming approach to capital rationing, 603
Linear regression analysis, 230
Linear relationships, 227
Liquidity ratios, 317, 391
Listing, 453
Loan Guarantee Scheme, 517
Loan stock, 481
Local authority deposits, 438
Logistical transactions, 47
Long range planning, 306
Long-term capital, 325
Long-term creditors, 311
Long-term plan, 151

Macroeconomics, 344
Management, 310
Management accounting, 7
Management accounts, 302
Management control action, 113
Management performance measures, 291
Managerial model, 303
Managerial performance, 205
Marginal cost, 27
Marginal costing, 18, 27
Market failure, 366
Market portfolio, 338
Market segmentation theory, 332
Market segmentation theory of interest rates, 332
Market values, 304
Master budget, 181, 182
Matching receipts and payments, 440
Material price variance, 94
Material total variance, 94
Material usage variance, 94
Material variances, 94
Materials mix and yield variances, 127
Maximum level, 425
Mergers, 367
Microeconomics, 344
Miller-Orr model, 434
Minimum level, 425
Mix variance (sales), 133
Mix variance materials, 127
Models, 248
Modigliani and Miller, 497
Monetary measures, 273
Monetary policy, 346
Monetary Policy Committee, 333
Money market hedges, 443
Money markets, 325
Monopoly, 367
Mortgages, 484
Motivating, 5, 6
Motivation, 201, 203, 207
Moving averages, 241
Multi-period capital rationing, 601
Multiplicative model, 245
Mutually exclusive packages, 215

Nationalised industries, 312
Negative correlation, 235
Net present value (NPV) method, 546
Net working capital, 382
NFIs, 275
Non-accounting style of evaluation, 206
Non-controllable costs, 158

Non-financial indicators, 65, 274
Non-financial objectives, 307
Non-monetary performance measures, 274
Non-profit-making organisations, 287
Not-for-profit organisations, 66, 288, 313, 527
Notional cost, 41
Notional interest, 44
NPMOs, 287

Objectives, 151
OFEX, 327
Offer for sale, 454
Offers for sale by tender, 455
Official aid schemes, 371
Open offer, 463
Operating and measurement, 153
Operating gearing, 501, 502
Operating statements, 120
Operating variance, 135
Operational variances, 135
Operational-level decisions, 6
Opportunity cost, 43
Opportunity costing, 43
Options, 441
Ordinary shares, 453
Organic growth, 530
Organising, 5, 6
Over-absorption of overheads, 25
Over-capitalisation, 386
Overdraft, 325, 512
Overdraft facility, 429
Overdraft financing, 512
Overhead absorption, 18, 24
Overhead Apportionment, 20
overhead recovery rates, 24
Overheads, 16
Overseas factor, 414
Overtrading, 388

Paasche indices, 265
Paasche price index, 265
Paasche quantity index, 265
Participation, 203
Payback method, 531
Pearsonian coefficient of correlation, 236
Percentage, 275
Performance evaluation, 205
Performance measurement
 financial, 273
 in non-profit-making organisations, 287
Performance measures, 272, 274
 flexibility, 286
 for labour, 283

for manufacturing businesses, 282
for materials, 282
for overheads, 283
for sales, 282
for services, 284
for the service sector, 284
non-profit-making organisations, 287
of individual managers, 291
profitability, 278
quality of service, 285
quantitative and qualitative, 274
resource utilisation, 286
using the standard hour, 283
Periodic budget, 218
Personal taxation, 474
Placing, 455
Planning, 5, 6, 150
Planning and control cycle, 150
Planning variances, 135
Polluter pays principle, 372
Pollution, 372
Position audit, 151
Positive correl, 235
Practical capacity, 85
Precautionary motive, 429
Predetermined absorption rate, 24
Pre-emption rights, 457
Preference shares, 465
Present value, 541
Price earnings ratio, 468
Price index, 256
Price relative, 263
Prices and incomes policy, 346
Principal budget factor, 168
Private Finance Initiative, 349
Privatisation, 370
Probability distribution, 587
Product life cycle, 55
Product moment correlation coefficient, 236
Production capacity, 84
Production volume ratio, 284
Production volume ratio, 85
Productivity, 281
Product-market mix, 530
Profit, 273
Profit centre, 157, 277
Profit conscious style of evaluation, 206
Profit margin, 280, 315, 316
    profit to sales ratio, 280
Profit maximisation, 303
Profit to sales ratio, 280
Profitability, 278, 305, 314
Profitability index, 597
Programming, 153
Proportional model, 245

Prospectus issue, 455
Public sector, 545
Public sector borrowing requirement, 348
Public sector debt repayment, 348

Qualitative controls, 351
Qualitative performance measures, 274
Quality of service, 285
Quality transactions, 47
Quantitative controls, 351
Quantitative performance measures, 274
Quantity discounts, 427
Quantity index, 256
Quantity variance, 133
Quarterly accounting, 576
Quick ratio, 384

Random variations, 239
Ratio analysis, 314
Ratio pyramids, 314
Ratios, 275
    activity, 284
    capacity, 284
    efficiency, 284
Reciprocal services, 20
Reconciling profits, 31
Redemption, 483
Redistribution of wealth, 357
Regional Enterprise Grants, 518
Regression, 238
Regulation of markets, 366
Relevant cost, 40
Reorder level, 424
Repeated distribution method, 21
Replacement decisions, 562
Reporting and analysis, 153
Residual income, 279
Resource utilisation, 65
Resource utilisation measures, 286
Responsibility accounting, 156, **276**
Responsibility centre, 156
Responsibility centres, 275
Responsibility reporting, 156
Restrictive practices, 368
Retentions policy, 472
Return on capital employed (ROCE), 278, 305, 315, 533
Return on investment, 278
Return on investment (ROI) method), 533
Revenue expenditure, 526
Reverse yield gap, 334
Revision variance, 135
Rights issues, 457

INDEX

Risk, 582
Risk-return trade-off, 333
Rolling budgets, 218
Rule-of-thumb models, 110

Safety stock, 425
Sales budget, 168
Sales forecasting, 237
Sales mix and quantity variances, 133
Sales volume variance, 106
Scatter diagrams, 233
Scrip dividends, 464
Scrip issue, 463, 464
Scrip issue (bonus issue), 464
Seasonal variations, 240
Secondary ratios, 315
Selling price variance, 105
Sensitivity analysis, 583
Separation theorem, 335
Service costing, 63,
Service department cost apportionment, 20
Service quality, 65, 285
Settlement discount, 403
Share ownership, 311
Shareholders, 309
Shareholders and management, 310
Short-term capital, 325
Short-term debt instruments, 439
Short-term deposits, 438
Short-term finance, 416
Short-term investments, 438
Signalling, 471
Simple indices, 257
Simulation model, 591
Simultaneous equation (algebraic) method, 21
Single loop feedback, 154
Single period capital rationing, 597
Sinking fund, 549
Small and medium-sized enterprises (SMEs), 510
Soft capital rationing, 596
Special dividend payment, 438
Speculation, 353
Speculative motive, 429
Spreadsheet packages, 248
Stakeholder, 308, 309
Standard costing, 80
    as a control technique, 81
    in the modern organisation, 88
    uses of, 81
Standard costs, 80
Standard hour, 84, **173**, 283
Standards, 82
    behavioural impact, 86

deriving, 82
types of, 86
Statistical control charts, 112
Statistical significance model, 111
Step-wise (elimination) method, 22
Stock Exchange, 326
Stock Exchange introduction, 455
Stock Exchange requirements, 375
Stock market ratios, 466
Stock splits, 464
Stock turnover, 385, 429
Stockless production, 428
Stocks, 422
Strategic analysis, 151
Strategic fund management, 392
Strategic level decisions, 6
Strategies, 151
Subjective judgement, 288
Sunk cost, 41
Supply side policies, 371
Surplus cash, 437
SWOT analysis, 528

Tactical-level decisions, 6
Target costing, 56
Taxation, 572
The high-low method, 227
Theoretical ex rights price, 458
Theory of constraints (TOC), 58
Throughput accounting, 59
Time series, 239
time series analysis, 239
Time series deflation, 260
Time value of money, 561
Timing of cash flows, 547
Top-down, 203
Total Factory Costs (TFC), 59
Total shareholder return, 305
Trade bill, 417
Trade credit, 416, 514
Trading cycle, 383
Transactions motive, 429
Treasury bills, 439
Treasury management, 445
Trend, 239

Uncertainty, 582
Under absorption of overheads, 25
Underwriters, 456
Unit cost measurements, 288
Unit cost measures, 64
Updated annual budgets, 219

V

Valuation, 304
Value for money, 288
Value of rights, 459
Variable costs, 41
Variable production overhead expenditure variance, 99
Variable production overhead total variance, 99
Variable production overhead variances, 99
Variance analysis, 94
Variance investigation models, 110
Variance trend, 109
Variances, 94, 95, 96, 98, 99, 100, 127
    in a standard absorption costing system, 123
    in a standard marginal costing system, 123
    interdependence between, 110
    investigating, 109
    reasons for, 108
    significance of, 109, 110
Vendor consideration issue, 463
Vendor placing, 463
Venture capital, 516
Venture capital trusts, 516, 518
Volume capacity, 84

W

Wage-price spiral, 359
Warrant, 489
Warrant conversion premium, 489
Weighted average cost of capital, 497, 543
Weighted average of price relative index, 263
Weighted average of quantity relative index, 263
Weighted average of relatives indices, 263
Weighted index numbers, 263
What if analysis, 249
Working capital cycle, 383
Working capital investment, 526
Working capital requirement, 390

Y

Yield curve, 332
Yield variance, 127

Z

Zero based budgeting (ZBB), 214, 215
Zero coupon bonds, 483

Review Form & Free Prize Draw – Paper 2.4 Financial Management and Control (6/06)

All original review forms from the entire BPP range, completed with genuine comments, will be entered into one of two draws on 31 January 2007 and 31 July 2007. The names on the first four forms picked out on each occasion will be sent a cheque for £50.

Name: _____   Address: _____

How have you used this Text?
(Tick one box only)

- [ ] Home study (book only)
- [ ] On a course: college _____
- [ ] With 'correspondence' package
- [ ] Other _____

Why did you decide to purchase this Text?
(Tick one box only)

- [ ] Have used BPP Texts in the past
- [ ] Recommendation by friend/colleague
- [ ] Recommendation by a lecturer at college
- [ ] Saw advertising
- [ ] Saw information on BPP website
- [ ] Other _____

During the past six months do you recall seeing/receiving any of the following?
(Tick as many boxes as are relevant)

- [ ] Our advertisement in *ACCA Student Accountant*
- [ ] Our advertisement in *Pass*
- [ ] Our advertisement in *PQ*
- [ ] Our brochure with a letter through the post
- [ ] Our website www.bpp.com

Which (if any) aspects of our advertising do you find useful?
(Tick as many boxes as are relevant)

- [ ] Prices and publication dates of new editions
- [ ] Information on Text content
- [ ] Facility to order books off-the-page
- [ ] None of the above

Which BPP products have you used?

Text	✓	Success CD	☐	Learn Online	☐
Kit	☐	i-Learn	☐	Home Study Package	☐
Passcard	☐	i-Pass	☐	Home Study PLUS	☐

Your ratings, comments and suggestions would be appreciated on the following areas.

	Very useful	Useful	Not useful
Introductory section (Key study steps, personal study)	☐	☐	☐
Chapter introductions	☐	☐	☐
Key terms	☐	☐	☐
Quality of explanations	☐	☐	☐
Case studies and other examples	☐	☐	☐
Exam focus points	☐	☐	☐
Questions and answers in each chapter	☐	☐	☐
Fast forwards and chapter roundups	☐	☐	☐
Quick quizzes	☐	☐	☐
Question Bank	☐	☐	☐
Answer Bank	☐	☐	☐
Index	☐	☐	☐

Overall opinion of this Study Text	Excellent ☐	Good ☐	Adequate ☐	Poor ☐

Do you intend to continue using BPP products?   Yes ☐   No ☐

On the reverse of this page are noted particular areas of the text about which we would welcome your feedback. The BPP author of this edition can be e-mailed at: julietgood@bpp.com

Please return this form to: Nick Weller, ACCA Publishing Manager, BPP Professional Education, FREEPOST, London, W12 8BR

Review Form & Free Prize Draw (continued)

TELL US WHAT YOU THINK

Because the following specific areas of the text contain new material and cover highly examinable topics etc, your comments on their usefulness are particularly welcome.

Please note any further comments and suggestions/errors below

Free Prize Draw Rules

1. Closing date for 31 January 2007 draw is 31 December 2006. Closing date for 31 July 2007 draw is 30 June 2007.
2. Restricted to entries with UK and Eire addresses only. BPP employees, their families and business associates are excluded.
3. No purchase necessary. Entry forms are available upon request from BPP Professional Education. No more than one entry per title, per person. Draw restricted to persons aged 16 and over.
4. Winners will be notified by post and receive their cheques not later than 6 weeks after the relevant draw date.
5. The decision of the promoter in all matters is final and binding. No correspondence will be entered into.